Denyze Toffoli, Geoffrey Sockett and Meryl Kusyk (Eds.)
Language Learning and Leisure

Studies on Language Acquisition

Series Editors
Luke Plonsky
Martha Young-Scholten

Volume 66

Language Learning and Leisure

Informal Language Learning in the Digital Age

Edited by
Denyze Toffoli, Geoffrey Sockett and Meryl Kusyk

DE GRUYTER
MOUTON

ISBN 978-3-11-221392-6
e-ISBN (PDF) 978-3-11-075244-1
e-ISBN (EPUB) 978-3-11-075251-9
ISSN 1861-4248

Library of Congress Control Number: 2023934430

Bibliographic information published by the Deutsche Nationalbibliothek
The Deutsche Nationalbibliothek lists this publication in the Deutsche Nationalbibliografie;
detailed bibliographic data are available on the internet at http://dnb.dnb.de.

© 2025 Walter de Gruyter GmbH, Berlin/Boston
This volume is text- and page-identical with the hardback published in 2023.
Typesetting: Integra Software Services Pvt. Ltd.
Printing and binding: CPI books GmbH, Leck

www.degruyter.com

Contents

Author biographies —— VII

Meryl Kusyk, Geoffrey Sockett, Denyze Toffoli
1 Introduction to Language Learning and Leisure —— 1

Section 1: The nature of informal second language learning

Mark Dressman
2 Toward an anthropology of Informal Digital Learning of English (IDLE) —— 21

Meryl Kusyk
3 Does informal mean implicit? —— 43

Robert Godwin-Jones
4 Smart devices and informal language learning —— 69

Section 2: Language outcomes

Christina Lyrigkou
5 Informal second language learning and EFL learners' spoken use of discourse markers —— 91

Kossi Seto Yibokou
6 Influence of television series on pronunciation —— 121

Section 3: Learner activities

Phil Benson
7 Mapping space, leisure and informal language learning in the lives of international students in Australia —— 143

Marlene Schwarz
8 Learner perspectives on informal L2 vocabulary learning —— 159

Miho Inaba
9 Mediation in informal language learning activities outside of the classroom —— 185

Stefanie Cajka, Ed Griffiths, Nikolay Slavkov, Eva Vetter
10 Linguistic risk-taking and informal language learning in Canada and Austria —— 207

Section 4: Psychological dimensions

Linlin Liu, Ju Seong Lee
11 Why does IDLE make EFL learners gritty? —— 241

Artem Zadorozhnyy, Baohua Yu
12 Preservice English language teachers and informal digital learning of English (IDLE) in Kazakhstan —— 269

Denyze Toffoli
13 Learner profiles and ISLL trajectories —— 291

Section 5: Engagement

Henriette L. Arndt
14 Behaviour, thoughts, and feelings —— 327

Geoffrey Sockett
15 Learner engagement and learner change under lockdown —— 359

Antonie Alm
16 Engaging with L2 Netflix —— 379

Geoffrey Sockett, Denyze Toffoli, Meryl Kusyk
17 Conclusion —— 409

Index —— 425

Author biographies

The majority of the contributors to this volume met initially at the first symposium on Informal Second Language Learning, held at the University of Oxford, UK in August 2018, organised by Henriette Arndt and Christina Lyrigkou. This led to the formation of an ad hoc international research group and eventually the proposal of a symposium for AILA 2020 in Gröningen, Netherlands (which was finally held online in 2021). It is the participants in this symposium who are the contributing authors to this volume. We would like to thank each of them individually for their contribution, as well as Marjolijn Verspoor and the whole of the organising team in Gröningen and finally de Gruyter, who approached us with the book project.

Antonie Alm (PhD, UCLA) is an Associate Professor at the University of Otago (New Zealand), where she teaches German, Intercultural Communication and Computer Assisted Language Learning. Her research interests are in the areas of L2 motivation and engagement, learner autonomy, informal language learning and, more recently, the use of machine translation in language education. Antonie is a member of several editorial review boards and serves as associate editor for CALL Journal and JALT CALL Journal. She is also vice-president of the New Zealand German Teachers' Association.

Henriette L. Arndt is a Postdoctoral Research Fellow at the Lund University Humanities Lab (Sweden). Before taking up her current position, she received a DPhil in Education and an MSc in Applied Linguistics and Second Language Acquisition from the University of Oxford, as well as a BA (Hons) in Liberal Arts and Sciences from Amsterdam University College. Dr. Arndt's research is focused on how individuals use and experience different languages in their everyday lives, with the goal of helping learners and educators to better understand informal practices in second language learning. She is particularly interested in the role of attitudes, motivation, and attention in informal learning. A big part of her work has also been methodological, focusing on the development and application of innovative quantitative and mixed research methods.

Phil Benson is a Professor in Applied Linguistics, and former Director of the Multilingualism Research Centre at Macquarie University in Sydney (Australia). His current research interests are in the spatial dimensions of language mobility and second language learning. He has published widely on autonomy and language learning beyond the classroom and is author of a recent Multilingual Matters book, *Language Learning Environments: Spatial Perspectives on SLA* (2021).

Stefanie Cajka is a Doctoral Candidate in Linguistics and she is currently working at the Language Teaching and Learning Research Unit (Centre for Teacher Education, University of Vienna, Austria). Her research interests include linguistic risk-taking, language learning environments, informal language learning, language teaching and learning research, and multilingualism.

Mark Dressman is Professor Emeritus of Curriculum and Instruction at the University of Illinois at Urbana-Champaign (USA). A teacher and researcher of English in both first- and second-language contexts, his interest in informal language learning began as a Fulbright Scholar (2014–2016) studying the English education of Moroccan first-year students in three public universities. He is a former editor of *Research in the Teaching of English* and former Chair of English at Khalifa University in Abu Dhabi, UAE. His most recent publications are the *Handbook of Informal Language Learning* (Dressman & Sadler 2020) and *English Language Learning in the Digital Age: Learner-Driven Strategies for Adolescents and Young Adults* (Dressman, Lee & Perrot 2023).

Author biographies

Robert Godwin-Jones, Ph.D., is Professor of World Languages and International Studies at Virginia Commonwealth University (USA) and past Director of the English Language Program there, as well as Director of the Instructional Development Center (Office of Information Technology). His research is principally in applied linguistics, in the areas of language learning and technology and intercultural communication. Most recently, he has worked in the areas of mobile-assisted language learning, open educational resources, and AI-based, informal language learning. He writes a regular column for the journal *Language Learning & Technology* on emerging technologies. Robert has published five books and numerous articles and book chapters, as well as regularly presenting at international conferences. His most recent book, co-edited with Richard Lin and I.J. Weng (2018) is *Internationalizing English Language Education in Globalized Taiwan*. ORCID: 0000-0002-2377-3204

Ed Griffiths is a Doctoral Candidate in Applied Linguistics at the Department of Education at Concordia University, Montreal (Canada).

Miho Inaba is a Senior Lecturer in Japanese Language at the School of Modern Languages, Cardiff University (UK). She has researched autonomous language learning in out-of-class contexts from the perspectives of sociocultural theory and leaners' motivation, and is the author of *Second Language Literacy Practices and Language Learning Outside the Classroom* (Multilingual Matters 2018). Her research papers have also appeared in *Social Networks in Language Learning and Language Teaching* (Bloomsbury 2020) and in international journals.

Meryl Kusyk is an Applied Linguistics Researcher and Teaching Faculty Member at the Karlsruhe University of Education (Germany). She is also the Director of her university's Language Learning Centre. Her PhD work explored the development of complexity, accuracy and fluency amongst French and German university students as well as their informal activity usage. Her current research interests include Informal Second Language Learning, dynamic usage-based approaches to language learning and affective factors involved in language learning (anxiety, enjoyment).

Ju Seong Lee is Associate Head and Assistant Professor of the Department of English Language Education at the Education University of Hong Kong, specializing in Computer Assisted Language Learning (particularly in Extramural CALL contexts), emotions and motivation in language learning, and English as an International Language. He is the author of *Informal Digital Learning of English: Research to Practice* (Routledge 2022) and a co-author of *English Education in the Digital Age: Learner-Driven Strategies for Adolescents and Young Adults* Dressman, Lee & Perrot 2023.

Linlin Liu is a doctoral student in the Department of English Language Education at the Education University of Hong Kong. Her research interests include Computer Assisted Language Learning, online teaching, and second language emotions.

Christina Lyrigkou has a PhD in Applied Linguistics (Open University, UK) and a MSc in Applied Linguistics and Second Language Acquisition (University of Oxford). The title of her PhD thesis (2021) is: *The role of informal second language learning in the spoken use of discourse markers by Greek adolescent learners of English*. Christina has presented her work in several conferences (AILA, BAAl SIG, EuroCALL, PTSLL) and co-organised the first symposium on Informal Second Language Learning (August 2018, University of Oxford). She is co-owner of an English language learning online platform and school that, among others, provides material for self-study based on informal sources. She is currently working as a materials developer and EFL teacher, informed by the outcomes of her research.

Marlene Schwarz is a secondary school teacher for English as a foreign language, a Researcher in Applied Linguistics and Language Learning, and an external Lecturer in teacher training at the

English department of the University of Vienna (Austria), where she also obtained her PhD. Her main interests lie in the areas of informal second language learning and vocabulary acquisition, for which she tries to combine both her research and teaching experience.

Nikolay Slavkov is a Professor at the Official Languages and Bilingualism Institute of the University of Ottawa (Canada) and Director of the Canadian Centre for Research and Studies in Bilingualism and Language Planning. He is interested in bilingualism and multilingualism from various perspectives, including social, pedagogical, linguistic, cognitive, and technological.

Geoffrey Sockett is Professor of Language Sciences at Université Paris-Cité (France) where he currently serves as Director of the Department of Language Sciences. His research interests include the Online Informal Learning of English, Complexity Theory and Course design for language learning. Author of *The Online Informal Learning of English* (Palgrave Macmillan 2014), he has published and spoken widely on the theme of Informal learning over the past ten years.

Denyze Toffoli is Professor of English and Applied linguistics at the Université Toulouse III – Paul Sabatier (France). She was previously Director of Institution-wide language provision (10 language centres) and Director of the Department of Applied Linguistics and Language Didactics at the Université de Strasbourg. She has published extensively on language learning and teaching in both French and English. Her primary research interests concern the individual learner and the interface between informal language learning and formal structures that can encourage autonomous lifelong foreign language practices. Her latest book is *Informal Learning and Institution-wide Language Provision: University Language Learners in the 21st Century* (Palgrave Macmillan 2020). ORCID: 0000-0002-0879-8761.

Eva Vetter has been a Professor of Language Teaching and Learning at the University of Vienna (Austria) since 2011. She is particularly interested in multilingualism with respect to linguistic minorities, historical multilingualism, language policy and language teaching and learning. Since 2010 she has been focussing more on educational aspects of multilingualism. http://homepage.univie.ac.at/eva.vetter/php/wordpress/

Kossi Seto Yibokou (Ph.D, University of Strasbourg, France) is an Associate Professor in English for Specialists of Other Disciplines at the University of Lorraine (Nancy, France) and is a member of the ATILF Laboratory (Didactique des langues et Sociolinguistique Team). The main focus of his research is the impact of informal activities on language learning (especially English), from a socio-phonetic-phonological point of view (pronunciation, accent, identity). He is also interested in technology-assisted language teaching and learning.

Baohua Yu is an Associate Professor at Lingnan University, Hong Kong. Her research focuses on digital storytelling, intercultural communication competence, cross-cultural psychology of international students, and technology-enhanced teaching and learning. Her work has been published in leading international journals such as *Re-CALL, Journal of Multilingual and Multicultural Development, Language Teaching, International Journal of Intercultural Relations and Higher Education*. lucyyu@ln.edu.hk

Artem Zadorozhnyy is a Postdoctoral Fellow at the Education University of Hong Kong. His research interests include the role of digital affordances in the linguistic development of EFL students, informal digital language learning, out-of-class language learning activities and the role of motivation in predicting positive academic and linguistic outcomes. He is also interested in research on the development of students' L2 digital literacies.

Meryl Kusyk, Geoffrey Sockett, Denyze Toffoli

1 Introduction to Language Learning and Leisure

Abstract: The introduction to *Language Learning and Leisure* provides two reviews of the literature in this area, overviewing first the field to date and second the contributions to the book itself. We begin with a short etymologically-based explanation of the choice of title of the book and a brief history of the genesis of the volume. The review of the field to date examines literature touching on informal or leisure-related language acquisition since the early examples in the 1980's and 90's. It analyses past publications according to five categories: what informal language learners do, where they do it, the prevalence of English, what is learnt (language development) and the relationship of informal and leisure learning to other types of learning. The presentation of the contributing chapters follows the organisation of the book, presenting the nature of informal second language learning and informal second language learning research, research into language outcomes, learner activities and strategies, psychological dimensions of informal second language learning and more specifically engagement.

Keywords: informal second language learning, leisure, informal practices, informal environments, learner activities, online / digital learning, English vs. other languages, language development, learning outcomes, review of the field

1 Introduction

The Liddell and Scott Greek lexicon[1] offers several insights into the origins of the word *leisure* (σχολή – *schole*). The primary descriptions offered (leisure, rest, idleness) seem, at first glance, to somewhat contrast with the secondary descriptions given (that in which leisure is employed, learned discussion, disputation, lecture . . . a group to whom lectures are given, school). It is interesting indeed that "school" should appear as an example of a place of leisure. However, considering the full

---

[1] http://www.perseus.tufts.edu/hopper/text?doc=Perseus:text:1999.04.0057:entry=sxolh/

Meryl Kusyk, Karlsruhe Univ of Education, Germany
Geoffrey Sockett, Univ Paris Cité, France
Denyze Toffoli, Univ Toulouse III – Paul Sabatier, France

https://doi.org/10.1515/9783110752441-001

spectrum of this lexicon entry we may infer the journey from "leisure" to "school" more clearly: time allowing for rest or idleness also allows for intellectual activity, which may lead to discussing ideas, rhetorical debate, the development of philosophies and worldviews, which over time may become sufficiently sophisticated so as to be associated with a physical place: a school. That the primary and secondary descriptions strike us as incongruent serves as a reminder that in the present age, school is most often thought of in the category of work and that intellectual undertakings are assumed to be distinct from relaxation and leisure.

One of Liddell and Scott's references in Plato's Laws finds Clinias and the Athenian discussing the study of physical sciences and mathematics in the following terms:

> Athenian: People should be setting problems like these for one another, competing in activities that are valuable to them, a much more refined pastime (σχολή – *schole: leisure*) for old men than draughts.
> Clinias: No doubt. After all there is not a great deal of difference between draughts and these subjects. (Paraphrased from *Laws* 7:820:c-d)[2]

While a leisure pursuit such as draughts may be helpful for certain mathematical reasoning skills, the central reflection of this book will be on the affordances of leisure activities for second language learning. With the relationship between study and play as a starting point for a collection of chapters on language learning and leisure, it may be helpful to keep in mind the following questions: Philosophically, to what extent are leisure and schooling, free time and learning, all part of the same system? How do listening to music, watching videos or playing video games – widespread leisure activities for many young people today – contribute to the process of developing an additional language?

The study of informal involvement with additional languages has emerged as a relevant area of research within SLA. With the rapid development and spread of internet-based technologies, contact with foreign languages outside the classroom has become commonplace, even for learners who cannot study abroad and may never have travelled. While this contact can take multiple forms, online contents are a major driving force because they present learners with unprecedented opportunities for exposure to and use of target languages, regardless of their physical location. The literature concerning informal language learning has grown substantially over the past decade and in 2018 an inaugural conference was organized by Henriette Arndt and Christina Lyrigkou at the University of Oxford entitled *(In)formal L2 learning: Integrating informal practices into formal contexts*. This first gathering of researchers was followed by a symposium at the AILA 2021 World

---

[2] http://www.perseus.tufts.edu/hopper/text?doc=Perseus%3Atext%3A1999.01.0166%3Abook%3D7

Congress of Applied Linguistics, *Learning through leisure: Informal L2 learning in the 21st century*. Serving as a venue for discussions on the current state of the field, the symposium also acted as a catalyst for the creation of this book.

As research in this area has grown over the past decade, so too has the variety of labels used to describe informal involvement with languages. Readers may be familiar, for example, with Online Informal Learning of English (OILE), Informal Digital Learning of English (IDLE) or Extramural English (EE). For the present volume we have chosen Informal Second Language Learning (ISLL), initially coined by Henriette Arndt (2019), as an umbrella term for these different varieties, each of which examines informal language usage from a particular perspective or within a certain context. OILE, IDLE and EE, for example, all identify phenomena linked specifically to the learning of English. In addition, OILE and IDLE are restricted to digital environments while EE includes both face-to-face interactions as well as the use of traditional media. In any collection of studies from a wide variety of contexts, such as here, it is important to be as terminologically inclusive as possible. Therefore, broader notions of learning "out of class" or "beyond the classroom", which may offer a more substantial role for teacher-suggested activities, also have their place in some of the studies presented under the ISLL umbrella. Nonetheless, the central idea of learning through leisure, suggesting learner agency and enjoyment in exploring the affordances of materials not specifically designed for learning, should be kept in mind when taking this collection as a whole.

In the following pages, we will present two overviews: firstly of informal second language learning in general, including its historical developments and some of its more significant publications; secondly of the chapters included in this volume, explaining the rationale behind the groupings and order of inclusion.

2 Overview of the field

A review of previous ISLL literature will give insights into the current state of research in the field. Since non-native speakers around the world increasingly have access to their additional languages through online leisure content and interactions, researchers who may have limited their study of SLA to the classroom in the past are now expanding their realm of investigation beyond the formal sphere. However, we would be remiss to assume that studies on language learning in leisure contexts are limited to this recent wave of research. For example, Spada (1986) compared informal interactive contact in an ESL context, such as conversations, with purely receptive exposure, such as watching television programs. She found that the informal interactive contact correlated to greater speaking fluency and improvement in grammatical fluency, especially when the interactions took place in multiple contexts. Within an EFL context, Pickard (1996) queried German L1 secondary students on their out-of-class activities and found that they favoured reading and listening activities as opposed to production activities such as speaking and writing. They also selected their activities based on personal preference rather than on teacher recommendation. Murphy (2005) investigated adult French, German & Spanish learners' exposure to their target languages outside of class and inventoried the activities they engaged in. She also noted students' tendency to focus on meaning as opposed to form during their usage events, as well as some students' wishes for more easily accessible content in the L2. Murphy concluded by affirming the role of informal activities as a "recognised and valued aspect of study" (2005: 311). Finally, Murray (2008) reported on the language learning stories of adult Japanese EFL learners who eventually became intermediate to advanced level English users. Through their life narratives, participants underscored the prominent role that popular culture played in their language development outside of the classroom.

While it is clear that informal language learning has been studied in the past, in the last 10–15 years it has become an area of research in its own right, with an increasing number of both publications and thematic strands in conferences appearing each year across the globe. Its propulsion can largely be attributed to the proliferation of broadband internet access as well as the arrival and growth of mobile technologies.

The major preoccupations of ISLL research will be reviewed briefly in the following pages. These may be categorised as what informal learners do and how they do it (activities, practices, habits, strategies, techniques, sources and usage), where they do it (informal landscapes, contexts, environments), the place of English (as related to other languages), the nature of the language development that ensues and the relationship between informal and other learning contexts.

2.1 What informal learners do and how they do it

Activities, practices, habits, sources and usage all touch on language users' involvement with the L2. These terms may refer to a certain type of activity (gaming, viewing films, series or videos, reading, social networking, writing fan fiction, listening to music, etc.) or the nature of that activity (productive, receptive, oral, written). Much of the initial research into ISLL sought to inventory these different activities and observe patterns such as the predominance of receptive over productive activities, frequency of activity use or the occurrence of informal usage profiles (Sundqvist 2009; Toffoli and Sockett 2010; Kusyk 2017).

Early ISLL research identified a broad range of informal practices as well as high frequencies of usage, alerting researchers to the arrival of a genuine phenomenon rather than just the favored pastimes of certain enthusiastic outliers. These initial findings also revealed a wide variety of informal user profiles and activity preferences, foreshadowing the complexity involved in investigating ISLL and its myriad variables. Current ISLL research may now shift its focus to the numerous individual pathways taken by learners on their L2 usage journeys. Toffoli (2020) began to examine this in association with several individual difference variables and continues that exploration in her chapter here. Important insights have also been offered by Sundqvist and Sylvén's (2016: 139) EE House, illustrating differing levels of effort involved in different activities, or Muñoz's (2020) study of the activities predominantly engaged in according to gender.

What informal learners do may also touch on individual practices, habits and usage – terms that have been used in the literature to refer to techniques or strategies employed by users in order to take charge of or influence their own learning. Much of this can be found under the label of, or in relation to, the concept of autonomy (Chan 2016, Hyland 2004, Lyrigkou 2019, Toffoli 2020). Some research has focused specifically on diversity of activities as an indicator of how such learners proceed (Ibatova 2019, Lee 2019a). Lai & Gu (2011) found that participants in their study "reported using a variety of technologies selectively to fulfill various learning purposes and needs at different stages of their learning" (326). Another example examining the "hows" of ISLL is provided by Ibrahim et al (2014) who found that "powerful shared intentions and thoughts guide actions, shared practice and sociocultural mediation" (29) in the strategic use of web-based material by 400 Indonesian university students to advance their English-language proficiency. Sundqvist & Sylvén (2014) have looked specifically at the self-reported strategies of digital gamers as related to speaking English. The complexity of how users avail themselves of the affordances provided by authentic L2 materials outside the classroom is only beginning to be explored in detail and this book will provide several examples that examine these individual differences further.

2.2 Where they do it

Research on ISLL has been conducted in many countries, including Austria (Trinder 2017; Schwarz 2020), Brazil (Cole and Vanderplank 2016), China (Lai 2017) Denmark (Hannibal Jensen 2016), France (Sockett 2014; Kusyk 2017; Yibokou 2019; Toffoli 2020), Germany (Kusyk 2017; Arndt 2019), Greece (Lyrigkou 2019), Hong Kong (Benson

2015), Kazakhstan (Zodorozhnyy 2022), Morocco (Dressman 2020), New Zealand (Alm 2015), Norway (Brevik 2019), Slovenia (Jurkovič 2019), South Korea (Lee 2019b; Pooley, Midgley and Farley 2019) and Sweden (Sundqvist 2009). While geographic location determines certain aspects of usage (internet quality or restrictions, explicit or implicit censorship, digital practices within communities), other locational terms are more conceptual than purely geographical, such as *landscape, ecology* or *environment*. The notion of environment is helpful in suggesting that informal practices occur in a system of exposure and interactions unique to each learner. From an ecological perspective, this personalized environment is not isolated but rather in constant interaction and overlap with other areas of the learner's routines, surroundings and community (Godwin-Jones 2019). Some researchers have taken a complex and dynamic systems view of informal L2 development and accordingly characterise the process of learning as navigation through a landscape of attractor and repeller states (states that the L2 system gravitates towards and resists, respectively, sometimes visualized metaphorically as valleys and hills – Kusyk 2017; Godwin-Jones 2018; Toffoli 2020). Finally, the different states of a system and the system's corresponding behavior may be influenced by the location or context, such as work, school or home, in which they are played out (Benson 2021).

The notion of place also underlies a variety of individual preferences. Many learners view informal learning as an opportunity to be alone in their own private worlds, even when surrounded by others on public transport for example. Others see informal activities as taking place in essentially social spaces where games are played together, media are shared and even viewing is discussed with friends. Virtual space has increasingly become a focus of study alongside that of physical space in language learning. Lamb and Murray's (2018) review of space, place and autonomy, and Benson's (2021) in-depth examination of spatial perspectives in SLA go some way to developing an understanding of how *spaces with the potential for learning* (such as public transportation with cell-phone connectivity) become *places for learning* (that is, places which learners target as functional for learning) as L2 users inhabit and travel through them, transforming and individualising them.

2.3 Why English and what about other languages?

The specificities of particular languages in relation to informal learning are another key dimension of this field of research. Indeed, the widespread geographical influence of English and its economic and socio-politial role in global affairs have also endowed it with a predominant cultural role throughout most of the world through music, audio-visual and other media. This means that much research into informal language learning relates to English. In the growing field of vlogging, leading YouTube channels such as *PewDiePie* or *Nikki Tutorials* are produced in English by highly proficient second language users (in this case Swedish and Dutch vloggers). Other languages with a strong cultural presence in the media, such as Japanese (Manga, Anime) or Korean (K-pop, K-dramas), have received attention (Armour and Iida 2016), while Spanish, in particular through the popularity of Telenovelas, is also an area of interest (Lerner 2013). Sundqvist (2020) mentions the learning of French, German, Spanish, Chinese, Japanese, Korean, Russian and Norwegian via informal and leisure-related activities.

Some studies that focus on languages other than English (Scholz 2017 and Vosburg 2017 for learning German; Silva and Brougère 2017 or Peters et al. 2019 for French), tend to be characterised by greater teacher involvement and may indeed even lean towards the category of formal learning using authentic documents. In the present volume, the majority of chapters concern English, but Japanese (Inaba), French (Cajka et al.) and German (Alm, Cajka et al.) are also studied as target languages. Although these examples may involve teacher-suggested or teacher-initiated activities, they aim to foster learner autonomy directly, acting as bridging activities that both connect classroom learners to the world beyond and bring authentic L2 usage habits into the formal sphere.

When viewed through the prism of individual preferences, the role of English as compared to other languages again reveals disparity. The mediating role of English to help negotiate the "linguistic distance" (Muñoz 2018) between two other languages was also acknowledged by Sockett (2014), whose informants reported learning some English when viewing Korean series with English subtitles, when subtitles in their own language did not exist. In this volume, Inaba explores the mediating role of English for Swedish learners of Japanese. Other individual choices can be observed with regard to captions and subtitling, for example, varying subtitle choice based on the type of show, viewing context or level of fatigue on a given day, as mentioned by Lyrigkou, Yibokou, Inaba and Alm in the present volume.

2.4 What they learn

As the term suggests, *Informal Second Language Learning* implies some kind of link between exposure to a target language and its subsequent development. It is therefore unsurprising that many studies have sought to investigate, characterise and quantify informal L2 users' language development. While measurement of language learning in a classroom setting may offer a degree of certainty and control for researchers, measuring development from informal contexts is challenging for a range of reasons, not least of which being that each learner is exposed to a unique range of inputs and interactions over a potentially long period of time and that they carry out their activities in private contexts.

Answering the question "why do some informal L2 users appear to learn more than others?" will likely be a focus of research into ISLL for many years to come. Indeed, this question is at the heart of the exploration of individual differences undertaken in this book. The contributions here do not study individual differences merely to see how different people develop the same skills, but more importantly to examine why so many develop them only partially and in such different ways. To be sure, these questions have been at the heart of SLA research since enquiry into the good language learner came to prominence nearly half a century ago (Naiman 1975). A complex range of internal and external factors means that each learner develops differently and recent studies have sought to explore this issue. For example, Kusyk's (2017) longitudinal case study revealed highly individualized learning trajectories and fluctuating levels of development with regard to informal learners' L2 complexity, accuracy and fluency. Other studies have aimed to identify the impact of factors such as time on task and opportunity to communicate on language development (Las Vergnas 2017), while Arndt (2019), Peng, Jager and Lowie (2021) and Lee (2022) have sought to develop models to express the relative impacts of a variety of individual factors on informal learning outcomes. Different chapters in this volume pay specific attention to engagement (Arndt, Sockett, Alm), grit and L2 enjoyment (Liu and Lee), beliefs and identities (Zadorozhnyy and Yu) and autonomy, competence and attachment (Toffoli).

2.5 Relationship to other forms of learning

As many individuals carry double L2 identities – those of both informal and classroom learners – the question of the relationship between formal and informal learning inevitably presents itself. While circumstances exist where there is little shared interface between the two realms (for example Cole and Vanderplank 2016), many teachers are confronted with an ever-growing number of students who are exposed to and interact with the L2 in their free time (Godwin-Jones 2019; Moffat 2022). Though some teachers appear to be unaware of the extent to which their students participate in informal activities (Toffoli and Sockett 2015), or even doubt the potential of such input for L2 development (see Zadorozhnyy and Yu, this volume), others seek out such activities and attempt to build bridges between the two spheres (Nunan and Richards 2015). The teacher's role in informal learning could be conceptualized along a scale of involvement, ranging from expressing general statements that acknowledge informal practices, to encouraging or inciting students to engage with them, to providing concrete suggestions or demonstrating how to use certain resources. Other approaches may include efforts to integrate informal practice or informal content into the classroom itself, including through bridging activities (Thorne and Reinhardt 2008; Reinhardt and Ryu 2013). For terminological clarity within the field, however, researchers and teachers should specify where the notional boundary between formal, non-formal[3] and informal is to be placed when designing their research or teaching scenarios (see Alm's reflection on "intraformal" in this volume).

In some cases, activities prescribed by teachers may resemble those which learners either already engage in of their own volition or could choose to engage in for pleasure. However, the learner's approach to viewing a video or playing an online game when asked to do so by a teacher is likely to be more form-focused, while doing this as a leisure activity usually implies a focus on meaning. There may also be (positive or negative) affective consequences to teacher-initiated activities, as suggested by Lee and Drajati (2019) and taken up in Liu and Lee's chapter in this volume.

Some researchers have questioned whether informal activities involving authentic materials (for example video tutorials about economics) and non-formal activities (learning applications such as Babbel or Duolingo) are similar enough in nature to be studied as a single phenomenon (Lai 2017). This question reflects the debate around the deliberate or incidental nature of informal learning. It is clearly possible to use materials from an informal context as learning resources, as every teacher has done when using authentic documents. The issue is to what extent this is done in an explicit attempt to learn the target language, or whether the focus of most informal activities, as suggested by the title of this book, is leisure. In the case of the latter, language acquisition resulting from the activity would seemingly be characterized as incidental, a by-product of understanding the contents of the materials involved. Alternatively, if ISLL can predominantly be described as a deliberate approach to self-directed autonomous learning, then it may be relevant to consider it alongside the use of non-formal learning applications. Kusyk extensively explores such questions related to the nature of learning in ISLL in her contribution here.

Many researchers in this field are also language teachers or teacher trainers, and as such, may observe the impact of the informal on the formal in daily classroom interactions. As mentioned above, informal activities may be targeted, suggested or encouraged by teachers as a means to improve the learners' L2. Current

---

[3] A framework designed for learning that takes place outside the classroom, such as a sports club, or, from an ISLL perspective, mobile applications specifically designed for language learning.

literature also suggests that the focus of contemporary formal L2 learning should be to facilitate access to the world of informal practices awaiting the learner at the end of their school day or academic degree (Sockett 2020; Toffoli 2020; Toffoli this volume; Alm this volume).

Whichever perspective is most resonant for a particular reader, it is clear that the influential role of a foreign language in the leisure activities of informal language learners represents an opportunity which teachers of other subjects – wishing that their students would engage with mathematics or geography content "for fun" in their free time – can only dream of.

3 Overview of the chapters

In the context of the overview presented above, this book begins by seeking to understand what is meant by informal learning. The three chapters under the heading "Nature of ISLL and ISLL research" are therefore an ideal starting point to situate ISLL within a range of theoretical and methodological perspectives in social science research.

3.1 The nature of ISLL and ISLL research

Mark Dressman's chapter "Toward an Anthropology of Informal Digital Learning of English" invites the reader to take up the tools of anthropology in order to develop the qualitative study of informal language learning, obtaining "thick" descriptions of individual practices in the field. It explores the epistemological positioning of ISLL research and argues for the use of qualitative approaches. Dressman details six qualities of ethnographic research that can be central to IDLE inquiries and proposes justifications for what many consider its weaknesses. Finally, he indicates how general knowledge can be constructed from this type of narrative. The chapter contains helpful methodological examples from the author's own experiences in Morocco. The reader will find several further examples of such qualitative approaches in chapters 7–10, 12–13, 15 and 16.

Meryl Kusyk's reflection "Does informal mean implicit? Exploring the nature of ISLL" offers a cognitivist foray into the essence of informal language learning itself. It presents a comprehensive overview of the constructs of implicit, explicit and incidental learning, before delving into the literature on five current denominations of ISLL (Online Informal Learning of English, Extramural English, etc.). The learning constructs are then juxtaposed with the ISLL varieties in an attempt to identify which type(s) of learning may be most prominent within each variety. Kusyk advocates for greater emphasis both on terminological clarity and the nature of the informal learning process, which she claims to be essential in this still emerging field.

In chapter 4, Robert Godwin-Jones focuses on the technological dimensions of ISLL, examining how recent advances such as Intelligent Personal Assistants (IPAs) can become part of the new and ever-changing terrain of informal additional language development. Giving detailed explanations of the affordances of these new technologies, he analyses their potential to meet both language acquisition and communication needs and situates them with regard to different theoretical SLA frameworks. Godwin-Jones reviews several studies where aspects of these intelligent technologies were tested with learners and examines the relevance and feasibility of future developments that have been suggested in the literature.

3.2 Language outcomes

The broad question of language outcomes is key to SLA-focused informal learning studies. Beyond viewing ISLL as a series of interesting activities in a variety of foreign languages, seeking to measure what may and may not be learned informally is a difficult but essential endeavour. Two important examinations of outcomes related to speaking are presented in these chapters. Christina Lyrigkou's study of pragmatic development, in particular discourse markers (DM), is a welcome addition to a field which has often focused on lexical acquisition as the primary outcome of informal exposure. Through the study of DM acquisitions, Lyrigkou also returns to the intentional/incidental and explicit/implicit debates analysed by Kusyk, bringing persuasive examples to illustrate her arguments. In common with Yibokou's chapter, which follows, Lyrigkou looks at the extent to which the orality of informal exposure can be detected in the language learners' speech.

Kossi Seto Yibokou's study of the influence of informal exposure on pronunciation also fills a long-standing gap in ISLL research. Returning first to a long-time hotly-debated topic among phoneticians as to whether media-viewing influences accent, he then studies ten specific markers of General American and Received Pronunciation British accents in learner speech. Like Lyrigkou and others, he also compares his results with learners' declared informal activities to seek potential relationships between practices and language outcomes. His overall findings highlight the large degree of variability in pronunciation on both an inter and intra-individual basis. For those researchers who adhere to a complex, dynamic systems approach to learning, these findings underscore the relevance of such a perspective.

3.3 Learner activities and strategies

Including research which does not relate exclusively to digital or online learning allows space for studies which take place within physical mobility contexts such as study abroad or migration, yet the nature of modern life is such that digital media interactions are inevitably present even in these circumstances. Chapters 7 through 10 offer examples of how learners go about their informal language development, examining both the strategies they employ and, in the cases of chapters 7 and 10, the importance of both physical and technological contexts.

In chapter 7, Phil Benson analyses the space through which informal learners move in a study-abroad context, offering insights into physical mobility rather than only the virtual mobility which so often characterises informal learning research. Following students around virtually in their daily geographical routines brings to light the particular difficulties international students face when seeking to maximise and seise L2 affordances, even in an environment that is assumed to be a linguistic immersion experience. Benson specifically addresses the question of leisure activities and finds that study-abroad students often lack the time and opportunities for leisure that may be more available to study-at-home students. The role that digital media takes on in the maintenance of contact with native languages and friends and families "back home", as well as the specific applications that are used for navigating life in a foreign country are quite different from those used by learners of the same language in at-home (EFL) learning contexts. As such, this study widens the scope of ISLL research to include the particular experience of the informal language learner abroad.

In chapter 8, Marlene Schwarz explores in detail how adolescent learners of English in Vienna approach vocabulary acquisition through ISLL. Via a series of in-depth group interviews, she focuses on learners' voices as they explain what vocabulary they pay attention to (or not), the strategies that they employ for comprehension and retention and how the new vocabulary from informal sources interfaces with that encountered in school. Beyond bringing significant new insights to ISLL, this study also points to new directions for studies in vocabulary acquisition, indicating qualitative methodologies for emic insights into learner experience as a necessary complement to more traditional quantitative research.

Miho Inaba's chapter (9) "Mediation in L2-related activities outside of the classroom: Case studies of learners of Japanese" invites the reader to use the lens of activity theory to understand learning outside the classroom. This perspective focuses more closely on the mediating artefacts which are at the heart of ISLL. The examples offered are drawn from five Swedish learners of Japanese and show the use of images from Mangas or Japanese-language subtitles from Anime as examples of such mediating artefacts. Of particular interest is the mediating role of a proficient L2 (in this case English) for the learning of a more linguistically distant L3 (Japanese).

In chapter 10, Stefanie Cajka, Ed Griffiths, Nikolay Slavkov and Eva Vetter, like Benson, also examine immersion and semi-immersion study contexts, and, like the other authors in this section, also examine *how* learners go about their out-of-class language learning, specifically addressing risk-taking and enlarging the scope of self-initiated risks. To do so they report on the development and use of a pedagogical initiative to encourage risk-taking for language development. The concept of physical and virtual mobility is taken one step further as the creation and implementation of a mobile application for student self-management of their own language risk-taking is explored. Their description of the iterative process of research and development to create the application itself reveals a particular attention to inclusion of learner perspectives. The project also highlights the nature of bridging activities that can be created to instigate engagement and life-long practices with additional languages.

3.4 Psychological dimensions

Varieties of context as well as both individual and social factors lead to the multifaceted manifestations of ISLL. This means both variability in learning outcomes, as seen in chapters 5 and 6 and in techniques and practices, as seen in chapters 7 through 10. In the remaining chapters, we will see how individual difference variables such as learner identity, motivation, autonomy, enjoyment, grit and engagement intrinsically differentiate learners from each other and how these differences impact their L2 learning. Chapters 14 through 16 specifically investigate the construct of engagement as it relates to additional language development in the informal sphere.

In chapter 11, Linlin Liu and Ju Seong Lee examine the relations between IDLE, enjoyment of the process of learning the target language and grit, which can be seen as the persistence necessary to continue the learning process. Working with data from 656 freshman students in mainland China, the authors take a quantitative approach to testing three hypotheses. Using Structural Equation Modelling, they demonstrate that L2 enjoyment in general mediated the relationship between IDLE and grit, but that classroom L2 enjoyment did not play such a mediating role. Their results suggest that EFL learners tend to exert more effort in learning English when their L2 enjoyment is enhanced through practice using IDLE activities. This positive link between IDLE and grit may indicate that learners who engage in IDLE more frequently are more likely to remain passionate and persist in learning and mastering the English language. It may also give some indications to teachers as to how to encourage language acquisition through enjoyable leisure activities in the target language.

In chapter 12, Artem Zadorozhnyy and Baohua Yu work specifically with the unique population of informal learners training to be language teachers in Khazakstan. While their results support many existing findings concerning learners improving their English using informal sources, they also uncover surprising contradictions in how some future teachers regard (or minimise) the importance of these activities for language development. Zadorozhnyy and Yu point to elements concerning teacher beliefs and ISLL, which should undoubtedly be addressed in L2 teacher training programmes, not just for English nor in central Asia alone.

Using a self-determination theory framework which she links to other psychological theories, Denyze Toffoli (chapter 13) examines articulations between several individual difference indicators linked to motivation (principally autonomy, attachment, self-direction and existing language skills) and learners' individual trajectories through the irregular (metaphorical) landscape of ISLL. She looks closely at the learning paths of nine students learning English in France and attempts to identify more general profiles of informal language learners, while recognising the eminently personal aspect of each of these trajectories.

3.5 Engagement

Henriette Arndt's work (chapter 14), introduces the construct of engagement, giving a thorough review of the literature in this area and enriching the three traditional vectors of cognitive, behavioural and affective engagement with a fourth, linguistic engagement. The latter can be seen as what has elsewhere been identified as "focus-on-form". Using a large-scale mixed-methods study Arndt examines the nature of these engagement dimensions with secondary school learners of English in Germany and teases out the different ways in which the four dimensions interact with each other. Her findings attest to the highly variable nature of engagement in ISLL even in a relatively homogenous population.

Geoffrey Sockett (chapter 15), also refers to the engagement construct to study how French university learners of English did or did not modify their practices of ISLL during the first Covid-19 lockdown. He sees the instances of such change as pivotal "phase transitions" in the dynamic system of additional language development. However, where Arndt distinguishes between cognitive and linguistic engagement, Sockett conflates the two and adds a social engagement dimension. His findings confirm both the relevance of engagement as a conceptual tool for understanding ISLL and, once again, the variability present in all such studies of individual differences.

In chapter 16, Antonie Alm also looks specifically at the role of engagement in the language learning process and introduces the notion of "willingness to engage." In contrast to the previous two authors, she analyses the learning of German by native English speakers, through an examination of how two very different students engage with Netflix. Finally, she defines a notion of *intraformal* learning, based on the satisfaction of the three basic needs of self-determination theory (autonomy, competence and relatedness) as a means to reconcile teacher-initiated pedagogy with learner-engaged activities. She sees such *intraformal* learning as a new "pedagogy of wellbeing" whose finality, rather than simply measurable additional language development, would be personal growth. In this, Alm seems to deconstruct the duality between formal and informal learning, situating the ultimate purpose of all learning in a lifelong and lifewide dimension that far exceeds the practicalities of communication, to enhance the self of the learner.

4 Conclusion

As the field of Informal Second Language Learning continues on its trajectory, new questions, themes and challenges are sure to arise. No longer in the early stages of ISLL research where findings overwhelmingly focused on activity type and frequency of use, this volume underscores issues such as methodological and theoretical approaches, the nature of informal learning, language learning outcomes, learning strategies and techniques and individual difference variables. Although the chapters have been grouped thematically, they do not represent a linear path and the reader could profitably approach them in order of preference. As editors, we hope that your reading will be a leisurely stroll deeper into the world of ISLL.

References

Alm, Antonie. 2015. Facebook for informal language learning: Perspectives from tertiary language students. *The Eurocall Review* 23(2). 3–18.

Arndt, Henriette L. 2019. *Informal second language learning: The role of engagement, proficiency, attitudes, and motivation*. Oxford: Oxford University Dissertation. https://ora.ox.ac.uk/objects/uuid:c579077d-61fd-4b94-bd57-de7063389122

Armour, William S. & Sumiko Iida. 2016. Are Australian fans of anime and manga motivated to learn Japanese language? *Asia Pacific Journal of Education* 36(1). 31–47.

Benson, Phil. 2015. Commenting to learn: Evidence of language and intercultural learning in comments on YouTube videos. *Language Learning & Technology* 19(3). 88–105.

Benson, Phil. 2021. *Language Learning Environments: Spatial Perspectives on SLA. Language Learning Environments*. Bristol: Multilingual Matters.

Brevik, Lisbeth. 2019. Gamers, Surfers, Social Media Users: Unpacking the role of interest in English. *Journal of Computer Assisted Learning* 35(5). 595–606.

Chan, Hoi Wing. 2016. Popular culture, English out-of-class activities, and learner autonomy among highly proficient secondary students in Hong Kong. *Universal Journal of Educational Research* 4(8). 1918–1923.

Cole, Jason & Robert Vanderplank. 2016. Comparing autonomous and class-based learners in Brazil: Evidence for the present-day advantages of informal, out-of-class learning. *System* 61. 31–42.

Dressman, Mark. 2020. Informal English learning among Moroccan youth. In Mark Dressman & Randall Sadler (eds.), *The Handbook of Informal Language Learning*, 303–318. Hoboken/Chichester: Wiley-Blackwell.

Godwin-Jones, Robert. 2018. Chasing the butterfly effect: Informal language learning online as a complex system. *Language Learning & Technology* 22(2). 8–27.

Godwin-Jones, Robert. 2019. Riding the digital wilds: Learner autonomy and informal language learning. *Language Learning & Technology* 23(1). 8–25.

Hannibal Jensen, Signe. 2016. Gaming as an English Language Learning Resource among Young Children in Denmark. *CALICO Journal* 34(1). 1–19.

Hyland, Fiona. 2004. Learning autonomously: Contextualising out-of-class English language learning. *Language Awareness* 13(3). 180–202.

Ibrahim, Che Wan Ida Rahimah, Vaughn Prain & Penelope Collet. 2014. Perceived learning strategies of Malaysian university students in web 2.0-based English as a second language informal learning. *GEMA Online Journal of Language Studies* 14(01). 29–42.

Jurkovič, Violeta. 2019. Online informal learning of English through smartphones in Slovenia. *System* 80. 27–37.

Kusyk, Meryl. 2017. *Les dynamiques du développement de l'anglais au travers d'activités informelles en ligne: une étude exploratoire auprès d'étudiants français et allemands.* [The dynamics of L2 English development through participation in online informal activities: an exploratory study of French and German university students.] Strasbourg: University of Strasbourg dissertation. https://phka.bsz-bw.de/frontdoor/deliver/index/docId/116/file/Kusyk_dynamiques_du_d%c3%a9veloppement_de_l'anglais_au_travers_d'activit%c3%a9s_informelles_en_ligne.pdf

Lai, Chun. 2017. *Autonomous Language Learning with Technology Beyond the Classroom*. NY: Bloomsbury Publishing.

Lai, Chun & Mingyue Gu. 2011. Self-regulated out-of-class language learning with technology. *Computer Assisted Language Learning* 24(4). 317–335.

Lamb, Terry & Garold Murray. 2018. Space, place and autonomy in language learning: An introduction. In Garold Murray & Terry Lamb (eds.), *Space, place and autonomy in language learning* (Routledge Research in Language Education), 1–6. Abingdon/New York: Routledge.

Las Vergnas, Olivier. 2017. Le e-learning informel? Des apprentissages diffus, noyés dans la participation en ligne. Symposium presented at the conference *La e-formation des adultes et des jeunes adultes*, Lille, 3–5 June, 2017.

Lee, Ju Seong. 2019a. Quantity and diversity of informal digital learning of English. *Language Learning & Technology* 23(1). 114–126.

Lee, Ju Seong. 2019b. An Emerging path to English in Korea: Informal digital learning of English. In Mark Dressman & Randall Sadler (eds.), *The Handbook of Informal Language Learning*, 289–301. Hoboken/Chichester: Wiley-Blackwell.

Lee, Ju Seong. 2022. *Informal Digital Learning of English*. New York/London: Routledge.

Lee, Ju Seong & Nur Arifah Drajati. 2019. Affective variables and informal digital learning of English: Keys to willingness to communicate in a second language. *Australasian Journal of Educational Technology* 15. 168–182.

Lerner, Ivonne. 2013. Not just hugs and tears: Israeli teenagers learn Spanish by watching telenovelas. Paper presented at the Annual Conference of the Israeli Association of Language and Society, Tel Aviv University, 30 June, 2013.

Lyrigkou, Christina. 2019. Not to be overlooked: agency in informal language contact. *Innovation in Language Learning and Teaching* 13(3). 237–252.

Moffat, Andrew. 2022. *Second Language Use Online and its Integration in Formal Language Learning*. Bristol: Multilingual Matters.

Murphy, Linda. 2005. Attending to form and meaning: the experience of adult distance learners of French, German and Spanish. *Language Teaching Research* 9(3). 295–317.

Murray, Garold. 2008. Pop culture and language learning: Learners' stories informing EFL. *Innovation in Language Learning & Teaching* 2(1). 2–17.

Muñoz, Carmen, Teresa Cadierno & Isabel Casas. 2018. Different starting points for early language learning: A comparative study of Danish and Spanish young learners of English. *Language Learning* 68(4). 1076–1109.

Muñoz, Carmen. 2020. Boys like games and girls like movies: Age and gender differences in out-of-school contact with English. *Revista Española de Lingüística Aplicada/Spanish Journal of Applied Linguistics* 33(1). 171–201.

Nunan, David & Jack C. Richards (eds.). 2014. *Language Learning Beyond the Classroom*. New York: Routledge.

Peng, Hongying, Sake Jager & Wander Lowie. 2021. A person-centred approach to L2 learners' informal mobile language learning. *Computer Assisted Language Learning* 35(9). 2148–2169.

Peters, Elke, Anne-Sophie Noreillie, Kris Heylen, Bram Bulté & Piet Desmet. 2019. The Impact of instruction and out-of-school exposure to foreign language input on learners' vocabulary knowledge in two languages. *Language Learning* 69(3). 747–782.

Pickard, Nigel. 1996. Out-of-class language learning strategies. *English Teaching Journal* 50. 150–159.

Pooley, Aaron William, Warren Midgley & Helen Farley. 2019. Informal language learning through mobile instant messaging among university students in Korea. *International Journal of Mobile and Blended Learning* 11(2). 33–49.

Reinhardt, Jonathan & Jieun Ryu. 2013. Using social network-mediated bridging activities to develop socio-pragmatic awareness in elementary Korean. *International Journal of Computer-Assisted Language Learning and Teaching* 3(3). 18–33.

Scholz, Kyle. 2017. Encouraging free play: Extramural digital game-based language learning as a complex adaptive system. *CALICO Journal* 34(1). 39–57.

Schwarz, Marlene. 2020. *Beyond the walls: A mixed methods study of teenagers' extramural English practices and their vocabulary knowledge*. Wien: University of Vienna dissertation.

Silva, Haydée & Gilles Brougère. 2017. Jouer pour apprendre une langue étrangère : Concert à 16 voix. *Synergies Mexique* 7. 51–62.

Sockett, Geoffrey. 2014. *The Online Informal Learning of English*. Basingstoke/New York: Palgrave Macmillan.

Sockett, Geoff. 2022. Learning Beyond the Classroom and Autonomy. In Hayo Reinders, Chun Lai & Pia Sundqvist (eds.), *The Routledge handbook of language learning and teaching beyond the classroom (Routledge international handbooks of education)*, 67–80. Abingdon/New York: Routledge.

Spada, Nina. 1986. The interaction between type of contact and type of instruction: Some effects on the L2 proficiency of adult learners. *Studies in Second Language Acquisition* 8. 181–200.

Sundqvist, Pia. 2009. *Extramural English Matters: Out-of-School English and its Impact on Swedish Ninth Graders' Oral Proficiency and Vocabulary*. Karlstad: Karlstad University dissertation.

Sundqvist, Pia. 2020. Sweden and informal language learning. In Mark Dressman & Randall Sadler (eds.), *The Handbook of Informal Language Learning*, 319–332. Hoboken/Chichester: Wiley-Blackwell.

Sundqvist, Pia & Liss Kerstin Sylvén. 2014. Language-related computer use: Focus on young L2 English learners in Sweden. *ReCALL* 26(1). 3–20.

Sundqvist, Pia & Liss Kerstin Sylvén. 2016. *Extramural English in Teaching and Learning – From Theory and Research to Practice* (New Language Learning and Teaching Environments). Basingstoke/New York: Palgrave Macmillan.

Thorne, Steve & Jonathan Reinhardt. 2008. Bridging activities, new media literacies, and advanced foreign language proficiency. *CALICO Journal* 25(3). 558–572.

Toffoli, Denyze & Geoffrey Sockett. 2010. How non-specialist students of English practice informal learning using web 2.0 tools. *ASp. La revue du GERAS* 58. 125–144.

Toffoli, Denyze. 2020. *Informal Learning and Institution-wide Language Provision: University Language Learners in the 21st Century*. Cham: Palgrave Macmillan.

Trinder, Ruth. 2017. Informal and deliberate learning with new technologies. *ELT Journal* 71(4). 401–412.

Vosburg, Donald. 2016. The Effects of group dynamics on language learning and use in an MMOG. *CALICO Journal* 34(1). 58–74.

Yibokou, Kossi Seto. 2019. *Apprentissage informel de l'anglais en ligne: Quelles conséquences sur la prononciation des étudiants français?* Strasbourg: Strasbourg University dissertation.

Zadorozhnyy, Artem. 2022. *Informal digital learning of English: The case of Kazakhstani pre-service teachers of English*. Hong Kong: Education University of Hong Kong dissertation.

Section 1: **The nature of informal second language learning**

Mark Dressman
2 Toward an anthropology of Informal Digital Learning of English (IDLE)

Abstract: This chapter makes an argument for the role of ethnographic play in the study of informal digital learning of English (IDLE) as a complement to the work of applied linguistic research. In most cases, the initial impulse to study IDLE is itself a result of researchers' playful observation of youth learning English from engagement with a wide variety of digital media. IDLE is therefore a fundamentally cultural, anthropological phenomenon requiring a range of methods to be understood in its fullest context. A review of the history of ethnography presents its key practices as complementary to the more quantitative approaches of applied linguistics research. These include participant observation; analysis of artefacts; narrative, thick description; case study; grand theorization; and confession. An ethnographic approach also provides a check on reductionism, implications for language pedagogy, and assistance in building general knowledge about IDLE as a global, contextualised phenomenon. The chapter concludes with a "confessional" account of studying IDLE ethnographically in Morocco, illustrating again the need for the playfulness of ethnographic research as a complement to the temperance of careful measurement and design.

Keywords: Confessional writing, ethnography, informal digital learning of English (IDLE), Morocco, thick description

1 Introduction

Idle: Old English *idel* "empty, void; vain; worthless, useless." From Proto-West Germanic **idla*-a word of unknown origin. Subsequent developments are peculiar to English: sense "not employed, not doing work" was in late Old English in reference to persons; from 1520s of things; from 1805 of machinery. Meaning "lazy, slothful" is from c. 1300. In Elizabethan English it could also mean "foolish, delirious, wandering in the mind." *Idle threats* preserves original sense.

–Online Etymology Dictionary
(https://www.etymonline.com/)

Mark Dressman, University of Illinois, USA

https://doi.org/10.1515/9783110752441-002

What a waste of time it is to wall-off work from play or play from work: in practice, it can't be done. Who has ever achieved anything of consequence that did not require vast, protean amounts of idleness, mostly in the beginning, but often throughout? Without play, work becomes labour: brutal, seemingly endless tedium that may complete its task but at an onerous price. By the same token, real play demands work: it demands energy, commitment, and focus, lest the game be lost, and the player vanquished.

So it is with Informal Digital Learning of English (IDLE), whose playful name is both its acronym and its description. It is an ancient word, a pejorative, Germanic word for being slothful, foolish, and wasting time; and later, for an engine standing still, waiting to be put into motion. IDLE, to be successful, demands idleness, at least at first; its experience, its investigation, and ultimately its understanding, demand the same. Patience and forgiveness are its price of admission; empathy and introspection are its lenses; voyeurism, experience, and knowing are its rewards.

2 The practice of anthropology

Of all the modern social sciences, anthropology's practices, or *habitus*, are the most in tune with IDLE's sensibilities, and the most likely to yield its idylls and its rewards. The others – linguistics, psychology, economics, history, political science, and so on – are either reductive or not relevant to its condition. Some forms of sociology – case studies and cultural studies, for instance – are also sympathetic, but these are essentially anthropological, ethnographic studies conducted in domestic, rather than "other," contexts. As a modern discipline, anthropology was born in the nineteenth century from two impulses – travel writing (Pratt 1992), or the desire to capture the experiences of exotic lands and cultures and convey them to an audience back home; and natural history (Boas 1904, 1909), or the desire to comprehend the order of the natural world and curate its relevant objects. These dual impulses – to play far afield and then report home and to work far afield at collecting and then preserve and catalogue in a laboratory setting – served a complementary function and are the genesis of anthropology's major practices and tropes today: ethnography; participant observation; the play of emic and etic perspectives; thick description; Grand Theory; and ultimately, introspection and confession.

In the beginning, anthropology took itself very, very seriously. Franz Boas, the founder of anthropology in the United States, assisted in the development of exhibitions for the Chicago Columbian Exposition based on the belief that remote cultures untouched by Western technology and culture would soon become extinct, and must be preserved – by which he meant *embalmed* – for future generations in museums before they disappeared (Truman 1893). Boas himself visited the Kwakiutl in British Columbia, collecting their artefacts, documenting their language, and studying their rituals and beliefs (Boas 1895). In the 1920s, a new generation of anthropologists, among them Boas's student Margaret Mead, and at the University of Oxford, Bronislaw Malinowski, expanded the scope of ethnography by spending extended lengths of time in settings and living among the people they were studying, after Malinowski chided his fellow anthropologists for their "armchair anthropology." This practice, known as *participant observation*, soon became the hallmark method of ethnographic research. Field notes taken during participant observation provided a diurnal record of ethnographers' experiences and enhanced the travel-writing aspect of reportage. Some anthropologists were also fine writers; *Argonauts of the Western Pacific* (1922), by Malinowski, can be read as both a scientific treatise and a gripping, heroic travelogue. Mead's account of teenage puberty and promiscuity, *Coming of Age in Samoa* (1928), became a best seller in the United States and propelled Mead into the position of public intellectual from the 1930s to her death in 1978.

At the start of WWII, many anthropologists were enlisted to serve as intelligence officers, providing humanizing insight into the cultures of people Allied troops were encountering as adversaries and as co- and non-combatants. A student of Franz Boas, Ruth Benedict, was enlisted by the U.S. Office of War Information to provide insights into Japanese culture. Unable to travel to Japan during the war, Benedict forensically read the artefacts of Japanese culture and society – newspapers, official statements, media, and popular culture – as well as other accounts of the culture itself to create a document that explained wartime practices that were puzzling to the U.S. military and in the post-war period, to policymakers. *The Chrysanthemum and the Sword* (1946), published after the war, remains a classic ethnography of Japanese culture.

As anthropology grew in standing, so did its hubris. The reading of artefacts was also taken up in France in the late 1940s by Claude Lévi-Strauss and others through the interpretive, Saussurean-based frame of structuralism, a semantic analytical process in which objects – language, ceremonial artefacts, rituals, architectural designs – were schematized as sets of binary relations (1949; 1969). A particularly striking example of structural analysis is "The Berber House or the World Reversed," by Pierre Bourdieu (1970), written from data collected during his own work in Algeria in the early 1960s. Structuralism for Lévi-Strauss was more than a method. Beyond Saussure's claim that the structure of language was the primary paradigm for all of semiology (the study of meaning), Lévi-Strauss argued that in fact structuralism was cosmological in its import – that it described relations between human culture and its geophysical situation, so that in conducting structural analyses of cultures, anthropologists were unlocking the secrets of humanity's connection to the universe itself (Eagleton 1983).

A similar although more earthly approach to ethnographic analysis was under development in the U.S. and U.K. in the same period. At the University of Manchester and later at the University of Chicago, Victor Turner developed a *symbolic* approach to the interpretation of human life events, based on his work with conflict and adolescent rites of passage among the Ndembu people in Zambia, that was more grounded in an empathic understanding of how individuals understood relations with others and the world through endemic cultural symbols than through structural binarism (1967). Although grounded in people's local understanding of their culture, Turner considered his descriptions of *liminality* and *communitas* to have broad implications culturally, and his theories have been taken up by anthropologists in many different settings (e.g., McLaren 1986). Turner's colleague at Chicago, Clifford Geertz, also focused on the symbolic interpretation of "local knowledge," but also stressed the interpretation of data through writing, using *thick description*, or detailed written descriptions of events and artefacts that stressed their interpretability (1983). Geertz's approach introduced writing itself as a tool or method of interpretive understanding of culture, and both drew from and contributed to a broad range of literary approaches to analysis then current in Europe, especially in France in the work of Roland Barthes (1972), Louis Althusser (1971), and Michel Foucault (1977), and more diffusely in the *cultural studies* movement at the University of Birmingham (Turner 2002) and elsewhere.

But then cracks in anthropology's façade of objective reportage began to appear. In 1967, Malinowski's personal diary of his fieldwork for *Argonauts* was published and instead of the empathetic, egalitarian portrait of "an ethnographer among the people" suggested in the book, Malinowski appeared narcissistic, peevish, and often contemptuous of the Trobriand islanders with whom he lived (Malinowski 1989). A decade later, Geertz's student Paul Rabinow published *Reflections on Fieldwork in Morocco* (1977), a confessional, tell-all account of his fieldwork for his dissertation that had already produced a more conventional ethnography. Rabinow rejected claims of objectivity and embraced his own subjective experience, describing in detail his personal relations with several informants, villagers, and one night spent with a local prostitute as an act of participant observation. In 1983, five years after Margaret Mead's death, Derek Freeman, a New Zealand anthropologist living in Samoa, published a "restudy" of *Coming of Age in Samoa*, in which he argued that Mead had fabricated a "myth" about adolescent sexuality and that, in fact, Samoan adolescents suffered the same sense of alienation from their elders as in the West. Freeman's book ignited a firestorm among anthropologists. Mead's defenders argued that Samoan society in the 1970s was radically different from the 1920s and that the conversion to Christianity of the now-elderly women Freeman interviewed, who had been Mead's original informants, coloured their memories of Mead and their adolescence. However, the damage to anthropology's claims of scientific objectivity had been done: the work of anthropology as key to unlocking universal truths about human culture now appeared to the scientific community as more like self-indulgent play.

3 IDLE and ethnography

Given anthropology's seeming fall from grace and authority at the end of the 20th Century, it might therefore be pertinent to ask why the study of IDLE needs or could benefit from ethnography and anthropology in the 21st. My answer is that the study of IDLE needs anthropology for the same reason that work needs play, and play needs work, or that all claims of objectivity require the tempering admission of some subjective component (and vice versa). To a far greater degree than any other social science discipline, anthropology has needed to face its claims of objectivity head-on, and in the process, it has arguably become a stronger, not weaker, form of social enquiry. Following the "scandals" of Malinowski, Rabinow, and Mead, the field of anthropology turned introspective, analysing in stringent detail the implications of ethnography as a written medium, of the ethnographer as a gendered, racial, linguistic subject, and of the play between emic (insider) and etic (outsider) points of view (e.g., Clifford and Marcus 1986). New practices of confessional writing and methodological reflexivity have added a level of sophistication and insight to cultural inquiry that has redefined rather than renounced anthropology's claims of scientific validity and reliability.

A more important and practical reason, however, is that the original impulse to study IDLE is itself the direct result of participant observation by researchers, either of their students, in my generation's case, or by a younger generation of researchers whose own proficiency in English as an L2 is due largely to watching captioned or subtitled television programs, listening to music, or chatting with co-players of MMORPGs. Thus, because IDLE is itself a cultural, anthropological phenomenon first discovered by researchers through experiences that are essentially ethnographic, coming to understand IDLE in all its facets demands the tools of anthropological inquiry, as humanly flawed as they might seem to be. IDLE is much more than a linguistic phenomenon or a new way to learn another language; it is a practice with a culture of its own whose participants across the world share some common traits, such as youthfulness and a specific setting, the digisphere. It has gendered, political, and geographic nuances as well, and it enables its participants to assume identities and engage in symbolic exchanges they otherwise could not imagine. More than a way to learn, it is an *experience* of learning, mediated through interactions with others and with texts that produce meaning within, and connection to, the world-at-large. These experiences require more than one-time interviews, questionnaires, testing, conversation analysis, or the reductive practices of coding to be understood (as valuable as these tools also are); they require immersive participation, introspection, and case study rendered in thick, descriptive narratives.

In the remainder of this chapter I will focus on two topics extending this argument. First, I will argue for four ways that the ethnographic study of IDLE, grounded in the rhetorical practices of anthropology, provides a critical and much-needed complement to the study of IDLE as a phenomenon within applied linguistics. Second and in conclusion, as an illustrative example I will provide a brief, "confessional" account of my own fieldwork studying IDLE in Morocco. In conclusion, I attempt to outline a future for the ethnography of IDLE and its complementary relationship to applied linguistics research.

4 The complementarity of ethnographic practice with applied linguistic research

4.1 Complementary research tools

Rather than focus on one specific feature of human behaviour, such as language or cognition, anthropology focuses on the totality of human behaviour within a specific context, with the goal of identifying and explaining routine patterns of behaviour and the forces that determine them. It is less focused on variables than on describing relations among variables narratively and reliably, often over time. It thus adds a fully narrative, diachronic dimension to the study of IDLE, and relies on a different range of tools. These include:

4.1.1 Participant observation: Playing with the emic and the etic

One of the chief benefits of participant observation is serendipitous experiences that yield insights into patterns of behaviour or relations among aspects of cultural life that would otherwise never be seen. Living among people for extended periods of time, trust develops, one is taken for granted, and guards are let down to reveal information that otherwise would remain concealed – not because the information is necessarily secret or forbidden in some way, but because it had not been considered to be "information" previously. Over extended periods of time, cycles or patterns of behaviour become apparent; one begins to see the same things happen again and again in the presence or absence of other events, and these patterns may explain much about the phenomenon under study.

In the case of IDLE, participant observation can be difficult because much of the activity of learning English digitally takes place online, at odd hours and in odd spaces, such as in learners' homes or on mobile phones. It may, however, be possible to "hang out" with students in online gaming parlours, playing with them, or to watch some downloaded episodes of a television program or a movie identified by an informant as critical to their learning, or to exchange formal lessons in English with them as a way of having deeper insight into the full range of a speaker's vocabulary, grammar, and pragmatics. The more one can idle within the daily life worlds of IDLErs, the more insight is gained into the motivations, the learning processes, and relations between the acquisition of English and the unfolding lives of learners.

A long-standing criticism of participant observation is that oftentimes the cultural insights developed from cultural immersion turn out in the end to be illusionary – that is, that the emic, "insider" perspective an ethnographer believed they had achieved was false, and that all along informants had not been completely forthcoming or that the ethnographer's own biases had coloured their perception. However, these problems are more common to ethnographers in the early stages of their work or when fieldwork is conducted for short periods of time. They are also sustained by the (false) assumption that cultures are unified, stable, and enduring patterns of behaviour that have only one accurate description, and by the idea that one is either entirely an "insider" or an "outsider" to them.

In reality, participation in one's own or other cultures almost always contains elements of reflexivity born of alienation or lingering doubt as well as elements of complete immersion, engagement, and empathy with others whatever the cultural setting. Our subject positions within any context are simultaneously emic and etic; we are normatively both insiders and outsiders within our own and other cultures, and the validity of our understanding and capacity to describe a phenomenon to others depends on the embrace of that mixed subjectivity (Dressman 2013).

4.1.2 Artefact collection and analysis

A core principle of anthropology and ethnographic research is that the objects that people make and the way in which they arrange the material goods of their lives, such as their homes, their clothing, their utensils and tools and their language, "says something" about them collectively as a culture that far exceeds the objects' concrete functionality. Understanding the symbolic nature of human life is thus key to understanding culture.

With respect to IDLE, relevant documents and artefacts include everything in a learner's cultural environment that might contribute in some way to language acquisition or perceptions of language acquisition. These artefacts and documents include videos the learner watches on YouTube or television programs or movies and songs or chat rooms, but they also include websites in English or another target language that the learner visits, or even environmental print in the learner's culture, books or magazines owned by a learner, as are rituals, procedures, published instructions, and the artefacts of formal classroom instruction. Examples of language production by the learner in the form of blog posts, written papers, notes, chats, and so on are also collectible. As sources of language input and output, all of these are collectible by an ethnographer, whose task will necessarily need to be selective in many cases due to the sheer volume of materials.

However, the task of ethnography since the 1940s has been less the curation of these than their forensic and symbolic analysis. There is an assumption in anthropology and many other areas of media studies and discourse analysis that beyond the stated, official, or literal meanings and uses, there is an underlying order and symbolic significance to the actions of individuals and their ordered material environment that requires interpretation. Sometimes, as in the case of Benedict's study of Japanese culture from a distance, the interpretation is broadly hermeneutic, and depends on an ethnographer's knowledge base and capacity intuitively to detect and then empirically to corroborate patterns of behaviour from a range of disparate data sources.

In other cases, such as the structuralist approach of Lévi-Strauss, the analysis is more systematic and relies on the coding of artefacts according to an externally validated scheme or practice, such as looking for binary pairs and aligning them in sets.[1] Document and artefact analysis are critical to the study of IDLE because they provide important insights into the underlying cultural and political dimensions of language learning, such as motivation within a specific culture and connections between language acquisition and an individual learner's identity.

---

[1] For an excellent example of structural analysis applied to media, I suggest *Television Culture* (2010), by John Fiske. For additional approaches to non-Saussurean semiotic analysis of non-linguistic artefacts, see "Multimodality and Language Learning" (Dressman 2020a).

4.1.3 Narrative and thick description

There is something inherent in the act of presenting events and their significance to an audience of readers outside the culture being described that pushes an ethnographer to focus carefully and self-critically, checking and rechecking data, and triangulating among notes, transcripts, and artefacts, to create a unified, "true" (Hemingway 1999) account of a distant world and the people in it. The re-creation of a world and its experiences through thick description is thus an act of analysis – an act of creation in itself – and a message and admonition to readers outside that world who might be inclined otherwise to judge that world on their own terms.

Narration and thick description are critical to the study of IDLE and the presentation of its experiences. Every digital learner of English has a story to tell about "how they did it." Those stories are often impressive and share both commonalities and peculiarities. Coding the transcripts of interviews or tabulating results of a large number of questionnaires ensures a level of objectivity in the interpretation of data but largely fails to describe processes or the play of general trends with individual difference. Most important, narration and thick description are a researcher's best tools for rendering the experience of informal digital learning of English to an audience removed from its culture and practices.

4.1.4 Longitudinal case study

A frequent criticism of ethnography is that it commits the dual sins of metonymy and synecdoche, i.e., that based on fieldwork conducted within a relatively short period of time, it produces a snapshot that both miniaturizes and only partially represents cultural reality, but that once distributed, becomes timeless and accepted as generalized knowledge. Although that may be the case in some instances (as in the case of Mead's study of Samoan teens), it is not always so; many anthropologists and ethnographers establish long-term relationships with informants and settings and may produce multiple ethnographies of the same setting over time. One such case is the work of Douglas Foley, who studied the education of Mexican-American high school students in a South Texas town in the late 1970s (Foley, da Mota, Post & Lozano 1977) and revisited the same school in the late 1980s (Foley 1990) to restudy the effects of desegregation on students there. Although many of the adults and all of the adolescents from his first study had moved on in the intervening period, Foley's understanding of the historical context and trajectory of the high school's culture over more than a decade provided his work with an insight and power it otherwise would not have had.

IDLE is also in deep need of longitudinal, ethnographic study. Learning a language is a lengthy process and although informants may be able to describe their learning process over time, memory is limited and reconstructive, not reproductive. Without longitudinal data collected from the same participants over a period of years, milestones in vocabulary acquisition, syntactic development, pronunciation, and expressiveness are difficult to assess and must rely instead on the testing of groups of participants at different ages and levels of proficiency. More significantly, continuity and connections to critical life events in learners' experiences are difficult to assess, as are the broader cultural and life outcomes of learners.

4.1.5 Grand theory

The term, "Grand Theory," refers to overarching, broad theories of society that attempt to bring many elements of a culture into relationship. Marxism is one example of a Grand Theory; Herbert Spencer's theory of Social Darwinism is another; Structuralism, Postmodernism, and Poststructuralism are others, as is Globalization. A wide range of twentieth century philosophers, from Wittgenstein (Monk 2012) to Lyotard (1984) and Foucault (1977), were dismissive of Metanarratives, Grand Narratives, and Grand Theories, describing them as reductive and controlling: in some cases lacking empirical support, and in others simply, dangerously, wrong. Indeed, such theories have an affinity to conspiracy theories, in both their frequent lack of empirical backing and tendency to "connect the dots" narratively in fanciful ways.

Yet, the making of theories and generalizations about the nature of cultures and the social order seems unavoidable and even necessary in some situations. Despite their protestations to the contrary, Wittgenstein, Lyotard, and Foucault are regarded as some of the Grandest Theorists of the Twentieth Century, whose ideas resonate today. Theories provide a means of interpreting the broader implications of findings and for finding the connectedness among disparate studies conducted in different settings. They go awry when researchers turn them into belief systems into which all findings must be fit, rather than as interesting heuristics or "hunches" to be sceptically tested and rejected or refined through empirical investigation.

Theory is critical to the development of IDLE as a field of research, because IDLE itself has implications for linguistics, for education, for the psychology of learning the and sociology of identity production, and for global media studies that extend far beyond the local study of how adolescents are learning English online. Worldwide, we are barely 30 years into the life of the World-Wide Web, and its implications for national and international politics, relations among countries and social groups, and globalism have been barely explored. The comparative study across nations, languages, religions, economies, and cultures of how (mainly) adolescents are teaching themselves English and other languages can contribute to broad, general, theoretical understanding of the impact of digital culture on the world itself. Theorization of these processes is inevitable, but responsible, ethical, and reliable theorization is not, unless the need for such responsible theorization is openly embraced by IDLE research.

4.1.6 Introspection and confession

These are anthropology's most recent and its most unique tools. Self-criticism in the form of statements of limitations in research studies has been a feature of applied linguistics and quantitative social science research for many years, but the need for researchers to place themselves and their own perceptions in relation to the phenomena they are studying has not. Confession in this context does not refer to embarrassing admissions of a researcher's foibles, or "sins," but rather to the reflexive admission that the research was not conducted with an exclusively emic, insider or etic, outsider perspective, and that complementarity and conflict between these played a role in the interpretation and presentation of findings.

This is important in the study of IDLE because of the limitations imposed by studying a process – language acquisition – that needs to be observed indirectly, though assessments, interviews and engagement in the learning process as a learner oneself or sometimes as a teacher. Introspection, or the self-questioning of motives, data collection techniques, choice of participants, and analytical and interpretive methods, only strengthens the quality of findings, and confession, or the public description of one's conflicts and practices, only strengthens and validates responsibly made research claims.

4.2 Checking reductionism

A central tendency of social sciences modelled on the paradigms of physical sciences has been the statistical reduction of complex behaviours to elemental constructs, i.e., to terms meant to capture the essence of a behaviour. In psychology, for example, differences in individuals' general ability to remember, solve problems, and learn is typically described as their *intelligence*, or I.Q.

Applied linguistics also makes use of many constructs, often presented as binarisms or sets of three or more categories. For example, since the 1970s, a distinction has often been made between the *acquisition* and the *learning* (Krashen 1976) of languages, which, in turn, has influenced distinctions made in informal language learning research between *incidental* (unconscious) and *intentional* (deliberate) language learning (Sjöholm 2001; Sockett 2014). But ethnographic studies of IDLE practices, especially from the detailed accounts of learners about how they developed proficiency in English, challenge this dichotomy. These studies contain accounts of learners initially "picking up" words and phrases from media but then, over time, becoming more strategic in their learning by taking notes, asking more advanced learners for assistance, consulting dictionary apps, and even reading materials explaining points of grammar and communication. These activities are independently and consciously performed but they are also very spontaneous and unrehearsed; they seem to defy the binary logic of incidental vs. intentional learning.

Similarly, a distinction among formal (classroom), informal (self-directed), and non-formal (independent programmed) learning is often made by applied linguists to describe clear differences among instructional contexts (Benson 2011). However, these are not distinctions made by learners interviewed in my research in Morocco (Dressman 2020b). Most of the participants in this study did make an implicit distinction between learning English at school or a language centre and learning on their own; but they viewed resources for learning outside school as a single reservoir, without distinction between resources that were pedagogical (non-formal), such as websites (e.g., WikiHow) or instructional YouTube videos, and the (informal) pleasures of social media, satellite television, or YouTube music videos. They were all enjoyed as pleasurable sources of English and of learning.

In another study, Rothoni (2018) studied the English literacy practices of 15 teenagers in Athens, Greece. Rothoni analysed written artefacts produced by her participants in both informal, online settings, and at school, and found a high degree of hybridity across their texts and their practices. Students actively used language and rhetorical approaches acquired informally through media in school, but they also used strategies and ways of speaking and writing promoted in school in their interactions on the internet.

These examples suggest that the ethnography of IDLE has a significant role to play in refining the terminology and categories of applied linguistics research. Theoretically, distinctions between acquisition and learning and between incidental and intentional learning are interesting to contemplate; but practically and from the emic perspective of learners, these distinctions often do not exist. From an etic, academic perspective, there are clear and compelling differences among formal, informal, and non-formal approaches to teaching a second language; but learners themselves do not make these distinctions. Pedagogically, the difference between how teachers see the task of learning and how learners see it, is vast; it holds implications for how well and how much students learn – and for how well research may contribute to learning's outcomes – that are profound.

4.2.1 Redesigning language pedagogy

The implications of IDLE for second and foreign language instruction are obviously great, and potentially revolutionary. If, in the digital age, adolescents and young adults are acquiring much of their proficiency in English through a wide range of media, and if these practices "solve" many of the limitations of classroom instruction such as lack of authentic materials and ubiquitous opportunities for meaningful communication and practice, then why is classroom curriculum necessary and how does it remain relevant? From this perspective, IDLE may be perceived – and its implications resisted – by English educators as an existential threat.

However, researchers of IDLE have not suggested that the rise of informal language learning means there is no longer a meaningful role for formal instruction. Cole and Vanderplank (2016), for example, in their study of Brazilian learners who were entirely autonomous in their English language learning (and who outperformed classroom learners), also noted that their participants' experiences were not generalizable to the entire population of Brazil. Other studies, such as Dressman (2020b) and Rothoni (2018) have noted the overlap and interaction between learning in and out of classrooms, especially literacy development.

Although the practices of IDLE have much to contribute to the development of students' autonomy and confidence as learners, as Dressman, Lee, and Perrot (2023) note, by adapting, or "taming" the practices of the digital wilds for classroom use, teachers also run the very great risk of destroying the properties that make them pedagogically powerful. In other words, if one of the attractive features of IDLE is that it is "not like school," then bringing it into a classroom context may remove its attraction.

One potential solution to this conundrum and to some teachers' reluctance to embrace the implications of IDLE is to have students and their teachers explore IDLE as a phenomenon themselves, ethnographically. For example, Sayer and Ban (2014), in their study of Mexican middle school students' learning of English through social media, concluded, "One clear implication is that teachers would benefit from taking a more ethnographic perspective towards their students, and find out what they like to do with English when she or he is not around" (328). Both Lee (2021) and Sundqvist and Sylvén (2016) have advocated a "30-Day Extramural English Challenge," in which teachers and students collaboratively record and analyse their daily engagement with English outside the classroom. Their goal is to invert the traditional instructional paradigm to make it "learner-cantered," according to Dressman, Lee, and Perrot (2023), in which curriculum is built from students' naturalistic, autonomous learning practices, in dialogue with applied linguistics research.

4.2.2 Building general knowledge

A long-standing assumption (of quantitative research) is that the only way to produce "scientific," valid, and generalizable knowledge is through the application of research designs that eliminate the possibility of bias through large sample sizes, experimental control, rigorous cross-checks, and elaborate statistical analysis. However, these claims ignore the fact that much scientific research in the physical sciences (in astronomy, biology, archaeology, and palaeontology, for example) is fundamentally *observational* rather than experimental, in which forensic analysis of single or small groups of subjects/objects is more often used to establish factual claims.

However, as I have argued elsewhere (Dressman 2009), research is fundamentally a *rhetorical activity*, in which data are used to make an argument about a phenomenon, subject to the scrutiny of others. In the case of ethnographic studies, key questions for determining validity, reliability, and generalizability include the frequency of patterns of behaviour observed and their comparison across a wide variety of contexts to identify instances of variation and consistency. Because ethnographic practices are relatively consistent across studies and focused on producing highly contextualized descriptions, they can be easily and reliably compared across a wide range of contexts to develop global, general knowledge about a phenomenon that is defensibly valid and reliable without the use of statistical analysis or massive sample sizes.

The study of IDLE across a wide range of regional and national contexts provides an excellent opportunity to develop a valid and reliable body of knowledge about the processes and practices of IDLE globally. In cities and countries as diverse as Greece (Rothoni 2018), Morocco (Dressman 2020b), Mexico (Sayer and Ban 2014), Hong Kong (Lai and Gu 2011), South Korea (Lee and Dressman 2018), Slovenia (Jurkovič 2019), Sweden (Sundqvist and Sylvén 2016), and Brazil (Cole and Vanderplank 2016), studies have been conducted that provide detailed, complex descriptions of how adolescents and young adults learn English informally. Some of these are purely ethnographic in method and others use mixed methods, in which ethnographic data collection (e.g., field notes from participant observation; interviews; document analysis) is combined with quantitative analysis of relations between, for example, the quantity and quality of learners' self-reported use of digital media and measures of proficiency. One salient feature of all of these studies, however, is that they include case studies of individual learners, sometimes as the central focus of analysis and sometimes as examples that illustrate quantitative findings.

The narratives of these case studies provide an invaluable resource for constructing global, general knowledge about the processes and practices of IDLE that would be difficult if not impossible to construct or observe through quantitative approaches. Either through coding or the use of constant-comparative analysis (Glaser 1965), these narratives can be compiled into a single data set yielding an extensive inventory of the steps and features of learners' learning processes as well as variables such as age, gender, socioeconomics, linguistic background, and so on. The number of cases may not permit claims of generality to be verified statistically, but other factors, such as the finding of similar patterns of practice and language development by researchers acting independent of one another in many different parts of the world, provide strong grounds for claims of validity and reliability.

4.3 An example: IDLE in Morocco

To illustrate the application of ethnographic tools to IDLE research, I will recount my own experiences studying IDLE in Morocco (Dressman 2020b). My first experience of informal digital learning of English came in 2006, on a summer trip to the country to establish research connections with university faculty there. I was checking my email in an Internet café in Kasba Tadla, a small town in central Morocco where I had taught as a Peace Corps Volunteer three decades before, and I overheard a Moroccan teen-ager struggling to communicate in English with someone in a live chatroom. I was impressed by the intensity and focus of his efforts and when he finished, I introduced myself speaking Moroccan Arabic as a former teacher of English at Lycée Moulay Ismail and asked about his background and whom he'd been talking to. He told me he was a "science" student at a new lycée in town and he was talking to his girlfriend, who lived in Spain. He had very limited English instruction at school, he explained, but it was the only language he and his girlfriend shared. He was desperate to talk to her, so he had begun to study English on his own.

The memory of this incident returned to me as I was planning three consecutive fall trips to Morocco between 2014 and 2016 as a Fulbright Scholar. My primary proposal was an action research project in which I was designing improved ways to teach English to first-year undergraduate majors in three public Moroccan universities, in which the enrolment for beginning courses was typically 100–150 students.

However, I also had a side project to interview students about their uses of the Internet and technology in learning.

The general quality of students' English in their first semester at the University, after three years of high-school instruction, was much better than I had anticipated, based on my experiences 35 years before teaching in Kasba Tadla. I had no problems communicating with the students in class and discovered that most students, while not "native" in their ability, were conversational, and that I seldom needed to repeat or rephrase what I said, in class or individually. The first year I conducted only 18 interviews, but the information these provided completely changed the focus of my research and led to a redesign of my interview protocol for the second year, in which I focused directly on how students were using digital and other resources to acquire English outside formal instruction.

The stories that students told me in my interviews and informal conversations with them about learning English from satellite television, YouTube, and many Internet sites were revelatory to me, but less so to my Moroccan counterparts. Most faculty in the English departments where I taught were indifferent or suggested that even if students were learning to speak English online, they were not learning it properly. A few others were hostile, and one told me indignantly that I was wasting my time because students today learned English exactly as she had 30 years before, from their textbooks and their teachers. Our disagreement led to a break at the beginning of my second visit in fall, 2015, and to a shift in my research plans and location and a refocusing of my efforts on documenting through interviews and other means the resources and strategies students were using to acquire English at the university, at home online, and at times in the street and cafes.

In fall 2015 I was able to conduct more than 100 additional interviews with students primarily at two universities, along with teaching a graduate class and assisting the teaching of several undergraduate courses. Clear patterns began to emerge in what students told me, and I began to gain some insight into how English figured into the identity production of these students in relation to their other two literate languages, Standard Arabic and French, as well as to the national lingua franca, Moroccan Arabic (Darija) and varieties of the Amazigh language, spoken at home by approximately half of the Moroccan population. However, many insights did not come from formal data collection practices but informally in conversations with students in cafes or chatting on Facebook, when working on special projects, such as with a group of students who met with me every Friday afternoon to "rewrite" the classic US play, "Our Town" (Wilder 1965), with a Moroccan setting and characters, or when driving and listening to local radio talk shows, especially "The Momo Morning Show," on HitRadio, a nation-wide FM station based in Rabat.

I learned, for example, how tied to context, purpose, and identity language choices are in Morocco. Every morning the banter of Momo and his sidekicks mixed Standard Arabic, Darija (Moroccan dialect), French, and a bit of English, depending on the topic and its relation to the speaker. Standard Arabic was always used to discuss the government and important news events; French was the language of discussions about the arts, civic engagement, and social issues; joking and personal topics were largely in Darija; and when discussing entertainment or to signify "coolness," Momo would throw in some English, often with a reference to Southern California or New York. When people called in, they typically alternated between French and Darija and Momo would respond similarly. The use of French in conversation on the radio was surprising to me, because I never heard it spoken at the university among students, who frequently told me in interviews and informally that they "hated French" and "never spoke it."

At the same time, news articles appeared online, and colleagues began to mention the possibility that soon the Ministry of Higher Education would require doctoral courses to be taught and dissertations written in English. On a hunch, I began to raise this issue with my informants and found, as I suspected, that they associated it with the elite classes of Moroccans who lived mainly in Casablanca and Rabat. The students I interviewed were attending public universities on bursaries or scholarships, while their wealthier peers attended private universities and institutes in-country or in France; their repudiation of French and embrace of English was strongly tied to their identity as "new" Moroccans not tied to the colonial past or its privileged elite. English was also tied to non-economic and social interests. Several male students with whom I spent time in cafes and working on special projects told me that it was easier to talk about "some things" in English than in Arabic, such as sex, because of Arabic's association with religion and traditional values.

My work with students as an assistant in courses taught by Moroccan instructors was also very valuable. I attended many meetings with faculty and administrators, which were typically conducted in a combination of Moroccan and Standard Arabic with many French words and phrases and occasionally some English. This echoed the multilingual practices of what I heard on radio and television and on billboards in the cities.

Enrolments in first-year classes were typically 100–150 students, although attendance was much lower, usually between 80–90 students. Given these class sizes, instructors typically lectured or worked through exercises with students, writing sentences on white boards and discussing possible grammatical constructions. Mostly these consisted of review of topics like the present perfect tense or conditionality. It seemed to me that students were not learning the language systematically, yet they also seemed enthusiastic about the lessons and took many notes; students told me that the structure of the lessons did help them to understand the structure of passages they read online or otherwise on their own.

At one university I had the opportunity to take over some classes for most of the semester, and designed a reading assessment in which students read short passages and gave short answers to questions of increasing difficulty that asked for literal responses in which they found information directly in the test; then questions in which they were required to combine two pieces of information to infer the correct response; and finally, critical questions, in which they were required to combine information in the text with information beyond the text to give a response. The passages were 100–150 words long and were written simply; however, most students read very slowly, taking sometimes 10 minutes to read a short passage. I also noticed that most "subvocalized," or read aloud softly as they worked; they seemed to be struggling, and the results of the assessment above the literal level were weak. I wondered if this was only a problem with their literacy in English or if it extended to their other literate languages, French and Standard Arabic, and if they had problems with writing as well as with reading. In my third semester, with the help of a Moroccan colleague I designed a reading test in three languages and a writing assessment in which students wrote essays in English, French, and Arabic in response to three equivalent prompts.

From these assessments I learned that the basic levels of literacy for the students were generally low across all three of their literate languages. Students scored highest in reading for the Standard Arabic test, followed by English and distantly by French, but the scores for all three assessments were generally low. The same results were found for the writing assessment, but with an unexpected twist: there was a great deal of *translingualism*, or translinguistic "sharing," across all essays. Students inserted English words and phrases within essays written in French and in Arabic, and vice versa, with more sharing between French and English than Arabic. Moreover, the sharing occurred at the level of words, of phrases, of idioms, of sentence structures, and of organization of the essays. Most significantly of all, there was a significant correlation between the amount of translingual sharing across the three essays and both the quantity and quality of the essays as measured by the TOEFL iBT Independent Writing Rubric (Educational Testing Service 2019): The greater the amount of translingualism in a writer's essays, the longer and better written the essays were. From these quantitative findings, in combination with field notes and other collected documents and artefacts, I have now begun to develop general insights into the relationship between formal and informal English acquisition and its relationship to language acquisition and use within multilingual cultural contexts.

5 Conclusion: The play of IDLE and the work of research

To a dedicated experimentalist or otherwise quantitative researcher, the preceding account of research likely appears seriously disorganized and messy. In the course of a curriculum development project, a researcher makes an interesting observation and decides to change course abruptly, revising research questions and instruments in process, following hunches, collecting data from disparate sources, and using a broad range of data to come to conclusions not simply about measured, carefully pre-defined phenomena, but about the broad social and cultural implications of the informal digital learning of English in Morocco. Where is the careful design, the linguistically framed research questions closely tied to validated instruments, the randomized selection of participants, and the narrow, objectively verified, conclusions? Is this research at all, or just some messing around?

Such criticisms, from a view of research grounded in the natural sciences, have merit, were the phenomena under study subject to the laws of physics or biochemistry or even, in many cases, linguistics. And yet, given the novelty of IDLE in Morocco, the context of students' learning both formally and informally, and the context in which IDLE could be observed and data collected, the messiness of the process was unavoidable. Indeed, I would argue that without the play of the investigative process, without following serendipitous leads and most of all without the expense of months of living and interacting within the environment in which students learned English both in and out of school, many critical insights would never have occurred, and the findings of the study would have been seriously distorted.

Without spending significant amounts of time in formal instructional settings, for example, the relationship between informal and formal learning would never have been seen. The relationship between learning other languages and the learning of English would also have been missed, and an image of IDLE in which students' learning/acquisition of English was contained within digital spaces would have been reinforced. Through participant observation and the documentation of language use across all contexts of Moroccan life, the integration of IDLE within the life worlds of students and its cultural and motivational significance for those students became apparent in ways that a purely quantified and pre-designed approach would have overlooked or dismissed.

Without the play of anthropology, the work of rigorous, systematic, applied linguistic research renders the study of IDLE a lifeless set of numbers documenting an interesting but possibly trivial phenomenon, easily dismissed by policy makers under the influence of educators with a stake in the maintenance of the status quo. With the play of anthropology comes narrative and theorizing and a view of English and its relationship to students' personal, cultural, and social identities with undeniable implications for educational policy and classroom teaching. On the other hand, without rigorous, carefully designed studies that complement and provide nuance and verification of ethnographic observations, the play of anthropology appears as simply playing around without serious intent. My argument in this chapter has been that the work of applied linguistics research needs the play of anthropology; but so, too, the playfulness of ethnographic research requires the temperance of measurement and careful design.

References

Althusser, Louis. 1971. *Lenin and Philosophy and Other Essays*. London: New Left Books.
Barthes, Roland. 1972. *Mythologies*. New York: Farrar, Strauss, and Giroux.
Benedict, Ruth. 1946. *The Chrysanthemum and the Sword*. New York: Houghton Mifflin.
Benson, Phil. 2011. Language learning and teaching beyond the classroom: An introduction to the field. In Phil Benson & Hayo Reinders (eds.), *Beyond the language classroom*, 7–16. Basingstoke/New York: Palgrave Macmillan.
Boas, Franz. 1904. The history of anthropology. *Science* 20(512). 513–523.
Boas, Franz. 1909. The relation of Darwin to anthropology. *Unpublished lecture delivered to commemorate the 50th Anniversary of the publication of the Origin of Species*. New York: Columbia University.
Bourdieu, Pierre. 1970. The Berber house or the world reversed. *Social Science Information* 9(2). 151–170.
Clifford, James & George E. Marcus. 1986. *Writing Culture: The Poetics and Politics of Ethnography: A School of American Research Advanced Seminar*. Berkeley: University of California Press.
Cole, Jason & Robert Vanderplank. 2016. Comparing autonomous and class-based learners in Brazil: Evidence for the present-day advantages of informal, out-of-class learning. *System* 61. 31–42.
Dressman, Mark. 2009. *Using Social Theory in Educational Research: A Practical Guide*. London: Routledge.
Dressman, Mark. 2013. Beyond disbelief: A confession of religion, technology and academic conceit. *Ethnography* 14(2). 255–274.
Dressman, Mark. 2020a. Multimodality and language learning. In Mark Dressman & Randall Sadler (eds.), *The Handbook of Informal Language Learning*, 39–55. Hoboken/Chichester: Wiley-Blackwell.
Dressman, Mark. 2020b. Informal English learning among Moroccan youth. In Mark Dressman & Randall Sadler (eds.), *The Handbook of Informal Language Learning*, 303–318. Hoboken/Chichester. Wiley-Blackwell.
Dressman, Mark, Ju Seong Lee & Laurent Perrot. 2023. *English Language Learning in the Digital Age: Learner-Driven Strategies for Adolescents and Young Adults*. Oxford: Wiley-Blackwell.
Eagleton, Terry. 1983. *Literary Theory: An Introduction*. Minneapolis: University of Minnesota Press.
Educational Testing Service. 2019. *TOEFL iBT Independent Writing Rubric*. Online: https://www.ets.org/s/toefl/pdf/toefl_writing_rubrics.pdf

Fiske, John. 2010. *Television Culture*, 2nd edn. London: Routledge.
Foley, Douglas E., Clarice Novaes da Mota, Donald E. Post & Ignacio Lozano. 1977. *From Peones to Politicos: Ethnic Relations in a South Texas Town, 1900 to 1977*. Austin: University of Texas Press.
Foley, Douglas E. 1990. *Learning Capitalist Culture: Deep in the Heart of Tejas*. University of Pennsylvania Press.
Foucault, Michel. 1977. *Discipline and Punish: The Birth of the Prison*. New York: Pantheon Books.
Geertz, Clifford. 1983. *Local Knowledge: Further Essays in Interpretive Anthropology*. New York: Basic Books.
Glaser, Barney. 1965. The constant comparative method of qualitative analysis. *Social Problems* 12(4). 436–445.
Freeman, Derek. 1983. *Margaret Mead and Samoa: The Making and Unmaking of an Anthropological Myth*. Cambridge: Harvard University Press.
Hemingway, Ernest. 1999. *Ernest Hemingway on Writing* (L. W. Phillips, ed.). New York: Touchstone.
Jurkovič, Violeta. 2019. Online informal learning of English through smartphones in Slovenia. *System* 80. 27–37.
Krashen, Stephen D. 1976. Formal and informal linguistic environments in language acquisition and language learning. *TESOL Quarterly* 10(2). 5–16.
Lai, Chun & Mingyue Gu. 2011. Self-regulated out-of-class language learning with technology. *Computer Assisted Language Learning* 24(4). 317–335.
Lee, Ju Seong. 2022. *Informal Digital Learning of English: Research to Practice*. New York: Routledge.
Lee, Ju Seong & Mark Dressman. 2018. When IDLE hands make an English workshop: Informal digital learning of English and language proficiency. *TESOL Quarterly* 52(2). 435–445.
Lévi Strauss, Claude. 1949. *Les Structures Élémentaires de la Parenté*. Paris: Presses Universitaires de France.
Lévi Strauss, Claude. 1969. *The Elementary Structures of Kinship*. Trans. J. H. Bell, J. R. von Sturmer & R. Needham. Boston: Beacon Press.
Lyotard, Jean-Francois. 1984. *The Postmodern Condition: A Report on Knowledge*. Minneapolis: University of Minnesota Press.
Malinowski, Bronislaw. 1922. *Argonauts of the Western Pacific: An Account of Native Enterprise and Adventure in the Archipelagoes of Melanesian New Guinea*. London: Routledge and Kegan Paul.
Malinowski, Bronislaw. 1989. *A Diary in the Strict Sense of the Term*. Stanford: Stanford University Press.
McLaren, Peter. 1986. *Schooling as a Ritual Performance: Towards a Political Economy of Educational Symbols and Gestures*. London: Routledge and Kegan Paul.
Mead, Margaret. 1928. *Coming of Age in Samoa*. New York: William Morrow and Company.
Monk, Ray. 2012. *Ludwig Wittgenstein: The Duty of Genius*. New York: Random House.
Pratt, Mary Louise. 1992. *Imperial Eyes: Travel Writing and Transculturation*. New York: Routledge.
Rabinow, Paul. 1977. *Reflections on Fieldwork in Morocco*. Berkeley: University of California Press.
Rothoni, Anastasia. 2018. The Complex relationship between home and school literacy: A Blurred boundary between formal and informal English literacy practices of Greek teenagers. *TESOL Quarterly* 52(2). 331–359.
Sayer, Peter & Ruth Ban. 2014. Young EFL students' engagements with English outside the classroom. *ELT Journal* 68(3). 321–329.
Sjöholm, Kaj. 2001. Incidental learning of English by Swedish learners in Finland. In Martin Gill, Anthony Johnson, Lena M. Koski, Roger Sell & Brita Wårvik (eds.), *Language, Learning, Literature: Studies Presented to Håkan Ringbom*, 77–89. Åbo: Åbo Akademi.
Sockett, Geoffrey. 2014. *The Online Informal Learning of English*. Basingstoke: Palgrave Macmillan.

Sundqvist, Pia & Liss Kerstin Sylvén. 2016. *Extramural English in Teaching and Learning: From Theory and Research to Practice*. Basingstoke: Palgrave Macmillan.
Truman, Benjamin. 1893. *History of the World's Fair: Being a Complete and Authentic Description of the Columbian Exposition from Its Inception*. Philadelphia: J. W. Keller and Co.
Turner, Graeme. 2002. *British Cultural Studies: An Introduction*, 3rd edn. London: Routledge.
Turner, Victor. 1967. *The Forest of Symbols: Aspects of Ndembu Ritual*. Ithaca: Cornell University Press.
Wilder, Thornton. 1965. *Our Town: A Play in Three Acts*. New York: Samuel French, Inc.

Meryl Kusyk
3 Does informal mean implicit?
Exploring the nature of informal second language learning

Abstract: A growing body of research on informal second language learning (ISLL) has shown that non-native speakers in various corners of the world can learn foreign languages via participation in online leisure activities such as television and video watching, playing video games or interacting on social media (Sockett 2014; Kusyk 2017a; Cole and Vanderplank 2016; Sundqvist 2009; Sundqvist and Sylvén 2016). During these usage events attention is primarily focused on meaning (rather than form) and often there is no intention to learn formal aspects of the language. At the same time, non-native speakers may be aware of the positive impact that informal activities can have on their L2 and may express a desire for their skills to improve as a "by-product" of participation (Kusyk 2017a). The question of which type(s) of learning would best characterize the cognitive processes at play in an ISLL context has not yet been thoroughly explored. The lack of intention to learn and the focus on meaning would seem to suggest that implicit processes may be at play, though the awareness of linguistic progress and a (peripheral) desire to improve would indicate that explicit aspects also play a role. Drawing on current literature in the field, this chapter examines different varieties of informal learning and situates them within the implicit-explicit & incidental-intentional learning discussion.

Keywords: Implicit learning, explicit learning, incidental learning, intentional learning, informal learning, ISLL varieties

1 Introduction

Better understanding the learning processes that underlie language development as well as how learned linguistic information is stored and represented in the mind, are principal lines of inquiry for language researchers. Within the field of second language acquisition (SLA), it has been hypothesized that fundamentally different types of learning take place when learning an L2. This notion was popularized by Krashen's *Acquisition versus Learning Hypothesis*, which stated that L2 *acquisition* takes place naturally and without conscious intervention, while L2 *learning* is effortful and involves attempts to learn the formal structure of the language system

---

Meryl Kusyk, Karlsruhe Univ of Education, Germany

(Krashen 1981, 1982).[1] Subsequently, language knowledge that has been *acquired* can be produced spontaneously, automatically and fluently while language knowledge that has been *learned* can only aid acquired knowledge in the form of a monitor, surveying output and intervening (correcting, editing, etc.), when sufficient attentional resources are present. Thus, Krashen considered the L2 learning endeavour as consisting of two fundamentally distinct systems – one unconscious and automatic (implicit), the other conscious and effortful (explicit).

While Krashen's work has since been criticized on theoretical and methodological grounds, on a conceptual level his acquisition-learning distinction continues to be a vibrant source of debate and inquiry. The idea that different systems underlie our ability to learn is one that has been studied in the fields of cognitive psychology, psycholinguistics and SLA. Research in these fields over the past several decades has contributed to a better understanding of the explicit and implicit processes (Krashen's 'learning' and 'acquisition', respectively) at play during both first and second language acquisition. Much still remains unknown, however, such as the extent to which explicit and implicit systems interact as well as how our implicit learning abilities change over time.

In addition to explicit and implicit learning, informal second language learning (ISLL) is a field of research that has gained considerable recognition in recent years. Known under a variety of labels – Extramural English, Informal Digital Learning of English, Language Learning Beyond the Classroom, to name a few – the field of ISLL investigates how individuals make language gains through exposure to and interaction with primarily leisure or meaning-based activities. Research on ISLL has grown rapidly over the past decade, with studies having been conducted in various parts of the world such as France (Sockett 2014; Kusyk 2017a), Sweden (Sundqvist & Sylvén 2016), South Korea (Lee 2019), Brazil (Cole & Vanderplank 2016), Denmark (Hannibal Jensen 2017) and Morocco (Dressman 2020b), among others. Researchers have examined a multitude of variables involved in the informal context, such as complexity, accuracy and fluency (Kusyk 2017a, 2017b, 2020), vocabulary development (Sundqvist 2009, 2019; Schwarz 2020), motivation and engagement (Arndt 2019), willingness to communicate and grit (Lee 2019), demotivation (Sundqvist & Olin-Scheller 2013), bridging possibilities with the formal sector (Henry et al. 2018), pronunciation (Yibokou 2019) and autonomy (Toffoli and Perrot 2017).

One variable that has not yet been studied within the ISLL context is the question of the *nature* of language learning. Based on findings from the field

---

[1] Except where specifically designated (for example, Krashen's *acquisition* versus *learning* distinction), the terms *learning* and *acquisition* are used interchangeably in this chapter.

within the last decade (see above), language usage in informal contexts would appear to align with both implicit and explicit modes of learning. On the one hand, some observed characteristics of informal language usage include a lack of intention to learn the L2 and a focus on meaning rather than language form. Sockett's (2011) definition of Online Informal Learning of English also acknowledges the potential lack of awareness of learning on the part of the individual L2 user. These characteristics would suggest that informal L2 learning might play out as an implicit process. Indeed, Williams (2009) argues that implicit learning is the typical learning mode in settings of incidental (non-intentional) learning. However, evidence for explicit learning also exists, as L2 users may have a peripheral (or even direct) intention to improve their language skills through informal usage and may also show awareness of learned items. In Sundqvist's definition of Extramural English, she acknowledges that "no degree of deliberate intention [. . .] is necessary on the part of the learner, even though deliberate intention is by no means excluded from the concept" (2009: 25). Participants of Extramural English may therefore, in theory, have clearly defined learning goals that they wish to achieve through their informal usage.

The present chapter addresses the following question with regard to the nature of informal language usage: can informal language learning / usage be best characterized as implicit learning, explicit learning or a combination of both? In order to answer this question, the terms explicit and implicit (regarding both learning and knowledge) will be reviewed. Two additional terms, intentional learning and incidental acquisition – the latter term showing particular relevance for the informal realm – will also be examined. Several informal language learning varieties will then be discussed with respect to these constructs and avenues for fruitful future investigations will be considered.

2 The implicit-explicit distinction

Before delving into the distinction between "explicit" versus "implicit", it is important to point out that the research community does not universally agree on a binary system view of learning, knowledge & memory. Shanks (2005) for example argues against a dissociation between implicit and explicit learning and contends that a single knowledge source underlies performance, while Baddeley (1997) critiques the dual system as overly simplistic and unable to account for the layered processes involved in learning (cf. Hulstijn 2015 for further discussion). However, due to its current prevalence in SLA and psycholinguistics research, the dual system approach shall be referenced here.

2.1 Explicit & implicit learning

The terms "explicit" and "implicit" can refer to learning, knowledge or memory, however only learning and knowledge will be dealt with in the present chapter. *Explicit learning* describes the processing of information whereby an individual consciously attempts to discover regularities within the input and the patterns that govern them (Hulstijn 2005). It involves making and testing hypotheses, is generally intentional in nature and can be characterized by the type of learning that goes on in educational establishments.

In contrast, the definition of *implicit learning*[2] is more layered and complex due to both the lack of consciousness and the lack of intention involved in the process. It is the primary form of learning that occurs when we learn our native language as an infant. According to N. C. Ellis "implicit learning is acquisition of knowledge about the underlying structure of a complex stimulus environment by a process which takes place naturally, simply and without conscious operations" (2008: 121). Individuals are unaware of the learning that has taken place and, in most cases, cannot verbalise what they have learned (R. Ellis 2009). Definitions of implicit learning also emphasize the unconscious mechanisms that guide the process, such as the automatic *tallying* that occurs while attending to a certain stimulus, thus resulting in knowledge about the distributional regularities in the input that is "subsymbolic, reflecting a statistical sensitivity to the structure of the learned material [. . .] learners remain unaware of the learning that has taken place, although it is evident in the behavioural responses they make" (R. Ellis 2009: 3). *Priming* refers to the preferential use or processing of a particular structure based on prior exposure to that structure (N. C. Ellis 2013). Priming can be observed across phonology, lexical choice, syntax and conceptual representation and has been shown to reveal various aspects of the implicit system.

While definitions of implicit learning emphasize its unconscious nature, certain discussions in the literature question whether or not it can be qualified as fully unconscious. Indeed, Baars' statement that "all learning requires conscious access to what is to be learnt" would suggest that the learning endeavour – whether implicit or explicit – calls for the presence of at least some level of consciousness (1997: 305). This statement finds support from the *Noticing Hypothesis* (Schmidt 1995), which contends that in order for language learning to occur, both attention towards and noticing of a language stimulus are necessary. For such

---

[2] Arthur Reber initially coined the term "implicit learning" in his 1965 MA thesis (Brown University). He chose "implicit" as a substitute for "unconscious" in an attempt to avoid any links with psychoanalysis and other psychological approaches that focus specifically on the unconscious (Reber 2015).

statements to be tested, however, it is important to clarify what is meant by certain constructs such as consciousness, awareness and noticing. Schmidt (1990) considers *consciousness* as *awareness*[3] and further distinguishes between two types of awareness: *awareness* as *noticing* and *metalinguistic awareness* (Schmidt 2001). The former involves conscious attention to certain features of an input stimulus and the latter involves awareness of the underlying rule system of a given language. While researchers would agree that implicit learning does not involve the latter type of metalinguistic awareness (R. Ellis 2009), the multifaceted and ambiguous nature of the construct of awareness makes it "one of the slipperiest to operationalize and measure in both second language acquisition (SLA) and non-SLA fields" (Leow et al. 2011: 61). As it is beyond the scope of this chapter to debate and investigate the term awareness and its associated constructs, the following definitions are used: *noticing* is considered to be the corresponding subjective experience that results from *attention* (that is, noticing is attention plus a certain degree of awareness (Schmidt 1995, 2001)). Attention is considered to consist of a variety of mechanisms such as alertness, orientation or detection; it is limited, selective and partially subject to voluntary control (Schmidt 2001). According to Baars' theatre metaphor in which the stage is our unconscious mind, attention is the spotlight and "only events in the bright spot on stage are strictly conscious" (1997: 303). Thus, attention controls access to awareness.

In contrast to Schmidt's (1995) *Noticing Hypothesis*, N. C. Ellis (2005) argues that while noticing is not necessary for the unconscious mechanisms of priming and tallying to take place, attention is. In other words, we do not automatically (unconsciously) tally everything in our stimulus environment, rather, only the stimuli that are attended to. In N. C. Ellis's view, attention is a first necessary, albeit conscious, step in the process of implicit learning, after which unconscious and automatic processing may take place. And while he argues that implicit learning without noticing is technically possible (see also Williams 2005), he nevertheless underscores its importance, especially in the initial registration of new information (N. C. Ellis 2002). Once registered, "there is scope for its implicit learning on every subsequent occasion of use" (N. C. Ellis 2005: 321). In other words, during subsequent usage events, noticing of the already-registered item in question is no longer necessary for implicit learning to occur: "mere usage in processing is enough for this implicit tallying, priming and strengthening to take place" (N. C. Ellis 2005: 321).

---

[3] In N. C. Ellis 1994a, 1994b, 1994c the terms awareness and consciousness are also used synonymously.

Investigating the role of implicit learning within SLA is an ongoing endeavour. There is currently no consensus as to whether it truly exists in L2 learning, as findings from studies offer evidence both for and against learning without awareness (see Leow 2015, for an overview). Despite the ongoing debate surrounding construct terminology as well as the operationalisation and measurement of awareness, the present chapter shall adopt the argument put forth by N. C. Ellis (2005), that is, in order for learning to occur, attention is needed. This implies that implicit learning is not fully unconscious at all levels as it does not signify unattended learning. However, once novel items have been registered, there is scope for implicit learning / processing during subsequent usage events.

2.2 Explicit & implicit knowledge

Explicit and implicit knowledge refer to the extent to which an individual is aware or unaware, respectively, of the rules, patterns and regularities that underlie a given stimulus (e.g., linguistic input) and whether they can verbalise them or not (Hulstijn 2005). According to R. Ellis "there is broad consensus that the acquisition of an L2 entails the development of implicit knowledge. However, there is no consensus on how this is achieved; nor is there consensus on the role played by explicit knowledge" (2005: 143). This statement highlights two key issues: how implicit knowledge is achieved in SLA and the potential interface between the implicit and explicit systems (and consequently, the effects they may have on each other). While it may appear intuitive to assume that explicit learning results in explicit knowledge and implicit learning results in implicit knowledge, this is not necessarily the case. According to Paciorek and Williams (2015), the presence of implicit knowledge presupposes the prior occurrence of implicit learning, except in cases in which prior explicit knowledge has been automatised. However, the claim that automatised explicit knowledge is the qualitative equivalent to implicit knowledge is a disputed one (Hulstijn 2002). Inversely, implicit acquisition does not necessarily directly lead to implicit knowledge as unconscious knowledge may emerge into awareness. In other words, we may reflect on knowledge that we have acquired implicitly and subsequently develop an explicit representation of it (R. Ellis 2009). Finally, instances of explicit learning usually lead to explicit knowledge (except, as previously mentioned, in cases of automatization of this knowledge).

R. Ellis (2005: 151) summarizes the primary differences between implicit and explicit knowledge. Implicit knowledge involves a feeling or intuition for what 'sounds right', thereby reflecting underlying knowledge of the patterns, categories and distributional regularities of the language. Language users are unable to explain why something is correct or incorrect; implicit knowledge is therefore said to be non-verbalizable and only evident in actual language use. Any attempt to verbalize or explain usage of a particular form involves the creation of a separate, explicit representation of the knowledge item, which can exist in varying degrees of specificity and exactness (R. Ellis 2005; Dienes & Perner 1999). Subsequently, it is possible that language users have both implicit and explicit knowledge of the same linguistic item (R. Ellis 2009). Explicit knowledge, on the other hand, is evident when an individual knows *why* a certain structure is grammatical or ungrammatical and can explain this in either general or metalinguistic terms. Implicit knowledge displays higher certainty and lower variability than explicit knowledge, while the latter often demonstrates inconsistency and imprecision. In terms of access to knowledge, implicit knowledge involves automatic access while explicit knowledge involves controlled access. However, this latter point has been disputed in the literature. Drawing on *Skill Acquisition Theory* and the ACT-R approach to learning, DeKeyser (2003) suggests that explicit knowledge can be fully automatized and can therefore function as an equivalent to implicit knowledge. Hulstijn (2002), however, argues that while access to explicit knowledge can be accelerated, automaticity of access remains fundamentally different in implicit compared to explicit knowledge. Finally, while acknowledging its controversial implications, R. Ellis (2005) suggests that although explicit knowledge is learnable at any age, implicit knowledge is subjected to the age-related constraints that form the basis of the sensitive / critical period hypothesis.

As much of the scientific inquiry dedicated to the study of implicit and explicit learning deals with the potential interactions between the two systems, the following section will briefly address the interface question.

2.3 The interface question

One of the main questions explored in the past three decades of research on the explicit and implicit learning systems examines the extent to which an interface exists between the two dimensions (Rebuschat 2015). Researchers have explored such questions as: does explicit L2 knowledge (e.g., in the form of learned or taught pedagogical rules) promote the development of implicit L2 knowledge and can explicit L2 knowledge be transformed into L2 implicit knowledge? Three main perspectives to this line of inquiry have emerged: the non-interface position, the weak interface position and the strong interface position.

Proponents of the *non-interface position* (Krashen 1982; Paradis 2004) contend that there is no direct interface between explicit and implicit knowledge and that the latter cannot be generated from the former through practice. Some researchers whose non-interface stance is based on neurophysiological reasoning (information in one area of the brain cannot physically transform itself into information stored in other neural regions) do not, however, deny the potential impact that dedicated practice can have on the creation of implicit knowledge. According to Hulstijn (2015: 36), it is conceivable that "through extensive practice with instances representing a certain grammatical regularity, guided by a declarative, conscious knowledge of that regularity, an implicit representation of it [. . .] gradually emerges elsewhere in the brain". The *strong interface position* claims that explicit knowledge can be derived from implicit knowledge and that explicit knowledge can be transformed into implicit knowledge through practice (R. Ellis 2005). Finally, the *weak interface position* acknowledges the possibility that explicit knowledge can indirectly contribute to the creation of implicit knowledge "by promoting certain processes in which implicit learning can occur (e.g., controlled practice) or by making certain features of the language salient" (Dörnyei 2009: 161).

None of these positions has achieved dominance or a full consensus within the scientific community, however their very existence has encouraged research and furthered collective knowledge of the constructs. Sidestepping the qualitative transformation aspects of the interface question, Dörnyei (2009: 171) points out that, "the key to L2 learning efficiency is the successful *co-operation* of the explicit and implicit learning systems" (author's emphasis). Thus, while it remains unclear if explicit learning may lead to implicit knowledge or if explicit knowledge can be converted into implicit knowledge, some scholars instead focus on ways in which the two systems can complement and compensate for one another (Dörnyei 2009).

3 Incidental & intentional L2 learning

In addition to explicit and implicit learning, two other learning constructs are widely used in the SLA literature: *intentional* and *incidental learning*. On a superficial level, intentional and incidental learning appear to correspond with explicit and implicit learning, respectively. Intentional learning refers to "any activity geared at committing lexical information to memory" (Hulstijn 2001: 271). Although intentional and explicit learning are often used in conjunction with one another, they are not synonymous: *intentional* connotes learning that is goal-related or motivationally focused while *explicit* refers to learning that involves online awareness and hypothesis formation but not necessarily a direct intention to learn (Hulstijn 2003).

In contrast, definitions of incidental acquisition centre on the *unintentional* aspects of language use. Rieder (2003) considers incidental acquisition as a process that does not involve the intention to learn but which also does not restrict the role that awareness (of the learning process) might play. Schmidt (1994) acknowledges the absence of intention to learn and proposes, in addition, that incidental acquisition involves learning one aspect of the linguistic input while paying attention to another. For example, learning formal aspects of the language (grammar, syntax) while concentrating on semantic aspects (communication, meaning). Loewan et al. (2009) define incidental acquisition as learning in the absence of intention but which may involve spontaneous conscious attention applied to certain aspects of the L2. The "acquisition as a side-effect" and unintentional nature of incidental acquisition may invite comparisons to the construct of implicit learning. However, it is important to not confound the two terms as they have traditionally involved different avenues of research and bodies of literature.[4] In addition, "while implicit learning may subsume incidental learning, incidental learning may involve both implicit and explicit learning primarily based on how learners interact differentially with the L2 data" (Leow 2015: 54). Thus, the incidental L2 learner does not use the language in order to learn it but may "pick up" certain aspects while paying attention to others and may experience degrees of awareness during usage.

Leow's (2015) above statement that incidental learning involves both explicit and implicit mechanisms would suggest that the term exists in a kind of conceptual grey zone. Rieder (2003: 26) also highlights its nebulous nature, in that it "is non-explicit in so far as it does not involve an explicit learning intention (the overall goal of the learner is text comprehension), but neither the process nor the product of such learning is necessarily implicit in the sense of non-conscious". Rieder (2003: 28) considers incidental vocabulary acquisition as a process that takes place without intention and that is achieved by:

- implicit learning (lack of intention and awareness)
  and / or
- explicit learning (lack of intention, presence of online awareness and potential hypothesis formation).

Delving deeper into her conceptual analysis, Rieder (2003) draws on N. C. Ellis' (1994a, 1994b, 1994c, 1997) account of implicit and explicit features of incidental vocabulary acquisition. In his perspective "both implicit and explicit learning mechanisms are involved in incidental vocabulary acquisition: while the acquisition of a

---

[4] The majority of literature produced on incidental acquisition in leisure (informal) contexts has focused on vocabulary acquisition, particularly from reading.

word's form, collocations and grammatical class information are said to involve implicit processes, acquiring a word's semantic properties and mapping word form to meaning are claimed to result from explicit learning processes" (Rieder 2003: 29). According to Rieder's (2003) analysis, N. C. Ellis also argues that the implicit and explicit features of incidental acquisition are distinct and dissociated from one another. The extent to which an interface between the explicit and implicit realms exists or doesn't exist has been extensively discussed in the literature (see above). Though there is no current consensus in the SLA or psycholinguistic communities regarding this question, it is interesting to note that later works of N. C. Ellis appear to consider, or even support, the possibility of an interface between the implicit and explicit domains: "the degree of influence of metalinguistic information on the nature of the processing is so profound that claims of interface and interaction seem fully justified" (2005: 325).

The construct of incidental learning is particularly relevant to the domain of ISLL as informal learning is generally characterized by interaction in meaning-focused activities (that is, the intention to learn the language itself is often absent) and by varying degrees of awareness. The following section presents a brief overview of the field of ISLL as well as some recent findings.

4 Informal second language learning

Research on ISLL has surged over the past decade, with reports of informal learning coming from across the globe. Due to the fact that language use in the informal sphere has now been observed by a multitude of researchers in diverse environments, several different labels have been invented to describe the phenomenon. This has led to a considerable amount of conceptual and terminological confusion in the literature. Indeed, it would appear as though ISLL suffers from the "jingle jangle" problem (Reschly and Christenson 2012), which occurs when both a single term is used inconsistently in the literature to describe different phenomena (jingle) and when different terms are used to study the same thing (jangle). For example, when ISLL researchers conduct literature searches for the term "informal", their results may very well pertain to "non-formal" or "formal-disguised-as-informal" (e.g., teacher-led) learning (jingle). On the other hand, different labels like "extramural" and "in the wild" both refer to the same type of informal learning that is fully autonomous and L2-user-initiated (jangle). Some of the current varieties that qualify themselves as "informal" SLA include Extramural English (EE), Online Informal Learning of English (OILE), Language Learning Beyond the Classroom (LBC), Out-of-class language learning (OOC) and Informal

Digital Learning of English (IDLE). In the following section the similarities and differences of each of these varieties will be discussed.

Generally speaking, diversity in a field of research allows for a comprehensive approach to investigating a given phenomenon, however the current diversity of terms used to describe participation in L2 activities in the informal sphere has blurred the borders between varieties in ways that have led to confusion and inconsistency. To be sure, within Education Sciences the construct "informal learning" is also notoriously ambiguous and faces challenges in its operationalization on several levels, including the conceptual level (what does informal refer to?), the methodological level (how does one measure it?) and the recognition / validation level (what value is attributed to it?) (Schugurensky 2007). It therefore comes as no surprise that the construct's application within SLA has also given rise to a certain level of ambiguity. Benson (2011a) has tried to contribute structure and clarity to the construct, outlining the different dimensions of his variety of ISLL, Language Learning Beyond the Classroom (LBC). He identifies location, degree of formality, degree of pedagogy and locus of control as points of departure for classifying the nuanced nature(s) of LBC and proposes descriptions and terms for each of these dimensions.

More recently, Reinders and Benson (2017) discussed dimensions of the informal sphere in light of recent developments and new findings in the field. They identified additional factors from current ISLL research that could help complement Benson's (2011a) original model such as mediation (in the form of resources used), sociality (the social relationships involved in language use), modality of use (the different language practices in effect), language skills and levels of competence needed for language use, as well as engagement trajectories (Chik 2014) and the variety of activities and the degree to which they are meaning-focused (Lai et al. 2015). In their discussion of relevant components of a potential LBC model Reinders and Benson (2017) also considered learning processes that may underlie LBC, including intentional versus incidental learning, explicit versus implicit learning and inductive versus deductive learning (though no further discussion or analysis was provided).

Though still in its early stages, research on informal L2 learning has covered much ground in the last two decades, particularly in the latter. Studies have investigated such variables as vocabulary (Sundqvist 2019; Sundqvist & Wickström 2015; Schwarz 2020; Hannibal Jensen 2017; Lee 2019), oral proficiency (Sundqvist 2009), complexity, accuracy & fluency (Kusyk 2017a, Kusyk 2017b), chunks (Kusyk & Sockett 2012; Kusyk 2017a, Sockett & Kusyk 2015), motivation, engagement and attitudes (Arndt 2019), proficiency (Lee & Dressman 2018), pronunciation (Yibokou 2019), autonomy (Godwin-Jones 2019; Toffoli & Perrot 2017), learning beliefs (Lai 2019) and willingness to communicate, motivation and grit (Lee & Drajati 2019; Lee & Drajati 2020), to name but a few. A recent review of the literature examined 30 ISLL articles and found that 70% focused on linguistic features, 16% focused on digital literacies and agency and 13% focused on affective and cultural aspects of ISLL (Soyoof et al. 2021). While the above examples as well as the scope of Soyoof et al.'s (2021) review are certainly non-exhaustive and do not cover the full diversity of issues examined within ISLL, they do point to a potential tendency to focus on the effects of informal exposure on the learning process. Studying gains in vocabulary development, fluctuations in complexity, accuracy and fluency or the acquisition of multiword expressions certainly provides important insight into the learning potential that informal activities hold for the L2 user. However, what has not yet been extensively explored in this regard are the deeper learning processes that underpin usage. The following section will therefore explore five different varieties of ISLL and, based on the above discussion of explicit, implicit, intentional and incidental modes of learning, consider the natures of learning that are likely to underlie them.

5 The nature of informal second language learning

One of the most recent definitions of informal second language learning comes from Dressman (2020a: 4) in the foreword to the first *Handbook of Informal Language Learning*:

> Informal language learning refers to any activities taken consciously or unconsciously by a learner outside of formal instruction that lead to an increase in the learner's ability to communicate in a second (or other, non-native) language [. . .] from in-the-moment "lessons" with friends and family members who speak a target language to environmental print to encounters as a tourist to subtitled or captioned video to chatrooms with friends and family, the chat of MMORPGs, or chat within spaces that are three dimensional and either virtual or augmented in their reality. [. . .] In short, the use of the term informal language learning includes all activities undertaken by learners outside a formally organized program of language instruction.

Dressman offers a global definition, encompassing factors such as the active, intentional steps an individual may take to learn the language,[5] both online / digital and

---

[5] It is unclear whether "non-formal" activities fit in this definition of "informal". According to Schugurensky (2007), non-formal activities are educational activities that occur outside of the school environment. Within an ISLL context this could conceivably take the form of self-initiated participation in a language learning application such as DuoLingo or Rosetta Stone, which is

in-person modalities, as well as both receptive and productive language usage. He deliberately goes beyond the more specific, distinct definitions of certain informal varieties in order to offer an all-inclusive portrait that takes into account the dynamic and diverse forms of interaction and usage that an L2 user may engage in. While this description offers an umbrella under which the different types of ISLL may find points of attachment, the present analysis of the nature of informal language learning will focus on just a selection of these individual varieties in order to assess the possible types of learning that may underlie them. These include Extramural English, Online Informal Learning of English, Language Learning Beyond the Classroom, Out-of-Class Language Learning and Informal Digital Language Learning.

5.1 Definitions

Extramural English (EE) is a term coined by Sundqvist from her 2009 dissertation on informal English learning in Sweden. She defines it as "the English that learners come in contact with or are involved in outside the walls of the classroom" (2009: 25). EE therefore investigates activities such as surfing the internet, playing video games and watching television, but it is not limited to the online or digital domain. Sundqvist addresses the question of intention, clarifying that "no degree of deliberate intention to acquire English is necessary on the part of the learner, even though deliberate intention is by no means excluded from the concept" (2009: 25).

The Online Informal Learning of English (OILE) has primarily been studied in French and German contexts and refers to "language development through online activities such as social networking, streaming and / or downloading television series or films, listening to music on demand and web browsing" (Toffoli and Sockett 2015: 1). Participation in these activities is self-directed and not associated with any formal educational or structured learning framework. L2 users may or may not be aware of any acquisition that takes place (Sockett 2011) and intention to learn the language is usually not the primary reason for L2 use (Kusyk 2017a). The researchers who coined the term OILE, Toffoli and Sockett, emphasize incidental acquisition as relevant to the underlying learning process, though no OILE study has attempted to specifically measure the construct (Toffoli and Sockett 2010; Sockett 2011).

---

arguably a wholly different nature of interaction than that of fully meaning-based participation with no intention to learn the language.

Language Learning Beyond the Classroom (LBC) is also a term that is prevalent in the literature. Benson (2011a) prefers it as an umbrella term (much as Dressman (2020a) uses "informal language learning" above) rather than labels such as extramural, informal, naturalistic, self-directed or autonomous, as he views LBC to be more inclusive than these latter terms. In his perspective, these alternative terms function better as specific descriptors of the four dimensions of his LBC model (location, formality, pedagogy, locus of control). Benson (2011a: 13) describes LBC as a field of inquiry that is "concerned with locations for language learning other than the classroom and with relationships between these locations and aspects of formality, pedagogy and locus of control". Importantly, there is a direct connection with the classroom: "LBC does not exclude the classroom but rather connects with it" (Reinders and Benson 2017: 563). It is worth mentioning that some authors use the term "beyond the classroom" seemingly as a general descriptor of activities that do not physically take place in the classroom, without explicitly referring to Benson's LBC model (Nunan and Richards 2015; Richards 2014).

Out-of-Class Language Learning (OOC) is a term that is often used in conjunction, or even synonymously, with LBC (Nunan and Richards 2015; Richards 2015; Reinders 2014; Benson 2011a; Benson and Reinders 2011). Indeed, in Nunan and Richard's (2015) *Language Learning Beyond the Classroom*, the term "out-of-class" is ubiquitous and is even featured in section titles, such as Part I, *Involving the Learner in Out-of-Class Learning*. In OOC the teacher appears to play a prominent role in suggesting (or even setting up) activities, pointing out metacognitive strategies, encouraging learner autonomy and acting as a general guide for activities outside of the classroom (Nunan 2015; Reinders 2014). According to Benson (2011b: 139), "out-of-class learning is typically initiated by the learner, makes use of authentic resources, and involves pleasure and interest, as well as language learning. In these respects, much out-of-class learning takes the forms of 'self-directed naturalistic learning', in which the learner engages in language use for pleasure or interest, but also with the broader intention of learning". Thus, OOC appears to have a strong link with the formal sector and usually involves a direct learning intention on the part of the L2 user.

Research on the Informal Digital Learning of English (IDLE) has been carried out in several countries, such as South Korea and Morocco, and is defined as "self-directed, informal English learning using a range of different digital devices (e.g., smartphones, desktop computers) and resources (e.g., web apps, social media) independent of formal contexts" (Lee 2017: 768). Lee (2020) aligns IDLE with OILE and EE in respect to their taking place independently of the formal sphere. Lee (2017) states that IDLE is theoretically underpinned by the construct of incidental acquisition but provides no further explanation of this relationship.

The role of intention to learn has not been explicitly addressed in IDLE, with "casual conversation" or "socializing" used as examples of IDLE practices (e.g., Lee 2019: 116; Lee 2020: 156). However, data from IDLE studies have also examined "form-focused" activities that demand attention to accuracy of linguistic forms, such as using translation software or online dictionaries (Lee 2017: 771). Interview data have also suggested that some IDLE participants engage in activities in order to improve their language skills, such as joining a TESOL community on Facebook or practicing one's spoken English (Lee 2017: 774). Thus it appears safe to assume that, just as with OILE and EE, intention to learn the language is not necessary, but may be present in IDLE.

The following subsection will take a closer look at each of these five varieties in terms of the explicit, implicit, incidental and intentional qualities they may feature.

6 Discussion

As a point of departure for a discussion on the intersection between the five different varieties of ISLL and the four different types of learning that may underlie them, Figure 1 presents an intention / awareness continuum that shows the absence (–) or presence (+) of these primary features within the different types of learning discussed above.[6]

Here, intentional learning is displayed as the most actively conscious type of learning in that it features both awareness and intention. Explicit learning appears next with the presence of consciousness (as per this construct's definition) and the possibility of both the presence or the absence of intention to learn. As the third construct on the continuum, incidental acquisition features a clear absence of intention to learn and individuals both may or may not experience awareness while learning. Incidental acquisition has been shown to feature both explicit and implicit qualities and due to its meaning-based and learning-as-a-side-effect qualities it has been referred to as "implicit-like". Finally, implicit learning is

---

6 This oversimplified continuum serves to present general differences between these four types of learning. The suggested absence of awareness in implicit learning refers to definitions that indicate a lack of "conscious operations" (N. C. Ellis 2008: 121) or those which underscore the importance of underlying unconscious mechanisms such as tallying (R. Ellis 2009) or priming (N. C. Ellis 2013). These definitions notwithstanding, it is important to recall the ambiguous nature of consciousness / awareness in implicit learning as well as the assertion that it qualifying it as fully unconscious may not be accurate (see Section 2.1).

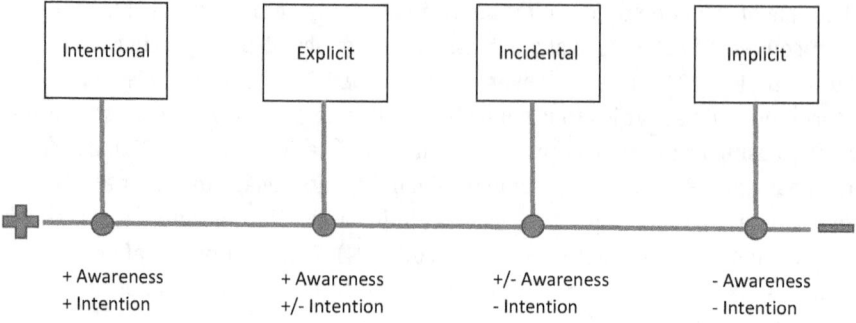

Figure 1: Intention-awareness continuum.

presented as the "least conscious" learning type in that there is a presumed absence of awareness and of intention to learn.

A more fine-grained examination of each learning type allows us to consider additional characteristics such as meaning-based interactions or frequency effects:
- Implicit learning involves meaning-based interaction, it is frequency-sensitive, there is no intention to learn, there is a lack of awareness (of learning & its results) and it is involved in the fine-tuning and strengthening of associations.
- Incidental learning involves meaning-based interaction, there is no intention to learn, there is a potential lack of awareness and it has shown to be beneficial for fine-tuning vocabulary knowledge (that is, enhancing already-met items rather than learning novel items).
- Explicit learning is conscious and can be intentional.
- Intentional learning involves active efforts to learn as well as an underlying motivational component.

Cross-checking these characteristics against the different versions of ISLL, it becomes clear that nearly all characteristics are in fact featured in informal learning contexts. Firstly, all five varieties of ISLL acknowledge that participation in the informal sphere may involve *meaning-based interaction* that is naturalistic, involves communication or emphasizes leisure. Both *intention to learn* and a *lack of intention to learn* are featured: while in EE and OILE (and presumably IDLE) no intention to learn is required on the part of the individual, in OOC intention is inherent in participation. LBC does not specifically address intention but in consideration of its use as an umbrella term for all varieties of ISLL and due to its clear connection to the classroom, intention would appear to play an important role. While *frequency effects* are important in implicit learning and incidental acquisition, they are not mentioned in the general descriptions of any of the five ISLL varieties.

However, several OILE studies have explored frequency effects in terms of participation levels (Kusyk 2017a) and chunk frequency in informal content (Sockett 2011). Indeed, though characteristics such as *fine-tuning* or *strengthening of associations* have not yet been studied within an ISLL context, the field of L2 incidental vocabulary learning has in recent years expanded its primary modality of choice (reading) to include television and movie viewing (both extensive and normal), thus aligning it even more closely with ISLL. Drawing on the comprehensive findings of incidental acquisition researchers (see for example Webb and Rodgers 2020; Rodgers 2013; Peters and Webb 2018; Uchihara et al. 2019) informal researchers could aim to investigate the fine-tuning or depth of knowledge for lexical items encountered in informal input. Finally, no ISLL study has specifically addressed the construct of *awareness*, thus no data exist on either the presence or absence of awareness in informal contexts. However, LBC and OOC appear to be contexts in which awareness would be present, due to their intentional learning undertones. This does not deny the possibility that some degree of implicit learning may take place in LBC and OOC, but it is unlikely to be the predominant form of learning due to their emphasis on intentional learning.

An additional perspective of the learning types at play in ISLL varieties can be seen in Figure 2. Here, circle size represents the suggested relevance for each informal context. The top row features EE, OILE and IDLE. Based on their descriptions, all three appear to rest on a similar learning-type foundation. Indeed, intention is likely to play a smaller role due to the emphasis on meaning-based activities (though

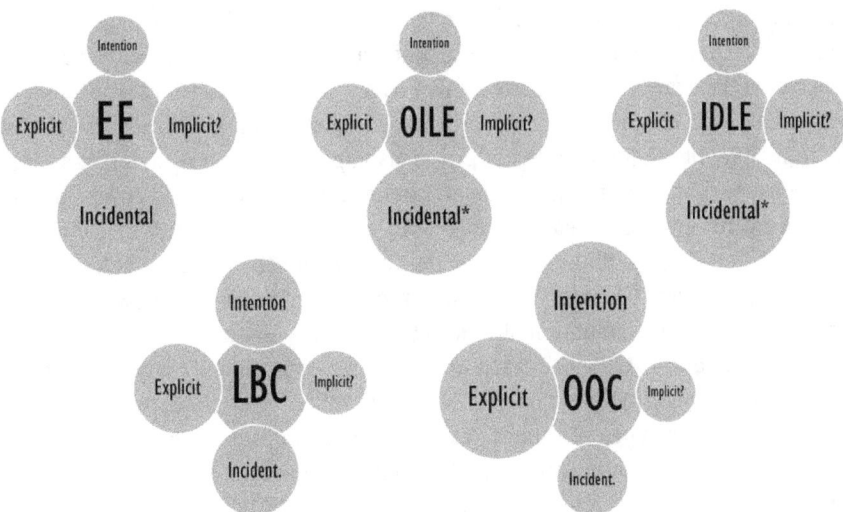

Figure 2: Varieties of ISLL and the potential learning types that may characterize them.

it is not excluded), while incidental learning may potentially play an important role. The asterisk serves as a reminder that both OILE and IDLE have mentioned incidental acquisition as a relevant learning framework in which these phenomena can be examined, though neither have specifically operationalized or measured the construct. It is safe to assume that explicit learning is experienced in all three informal varieties, since intention to learn is not ruled out and any instance of intentional learning would inherently imply that awareness is consciously directed towards a given stimulus. Implicit learning is marked with a question mark as no ISLL study to date has attempted to target the construct of awareness. However, informal L2 users have been known to spend extraordinary amounts of time on certain activities (Kusyk 2017a; Cole and Vanderplank 2016), which could provide fruitful opportunities for implicit learning to occur.

The remaining two informal varieties, LBC and OOC, are featured on a separate row so as to highlight their differences with EE, OILE and IDLE. The primary distinction between the two levels concerns the role of intention and the formal sphere. Indeed, OOC directly emphasizes both the role of the classroom as well as the intention upon the part of the individual to learn the language. LBC also calls attention to "connecting" with the formal sphere. As LBC aims at inclusion of all informal varieties, its representational graphic is more evenly distributed, with the exception of implicit learning which may be slightly minimized due to the aforementioned link with formal learning.

It is clear from the present analysis and discussion that teasing out the nature(s) of informal L2 learning is a complex endeavour, involving much overlap and speculation. Indeed, the above analysis is based on already-existing definitions, descriptions and findings. In order to truly investigate how learning takes place in an informal context a study must have this objective firmly embedded in its design. This chapter nevertheless explores the question of which type(s) of learning may best characterize the processes at play during informal second language usage. The present discussion of current ISLL literature has revealed that, until now, the nature of learning has largely been ignored in the field. Indeed, Reinders and Benson (2017) is one of the few papers that directly refers to the learning processes that may accompany informal activity usage, however, these processes are merely mentioned and not thoroughly discussed. This is also the case for OILE and IDLE with regard to incidental acquisition. Despite the existing ambiguity surrounding the nature of learning in ISLL, it would appear as though multiple learning types – implicit, explicit, incidental, intentional – may come into play within a specific variety and perhaps even during a given period of activity usage. Indeed, given the overlap between the informal varieties, the dynamic relationships that L2 users have with their activities, their fluctuating reasons for participating as well as the changing contexts in which the L2 is used, it is debatable as to whether an individual's informal usage could be restricted to just one variety.

It is important to note that a number of additional ISLL labels were not included in the present analysis. These include Out-of-School Contact (Munoz et al. 2018), Language Learning in the Digital Wilds (Godwin-Jones 2019; Sauro and Zourou 2019), Autonomous Language Learning with Technology (Lai 2017) and Fully Autonomous Self-Instructed Learners (Cole and Vanderplank 2016), among others. Moving forward, it will be important for ISLL as a field of research to sort through the conceptual and terminological haziness, identify both overlap and points of divergence and arrive at a coherent, consistent use of terms.

7 Looking forward: The nature of learning & knowledge in future ISLL research

It is clear that ISLL as an area of research would benefit from knowing more about *how* learning takes place in informal environments. Such investigations can help contribute to answering overarching questions in the field of SLA, such as the availability of implicit L2 learning, under which conditions it may occur, the role of explicit learning in SLA or the relationship between the explicit and implicit systems. As mentioned above, in order to produce reliable, generalizable findings, ISLL researchers need to design studies that specifically target the nature of learning. They must also be clear on the definitions, terms and labels they use when operating within the framework of a given ISLL variety (see previous section). To be sure, operationalizing "slippery" (Leow 2015) constructs such as awareness is an exceptional challenge. The researcher must also take care not to conflate terms and only answer those research questions that have been asked. According to R. Ellis (2009: 6), studies on explicit and implicit *learning* in SLA often actually investigate the constructs in reference to the *knowledge* that has resulted from task conditions (designed to favour either explicit or implicit learning). Thus, by examining the product of learning, the process of learning is inferred. And yet, in order to demonstrably show that implicit learning has taken place at both the process and product levels, researchers need to ensure that learners really were unaware, that even low levels of awareness were accounted for, that learners processed the stimulus with very low cognitive effort and that learners did not use any strategies to remember the targeted stimulus (Leow 2015: 62).

Measuring explicit learning and knowledge is, to be sure, far simpler than attempting to identify implicit learning and knowledge, due to the former's presence of awareness. A learner can verbalize their knowledge and demonstrate

awareness through specific explanations. While measuring the implicit system proves to be a challenging endeavour, various methodological approaches could be adopted which aim to report on the implicit (or incidental) system as it operates in the informal realm. These include:
- A focus on fluency, as fluent (automatic) speech is largely automatized and draws on implicit knowledge (Foster 2021; Dörnyei 2009).
- A focus on frequency effects such as collocations and formulaic knowledge, as their use also draws on implicit knowledge (Foster 2021; Dörnyei 2009).
- Employing timed (oral) grammaticality judgment tests, which draw on implicit knowledge (R. Ellis 2005).
- Employing think-aloud protocols, which target online awareness (that is, the *process* of implicit learning; Paciorek and Williams 2015).
- Conducting longitudinal studies, as short duration studies may inherently be biased against implicit learning (R. Ellis 2009).

Findings from studies employing the above measures could provide great insight into the nature of the informal learning process.

Finally, due to the intricate interplay of variables at play "in the wild", it may be useful to adopt a complex and dynamic systems theory approach to the study of ISLL (Larsen-Freeman 1997; Kusyk 2017a, 2017b; Godwin-Jones 2018). This framework emphasizes the dynamic interactions between a multitude of variables over the trajectory of a given system, which could be helpful for studying individuals who participate in a variety of activities (including varying modalities) and have fluctuating levels of motivation, engagement, and affect for the target material. Similarly, this approach may be useful for studying the different types of learning mentioned in this chapter as it is clear that they also involve a high degree of complexity and a multitude of variables (e.g., the construct of awareness or the "conceptual grey zone" of incidental learning). Finally, as the binary distinction of explicit and implicit learning and knowledge has been critiqued as overly simplistic (Baddeley 1997), complex and dynamic systems theory could be a relevant framework for investigating the potential interactions between these different systems.

8 Conclusion

To date, the field of ISLL has not yet thoroughly explored *which* types of learning are at play during informal activity usage. This chapter therefore set out to discuss the nature of informal second language learning through the lens of four learning constructs: explicit, implicit, intentional and incidental learning. To begin, these constructs were reviewed and briefly discussed. As the awareness / intention continuum (Figure 1) shows, the borders between some constructs are porous and certain characteristics are shared. The latter half of this chapter dealt with informal second language learning and specific varieties within this field. Like the learning constructs above, the five informal varieties presently examined – EE, OILE, LBC, OOC, IDLE – also demonstrate considerable overlap as well as some conceptual and terminological confusion. It is clear that, moving forward, the greater field of ISLL must clarify the labels it uses and be more specific as to how learning proceeds within a given variety. Only then can future studies address the specific nature(s) of learning within each variety. The present analysis suggests that all four learning types may be present in each of the five ISLL varieties and that it is possible that a given individual may participate in multiple informal varieties during their L2 usage. The current lack of data on the nature of ISLL could be addressed by carrying out specifically designed studies that target clearly defined learning constructs. In closing, we may consider the words of the founding father of implicit learning, Arthur Reber, who reminds us that "virtually everything cognitively interesting that people do is a complex blend of consciously controlled processing that is declarative in nature AND implicit, automatic functioning that lies largely outside of awareness" (2003: 488).

References

Arndt, Henriette. 2019. Informal second language learning: The role of engagement, proficiency, attitudes, and motivation. Oxford: University of Oxford dissertation. https://ora.ox.ac.uk/objects/uuid:c579077d-61fd-4b94-bd57-de7063389122

Baars, Bernard J. 1997. In the theatre of consciousness: Global workspace theory, a rigorous scientific theory of consciousness. *Journal of Consciousness Studies* 4(4). 292–309.

Baddeley, Alan D. 1997. *Human Memory: Theory and Practice*. Revised edition. Hove: Psychology Press.

Benson, Phil. 2011a. Language learning and teaching beyond the classroom: An introduction to the field. In Phil Benson & Hayo Reinders (eds.), *Beyond the Language Classroom*, 7–16. Basingstoke: Palgrave Macmillan.

Benson, Phil. 2011b. *Teaching and Researching Autonomy in Language Learning*. Harlow: Routledge.

Benson, Phil & Hayo Reinders (eds.). 2011. *Beyond the Language Classroom*. Basingstoke: Palgrave Macmillan.

Chik, Alice. 2014. Digital gaming and language learning: Autonomy and community. *Language Learning & Technology* 18(2). 85–100.

Cole, Jason & Robert Vanderplank. 2016. Comparing autonomous and class-based learners in Brazil: Evidence for the present-day advantages of informal, out-of-class learning. *System* 61. 31–42.

DeKeyser, Robert. 2003. Explicit and implicit learning. In Catherine Doughty & Michael Long (eds.), *The Handbook of Second Language Acquisition*, 313–348. Oxford: Blackwell.

Dienes, Zoltan & Josef Perner. 1999. A theory of implicit and explicit knowledge. *Behavioral and Brain Sciences* 22(5). 735–808.

Dörnyei, Zoltan. 2009. *The Psychology of Second Language Acquisition*. Oxford: Oxford University Press.

Dressman, Mark. 2020a. Introduction. In Mark Dressman & Randall Sadler (eds.), *The Handbook of Informal Language Learning*, 1–12. Hoboken/Chichester: Wiley Blackwell.

Dressman, Mark. 2020b. Informal English learning among Moroccan youth. In Mark Dressman & Randall Sadler (eds.), *The Handbook of Informal Language Learning*, 303–318. Hoboken/Chichester: Wiley Blackwell.

Ellis, Nick C. 1994a. Consciousness in second language learning: Psychological perspectives on the role of conscious processes in vocabulary acquisition. *AILA Review* 11. 37–56.

Ellis, Nick C. 1994b. Introduction: implicit and explicit language learning – an overview. In Nick C. Ellis (ed.). *Implicit and Explicit Learning of Languages*, 1–31. London: Academic Press.

Ellis, Nick C. 1994c. Vocabulary acquisition: the implicit ins and outs of explicit cognitive mechanisms. In Nick C. Ellis (ed.). *Implicit and Explicit Learning of Languages*, 211–282. London: Academic Press.

Ellis, Nick C. 1997. Vocabulary acquisition: word structure, collocation, word-class. In: Norbert Schmitt & Michael McCarthy (eds.). *Vocabulary: Description, Acquisition and Pedagogy*, 122–139. Cambridge: Cambridge University Press.

Ellis, Nick C. 2002. Reflections on frequency effects in language processing. *Studies in Second Language Acquisition* 24(2). 297–339.

Ellis, Nick C. 2005. At the interface: Dynamic interactions of explicit and implicit language knowledge. *Studies in Second Language Acquisition* 27(2). 305–352.

Ellis, Nick C. 2008. Implicit and explicit knowledge about language. In Jasone Cenoz & Nancy Hornberger (eds.), *Encyclopedia of Language and Education*, 119–131. Vol 6. New York: Springer.

Ellis, Nick C. 2013. Second language acquisition. In Graeme Trousdale & Thomas Hoffmann (eds.), *Oxford Handbook of Construction Grammar*, 365–378. Oxford: Oxford University Press.

Ellis, Rod. 2005. Measuring implicit and explicit knowledge of a second language: A psychometric study. *Studies in Second Language Acquisition* 27(2). 141–172.

Ellis, Rod. 2009. Implicit and explicit learning, knowledge and instruction. In Rod Ellis, Shawn Loewen, Catherine Elder, Rosemary Erlam, Jenefer Philp & Hayo Reinders (eds.), *Implicit and Explicit Knowledge in Second Language Learning, Testing and Teaching*, 3–25. Bristol: Multilingual Matters.

Foster, Pauline. 2021. Implicit learning and morphosyntactic attainment in a second language: The interplay of age of onset, context of learning, phonological short-term memory, & implicit pattern learning. *ESRC Special SLA Lecture Series*. https://www.youtube.com/watch?v=SclZWgEfkCg. (accessed 28 May 2021)

Godwin-Jones, Robert. 2018. Chasing the butterfly effect: Informal language learning online as a complex system. *Language Learning & Technology* 22(2). 8–27.

Godwin-Jones, Robert. 2019. Riding the digital wilds: Learner autonomy and informal language learning. *Language Learning and Technology* 23(1). 8–25.

Hannibal Jensen, Signe. 2017. Gaming as an English language learning resource among young children in Denmark. *CALICO Journal* 34(1). 1–19.

Henry, Alastair, Helena Korp, Pia Sundqvist & Cecilia Thorsen. 2018. Motivational strategies and the reframing of English: Activity design and challenges for teachers in contexts of extensive extramural encounters. *TESOL Quarterly* 52(2). 247–273.

Hulstijn, Jan. 2001. Intentional and incidental second language vocabulary learning: A reappraisal of elaboration, rehearsal and automaticity. In Peter Robinson (ed.), *Cognition and Second Language Instruction*, 258–287. Cambridge: Cambridge University Press.

Hulstijn, Jan. 2002. Towards a unified account of the representation, processing and acquisition of second language knowledge. *Second Language Research* 18(3). 193–223.

Hulstijn, Jan. 2003. Incidental and intentional learning. In Catherine Doughty & Michael Long (eds.), *The Handbook of Second Language Acquisition*, 349–81. London: Blackwell.

Hulstijn, Jan. 2005. Theoretical and empirical issues in the study of implicit and explicit second language learning: An introduction. *Studies in Second Language Acquisition* 27(2). 129–140.

Hulstijn, Jan. 2015. Explaining phenomena of first and second language acquisition with the constructs of implicit and explicit learning. The virtues and pitfalls of a two-system view. In Patrick Rebuschat (ed.), *Implicit and Explicit Learning of Languages*, 25–46. Amsterdam: John Benjamins.

Krashen, Stephen. 1981. *Second Language Acquisition and Second Language Learning*. Oxford: Pergamon Press.

Krashen, Stephen. 1982. *Principles and Practice in Second Language Acquisition*. Oxford: Pergamon Press.

Kusyk, Meryl. 2017a. *Les dynamiques du développement de l'anglais au travers d'activités informelles en ligne: une étude exploratoire auprès d'étudiants français et allemands*. [The dynamics of L2 English development through participation in online informal activities: an exploratory study of French and German university students.] Strasbourg: University of Strasbourg dissertation. https://phka.bsz-bw.de/frontdoor/deliver/index/docId/116/file/Kusyk_dynamiques_du_d%c3%a9veloppement_de_l'anglais_au_travers_d'activit%c3%a9s_informelles_en_ligne.pdf

Kusyk, Meryl. 2017b. The development of complexity, accuracy and fluency in L2 written production through informal participation in online activities. *CALICO Journal* 34(1). 75–96.

Kusyk, Meryl. 2020. Informal English learning in France. In Mark Dressman & Randall Sadler (eds.), *The Handbook of Informal Language Learning*, 333–348. Hoboken/Chichester: Wiley-Blackwell.

Kusyk, Meryl & Geoffrey Sockett. 2012. From informal resource usage to incidental language acquisition: Language uptake from online television viewing in English. *ASp. La revue du GERAS* 62. 45–65.

Lai, Chun, Weimin Zhu & Gang Gong. 2015. Understanding the quality of out-of-class English learning. *TESOL Quarterly* 49(2). 278–308.

Lai, Chun. 2017. *Autonomous language learning with technology: Beyond the classroom*. London: Bloomsbury.

Lai, Chun. 2019. Learning beliefs and autonomous language learning with technology beyond the classroom. *Language Awareness* 28(4). 291–309.

Larsen-Freeman, Diane. 1997. Chaos/complexity and second language acquisition. *Applied Linguistics* 18. 141–165.

Lee, Ju Seong. 2017. Informal digital learning of English and second language vocabulary outcomes: Can quantity conquer quality? *British Journal of Educational Technology* 50(1). 767–712.

Lee, Ju Seong. 2019. Quantity and diversity of informal digital learning of English. *Language Learning & Technology* 23(1). 114–126.

Lee, Ju Seong. 2020. The role of informal digital learning of English and a high-stakes English test on perceptions of English as an international language. *Australasian Journal of Educational Technology* 36(2). 155–168.

Lee, Ju Seong & Nur Arifah Drajati. 2019. Affective variables and informal digital learning of English: Keys to willingness to communicate in a second language. *Australasian Journal of Educational Technology* 35(5). 168–182.

Lee, Ju Seong & Nur Arifah Drajati. 2020. Willingness to communicate in digital and non-digital EFL contexts: Scale development and psychometric testing. *Computer Assisted Language Learning* 33(7). 688–707.

Lee, Ju Seong & Mark Dressman. 2018. When IDLE hands make an English workshop: Informal digital learning of English and language proficiency. *TESOL Quarterly* 52(2). 435–445.

Leow, Ronald. 2015. Implicit learning in SLA. In Patrick Rebuschat (ed.), *Implicit and Explicit Learning of Languages*, 47–67. Amsterdam: John Benjamins.

Leow, Ronald, Ellen Johnson & Germán Zárate-Sández. 2011. Getting a grip on the slippery construct of awareness: Toward a finer-grained methodological perspective. In Cristina Sanz & Ronald Leow (eds.), *Implicit and Explicit Conditions, Processes and Knowledge in SLA and Bilingualism*, 61–72. Washington: Georgetown University Press.

Loewen, Shawn, Rosemary Erlam & Rod Ellis. 2009. The incidental acquisition of third person -s as implicit and explicit knowledge. In Rod Ellis, Shawn Loewen, Catherine Elder, Rosemary Erlam, Jenefer Philp & Hayo Reinders (eds.), *Implicit and Explicit Knowledge in Second Language Learning, Testing and Teaching*, 262–280. Bristol: Multilingual Matters.

Muñoz, Carmen, Teresa Cadierno & Isabel Casas. 2018. Different starting points for English language learning: A comparative study of Danish and Spanish young learners. *Language Learning* 68(4). 1076–1109.

Nunan, David. 2015. Beyond the classroom: A case for out-of-class language learning. *National Symposium on Japanese Language Education*. 1–10. https://nsjle.org.au/nsjle/media/2014-NSJLE-05-DAVID-NUNAN.pdf

Nunan, David & Richards, Jack C (eds.). 2015. *Language Learning Beyond the Classroom*. New York: Routledge.

Paciorek, Albertyna & John N. Williams. 2015. Semantic implicit learning. In Patrick Rebuschat (ed.), *Implicit and Explicit Learning of Languages*, 69–89. Amsterdam: John Benjamins.

Paradis, Michel. 2004. *A neurolinguistics Theory of Bilingualism*. Amsterdam: John Benjamins.

Peters, Elke & Stuart Webb. 2018. Incidental vocabulary acquisition through viewing L2 television and factors that affect learning. *Studies in Second Language Acquisition* 40. 551–577.

Reber, Arthur S. 2003. Implicit learning. In Lynn Nadel (ed.), *Encyclopedia of Cognitive Science*, 486–491. London: Nature.

Reber, Arthur S. 2015. Foreword. In Patrick Rebuschat (ed.) *Implicit and Explicit Learning of Languages*, VII-VIII. Amsterdam: John Benjamins.

Rebuschat, Patrick. 2015. Introduction: Implicit and explicit learning of languages. In Patrick Rebuschat (ed.) *Implicit and Explicit Learning of Languages*, XIII-XXII. Amsterdam: John Benjamins.

Reinders, Hayo. 2014. Personal learning environments for supporting out-of-class language learning. *English Teaching Forum* 4. 14–27.

Reinders, Hayo & Phil Benson. 2017. Research agenda: Language learning beyond the classroom. *Language Teaching* 50(4). 561–578.

Reschly, Amy L. & Sandra L. Christenson. 2012. Jingle, jangle, and conceptual haziness: Evolution and future directions of the engagement construct. In Sandra L. Christenson, Amy L. Reschly & Cathy Wylie (eds.), *Handbook of Research on Student Engagement*, 3–20. Boston: Springer.

Richards, Jack C. 2015. The changing face of language learning: Learning beyond the classroom. *RELC Journal* 46(1). 5–22.

Rieder, Angelika. 2003. Implicit and explicit learning in incidental vocabulary acquisition, *VIEWS* 12(2). 24–39.

Rodgers, Michael. 2013. *English language learning through viewing television: An investigation of comprehension, incidental vocabulary acquisition, lexical coverage, attitudes, and captions.* Victoria: University of Wellington dissertation.

Sauro, Shannon & Katerina Zourou. 2019. What are the digital wilds? *Language Learning & Technology* 23(1). 1–7.

Schmidt, Richard. 1990. The role of consciousness in second language learning. *Applied Linguistics* 11. 129–158.

Schmidt, Richard. 1994. Deconstructing consciousness in search of useful definitions for applied linguistics. *AILA Review* 11. 11–26.

Schmidt, Richard. 1995. Consciousness and foreign language learning: A tutorial on the role of attention and awareness in learning. In Richard Schmidt (ed.), *Attention and Awareness in Foreign Language Learning*, 1–63. Honolulu: University of Hawai'i Press.

Schmidt, Richard. 2001. Attention. In P. Robinson (ed.), *Cognition and Second Language Instruction*, 3–32. Cambridge: Cambridge University Press.

Schugurensky, Daniel. 2007. Vingt mille lieues sous les mers: les quatre défis de l'apprentissage informel. *Revue française de pédagogie* 160. 13–27.

Schwarz, Marlene. 2020. *Beyond the walls: A mixed methods study of teenagers' extramural English practices and their vocabulary knowledge.* Wien: University of Vienna dissertation.

Shanks, David R. 2005. Implicit learning. In K. Lamberts & R. Goldstone (eds.), *Handbook of cognition*, 202–220. London: Sage Publications.

Sockett, Geoffrey. 2011. From the cultural hegemony of English to online informal learning: Cluster frequency as an indicator of relevance in authentic documents. *ASp, la revue du GERAS* 60. 5–20.

Sockett, Geoffrey. 2014. *The Online Informal Learning of English.* Basingstoke: Palgrave Macmillan.

Sockett, Geoffrey & Meryl Kusyk. 2015. Online informal learning of English: frequency effects in the uptake of chunks of language from participation in web-based activities. In Teresa Cadierno & Søren Eskildsen (eds.), *Usage-based Perspectives on Second Language Learning*, 153–177. Berlin: De Gruyter Mouton.

Soyoof, Ali, Barry Lee Reynolds, Boris Vazquez-Calvo & Katherine McLay. 2021. Informal digital learning of English (IDLE): A scoping review of what has been done and a look towards what is to come. *Computer Assisted Language Learning*, 1–33. https://doi.org/10.1080/09588221.2021.1936562

Sundqvist, Pia. 2009. *Extramural English Matters: Out-of-School English and its Impact on Swedish Ninth Graders' Oral Proficiency and Vocabulary.* Karlstad: Karlstad University dissertation.

Sundqvist, Pia. 2019. Commercial-off-the-shelf games in the digital wild and L2 learner vocabulary. *Language Learning & Technology* 23(1). 87–113.

Sundqvist, Pia & Cristina Olin-Scheller. 2013. Classroom vs. Extramural English: Teachers Dealing with Demotivation. *Lang. Linguistics Compass* 7. 329–338.

Sundqvist, Pia & Liss Kerstin Sylvén. 2016. *Extramural English in Teaching and Learning – From Theory and Research to Practice.* London: Palgrave Macmillan.

Sundqvist, Pia & Peter Wickström. 2015. Out-of-school digital gameplay and in-school L2 English vocabulary outcomes. *System* 51. 65–76.

Toffoli, Denyze & Laurent Perrot. 2017. Autonomy and the online informal learning of English (OILE): Relationships between learner autonomy, L2 proficiency, L2 autonomy and digital literacy. In Marco Cappellini, Tim Lewis & Annick Rivens Mompean (eds.), *Learner Autonomy and Web 2.0*, 198–228. Sheffield: Equinox.

Toffoli, Denyze & Geoffrey Sockett. 2010. How non-specialist students of English practice informal learning using web 2.0 tools. *ASp, la revue du GERAS* 58. 125–144.

Toffoli, Denyze & Geoffrey Sockett. 2015. University teachers' perceptions of online informal learning of English (OILE). *Computer Assisted Language Learning* 28(1). 7–21.

Uchihara, Takumi, Stuart Webb & Akifumi Yanagisawa. 2019. The effects of repetition on incidental vocabulary learning: A meta-analysis of correlational studies. *Language Learning* 69(3). 559–599.

Webb, Stuart & Michael Rodgers. 2020. Incidental vocabulary learning through viewing television. *ITL – International Journal of Applied Linguistics* 171(2). 191–220.

Williams, John N. 2005. Learning without awareness. *Studies in Second Language Acquisition* 27. 269–304.

Williams, John N. 2009. Implicit learning in second language acquisition. In William C. Ritchie & Tej K. Bhatia (eds.), *The new handbook of second language acquisition*, 319–353. Bingley: Emerald.

Yibokou, Kossi Seto. 2019. *Apprentissage informel de l'anglais en ligne: quelles conséquences sur la prononciation des étudiants français?* Strasbourg: Strasbourg University dissertation.

Robert Godwin-Jones
4 Smart devices and informal language learning

Abstract: There has recently been a growth in consumer products that incorporate intelligent personal assistants (IPAs), such as Siri, featuring voice recognition/synthesis in multiple languages. The always-available status of smart devices, along with their ever-increasing functionality through advances in AI, holds the promise of new options for language learning/maintenance, and especially for autonomous learning. This chapter looks at opportunities for IPAs to engage L2 user-learners in social and recreational activities that foster informal language learning. The most obvious role is for the IPA to function as an expert L2 learning resource and as a conversation partner. As in entertainment-oriented activities such as watching videos in the L2, IPA interactions can foster incidental language learning. The human-machine interface involved in conversing with an IPA is complex and can be best investigated through frameworks that take into account the dynamic and contextually determined relationship between digital devices and human users. Those include ecological theories such as sociomaterialism and complex dynamic systems.

Keywords: Intelligent assistants, voice technologies, informal language learning, artificial intelligence

1 Introduction

Intelligent personal assistants (IPAs), such as Siri, Google Assistant, or Alexa have been available for some time on smartphones and more recently have become integrated into a variety of consumer products. Those include wearable devices (smartwatches, earbuds), home appliances (speakers, entertainment hubs), and car dashboards. These "smart" devices, built on AI systems (artificial intelligence), have gained their "intelligence" through machine learning and large collections of data. They are networked, connected to the Internet through wireless networks, and operate autonomously, synching personalized data continuously. Using voice technologies, IPAs provide access to a variety of services, including Internet queries, news/weather reports, music playback, and personal scheduling.

Robert Godwin-Jones, Virginia Commonwealth University, USA

https://doi.org/10.1515/9783110752441-004

Voice services are available in multiple languages, although the most advanced research and cutting-edge features are available first only in English (Petrović and Jovanović 2021). Advances in voice recognition and in more naturally sounding synthetic voices have grown at a fast pace, as companies fast-track technical advances to further expand services and commercial opportunities (Bajorek 2020; Godwin-Jones 2019). Technical progress in AI has come through the expanded use of recurrent artificial neural networks (see Godwin-Jones 2021). Large language models enabled through those advances, have led to significant breakthroughs in natural language processing/understanding, integrated into IPAs.

The voice capabilities of IPAs make such devices of obvious interest to language learners and teachers. Translation services, for example, are widely used by learners (Slayter and Forget 2020). Users also can easily change the default language of the device/service, offering practice in hearing and speaking the second language (L2). This can provide the opportunity to test out pronunciation, vocabulary use, and syntax as speech is recognized and responded to by the device. In fact, a number of studies have explored using IPAs for these purposes (for overviews, see Bibauw et al. 2022; de Barcelos Silva et al. 2020; Dizon 2017; Kukulska-Hulme and Lee 2020). The overwhelming preponderance of research in the use of IPAs for language learning has taken place in formal instructional settings (Alm and Nkomo 2020). There are few studies which explore the use of IPAs from the perspective of informal or recreational use.

Given the rise of smart devices, L2 user-learners in many cases may have access to voice services in a variety of settings. Their presence as a ubiquitous digital companion offers a further expansion of the intimate human-machine relationship which began with the arrival of the iPhone in 2007 (Godwin-Jones 2017). Smartphones like the iPhone represent a dramatic improvement over earlier mobile devices, in that they provide a much-improved user interface, along with persistent and individualized access to mobile versions of social media and other software programs (apps). The always-available status of smart devices holds the promise of new options for language learning/maintenance, and especially for autonomous learning. The most obvious role is for the IPA to function as an expert L2 learning resource and as a conversation partner. We are already seeing uses of IPAs that go beyond transactional usage and point to more meaningful (and social) relationships than that of assistant (Dizon 2021). Surveys have shown that IPA users have moved beyond information retrieval, using the service for "fun" (68% of respondents in Nielson 2018).

This chapter looks at what opportunities exist – and are under development – for IPAs to engage L2 user learners in social and recreational activities that foster informal language learning. The increasing sociopragmatic capabilities added to IPAs hold promise for serving as virtual companions with whom users will engage as a leisure-time activity. As in entertainment-oriented activities such as watching videos in the L2, IPA interactions can foster incidental language learning. The human-machine interface involved in conversing with an IPA is complex and can be best investigated through frameworks that take into account the dynamic and contextually determined relationship between digital devices and human users. Those include, as discussed below, ecological theories such as sociomaterialism (Guerrettaz et al. 2021) and complex dynamic systems (Kusyk 2017).

2 Rule-based chatbots and spoken dialogue systems

In their conversational interface, IPAs have a considerable history beginning with text chatbots (Lee et al. 2020; Shum, He, and Li 2018). The earliest was ELIZA (1966), which simulated a therapist in conversation with a patient. As is the case in the vast majority of subsequent chatbots, ELIZA was based on a script and used pattern matching to formulate responses to user input. In the 1970s and 1980s spoken dialogue systems were developed by companies for informational access purposes, particularly through the telephone. These are scripted systems which feature voice recognition and text-to-speech. They use simple dialogue management mechanisms. Experimentation with such systems for language learning began in the 1980s (see Alm and Nkomo 2020; Bibauw, François, and Desmet 2019). Subsequently, chatbots and spoken dialogue systems have played significant roles in computer-assisted language learning (CALL). Bibauw, François, and Desmet (2019) provide a comprehensive overview. Considerable work in this area has been done in tutorial CALL (Heift and Schulze 2015) where the voice system plays the role of tutor. Such systems have typically been used in instructed SLA (second language acquisition), although the systems are sometimes available outside the classroom or laboratory setting. In any case, they represent a form of explicit language learning.

Recently, a good deal of attention has been paid in CALL research to SLA dedicated voice and text dialogue applications. Like conventional chatbots, these are rule-based systems. A number of these have been released in recent years, generally as independent systems, not associated with intelligent tutoring systems. They are different from IPAs in that they are developed specifically for language learning purposes. That is the case for language learning bots from Duolingo (https://www.duolingo.com/), Eggbun/Lanny (https://web.eggbun.net/), and Mondly (https://www.mondly.com/; Alm and Kmono 2020). Others are general purpose chatbots, configured to be used for SLA, such as Cleverbot (Fryer et al. 2020). Fryer et al. (2017) and Fryer et al. (2020) provide useful reviews. Some systems, such as Mondly, are multimodal, featuring text and image display alongside voice services. Moving more adventurously in that direction are robots incorporating chat and voice. Randall (2019), Kim et al. (2019), and Jones (2016) provide surveys of what is sometimes labeled robot-assisted language learning or RALL.

3 AI-based voice systems

Most spoken dialogue systems for language learning lack sustainability, remaining at the proof of concept or prototype stages (Bibauw, François, and Desmet 2019). Moreover, rule-based voice systems have severe limitations in terms of range and performance. Because they are scripted, they function only within particular domains of language and human experience. Outside of those domains, they cannot provide appropriate responses. Even within the targeted domains, generated utterances tend to be repetitive or overly general (Höhn 2019). In contrast to domain-specific voice systems, IPAs are designed to function in a wide variety of domains. That does not mean, however, that users will have satisfactory responses to queries or conversations. Depending on the topic, IPAs will use default or fallback responses, repeat statements, give vague answers, express ignorance or lack of understanding, or simply read from a web page. While IPAs have some degree of personalization through user profiles, that does not currently go beyond general settings and access to user-subscribed services. For language learners, there is an additional limitation. Voice systems are trained on collected human samples, which mostly include "standard" language output. That translates into a built-in bias which problematizes recognition of ungrammatical, dialectical, or regional forms. In that way, IPAs reinforce native speaker privilege (Kukulska-Hulme and Lee 2020; Peng, Jager, and Lowie 2020), which has increasingly become a concern in applied linguistics (Ortega 2019). Studies targeting the use of IPAs for pronunciation or speaking practice have shown mixed results in terms of voice recognition of learner language (Fryer et al. 2017; Moussalli and Cardoso 2016; Underwood 2017). Gender and race bias has also been raised as in issue with IPAs (Bajorek 2019).

In spite of those limitations, studies have shown the usefulness of IPAs for independent language learning, especially at novice levels (Bibauw et al 2022). Learners find them convenient and easy to use (Coniam 2008; Moussalli and Cardoso 2016), enjoy their interactions (Friar and Carpenter 2006; Underwood 2017), evince less anxiety in speaking (Tai and Chen 2020; Fryer et al. 2017), thus enhancing their willingness to communicate (Alm and Nkomo 2020; Tai and Chen 2020). Alm and Kmono (2020) report that many learners feel more comfortable conversing with a machine than with a person. They report that while learners found the experience of using voice systems intriguing and enjoyable, they also were often frustrated with their limitations. IPAs have been used, as one might expect, to practice pronunciation (Liakin, Cardoso, and Liakina 2015; Dizon 2020; Moussalli and Cardoso 2020), in conversational exchanges (Alm and Nkomo 2020; Dizon 2020), but also for reading and writing (Bailey 2019; Dokukina and Gumanova 2020). Those latter areas of language use – and other studies using IPAs – customize the voice capabilities, typically through the use of add-on "skills", most often to Amazon's Alexa (Schwartz 2019). A number of skills are available for Alexa specifically intended for language learning (Maria 2021). Those include general applications such as Daily-Dose or My Linguist to language-specific areas such as Chineasy, Weather in Russian, or German Articles (see Maria 2021). Dizon (2017) used the storytelling skill "Earplay" to have students engage in interactive storytelling.

Overall studies of IPAs for SLA show mixed results in terms of user experience. García Botero et al. (2019) summarize published studies as showing overall a favorable reception of IPA use. Dizon (2020) cautions that most studies have limitations in that the user base is small. That study showed, as have others, that interest in IPA use was most pronounced for already motivated learners and that student interest declined over time. In terms of learning effectiveness, results too are mixed. Dizon (2020) showed improvement in speaking ability. Other studies have shown improvements in reading (Dokukina and Gumanova 2020). Bibauw et al. (2022) found that language gains diminished for higher proficiency users. Ideal candidates according to the authors are students with some foundational knowledge of the L2 but who are hindered by learning anxiety and by a lack of opportunity to practice the target language. Bibauw, François, and Desmet (2019) point out that the results of voice system projects may be skewed, in that assessments of effectiveness are often done by the originators of the system themselves, raising the possibility of confirmation bias.

4 Incidental and informal language learning

Dizon (2020) points out that little research has been done on the autonomous use of IPAs for language learning. Alm and Nkomo (2020) label that area of research "underexplored" (52). Yet, the use of voice systems for informal learning seems to many to be the most natural and logical use in terms of language learning opportunities (Fryer, Nakao, and Thompson 2019; Dizon 2021; Petrović and Jovanović 2021). IPAs offer access to conversational exchanges with partners of infinite patience and provide linguistic and informational resources beyond the typical L2 instructor or native speaker. In that way, conversational agents can be conceived to be expert speakers of the L2, who, in contrast to human partners, are continuously available. They allow learners to try out their pronunciation, new vocabulary, or learned linguistic patterns. Stewart and File (2007) point out that especially at early stages of learning, learners can benefit from more opportunities for trial and error in speaking. In learning contexts in which other speakers of the L2 are not readily available, IPAs can be a valuable resource for language practice. That is likely a reality for many English learners, given the worldwide interest in learning English in foreign language contexts (see Godwin-Jones 2020; Qian et al. 2020).

IPAs, even though machines, can supply a context for social engagement through the L2. That indeed is the great potential of IPAs for SLA, to be exposed to L2 use in conversational contexts. That necessarily involves not just lexis and syntax, but social practices as well, such as the use of adjacency pairs (greeting-greeting; compliment-thanks), conversational practices such as turn-taking, and speech acts (requesting, apologizing). In their existing configurations, however, mainstream IPAs are not optimized to serve as conversational partners. They are designed to function as transactional agents, responding to user requests and inquiries as efficiently as possible, in other words, with minimal verbal output. They are not meant to engage in multiturn conversations. Although they are programmed to observe basic politeness conventions in a given language, their pragmatic competence and capabilities in terms of conversation management are limited. It is not surprising, given that situation, that learners would lose interest in IPAs for language learning once the novelty effect wears off (see Fryer 2017; Fryer, Nakao, and Thompson 2019).

In order to optimize IPAs' role as conversation partners, several developments are necessary, some of which are already beginning to appear. First, the human-machine relationship needs to be more meaningful and persistent. An important component of that more permanent connection is a record of interactions, which can serve as a data source to inform future exchanges. That would allow for the avoidance of repetitive exchanges as well as the opportunity to build on information collected, so as to continue conversations from where they left off. User profiles of that kind have long been a standard feature of intelligent language tutors (Heift and Schulze 2015). That functionality is particularly important considering usage patterns with mobile devices, which will vary in duration but are likely to be short and intermittent.

An illustration of how that kind of user profile would benefit exchanges is demonstrated in a voicebot developed by Microsoft Asia and widely used for Chinese speakers, XiaoIce (literally small ice). It is more significantly personalized than IPAs, with the capability of extended conversations, with examples in studies of multiple conversational turns, with some conversations lasting up to half an hour

(Dokukina and Gumanova 2020; Shum, He, and Li 2018). Zhou (2020) describes a project in which XiaoIce was used over a period of two months, resulting in users engaging the system as a habitual conversation partner, conversing on users' preferred topics. The AI behind XiaoIce is able to ascertain through conversation the topics likely to be of interest to the user, and to be proactive in offering suggestions to further the conversation along lines of potential user interest. Allowing the bot to initiate conversation extends the interaction beyond a simple transaction and more closely resembles human communication. Additionally, by encouraging conversation around particular topics, the exchanges are likely to be more motivating, leading to more contact with the target language as well as possible repetitions in context of key expressions in particular domains, a key component of usage-based language learning (Ellis 2017).

A second quality that enhances bot capabilities to engage in conversation is to de-emphasize or disguise to the extent possible the bot's identity as a machine. That can mean endowing the bot with a particular personality, enabling the establishment of an affective relationship with the user, and adding nonverbal communicative options. This kind of chatbot, designed for human companionship is known as a social bot. XiaoIce has been developed to move in that direction, having been programmed to exhibit a particular profile, which varies depending on the country and language in which the system is being used. For China, the personality is that of a young female. As a social bot, it is intended not just to supply information, but to offer companionship, and even emotional support. Cleverbot, similarly, was designed for companionship (Fryer et al. 2020). Meng and Dai (2021) discuss how AI-based chatbots are being programmed to pick up on social cues. That information can be conveyed by voice through word choice or prosody, but also through nonverbal means such as facial expressions. Conversing with a social bot in the L2 could become for some users a habitual leisure time activity, carried out at home, in the car, or in other venues in which the user is likely alone, and perhaps engaged in activities not requiring focused attention (i.e. sweeping the floor). Exchanges with the bot would be more fulfilling to the extent that it is aware of the user's interests, so as to carry out conversations in areas such as sports, hobbies, favourite authors, or other topics. In the process, it is likely that repeated conversations covering the same topic would reuse vocabulary from that domain, or repeat common lexicogrammatical constructions, potentially leading to incidental language development.

Camera and sensors integrated into bots are becoming increasingly capable of reading and responding to human emotional displays. That capability has been explored extensively in prototypes using robots in educational settings (see Randall 2019; Kim et al. 2019). Robots, especially in use with children, have been engineered to change expressions to display empathy. Alemi (2020) found that the engaging personality programmed into a robot served to enhance children's learning of speech acts, namely requests and giving thanks. The robot in that study was designed to make mistakes, allowing the children to offer corrections. For adults, as Meng and Dai (2021) caution, that kind of personification and emotional connection, when offered by machines, might well be received as scripted and ingenuine. Experiments with robot pets, such as Sony's Aibo dog, have shown that in certain contexts (such as with older adults) the robot animals serve as welcome companions (Coghlan et al. 2018).

A third direction in transforming bots into more attractive companions for humans, and especially for L2 users, is to endow them with specific recreational capabilities. Experimentation has been done, for example, with voice systems in storytelling (Bailey 2019; Bailey, Southam, and Costley 2021). Seering et al. (2019) suggest a number of additional socially oriented roles chatbots could be configured to take on. The most likely direction for leisure-time use of voice is through gamification. Given their popularity, games are one of the more exciting avenues for voice-based role play and cultural simulations. The meta-analysis by Bibauw et al. (2022) finds that "dialogue-based CALL applications that used some form of gamification had a significantly stronger impact on L2 development" (13). The author advocates for the integration of game elements in dialogue systems, in part for motivational purposes. While peer chat functionality has long been part of digital gaming environments, some immersive systems feature chatbots as an integral component. Wang et al. (2017) added a chatbot to an immersive English language environment in a 3D virtual world with positive results. Games using augmented reality (AR) often feature spoken exchanges with non-playing characters, which has been used for language learning in games such as Mentira (Holden and Sykes 2011) or in simulations such as Explorez! (Perry 2015). Mondly's AR environment integrates a chatbot through an avatar who uses gestures and facial expressions in spatial interactions with projected objects and changes its appearance depending on the topic of conversation (Fryer et al. 2020). The authors point to the potential of such simulated environments to support pragmatic language development. Sykes and González-Lloret (2020) list games as one of the optimal environments for the development of interactional pragmatics. As do other forms of immersive environments, chatbots offer affordances for contingent and interpretive experiences leading to potential L2 development.

5 Conversations-for-learning

Although there has been experimentation with the use of IPAs for language learning, it has been limited. Most projects in CALL involving voice have used role-based, limited-domain dialogue systems. As argued in Bibauw, François, and Desmet (2019), such an approach provides more control over interactions, leading to more predictable exchanges, as the system is likely to produce fewer non sequiturs or general, fallback utterances. System constraints can range from controlling the conversational flow (using pre-determined choices or a question and answer format, for example) or using other implicit or explicit conversation management mechanisms. Bibauw, François, and Desmet (2019) offer a typology of constraints used in dialogue-based CALL. Scripted dialogue systems will also normally be able to provide error analysis and feedback, thus providing the kind of "controlled practice" often seen as necessary in SLA (Dörnyei 2013: 164). This approach also aligns with task-based language learning, as normally there will be a specific goal to be achieved through dialogue (Bibauw, François, and Desmet 2019). Such systems can track error histories and user profiles, useful for assessment of learning discrete linguistic patterns in terms of vocabulary or grammar.

Voice systems lacking the constraints typically incorporated into CALL systems are less predictable in terms of user experience and learning potential. Free flowing conversations with a bot can be a frustrating experience, as many studies have shown. Bibauw, François, and Desmet (2019) argue that "free dialogue should not be seen as the ultimate target of dialogue-based CALL" (856). That position is echoed in other studies of voice systems in CALL (Fryer, Nakao, and Thompson 2019; Höhn 2019). I would argue, however, that open-ended conversations with a spoken dialogue system should not be quickly dismissed as a viable alternative to scripted systems. That will especially be the case as IPAs gain more capabilities through integration of powerful AI systems and through enhancements in conversation management. In particular, as discussed below, hybrid systems, built upon extending existing large language models, have the potential to combine the advantages of language practice through open-ended conversation with features enhancing both learner motivation and implicit, usage-based learning.

One of the main arguments to be made in favour of IPA use for SLA is access. Using a mainstream IPA, deployed through a dedicated app or a commonly used messaging system shifts the dynamics of exchanges from an artificial academic setting to an experience integrated into everyday life. That is likely to make the service more universally available (for example, through a variety of smart devices), and to enhance motivation and lead potentially to more frequent use. However, that scenario is only likely if the voice system can engage coherently and meaningfully in virtually any domain of human activity. Also, as discussed above, the bot needs to be capable of building and using a personal profile of the user, which is capable of calling on past exchanges to inform new conversations. Needed also is a greater competence in conversation management, including awareness of pragmatic aspects of language use. Important as well are capabilities that enhance the naturalness and attractiveness of synthetic voices, such as more sophisticated paralinguistic features, like intonation and tone.

We have seen that XiaoIce already exhibits many of these attributes. Mainstream IPAs are moving in these directions as well. One of the major developments that will enable more knowledge in bots is the continuing development of ever more extensive large language models (LLM), which can provide the wide knowledge base necessary. There are AI systems such as GPT-3 (from OpenAI) which use immense language data collection and neural network processing to enable interactions with users in a great number of domains (Godwin-Jones 2021). With only a few prompts, systems such as GPT-3 can generate extensive output on virtually any topic in language that is remarkable in its resemblance to human generated speech. Several voice systems have used GPT-3 as a backend for voice-bots (Ultra Hal from zabaware.com; Emerson from quickchat.ai). Blender from Facebook is an open-domain chatbot also built on a LLM and capable of discussing a wide variety of topics (Romero 2021). It remembers the content and context of previous discussions, keeping a separate record for each user. It is also capable of adding knowledge on the fly through web search results and integrating that information into a currently active dialogue.

In terms of the mechanisms of conversational exchange, that is also an area in which considerable progress has been made. All IPAs have improved in sounding less robotic. The voice system used in Google's Duplex (an add-on to Google Assistant), for example, can be indistinguishable from human voices, making use of hesitations and disfluencies in a chatty tone of voice (González-Lloret 2019). Amazon's Alexa has enabled a range of voices, as well as a long-form speaking style. That system has also incorporated a variety of emotional tones, incorporating human nuances of feelings such as happiness or excitement (Schwartz 2021). Alexa has built more conversational management capabilities, a direction other IPAs will surely move towards as well.

One of the developments that has added considerably to IPA capabilities is the growth of third-party add-ons. Apple has done that to a limited extent for Siri, but both Alexa and Google Assistant have APIs (application programming interface) that enable powerful extensions to baseline functionality. As previously discussed, such "skills" can be used to create apps for dedicated language learning. However, they can also be used to add capabilities to IPAs generally that enhance language learning potential. Kiy, Wegner, and Lucke (2019) present a prototype of a virtual tutor for SLA built on top of Amazon's deep learning infrastructure. The system uses accepted and widely-used technology standards to maintain and update user profiles, making learning objects available, and creating a recommendation system based on user actions. Stasaski and Ramanarayanan (2020) developed an English language learning system built upon extending an LLM (in this case, XLNet) and "fine-tuned it for the purposes of generating natural language feedback on pragmatic appropriateness for dialogic text" (1).

Höhn (2019) uses conversation analysis in a Wizard of Oz implementation of a chatbot (expert speaker taking on the role of the computer) to create a corpus that can be used in an automated system. As is done in Stasaski and Ramanarayanan (2020), the corpus created was annotated for pragmatic as well as dialogic metadata. Such corpora could be used to supplement and fine-tune an AI system. The system Höhn (2019) proposes offers an attractive model for enhancing the language potential of voice systems such as IPAs. It features an individual *interaction profile*, which keeps track of conversations and enables *backlinks* to specific language patterns in previous conversations, which might offer *embedded corrections*. In that way, conversations can flow in a normal manner, while enabling implicit language learning. The system does not function as a tutor, but as an *artificial companion*. How the system interacts with the user can be negotiated individually, so that options could be supplied to request features such as explicit error correction or to keep track of items used in a non-standard way in patterns such as idioms or collocations. Höhn (2019) advocates the integration of machine translation as a means to identify and normalize non-standard language use. Huang et al. (2018) describe how that can be implemented in a chatbot for language learning.

The bot Höhn (2019) outlines can function in different ways, depending on user choice. Höhn (2019) points out that traditionally in voice systems developed for SLA, the role assigned is inevitably that of tutor. If, however, we want to enable *conversation-for-learning*, as Höhn puts it, we need computational simulations other than roles mimicking the classroom setting. This is where systems like GPT-3 come to the fore. Such pre-trained generative systems are capable of taking on multiple identities. That has been aptly demonstrated by the great variety of texts generated by GPT-3 (Vincent 2020). With prompts, the system can be instructed to take on identities such as a famous writer, noteworthy scientist, or any public figure. Roles could include a language teacher ("please correct errors") or specific cultural identities (a barista in Seattle, for example), thus enabling a variety of role-playing scenarios. In fact, after GPT-3 was released, a startup, Learn from Anyone, announced tutoring services based on GPT-3's ability to mimic famous figures (Godwin-Jones 2021). The idea of celebrity chatbots has been raised before in voice studies (Fryer et al. 2020). One could imagine as well LLMs being integrated into *global simulations* (Dupuy 2006), which offer a contextualized, immersive environment for language learning in which students enact roles and use discourse appropriate to characters assigned to them in the simulation.

6 IPAs and SLA theory

The system outlined above provides a model quite different from the SLA theories normally used in studies on voice systems. The *conversation-for-learning* model takes a holistic view of language development, looking at patterns learned implicitly and over time. This contrasts with skill acquisition theory (DeKeyser 2007), the foundation on which most of the form-focused and error correction emphasis in dialogue-based CALL is based. Interactionist theory (Chapelle 2006; Kramsch 1986; Long 1996) has also been explicitly evoked in studies involving voice systems. That has, in fact, been shown to be a viable approach to understanding chatbot interactions. Bots allow users to interact in meaningful exchanges, while encouraging modification of output as needed. That occurs through a form of negative feedback when the system requests repetition or reformulation – or does not respond at all. That process makes users aware of gaps in their ability to generate comprehensible output in the L2, whether that be due to pronunciation, structure, or vocabulary. In that way, learners are pushed to modify output in line with the output hypothesis (Swain 2005). Moussalli and Cardoso (2020) found that when students were not understood by the IPA they tended to follow the same interactional pattern, in this order: 1) repeat, 2) rephrase, 3) abandon. That finding makes it clear that the interaction with IPAs is quite different from that with human interlocutors, where abandoning attempts to communicate is not normally an option. In actual conversation, partners in the exchange will likely aid the speaker, through verbal encouragement or nonverbal means (body language, affect displays). Alternatively, the conversation partner might change the topic or use other methods to maintain the conversation and to provide emotional support.

Perhaps as a consequence of the relatively small number of studies of IPA usage, there has not been research in this area that has used approaches and frameworks commonly seen in studying informal language learning in recent years, namely ecological SLA (Chun 2016), encompassing complex dynamic systems (Kusyk 2017; Sockett 2014) and sociomaterialism (Guerrettaz, Engman, and Matsumoto 2021). These have in common that they consider second language development as a nonlinear process of interaction between a dynamically changing set of learning resources (the context/environment) and the ever-changing needs, preferences, and learning trajectory of the student. Second language development is seen as a broad "language learning system", which encompass all possible language learning opportunities, formal and informal, implicit and explicit (Magno e Silva 2018: 230). In the case of IPA use, we have a potentially omnipresent voice-activated agent whose capabilities are in constant flux, determined by technological advances as well as by input supplied by the user, input which the cloud forwards on to the AI system as data. That data is integrated into the system, helping the machine learn and improve performance. In a reciprocal process, the user is affected by the voice system and in turn transforms it. Reinhardt (2020) points to the transformation in the nature of CALL "tools" in recent decades, leading to the need to recognize "the socially networked and interconnected nature of the use of tools" (235). We think of social networks as human communities, but the rise of smart devices and our reliance on their services for communication, companionship, and entertainment, should lead us to reconsider that view.

Examining the new intimate and dynamic relationship between objects and humans has been the focus of sociomaterialism, increasingly recognized as a useful approach for understanding the dynamics of learning materials within SLA (Guerrettaz, Engman, and Matsumoto 2021). A recent study of an augmented reality app (Thorne, Hellermann, and Jakonen 2021) demonstrates how the dynamic relationship between human and non-human actors plays out in informal language learning. From a sociomaterialist perspective, the use of voice systems in SLA represents an *emergent assemblage*, where use is dynamic and contingent, constituting an *entanglement* of people and objects. Using sociomaterialist theory, Tietjen et al. (2021) advocates for the examination of linguistic interactions at the micro, meso, and macro levels, as does Levine (2020) in his concept of "human ecological language pedagogy" (1). That involves zeroing in on the particular dynamics of an interaction, such as the use of voice systems, but also zooming out to analyze the "histories, cultures, and communities within which the emergent activity resides" (6). From this perspective, studies of voice systems should take into consideration the physical setting and individual context of the interaction, but also encompass macro level topics such as privacy and ethical issues (built-in language bias, privacy concerns) in the use of IPAs and similar systems. The practice of LLMs, for example, to collect online data indiscriminately raises serious ethical concerns (Bender et al. 2021; Godwin-Jones 2021).

Applying complexity theory and socialmaterialist frameworks to understanding the dynamics of voice systems in SLA shows that the process is not as straightforward as it might seem, namely learners simply using the IPA to practice listening comprehension, speaking, and other aspects of developing L2 proficiency. Such activities do not occur in isolation. There are multiple variables at play. Environmental issues (background noise, for example) may affect communication. Learner language may impede comprehension, leading potentially to broken conversations. The ability of the system to access some user information in the exchange may be limited by regulatory means, as in the case in Europe (Sayers et al. 2021). The learner's native language comes into play as well. Studies have pointed to the fact that IPAs have been designed to be monolingual (Dizon 2020), although this is beginning to change.

The changing environment of constantly evolving capabilities of IPAs makes it problematic to learn from past studies in terms of affordances for SLA. Assessing language learning is especially difficult in informal settings, due to the difficulties of data collection and to the multitude of variables an L2 user may experience (Peng, Jager, and Lowie 2021). That variety of sources and resources is more pronounced than ever in online environments, and especially in mobile spaces. Activities with smart devices are typified by the dynamic relationship of learner attributes and learning resource, as accessed at a specific time and place. The assemblage of humans and digital resources is in an emergent, coevolving relationship (Tietjen et al. 2021). Peng, Jager, and Lowie (2020) point out that in studies of mobile-assisted language learning, scant attention has been paid to uncontrolled variables. More so in comparison to other areas of CALL, that makes the usefulness of results from pre- and post-tests questionable for measuring learning in the context of IPA or mobile use. Data mining techniques may be useful in identifying clustering patterns (see Lee et al. 2020; Peng, Jager, and Lowie 2020), but in most cases qualitative studies are likely to yield the most revelatory results.

7 Conclusion

According to Dizon (2021) voice bots are poised to dominate how humans interact with smart devices; for Sejnowski (2020), "keyboards will become obsolete, taking their place in museums alongside typewriters" (30038). For L2 learners, that means that a potential conversation partner, sympathetic listener, or richly informed assistant will be available – in many cases no matter where one might be. While interactions with a bot do not duplicate human conversation or replace the need for human contact, they do offer learners, in the absence of human partners, a significant resource, alongside others available in online or informal settings. The dynamics of that process need to be understood not from the perspective of linear development or cause and effect, but rather as part of a complex web of interactions the L2 user-learner has with both people and non-human actors, whether they be smart devices, physical objects in the environment, or other digital resources (see Thorne, Hellermann, and Jakonen 2021). Most useful in understanding that process is to trace individual learning trajectories, examining the learner's initial conditions, then following the resources encountered in order to untangle the different assemblages of resource, user, and environment that may have contributed as either positive or negative factors (Godwin-Jones 2018). The process of *retrodictive qualitative modeling* is one option (Dörnyei 2014), looking at what resources and approaches were used at different stages of the learning process.

By themselves, smart devices do not appear to provide what is necessary for L2 development in most situations and for most users. Research on the use of IPAs for L2 has shown largely positive outcomes, but studies have been limited in terms of scope and duration. Almost all have been linked to classroom-based learning. We need more longitudinal studies in naturalistic settings, for different sets of learners at different proficiency levels. That might involve studies that follow learners' informal use of IPAs over time, with periodical assessments of their language skills. Important in such research would be to maintain a holistic perspective on language development, accounting for multiple variables in terms of L2 encounters. Useful for that purpose might be learner language diaries or other mechanisms for users to record their learning activities. More studies on voice systems integrated into other devices such as wearables would be informative, particularly as more become available, such as smart glasses. Blyth and Sykes (2020) call for more research that combines cutting-edge technology such as AI and pragmatic language learning. One of the areas of growing interest along those lines is likely to be immersive environments with integrated voice capabilities. Multiple modalities in general is an important area of future development and research. One of the features that would help render IPAs more useful for L2 learners is visual feedback. Some IPAs are built into visual displays of some kind, with options for text display and images. Dedicated voice systems for SLA, or intelligent tutors incorporating voice technology, are often multimodal, with, for example, the capacity to display transcripts of conversations in real time. On the other hand, a recent meta-analysis (Bibauw et al. 2022) showed slim evidence of the benefits of multiple modes in terms of dialogue-based CALL. The utility of incorporating visual, auditory, or video capabilities into dialogue systems for SLA is a fruitful topic for future research. In studying the use of IPAs in language learning, CALL researchers are well advised to follow the advice given in Bibauw, François, and Desmet (2019) not to look at their use solely from the perspective of CALL or to examine them as totally new phenomena, but to be aware of the considerable base of research in other fields looking at voice technologies and spoken dialogue systems.

A cautionary note should be added to the potential of smart devices for informal language learning, namely the ethical issues and privacy concerns they bring with them. Ethics have been particularly raised in connection with the development of LLMs (Godwin-Jones 2021). Although systems have filters in place to attempt to eliminate the worst derogatory or demeaning language, language collected does not at all represent populations in general and so is far from being representative (Mayfield et al. 2019). Another concern is the fact that work on voice systems has been focused primarily on English, with work in other languages lagging considerably behind. That is especially the case for languages for which there are no large corpora available. Projects such as that described in Doumbouya, Einstein, and Piech (2021), which collected voice data to create voice recognition systems for West African languages, are therefore very welcome. The view expressed in Dizon (2017), that "the ability to have authentic communication between people and machines via AI has the potential to transform language learning" (815) may be on the horizon for English user-learners but is likely to be delayed for learners of other languages.

References

Alm, Antonie & Larian M. Nkomo. 2020. Chatbot experiences of informal language learners: A sentiment analysis. *International Journal of Computer-Assisted Language Learning and Teaching* 10(4). 51–65.

Bailey, Daniel. 2019. Chatbots as conversational agents in the context of language learning. *Proceedings of the Fourth Industrial Revolution and Education*, 32–41.

Bailey, Daniel, Ashleigh Southam & Jamie Costley. 2021. Digital storytelling with chatbots: Mapping L2 participation and perception patterns. *Interactive Technology and Smart Education* 18(1). 85–103.

Bajorek, Joan Palmiter. 2019. May 10. Voice recognition still has significant race and gender biases. *Harvard Business Review*. https://hbr.org/2019/05/voice-recognition-still-has-significant-race-and-gender-biases

Bajorek, Joan Palmiter. 2020. January 28. CES 2020? 3 Takeaways with Big Implications to Voice's Future. https://medium.com/versa-agency/ces-2020-3-takeaways-with-big-implications-to-voices-future-d9494a9e59a9

Bender, Emily M., Timnit Gebru, Angelina McMillan-Major & Shmargaret Shmitchell. 2021. On the dangers of stochastic parrots: Can language models be too big? In *FAccT '21: Proceedings of the 2021 Association for Computing Machinery (ACM) Conference on Fairness, Accountability, and Transparency*, 610–623. New York: Association for Computing Machinery.

Bibauw, Serge, Wim Van Den Noortgate, Thomas François & Piet Desmet. 2022. Dialogue systems for language learning: a meta-analysis. *Language Learning & Technology* 26(1). 1–24.

Bibauw, Serge, Thomas François & Piet Desmet. 2019. Discussing with a computer to practice a foreign language: research synthesis and conceptual framework of dialogue-based CALL. *Computer Assisted Language Learning* 32(8). 827–877.

Blyth, Carl & Julia Sykes. 2020. Technology-enhanced L2 instructional pragmatics. *Language Learning & Technology* 24(2). 1–7. http://hdl.handle.net/10125/44718

Chapelle, Carol. 2006. Interactionist SLA theory in CALL research. In Joy L. Egbert & Gina Mikel Petrie (eds.), *CALL research perspectives*, 65–76. London: Routledge.

Chun, Dorothy. 2016. The role of technology in SLA research. *Language Learning & Technology* 20(2). 98–115.

Coniam, David. 2008. Evaluating the Language Resources of Chatbots for Their Potential in English as a Second Language. *ReCALL* 20(1). 98–116.

Coghlan, Simon, Jenny Waycott, Barbara Barbosa Neves & Frank Vetere. 2018. Using robot pets instead of companion animals for older people: a case of "reinventing the wheel"? In *Proceedings of the 30th Australian Conference on Computer-Human Interaction*, 172–183. New York: Association for Computing Machinery.

DeKeyser, Robert (ed.). 2007. *Practicing in a second language: Perspectives from applied linguistics and cognitive psychology*. Cambridge: Cambridge University Press.

Dizon, Gilbert. 2017. Using intelligent personal assistants for second language learning: A case study of Alexa. *TESOL Journal* 8(4). 811–830.

Dizon, Gilbert. 2020. Evaluating intelligent personal assistants for L2 listening and speaking development. *Language Learning & Technology* 24(1). 16–26. https://doi.org/10125/44705

Dizon, Gilbert. 2021. Affordances and Constraints of Intelligent Personal Assistants for Second-Language Learning. *RELC Journal*. OnlineFirst. https://doi.org/10.1177/00336882211020548

Dokukina, Irina & Julia Gumanova. 2020. The rise of chatbots – new personal assistants in foreign language learning. *Procedia Computer Science* 169. 542–546.

de Barcelos Silva, Allan, Marcio Miguel Gomes, Cristiano André da Costa, Rodrigo da Rosa Righi, Jorge Luis Victoria Barbosa, Gustavo Pessin, Geert De Doncker & Gustavo Federizzi. 2020. Intelligent personal assistants: A systematic literature review. *Expert Systems with Applications* 147. 1–14.

Doumbouya, Moussa, Lisa Einstein & Chris Piech. 2021. Using Radio Archives for Low-Resource Speech Recognition: Towards an Intelligent Virtual Assistant for Illiterate Users. *Proceedings of the AAAI Conference on Artificial Intelligence* 35(17). 14757–14765.

Dörnyei, Zoltan. 2013. Communicative language teaching in the twenty-first century: The principled communicative approach. In Jane Arnold and Tim Murphey (eds.), *Meaningful Action*, 161–171. Cambridge: Cambridge University Press.

Dörnyei, Zoltan. 2014. Researching complex dynamic systems: 'Retrodictive qualitative modelling' in the language classroom. *Language Teaching* 47(1). 80–91.

Dupuy, Beatrice. 2006. *Global simulation: Experiential learning and preparing students at home for study abroad*. The American Association of University Supervisors, Coordinators and Directors of Foreign Languages Programs (AAUSC). 134–156. http://hdl.handle.net/102015/69636

Ellis, Nick C. 2017. Cognition, corpora, and computing: Triangulating research in usage-based language learning. *Language Learning* 67(S1). 40–65.

Fryer, Luke, Mary Ainley, Andrew Thompson, Aaron Gibson & Zelinda Sherlock. 2017. Stimulating and sustaining interest in a language course: An experimental comparison of Chatbot and Human task partners. *Computers in Human Behavior* 75. 461–468.

Fryer, Luke, David Coniam, Rollo Carpenter & Diana Lăpușneanu. 2020. Bots for language learning now: Current and future directions. *Language Learning & Technology* 24(2). 8–22. http://hdl.handle.net/10125/44719

Fryer, Luke, Kaori Nakao & Andrew Thompson. 2019. Chatbot learning partners: Connecting learning experiences, interest and competence. *Computers in Human Behavior* 93. 279–289.

García Botero, Gustavo, Frederik Questier & Chang Zhu. 2019. Self-directed language learning in a mobile-assisted, out-of-class context: Do students walk the talk? *Computer Assisted Language Learning* 32(1–2). 71–97.

Godwin-Jones, Robert. 2017. Smartphones and language learning. *Language Learning & Technology* 21(2). 2–11. https://scholarspace.manoa.hawaii.edu/bitstream/10125/44607/1/21_02_emerging.pdf

Godwin-Jones, Robert. 2018. Chasing the butterfly effect: Informal language learning online as a complex system. *Language Learning & Technology* 22(2). 8–27. https://doi.org/10125/44643

Godwin-Jones, Robert. 2019. In a world of SMART technology, why learn another language? *Educational Technology & Society* 22(2). 4–13. https://drive.google.com/file/d/1dZ0gydJh2aLzviY5Z_fkrmCS7rG6rUmq/view

Godwin-Jones, Robert. 2020. Towards transculturality: English as a lingua franca in intercultural communication and in online language learning. *Languages and International Studies* 23. 23–54.

Godwin-Jones, Robert. 2021. Big data and language learning: Opportunities and challenges. *Language Learning & Technology* 25(1). 4–19. http://hdl.handle.net/10125/44746

González-Lloret, Marta. 2019. Technology and L2 pragmatics learning. *Annual Review of Applied Linguistics* 39. 113–127.

Guerrettaz, Anne Marie, Mel M. Engman & Yumi Matsumoto. 2021. Empirically defining language learning and teaching materials in use through sociomaterial perspectives. *Modern Language Journal* 105(1). 3–20.

Heift, Trude. & Mat Schulze. 2015. Tutorial computer-assisted language learning. *Language Teaching* 48(4). 471–490.

Höhn, Sviatlana. 2019. *Artificial Companion for Second Language Conversation*. Berlin: Springer International Publishing.

Holden, Christopher L. & Julie M. Sykes. 2011. Leveraging mobile games for place-based language learning. *International Journal of Game-Based Learning* 1(2). 1–18.

Huang, Jin-Xia, Oh-Woog Kwon, Kyung-Soon Lee & Young-Kil Kim. 2018. Improve the chatbot performance for the DBCALL system using a hybrid method and a domain corpus. In Taalas, Peppi, Juha Jalkanen, Linda Bradley & Sylvie Thouësny (eds.), *Future-Proof CALL: Language Learning Exploration Encounters–Short Papers from EUROCALL*, 100–105. Dublin: Research-publishing.net.

Kim, Na-Young, Yoonjung Cha & Hea-Suk Kim. 2019. Future English learning: Chatbots and artificial intelligence. *Multimedia-Assisted Language Learning* 22(3). 32–53.

Kiy, Alexander, Dustin Wegner & Ulrike Lucke. 2019. Learning Smart in Home. *eleed* 13(1). https://eleed.campussource.de/archive/13/4893/

Kramsch, Claire. 1986. From language proficiency to interactional competence. *The Modern Language Journal* 70. 366–372.

Kukulska-Hulme, Agnes & Helen Lee. 2020. Intelligent assistants in language learning: An analysis of features and limitations. In Karen-Margrete Frederiksen, Sanne Larsen, Linda Bradley & Sylvie Thouësny (eds.), *CALL for widening participation: short papers from EUROCALL 2020*, 172–176. Research-publishing.net. https://doi.org/10.14705/rpnet.2020.48.1184

Kusyk, Meryl. 2017. The development of complexity, accuracy, and fluency in L2 written production through informal participation in online activities. *CALICO Journal* 34(1). 75–96.

Lee, Jang Ho, Hyejin Yang, Dongkwang Shin & Heyoung Kim. 2020. Chatbots. *ELT Journal* 74(3). 338–344.

Levine, G. 2020. A human ecological language pedagogy. *Modern Language Journal* 104(S1). 1–130.

Liakin, Denis, Walcir Cardoso & Natallia Liakina. 2015. Learning L2 pronunciation with a mobile speech recognizer: French /y/. *CALICO Journal* 32(1). 1–25. https://doi.org/10.1558/cj.v32i1.25962

Long, Michael. 1996. The role of the linguistic environment in second language acquisition. In William C. Ritchie & Tej K. Bhatia (eds.), *Handbook of second language acquisition*, 413–666. San Diego: Academic Press.

Magno e Silva, Walkyria. 2018. Autonomous learning support base. In Garold Murray & Terry Lamb (eds.), *Space, place, and autonomy in language learning*, 219–232. London: Routledge.

Maria, Anna. 2021. *Got an Alexa? You've Got a Polyglot Tutor That Can Teach You a Language*. FluentU. https://www.fluentu.com/blog/can-alexa-teach-languages/

Mayfield, Elijah, Michael Madaio, Shrimai Prabhumoye, David Gerritsen, Brittany McLaughlin, Ezekiel Dixon-Román & Alan W. Black. 2019. Equity beyond bias in language technologies for education. In Helen Yannakoudakis, Ekaterina Kochmar, Claudia Leacock, Nitin Madnani, Ildikó Pilán & Torsten Zesch (eds.), *Proceedings of the Fourteenth Workshop on Innovative Use of NLP for Building Educational Applications*, 444–460. Florence: ACL. https://www.aclweb.org/anthology/W19-4400.pdf

Meng, Jingbo & Yue Nancy Dai. 2021. Emotional support from AI chatbots: Should a supportive partner self-disclose or not? *Journal of Computer-Mediated Communication* 26(4). 1–16. https://doi.org/10.1093/jcmc/zmab005

Moussalli, Souheila & Walcir Cardoso. 2016. Are commercial 'personal robots' ready for language learning? Focus on second language speech. In Salomi Papadima-Sophocleous, Linda Bradley & Sylvie Thouësny (eds.), *CALL communities and culture – short papers from EUROCALL 2016*, 325–329. Dublin: Research-publishing.net.

Moussalli, Souheila & Walcir Cardoso. 2020. Intelligent personal assistants: can they understand and be understood by accented L2 learners? *Computer Assisted Language Learning* 33(8). 865–890.

Ortega, Lourdes. 2019. SLA and the study of equitable multilingualism. *The Modern Language Journal* 103. 3–38.

Peng, Hongying, Sake Jager & Wander Lowie. 2020. Narrative review and meta-analysis of MALL research on L2 skills. *ReCALL* FirstView. 1–18. https://doi.org/10.1017/S0958344020000221

Peng, Hongying, Sake Jager & Wander Lowie. 2021. A person-centred approach to L2 learners' informal mobile language learning. *Computer Assisted Language Learning* 35(9). 2148–2169 https://www.tandfonline.com/doi/pdf/10.1080/09588221.2020.1868532

Perry, Bernadette. 2015. Gamifying French language learning: A case study examining a quest-based, augmented reality mobile learning-tool. *Procedia – Social and Behavioral Sciences* 174. 2308–2315.

Petrović, Jasna & Mlađan Jovanović. 2021. The Role of chatbots in foreign language learning: The present situation and the future outlook. In Endre Pap (ed.), *Artificial Intelligence: Theory and Applications*, 313–330. Berlin: Springer.

Qian, Yao, Rutuja Ubale, Patrick Lange, Keelan Evanini, Vikram Ramanarayanan & Frank K. Soong. 2020. Spoken language understanding of human-machine conversations for language learning applications. *Journal of Signal Processing Systems* 92(8). 805–817.

Ramanarayanan, Vikram. 2020. Design and development of a human-machine dialog corpus for the automated assessment of conversational English proficiency. In *Proceedings from INTERSPEECH, Shanghai, October 25–29, 2020*, 419–423. http://www.interspeech2020.org/uploadfile/pdf/Mon-1-10-5.pdf

Randall, Natasha. 2019. A survey of robot-assisted language learning (RALL). *ACM Transactions on Human-Robot Interaction* 9(1). 1–36.

Reinhardt, Jon. 2020. Metaphors for social media-enhanced foreign language teaching and learning. *Foreign Language Annals* 53(2). 234–242.

Romero, Alberto. 2021. July 26. Better Than GPT-3 – Meet BlenderBot 2.0: Facebook's Latest Chatbot. *Towards data science*. https://towardsdatascience.com/better-than-gpt-3-meet-blenderbot-2-0-facebooks-latest-chatbot-8941f100d146

Sayers, Dave, Rui Sousa-Silva, Sviatlana Höhn, Lule Ahmedi, Kais Allkivi-Metsoja, Dimitra Anastasiou & Štefan Beňuš. 2021. *The dawn of the human-machine era: A forecast of new and emerging language* technologies. Report for EU COST Action CA19102 'Language in The Human-Machine Era'. https://doi.org/10.17011/jyx/reports/20210518/1

Schwartz, Eric. 2019. 20 Alexa skills you should try. *Voicebot*. https://voicebot.ai/2019/12/25/20-alexa-skills-you-should-try/

Schwartz, Eric. 2021. May 18. Google upgrades conversational AI intuition and flexibility at Google I/O 2021 with LaMDA and MUM. *Voicebot*. https://voicebot.ai/2021/05/18/google-upgrades-conversational-ai-intuition-and-flexibility-at-google-i-o-2021-with-lamda-and-mum/

Seering, Joseph, Michal Luria, Geoff Kaufman & Jessica Hammer. 2019. Beyond dyadic interactions: Considering chatbots as community members. In *Proceedings of the 2019 CHI Conference on Human Factors in Computing Systems*, 1–13. Association for Computing MachineryNew YorkNYUnited States.

Sejnowski, Terrence J. 2020. The unreasonable effectiveness of deep learning in artificial intelligence. *Proceedings of the National Academy of Sciences* 117(48). 30033–30038.

Shum, Heung-Yeung, Xiaodong He & Di Li. 2018. From Eliza to XiaoIce: challenges and opportunities with social chatbots. *arXiv preprint arXiv:1801.01957*. https://doi.org/10.48550/arXiv.1801.01957

Sockett, Geoffrey. 2014. *The online informal learning of English*. New York: Palgrave Macmillan.

Stasaski, Katherine & Vikram Ramanarayanan. 2020. Automatic feedback generation for dialog-based language tutors using transformer models and active learning. Paper presented at the 34th Conference on Neural Information Processing Systems, Vancouver, December 6–12, 2020. http://vikramr.com/pubs/Active_Learning_for_Dialogue_Feedback.pdf

Stewart, Iain & Portia File. 2007. *Computer Assisted Language Learning* 20(2). 97–116.

Swain, Merrill. 2005. The output hypothesis: theory and research. In Eli Hinkel (ed.), *Handbook of Research in Second Language Teaching and Learning*, 495–508. Mahwah, NJ: Lawrence Erlbaum.

Sykes, Julie & Marta González-Lloret. 2020. Exploring the interface of interlanguage (L2) pragmatics and digital spaces. *CALICO Journal* 37(1). i–xv.

Tai, Tzu-Yu & Howard Hao-Jan Chen. 2020. The impact of Google Assistant on adolescent EFL learners' willingness to communicate. *Interactive Learning Environments*. 1–18. https://doi.org/10.1080/10494820.2020.1841801

Thorne, Steven L., John Hellermann & Teppo Jakonen. 2021. Rewilding language education: Emergent assemblages and entangled actions. *The Modern Language Journal* 105(S1). 106–125.

Tietjen, Phil, Saliha Ozkan Bekiroglu, Koun Choi, Michael M. Rook & Scott P. McDonald. 2021. Three sociomaterial framings for analysing emergent activity in future learning spaces. *Pedagogy, Culture & Society*. 1–20. https://doi.org/10.1080/14681366.2021.1881593

Underwood, Joshua. 2017. Exploring AI language assistants with primary EFL students. In Kate Borthwick, Linda Bradley & Sylvie Thouësny (eds.), *CALL in a Climate of Change: Adapting to Turbulent Global Conditions – short papers from Eurocall 2017*, 317–321. Research-publishing.net. https://doi.org/10.14705/rpnet.2017.eurocall2017.733

Vincent, James. 2020. June 30. OpenAI's latest breakthrough is astonishingly powerful, but still fighting its flaws. *The Verge*. https://www.theverge.com/21346343/gpt-3-explainer-openai-examples-errors-agi-potential

Wang, Yi Fei, Stephen Petrina & Francis Feng. 2017. VILLAGE – Virtual Immersive Language Learning and Gaming Environment: Immersion and presence. *British Journal of Educational Technology* 48(2). 431–450.

Section 2: **Language outcomes**

Christina Lyrigkou
5 Informal second language learning and EFL learners' spoken use of discourse markers

Abstract: There is a literature gap regarding the effect of informal second language learning (ISLL) in pragmatic performance. The current chapter reports on the findings of a longitudinal study which tracked the use of discourse markers (DMs) in the spoken productions of 52 Greek adolescent learners of English at four time-points over five months. Statistical analysis (Generalized Linear Mixed-effects Modelling) and thematic qualitative text analysis revealed the determining role of leisure-oriented ISLL in broad and frequent DM use. Discussing the findings in light of the explicit/implicit debate, this study makes important contributions to the fields of ISLL and interlanguage pragmatics.

Keywords: informal learning, L2 pragmatics, discourse markers

1 Introduction

Research on informal second language learning (ISLL) and its different conceptualisations (e.g., Online Informal Learning of English, Sockett 2014; Extramural English, Sundqvist and Sylven 2016; Informal Digital Learning of English, Lee and Dressman 2018) has looked into learners' out-of-class engagement with English. Engagement is self-initiated rather than guided by the teacher or researcher and takes place through a variety of activities. Findings of research to date suggest that ISLL is widespread among learners, particularly in the form of receptive activities, such as TV watching (Kusyk 2017; Lai, Hu, and Lyu 2018; Jurkovič 2019).

In terms of language outcomes, findings suggest a positive relationship between activity engagement and various second language (L2) aspects, such as vocabulary knowledge and production (e.g., Peters 2018; Sundqvist 2019), written complexity and accuracy (Kusyk 2017, 2020), spoken proficiency (e.g., Lee 2019), reading (Brevik 2016) and listening skills (Lindgren and Muñoz 2013). Although ISLL has evolved into a productive and promising field, an area that has not been sufficiently addressed is the effect of ISLL on L2 pragmatics and, in particular, the

Christina Lyrigkou, The Open University, UK

https://doi.org/10.1515/9783110752441-005

spoken use of discourse markers (DMs). More specifically, the question that this study addresses is whether and how different ISLL activities can promote the use of DMs in speech. The present study brings together the two fields with the aim to investigate the effects of ISLL on learner spoken DM use.

2 Literature review

This section looks into previous research in learner DM use and draws attention to the factor of ISLL which has been given little consideration in DM research, but which could be positively associated with broad and frequent DM use, as this study argues.

2.1 Learner spoken use of discourse markers

Being pragmatically competent in the L2 is an indispensable part of successful communication and social interaction, and entails being able to comprehend and produce pragmatic norms and sociocultural conventions in order to achieve communication goals (Taguchi 2019). A pragmatically competent L2 speaker employs DMs (e.g., *so, well, like, you know, I mean*) in order to structure their discourse as well as involve the listener in the construction of the message (Aijmer 2002; House 2013), ensuring spontaneous communication flows smoothly and efficiently (Crystal 1988) and preventing misunderstandings (Romero-Trillo 2020). DMs are multifunctional; at the textual level, DMs manage the conversation by creating coherence, and at the interpersonal level, they establish a social rapport between speaker and hearer (Haselow 2017).

Although DMs render a learner's spoken discourse more natural sounding and unrehearsed (McCarthy and McCarten 2018; Jakupčević 2019), the characteristics of DMs may render their acquisition problematic. For example, DMs may go unnoticed by the learner-hearer of the utterance given their low lexical value, i.e., DMs do not embody a concept (like content words do) but rather function as instructions for how to interpret the message (Blakemore 2002). Furthermore, because of their syntactical optionality, omission of DMs does not render the utterance of a speaker grammatically erroneous (Gilquin 2016) and, therefore, is less likely to cause communication breakdown as opposed to overt errors (e.g., wrong word choice). Hence, a learner might not always become aware of "pragmatic misunderstandings" (Polat 2011: 3745) that could be caused by omitting or misusing DMs, such as sounding authoritative, rude, or awkward (Svartvik 1980).

Apart from measuring the frequency (total number of tokens) and range (total number of types) of DMs in learners' oral productions, studies have also examined whether and the extent to which different factors influence DM use (Müller 2005; Neary-Sundquist 2014; Ament, Pérez Vidal, and Barón Parés 2018). Among several factors that have been investigated (formal instruction, spoken proficiency, motivation, first language [L1] transfer, age, gender), studies have underscored the importance of exposure to input that contains DMs and interactions with members of the speech community (Liao 2009; Gilquin 2016; Diskin 2017).

Frequent exposure to input and repeated usage of the language through interaction can trigger learning mechanisms, such as pattern finding and entrenchment (Tomasello 2009), which can drive L2 acquisition, according to usage-based approaches to language learning (Verspoor and Behrens 2011; Ellis 2019). Drawing on the Noticing Hypothesis (Schmidt 1990), increased opportunities to notice and process the input are considered a prerequisite for the acquisition of L2 pragmatics (Alcón Soler 2005; Taguchi and Roever 2017). DMs are widely used by L1 speakers and are frequent in spoken input and social interactions (Aijmer 2002; Fung and Carter 2007; D'Arcy 2017); therefore, exposure to such input and language use by learners can reinforce their DM use.

The majority of studies in spoken DM use have looked into English as a Second Language (ESL) contexts (e.g., Immigrant or Study Abroad studies). Findings have revealed that learners who felt more acculturated to the local community, such as by interacting with others or using L2 media (e.g., TV), had more frequent and/or broader DM use than learners with limited L2 exposure and opportunities for interaction (Liao 2009; Liu 2016). Others have shown that L2 exposure and socialisation, often measured through length of residence in the L2 country, played a more determining role in DM use than learner proficiency (Diskin 2017) or formal instruction (Hellermann and Vergun 2007).

Learners' exposure to naturalistic input and interactions in English as a Foreign Language (EFL) contexts, such as in their non-English speaking home country, has been studied only in the traditional sense. For example, studies have looked into learners' number of visits to and length of stay in English-speaking countries, and their contact with "native speakers" (e.g., Müller 2005; Gilquin 2016; Davydova, Tytus, and Schleef 2017). Findings posit that unless there is increased exposure to ESL contexts, EFL learners' acquisition of DMs will remain constrained. Martín-Laguna's (2019: 41) assertion reflects the widely held view that EFL students are in a disadvantageous position: "In foreign language settings, opportunities for contact with the language outside of the classroom are limited, and pragmatic development is closely interrelated to what happens in the classroom". However, a factor that has been largely neglected in DM research is whether and how learners engage with the language outside the classroom in the EFL context (i.e. without necessarily spending time in an English-speaking country). In other words, DM research has not examined in depth EFL learners' informal second language learning (ISLL).

2.2 Informal second language learning and DM use

Two studies (Vickov 2015; Gilquin 2016) have examined DM use and informal second language learning. Vickov (2015) investigated the written DM frequency of 200 Croatian EFL learners in primary and secondary schools, and three out-of-school activities: surfing English websites, watching English TV, and reading English literature. Data on DM frequency were collected through a written test (formal letter to a magazine editor). Questionnaires were administered to gather information on students' ISLL. The findings report positive correlations between written DM frequency and all three out-of-school activities for primary school students (and of lower proficiency), but correlations were non-significant for secondary school students (and of higher proficiency). Although the study is promising, the lack of convincing results for the whole sample renders the effect of ISLL in DM use inconclusive. Furthermore, the researcher provided only a limited scope of participants' ISLL, especially since the three activities studied were of a receptive nature whereas the language examined involved production. Vickov's (2015) focus on written DM use still leaves the question regarding the effect of ISLL on spoken DM use unanswered.

In a corpus-based study of 554 university EFL learners from different L1 backgrounds, Gilquin (2016) compared the spoken DM use of learner populations whose home-country was more EFL-like to the spoken DM use of those whose country was more ESL-like in terms of L2 exposure. The different populations were placed on a continuum of those whose country resembled more an ESL or EFL environment based on the status and use of English in traditional media and the internet in each country. For example, the Greek population was placed towards the ESL end of the continuum as the author perceived that Greeks had extensive access to English input through media, whereas the Chinese population was towards the EFL end, as use of English media was considered limited. The study demonstrated a tendency for learners in more ESL-like contexts (e.g., where TV is not dubbed, such as Sweden) to use DMs more frequently than those in EFL-like countries, where English is not as omnipresent. However, an unexpected finding, according to the author, was that the Greek population had low DM frequency despite being placed at the ESL end of the continuum. More objective evidence regarding learners' ISLL could have been provided had data been collected from participants' own accounts of ISLL rather than resorting to information about the status of English in the learner's country.

An important reason why the effect of ISLL on EFL learners' spoken DM use merits further and more thorough investigation is that DMs are present in English language media which, as ISLL literature has shown, are widely used by EFL learners outside the class and engagement in which is positively related to language outcomes. DM research into English media discourse has documented the repetitive presence of DMs in TV and film dialogue (Quaglio 2009; Bednarek 2018; Pettersson-Traba 2018). This is related to the desire of some showrunners to make TV dialogue sound as natural as unscripted conversation ("staged orality", Bednarek 2018: 125). In ISLL literature, regular TV watching has been related to language gains (Sockett and Kusyk 2015) and it might lead to picking up words and phrases that are frequent and salient in the input (Vanderplank 2019). The same might be assumed for DMs.

Research has also examined the presence of DMs in online videos (Tolson 2010; Frobenius 2014; Uicheng and Crabtree 2018), digital written communication, such as texting and chatting (Tagg 2012; Asprey and Tagg 2019), and written media, such as blogs (Lutzky and Gee 2018) and social media posts (Wikström 2014). EFL learners have been found to often engage with these resources (Codreanu and Combe 2020; Ewert 2020). The question therefore remains as to whether and which ISLL activities, involving those resources, have an effect on learners' spoken DM use. Furthermore, what is the contribution of ISLL when factors such as formal instruction and spoken proficiency are taken into consideration? These issues are addressed in the present study. It could be speculated that engagement with written input might not have an effect on spoken DM use; it might be that, as with Vickov's (2015) study where exposure to spoken input did not always transfer to increased written DM use, exposure to written input might not transfer to increased spoken DM use.

2.3 The explicit-implicit debate

Because of the different purposes for engaging in ISLL, a hotly contested issue in the literature is the explicit-implicit debate or the intentional learning – incidental acquisition debate (Dressman 2020). On the one hand, informal learning, as conceptualised by Sockett (2014), is motivated by leisure and therefore any linguistic gains are "incidental" (Sockett 2014: 8). Language gains that arise might not be the primary or conscious intention of the learner; attention is primarily paid to meaning rather than form (e.g., the plot of the TV show and not necessarily the grammatical structures used by the actors).

On the other hand, the boundaries between intentional and incidental learning during ISLL are considered to be blurred (Dressman 2020; Kukulska-Hulme and Lee 2020). Instances where the learner's focus might shift from being immersed in the activity to attention to a linguistic feature and intentional practice

(Dressman 2020) may exist. The work by Vanderplank and Cole (Vanderplank 1990, 2016; Cole 2015; Cole and Vanderplank 2016) in particular has shown that explicit attention to linguistic details and active processing of language during ISLL (e.g., pausing, rewinding, and looking up words when watching captioned TV) is critical in order for input to become intake. Given the blurred distinction between picking up language and learning it intentionally, Hubbard (2020) views intentional learning and incidental acquisition during ISLL not as discrete categories, but as a continuum.

It is important to investigate learner practices during input exposure in ISLL to understand whether and how DM use can be reinforced during ISLL. Based on theories of pragmatic learning, although noticing is an important pre-requisite, it is not a sufficient condition for L2 pragmatic acquisition. Noticing should be followed by subsequent processing of input (Kasper and Rose 2002). This takes the form of accessing and selecting pragmatic knowledge in order to incorporate it into one's own productions (Li 2019). Therefore, the following can be considered crucial for driving DM acquisition: frequent exposure to input where constructions such as DMs are frequent, combined with noticing these features in the input and subsequently processing them through active use.

2.4 Research questions

This study examined the following research questions (RQs):

RQ1: How does learners' reported ISLL impact their DM use?
RQ2: How do different types of DM users reportedly engage with spoken input during their ISLL?

3 Methodology

The methodology implemented in the study is detailed below. It includes descriptions of sample recruitment, data collection and data analysis.

3.1 Sample

The study draws from a longitudinal PhD project on 52 adolescent (13–17 years old) EFL learners of English in Greece. The population receives additional, non-compulsory English lessons outside the official school system in private language schools with the aim of preparing students for English language certification exams (Mattheoudakis and Alexiou 2009). Being able to communicate successfully in English is considered vital, not only because Greek is a lesser spoken language globally, but also due to the increasingly high status of English in the Greek job market, especially taking into consideration Greece's economic dependence on the tourism industry (Angouri, Mattheoudakis, and Zigrika 2010; Kantaridou and Xekalou 2021). Therefore, the incentive to use and speak English is not restricted to those who wish to work or study internationally.

Greek learners of English might struggle to learn to speak natural English and communicate because of the restrictions of formal educational settings. Due to the exam and certificate-centredness of EFL education in Greece (Mitsikopoulou, Karavas, and Papadopoulou 2017), the focus is not on using the language communicatively in real-life settings (Sifakis 2018). Although studies have shown that Greek EFL learners have informal encounters with English through films, TV,[1] radio and the Internet (Rothoni and Mitsikopoulou 2019), the effect of ISLL on their spoken communication is not yet clear. Using DMs is associated with successful spoken communication (Blakemore 2002) and examining the relationship between ISLL and DM use can provide useful insights.

Students (n = 33 female, n = 19 male) were recruited from six classes of four English language schools in Athens and Patras, Greece. Participants attended English lessons two to three times a week, in addition to their morning schooling, with the aim to sit CEFR B2 and C2 proficiency level examinations. The study took place in the academic year 2018–2019 (November to April), and all data were collected inside the schools.

3.2 Instruments and data collection

Instruments were employed iteratively at four times during the five-month period of the school year. Speaking activities were used to collect data on learners' DM use and spoken proficiency. Each student participated in one-to-one, 10-minute speaking activities with the researcher, which included a video-clip description, picture description and short discussion based on topics such as sports, social media, and holidays. Spoken performance was audio-recorded. Activities

---

[1] In Greece, English-speaking TV and cinema are not dubbed but broadcast in the original language with Greek subtitles. Greek subtitles became available on Netflix in December 2017 (https://about.netflix.com/en/news/netflix-is-now-truly-greek).

comprised engaging content for adolescents, thereby encouraging participants to speak, and, potentially, produce DMs. The study followed previous research which has employed a combination of activities to elicit spoken DMs (e.g., Buysse 2017).

Data on ISLL were collected through questionnaires and semi-structured interviews with each student. During piloting, it appeared that students would neglect to complete an online questionnaire; therefore, paper copies were handed out. Providing reliable time estimates might prove challenging, especially when an ISLL activity is scattered throughout the day or week, taking place at several intervals. In an attempt to ensure reliability of responses, the items did not include frequency scales. Instead, the time span was limited to activities undertaken in the last 24 hours and participants were asked to indicate whether or not they had engaged in a certain activity during that period. The questionnaire comprised closed-ended questions about type of ISLL, i.e., whether or not students had participated in different out-of-class activities in the last 24 hours, and purposes for ISLL, i.e. whether each activity was leisure-oriented, learning-oriented or both. The following questions gauged whether responses reflected students' typical practices: "Are all of the above answers typical of your contact with English outside the class?", "If you answered 'No', what was different this time and why?". The inventory of different activities included in the questionnaire was informed by a pilot study. Questionnaire completion was piloted to not exceed 10 minutes. The purpose of the questionnaire was to collect initial, general data on students' ISLL, which were then validated by and explored further in subsequent interviews. The main purpose of the interview was to elicit richer data on the questionnaire responses and track any changes over time, as well as elicit data on students' behaviours during ISLL, such as intentional learning practices.

The study adhered to ethical guidelines that specify voluntary participation and informed consent (BAAL 2016). Participants had the right to withdraw, as multiple iterations of data collection throughout the school year could be perceived as intrusive. Data collection was scheduled to cause minimum obstruction to the lesson flow so as not to affect non-participants who continued their lessons as normal. Ethical considerations were outlined in participation leaflets and orally at each time-point. Data collection commenced only after student and/or parental consent was granted through consent forms. Participants were anonymised and personal data remained confidential. Data from five participants who withdrew during the study were not retained.

3.3 Data processing

The markers under examination were *so, well, just, like, I don't know, actually/in fact, you know, I mean, kind of/sort of,* and the category of general extenders (e.g., *and stuff, or something, and things like that*). The criteria for including those markers were their being amongst the most commonly studied DMs in spoken learner English (e.g., Müller 2005; Buysee 2011) and their use by more than one participant in the sample. All instances of the selected items were identified on the transcripts of participants' audio-recordings; discursive uses (i.e., lexical item has DM function) were distinguished from canonical uses (i.e., lexical item has non-DM function) based on criteria such as syntactic optionality, procedural meaning, and fulfilment of non-propositional functions (Müller 2005). Unclear tokens due to, for example, inaudible speech, were not included in subsequent analysis. The following aspects were measured: DM range and DM frequency. DM range is the total number of DM types used. It must be noted that students may have used a range of other DMs not covered in this study. DM frequency is the total number of DM tokens used, divided by the individual's total word count, and normalised by 1,000 following the typical procedure employed in DM research (Buysse 2012). Identifying and coding DMs in participants' transcripts was performed twice by the researcher and once by a second coder (an experienced EFL teacher). Intra-coder reliability (ICC = .911) and inter-coder reliability (ICC = .961) were achieved, since an ICC value of .70 or higher is desirable (Meyers, Gamst, and Guarino 2013). Audio-recordings of learners' spoken performance were listened to by two professional IELTS raters who provided spoken proficiency scores based on the IELTS rubrics; inter-rater reliability was achieved (ICC = .902).

Collected data for ISLL were qualitative and therefore data processing was necessary to extract numerical values for subsequent quantitative analysis to answer RQ1. Data processing was conducted through thematic qualitative text analysis (Kuckartz 2014) and the resulting categories were then assigned numerical codes. Students' responses to the questionnaire at every time-point were studied alongside their responses to the corresponding interview to triangulate and merge data regarding the different ISLL activities. For every informal L2 activity the following information was coded: skills practised, purpose and frequency of activity engagement.

The coding of language skills was based on the traditional model of four skills: speaking, writing, listening/watching[2] and reading (Council of Europe 2001). Given the overlap of skills within one activity, the study also considered the organisation into modes of communication: reception, production, and interaction (Council of Europe 2018).

---

2 For descriptive purposes, listening and watching were studied together.

Data on the aspect of "purpose" were coded deductively based on whether the activity was leisure-oriented, learning-oriented or both. An activity was coded leisure-oriented if the student's primary reason for engagement was to communicate, entertain themselves, relax or seek information, as suggested by Sockett (2014). Although language learning outcomes were acknowledged by students, language learning was not the primary reason for performing the activity. An activity was coded as learning-oriented if it was considered as formal practice (e.g., speaking for exam preparation). An activity was coded as both leisure- and learning-oriented if the student reported engaging both for leisure and formal learning practice, that is, with the explicit aim to practise aspects of the language while entertaining themselves or seeking information.

Data on "frequency" were coded based on whether the activity was performed on a frequent basis, on occasion or was never carried out. Details in the data pointed towards the three frequency categories. Engagement in an activity was coded as frequent if the participant asserted that it was typical of their ISLL. Although not explicitly asked so as to avoid inaccurate estimates, some participants gave further details, such as the number of times they engaged in the activity during the week or day. Engagement "on occasion" was coded for activities that took place due to a particular event at the respective time-point and if the participant stated they were not typical of their ISLL. If a participant reported that they had not engaged in an activity during the respective time-point, it was coded as "never". When all information was coded for every activity for every student for every time-point, a final list was devised for the full sample of all identified activities depicted by purpose.

3.4 Data analysis

To answer RQ1, data were analysed quantitatively. Descriptive statistics were used to examine students' DM range and DM frequency at each time-point. To obtain an overall picture, data were aggregated from all time-points (average across Time 1–Time 4). Data exploration revealed an extreme outlier, who was removed from subsequent quantitative analysis (n = 51). Non-parametric equivalents of statistical procedures were used because DM range and DM frequency were not normally distributed.

The next step was to examine the effect of informal second language learning on DM use. Due to the iterative data collection and because participants were recruited from six classes in four language schools, the study used Generalized Linear Mixed-Effect Modelling (GLMM), which is a regression-type analysis (McNeish and Matta 2018). GLMMs were chosen as they accommodate repeated measures and all possible levels of dependency at once (i.e., within-subject, within-class, within-school correlation; Cunnings and Finlayson 2015). Initial analysis indicated that although there was significant variability among participants in terms of DM use and ISLL, there was no statistically significant variability in students' trajectories over time (Curran, Obeidat, and Losardo 2010), meaning that the sample as a whole followed a similar trajectory over time regarding their DM use and ISLL. Different GLMMs were created with the following fixed effects (i.e., predictors): overall engagement in all activities, overall engagement in activities by purpose, and engagement in each activity separately.

The fixed effects that stood out from this analysis were included in subsequent GLMMs, where the following fixed effects were added: spoken proficiency, aspects of formal instruction (previous years of formal instruction, class level and school attended), age and gender, to examine the contribution of ISLL when those factors were taken into consideration. For fitting GLMMs, the study followed the recommendations of Harrison et al. (2018).

To answer RQ2, data were analysed through qualitative thematic text analysis for an examination of the reported behaviours of students when they engaged with language input in their ISLL. Data were analysed from student interviews, where participants provided more detailed descriptions of the activities in which they engaged and, in particular, of the ways in which they engaged with the language they encountered during their ISLL (e.g., noticing linguistic items). Data were coded inductively based on patterns in responses of students in different DM user sub-groups (more details regarding the emergence of DM user sub-groups can be found in the Results section).

4 Results

This section presents the quantitative and qualitative results that address each RQ.

4.1 Quantitative results

Overall, students (n = 51) exhibited narrow DM range in their discourse, given that the majority employed a mean of around 3 out of the 10 DM types (M = 2.47, SD = 1.58). In terms of DM frequency, they employed on average 14.07 DM tokens per 1000 words (SD = 9.77). The results of Spearman rho correlations showed that there was a positive, strong correlation between DM range and DM frequency (r_s = .906, p < .001), indicating that students who used a wider range of DM types were also likely to employ a larger number of DM tokens, and vice versa.

Students were categorised into different sub-groups based on their DM range to enable a closer look into different types of DM users. Dividing the sample into sub-groups was guided by the distribution of the data itself, which revealed somewhat clearly defined categories of users: those at the top end of the distribution with regard to their DM range, who employed half or more than half of the DM types under examination (5 or more out of 10, "considerable DM users"), those at the low end, who did not employ any of the 10 DM types ("non-DM users"), and those whose DM range was in-between the two contrasting ends ("limited DM users" and "moderate DM users"). Creating the two sub-groups of limited and moderate DM users was deemed necessary as it was considered inappropriate to identify as equal type of user those who had employed 1 or 2 DM types ("limited DM users") and those with 3 or 4 ("moderate DM users"). Overall, as shown in Figure 1, most participants were either limited DM users (41.2%) or moderate DM users (35.3%), whereas fewer students were either considerable DM users (17.6%) or non-DM users (5.9%).

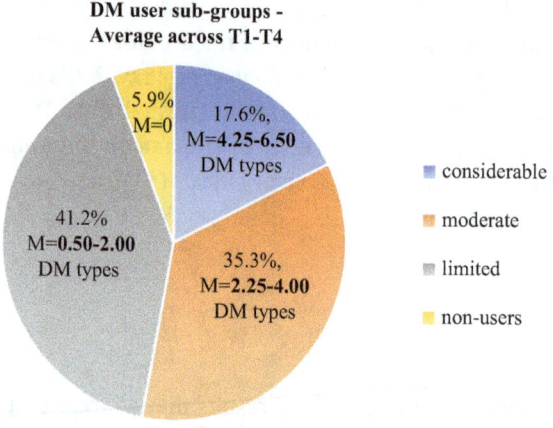

Figure 1: Percentage of students in each DM user sub-group for the average time measure (Time 1 through Time 4).

Participants were found to engage in 23 ISLL activities, identified based on purpose of engagement, i.e., leisure-oriented (15 activities), learning-oriented (4 activities) and both leisure-and-learning-oriented (4 activities). Activities that involved listening/watching and reading were carried out by all participants, while fewer students reported writing (N = 46, 90.2%) and speaking (N = 39, 76.5%). Leisure-oriented activities were carried out on a frequent basis by most participants, whereas learning-oriented activities were carried out by fewer participants, and mostly on occasion. Unlike L2 speaking and L2 writing, which were generally carried out on occasion (e.g., speaking/writing to co-players in digital games), the majority of students engaged in most L2 listening/watching activities frequently. Only a few reading activities were carried out frequently by the majority of participants (e.g., reading song lyrics). Appendix A details students' engagement in all identified activities.

Random-intercept GLMMs were fitted to examine the impact of ISLL on DM use when time (repeated measures) and individual variation were taken into account. Each model had each of the two aspects of DM use as the dependent variable and overall engagement in all 23 activities as a fixed effect. There was no significant effect of overall engagement on DM range and DM frequency (all p's > .05). Separate analyses were conducted for engagement by purpose. Random-intercept GLMMs were fitted with the three types of engagement by purpose as fixed effects. There was no significant effect of any type of engagement by purpose (leisure-oriented, learning-oriented, both leisure-and-learning-oriented) on DM range and DM frequency (all p's > .05).

Because engaging in more ISLL activities did not have an impact on DM use, the next step was to examine whether engaging in certain activities had a significant effect. Random-intercept GLMMs were constructed with each of the two aspects of DM use as the dependent variable and each ISLL activity as fixed effects to examine which of the 23 activities was the strongest predictor of DM range and DM frequency. Collinear variables (Phi and Cramer's V values were above .500) were linearly combined into a single variable (i.e. activity), following Neys (2017). Appendix B summarises the results of two random-intercept GLMMs for DM range (Appendix B, Table 1) and DM frequency (Appendix B, Table 2) with engagement in each of the 23 ISLL activities as fixed effects. The results revealed that leisure-oriented speaking/interacting (activities 1 and 3 combined) had a significant, positive effect on DM range, $F(2,82) = 6.66$, $p = .002$, and leisure-oriented TV/film watching without subtitles/captions (activity 10) had a significant, positive effect on DM frequency, $F(1,141) = 8.33$, $p = .005$. None of the remaining activities had a significant, positive effect on DM use (all p's > .05).

The results of pairwise comparisons (with sequential Bonferroni correction) showed significant differences in DM use depending on frequency of carrying out an activity. More specifically, students who spoke to themselves or interacted (by speaking) with L1/L2 others for leisure frequently (activities 1 and 3) had wider DM range than students who spoke on occasion ($\beta = .72$, $SE = .23$, $p = .007$) or never engaged in those activities ($\beta = .88$, $SE = .24$, $p = .001$). Students who watched TV/films without subtitles/captions for leisure frequently (activity 10) had higher DM frequency than students who never engaged in the activity ($\beta = .54$, $SE = .19$, $p = .005$).

Results of subsequent analysis revealed that when spoken proficiency, aspects of formal instruction, age and gender were also taken into consideration, the only significant predictors for DM use were the ISLL activities which stood out in the previous analysis. More specifically, leisure-oriented speaking/interacting was a significant predictor of DM range, $F(2,130) = 5.39$, p = .006, and DM frequency, $F(2,140) = 4.09$, p = .019. Leisure-oriented TV/film watching without subtitles/captions was a significant predictor of DM frequency, $F(1,161) = 6.71$, p = .010. None of the remaining factors (i.e. spoken proficiency, aspects of formal instruction attended, age and gender) had a significant effect on DM range (all p's > .05) and DM frequency (most p's > .05), except for a marginally negative effect of age on DM frequency, $F(1,40) = 4.10$, p = .05.

4.2 Qualitative results

Students who reported carrying out all three key activities frequently throughout the 5-month period of the study were either considerable or moderate DM users. In terms of speaking/interacting, those students emphasised reasons such as keeping in touch with L1 (Greek) or L2 friends, getting to know other L2 speakers or talking to themselves for fun. Some engaged in spoken communication in English with their Greek friends despite sharing the same L1 (*"Like me, she would rather have English as her mother tongue, instead of Greek, and we talk a lot, at school, but we also send WhatsApp recordings in English all the time"*, considerable user S45).

Others maintained frequent contact with L2 speaking peers from various language backgrounds through technology. For example, one considerable DM user spoke frequently via Snapchat video-calls to an American friend who she was initially pen-pals with. Or one moderate DM user spoke with friends she had made online through a fandom of her favourite singer on Instagram (*"I have these international friends and we call each other; we FaceTime for many hours [. . .] They are from the USA, the UK, Italy and Dubai"*).

With regard to leisure-oriented TV/film watching without subtitles/captions, not using subtitles nor captions was partly a conscious choice but also shaped by the technology, such as the low quality of captions offered by the source or the lack of their availability in the source (*"When I started using Netflix, there weren't any subtitles in Greek, so it started like that and then I got used to it and now I don't even need English subtitles, so I watch everything without subtitles"*, considerable user S1).

Qualitative analysis revealed differences between considerable/moderate DM users and limited/non-DM users regarding their engagement with spoken input during ISLL. Limited DM users mainly claimed to notice specific, isolated words or expressions encountered in songs, games, videos, and TV/films (e.g., *"flexing"*, "*heads up*"). Besides noticing individual lexical items, considerable/moderate DM users also made more general comments about noticing how language was spoken in informal sources. Those students mentioned that they paid attention to the way speakers expressed themselves more generally; what appears to be a focus on the bigger picture ("*I see how English people speak and how they say different things and I see everything in 'context' and I understand it better*", considerable user S11; "*I like to listen to the way the actors express themselves and how they use the language*" considerable user S43; "*Listening to actors talking and how they say different expressions. . . it sticks to you more*", considerable user S1).

Another difference was that only considerable/moderate DM users mentioned actively using in a productive way the language encountered in speech during their ISLL. This took the form of repeating lines from a favourite film, imitating accents, or using words/expressions encountered during ISLL. Such language was reported as being subsequently incorporated into students' own spoken productions ("*I take lines from my favourite movies and repeat them and mimic the voice of the actor [. . .] I often speak to my friends like that*", considerable user S14).

Interesting findings regarding DM users' engagement with spoken input during ISLL were further revealed when students were asked specifically about their DM use.[3] Most limited DM users regarded formal contexts (i.e., teachers, speaking lessons, textbooks) as the main source of learning and/or using DMs, whereas most considerable/moderate DM users attributed their learning of DMs to their ISLL. However, it was only students who attributed their learning of DMs to their ISLL who reported noticing DMs in the spoken input ("*You encounter these words mainly on YouTube and the Internet because the teacher doesn't say these words at school, she doesn't say 'I mean', 'you know what I mean' and so on. The only time she's going to say these words is to tell us not to use them*", moderate user S35; "*From the girls I talk to who are American [. . .] I heard them saying 'like' and I remember how I first talked to them and how I speak now, so it's definitely because of them*", moderate user S37).

Despite reporting having noticed DMs in informal input, considerable/moderate users perceived their DM learning to be incidental. In other words, those students reported that they did not deliberately practise the DMs they encountered in informal sources, but regarded their DM use to be a result of frequent receptive exposure to speech ("*If you listen to how English people talk and the words they use, at some point while you're speaking, you wind up using them too, so it's out of habit*", considerable user S11; "*I'm watching all these movies and mainly

---

[3] All participants were asked except for non-DM users, who had not used any of the examined DMs.

without subtitles [. . .] and because I have this habit of remembering the actors' lines, I think that these words have in some way permeated my speech", moderate user S15). Limited DM users, on the other hand, implied that learning/use of DMs was intentional. Those students claimed deliberately using DMs because they had been explicitly instructed by their teacher to employ them for instrumental reasons, such as better performance at the exams (*"She says that in the exams we will have a discussion with the examiners and that we have to be spontaneous, to say 'well', so I think I learned it from her"*, limited user S8). Those students did not mention noticing DMs in spontaneous speech.

5 Discussion

The results of the study are discussed in this section and are interpreted in light of previous research, while pointing to their contribution to existing knowledge and their implications for practice.

5.1 Effect of ISLL on spoken DM use

The study indicated three leisure-oriented activities that when performed frequently likely reinforced spoken DM use: speaking to oneself, interacting by speaking with L1/L2 others and watching TV/films without subtitles/captions. Previous research has shown the importance of certain ISLL activities in vocabulary knowledge (e.g., Peters 2018) and written accuracy (e.g., Kusyk 2020). This study has provided further evidence by identifying activities that can promote pragmalinguistic use. The fact that a few students reported engaging in all three activities at each time-point, contrary to the majority of participants for whom such engagement was rare, can explain most participants' more limited DM use.

In L2 pragmatics there is only limited and tentative evidence regarding the positive effect of ISLL on DM use. Building on Vickov (2015), who reported positive correlations between ISLL and written DM use, present findings add to existing knowledge by demonstrating links between ISLL and spoken DM use. This study showed that an activity which is simply receptive (i.e., TV watching), such as the ones studied by Vickov (2015), only contributed to spoken DM frequency, compared to productive activities (i.e., speaking/interacting) which had an effect on spoken DM range. This disparity might be explained by the possibility that different aspects of DM use in different registers (written vs. spoken) might be affected by engagement in different activities. This working hypothesis could be tested in the future. The study also extends the perspective of previous DM research that has either relied on assumptions about the status of the English language in EFL contexts (Gilquin 2016) or has studied exposure to authentic input in the traditional sense, such as the number of times students have been to an English-speaking country, the length of time spent there or L2 exposure within that country (Müller 2005; Beeching 2015; Liu 2016).

The finding that broad and frequent DM use was related to frequency of engagement in three activities rather than frequency of overall engagement or frequency of engagement in any of the remaining activities points to the importance of type of activity engagement in addition to frequency. This is in line with studies which have shown that frequency of engagement alone is not associated with language outcomes (Cole and Vanderplank 2016; Lee 2019). The study adds to previous knowledge by specifying those three activity types that impact broad and frequent spoken DM use. Engagement in the remaining twenty activities might not have involved the characteristics of the three key activities (frequent exposure to spoken input, spoken production and interaction). For example, some activities were carried out on occasion and therefore not with the optimal frequency that could encourage frequent exposure to and/or use of DMs. Of the activities that were carried out frequently, spoken DMs might not have been frequent in the input (e.g., when reading online articles) due to differences in discourse modality and formality.

There are various reasons, albeit speculative, why those activities stood out. Students who interacted with L1/L2 others were likely to be exposed to DMs used by their interlocutors. DMs are frequent in spoken, naturalistic social interactions given their various functions in discourse (Aijmer 2002; Fung and Carter 2007; D'Arcy 2017). Spoken interactions could also have reinforced production of DMs; previous research has highlighted the importance of social interaction in DM acquisition (Müller 2005; Hellermann and Vergun 2007; Romero-Trillo 2012). The study showed that English spoken interaction can range from talking in English to speakers of different L1s (not necessarily English) to talking to others of the same L1 as the speaker's (i.e., Greek) to even talking to oneself (e.g., imitating language heard elsewhere). Hence, the study broadens the perspective of previous research which has studied L2 interaction either with "native speakers" or taking place within a country where the L2 is dominant (Sankoff et al. 1997; Müller 2005; Polat 2011; Magliacane 2020).

Watching TV/films without subtitles/captions might have provided opportunities for exposure to authentic input where DMs were likely to be frequent. Although no data were collected from out-of-class DM input, it is not unreasonable to surmise that students were exposed to DMs in TV/film dialogue given the repetitive presence of DMs in such dialogue (Quaglio 2009; Bednarek 2018; Pettersson-Traba 2018). The finding that TV/film watching contributed to frequent DM use accords with findings from previous smaller-scale studies conducted in ESL contexts (Liao 2009; Liu 2016); this study extends such claims to the EFL context.

Frequent DM use was associated with watching TV/films without rather than with the use of subtitles/captions, supporting previous research that has documented a positive relationship between out-of-class, non-subtitled TV/film watching and vocabulary knowledge (Peters 2018). Watching without subtitles/captions might direct the viewer's attention from both reading and listening to only listening and consequently to linguistic features, such as DMs, that are prevalent in spoken TV/film discourse but might be absent from subtitles/captions. This interpretation is motivated by the findings of previous research which has documented the absence of DMs from subtitles/captions due to brevity purposes (Chaume 2004; Bruti and Zanotti 2014), difficulties in translating (Cuenca 2008) and low quality of subtitles/captions (Vanderplank 2016), especially in material downloaded illegally for free, as some participants reported doing. Understanding the nature of the source is important because it can shed light onto the suitability for the activity to encourage DM exposure and use.

Finally, factors which have previously been linked to higher DM frequency and/or broader DM range, such as high spoken proficiency (Wei 2011; Neary-Sundquist 2014) and increased exposure to input in formal instruction (Ament, Pérez Vidal, and Barón Parés 2018), were found to have no effect on those aspects of DM use presently, further strengthening the potential of ISLL.

5.2 Engagement with spoken input during ISLL

This study reinforced the importance of noticing and subsequently processing the input because it suggested that it was a specific form of noticing and input processing that distinguished the broader from the more limited DM users. Whereas limited DM users mentioned having noticed lexical items in isolation, considerable/moderate DM users reportedly also focused on the overall spoken production. According to Schmidt (2010), attention to linguistic forms together with social and contextual features is necessary for the acquisition of L2 pragmatics. It might be necessary to be attentive to longer stretches of speech and the way spoken discourse unfolds, owing to the polysemy and multifunctionality of DMs (Beeching 2016), the fact that certain pragmatic functions of DMs have been found to be less salient than others (Müller 2005) and the fact that DMs function as instructions of how to interpret the message rather than embody a concept (Haselow 2017).

Furthermore, it appeared that broad and frequent DM use was related to input processing practices that were productive (e.g., embedding aspects of spoken discourse, such as accent, lexical items, longer stretches of speech, into one's own spoken productions) rather than simply receptive (e.g., looking up the meaning of lexical items). This is well substantiated by the notion that "efficiency in performing pragmatic functions" requires sustained practice besides exposure (Taguchi 2015b: 34). As this study showed, producing language through frequent and constant spoken interaction with L1/L2 others and speaking to oneself, imitating actors, and repeating lines from TV/films, were habits of considerable/moderate DM users.

Noticing and processing input from informal sources might be of great importance to DM acquisition given the limited representation of pragmalinguistic features in the classroom input (Taguchi 2015a), and the artificial type of classroom interaction (González-Lloret 2019). With no student mentioning having noticed DMs in their teacher's use of the language, but rather when the teacher explicitly instructed students to use certain DMs, it can be argued that noticing and processing spoken input might be encouraged more during ISLL because of the personally relevant, leisure-oriented nature of engagement with the language (Cole and Vanderplank 2016).

5.3 Intentional learning or incidental acquisition?

One final finding was the blurred boundaries between incidental acquisition and intentional practices. DM acquisition might have been incidental: students who engaged in the three key activities claimed to have done so without the primary intention to learn, but for leisure. When ISLL is motivated by leisure, any linguistic outcome is a "side-effect" of other activities (Toffoli 2020: 127), and hence "incidental" (Sockett 2014: 8). Furthermore, although students who attributed their DM learning/use to their ISLL mentioned noticing DMs in the input, they implied that they had picked them up. In other words, there was no indication in students' statements that they engaged in the activities to learn DMs, nor that they purposefully and deliberately practised them. Students expressed an awareness of learning outcomes in terms of DM use; thus, it can be argued that DM acquisition might have been "incidental explicit", which, as defined by Rieder (2003: 28), takes place "without learning intention" but encompasses a conscious process, i.e., individuals are aware that learning has taken place.

Although ISLL that contributed to broad and frequent DM use was motivated by leisure purposes and was not learning oriented, there is evidence to suggest the importance of intentional practices that involved active noticing and subsequent processing of spoken input. With these findings, this study contributes to the ISLL field by offering some insight into the explicit-implicit debate (Dressman 2020). This study supports Hubbard's position (2020) who views intentional learning and incidental acquisition during ISLL as a continuum. It also argues that explicit attention to spoken language and active use are critical, corroborating Vanderplank and Cole's work (Cole 2015; Cole and Vanderplank 2016; Vanderplank 2019), who posit that in order for linguistic gains to occur and for input to become intake from informal L2 sources, there needs to be a focus on linguistic details and active use. Students did not mention explicitly targeting DMs through their intentional practices, but it can be argued that DMs could have been included in the spoken input students reportedly processed. Although previous research has focused on lexico-grammatical knowledge, this study adds to the literature by showing that intentional practices during ISLL are also crucial for pragmatic performance.

The present findings have implications for practice, such as encouraging learners to develop strategies in order to benefit pragmalinguistically during their ISLL, especially since DM use is associated with pragmatically successful communication and natural sounding discourse. This can be achieved through experience sharing inside the class and strategy instruction. Given that adolescents are more susceptible to peer suggestions and because activities which contributed to DM use were personally relevant and self-initiated rather than imposed by a teacher, the teacher's role should be one of guidance and dialogue building rather than interference. For example, teachers can encourage broader DM users to share details of their out-of-class habits with more limited DM users, with a focus on those key activities that promote DM use, such as outlets for accessing L2 others. Ways to benefit from informal sources pragmalinguistically can be shown through strategy instruction or showcasing practices of broader DM users, such as paying attention to longer stretches of speech and repeating lines from favourite TV shows.

6 Conclusion

Despite previous tentative evidence with regard to written DM use, ISLL has not been examined sufficiently in spoken DM use in EFL contexts, as the latter have been conceptualised in a limited way in DM research. By bringing together the fields of ISLL and L2 pragmatics this study has shown that the potential of ISLL rises beyond gains in vocabulary knowledge or the four language skills, with many exciting and promising opportunities for future research. Regarding limitations, the study did not examine the language that learners were exposed to or used during their ISLL activities, which could provide more definite answers about their DM acquisition and the implicit-explicit debate. Creating various sub-corpora of data from participants' favourite TV series, interactions with friends or voice-recordings of speaking to themselves will enable the analysis of DM data from participants' ISLL. Potential challenges to be overcome concern data collection and ethical considerations given the private and highly individualised nature of underage participants' ISLL. Another limitation is that the study looked into the quantity of certain DM types and not the quality, such as functions signalled by DMs. Future research can include a wider DM repertoire and assess quality of DM use as well as how ISLL contributes to that aspect.

Appendices

Appendix A

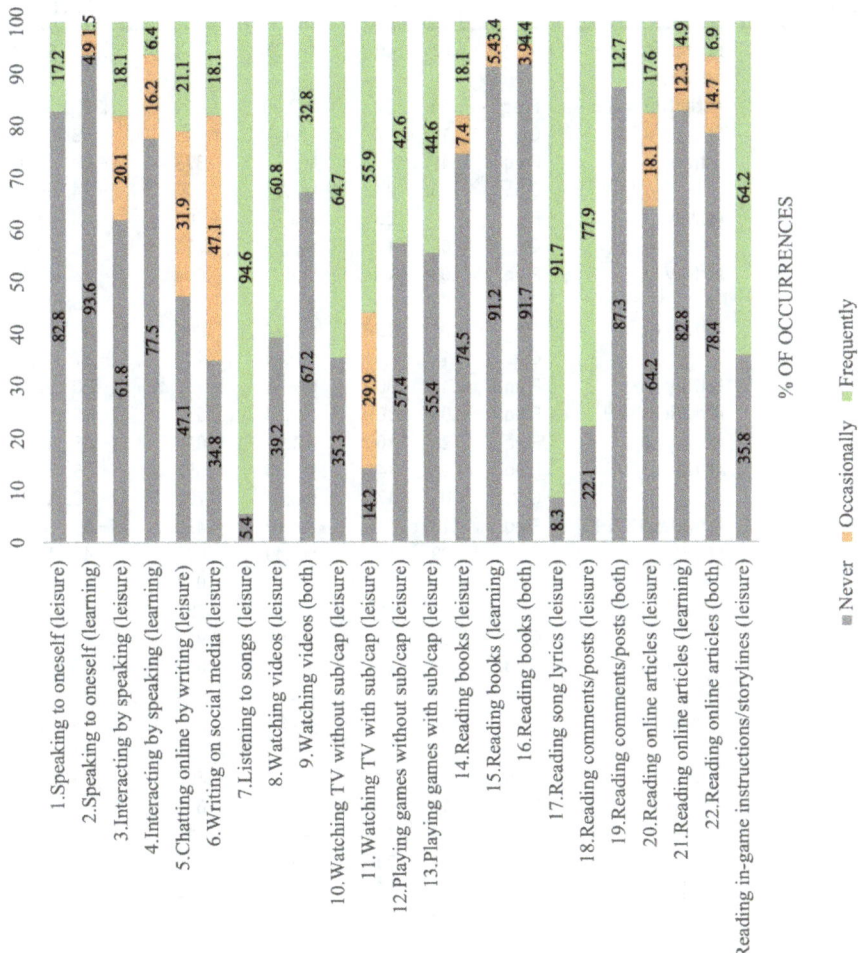

Students' overall engagement (average Time 1 through Time 4) in the 23 identified activities by purpose

Appendix B

Table 1: Random-intercept GLMM for DM range with ISLL activities as fixed effects.

Parameters			β	SE	Test	p	95% CI
Fixed effects	Intercept		1.01	.40	t=2.53	.013	[.22, 1.81]
	Activities						
	Activities 1 & 3	**Freq.**	**.88**	**.24**	**t=3.60**	**.001**	**[.39, 1.37]**
		Occ.	.16	.17	t=.95	.345	[−.18, .51]
	Activity 2	Freq.	.40	.45	t=.90	.373	[−.49, 1.29]
		Occ.	.26	.20	t=1.27	.207	[−.14, .66]
	Activity 4	Freq.	.17	.26	t=.67	.506	[−.34, .68]
		Occ.	−.04	.14	t=−.26	.799	[−.32, .25]
	Activity 5	Freq.	.09	.19	t=.46	.644	[−.28, .46]
		Occ.	.02	.14	t=.15	.880	[−.25, .29]
	Activity 6	Freq.	−.05	.19	t=−.24	.808	[−.43, .34]
		Occ.	−.11	.13	t=−.84	.404	[−.37, .15]
	Activity 7	Freq.	−.44	.30	t=−1.43	.156	[−1.04, .17]
	Activities 8 & 9	Freq.	−.04	.16	t=−.24	.812	[−1.04, .17]
	Activity 10	Freq.	.28	.16	t=1.69	.094	[−.05, .60]
	Activity 11	Freq.	−.06	.14	t=−.45	.652	[−.35, .22]
		Occ.	.05	.17	t=.26	.794	[−.30, .39]
	Activities 12 & 13	Freq.	−.10	.14	t=−.69	.490	[−.38, .18]
	Activity 14	Freq.	−.09	.17	t=−.49	.628	[−.43, .26]
		Occ.	−.57	.27	t=−2.11	.037	[−1.11, −.04]
	Activity 15	Freq.	.14	.45	t=.31	.757	[−.75, 1.03]
		Occ.	.03	.24	t=.10	.917	[−.44, .49]
	Activity 16	Freq.	−.06	.27	t=−.23	.817	[−.58, .46]
		Occ.	.08	.28	t=.27	.789	[−.48, .63]
	Activity 17	Freq.	.29	.24	t=1.21	.228	[−.18, .75]
	Activities 18 & 19	Freq.	−.27	.19	t=−1.41	.161	[−.64, .11]
	Activity 20	Freq.	.09	.17	t=.52	.606	[−.25, .43]
		Occ.	−.10	.20	t=−.49	.626	[−.48, .29]
	Activity 21	Freq.	−.14	.37	t=−.37	.712	[−.87, .59]
		Occ.	−.03	.20	t=−.14	.890	[−.43, .37]
	Activity 22	Freq.	−.06	.21	t=−.27	.785	[−.47, .36]
		Occ.	−.12	.18	t=−.67	.502	[−.47, .23]
	Activity 23	Freq.	−.13	.15	t=−.85	.396	[−.44, .17]

Table 1 (continued)

Parameters		β	SE	Test	p	95% CI
Random effects	Residual	.73	.20	Z=3.66	<.001	[.43, 1.24]
	Time 1	.56	.16	Z=3.45	.001	[.32, .99]
	Time 2	.55	.16	Z=3.52	<.001	[.31, .96]
	Time 3	.49	.15	Z=3.23	.001	[.27, .91]
	Time 4					
	Intercept (participant)	.21	.09	Z=2.38	.017	[.09, .47]
AICC			423.09			

Note: Activities are detailed in Appendix A; β=estimate; SE=standard error; CI=confidence interval; AICC=Akaike Information Criterion Corrected; Freq.=engaging in the activity frequently; Occ.= engaging in the activity on occasion, "Never engaging in the activity" was the reference category; Significant positive fixed effects are in bold.

Table 2: Random-intercept GLMM for DM frequency with ISLL activities as fixed effects.

Parameters			β	SE	Test	p	95% CI
Fixed effects	Intercept		2.56	.47	t=5.44	<.001	[1.63, 3.49]
	Activities						
	Activities 1 & 3	Freq.	.53	.32	t=1.68	.097	[−.10, 1.17]
		Occ.	−.08	.18	t=−.46	.643	[−.44, .27]
	Activity 2	Freq.	.28	.48	t=.59	.556	[−.66, 1.23]
		Occ.	.08	.24	t=.35	.724	[−.38, .55]
	Activity 4	Freq.	.06	.30	t=.21	.832	[−.53, .65]
		Occ.	.01	.15	t=.07	.945	[−.28, .30]
	Activity 5	Freq.	.17	.24	t=.73	.469	[−.30, .64]
		Occ.	.20	.15	t=1.28	.203	[−.11, .50]
	Activity 6	Freq.	−.16	.22	t=−.73	.470	[−.60, .28]
		Occ.	−.26	.13	t=−1.96	.052	[−.51, .00]
	Activity 7	Freq.	−.60	.36	t=−1.67	.098	[−1.30, .11]
	Activities 8 & 9	Freq.	.18	.16	t=1.10	.276	[−.14, .50]
	Activity 10	**Freq.**	**.54**	**.19**	**t=2.89**	**.005**	**[.17, .91]**
	Activity 11	Freq.	−.20	.19	t=−1.06	.292	[−.57, .17]
		Occ.	.11	.21	t=.52	.604	[−.31, .53]
	Activities 12 & 13	Freq.	−.06	.16	t=−.34	.731	[−.38, .27]
	Activity 14	Freq.	.15	.22	t=.69	.494	[−.29, .59]
		Occ.	−.53	.25	t=−2.18	.031	[−1.02, −.05]
	Activity 15	Freq.	.84	.48	t=1.75	.083	[−.11, 1.78]
		Occ.	−.27	.25	t=−1.11	.269	[−.76, .22]
	Activity 16	Freq.	.15	.28	t=.53	.595	[−.41, .71]
		Occ.	.01	.26	t=.02	.982	[−.50, .52]

Table 2 (continued)

Parameters			β	SE	Test	p	95% CI
	Activity 17	Freq.	.43	.27	t=1.60	.113	[−.10, .96]
	Activities 18 & 19	Freq.	−.29	.23	t=−1.27	.207	[−.74, .16]
	Activity 20	Freq.	−.01	.19	t=−.04	.971	[−.39, .37]
		Occ.	−.24	.19	t=−1.27	.207	[−.61, .13]
	Activity 21	Freq.	−.76	.40	t=−1.90	.059	[−1.55, .03]
		Occ.	.10	.21	t=.45	.656	[−.33, .51]
	Activity 22	Freq.	−.18	.23	t=−.78	.435	[−.64, .28]
		Occ.	−.09	.19	t=−.50	.618	[−.46, .28]
	Activity 23	Freq.	−.12	.17	t=−.68	.498	[−.45, .22]
Random effects	Residual		.31	.09	Z=3.57	<.001	[.18, .54]
	Time 1		.27	.08	Z=3.33	.001	[.15, .49]
	Time 2		.27	.08	Z=3.29	.001	[.15, .49]
	Time 3		.18	.07	Z=2.65	.008	[.09, .39]
	Time 4						
	Intercept (participant)		.47	.12	Z=3.87	<.001	[.29, .79]
AICC			433.33				

Note: Activities are detailed in Appendix A; β=estimate; SE=standard error; CI=confidence interval; AICC=Akaike Information Criterion Corrected; Freq.=engaging in the activity frequently; Occ.= engaging in the activity on occasion, "Never engaging in the activity" was the reference category; Significant positive fixed effects are in bold.

References

Aijmer, Karin. 2002. *English Discourse Particles. Evidence from a Corpus*. Amsterdam: John Benjamins.

Alcón Soler, Eva. 2005. Does instruction work for learning pragmatics in the EFL context? *System* 33. 417–435.

Ament, Jennifer, Carmen Pérez Vidal & Júlia Barón Parés. 2018. The effects of English-medium instruction on the use of textual and interpersonal pragmatic markers. *Pragmatics* 28(4). 517–545.

Angouri, Jo, Marina Mattheoudakis & Maria Zigrika. 2010. Then how will they get the much-wanted paper? A multifaceted study of English as a foreign language in Greece. *Advances in research on language acquisition and teaching: Selected papers (Proceedings of the 14th International Conference of Greek Applied Linguistics Association)*, 179–194. Athens: Greek Applied Linguistics Association.

Asprey, Esther & Caroline Tagg. 2019. The pragmatic use of vocatives in private one-to-one digital communication. *Internet Pragmatics* 2(1). 83–111.

BAAL. 2016 *Recommendations on Good Practice in Applied Linguistics*. 3rd edn. Available online at: www.baal.org.uk

Bednarek, Monika. 2018. *Language and Television Series: A linguistic approach to TV dialogue*. Cambridge: Cambridge University Press.

Beeching, Kate. 2015. Variability in native and non-native use of pragmatic markers: The example of well in role-play data. In Kate Beeching & Helen Woodfield (eds.), *Researching Sociopragmatic Variation: Perspectives from Variational, Interlanguage and Contrastive Pragmatics*, 174–197. New York: Palgrave Macmillan.

Beeching, Kate. 2016. *Pragmatic Markers in British English: Meaning in Social Interaction*. Cambridge: Cambridge University Press.

Blakemore, Diane. 2002. *Relevance and Linguistic Meaning. The Semantics and Pragmatics of Discourse Markers*. Cambridge: Cambridge University Press.

Brevik, Lisbeth M. 2016. The Gaming Outliers: Does out-of-school gaming improve boys' reading skills in English as a second language? In Eyvind Elstad (ed.), *Educational technology and Polycontextual bridging*, 39–61. Rotterdam/Boston/Taipei: Sense Publishers.

Bruti, Silvia & Serenella Zanotti. 2014. Fansubbing in close-up: A study of interjections and discourse markers. In Rachele Antonini & Chiara Bucaria (eds.), *Non-Professional Interpreting and Translation in the Media*, 231–256. Bern: Peter Lang.

Buysse, Lieven. 2012. So as a multifunctional discourse marker in native and learner speech. *Journal of Pragmatics* 44. 1764–1782.

Buysse, Lieven. 2017. The pragmatic you know in learner Englishes. *Journal of Pragmatics* 121. 40–57.

Chaume, Frederic. 2004. Discourse markers in audiovisual translating. *Meta: journal des traducteurs/ Meta: Translators' Journal* 49(4). 843–855.

Codreanu, Tatiana & Christelle Combe. 2020. Vlogs, video publishing, and informal language learning. In Mark Dressman & Randall William Sadler (eds.), *The Handbook of Informal Language Learning*, 153–168. Hoboken/Chichester: Wiley-Blackwell.

Cole, Jason. 2015. *Foreign language learning in the age of the Internet: A comparison of informal acquirers and traditional classroom learners in central Brazil*. Oxford: University of Oxford dissertation.

Cole, Jason & Robert Vanderplank. 2016. Comparing autonomous and class-based learners in Brazil: Evidence for the present-day advantages of informal, out-of-class learning. *System* 61. 31–42.

Council of Europe. 2001. *The Common European Framework of Reference for Languages Languages – Learning, Teaching, Assessment*. Cambridge: Cambridge University Press.

Council of Europe. 2018. *The Common European Framework of Reference for Languages – Learning, Teaching, Assessment: Companion Volume with New Descriptors*. Strasbourg: Council of Europe Publishing. https://rm.coe.int/cefr-companion-volume-with-new-descriptors-2018/1680787989 (accessed March 29, 2021)

Crystal, David. 1988. Another look at, well, you know. *English Today* 13. 47–49.

Cuenca, Maria-Josep. 2008. Pragmatic markers in contrast: The case of well. *Journal of Pragmatics* 40(8). 1373–1391.

Cunnings, Ian & Ian Finlayson. 2015. Mixed effects modeling and longitudinal data analysis. In Luke Plonsky (ed.), *Advancing quantitative methods in second language research*, 159–181. New York: Routledge.

Curran, Patrick J., Khawla Obeidat & Diane Losardo. 2010. Twelve frequently asked questions about growth curve odelling. *Journal of Cognition and Development* 11(2). 121–136.

D'Arcy, Alexandra. 2017. *Discourse-Pragmatic Variation in Context. Eight Hundred Years of LIKE*. Amsterdam: John Benjamins.

Davydova, Julia, Agnieszka Ewa Tytus & Erik Schleef. 2017. Acquisition of sociolinguistic awareness by German learners of English: A study in perceptions of quotative be like. *Linguistics* 55(4). 783–812.

Diskin, Chloé. 2017. The use of the discourse-pragmatic marker *like* by native and non-native speakers of English in Ireland. *Journal of Pragmatics* 120. 144–157.

Dressman, Mark. 2020. Introduction. In Mark Dressman & Randall William Sadler (eds.), *The Handbook of Informal Language Learning*, 1–12. Hoboken/Chichester: Wiley-Blackwell.

Ellis, Nick C. 2019. Essentials of a theory of language cognition. *The Modern Language Journal* 103. 39–60.

Ewert, Doreen E. 2020. Extensive reading for statistical learning. In Mark Dressman & Randall William Sadler (eds.), *The Handbook of Informal Language Learning*, 395–404. Hoboken/Chichester: Wiley-Blackwell.

Frobenius, Maximiliane. 2014. Audience design in monologues: How vloggers involve their viewers. *Journal of Pragmatics* 72. 59–72.

Fung, Loretta & Ronald Carter. 2007. Discourse markers and spoken English: Native and learner use in pedagogic settings. *Applied Linguistics* 28(3). 410–439.

Gilquin, Gaëtanelle. 2016. Discourse markers in L2 English: From classroom to naturalistic input. In Olga Timofeeva, Anne-Christine Gardner, Alpo Honkapohja & Sarah Chevalier (eds.), *New Approaches to English Linguistics: Building Bridges*, 213–249. Amsterdam: John Benjamins.

González-Lloret, Marta. 2019. Technology and L2 pragmatics learning. *Annual Review of Applied Linguistics* 39. 113–127.

Harrison, Xavier A., Lynda Donaldson, Maria Eugenia Correa-Cano, Julian Evans, David N. Fisher, Cecily E. D. Goodwin, Beth S. Robinson, David J. Hodgson & Richard Inger. 2018. A brief introduction to mixed effects modelling and multi-model inference in ecology. *PeerJ* 6. 1–32. doi: 10.7717/peerj.4794

Haselow, Alexander. 2017. *Spontaneous Spoken English. An Integrated Approach to the Emergent Grammar of Speech*. Cambridge: Cambridge University Press.

Hellermann, John & Andrea Vergun. 2007. Language which is not taught: The discourse marker use of beginning adult learners of English. *Journal of Pragmatics* 39(1). 157–179.

House, Juliane. 2013. Developing pragmatic competence in English as a lingua franca: Using discourse markers to express (inter)subjectivity and connectivity. *Journal of Pragmatics* 59. 57–67.

Hubbard, Philip. 2020. Leveraging technology to integrate informal language learning within classroom settings. In Mark Dressman & Randall William Sadler (eds.), *The Handbook of Informal Language Learning*, 405–420. Hoboken/Chichester: Wiley-Blackwell.

Jakupčević, Eva. 2019. Young language learners' use of discourse markers in L2 narratives. *English Teaching & Learning* 43(2). 1–18.

Jurkovič, Violeta. 2019. Online informal learning through smartphones in Slovenia. *System* 80. 27–37.

Kantaridou, Zoe & Eleanna Xekalou. 2021. The L2 motivational self system profile of Greek adolescents. *Research papers in language teaching and learning* 11(1). 268–283.

Kasper, Gabriele & Kenneth R. Rose. 2002. *Pragmatic Development in a Second Language*. Oxford: Blackwell.

Kuckartz, Udo. 2014. *Qualitative Text Analysis: A Guide to Methods, Practice & Using Software*. London: Sage Publications.

Kukulska-Hulme, Agnes & Helen Lee. 2020. Mobile collaboration for language learning and cultural learning. In Mark Dressman & Randall William Sadler (eds.), *The Handbook of Informal Language Learning*, 169–180. Hoboken/Chichester: Wiley-Blackwell.

Kusyk, Meryl. 2017. The development of complexity, accuracy & fluency in L2 written production through informal participation in online activities. *CALICO Journal* 34 (1). 75–96.

Kusyk, Meryl. 2020. Informal English learning in France. In Mark Dressman & Randall William Sadler (eds.), *The Handbook of Informal Language Learning*, 333–348. Hoboken/Chichester: Wiley-Blackwell.

Lai, Chun, Xiao Hu & Boning Lyu. 2018. Understanding the nature of learners' out-of-class language learning experience with technology. *Computer Assisted Language Learning* 31(1–2). 114–143.

Lee, Ju Seong. 2019. Quantity and diversity of informal digital learning of English. *Language Learning & Technology* 23(1). 114–126.

Lee, Ju Seong & Mark Dressman. 2018. When IDLE hands make an English workshop: Informal digital learning of English and language proficiency. *TESOL Quarterly* 52(2). 435–445.

Li, Shuai. 2019. Cognitive approaches in L2 pragmatics research. In Naoko Taguchi (ed.), *The Routledge Handbook of Second Language Acquisition and Pragmatics*, 113–127. Abingdon: Routledge.

Liao, Silvie. 2009. Variation in the use of discourse markers by Chinese teaching assistants in the U.S. *Journal of Pragmatics* 41(7). 1313–1328.

Lindgren, Eva & Carmen Muñoz. 2013. The influence of exposure, parents, and linguistic distance on young European learners' foreign language comprehension. *International Journal of Multilingualism* 10(1). 105–129.

Liu, Binmei. 2016. Effect of L2 exposure: From a perspective of discourse markers. *Applied Linguistics Review* 7(1). 73–98.

Lutzky, Ursula & Matt Gee. 2018. I just found your blog: The pragmatics of initiating comments on blog posts. *Journal of Pragmatics* 129. 173–184.

Magliacane, Annarita. 2020. Erasmus students in an Irish study abroad context: A longitudinal analysis of the use of *well* and *like*. *Study Abroad Research in Second Language Acquisition and International Education* 5(1). 92–120.

Martín-Laguna, Sofia. 2019. Exploring case stories in the development of textual discourse-pragmatic markers in formal English language classrooms. In Patricia Salazar-Campillo & Victòria Codina-Espurz (eds.), *Investigating the Learning of Pragmatics across Ages and Contexts*, 40–53. Leiden: Brill.

Mattheoudakis, Marina & Thomai Alexiou. 2009. Early foreign language instruction in Greece: Socioeconomic factors and their effect on young learners' language development. In Marianne Nikolov (ed.), *Contextualising the age factor*, 227–251. Clevendon: Multilingual Matters.

McCarthy, Michael & Jeanne McCarten. 2018. Now you're talking! Practising conversation in second language learning. In Christian Jones (ed.), *Practice in Second Language Learning*, 7–29. Cambridge: Cambridge University Press.

McNeish, Daniel & Tyler Matta. 2018. Differentiating between mixed-effects and latent-curve approaches to growth modelling. *Behavior Research Methods* 50. 1398–1414.

Meyers, Lawrence S., Glenn Gamst & A. J. Guarino. 2013. *Applied Multivariate Research: Design and Interpretation*, 2nd edn. Thousand Oaks: Sage Publications.

Mitsikopoulou, Bessie, Evdokia Karavas & Smaragda Papadopoulou. 2017. KPG e-school: The diffusion and implementation of an educational innovation. In Evdokia Karavas & Bessie Mitsikopoulou (eds.), *Developments in Glocal Language Testing: The Case of the Greek National Foreign Language Exam System*, 297–326. Oxford: Peter Lang.

Müller, Simone. 2005. *Discourse Markers in Native and Non-native English Discourse*. Amsterdam: John Benjamins.

Neary-Sundquist, Colleen. 2014. The use of pragmatic markers across proficiency levels in second language speech. *Studies in Second Language Learning and Teaching* 4(4). 637–663.

Neys, Joyce. 2017. Multicollinearity. In Mike Allen (ed.), *The SAGE Encyclopedia of Communication Research Methods*, 1036–1037. Thousand Oaks: SAGE Publications.

Peters, Elke. 2018. The effect of out-of-class exposure to English language media on learners' vocabulary knowledge. *ITL–International Journal of Applied Linguistics* 169. 142–168.

Pettersson-Traba, Daniela. 2018. Revisiting *you know* and *I mean*: Some notes on the functions of the two pragmatic markers in contemporary spoken American English. *Research in Corpus Linguistics* 6. 67–81.

Polat, Brittany. 2011. Investigating acquisition of discourse markers through a developmental learner corpus. *Journal of Pragmatics* 43. 3745–3756.

Quaglio, Paulo. 2009. *Television Dialogue: The Sitcom Friends vs. Natural Conversation*. Amsterdam: John Benjamins.

Rieder, Angelika. 2003. Implicit and explicit learning in incidental vocabulary acquisition. *VIEWS* 12(2). 24–39.

Romero-Trillo, Jesús. 2012. Pragmatic markers. In Carol Chapelle (ed.), *Encyclopaedia of Applied Linguistics*. Oxford: Wiley-Blackwell.

Romero-Trillo, Jesús. 2020. Pragmatic markers. In Carol Chapelle (ed.), *The Concise Encyclopaedia of Applied Linguistics*. Oxford: Wiley-Blackwell.

Rothoni, Anastasia & Bessie Mitsikopoulou. 2019. Visual representations of English language learning and literacy in Greece. In Sangeeta Bagga-Gupta, Anne Golden, Lars Holm, Helle Pia Laursen & Anne Pitkänen-Huhta (eds.), *Reconceptualizing Connections between Language, Literacy and Learning*, 231–252. Cham: Springer.

Sankoff, Gillian, Pierrette Thibault, Naomi Nagy, Hélène Blondeau, Marie-Odile Fonollosa & Lucie Gagnon. 1997. Variation in the use of discourse markers in a language contact situation. *Language Variation and Change* 9. 191–218.

Schmidt, Richard W. 1990. The role of consciousness in second language learning. *Applied Linguistics* 11. 129–158.

Schmidt, Richard W. 2010. Attention, awareness, and individual differences in language learning. In W. M. Chan, S. Chi, K. N. Cin, J. Istanto, M. Nagami, J. W. Sew, T. Suthiwan & I. Walker (eds.), *Proceedings of CLaSIC 2010*, 721–737. Singapore: National University of Singapore.

Sifakis, Nicos. 2018. ELF as an opportunity for foreign language use, learning and instruction in Greece and beyond. In Zoi Tatsioka, Barbara Seidlhofer, Nicos Sifakis & Ferguson Gibson (eds.), *Using English as a Lingua Franca in Education in Europe. English in Europe: Volume 4*, 13–27. Berlin/Boston: De Gruyter Mouton.

Sockett, Geoffrey. 2014. *The Online Informal Learning of English*. Basingstoke: Palgrave Macmillan.

Sockett, Geoffrey & Meryl Kusyk. 2015. Online informal learning of English: Frequency effects in the uptake of chunks of language from participation in web-based activities. In Teresa Cadierno and Søren Wind Eskildsen (eds.), *Usage-based Perspectives on Second Language Learning*, 153–177. Berlin/Boston: De Gruyter Mouton.

Sundqvist, Pia. 2019. Commercial-off-the-shelf games in the digital wild and L2 learner vocabulary. *Language Learning and Technology* 23(1). 87–113.

Sundqvist, Pia & Liss Kerstin Sylvén. 2016. *Extramural English in teaching and learning: From theory and research to practice*. Basingstoke: Palgrave Macmillan.

Svartvik, Jan. 1980. Well in conversation. In Sidney Greenbaum, Geoffrey Leech & Jan Svartvik (eds.), *Studies in English linguistics for Randolph Quirk*, 167–177. London: Longman.

Tagg, Caroline. 2012. *The Discourse of Text Messaging*. London: Continuum.

Taguchi, Naoko. 2015a. Contextually speaking: A survey of pragmatic learning abroad, in class, and online. *System* 48. 3–20.

Taguchi, Naoko. 2015b. Instructed pragmatics at a glance: Where instructional studies were, are, and should be going. *Language Teaching* 48. 1–50.

Taguchi, Naoko. 2019. Second language acquisition and pragmatics. In Naoko Taguchi (ed.), *The Routledge Handbook of Second Language Acquisition and Pragmatics*, 1–14. Abingdon: Routledge.

Taguchi, Naoko & Carsten Roever. 2017. *Second Language Pragmatics*. Oxford: Oxford University Press.

Toffoli, Denyze. 2020. *Informal Learning and Institution-wide Language Provision: University Language Learners in the 21st Century*. Cham: Palgrave Macmillan.

Tolson, Andrew. 2010. A new authenticity? Communicative practices on YouTube. *Critical Discourse Studies* 7(4). 277–289.

Tomasello, Michael. 2009. The usage-based theory of language acquisition. In Edith L. Bavin (ed.), *The Cambridge handbook of child language*, 69–88. Cambridge: Cambridge University Press.

Uicheng, Kanokrat & Michael Crabtree. 2018. Micro discourse markers in TED Talks: How ideas are signaled to listeners. *PASAA* 55. 1–31.

Vanderplank, Robert. 1990. Paying attention to the words: Practical and theoretical problems in watching television programmes with unilingual (CEEFAX) subtitles. *System* 18(2). 221–234.

Vanderplank, Robert. 2016. *Captioned Media in Foreign Language Learning: Subtitles for the Deaf and Hard-of-Hearing as Tools for Language Learning*. London: Palgrave Macmillan.

Vanderplank, Robert. 2019. Gist watching can only take you so far: Attitudes, strategies and changes in behaviour in watching films with captions. *The Language Learning Journal* 47(4). 407–423.

Verspoor, Marjolijn H. & Heike Behrens. 2011. Dynamic systems theory and a usage-based approach to second language development. In Marjolijn H. Verspoor, Kees de Bot & Wander Lowie (eds.), *A dynamic approach to second language development: Methods and techniques*, 25–38. Amsterdam: John Benjamins.

Vickov, Gloria. 2015. Discourse marker acquisition and out-of-school activities: Evidence from EFL writing. *TEM Journal* 4(2). 207–218.

Wei, Ming. 2011. Investigating the oral proficiency of English learners in China: A comparative study of the use of pragmatic markers. *Journal of Pragmatics* 43. 3455–3472.

Wikström, Peter. 2014. & she was like O_O: Animation of reported speech on Twitter. *Nordic Journal of English Studies* 13(3). 83–111.

Kossi Seto Yibokou
6 Influence of television series on pronunciation
French learners of English

Abstract: This study seeks to explore the impact of informal out-of-class exposure to authentic input on English as a second language learners' pronunciation. Data was collected from 20 French students who participated in a pronunciation task followed by a questionnaire about their formal (classroom) and informal (leisure) activities in English. The results of the acoustic analysis show that the participants' pronunciation is composed of mixed phonological features akin to British, American and French accents. Although there are individual differences in their productions, all participants tend to unconsciously imitate phonological features from the videos they watch. From the data provided in a questionnaire, I argue that the elements of American English found in their pronunciation emanate from informal exposure, mainly by watching American television series, whilst the British phonological aspects come from the formal sphere. It is further hypothesized that viewing activities might allow learners to understand, pick up sociolinguistic elements and speak the varieties of English accents (World Englishes) they are exposed to through their leisure activities. From a pedagogical standpoint, these results could encourage teachers and learners to value and take advantage of such informal language practices.

Keywords: individual differences, informal media exposure, leisure activities, phonetic imitation, pronunciation

1 Introduction

Online Informal Learning of English (OILE) can be defined as: "emerging from a communicative intention, implying that it does not take place according to a set timetable or as an organized learning activity and indeed that the learner may not necessarily be aware that learning is taking place" (Sockett 2011: 7). Studies that have been conducted within the field of informal language learning in France have shown many benefits for English language learners, ranging from vocabulary development to effects on learning strategies and autonomy (Toffoli and Sockett 2010;

Kossi Seto Yibokou, Université de Lorraine, France

https://doi.org/10.1515/9783110752441-006

Sockett 2014; Toffoli and Sockett 2015a; Toffoli and Perrot 2017). Elsewhere, studies that analyzed the informal practices of English learners yielded similar results, indicating that activities performed in informal contexts have great potential for language learning. In the Brazilian context, Cole and Vanderplank (2016) have shown a higher level of linguistic performance of "fully autonomous self-instructed learners" (FASILs) over their "classroom trained" (CTL) counterparts. Chik (2014) and Sundqvist (2015) have also shown a link between English vocabulary acquisition and video game practices in Hong Kong and Sweden respectively. Other studies have examined Austrian students' perceptions of the usefulness of informal practices in the classroom (Trinder 2017), the relationship between language acquisition, quantity, and diversity of Informal Digital Learning of English (IDLE) activities in South Korea (Lee and Lee 2019; Lee 2022) and Tunisian students' acquisition of Italian through broadcast programs (Narcy-Combes and Boughnim 2011). While the question of informal activities influencing learners' pronunciation has been raised on many occasions (Cole and Vanderplank 2016; Kusyk 2017), none of these publications were devoted to the phonetic analysis of respondents' oral productions. For instance, although Narcy-Combes and Boughnim (2011) and Lee (2017) recorded learners' speaking during data collection, the recordings were not subjected to phonetic or phonological analyses and only aspects such as fluency were considered. At the same time, whilst earlier sociolinguistic work refutes the impact of television on pronunciation (Chambers 1998), current research has shown that informal activities, especially television watching, do influence native speakers' pronunciation (Stuart-Smith et al. 2013). The present study aims to consider the case of the L2 context by specifically looking for any influence that viewing videos (films and series) might have on the pronunciation of English by French native speakers.

2 Background and objective

This research originated from observations according to which English teachers in France perceive their learners' pronunciation of English as tending increasingly towards American accents (Toffoli and Sockett 2015b). Remarks such as "[students] use current idiomatic expressions with appropriate pronunciation" and "demonstrate better pronunciation in general" are examples given (Toffoli and Sockett 2015b: 14). Thus, the need to conduct research exploring this phenomenon more precisely became apparent as can be seen from the following remarks: "In the future, the effect of OILE on oral production, which is attested by some teachers [. . .], should also be investigated empirically" (Kusyk and Sockett 2012: 16), or "we still know little about many aspects of the OILE phenomenon, such as its impact on speaking" (Sockett and Kusyk 2013: 89). After conducting acoustic and perceptual analyses of British English posterior vowels in two French speakers, Exare (2009) claims that "the massive exposure of our young students (through movies and songs in particular) to varieties of English such as American (rhotic) English certainly has an impact on this propensity for rhotic realizations" (Exare 2009: 8). In line with these assumptions, but in a different linguistic context, Rindal (2010) examined Norwegian learners' production and perception of American and British English and noted that "It is difficult to avoid the impression that learners' pronunciation is influenced by spoken media, seeing as there is limited access to AmE elsewhere. More research is needed to investigate this suggested link between spoken media and L2 [second/foreign language] pronunciation" (Rindal 2010: 256).

From the above remarks and questions, it becomes clear that the relation between audiovisual informal activities and pronunciation has not yet been established by studies in second language acquisition (SLA). Our study intends to fill this gap. The aim of this exploratory research is to investigate the effects advanced by researchers and English teachers in the literature cited above. It also attempts an examination of the different relationships between French learners' out-of-class informal activities, especially the watching of TV series, and some English pronunciation features.

3 Informal media exposure and pronunciation

As far as pronunciation is concerned, several studies have shown the impact of media on the phonological system of native-speakers (Stuart-Smith et al. 2011, 2013). However, rare are the studies that demonstrate the impact of exposure to out-of-class informal media on the phonological system of second/foreign language (L2) learners. Indeed, some researchers consider phonological acquisition to be the pure product of live interactions and remain skeptical of or even refute any effect of the media, qualified as non-interactive sources, on phonetic acquisition (Chambers 1998; Labov 2001). Moreover, the impact of real physical interactions on phonological acquisition has been considerably documented and it has been shown, for example, that during face-to-face interactions, speakers imitate each other gesturally, lexically, syntactically, rhythmically, phonetically, phonologically (Schmale, Seidl, and Cristia 2015). In the same vein, Chambers (1998) published an article entitled *"TV makes people sound the same"*, in which he presented evidence that showed that television does not influence phonetic-phonological acquisition: "sociolinguists see some evidence for the mass media playing a role in the spread of vocabulary items. But in the deeper reaches of language change – sound changes and grammatical changes – the media have no significant effect at all" (Chambers 1998: 124). Chambers supports the idea that phonological or accent changes within a community of individuals are the exclusive consequence of human interaction, and that television does not have an impact on the pronunciation of viewers. According to him: "It may be that the media diffuse tolerance towards accent and dialect. But the changes themselves must be conveyed in face-to-face interactions among peers" (Chambers 1998: 129). Therefore, it should be understood that television does not cause viewers to speak with the accents they are exposed to. Chambers based his assumptions on several examples from empirical research to refute the impact of media on pronunciation, which he calls "linguistic science fiction" (Chambers 1998: 125). These include the fact that African Americans never speak like their white counterparts despite heavy media consumption (Chambers 1998: 126) or a hearing child of deaf parents who could not speak despite being regularly exposed to television (Chambers 1998: 126–127).

However, contrary to the above arguments, there is considerable research showing the impact of television on viewers' phonological systems. Mitterer and McQueen's (2009) results on the perception of English words pronounced with Australian and Scottish accents by Dutch learners show learners' willingness to imitate accents from non-interactive recorded sources. Sanchez, Miller and Rosenblum (2010) also found that audio-visual sources influenced participants' Voice Onset Time of plosives in two phonetic imitation tests. Stuart-Smith and colleagues (2011) had two groups of Scottish speakers perform imitation tests (perception-categorization, production) under two different conditions. The control group interacted directly with a native speaker of Standard British English (SBE), while the first group watched videos of the latter session. In both conditions, all participants showed phonetic imitation, indicating that media influences phonological acquisition:

> Sometimes experiencing speech without the possibility for interaction, e.g., engaging with a favourite Television show, is related to language change. [. . .] It is also clear that many kinds of rapid perceptual learning are possible from non-interactive recorded speech. Exposure to non-interactive recorded speech can trigger short-term shifts in speech perception and production. Speakers can also show short-term shifting even towards a virtual interlocutor (Stuart-Smith et al. 2011: 1914).

In another study, Stuart-Smith and colleagues (2013) show that active and motivated viewing of television series accelerates accent change in a language. They found that not only do young people in Glasgow, Scotland, who regularly watch the series *East Enders* become emotionally attached to the characters in the series, but they also take in elements of the London accent (Cockney). In this study, two pronunciation factors were identified. Glasgow speakers begin to use /f/ and /v/ in place of the unvoiced dentate fricative /θ/ and voiced dentate fricative /ð/ respectively (think: /fɪŋk/

instead of /θɪŋk/; this: /vɪs/ instead of /ðɪs/) and to replace the lateral approximant /l/ with the posterior closed vowel /ʊ/ of the word "good" (milk: /mʊk/ instead of /mɪlk/). This latter phenomenon is called L-vocalization (Stuart-Smith et al. 2013: 501). Further, Ota and Takano (2014) also identified a similarity between the intonation system of two distinct dialects spoken in two geographically distant cities in Japan (Hokkaido in the far north and Kagoshima in the far south), and that of the Japanese spoken in the media, which originates from the capital city of Tokyo in the centre (143–145). They also found that young people in these regions identify themselves with cartoon characters and imitate them on a phonological level (151).

The debate about the influence of the media on linguistic change continues to generate strong reactions among sociolinguists. In light of theories of phonetic imitation, Markham (1997), argues that audiovisual media also promotes phonetic imitation and thus facilitates the acquisition of pronunciation, while Androutsopoulos (2014) notes that:

> Despite a fair amount of relevant scholarship in sociolinguistics and neighbouring fields, the role of media in processes of linguistic change is not yet fully understood. [. . .] The predominant position in variationist sociolinguistics, i.e. that the media play no role in systemic language change [. . .] is increasingly perceived as unsatisfactory (2014: 3).

A few studies have also reported impacts of extracurricular video viewing on second language acquisition. Maeda (2009) conducted a study to find out which variety of English Japanese learners prefer to learn and which one(s) influence their pronunciation. She recorded 65 students from two universities in the Kanto area (Kanagawa and Tokyo), reading short stories and administered a questionnaire about their exposure and attitudes to English varieties. Phoneticians (American, British, and Japanese) judged the characteristics of the participants with regard to American, British, Australian, Japanese and mixed varieties of English. Most students preferred to learn the pronunciation of American English, a minority wanted the British English pronunciation, whilst only a few showed no preference, as they wanted to be easily and simply understood. The results indicate that the pronunciation of most students is influenced much more by American than by British English. Some words are pronounced more with elements of British English (e.g., "new") while others were mixed (e.g., "tune" is pronounced as "turn"). Influences from Japanese and some traces of Australian English were also noted.

In line with this work, Navrátilová (2013) examined the pronunciation of Czech pupils to explore the influences of out-of-class exposure to English input via viewing and listening. According to the author, in the Czech Republic, most films shown on screens are American and students in primary and secondary schools are exposed to the English language not only in class but also during their free time. They mostly watch in original version (English) because the country does not have the means to dub films, and the youth have sufficient English levels to understand the films without subtitles. The oral productions of the respondents were subjected to a perception test by pronunciation professionals. The results showed that the participants pronounced with a mixture of American and British varieties of English, but with a slight predominance of the American accent. This mixture of pronunciation is also noticed within words containing the same target phonemes. For example, the words "somebody" and "lot" are pronounced in the British accent while "God" is pronounced in the American accent. The authors attribute these results to the notion of frequency of exposure, as "God" would appear more frequently in the American television series. The results of the questionnaire also indicated that students "spent more time watching the television in English than they spent in English lessons at school" (Navrátilová 2013: 24–25).

Furthermore, Rindal and Piercy (2013) examined the pronunciation of English among Norwegian teenagers and using auditory analysis, they found a mixed production of linguistic features of American and British English, and some pronunciation elements forming a hybrid L2 accent. However, American English was the dominant pronunciation, and the authors suggested an influence of American media. Although many learners aimed for a native accent, a minority stated that they wanted to avoid native accents and use a neutral variety of English. Nevertheless, they point to a high degree of variability in participants' pronunciation, which would contribute to the increasing diversity in the development of English as a world language.

Finally, from a sociolinguistic perspective, speaking a language with an accent results from involuntary or voluntary vocal imitation according to Markham (1997: 50). Also, for Moyer (2013), the adoption of a particular accent is related to a question of identity but also to the symbolic value of a language (18). Whether voluntary or involuntary, direct or mediated, vocal imitation is characterized by a number of factors sometimes acting simultaneously. These may include intelligibility (the effort to be understood by the speaker), relationship (friendship, admiration . . .), identity and style (the desire to identify with a community of speakers, e.g., Uptalk or creaky voicing . . .) or geographical origin. These factors are also governed by the notion of individual differences (Dörnyei and Skehan 2003; Ellis 2004).

As seen in this literature review, the influence of the media on pronunciation has been shown in other countries and other contexts, but not yet in France. Through these few examples, one can clearly see the influence of media on pronunciation to varying degrees, despite the assumptions from some researchers (e.g., Chambers 1998). But, because studies have yielded conflicting results, more work is needed to ascertain the impact of out-of-class informal media exposure on English learners' pronunciation. This chapter reports on the first study which aims to fill the gap in the literature regarding informal media influence on learners' pronunciation in France.

4 Method

The participants in this research are young French women (11) and men (9) between 18 and 33 years of age at the time of the study. They were randomly selected from various language resource centers of the University of Strasbourg, France, as these are the ideal places to constitute a *Langues pour Specialistes d'Autres Disciplines* (LanSAD[1]) sample (Poteaux 2014; Toffoli and Sockett 2015a). To ensure anonymity, we labeled the participants 'loc' as in *locuteur*[2] in French (loc1, loc2, loc3 to loc20). The participants are both undergraduates and graduates enrolled in different disciplines (history, engineering, math and physics, arts, biology, linguistics, etc.). French is their first language, and they study English as their first foreign language, alongside other foreign languages (German, Spanish, Italian, Russian and Chinese). Their English levels varied from A2 to C1 according to the Common European Framework of Reference (Council of Europe 2018). At the time of this study, they had been learning the language for between 5 and 23 years, including 7 months to 4 years at university. They take a few hours of English classes, usually between one and two hours per week. This target audience obviously differs from English majors in that they are not taught phonetics, phonology, or English literature, for example.

Our corpus is composed of voice recordings of oral productions of 24 words embedded each time in a carrier phrase (ex: It is *city* please) which is pronounced five times by every participant. The total number of productions analyzed amounts to 2900 items, that is, 145 productions per speaker. Among these words, there are 10 target variables whose pronunciation differs markedly between standard British and American accents (Cruttenden 2014; Hughes, Trudgill and Watt 2012;). For example, the target sound of the word **hot** is the vowel /ɑ/ in American English and /ɒ/ in British English. Table 1 below lists all the variables that are contained in the words presented, together with their General American (GA) and Received Pronunciation (RP) phonetic transcription.

---

[1] Language for Specialists of Other Disciplines is the teaching of foreign languages to students who are not majoring in languages but in other disciplines.
[2] speaker.

Table 1: Target variables for the acoustic analyses.

Categories	Words	RP transcription	GA transcription
Rhoticity	**more**	/mɔː/	/mɔr/
Intervocalic /t/	**city**	/ˈsɪti/	/ˈsɪri/
<i> and <y> vowels	**Vitamin, dynasty**	/ˈvɪtəmɪn/, /ˈdɪnəsti/	/ˈvaɪrəmɪn/, /ˈdaɪnəsti/
GOAT vowels	**joke**	/dʒəʊk/	/dʒoʊk/
Yod-dropping	**tune**	/tjuːn/	/tuːn/
<ei> et <e> vowels	**Leisure, evolution**	/ˈleʒə(r)/, /ˌiːvəˈluːʃ(ə)n/	/ˈliːʒɚ/, /ˌevəˈluʃ(ə)n/
Vocal nasalization	**hand**	/hɑːnd/	/hænd/
LOT vowel	**top**	/tɒp/	/tɑːp/
Number of (stressed) syllables	**necessary**	/ˈnesəs(ə)ri/	/ˈnesəˌseri/
Principal stress	**locate**	/ləʊˈkeɪt/	/ˈloʊˌkeɪt/

The recordings were made in the anechoic chamber of the *Institut de Phonétique de Strasbourg, France* (IPS[3]) in order to enhance the sound quality for the acoustic analysis process. The audio signals of the phonetic elements under study were acoustically analyzed with Praat software by taking into consideration the duration of the sound (in milliseconds), its intensity, fundamental frequencies and the first four formants (in Hertz). This analysis allows for more precision in the identification of the produced sounds, as compared to simple auditory analysis, although listening was also very helpful. Figure 1 below shows an example of the pronunciation of the letter in the <vi> syllable of the word vitamin. The red box highlights the production of the diphthong [aɪ] (/ˈv[aɪ]təmɪn/) whereas the blue box indicates the production of the monophthong [ɪ] (/ˈv[ɪ]təmɪn/).

The experimental procedure consisted of three steps and lasted approximately 30 to 45 minutes per participant. First, each participant introduced themselves in English (name, age, residence, hobbies, etc.). This introduction was intended to generate spontaneous speech as a control. Second, they read the phrases with the target words and sounds. The order of the phrases was randomized for each speaker, in order to minimize the effect of fatigue on the items at the end of the list. Third, participants filled out a paper questionnaire about their contact with the English language, their activities in English in formal and informal contexts, and factors that they think they could have affected their English pronunciation. The questionnaire, apart from collecting some identity-related information, also targeted practices such as watching series in English, as well as other elements that may have had significant effects on their pronunciation. Thus, learners were asked: to estimate the duration (in years) of their contact

---

3 Phonetic Institute of Strasbourg, France.

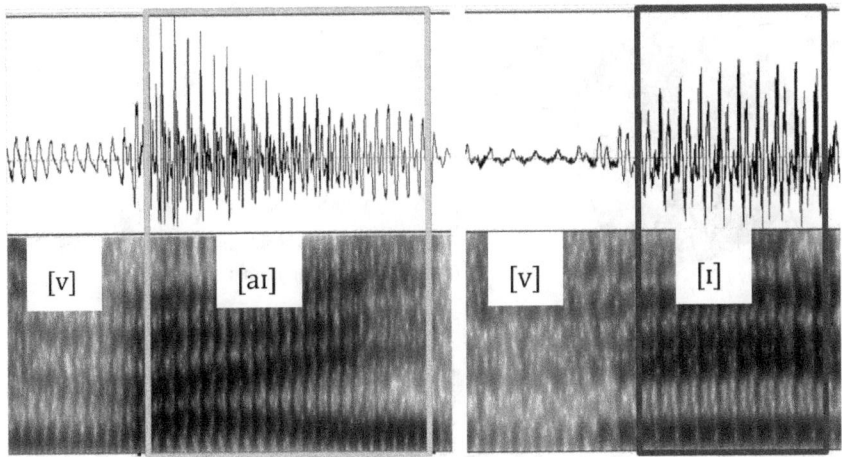

Figure 1: Acoustic analysis of the syllable "vai" in the word "vitamin".

with English, to identify the accents of English teachers they had had since secondary school, whether they had ever spent time in an English-speaking country (and for how long), whether they consciously imitated a particular accent they were exposed to in English (and which one). They were also asked to estimate the amount of time they spent each week watching series in English, to indicate the purpose of watching the series, and to list the titles of the series.

5 Findings and analysis

The overall results for the 20 speakers are presented in this section. It may be observed that the percentages for the two reference accents are quite close: the features of the British accent represent 44% and 45% for those of the American accent. The remaining features are put under the label 'other' (11%) as shown below (Figure 2).

On a group level, the first notable result from our data is the variability in the participants' pronunciation (Yibokou, Toffoli and Vaxelaire 2019). The first variability is inter-individual as the overall productions differ from one participant to the other.

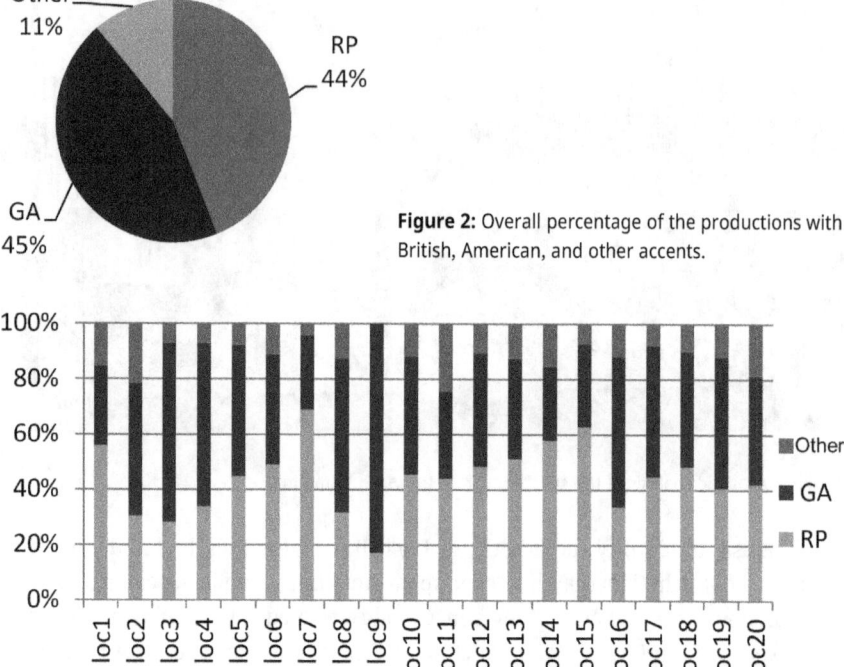

Figure 2: Overall percentage of the productions with British, American, and other accents.

Figure 3: Percentage of the productions with British, American, and other accents for each speaker (100% = 145 productions per speaker).

As can be seen in Figure 3 above, the percentages of productions per speaker were quite variable (interindividual variability). Participants pronounced the words with a mixture of accents including American, British, and other accents including French. In broad terms, British accent features were dominant in half of the participants (loc 1, 7, 13, 14, 15 with over 50% and loc 6, 11, 12, 18, 20), while the other half produced more American accent features (loc 2, 3, 4, 5, 8, 9, 10, 16, 17, 19). Similar percentages were obtained in some speakers. This is for example the case of the pairs of speakers 5 and 17, 12 and 18 who produced the same percentages. Sometimes they had identical percentages for a specific feature (e.g., loc 4 and 16 each had 34% for the British features but the other items were quite different). Speakers 2 and 11 were the only ones whose 'other' productions exceeded 20%. Finally, speaker 9 was the only participant who did not produce any 'other' accent features and in whom American accent features were the highest (83%). It should be noted that among the 10 phenomena studied that make the phonetic-phonological difference between the American accent and the British accent, rhoticity, flap, and vowel nasalization were the most frequently produced by all participants.

The intra-individual variability observed in the productions of our group can also be seen on two levels:
- Inter-word variability consists of pronouncing some words with one accent and other words with a different accent. Example: /ˈsɪri/ (city) but /ˈpɑːti/ (party) for speaker 4, or /ˈpɑːti/ and /ˈpɑrɾi/ (party) for speaker 17.
- Intra-word variability occurs when two different segmental elements are found within the same word. Example for vitamin: /ˈvaɪtəmɪn/ (speakers 1 & 7) or /ˈvɪɾəmɪn/ (speakers 14 & 15).

Table 2 summarizes the different phonetic and phonological productions for all the participants. It is worth noting that the intervocalic /t/ has yielded the highest number of different productions, namely: [tʰ]; [t̪s]; [tʃ]; [d]; [ɾ]; [t] & [ʔ], with the flap ([ɾ]) being dominant.

Table 2: The phonetic variables studied and the participants' productions.

Phonetic variable	Words	British and American phonetic transcription	Target phonemes produced by the participants
Intervocalic /t/	city	/ˈsɪti/; /ˈsɪri/	[t̪], [ɾ], [tʰ], [d], [t̪s], [t], [tʃ], [ʔ]
	vitamin	/ˈvɪtəmɪn/; /ˈvaɪɾəmɪn/	[t̪], [ɾ], [tʰ], [d], [t̪s], [t], [ʔ]
	party	/ˈpɑːti/; /ˈpɑːɾi/	[t̪], [ɾ], [tʰ], [d], [t̪s], [t], [ʔ], [tʃ]
Rhoticity	more	/mɔː/; /mɔr/	[ɔː], [ɔr]
	organisation	/ˌɔːgənaɪˈzeɪʃ(ə)n/; /ˌɔrgənɪˈzeɪʃ(ə)n/	[ɔː], [ɔr]
	dark	/dɑːk/; /dɑɹk/	[ɑː], [ɑɹ]
	bird	/bɜːd/; /bɝːd/	[ɜː], [ɝː], [ɜɹ]
	actor	/ˈæktə/; /ˈæktɚ/	[ə], [ɚ], [ɔ]
	leisure	/ˈlɛʒə/; /ˈliːʒɚ/	[ə], [ɚ]
Yod-dropping	tune	/tjuːn/; /tuːn/	[uː], [y], [juː]
	new	/njuː/; /nuː/	[uː], [juː]
	evolution	/ˌiːvəˈljuːʃən/; /ˌɛvəˈluːʃən/	[uː], [y], [juː]
Lot vowel	hot	/hɒt/; /hɑːt/	[ɒ], [ɔ], [ɑː]
	top	/tɒp/; /tɑːp/	[ɒ], [ɔ], [ɑː]

Table 2 (continued)

Phonetic variable	Words	British and American phonetic transcription	Target phonemes produced by the participants
Goat vowel	joke	/dʒəʊk/; /dʒoʊk/	[əʊ], [oʊ], [ɔ], [o]
	road	/rəʊd/; /roʊd/	[əʊ], [oʊ], [ɔ], [o]
<i> and <y> vowels	dynasty	/ˈdɪnəsti/; /ˈdaɪnəsti/	[ɪ], [aɪ]
	vitamin	/ˈvɪtəmɪn/; /ˈvaɪrəmɪn/	[ɪ], [aɪ]
	organisation	/ˌɔːgənaɪˈzeɪʃ(ə)n/; /ˌɔːrgənɪˈzeɪʃ(ə)n/	[aɪ], [ə], [ɪ]
	legalisation	/ˌliːgəlaɪˈzeɪʃ(ə)n/; /ˌligələˈzeɪʃ(ə)n/	[aɪ], [ə], [ɪ]
<ei> & <e> vowels	leisure	/ˈlɛʒə/; /ˈliːʒɚ/; /ˈleɪʒɚ/	[ɛ], [eɪ], [iː], [e]
	evolution	/ˌiːvəˈljuːʃən/; /ˌɛvəˈluːʃən/	[iː], [ɛ], [e]
Vocalic nasalisation	band	/band/; /bænd/	[a], [æ], [ã], [æ̃]
	hand	/hand/; /hænd/	[a], [æ], [ã], [æ̃]
Stress placement	donate	/dəʊˈneɪt/; /ˈdoʊneɪt/	Syllable 1, syllable 2, flat
	locate	/ləʊˈkeɪt/; /ˈloʊkeɪt/	Syllable 1, syllable 2, flat
Number of stressed syllables	mili**tary**	/ˈmɪlɪtᵊri/; /ˈmɪlɪˌtɛri/	[təri], [tɛri], [tɑri], [tri]
	neces**sary**	/ˈnɛsəsᵊri/; /ˈnɛsəˌsɛri/	[səri], [sɛri]

Regarding the salient results of the questionnaire, the participants estimated the amount of time they spent using English outside the classroom at somewhere between 4 and more than 24 hours per week. The data relating to the accents of their English teachers reveal that their teachers are mostly French and British nationals who speak with French, near-British or British accents. Moreover, none of the participants had lived for more than three months in an English-speaking environment. Whilst many of them declared to not intentionally imitate any accent, they reported that their pronunciation is mainly influenced by the media, as indicated in their responses (see citations in Table 3 below). This result is of note since it corroborates the concept of unconscious vocal imitation put forward by Markham (1997). The participants claimed not to imitate any accent yet traces of the phonological features they had been exposed to are found in their speech.

Table 3: Influence of media on the participants' pronunciation.

Speaker1	media in general
Speaker2	American films, series and music
Speaker3	the influence of American media
Speaker5	series
Speaker6	I watch a lot of American tv series
Speaker7	I watch American tv series
Speaker8	music and series
Speaker9	because I watch a lot of American film and series
Speaker11	films and music
Speaker15	tv series

In line with the aforementioned media, the viewing of American television series and films were the leading activities that the participants engaged in. Watching the videos with French subtitles was the dominant viewing mode (37% of the total estimated viewing time), followed by English only (no subtitles, 31%), English with captions (29%) and finally the dubbed versions (French only, 3%). These activities are primarily carried out online (streaming and downloading) and for pleasure and leisure purposes. Participants also indicated that the plots or the narratives in the films and series are the main reason for the viewing. The first 20 most frequently watched series in this sample are indicated in Figure 4 below. The figures on top of the bars represent the number of participants that watch a particular television series.

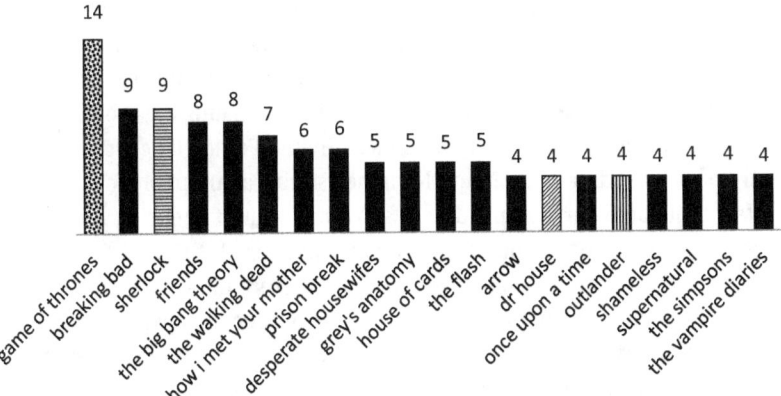

Figure 4: The first 20 most frequently watched series from the list provided by the participants.

As can be seen in Figure 4, different English accents are spoken in the series watched by the participants. A mixture of accents is spoken in *Game of thrones* including American and a number of United Kingdom accents (dotted bar). The British accent is mainly represented in *Sherlock Holmes* (horizontal striped bar). The series *Outlander* is mainly with Scottish English (vertical striped bar). In *Dr. House* (oblique striped bar), Hugh Laurie speaks with a mixture of British and American English. Aside from those series, all the remaining solely contain American accent input (black bars). Let us also remember that even though some actors speak with different accents (Australian, Canadian, Scottish, Indian, etc.) in some of the series, the American accent is still the most prevalent oral input for our participants.

6 Discussion

The results of this study show individual differences in the way participants react to the phonological input they are exposed to (Yibokou, Toffoli and Vaxelaire 2019), while the intra-individual variability could be an indication of inconsistency in their pronunciation. In addition, there is a general tendency to unconsciously imitate various accents (Markham 1997). Unlike conscious imitation where one would intentionally make an effort to speak with a particular accent, unconscious imitation of the American accent that was observed in this study did happen even though the participants were supposed to speak with a British accent, considering their formal English teachers' accents and courses. The pronunciation repertoire of our sample does show that it is composed of a mixture of American, British, French, and other accents, including Cockney, with one participant who excessively watched series with the London accent. For example, he pronounced "city" with the glottal stop in place of the intervocalic /t/ as [ciʔi]. Concerning the rhotic productions, I argue that it might be directly influenced by the French language, since all the "r"s are pronounced in all positions. Nonetheless, this assumption does not support the fact that some participants do not show any sign of rhoticity. It could be that during word repetitions, the participants remember all the varieties of pronunciation they have been exposed to, during the different informal activities they engage in. This could possibly justify the mixing of productions which may likely stem not only from exposure to the trans/mid-Atlantic accent (Modiano 1998), but also to other accents from around the world. This mixture of English accents which I refer to as inter-pronunciation is considered here as a sort of interlanguage that is developing within the English phonological system of these learners. In our case, this interlanguage only concerns pronunciation aspects rather than lexicon and grammar (with reference to Selinker 1972).

I hypothesize that watching American series is the one out-of-class activity influencing the adoption of several markers of General American accent in the English our participants speak. This is because formal coursework was mostly delivered by teachers with British or near-British accents, and because it is believed that the participants had little if any interaction with native American-English speakers given the fact that they reside in France and had spent less than 3 months in an English-speaking country.

Also, the observation that participants with the highest amount of exposure time also show a high number of components of the American accent should be subject to further scrutiny. I am conscious that the adoption of American and/or British accent features does not emanate solely from one source (de Bot, Lowie and Verspoor 2007; Cameron and Larsen-Freeman 2007). It comes rather from the interaction and influence of an array of factors including formal, informal and non-formal exposure to the language through all kinds of direct and indirect interactions with native and/or non-native speakers of English (teachers, friends, families, TV series, films, video clips, TV news, sports, video games, music, etc.).

As far as learning and teaching are concerned, online informal activities could constitute a good opportunity for English learners, particularly specialists of non-language disciplines who are not offered pronunciation courses or who cannot afford immersive programs in Anglophone environments, to be exposed to authentic English pronunciation. These activities also give them the opportunity to pick up sociocultural elements with which they can communicate in the target language, such as jokes and idioms. Teachers could show learners how to work with captions while watching films and series for instance, in order to "tune in to" their phonological categories (see Vanderplank 2016, 2019). Providing L2 learners with varieties of oral and aural input would diversify their soundscape and widen their capacity to understand the various accents they are being exposed to (Miras 2021: 87). Through a mediation approach, teachers could thus focus on intelligibility and comprehensibility rather than phonetic and phonological correction and accept learners' inter-pronunciation which is no longer restricted to a couple of standard varieties of English.

The online informal activities that learners engage in is contributing to a more positive image of the English language in Europe and in France, despite sometimes strong opposition from some French authorities (Deneire 2015). From a phenomenological perspective, these observations can be treated in isolation, but it is more likely that these pronunciation features result from the conscious or unconscious imitation of accents due to the frequency of their exposure to media input, especially television series (Markham 1997; Yibokou Forthcoming). However, from a complexity point of view, where other factors are necessarily also at play, further research is needed to understand this phenomenon and to ascertain the cognitive strategies at work for these learners. In-depth qualitative data, statistical correlation between variables, learner trajectories, or ecological data collection are some of the examples of methodological approaches that could be implemented. For now, this Globish[4] (Global English – Nerrière 2004) portrays the English accents that French students are acquiring in extramural contexts, and it appears to be an inevitable consequence of learners being simultaneously exposed to several accents through a rich soundscape.

7 Conclusion

The results presented in this chapter suggest that television series play a major role in the adoption of a more American accent by learners, as had been noted by English teachers in French universities (Toffoli & Sockett 2015b). This study also corroborates the results of other research concerning the impact of media on English language learners' pronunciation in other countries (Maeda 2009; Navrátilová 2013; Rindal and Piercy 2013). For now, this research has shed light on the English phonological repertoire of French learners and has thus filled the literature gap about the impact of media on the adoption of accent features learners are exposed to in the French context. Even though the data collected does not allow for any categorical conclusion, the participants might be un/consciously imitating the accents they are being exposed to. This could also be related to cultural affiliation and identity as indicated by Markham (1997) and Moyer (2013). The argument made here is that speech patterns are far more malleable than past sociolinguistic research (Chambers 1998) suggested. Further analyses will be needed with a larger sample of individuals and on a wider panel of segmental and supra-segmental elements. One could also consider recording speakers in an ecological environment (spontaneous speech) for possible comparison with reading. For further research, it would be particularly helpful to conduct in-depth qualitative analyses (longitudinal or retrodictive) that would help to better understand this phenomenon. This would allow us to investigate a possible correlation between the frequency of exposure to the series and the pronunciation of the learners-viewers. These analyses would also allow insights into the relationships between such pronunciation phenomena and the range of individual differences (engagement types, aptitudes etc.) which are the focus of other chapters in this collection.

---

[4] A subcategory of English developed by Jean-Paul Nerrière (2004). It uses common and simple words and expressions, no idiomatic expressions, and jokes, to facilitate communication and understanding between native and non-native, non-native and non-native speakers of English.

References

Androutsopoulos, Jannis. 2014. Mediatization and sociolinguistic change. Key concepts, research traditions, open issues. In Jannis Androutsopoulos (ed.), *Mediatization and sociolinguistic change*, 3–48. Berlin: De Gruyter.

Cameron, Lynne & Diane Larsen-Freeman. 2007. Complex systems and applied linguistics. *International Journal of Applied Linguistics* 17(2). 226–239.

Chambers, John Kenneth. 1998. TV makes people sound the same. In Laurie Bauer & Peter Trudgill (eds.), *Language Myths*, 123–131. New York: Penguin.

Chik, Alice. 2014. Digital gaming and language learning: Autonomy and community. *Language Learning & Technology* 18(2). 85–100.

Cole, Jason & Robert Vanderplank. 2016. Comparing autonomous and class-based learners in Brazil: Evidence for the present-day advantages of informal, out-of-class learning. *System* 61. 31–42.

Council of Europe. 2018. *Common European Framework of Reference for Languages: Learning, Teaching, Assessment. Companion Volume*. Strasbourg: Council of Europe.

Cruttenden, Alan. 2014. *Gimson's pronunciation of English*. New York: Routledge.

de Bot, Kees, Wander Lowie & Marjolijn Verspoor. 2007. A dynamics systems theory approach to second language acquisition. *Bilingualism: Language and Cognition* 10(1). 7–22.

Deneire, Marc. 2015. Images of English in the French press. In Andrew Linn, Neil Bermel & Gibson Ferguson (eds.), *Attitudes towards English in Europe: Language and Social Life*, 55–69. Berlin, Boston: De Gruyter Mouton.

Dörnyei, Zoltán & Perter Skehan. 2003. Individual differences in second language learning. In Catherine Doughty & Michael Long (eds.), *The Handbook of Second Language Acquisition*, 589–630. Oxford: Blackwell.

Ellis, Rod. 2004. Individual differences in second language learning. In Alan Davies & Catherine Elder (eds.), *The Handbook of Applied Linguistics*, 525–551. Oxford: Blackwell Publishing Ltd.

Exare, Christelle. 2009. La mise en place de trois voyelles postérieures en anglais langue étrangère. Analyse acoustique et perspective de quelques interférences pour des pistes de correction phonétique. *Recherche et Pratiques Pédagogiques en Langues de Spécialité. Cahiers de l'Apliut* XXVIII (3). 68–84. https://doi.org/10.4000/apliut.122

Hughes, Arthur, Peter Trudgill & Dominic Watt. 2012. *English Accents and Dialects*, 5th edn. London: Hodder Education.

Kusyk, Meryl. 2017. *Les dynamiques du développement de l'anglais au travers d'activités informelles en ligne : une étude exploratoire auprès d'étudiants allemands et français*. Strasbourg: Université de Strasbourg dissertation.

Kusyk, Meryl & Geoffrey Sockett. 2012. From informal resource usage to incidental language acquisition: language uptake from online television viewing in English. *ASp. La Revue Du GERAS* 62. 45–65.

Labov, William. 2001. *Principles of Linguistic Change: Social Factors*. Vol. 2. Oxford: Wiley-Blackwell.

Lee, Ju Seong. 2017. Informal digital learning of English and second language vocabulary outcomes: Can quantity conquer quality? *British Journal of Educational Technology* 50(2). 767–778. https://doi.org/10.1111/bjet.12599

Lee, Ju Seong. 2021. *Informal Digital Learning of English: Research to Practice*. London: Taylor & Francis.

Lee, Ju Seong & Kilryoung Lee. 2019. Perceptions of English as an international language by Korean English-major and non-English-major students. *Journal of Multilingual and Multicultural Development* 40(1). 76–89. https://doi.org/10.1080/01434632.2018.1480628

Maeda, Margaret. 2009. What varieties of English pronunciation are Japanese learners learning? *Studies in Language, Kanagawa University* 32. 1-31.

Markham, Duncan. 1997. *Phonetic imitation, accent, and the learner*. Lund: Lund University Press.

Miras, Grégory. 2021. *Didactique de la prononciation en langues étrangères: De la correction à une médiation*. Paris: Didier.

Mitterer, Holger & James McQueen. 2009. Foreign subtitles help but native-language subtitles harm foreign speech perception. *PloS one* 4 (11)e7785. 1-5. https://doi.org/10.1371/journal.pone.0007785

Modiano, Marko. 1998. The emergence of mid-Atlantic English in the European Union. In Hns Lindquist, Staffan Klintborg, Magnus Levin & Maria Estling (eds.), *The Major Varieties of English: Papers from MAVEN 97*, Vaxjo 20-22 November 1997,241-248. Hogskolon I Vaxjo, Sweden.

Moyer, Alene. 2013. *Foreign Accent: The Phenomenon of Non-native Speech*. Cambridge: Cambridge University Press.

Narcy-Combes, Jean-Paul & Amel Boughnim. 2011. Télévision et apprentissage de l'italien dans un contexte plurilingue : Pistes pour l'enseignement des langues étrangères à l'école élémentaire. *Recherches en Didactique des Langues et des Cultures. Les Cahiers de l'Acedle* 8. 8-11. https://doi.org/10.4000/rdlc.2288

Navrátilová, Mariana. 2013. *Aspects of Pronunciation Teaching: The Influence of American Media on Pronunciation of Czech Students*. Brno: Masarykova univerzita dissertation. https://is.muni.cz/th/385293/pedf_b/

Nerrière, Jean-Paul. 2004. *Parlez Globish. L'anglais Planétaire du Troisième Millénaire*. Paris: Eyrolles.

Ota, Ichiro & Shoji Takano. 2014. The media influence on language change in Japanese sociolinguistic contexts. In Jannis Androutsopoulos (ed.), *Mediatization and sociolinguistic change*, 171-203. Berlin: De Gruyter.

Poteaux, Nicole. 2014. Les langues étrangères pour tous à l'université: regard sur une expérience (1991-2013). *Les Dossiers des Sciences de l'Éducation* 32. 17-32.

Rindal, Ulrikke. 2010. Constructing identity with L2: Pronunciation and attitudes among Norwegian learners of English. *Journal of Sociolinguistics* 14(2). 240-261.

Rindal, Ulrikke & Caroline Piercy. 2013. Being 'neutral'? English pronunciation among Norwegian learners. *World Englishes* 32(2). 211-229. https://doi.org/10.1111/weng.12020

Sanchez, Mari, Rachel M. Miller & Lawrence D Rosenblum. 2010. Visual influences on alignment to voice onset time. *Journal of Speech, Language, and Hearing Research* 53(2). 262-272.

Schmale, Rachel, Amanda Seidl & Alejandrina Cristia. 2015. Mechanisms underlying accent accommodation in early word learning: Evidence for general expansion. *Developmental science* 18(4). 664-670.

Selinker, Larry. 1972. Interlanguage. *International Review of Applied Linguistics in Language Teaching* 10 (1-4). 209-232.

Sockett, Geoffrey. 2011. From the cultural hegemony of English to online informal learning: Cluster frequency as an indicator of relevance in authentic documents. *ASp. La Revue Du GERAS* 60. 5-20.

Sockett, Geoffrey & Meryl Kusyk. 2013. L'apprentissage informel en ligne: nouvelle donne pour l'enseignement-apprentissage de l'anglais. *Recherche et Pratiques Pédagogiques en Langues de Spécialité. Cahiers de l'Apliut* 32(1). 75-91. https://doi.org/10.4000/apliut.3578

Sockett, Geoffrey. 2014. *The Online Informal Learning of English*. Basingstoke: Palgrave Macmillan.

Stuart-Smith, Jane, Gwilym Pryce, Claire Timmins & Barrie Gunter. 2013. Television can also be a factor in language change: Evidence from an urban dialect. *Language* 89(3). 501-536.

Stuart-Smith, Jane, Rachel Smith, Tamara Rathcke, Francesco Li Santi & Sophie Holmes. 2011. Responding to accents after experiencing interactive or mediated speech. *International Congress of Phonetic Sciences* 17. 1914–1917.

Sundqvist, Pia. 2015. About a boy: A gamer and L2 English speaker coming into being by use of self-access. *Studies in Self-Access Learning Journal* 6(4). 352–364. https://doi.org/10.37237/060403

Toffoli, Denyze & Laurent Perrot. 2017. Autonomy, the online informal learning of English (OILE) and learning resource centres (LRCs): Relationships between learner autonomy, L2 proficiency, L2 autonomy and digital literacy. In Marco Cappellini, Tim Lewis & Annick Rivens Mompean (eds.), *Learner Autonomy and Web 2.0*, 198–228. Sheffield: Equinox.

Toffoli, Denyze & Geoffrey Sockett. 2010. How non-specialist students of English practice informal learning using web 2.0 tools. *ASp. La Revue Du GERAS* 58. 125–144.

Toffoli, Denyze & Geoffrey Sockett. 2015a. L'apprentissage informel de l'anglais en ligne (AIAL): Quelles conséquences pour les centres de ressources en langues? *Recherche et Pratiques Pédagogiques en Langues de Spécialité. Cahiers de l'Apliut* 34(1). 147–165.

Toffoli, Denyze & Geoffrey Sockett. 2015b. University teachers' perceptions of online informal learning of English (OILE). *Computer Assisted Language Learning* 28(1). 7–21. https://doi.org/10.1080/09588221.2013.776970

Trinder, Ruth. 2017. Informal and deliberate learning with new technologies. *Elt Journal* 71(4). 401–412. https://doi.org/10.1093/elt/ccw117

Vanderplank, Robert. 2016. 'Effects of' and 'effects with' captions: How exactly does watching a TV programme with same-language subtitles make a difference to language learners? *Language Teaching* 49(2). 235–250.

Vanderplank, Robert. 2019. 'Gist watching can only take you so far': attitudes, strategies and changes in behaviour in watching films with captions. *The Language Learning Journal* 47(4). 407–423.

Yibokou, Kossi Seto, Denyze Toffoli & Béatrice Vaxelaire. 2019. Variabilité inter-individuelle et intra-individuelle dans la prononciation d'étudiants français qui pratiquent l'apprentissage informel de l'anglais en ligne. *Lidil* 59. doi: https://doi.org/10.4000/lidil.6369

Yibokou, Kossi Seto. Forthcoming. Explorer les facteurs intervenant dans l'imitation de l'accent américain chez des étudiants français. In Pergia Gkouskou, Nadejda Kriajeva & Dana Martin (eds.), *L'accent – investigations sur un phénomène linguistique, social et identitaire*. Clermont-Ferrand: Presse Universitaire Blaise Pascal.

Section 3: Learner activities

Phil Benson
7 Mapping space, leisure and informal language learning in the lives of international students in Australia

Abstract: Drawing on a spatial approach to language learning environments, this chapter explores relationships between informal language learning and the uses of urban space in study abroad. Discussing data from two studies of international students' language learning in Sydney, it suggests that informal language learning in study abroad is shaped by students' everyday routines, which are in turn shaped partly by the demography of a global, leisure-oriented city and partly by the students' agency. Revisiting the data from the perspective of informal language learning and leisure, the chapter also suggests that study abroad may involve a reconfiguration of relationships between study, work and leisure.

Keywords: second language learning, informal learning, space, language learning environments, international students, Australia

1 Introduction

Growing recreational use of online materials as language learning resources has inspired a recent wave of interest in informal language learning (Dressman and Sadler 2020; Lai 2017; Reinders, Lai and Sundqvist 2022; Sockett 2014; Steel and Levy 2013). Whereas earlier work on informal language learning beyond the classroom examined a range of online and offline environments (Benson and Reinders 2011), the recent emphasis on online resources is signalled in terms such as 'Online Informal Learning of English' (OILE – Sockett 2014) and Informal Digital Learning of English (IDLE – Lee and Dressman 2017; Soyoof et al. 2021). These terms also signal an emphasis on what have traditionally been called 'English as a foreign language' (EFL) environments (Wilkins 1972), which might now be redefined as environments that are supportive of online access, but less supportive of offline access to the target language. In such environments, the Internet and global telecommunication networks now provide unprecedented access to language resources, allowing learners to reach high levels of foreign language competence without the direct contact with

Phil Benson, Macquarie University, Australia

expert speakers that was assumed to be a feature of 'English as a second language' (ESL) environments (Cole and Vanderplanck 2016).

The widespread use of social media and online popular culture materials in English language learning also prompts interest in the relationship between learning and leisure. It has long been assumed that informal situations in which learners are relaxed and free of stress are conducive to language learning (Krashen 1982). Current research on informal online language learning can also draw on work in the wider field of digital literacies, that suggests a blurring of the boundaries between study and leisure in learning that emerges from deep and pleasurable engagement with online resources (Buckingham 2008, Gee 2007; Lankshear and Knobel 2008). The aim of this chapter is to explore relationships between informal language learning and leisure in the under-researched context of study abroad, which, being closer to the traditional ESL environment, is rich in affordances for both online and offline informal language learning.

Adopting the spatial perspective on language learning environments elaborated in Benson (2021), the chapter begins by discussing study abroad at two levels of scale: first, the global scale on which study abroad is seen as an outcome of processes that have fundamentally transformed the landscapes of cities such as Sydney, and, second, the local scale on which individual study abroad participants map out their learning environments in online and offline worlds. The chapter then discusses data from two studies of international students in Sydney, which are revisited here from the perspective of informal language learning and leisure. (Benson 2022; Benson, Chappell and Yates 2018; Chappell, Benson and Yates 2018).

2 Study abroad in a global context

Study abroad refers, here, to the situation in which a language learner travels to a country other than the one in which they have hitherto learned a language, either independently as an individual or as a part of a group, in order to gain practical experience of using a language or to gain educational qualifications through the medium of the language (Benson et al. 2013; Howard 2019; Kinginger 2009; Mitchell, Tracey-Ventura and McManus 2015). The duration of study abroad sojourns varies from a few weeks to several years, which has implications for the relationship between informal language learning and leisure. Where participants conceptualize a short-term study abroad program as a vacation, there appear to be negative effects on language learning. However, longer periods of study abroad are often undertaken with the more serious intent of obtaining higher or vocational education qualifications, and ultimately migration. This is especially the case in Australia, where 'international education' through the medium of English has become a major industry, involving university degrees, vocational education, and short-term preparatory English courses in both the private and public sectors (Gomes 2018; Robertson 2013). International students studying English in Sydney are typically engaged in the serious business of enhancing their social mobility. However, their learning also has a relationship to leisure, as the international education industry is linked to the development of the city as an increasingly leisure-oriented urban environment.

The deregulation of financial markets since the early 1990s has profoundly changed the global landscape of language learning (Benson 2021; Block, Gray and Holborow 2012). Accelerated global mobility has put languages into motion on an unprecedented scale, leading to a rapid increase in the demand for language services of all kinds, which are estimated to have doubled in value between 2009 and 2018 (Mazereanu 2019). A global rise in the number of IELTS test takers (1.7 million in 2011 to more than 3 million in 2017), is one indicator of the growth in demand for English language teaching services (IELTS 2012 2017). The rise of informal online language learning has been one effect of the accelerated mobility of information. An effect of the accelerated mobility of people and things has been a proliferation and diversification of offline settings for informal language learning, including the rise of global cities as sites for language study abroad.

The global rise of international education and study abroad is mainly a consequence of falling costs of overseas travel, but the emergence of cities such as Sydney as sites for study abroad is equally a consequence of the urban de-industrialization that has accompanied financial deregulation in the wealthier parts of the world. As industrial production has increasingly shifted from higher-income to lower-income countries, the urban economies of the wealthier nations have come to rely more and more on financial and business services, education, tourism and leisure industries. For Sydney and other cities around the world, language has become an economic asset, especially in education, where English-speaking cities leverage their language advantage to provide educational qualifications to the socially-mobile populations of the nations to which industrial production has shifted. International education and study abroad have become major economic activities that are tied into what Australian urban historian Seamus O'Hanlon calls the development of Sydney as "a post-industrial finance-and-leisure-oriented city reaching out to the world" (O'Hanlon 2018: 172).

At the time of writing, Australia is emerging from a second wave of Covid-19 lockdowns, which have been most prolonged in its two largest and most globally-connected cities, Sydney and Melbourne. Since the beginning of the pandemic, very few international students have entered Australia due to stringent restrictions on overseas travel. Before the pandemic, however, international education ranked fourth among Australia's export industries, behind the iron ore, coal and gas exports that are the main sources of Australia's wealth. As Sydney and Melbourne are the main destinations for international students, international education is undoubtedly Australia's leading *urban* export industry. In 2019, the number of international students in the country reached a peak of 750,000, including 170,000 students taking short English courses, known as English Language Intensive Courses for Overseas Students (ELICOS – Australian Government 2021). The numbers for New South Wales (of which the vast majority study in Sydney) were 265,000 international students, including 65,000 ELICOS students. To put these numbers in perspective, in 2019, international students made up approximately 3% of the population of Australia, 5% of the population of Greater Sydney.

Sydney is marketed to international students as an attractive, cosmopolitan, leisure-oriented site for overseas study in which opportunities for using English abound. The following examples are culled from the websites of English language colleges in the city: *"Life beyond the classroom is always comfortable and exciting"*; *"Australians are . . . always happy to talk so it's a great place to improve your English."*; *"If you're going to be living here for a few months (or years) get to know – and speak with – the natives!"* (Chappell et al. 2018). However, the popular idea of study abroad participants "immersing" themselves in an English-speaking environment is a problematic one. The "studentification" of the city, especially the presence of large numbers of international students in the inner city, contributes to the city's "global feel" (O'Hanlon 2018: 73). As part-time workers, international students also contribute a great deal to the urban economy, especially in the retail, hospitality and tourism sectors. The key role of international students in the economy of the city is most evident in the inner-city districts in which they are most concentrated. The City of Sydney accounts for less than 5% of the population of Greater Sydney, but more than 50% of its international students. The proportion of international students at Sydney's most centrally located universities ranges from 33% at the University of Science and Technology to 43% at the University of Sydney (Ferguson and Sherrell 2021). Including both long-term students in higher and vocational education and short-term ELICOS students, international students make up approximately 40 to 50% of the inner-city population. Inner-city Sydney is, in this sense, a point of extreme spatial concentration for global language mobility. A main concern of our research on international students learning English in Sydney has been to understand how the spatiality of their experience of study abroad shapes their informal language learning practices in such an environment.

3 Theoretical framework

Study abroad is often conceptualized as a context in which informal language use outside the classroom plays a more important role than the classroom instruction that tends to dominate language learning "at home" (Collentine and Freed 2004). In practice, however, students on intensive study abroad programs often spend more time in the language classroom than they would at home. The idea that study abroad necessarily involves "immersion" in the target language is also challenged, especially in global cities that are host to large numbers of students and tourists (Coleman 2015). In Sydney, ELICOS students taking short English courses typically spend 25 hours per week in the classroom. Many work at part-time jobs to finance their studies and because they tend to live and work close to their English language colleges, they are often immersed in an international student environment in which they spend a good deal of their time with co-nationals. In our research program on international students' informal language learning in Sydney, however, we have treated the nature of the language learning environment as a problem to be resolved at the level of the individual. We also view study abroad not so much as a contrasting contextual condition to study at home, but as a sequential stage in language learning careers that either follows or interrupts a period of study at home (Benson 2011). From this perspective, study abroad typically involves a transition in which participants must, in effect, map out new learning environments that are conducive to new relations between formal in-class and informal out-of-class learning (Kashiwa and Benson 2018). Crucially, study abroad participants are not immersed in the target language in the way that a swimmer is immersed in water. From an ecological perspective, informal language learning emerges from the learner's interaction with language resources in the environment (van Lier 2004). However, we conceptualize these resources as being both relatively scarce and spatially located. In effect, informal out-of-class language learning in study abroad involves effort on the learner's part and, in particular, agentive uses of urban space within the constraints of busy spatiotemporal routines (Benson 2021).

In an exploratory interview study with 10 recently arrived ELICOS students who were studying at an inner city private language school, we identified six main themes in the experience of study abroad in Sydney: the settings in which students lived, studied, worked and spent their leisure time; journeys from one setting to another; the ways in which social networks were shaped by these settings and their locations relative to each other; uses of information technology across physical settings; constraints of finance, time and purpose for studying English; and the students' agency in determining the settings in which they lived, studied, worked and spent their leisure time, and in shaping these settings as settings for language learning (Chappell et al. 2018). The primary constraint on these students' informal language learning lay in a visa system which requires ELICOS students to be enrolled in a full-time language course, but also allows them to work part-time for up to 40 hours per fortnight. The financial cost of studying in Sydney was a shared theme across the interviews, and all of the students had taken part-time jobs to finance their studies. In consequence, their daily lives in the city were shaped by tightly organized spatiotemporal routines, involving travel between home, college and work, which left limited time for leisure activities. Within this shared framework, each student had mapped out an individualized spatiotemporal routine within which they accessed English-language resources in the environment. A student's language learning environment was, thus, conceptualized as the configuration of settings that the student mapped out in the course of their daily lives, and the language resources that these settings afforded.

4 Methodology

In a follow-up study with 11 recently-arrived ELICOS students, we attempted to address the geography of international students' language learning environments more directly by asking participants to track their movements over the course of a week, using an online GPS-enabled diary app, *Diaro* (http://diaroapp.com; Benson et al. 2018). The participants then consulted their diaries during a stimulated recall interview, in which they were prompted to recount their activities and reflect on their use of languages over the week. The methodology of the study drew on the use of logs and online tools to measure learners' language use outside the classroom in study abroad (Ranta and Meckelborg 2013; Dewey 2017; García-Amaya 2017), but our goal was not to quantify students' use of English, but to explore how their learning interacted with the environmental conditions of their daily lives.

Six of the participants were studying at the Macquarie University English Language Centre in Sydney's northwestern suburbs and five were studying at an inner-city English-language college in the Sydney City Centre. All were adults, six male and five female, aged 20–40 and of nine different nationalities. Nine intended to remain in Sydney after completing their courses, either to enter higher or vocational education or to obtain professional work; the other two were exchange students. At a briefing session, the participants downloaded *Diaro* to their mobile phones and were asked to keep an hourly record of their activities for the next seven days. Each entry was to include a brief note of the activity they were engaged in, who they were with and what language(s) they were using. The date, time and location of the entry were automatically recorded. The participants were also encouraged to take and attach photographs to their diary entries. All of the participants completed the task. Although there were some gaps in their record keeping, the data were sufficiently detailed for the participants to recall and talk about their activities in depth. The diary data were not accessed directly by the research team, but were used by the participants during stimulated recall interviews (Gass and Mackey 2000) that took place two to three days after they had completed the task. The interviews were conducted in English by the project research assistant (a female Japanese graduate student) and lasted approximately one hour. The interview data were read and re-read by the research team members who wrote up a narrative for each participant, describing their weekday and weekend activities, with a focus on their language use. The main locations of the students' activities were also superimposed on a map of Sydney.

Benson et al. (2018) reports an individual case study of one student's week. The following section which reports data from two additional students, Sonja and Odval, will illustrate the variation among the language learning environments that individual participants had mapped out. Sonja and Odval studied at the same college in the inner city and both were adults in their mid-thirties, who had been studying English in Sydney for more than a year with the goal of entering a Masters course. Unlike most students in Sydney, Sonja and Odval attended college only two days per week, which left them more time for part-time work and leisure activities. The following section includes a schematic map of what I call the shared experience of study abroad in Sydney. It also includes maps and brief narratives to illustrate the very different individual language learning environments that Sonja and Odval mapped out for themselves. The concluding section discusses their experiences from the perspective of informal language learning and leisure.

5 Experiences of study abroad in Sydney

5.1 The shared experience

Figure 1 aims to map, diagrammatically, the shared environment of all of the participants in the two studies referred to in this chapter; it represents, perhaps, a more or less universal experience of English-language study abroad in Sydney. The map is dominated on the right-hand side by daily journeys between home and college, college and part-time work, and work and home. Much of the day, especially on weekdays, is distributed among these three settings or travel from one setting to another. Viewed as a setting for language learning, the college is not only the site for English lessons (typically four to five hours per day, five days per week) but also a site for informal use of English with fellow students and

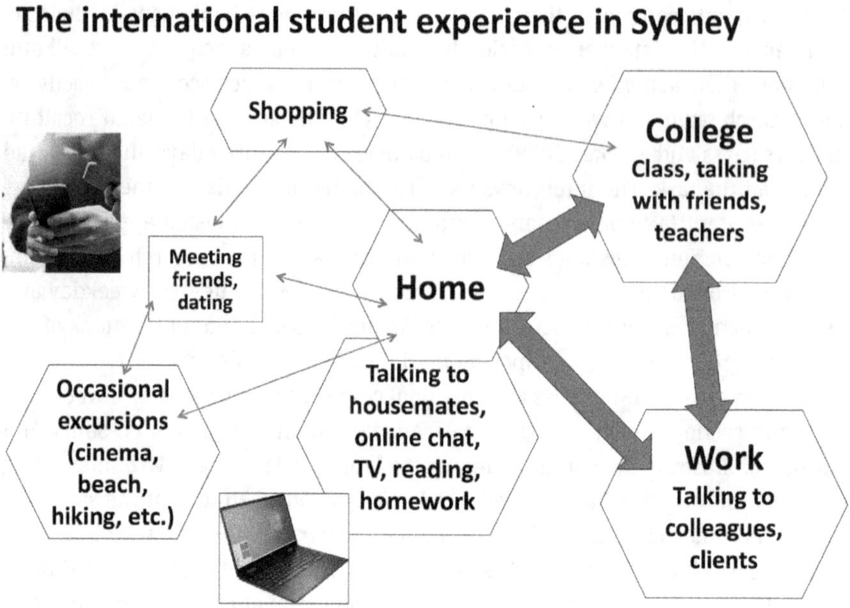

The international student experience in Sydney

Figure 1: The shared experience of study abroad.

teachers. A Vietnamese student in our first study, for example, described how she cooked Vietnamese dishes at home to share with a teacher and a small group of students who stayed in the classroom to eat lunch. However, both in and out of class, there is often tension between opportunities to use English and opportunities to use a first language with co-national students. Most of the students in our studies lived in shared houses with other international students or temporary migrants and most had strategically avoided sharing with co-nationals. While there was some interaction in English among housemates, this was often limited by their different schedules and the fact that they were generally either busy or tired while at home. The home was mainly a place to do English homework, surf the Internet and watch TV. The Vietnamese student mentioned above also described how her housemates strategically made time to watch lifestyle TV shows together, which provided ready topics for English conversation. Part-time work could also be a site for informal use of English, also several students had jobs in which they either worked with co-nationals or had little communication with co-workers. Students also ranked part-time jobs in terms of the affordances they offered for informal language learning, with jobs that brought them into contact with Australian co-workers or members of the public being favoured, and changing one's part-time job was seen as one of the best ways of improving the language learning environment.

The left-hand side of Figure 1 represents more occasional shopping trips, meetings with friends, visits to the cinema, excursions, and so on. However, the time devoted to such activities was limited by the demands of study and part-time work, with a number of the students having both weekday and weekend jobs. The overall picture that emerges is one of a shared language learning environment that is dominated by home, college and part-time work. The students that we interviewed typically had to fit informal language learning into the daily routines of busy lives, seeking out opportunities and resources in the locations in which they found themselves over the course of the day. One important theme that emerged in the accounts of many students, however, was the strategic management of these spaces and their uses of them for language learning purposes. It is also worth noting that students accessed online resources in two ways. Much of their use of the Internet and broadcast media took place at home and appeared to replicate existing preferences for international content; there was little evidence of use of the Internet or other media to access Australian content (see also Gomes 2015). Some students also spent time at home using the Internet to talk to family and friends back home. However, a number of students also reported making agentive use of mobile devices outside the home, especially online dating and meetup apps, maps and messaging services to arrange meetings with friends. It seems likely that our data did not fully capture the use of mobile devices for informal language learning while on the move, or indeed the learning that took place when travelling from setting to setting. These are topics that deserve further research in the context of study abroad.

Within this broad picture there is considerable variation among individual language learning environments, illustrated here by two participants, Sonja and Odval.

5.2 Sonja

In Figures 2 and 3, the background map represents the geographical environment in which each participant maps out their own individual environment for learning and using English. The boxes superimposed on the map show the approximate location of the main settings in this environment, and the lines represent the journeys made between them. The structure of lines and boxes represents, schematically, the unique pathway, or configuration of settings that each assembled as an environment for learning English. For readers who do not know Sydney, it may be helpful to know that the map covers approximately a quarter of the Greater Sydney area and that the distance between the 'home' and 'weekend work' boxes in Figure 1 is approximately 30 kilometres as the crow flies, a journey of around 90 minutes by public transport. The inner city is located beneath the 'school' and 'leisure' boxes on the lower right of the map.

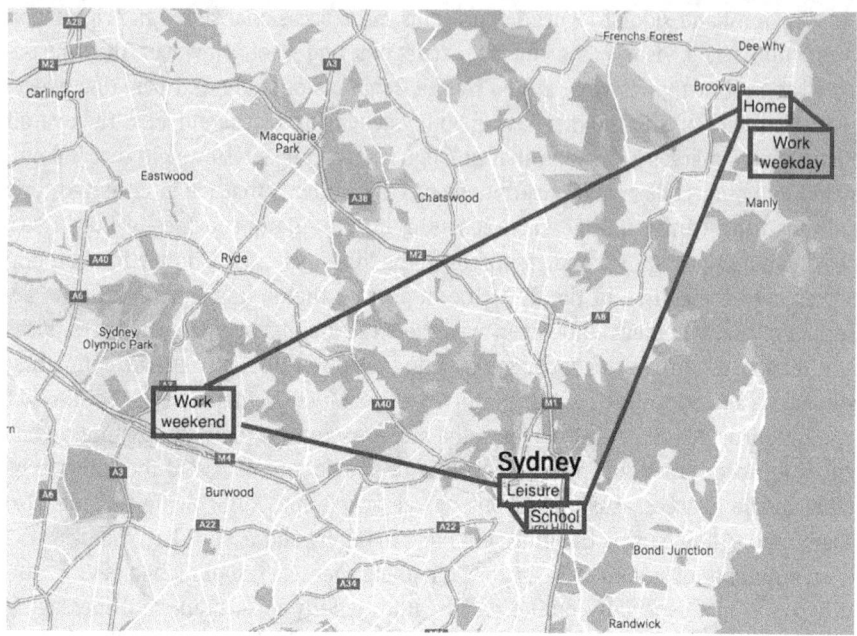

Figure 2: Sonja's language learning environment.

Sonja was a Serbian woman in her mid-thirties at the time of the study. She had been living in Sydney for more than a year, after working for six years on cruise ships. She had a high level of proficiency in spoken English but was studying in the hope of obtaining entry into an MBA program. Sonja lived in the Northern Beaches area, where she lived with an English-speaking South African family. She studied at a private sector English college two days per week and had a morning and afternoon childcare job at a local school three days per week. She also had a weekend job, three days per fortnight, in the play centre of a large department store in the west of the city. Sonja's daily routines were structured by the locations of her home, school and workplaces, which involved long journeys by public transport. However, in each case, the choice of location was strategically related to opportunities for informal English language learning. She had chosen to live in the suburbs, rather than the inner city, because it gave her the opportunity to lodge with an English-speaking family. She had also chosen to work in childcare, because it gave her opportunities to interact with English-speaking children as well as colleagues.

Although she only attended class for two days per week, Sonja had relatively little leisure time due to her part-time jobs and long commutes. She spent much of her time at home working on college assignments and studying academic

English, but she made a point of watching an English-language movie or TV show every night. She also spent some of her leisure time at the gym, on the beach, hiking and meeting friends, mostly in the inner city in the area close to her college. Like several of the female participants in our studies, Sonja also used an online dating app as a means of arranging casual meetings with native speakers of English. She also made good use of her time spent commuting to read English books; her preferences were for history and politics and, at the time of the interview, she was reading the autobiography of Nelson Mandela.

In sum, Sonja had mapped out an expansive spatial environment within the urban geography of Sydney that was rich in affordances for informal English language learning. She had, in effect, strategically shaped her everyday routine so that it would be conducive to informal learning. Her day-to-day interactions were mostly with English speakers and in her leisure activities, she rarely used Serbian despite the presence of a relatively large Serbian-speaking community in the city. This was in accordance with her strategic goals for living and studying in Sydney. "Luckily", she said, "I have only one Serbian family that I'm in touch with here in Sydney, I see them like every couple months . . . I don't want to be one of those people who stay in their own community and don't learn English at all."

5.3 Odval

Odval was one of several students who were both less resourceful and less expansive in their use of the space of the city than Sonja. Odval was a Mongolian woman in her mid-thirties. At the time of the study, she had spent four years studying in Australia with the aim of studying for a postgraduate degree. She self-assessed her spoken English as intermediate level, which was corroborated by her use of English in the interview, but said that she had a much higher level in the other skills. As Figure 3 shows, she lived much of her life in the inner city, making little use of other areas of the city. Odval lived in Waterloo, an inner-city suburb to the south of the city centre, where she shared a room with a Mongolian friend. She attended the same college as Sonja for two days per week and had a day-care job, also in Waterloo, looking after the child of a Mongolian friend. Her living and work arrangements, thus, meant that she made little use of English outside the language college. In her leisure time, Odval went to the cinema in Newtown, an inner west suburb close to the University of Sydney, once a week, met Mongolian friends, went shopping, and went to the gym and swimming pool. At home, she watched movies and was a voracious reader, telling us that she had recently read the seven books of the *Harry Potter* series in a month. She also chatted regularly online with

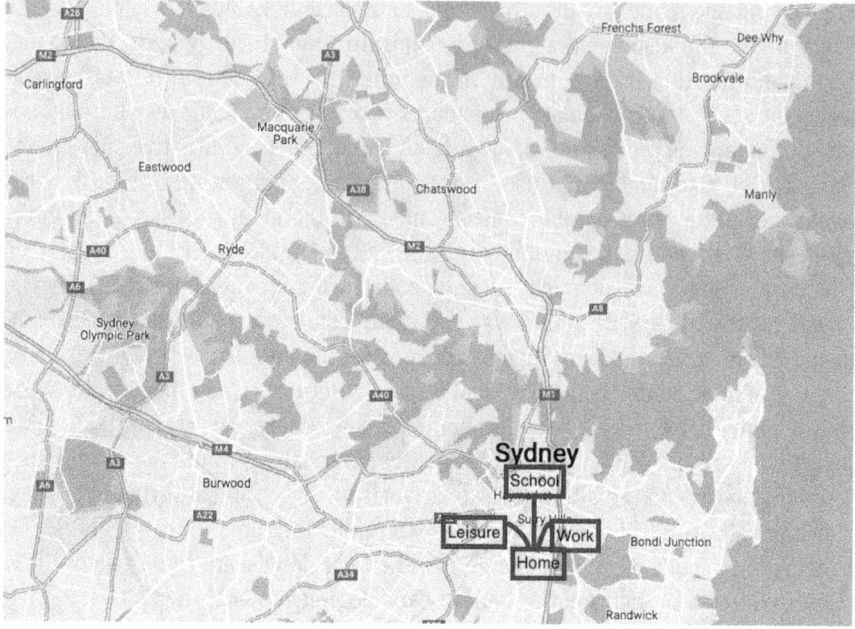

Figure 3: Odval's language learning environment.

a friend in China, using Chinese. By her own account, Odval used Mongolian frequently in Sydney – although the Mongolian-speaking community is relatively small it is concentrated in the inner city. She spoke little English outside school, but said that she was making more effort to engage in casual talk. She said that she had been making an effort to initiate talk with sales assistants when shopping and was also considering finding a room with a non-Mongolian roommate. But as Odval told the interviewer, "Ah yeah, yeah, I thought I'm just going to Sydney, to speak English every day every time, is not really".

It would be unfair to compare Odval's efforts to map out an environment conducive to English language learning with those of Sonja. Clearly, Sonja was more successful in this respect, but it is difficult to say why this was so, without further in-depth research. It is, perhaps, worth noting that Sonja was the exception to the rule in her expansive use of the space of the city, while Odval's was closer to the default environment of the participants in our study, which tended to be circumscribed by the area close to the place of study, and consequently more conducive to social networking with co-nationals. This question of why such differences exist, however, was beyond the scope of the study, which aimed only to understand how the availability of opportunities for informal language learning intersected with the participants' everyday lives and their uses of the space of the city. The strong conclusions that we can draw from a comparison of Sonja's and Odval's language learning environments are, first, that each student maps out a unique language learning environment; second, that the spatiality of these environments is shaped by the students' everyday spatiotemporal routines; and, third, that these routines are in turn shaped, partly by the demography of the city and partly by the students' agency. The uniqueness of language learning environments is clearly related to each student's positioning in the demographic space of the city, but because the student's agency can also affect this positioning, agency is, perhaps, the more important factor. The no doubt complex reasons behind variations in study abroad participants' capacities for, and willingness to, engage in agentive uses of space for the purpose of informal language learning is deserving of further research.

6 Informal language learning and leisure in study abroad

In conclusion, although leisure was not a focal issue in the studies I have reported in this chapter, the data provides some cause for comment on this issue. In the current literature on informal language learning there is a justified assumption that much informal learning takes place in the learner's leisure time and in the context of leisure activities. However, the discussion of the spatiality of informal learning in study abroad might also be turned back on the typical study 'at home' context of much of the current research. That is to say, in both cases, there is a broad framework within which language learning environments are mapped out and considerable variations in individual mappings. I would suggest tentatively that study-at-home environments are shaped largely by the restricted availability of target language resources in the local geographical environment and their abundance in the online environment. If I am right on this point, I would also suggest, again tentatively, that in the at-home context, informal language learning is, in a sense, channelled into the learners' leisure time and their use of online resources that combine learning with leisure. Whether these comments are valid or not, study abroad seems to present a very different case in several respects.

Firstly, because study-abroad participants so often travel overseas in order to experience the target language in the local geographical environment, the use of online resources remains in play but takes a back seat to direct engagement with the target language, especially in the context of interaction with target language speakers. Gomes' (2015) finding that international students in Australia do not significantly engage with local broadcast and online media is understandable, therefore, if we assume that the primary orientation in informal language learning shifts to engagement with target language resources in the local environment. Moreover, it seems that study-abroad participants do engage in innovative uses of mobile online resources to navigate local environments. The apparently widespread use of online dating apps as a resource to meet English speakers in Sydney is a case in point, although I stress that the use of mobile devices in study abroad calls for more research. A theme that emerges strongly, however, is that study abroad involves not only a reconfiguration of the students' language learning environment in a new geographical setting, but also a reconfiguration of its elements in relation to notions such as work, study and leisure.

Several points seem to be worth exploring further. First, I have observed several times that international students lead busy lives, largely because full-time study and part-time work take up so much of their time. Their lives seem to leave little time for conventional leisure activities such as trips to the cinema, days on the beach, meeting friends, or even browsing the Internet. Moreover, it seems that such leisure activities are often carried out with co-nationals using the students' first languages. They are not so much an opportunity to use English informally, as an opportunity to re-connect with a feeling of cultural familiarity. Second, because international students in Sydney have so many opportunities to use their first languages with co-nationals, there can be tension between engaging in informal English language learning and leisure time with friends. Sonja, for example, deliberately limits the time she spends with Serbian friends, in favour of creating opportunities for informal use of English. In this sense, informal language learning involves as much work as leisure, and, indeed, in Sonja's case, it largely takes place in the context of paid work. Odval seems to be either less capable of, or less willing to carry out the kind of work that is needed for informal language learning in Sydney and, in consequence, much of her informal learning takes place with media, as it might do at home.

However, at the same time, we see a kind of purposive mingling of study, work and leisure in the context of informal language learning. For example, when Sonja chats with children in English at work is this work or leisure? When a student spends her lunch break in the classroom eating and chatting with her teacher and other students in English, is she studying or enjoying her leisure time? When Sonja uses an online dating app to arrange a meeting over coffee with a speaker of English is this study or leisure? There are no clear answers to these questions, other than that informal language learning in study abroad seems to break down distinctions between study, work and leisure in interesting and unexpected ways.

References

Australian Government. 2021. *International Student Data*. Department of Education and Skills Training. https:///internationaleducation.gov.au/research/international-student-data/Pages/default.aspx/ internationaleducation.gov.au/research/international-student-data/Pages/default.aspx (accessed 15 October 2021).

Benson, Phil. 2021. *Language Learning Environments: Spatial Perspectives on SLA*. Bristol: Multilingual Matters.

Benson, Phil. 2022. Mapping language learning environments. In Hayo Reinders, Chun Lai & Pia Sundqvist (eds.), *Routledge Handbook of Language Learning Beyond the Classroom*. London: Routledge.

Benson, Phil, Gary Barkhuizen, Peter Bodycott & Jill Brown. 2013. *Second Language Identity in Narratives of Study Abroad*. Basingstoke: Palgrave Macmillan.

Benson, Phil, Phil Chappell & Lynda Yates. 2018. A day in the life: Mapping international students' language learning environments in multilingual Sydney. *Australian Journal of Applied Linguistics* 1(1). 20–32.

Benson, Phil & Hayo Reinders (eds.). 2011. *Beyond the Language Classroom*. Basingstoke: Palgrave Macmillan.

Block, David, John Gray & Marnie Holborow. 2012. *Neoliberalism and Applied Linguistics*. London: Routledge.

Buckingham, David (ed.). 2008. *Youth, Identity, and Digital Media*. Cambridge: MIT Press.

Chappell, Phil, Phil Benson & Lynda Yates. 2018. ELICOS students' out-of-class language learning experiences: An emerging research agenda. *English Australia Journal* 33(2). 43–48.

Coleman, Jim. 2015. Social circles during residence abroad: What students do, and who with. In Rosamund Mitchell, Nicole Tracy-Ventura & Kevin McManus (eds.), *Social Interaction, Identity and Language Learning During Residence Abroad*, 33–52. (Eurosla Monographs Series 4). Amsterdam: European Second Language Association.

Collentine, Joseph & Barbara Freed. 2004. Learning context and its effects on second language acquisition: Introduction. *Studies in Second Language Acquisition* 26(2). 153–171.

Dewey, Dan P. 2017. Measuring social interaction during study abroad: Quantitative methods and challenges. *System* 71. 49–59.

Dressman, Mark & Randall Sadler (eds.). 2020. *The Handbook of Informal Language Learning*. Hoboken/Chichester: Wiley Blackwell.

Ferguson, Hazel & Henry Sherrell. 2021. *Overseas Students in Australian Higher Education: A Quick Guide*. Canberra: Parliament of Australia. https://www.aph.gov.au/About_Parliament/Parliamentary_Departments/Parliamentary_Library/pubs/rp/rp2021/Quick_Guides/OverseasStudents. (accessed 12 October 2021)

García-Amaya, Lorenzo. 2017. Detailing L1 and L2 use in study abroad research: Data from the daily linguistic questionnaire. *System* 71. 60–72.

Gass, Susan & Alison Mackey. 2000. *Stimulated Recall Methodology in Second Language Research*. Mahwah: Lawrence Erlbaum.

Gee, James Paul. 2007. *Good Video Games and Good Learning: Collected Essays on Video Games, Learning and Literacy*. New York: Peter Lang.

Gomes, Catherine. 2015. Negotiating everyday life in Australia: Unpacking the parallel society inhabited by Asian international students through their social networks and entertainment media use. *Journal of Youth Studies*, 18(4). 515–536.

Gomes, Catherine. 2018. *Siloed Diversity: Transnational Migration, Digital Media and Social Networks.* Basingstoke: Palgrave Macmillan.

Howard, Martin (ed.). 2019. *Study Abroad, Second Language Acquisition and Interculturality.* Bristol: Multilingual Matters.

IELTS. 2012. Demand for IELTS increases around the world. https://www.ielts.org/news/2012/demand-for-ielts-increases-around-the-world. (accessed 12 October 2021)

IELTS. 2017. IELTS numbers rise to three million. https://www.ielts.org/news/2017/ielts-numbers-rise-to-three-million-a-year. (accessed 12 October 2021)

Kinginger, Celeste. 2009. *Language Learning and Study Abroad: A Critical Reading of Research.* New York: Palgrave Macmillan.

Krashen, Stephen. 1982. *Principles and Practice in Second Language Acquisition.* New York: Prentice-Hall.

Lai, Chun. 2017. *Autonomous Language Learning with Technology Beyond the Classroom.* London: Bloomsbury.

Lankshear, Colin & Michele Knobel (eds.). 2008. *Digital Literacies: Concepts, Policies and Practices.* New York: Peter Lang.

Lee, Ju Seong & Mark Dressman. 2018. When IDLE hands make an English workshop: Informal digital learning of English and language proficiency. *TESOL Quarterly* 52(2). 435–445.

Mazereanu, E. 2019. Market size of the global language services industry, 2009–2021. statista.com/statistics/257656/size-of-the-global-language-services-market. (accessed 21 October 2021)

Mitchell, Rosamond, Nicole Tracy-Ventura & Kevin McManus (eds.). 2015. *Social Interaction, Identity and Language Learning During Residence Abroad.* (Eurosla Monographs Series 4). Amsterdam: European Second Language Association.

O'Hanlon, Seamus. 2018. *City Life: The New Urban Australia.* Sydney: NewSouth Publishing.

Ranta, Leila & Amy Meckelborg. 2013. How much exposure to English do international graduate students really get? Measuring language use in a naturalistic setting. *The Canadian Modern Language Review* 69(1). 1–33.

Reinders, Hayo, Chun Lai & Pia Sundqvist (eds.). 2022. *The Routledge Handbook of Language Learning and Teaching Beyond the Classroom.* London: Routledge.

Robertson, Shanthi. 2013. *Transnational Student-Migrants and the State: The Education-Migration Nexus.* Basingstoke: Palgrave.

Sockett, Geoffrey. 2014. *The Online Informal Learning of English.* Basingstoke: Palgrave Macmillan.

Soyoof, Ali, Barry Lee Reynolds, Boris Vazquez-Calvo & Katherine McLay. 2021. Informal digital learning of English (IDLE): A scoping review of what has been done and a look towards what is to come. *Computer Assisted Language Learning.* Published online: 28 Jun 2021, available at: https://doi.org/10.1080/09588221.2021.1936562

Steel, Caroline & Mike Levy. 2013. Language students and their technologies: Charting the evolution 2006–2011. *ReCALL* 25(3). 306–320.

Van Lier, Leo. 2004. *The Ecology and Semiotics of Language Learning: A Sociocultural Perspective.* Boston: Kluwer Academic.

Wilkins, David. 1972. *Linguistics and Language Teaching.* London: Edward Arnold.

Marlene Schwarz
8 Learner perspectives on informal L2 vocabulary learning

Abstract: Previous research has shown that engaging in informal leisure activities in the L2 has positive effects on learners' vocabulary knowledge. However, most studies have had a strong quantitative focus which can provide information on the outcomes of informal learning but does not offer many insights into its processes. This chapter presents qualitative findings on learners' practices and perspectives on informal L2 vocabulary learning. The analysis is based on group interviews that were conducted as part of a larger mixed methods study with Austrian adolescents. Findings show that there are some common strategies learners use when they encounter new lexical items in informal activities, but that only few words with specific characteristics warrant closer strategic attention in their view.

Keywords: vocabulary learning, learner perspectives, extramural English, vocabulary learning strategies, qualitative vocabulary research

1 Introduction

Since most recreational leisure activities are firmly located in the private sphere, related practices of informal language learning and use cannot be readily observed. The "private and individualised nature" (Sockett 2014: 110) of such L2 activities presents obvious challenges in terms of research methodology, which makes it surprising that one source of information has only been tapped in a few studies so far: learners' own accounts of and beliefs about *informal second language learning* (ISLL), or more specifically *extramural English* (EE; Sundqvist 2009; Sundqvist and Sylvén 2016) in the case of the present study. As learners are arguably the most important stakeholders in informal learning processes, qualitative explorations giving room to their voices as independent agents are highly informative and worthwhile. To date, relatively few studies have included such a qualitative focus on learner views, although it presents a valuable counterpart to quantitative data on practices of ISLL and enhances our understanding of this complex phenomenon.

Marlene Schwarz, Universität Wien, Austria

https://doi.org/10.1515/9783110752441-008

This study focuses on engagement with extramural English among 15- to 16-year-old Austrian adolescents and its relation to informal L2 vocabulary learning. Extramural English refers to all L2 contact outside the walls of educational institutions. It thus encompasses all learner-initiated, informal language activities outside schools and other instructed language teaching environments, whether online or offline (Sundqvist 2019). Although such informal activities clearly also exist in other languages (see, for instance, Inaba (chapter 9), Alm (chapter 16) or Cajka et al. (chapter 10) in this volume and are then referred to as *extramural L$_n$* (Sundqvist 2019), the present study, like much previous research, is concerned with exposure to English due to its widespread use in media productions and online platforms. More specifically, it concentrates on learner perspectives on informal vocabulary acquisition, as little is known about how learners handle unknown vocabulary in extramural activities and how such learning opportunities benefit lexical development. The analysis draws on six focus group interviews with a total of 30 Austrian upper secondary school students, which were carried out as part of a larger mixed methods study.

In the following, an overview of the field of informal L2 vocabulary learning will be given before introducing the larger project from which the data were taken. The chapter will then explore learners' accounts of informal L2 vocabulary learning with regard to four themes: their evaluations of (vocabulary) learning from extramural activities, strategies for dealing with unknown words, characteristics of lexical items that warrant strategic attention, and factors that aid the retention of informally learned vocabulary.

2 Previous research on informal L2 English vocabulary learning

Over the last two decades informal practices of language learning and use have attracted growing attention. Although researchers have attempted to gauge the effects of extramural exposure on various areas of language competence and skills, vocabulary has been a prominent focus. By now there is a substantial body of research on extramural activities and English vocabulary acquisition for learners at primary (e.g., De Wilde et al. 2020; Jóhannsdóttir 2017; Puimège and Peters 2019), secondary (e.g., Peters, Noreillie, Heylen, Bulté, and Desmet 2019; Sundqvist 2009; Verspoor, De Bot, and Van Rein 2011) and tertiary (e.g., Kusyk and Sockett 2012; Lee 2019a, 2019b; Peters 2018) levels.

Overall, these studies point to a positive relationship between engagement with extramural English and vocabulary knowledge, in particular vocabulary size, for diverse groups of learners. Learners of all ages and from different contexts frequently engage with EE through popular media and thus have previously unprecedented opportunities for incidental vocabulary learning in their leisure time (Dressman 2020; Nunan and Richards 2015). Studies on young language learners without formal English instruction have established that children can acquire English vocabulary solely based on the input they receive outside school (De Wilde et al. 2020; Persson and Prins 2012; Puimège and Peters 2019). At secondary school level, data from Sweden (Olsson 2012; Olsson and Sylvén 2015; Sundqvist 2009), the Netherlands (Verspoor et al. 2011) and the Flemish region of Belgium (Peters 2018; Peters et al. 2019) show that exposure to English outside school benefits vocabulary development. These results are perhaps hardly surprising as these countries are known for their early exposure to English through English-language TV broadcasts with L1 subtitles (Media Consulting Group 2009). However, the evidence regarding the effects of subtitled TV is inconclusive, with positive effects in some studies (Puimège and Peters 2019) but not in others (De Wilde et al. 2020; Peters et al. 2019). Moreover, similar results on types and frequency of engagement with extramural English have been found in other countries all around the world (e.g., Lai, Zhu, and Gong 2015; Lamb 2004; Lyrigkou 2018; Nightingale 2016), and the quantitative strand of the present study (Schwarz 2020) showed that there is a statistically significant relation between extramural engagement and vocabulary size also in the Austrian context, even though all TV broadcasts are commonly dubbed. These findings suggest that subtitled television is not the decisive source of English input anymore, particularly since learners have a wide range of online resources at their disposal.

In terms of influencing factors, a study by Lee (2019a; 2019b) suggests that rather than the quantity it is the quality of informal activities, defined as the inclusion of diverse activities focusing on both meaning and form, that is related to vocabulary knowledge. Furthermore, in a comparative study of learners at upper secondary school and university, Peters (2018) showed that length of formal instruction is not as good a predictor of vocabulary size as exposure to EE, which is a highly interesting finding supported by previous studies focusing on specific aspects of lexical knowledge such as collocations (González-Fernández and Schmitt 2015) or phrasal verbs (Schmitt and Redwood 2011). Peters et al. (2019) further corroborate this result by showing that Flemish learners of French and English have significantly larger English vocabulary sizes despite a longer period of instruction for French. Studies investigating the effect of gender (e.g., De Wilde, Brysbaert, and Eyckmans 2021; Peters 2018; Puimège and Peters 2019; Sundqvist 2009) have produced mixed results: while some reported an advantage for boys (Puimège and Peters 2019; Sundqvist 2009), others found no difference (De Wilde et al. 2021; Peters 2018). Lastly, socioeconomic background in terms of parental education was included in some studies (e.g., De Wilde and Eyckmans 2017; Persson and Prins 2012) but did not show any statistically significant effects.

This synthesis of currently available research suggests that informal engagement with extramural English has an impact on vocabulary development, which may even be more profound than the effects of formal English instruction. However, what is sorely lacking so far is research on the learners' perspectives on informal L2 vocabulary learning. Learners' emic views on EE and its potential for ISLL have been considered in select studies (e.g., Anioł 2011; Arndt 2019; Grau 2009; Ingvarsdóttir and Jóhannsdóttir 2017; Lai 2015), but previous research specifically on informal vocabulary learning has not yet taken them into account. This tendency is indicative of the whole field of vocabulary research as Webb (2020: 7) states in his introduction to the *Routledge handbook of vocabulary studies*:

> Within applied linguistics and other research disciplines, studies are often classified by design with the most common classification being quantitative and qualitative studies. Within lexical studies this categorisation does not really apply, however, because there are very few qualitative studies of vocabulary (notable exceptions include Gu 2003; Haastrup & Henriksen 2000). This is a major limitation of the research on vocabulary. Although we can learn much through quantitative studies of words, there is also a great deal that is unaccounted for that deserves attention.

To date, qualitative methods in lexical research, such as interviews, have mostly been used in single-learner case studies (e.g., Fitzpatrick 2012), as an alternative method of testing lexical knowledge (e.g., Pellicer-Sánchez and Schmitt 2010; Schmitt 1998) or to validate the results of vocabulary tests (e.g., Pellicer-Sánchez and Schmitt 2012), and in research on vocabulary learning strategies (e.g., Bytheway 2015; Moir and Nation 2002). However, as this chapter aims to show for the sub-field of informal vocabulary learning, qualitative data can be used to gain a different perspective on L2 vocabulary acquisition through the learners' eyes. By giving learners a voice and taking their personal accounts and theories seriously, useful insights can be gained on how they cope with unknown vocabulary in authentic input, which factors influence strategic attention, and which strategies they actually use.

3 Introducing the study

The findings on informal L2 vocabulary learning presented in this chapter form part of a larger mixed methods study with adolescent learners of English in Vienna, Austria (Schwarz 2020). The project was one of the first to explore teenagers' informal English practices outside school in the Austrian context and focused on investigating the relationship between learners' extramural activities and their vocabulary knowledge. A major aim of the study was to connect quantitative results on the relation between extramural English and receptive and productive vocabulary size with more qualitative insights into students' actual informal practices of using and learning vocabulary in out-of-school contexts.

In keeping with these aims, the cross-sectional study used a fully integrated sequential mixed methods design consisting of a larger quantitative strand followed by a more in-depth qualitative exploration to confirm, complement and enhance the quantitative data (Creamer 2018; Creswell, Plano Clark, Gutmann, and Hanson 2003). Overall, 224 tenth-grade learners of English attending seven different academic secondary schools (*Gymnasien*) in Vienna participated in the quantitative strand, 30 of which subsequently also participated in the six focus group interviews that formed the qualitative strand of this study.

In the quantitative strand, data were collected using several instruments: an extensive *Extramural English Questionnaire* was used to gather information on students' informal engagement with EE, their reasons and strategies for doing so, as well as demographic data and their language background. The questionnaire was complemented by a structured online language diary,[1] which students were asked to fill in retrospectively at the end of each day for one week to estimate the extent of contact with English. In addition, two vocabulary tests by Meara (2015) and Meara and Fitzpatrick (2000) were used to measure receptive and productive vocabulary size.

However, the focus of this chapter is on the learners' own perspectives as expressed in focus groups. The interview guide covered five main topic areas sequenced from the general to the more specific: the significance of English in participants' everyday lives, extramural activities in the larger sample and participants' own use of these, the significance of EE for learning English, EE and vocabulary acquisition and the relationship between EE and school. In addition to questions on the specific qualitative research interests, first descriptive results of the quantitative part of the study were also included with some questions. This inclusion of quantitative results in the focus groups allowed for checking their validity and discussing them with participants in further depth. After the completion of qualitative data collection in June 2017, the six interviews with a total time of 5.5 hours were transcribed and subjected to a qualitative content analysis in several iterative stages. In the final stage of analysis, inferences drawn from the separate analyses of the quantitative and qualitative data were then compared

---

[1] The original German-language version of the *Extramural English Online Language Diary* is included in Appendix A of Schwarz (2020) or available from the author upon request.

and integrated to gain a more comprehensive understanding of the phenomenon of extramural language use and the processes of learning vocabulary informally. The presentation and discussion of selected findings in the next sections will mainly focus on learners' voices in the interviews, but in the spirit of the original mixed methods research project some quantitative results will be included where necessary. However, before presenting the results on the learners' views on informal vocabulary learning from extramural English, it is necessary to introduce the protagonists of the study in greater detail.

3.1 Participant characteristics and selected quantitative results

Of 224 teenagers taking part in the study, 23 had to be excluded according to pre-determined criteria (e.g., L1 English or extended stays in English-speaking countries). Thus 201 participants remained in the quantitative sample, but due to absences on the day of data collection only 189 students completed the *Extramural English Questionnaire* on which the following description is based. Of these, 109 (58.0%) were female and 79 (42.0%) male and the vast majority (85%) were born in Austria. However, more than half of the participants (54.8%) were bi- or multilingual, meaning that they regularly spoke more than one language at home.[2] For 50.5% German was the main home language, whereas the remaining participants only used it sometimes. Concerning English, the vast majority began studying it in primary school, as is typical for the Austrian context, and had been studying English as a school subject for an average of 7.75 years. Over 90% of the participants rated their English proficiency as CEFR level B1 or higher on a CEFR-based self-assessment scale which corresponds to the curriculum goal, as students in academic upper secondary schools are supposed to reach CEFR level B1 at the end of tenth grade.

Data on informal L2 engagement show that over 95% of the participants come in contact with English on an almost daily basis and that Viennese teenagers'

---

[2] Participants listed a total of 33 languages, which are spoken at home to at least some extent. In addition to German, the most frequently spoken home languages are Serbian (6.9%), Turkish (5.5%), Arabic (3.6%), Albanian (3.3%) and Bosnian (2.2%), but Armenian, Azerbaijani, Bambara, Bengali, Bulgarian, Chechen, Chinese, Croatian, Dari, Farsi, Finnish, French, Hindi, Hungarian, Italian, Korean, Kurdish, Luxembourgish, Macedonian, Malayalam, Pashto, Polish, Romanian, Russian, Slovakian and Spanish were also named. At school, most participants study Latin and one Romance language (French, Italian or Spanish) in addition to English.

preferred EE activities coincide with their generally preferred leisure activities. Listening to music, reading posts on social media, and watching audiovisual online content in the form of films, series or video clips are the most popular activities, but the range of activities participants engage in is highly individualised and varied as each of the activities listed in the detailed list of the *Extramural English Questionnaire* is done at least a few times a month by at least one of the participants and some participants engage in additional 'niche activities'. Hence, students' engagement with EE appears to be determined by specialised interests and personal preferences to a large extent. The most common activities are mainly carried out in online contexts and mostly involve receptive language use, while more infrequent activities and specialised niche activities, such as fan fiction writing or computer programming, often also entail language production. The results concerning the most frequent EE activities are similar to those of other studies focusing on European adolescents (Arndt 2019; Ingvarsdóttir and Jóhannsdóttir 2017; Lyrigkou 2018; Nightingale 2016; Olsson 2012; Peters 2018; Sundqvist 2009), but also to results on teenagers' informal practices in very different parts of the world such as China (Lai et al. 2015), Indonesia (Lamb 2004) or Japan (Barbee 2013). These studies also found that extramural exposure to English mainly revolves around digital media such as music, TV programmes, films, series, video clips and games, although the exact order of popularity varies. Similarly, research has shown that much informal contact with English happens online (Kusyk 2017; Lee and Dressman 2018; Sockett 2014; Sockett and Toffoli 2012).

Concerning the extent of informal language contact, 127 participants (68.3%) reported using English more for leisure activities than for lessons at school and the diary data suggest that students spend a large part of their leisure time with English for a mean time of approximately 4 hours per day. This remarkable finding may seem surprising but is supported by further analyses with regard to time use on weekends and the role of music, as well as by students confirming this estimate in the focus group interviews. The estimate is also in line with previous findings on Swedish teenagers, which indicate that the amount of time spent with EE is on the rise: Sundqvist (2009) found a daily mean time of 2 hours and 38 minutes, in Olsson (2012) it was 2 hours and 54 minutes and in Olsson and Sylvén (2015) students attending regular English classes spent 5 hours and 36 minutes with EE per day, whereas for students attending specialised CLIL language programmes the estimate was over 7.5 hours.

This chapter focuses on the smaller qualitative sub-sample, which included 30 individuals in six separate focus groups. Overall, the qualitative sample showed a similar picture concerning background variables but gender was more equally distributed with a total of 15 boys and 15 girls taking part and 12 interviewees (40.0%) came from bi- or multilingual families. 19 learners (63.3%) indicated that they use English more frequently in their spare time than at school, which is similar to the larger quantitative sample.

In the following presentation of results, all interviewees are designated using pseudonyms of their own choice. Furthermore, all quotes have been translated to English as the focus groups were conducted in German to ensure that participants felt comfortable and could fully express their thoughts. Care was taken to stay as close as possible to participants' original word choice and reflect their language use.

4 Learner accounts of the informal vocabulary learning process

The qualitative analysis of the interview data was guided by the research questions listed below, but also allowed for data-driven themes to emerge, which was especially relevant for questions three and four.

RQ 1: How do participants evaluate the role of extramural activities in informal L2 (vocabulary) learning?

RQ 2: Which strategies are used to discover the meanings of unknown words encountered during informal leisure activities?

RQ 3: Which words and lexical phrases warrant strategic attention in participants' views?

RQ 4: Which factors help participants to remember words and phrases encountered in extramural activities?

Before presenting the findings, it is important to clarify that students were made aware in the interviews that learning did not have to be intentional, but in this case rather meant 'picking something up' incidentally while engaging in an activity. Still, conceptions of learning are highly individualised and the interview data reveal diverse, multi-layered and sometimes even conflicting views, as is frequently the case for learner beliefs (Kalaja, Barcelos, Aro, and Ruohotie-Lyhty 2016).

4.1 Evaluating the potential of extramural English for informal vocabulary learning

Over two thirds of the interviewees believe that their overall language development benefits from engagement with extramural English, with 17 students across focus groups explicitly expressing this opinion and a further five implicitly agreeing with their peers.[3] These students believe that out-of-school engagement with English plays an essential role in their language development, some even more than teaching at school:

> **Mito**: I think what we do at school, that that's somehow a smaller part of what you learn from English. I mean, if (.) I mean, you learn something, but somehow, only with what you learn at school, I don't know, I think that (.) well, you rather learn the largest part in your free time.
>
> **Anna**: Yes, it's really like that.
>
> **Unidentified female student**: Mhm.
>
> **Anna**: I don't know, if I only had contact with English at school, I wouldn't even know a quarter of what I know today.[4]

In contrast, five participants are not as certain about learning from EE and express mixed views, which appear to be due to their conception of language learning as acquisition of new knowledge rather than expanding existing knowledge or practising skills, or to a lack of engagement with EE on their part. Finally, only two participants voice a negative opinion: both are gamers who argue that most of the international contacts they communicate with while gaming do not speak English well, which leads one of them to the conclusion that he is more likely to 'unlearn' the language rather than learn anything new.

Concerning the question of how their language development benefits from informal engagement with English, vocabulary was named most frequently by far, with 14 participants referring to it. This result may, however, be at least partially biased. Since all interviewees had also taken part in the quantitative strand, they were aware of the study's focus on vocabulary, which could have influenced their responses. Yet, several other benefits of extramural English for language

---

[3] Implicit agreement here means that these five students did not verbally respond to the question about learning from EE input, although they might have agreed via gestures such as nodding. However, these students expressed support for the idea of learning in other parts of the interview.

[4] Quotations from the interviews include the following transcription symbols: (.) for short pauses, x for parts that are not clearly understandable, and @ for laughter.

development also point to lexical learning: five students mention that idioms and phrases can be picked up from extramural input. Another five refer to 'casual and colloquial English' or slang terms, mainly regarding lexical expressions. Furthermore, in line with Nation's (2001) taxonomy of word knowledge, both pronunciation and spelling, mentioned by seven and five participants respectively, can also be considered aspects of lexical knowledge. Interestingly, in previous research not focusing on vocabulary acquisition "[v]ocabulary emerged as the most prominent aspect learned by students of English out-of-school" (Kalaja, Alanen, Palviainen, and Dufva 2011: 52) as well. In addition to lexis, several participants referred to developing their procedural knowledge and to a feeling for what 'sounds right'. Lai (2015: 274) reports a similar finding for university students in Hong Kong who also stated that using English outside class "gave them a stronger sense of the language in terms of how the language is actually used." Lastly, some interviewees in this study stated that they gain better comprehension skills, practise their speaking abilities or even learn new grammatical structures through extramural activities.

When participants use the term *learning* in relation to vocabulary they mostly refer to discovering the meaning of previously unknown words or phrases and thus to knowledge of the form-meaning link (e.g., Nation 2001). This finding indicates that for these teenagers, vocabulary learning usually equates to learning new words, i.e. expanding vocabulary size, rather than to learning more about individual words, i.e. improving depth of word knowledge, although a few such examples are given as well. Other aspects of word knowledge relating to form, such as discovering a misunderstanding with regard to spelling or pronunciation or a previously unknown word form, are mentioned in these instances. With respect to aspects of word use, participants' statements indicate a strong belief that exposure to native speakers and particularly 'natural' everyday language in contrast to 'school English' (Grau 2009; Ranta 2010) helps them acquire typical grammatical patterns and collocations which make their own L2 production sound more 'natural' as well.

> **Susi**: Well, generally, like how you say something that it sounds right (.) in English
>
> **Interviewer**: @@@ yes, so having a feeling for the language so to say
>
> **Unidentified female student**: Yes.
>
> **Mito**: Yes, it's often like that, if you see some kind of phrase in a movie somehow and then you think to yourself "Ah, interesting, you can say it like that, too", which you wouldn't think of yourself (.) but that one says it like that somehow and then you just know it.

Participants were also able to provide examples of lexical learning from EE during the interviews. Audiovisual media like series and video clips were frequently mentioned as sources of learning. For instance, John learned the word *turmoil* from a video about the USA, Paul picked up *vanguard* from the fantasy series *Game of Thrones* and Elisa looked up the word *inception* because she wanted to understand the title of the movie of the same name. Participants can also acquire formal word knowledge aspects from audiovisual input, for instance, Kira reports discovering the pronunciation of *hovercraft* through the movie *The Hunger Games*. Other students report learning words from written texts: Anna picked up the word *fiscal* from an introductory book on economics and Kirito learned *perennial* from a novel. To a lesser extent, teenagers also learn words from their peers as the next two examples show: Pinguin reports learning the word *discombobulated* from a cousin and then teaching it to all his other friends because he thinks that it is fun. In an example of a collaborative activity, Louise helped a friend create a character for the fantasy role-playing game *Dungeons & Dragons* and acquired the word *deception* in the process of doing so. In addition, several students mention picking up swearwords and youth slang, mostly in the context of social media; however, as the examples above clearly show, teenagers do not only learn colloquial terms and informal register words from their extramural activities but also encounter and memorise relatively formal and infrequent vocabulary or even specialised technical terms.

Having established that most interviewees strongly believe that their vocabulary development benefits from engaging in English-language leisure activities, the next question centres on what participants actually do when they encounter new vocabulary in the course of their free time.

4.2 Using strategies to discover the meaning of new words

Data on strategies for dealing with unknown vocabulary were collected in both the quantitative and qualitative strands of the present study. In the *Extramural English Questionnaire*, the students were provided with a list of eight options based on Schmitt's (1997) taxonomy of discovery strategies.[5] The quantitative results were then discussed with participants in the focus group interviews in a process similar to member checking (Creswell and Miller 2000) and a comparison shows that both the quantitative and qualitative results strongly overlap. In the larger sample, learners report using three main strategies when encountering unknown English words in extramural contexts: (1) guessing from context, (2) consulting (online) dictionaries and (3) thinking about other languages.

---

[5] See appendix for an overview of the questions on vocabulary learning strategies together with descriptive results.

In the interviews, guessing from context also clearly emerges as the default option across all six focus groups. It is the preferred method for dealing with new vocabulary in all kinds of input, whether written, spoken, or audiovisual. Some students even question whether lexical inferencing (Haastrup 1991) can count as a strategy because it happens automatically for them:

> **Marie**: You just read a text and then comes such a word where 'Ah, okay', I don't even, I think that somehow happens completely naturally, at once, totally normal, kind of you see a word, you don't know what it is, normal reaction, quickly think about it, do I know it, do I not know it, does it interest me, go on.

While this process may be more or less automatic for different students, inferencing is seen as particularly adequate for some of the most frequent activities. When watching series, films or videos the additional visual cues are considered particularly helpful for guessing:

> **Emma**: Well, if it's a series for instance, then out of context, perhaps there is a picture there or so, then you understand it, in a text also from context, but then I also sometimes ask my brother, but really rarely, if he is sitting next to me or so then I ask him about the word, well, yes.

Moreover, students only have very little time to find out about the meaning of a new word if they do not want to continuously pause videos, hence other strategies take too much time and are seen as impractical. Thus, inferring from context is regarded as the most viable option in many cases, particularly as teenagers may encounter a large amount of vocabulary they do not understand. The only problem students identify with guessing from context is that they only gain a rough idea of a new word's meaning and cannot use it, but arguably in many contexts approximate comprehension is sufficient for understanding the content, especially when engaging in extramural activities for entertainment purposes.

In addition to guessing from context, some participants also report thinking about other languages and using dictionaries. Comparing a new word to other languages in their repertoire is preferred by a number of interviewees, with most implying that only if guessing and comparing do not resolve the problem, then they might use further resources like dictionaries.[6]

---

[6] Participants did not always specify which other languages they use for comparative purposes, but those who did most often referred to Latin and the Romance languages studied at school.

> **Elisa**: Especially in relation to context, if you can't infer it from that, then I quickly look it up in the dictionary.
>
> **Johannes**: Yes, me too.
>
> **Elisa**: or I link it to other languages.
>
> **Louise**: Yes, I always think like that
>
> **Johannes**: At first you always think about it
>
> **Marie**: Exactly, like French, what is it in French.

Dictionaries, usually in the form of online platforms and apps, are a highly controversial topic in the group interviews: some participants see dictionaries as an easy and fast option to discover a new meaning and regard it as less strenuous than thinking themselves, whereas others see it as the very last resort that is only used when all other strategies fail.

> **Anna**: well, if I can manage, then I can manage and if it's really like somehow the main word of the whole text, then (.) then I think about everything I can do before looking it up, because I am too lazy for that @ to look up an English word, because that's stupid and too much of an effort. But if I then really don't know, then as the last possibility, then I look it up.

In contrast to Anna, some participants actually favour dictionary use: as mentioned, these students regard thinking about word meaning as more strenuous than looking a word up or they point out that while inferences may be incorrect, dictionaries definitely provide them with correct definitions or translations. In times of smartphones, another advantage of online dictionaries and apps is that they are always at hand and can be accessed very quickly:

> **Maria**: I always do it like that. I watch something, read something or whatever, then I take out my phone and type the word in
>
> **Paul**: Yeah it, that's really fast.
>
> **Maria**: because that's just the quickest. Because rarely there is someone beside you who, of whom you know that he knows that word or that he has a larger language use than yourself, well vocabulary.

Interestingly, asking someone for help with the meaning of new English words is a relatively unpopular strategy: while a few students state that they like being able to ask others and sometimes do so like Emma in the quote on page 170, most participants do not make use of such social strategies. Reasons given include the lack of other proficient English speakers in close proximity, as teenagers do many recreational leisure activities on their own. Clearly, smartphones could also be used to contact others, but waiting for replies simply takes too long in their opinion. In addition, students also report inhibitions to ask others because it could be embarrassing for them; hence, impersonal technological options like dictionaries are preferable in this case. Similarly, the remaining strategies listed in the questionnaire, i.e. identifying the part of speech and analysing word parts, are rarely employed by participants because they are seen as taking too much time and requiring too much cognitive effort.

It thus becomes clear that guessing from context is the default option for dealing with unknown vocabulary in extramural activities for most participants. Only if this strategy fails do the students resort to other options such as thinking about other languages and using dictionaries. Overall, these results are similar to previous research using large-scale surveys among university students: Schmitt (1997) found that using bilingual dictionaries was most common, followed by guessing from context, whereas in Fan (2003) students preferred guessing over dictionary strategies. Still, in both studies these two strategies were used most frequently to discover the meanings of unknown lexical items, which shows that although the technical options available to students today may have evolved, the results concerning discovery strategies are still rather similar. In the present study, the fact that many interviewees only use resources such as dictionaries if guessing from context is not successful or sufficient raises a further question, namely, what makes some new words noteworthy and interesting enough to use additional discovery strategies?

4.3 Characteristics of lexical items that receive strategic attention

Learners' statements in the focus group interviews shed light on factors that contribute to the prominence of unknown words in extramural input and make them worthy of further strategic behaviour beyond guessing from context. Overall, however, unknown English words that are considered irrelevant, aptly described as "random talk" by Elisa, are not worth looking up or reflecting upon for most participants. If new words are deemed unimportant, participants simply ignore them as explained by Anna:

> **Interviewer**: Mhm. But just now (.) how did you put it so nicely, if I if I can manage – does that mean that you, that you can't think of it in that moment or so, but that you get it from context, that you roughly understand the sense?
>
> **Anna**: Not even, some- sometimes not even that, but only if it simply is an irrelevant word,
>
> **Interviewer**: I see
>
> **Anna**: then I completely ignore it.

I thus argue that it is an individual student's perception of a new lexical item's importance that determines the amount of strategic attention it will be given. A first characteristic contributing to perceived importance can be inferred from the discussions of guessing from context, namely, that new lexical items are only worth the effort of looking them up if they are essential for understanding the content *and* cannot be easily inferred from context:

> **Interviewer**: Which words do you look up then? For which ones is the motivation there to look up the meaning?
>
> **Elisa**: If you (.) if the context doesn't help you either
>
> **Louise**: Yes, if it's important to understand the sentence, if it interests you I think.

Hence, the relevance of a word appears to depend, firstly, on how essential it is for being able to follow the content and, secondly, on how much information is provided by co-text and (multimodal) context. Research on lexical inferencing has also found positive results for the availability of local textual cues on vocabulary learning (e.g., Qian 2005; Van Zeeland 2014). In contrast, salience, i.e. the noticeability of a word in input (Ellis 1999), has received little attention so far and recent studies have produced mixed results: while Elgort and Warren (2014) showed a positive effect of keyness on incidental vocabulary acquisition from reading, Peters and Webb (2018) found no such effect for word relevance in their study on lexical learning from television viewing.[7]

Another characteristic that makes looking up lexical items worthwhile is repeated encounters with the same word. The idea that words that are encountered repeatedly merit further investigation is expressed in two separate groups. In one group, Mito seems to have reflected on his practices relating to unknown vocabulary during the interview and makes this statement after a lengthy discussion on the topic:

> **Mito**: I actually do it, I now realise, usually like this, if I somehow if I just see a word, then I usually skip over it while reading, but if I somehow with certain words if I realise that I have actually skipped over them quite often lately, ehm (.), then I think 'Well it's about time now to look this up because it's worth it' (.) I mean, I actually look up quite a lot, because I always get ah, see, new words again, where I think to myself 'Ah, I've actually already asked myself several times, x that I don't know that', yes.

---

7 While the operationalisations of *keyness* and *word relevance* are not exactly the same, as the first is a statistical measure relating to corpus frequency (Elgort & Warren 2014) and the second refers to a summary of ratings in relation to relevance for content comprehension (Peters & Webb 2018), they were both used as measures of word salience in a given text in the two studies.

From Mito's statement we can conclude that repeated encounters are another factor contributing to the perceived importance of new vocabulary: if unknown words are met several times in EE input, they become worth looking up. Although the central role of frequency of exposure is a known factor in vocabulary learning research (see Peters 2020; Webb 2007, 2014 for reviews), this relation between the number of encounters and the use of strategic behaviour is an interesting insight.

Finally, the last feature that prompts participants to reflect on words is that they spark their interest. For DJ that means that unknown words 'get stuck in his head' and this sentiment of being annoyed by unknown words is also well known to two other participants, but none can explain why that is the case in the course of the interviews. For Vanessa, on the other hand, the conspicuousness of unknown words is clearly linked to formal properties:

> **Vanessa**: I do not pay a lot of attention to understanding all the words
>
> **Interviewer**: Completely fine.
>
> **Vanessa**: but well if a word sounds or looks interesting, then I look it up, yes.

Thus, although participants' statements remain rather vague in this regard, some appear to be attracted by formal properties such as spelling or pronunciation, whereas others report wanting to know the exact meaning of words that 'get stuck' in their heads for unknown reasons. This finding highlights the fact that the salience of new lexical items cannot only be achieved through relevance for comprehension, but also through affective factors and formal properties, such as pronunciation, distinctiveness of word form or part of speech (Ellis 1999).

With regard to vocabulary that warrants further strategic behaviour in addition to contextual inferencing, three characteristics thus emerge from the focus group interviews: unknown lexical items become worth looking up (1) if they are crucial for understanding the content *and* difficult to infer from context, (2) if they are encountered repeatedly during extramural activities, or (3) if they somehow arouse learners' interest. Similar factors also play a role in relation to the ease of memorising and recalling new vocabulary that was learned informally.

4.4 Factors that aid the retention of informally acquired vocabulary

The final aspect related to students' accounts of lexical learning regards the extent to which they retain knowledge of informally acquired words and what helps to remember them. Although this topic was less of a focus in the interviews, interesting findings emerged indicating that individual learners' beliefs generally align: participants' preferred strategies are also those that they see as most helpful for long-term memorisation.

In the course of the interviews, some participants emphasise that memorising new words, both in general and from their EE activities, is a difficult endeavour. This sentiment is shared by Paul, who argues that learning is complicated by the fact that most unknown words are not encountered frequently enough:

> **Paul**: But most of the words that you do not know, they also do not come up that often. I mean, if you haven't really encountered them until now, perhaps you won't encounter them that often.

While this statement is very insightful and true for a large proportion of low-frequency vocabulary (see also Cobb 2007), other participants are more optimistic and maintain that they do remember new words picked up from EE.

A first finding on what supports learning and retention from participants' points of view is their motivation for understanding the content, especially in contrast to lessons at school. Students do these activities of their own volition and argue that because they are genuinely interested in the content, they are also more interested in the language expressing it. This is particularly true if understanding the vocabulary is necessary to follow content, as discussed in the previous section. In addition, students also point out that they come in contact with a wide variety of vocabulary due to their different interests:

> **Walküre**: I also think that the vocabulary expands itself quite a lot, if you if you (.) well because you spread your leisure activities over a lot of things (.) that you learn words that now you maybe don't study at school because they're not important, but that you might need later on perhaps
>
> **Unidentified male student**: Yes.
>
> **Walküre**: because now you are interested in it yourself and you need it or so.

Regarding factors that aid the retention of specific words, the main factor mentioned in five of six focus groups is the repetition effect. Many students argue that hearing and seeing words several times helps to remember them:

> **Jane**: it's also an advantage somehow if you also see the words that you hear and you can see how to spell them. The grammar also improves somehow and I also remember how words are spelled, mostly if they appear several times, if I often hear and often see them, then it's in my vocabulary.

Several students also assert that coming across words and expressions repeatedly in different contexts helps them understand their meaning and learn them incidentally:

> **Kira**: and I think 'Why is this word suddenly at school and in a series right the next day' and that's how it works for me and then at some point I understand it, for instance from these three different text contexts where the word appears I know quite accurately what it means.

This finding is in line with participants' overall belief that repetition aids informal language learning and with the literature on the effect of repeated exposure on incidental vocabulary learning (see Webb 2014 for a review). Indeed, repeated encounters with the same words or lexical phrases increase their salience and memorability, while repeatedly engaging in an activity, like for instance listening to the same song or playing the same game more than once, is also regarded as helpful. In addition, Kira expresses the idea that EE benefits language development because it triggers previous knowledge or because students have to use already existing 'school knowledge' in their extramural activities. Similar to recommendations on fluency-focused vocabulary development (Nation 2013; Schmitt 2010), some learners assert that this 'recycling' of language structures outside school helps to consolidate their language competence and thus supports vocabulary learning.

Participants also report that the salience of words in context and their importance for understanding the content plays a role; however, as discussed, these factors seem to make a difference especially in terms of strategy use. In this regard, participants in the focus groups argue for the beneficial effects of their preferred strategies and thus opinions differ widely again. Some students argue that inferring the meaning of words from context helps to remember them best, while others contend that looking words up in dictionaries makes memorising them easier. These differences in opinion also relate to different notions of what it means to know a word and to what the goal of memorising a new word is. Supporters of dictionaries argue that looking up definitions helps them to discover the exact meaning and aids in dealing with multiple word meanings, thus also helping to understand a given word in different contexts. Those who prefer guessing argue that although inferring from context may not be sufficient for being able to explain the exact meaning of a word, they can nevertheless understand and to a certain extent use it. In addition, proponents of guessing seem to argue that the invested mental effort helps to retain at least a vague meaning for these words, an argument similar to the Involvement Load Hypothesis (Laufer and Hulstijn 2001), which also posits that deeper processing leads to higher retention. Indeed, research on the relationship between successful lexical inferencing and gains in vocabulary knowledge has shown that guessing can contribute to incidental vocabulary learning from reading (Elgort 2017; Pulido 2007; Wesche and Paribakht 2010) and listening (Van Zeeland 2014), although this is certainly not always the case. However, research also indicates that dictionary use enhances vocabulary learning from reading (Knight 1994; Laufer and Hill 2000; Laufer and Rozovski-Roitblat 2015; Peters 2007). Studies that have directly compared guessing and dictionary strategies have produced mixed results with some finding little difference in relation to retention rates (Mondria 2003), whereas others found an advantage for guessing (Alahmadi and Foltz 2020) or for dictionary use (Knight 1994; Zou 2016). In the present study, participants' evaluations of whether lexical inferencing or using dictionaries is more useful depend on their personal preferences and on their conception of the learning aim: if it is enough to roughly remember what a word means, then guessing is seen as useful, but if the aim is being able to explain or translate a given word's meaning, dictionaries are the better option.

This discussion of factors that aid the retention of informally learned words again highlights the fact that participants believe in the benefits of extramural activities for vocabulary development even though they disagree on what exactly helps to remember novel lexical items. In accordance with the literature, many learners across groups stress the role of frequency of exposure, but there is great disagreement on the role of different discovery strategies, with most students arguing for the benefits of their own preferred strategy. Interestingly, the only memory strategy mentioned from Schmitt's (1997) taxonomy was actively trying to use the new lexical items productively, but this strategy does not seem to be widespread as it was only mentioned in one group.

5 Conclusion

This contribution is a first attempt to highlight the importance of learner voices in research on informal L2 vocabulary learning as a source that can provide access to adolescents' private worlds. The interview data show that 15- to 16- year-old Viennese teenagers are able to give useful insights into their extramural vocabulary learning strategies and more general beliefs regarding ISLL.

With regard to the four research questions, the majority of the learners evaluate the role of extramural activities in English language learning in general, and vocabulary learning in particular, very positively with only a few students expressing mixed or negative opinions. For Austrian teenagers, acquiring new vocabulary appears to be the most obvious linguistic benefit of engaging in English-language leisure activities and mostly refers to expanding vocabulary size rather than depth. Moreover, examples of lexical learning indicate that students do not only pick up frequently used words or youth slang, but also infrequent vocabulary in a rather formal register.

Adolescents' reports also show that when they encounter an unknown lexical item during their informal leisure activities, they are most likely to try and guess its meaning from context, or, if the content is seemingly irrelevant they might ignore it all together. Yet, while inferring from context emerged as the default method for most participants across all focus groups, there are some who prefer using online dictionaries as it is fast and provides them with the exact meaning. The majority, however, see dictionaries as a last resort to be used when inference and comparisons to other languages fail; for these students, words and phrases only warrant further strategic attention if they are (1) crucial for understanding the content and difficult to infer from context, (2) encountered repeatedly during their extramural activities, or (3) interesting in some way and thus capture their attention. Finally, the most prominent factor that helps participants remember words and phrases is frequency of exposure: repeated encounters both during leisure activities and at school are seen as particularly useful for long-term retention. In addition, students' beliefs in this respect align with their preferred discovery strategy: those who prefer lexical inferencing over dictionary use also argue for benefits in terms of memorisation and vice versa.

Although this study focused on informal second language vocabulary acquisition only, it shows the value of qualitative data for lexical research more generally. By allowing learners to share their experiences of vocabulary learning, we can gain a new perspective on L2 vocabulary acquisition, tap an additional source of data on the inherently private phenomenon of learning and explore individual differences that are all too often obscured by quantitative instruments. In relation to vocabulary research in the emerging field of ISLL, I agree with Schmitt (2019: 267) that the next step should be "[h]aving finer-grained detail about the nature of extramural exposure, and studying how this directly leads to L2 acquisition". Clearly, for such purposes, regular interviews with individual learners over longer periods of time, ideally coupled with direct observations of their actual practices, would be preferable to conducting a round of focus groups. However, one first step towards capturing a more complete picture of the phenomenon of informal second language vocabulary learning is to give learners a voice and include their perspectives in research.

6 Appendix

Quantitative results on vocabulary learning strategies based on the *Extramural English Questionnaire*

Table 1: Frequency of use for vocabulary learning strategies to discover new meanings during leisure time activities based on Schmitt (1997).

	almost never (%)	rarely (%)	often (%)	very often (%)	N
I think about what kind of a word it is (verb, noun . . .).	44.15	35.11	14.89	5.85	188
I try to separate the word into parts that I might now.	19.68	28.72	38.3	13.3	188
I think about if I know a similar word in other languages that I know.	12.77	17.02	40.96	29.26	188
If it comes up in a film or series, I try to guess its meaning with the help of the images and the story line.	7.98	8.51	42.55	40.96	188
If it comes up in a text, I try to guess its meaning from context.	2.66	7.98	43.62	45.74	188
I look it up in a dictionary (also online or on the phone).	9.14	15.59	27.96	47.31	186
I ask somebody (parents, siblings, friends, . . .) what the word means.	29.26	30.85	27.13	12.77	188
I don't do anything.	59.68	27.96	8.06	4.3	186

References

Alahmadi, Alaa & Anouschka Foltz. 2020. Exploring the effect of lexical inferencing and dictionary consultation on undergraduate EFL students' vocabulary acquisition. *PloS one* 15(7). https://doi.org/10.1371/journal.pone.0236798

Anioł, Magdalena. 2011. New media and new literacies: Mapping extracurricular English language competences of Polish and Norwegian adolescents. In Maria Kaczmarek (ed.), *Health and Wellbeing in Adolescence: Part Two. Media*, 101–124. Poznań: Bogucki Wydawnictwo Naukowe.

Arndt, Henriette L. 2019. *Informal second language learning: The role of engagement, proficiency, attitudes, and motivation*. Oxford: University of Oxford dissertation.

Barbee, Matthew. 2013. Extracurricular L2 input in a Japanese EFL context: Exposure, attitudes, and motivation. *Second Language Studies* 32(1). 1–58.

Bytheway, Julie. 2015. A taxonomy of vocabulary learning strategies used in massively multiplayer online role-playing games. *CALICO Journal* 32(3). 508–527.

Cobb, Tom. 2007. Computing the vocabulary demands of L2 reading. *Language Learning & Technology* 11(3). 38–63.

Creamer, Elizabeth G. 2018. *An Introduction to Fully Integrated Mixed Methods Research.* Thousand Oaks: Sage Publications.

Creswell, John W. & Dana Miller. 2000. Determining validity in qualitative inquiry. *Theory into Practice* 39(3). 124–130.

Creswell, John W., Vicki L. Plano Clark, Michelle L. Gutmann & William E. Hanson. 2003. Advanced mixed methods research designs. In Abbas Tashakkori & Charles Teddlie (eds.), *Handbook of Mixed Methods in Social and Behavioral Research*, 209–240. Thousand Oaks: Sage Publications.

De Wilde, Vanessa, Marc Brysbaert & June Eyckmans. 2020. Learning English through out-of-school exposure: Which levels of language proficiency are attained and which types of input are important? *Bilingualism: Language and Cognition* 23. 171–185.

De Wilde, Vanessa, Marc Brysbaert & June Eyckmans. 2021. Formal versus informal L2 learning: How do individual differenes and word-related variables influence French and English L2 vocabulary learning in Dutch-speaking children? *Studies in Second Language Acquisition* 44(1). 87–111.

De Wilde, Vanessa & June Eyckmans. 2017. Game on! Young learners' incidental language learning of English prior to instruction. *Studies in Second Language Learning and Teaching* 7(4). 673–694.

Dressman, Mark. 2020. Introduction. In Mark Dressman & Randall Sadler (eds.), *The Handbook of Informal Language Learning*, 1–12. Hoboken/Chichester: Wiley-Blackwell.

Elgort, Irina. 2017. Incorrect inferences and contextual word learning in English as a second language. *Journal of the European Second Language Association* 1(1). 1–11.

Elgort, Irina & Paul Warren. 2014. L2 vocabulary learning from reading: Explicit and tacit lexical knowledge and the role of learner and item variables. *Language Learning* 64(2). 365–414.

Ellis, Rod. 1999. Factors in the incidental acquisition of second language vocabulary from oral input. In Rod Ellis (ed.), *Learning a Second Language Through Interaction*, 35–61. Amsterdam: John Benjamins.

Fan, May Y. 2003. Frequency of use, perceived usefulness, and actual usefulness of second language vocabulary strategies: A study of Hong Kong learners. *The Modern Language Journal* 87(2). 222–241.

Fitzpatrick, Tess. 2012. Tracking the changes: Vocabulary acquisition in the study abroad context. *The Language Learning Journal* 40(1). 81–98.

González-Fernández, Beatriz & Norbert Schmitt. 2015. How much collocation knowledge do L2 learners have? The effects of frequency and amount of exposure. *International Journal of Applied Linguistics* 166(1). 94–126.

Grau, Maike. 2009. Worlds apart? English in German youth cultures and in educational settings. *World Englishes* 28(2). 160–174.

Haastrup, Kirsten. 1991. *Lexical Inferencing Procedures or Talking about Words: Receptive Procedures in Foreign Language Learning with Special Reference to English.* Tübingen: Gunter Narr Verlag.

Ingvarsdóttir, Hafdís & Ásrún Jóhannsdóttir. 2017. Learning and using English: The views of learners at the end of compulsory education. In Birna Arnbjörnsdóttir & Hafdís Ingvarsdóttir (eds.), *Language Development across the Life Span: The Impact of English on Education and Work in Iceland*, 79–94. Cham: Springer.

Jóhannsdóttir, Ásrún. 2017. English exposure and vocabulary proficiency at the onset of English instruction. In Birna Arnbjörnsdóttir & Hafdís Ingvarsdóttir (eds.), *Language Development across the Life Span: The Impact of English on Education and Work in Iceland*, 57–78. Cham: Springer.

Kalaja, Paula, Riikka Alanen, Åsa Palviainen & Hannele Dufva. 2011. From milk cartons to English roommates: Content and agency in L2 learning beyond the classroom. In Phil Benson & Hayo Reinders (eds.), *Beyond the Language Classroom*, 47–58. Basingstoke: Palgrave Macmillan.

Kalaja, Paula, Ana M. F. Barcelos, Mari Aro & Maria Ruohotie-Lyhty. 2016. *Beliefs, Agency and Identity in Foreign Language Learning and Teaching*. London: Palgrave Macmillan.

Knight, Susan. 1994. Dictionary use while reading: The effects on comprehension and vocabulary acquisition for students of different verbal abilities. *The Modern Language Journal* 78(3). 285–299.

Kusyk, Meryl. 2017. The development of complexity, accuracy and fluency in L2 written production through informal participation in online activities. *CALICO Journal* 34(1). 75–96.

Kusyk, Meryl & Geoffrey Sockett. 2012. From informal resource usage to incidental language acquisition: Language uptake from online television viewing in English. *ASp. La revue du GERAS* 62. 45–65.

Lai, Chun. 2015. Perceiving and traversing in-class and out-of-class learning: Accounts from foreign language learners in Hong Kong. *Innovation in Language Learning and Teaching* 9(3). 265–284.

Lai, Chun, Weimin Zhu & Gang Gong. 2015. Understanding the quality of out-of-class English learning. *TESOL Quarterly* 49(2). 278–308.

Lamb, Martin. 2004. 'It depends on the students themselves': Independent language learning at an Indonesian state school. *Language, Culture and Curriculum* 17(3). 229–245.

Laufer, Batia & Monica Hill. 2000. What lexical information do L2 learners select in a CALL dictionary and how does it affect word retention? *Language Learning & Technology* 3(2). 58–76.

Laufer, Batia & Jan H. Hulstijn. 2001. Incidental vocabulary acquisition in a second language: The construct of task-induced involvement. *Applied Linguistics* 22(1). 1–26.

Laufer, Batia & Bella Rozovski-Roitblat. 2015. Retention of new words: Quantity of encounters, quality of task, and degree of knowledge. *Language Teaching Research* 19(6). 687–711.

Lee, Ju S. 2019a. Informal digital learning of English and second language vocabulary outcomes: Can quantity conquer quality? *British Journal of Educational Technology* 50(2). 767–778.

Lee, Ju S. 2019b. Quantity and diversity of informal digital learning of English. *Language Learning & Technology* 23(1). 114–126.

Lee, Ju S. & Mark Dressman. 2018. When IDLE hands make an English workshop: Informal digital learning of English and language proficiency. *TESOL Quarterly* 52(2). 435–445.

Lyrigkou, Christina. 2018. Not to be overlooked: Agency in informal language contact. *Innovation in Language Learning and Teaching* 16(4). 1–16.

Meara, Paul. 2015. "V_YesNo: a Yes/No vocabulary test for English (v1.01)". http://www.lognostics.co.uk/tools/V_YesNo/V_YesNo.htm (accessed 18 November, 2015)

Meara, Paul & Tess Fitzpatrick. 2000. Lex30: An improved method of assessing productive vocabulary in an L2. *System* 28(1). 19–30.

Media Consulting Group. 2009. "Study on the use of subtitling: The potential of subtitling to encourage foreign language learning and improve the mastery of foreign languages". https://publications.europa.eu/en/publication-detail/-/publication/e4d5cbf4-a839-4a8a-81d0-7b19a22cc5ce/language-en (accessed 17 July, 2018)

Moir, Jo & I.S.P. Nation. 2002. Learners' use of strategies for effective vocabulary learning. *Prospect* 17 (1). 15–35.

Mondria, Jan-Arjen. 2003. The effects of inferring, verifying and memorizing on the retention of L2 word meanings: An experimental comparison of the "meaning-inferred method" and the "meaning-given method". *Studies in Second Language Acquisition* 25(4). 473–499.

Nation, I.S.P. 2001. *Learning Vocabulary in Another Language*. Cambridge: Cambridge University Press.

Nation, I.S.P. 2013. *Learning Vocabulary in Another Language*, 2nd edn. Cambridge: Cambridge University Press.

Nightingale, Richard. 2016. *The effect of out-of-school media contact on language attitudes in multilingual adolescents: A complex psycho-sociolinguistic system*. Castelló de la Plana: Jaume I University dissertation.

Nunan, David & Jack C. Richards. 2015. Preface. In David Nunan & Jack C. Richards (eds.), *Language Learning Beyond the Classroom*, xi–xvi. New York: Routledge.

Olsson, Eva. 2012. "Everything I read on the internet is in English": On the impact of extramural English on Swedish 16-year-old pupils' writing proficiency. *ROSA Report* 15. http://www.kultur.gu.se/digitalAssets/1325/1325748_olsson-eva-lic.pdf (accessed 7 July, 2014)

Olsson, Eva & Liss K. Sylvén. 2015. Extramural English and academic vocabulary: A longitudinal study of CLIL and non-CLIL students in Sweden. *Apples – Journal of Applied Language Studies* 9(2). 77–103.

Pellicer-Sánchez, Ana & Norbert Schmitt. 2010. Incidental vocabulary acquisition from an authentic novel: Do Things Fall Apart? *Reading in a Foreign Language* 22(1). 31–55.

Pellicer-Sánchez, Ana & Norbert Schmitt. 2012. Scoring yes-no vocabulary tests: Reaction time vs. nonword approaches. *Language Testing* 29(4). 489–509.

Persson, Liv & Tineke Prins. 2012. Learning English inside and outside the classroom. In Nel De Jong, Kasper Juffermans, Merel Keijzer & Laurent Rasier (eds.), *Papers of the Anéla 2012 Applied Linguistics Conference*, 3–13. Delft: Uitgeverij Eburon.

Peters, Elke. 2007. Manipulating L2 learners' online dictionary use and its effect on L2 word retention. *Language Learning & Technology* 11(2). 36–58.

Peters, Elke. 2018. The effect of out-of-class exposure to English language media on learners' vocabulary knowledge. *ITL - International Journal of Applied Linguistics* 169(1). 142–168.

Peters, Elke. 2020. Factors affecting the learning of single-word items. In Stuart Webb (ed.), *The Routledge Handbook of Vocabulary Studies*, 125–142. Abingdon: Routledge.

Peters, Elke, Ann-Sophie Noreillie, Kris Heylen, Bram Bulté & Piet Desmet. 2019. The impact of instruction and out-of-school exposure to foreign language input on learners' vocabulary knowledge in two languages. *Language Learning* 69(3). 747–782.

Peters, Elke & Stuart Webb. 2018. Incidental vocabulary acquisition through viewing L2 television and factors that affect learning. *Studies in Second Language Acquisition* 40. 551–577.

Puimège, Eva & Elke Peters. 2019. Learners' English vocabulary knowledge prior to formal instruction: The role of learner-related and word-related factors. *Language Learning* 69(4). 943–977.

Pulido, Diana. 2007. The effects of topic familiarity and passage sight vocabulary on L2 lexical inferencing and retention through reading. *Applied Linguistics* 28(1). 66–86.

Qian, David D. 2005. Demystifying lexical inferencing: The role of aspects of vocabulary knowledge. *TESL Canada Journal* 22. 34–54.

Ranta, Elina. 2010. English in the real world vs. English at school: Finnish English teachers' and students' views. *International Journal of Applied Linguistics* 20(2). 156–177.

Schmitt, Norbert. 1997. Vocabulary learning strategies. In Norbert Schmitt & Michael McCarthy (eds.), *Vocabulary: Description, Acquisition and Pedagogy*, 199–227. Cambridge: Cambridge University Press.

Schmitt, Norbert. 1998. Tracking the incremental acquisition of second language vocabulary: A longitudinal study. *Language Learning* 48(2). 281–317.

Schmitt, Norbert. 2010. Key issues in teaching and learning vocabulary. In Rubén Chacón-Beltrán, Christián Abello-Contesse & María d. M. Torreblanca-López (eds.), *Insights into Non-native Vocabulary Teaching and Learning*, 28–40. Bristol: Multilingual Matters.

Schmitt, Norbert. 2019. Understanding vocabulary acquisition, instruction, and assessment: A research agenda. *Language Teaching* 52(2). 261–274.

Schmitt, Norbert & Stephen Redwood. 2011. Learner knowledge of phrasal verbs: A corpus-informed study. In Fanny Meunier, Sylvie de Cock, Gaëtanelle Gilquin & Magali Paquot (eds.), *A Taste for Corpora: In Honour of Sylviane Granger*, 137–207. Amsterdam: John Benjamins.

Schwarz, Marlene. 2020. *Beyond the walls: A mixed methods study of teenagers' extramural English practices and their vocabulary knowledge*. Wien: University of Vienna dissertation.

Sockett, Geoffrey. 2014. *The Online Informal Learning of English*. New York: Palgrave Macmillan.

Sockett, Geoffrey & Denyze Toffoli. 2012. Beyond learner autonomy: A dynamic systems view of the informal learning of English in virtual online communities. *ReCALL* 24(2). 138–151.

Sundqvist, Pia. 2009. *Extramural English matters: Out-of-school English and its impact on swedish ninth graders' oral proficiency and vocabulary*. Karlstad: Karlstad University dissertation.

Sundqvist, Pia. 2019. Commercial-off-the-shelf games in the digital wild and L2 learner vocabulary. *Language Learning & Technology* 23(1). 87–113.

Sundqvist, Pia & Liss K. Sylvén. 2016. *Extramural English in Teaching and Learning: From Theory to Practice*. London: Palgrave Macmillan.

Van Zeeland, Hilde. 2014. Lexical inferencing in first and second language listening. *The Modern Language Journal* 98(4). 1006–1021.

Verspoor, Marjolijn H., Kees De Bot & Eva Van Rein. 2011. English as a foreign language: The role of out-of-school language input. In Annick De Houwer & Antje Wilton (eds.), *English in Europe Today: Sociocultural and Educational Perspectives*, 147–166. Amsterdam: John Benjamins.

Webb, Stuart. 2007. The effects of repetition on vocabulary knowledge. *Applied Linguistics* 28(1). 46–65.

Webb, Stuart. 2014. Repetition in incidental vocabulary learning. In Carol A. Chapelle (ed.), *The Encyclopedia of Applied Linguistics*. Oxford: Blackwell.

Webb, Stuart. 2020. Introduction. In Stuart Webb (ed.), *The Routledge Handbook of Vocabulary Studies*, 1–12. Abingdon: Routledge.

Wesche, Marjorie & Tahereh Paribakht. 2010. *Lexical Inferencing in a First and Second Language: Cross-linguistic Dimensions*. Bristol: Multilingual Matters.

Zou, Di. 2016. Comparing dictionary-induced vocabulary learning and inferencing in the context of reading. *Lexikos* 26. 372–390.

Miho Inaba
9 Mediation in informal language learning activities outside of the classroom
Case studies of learners of Japanese

Abstract: This chapter aims to examine the manner in which language learners undertake their informal language learning in out-of-class contexts. The cases of five Japanese language learners in a beginner course at a Swedish university were chosen because they provided us with insightful examples of learners of a non-English language with limited proficiency in that language. The data was collected through semi-structured interviews on the participants' background and their language learning diaries. Utilising Activity Theory, which is one of the strands of Vygotskyan sociocultural theory, the analysis found that students strategically engaged in informal language learning activities involving Japanese pop culture (e.g., watching anime) using subtitles and the features of multimodal media. It was also revealed that students still paid attention to the language while engaging in these activities, and linguistic knowledge acquired in Japanese classes was utilised to enhance their enjoyment of pop culture material. Based on these findings, this chapter also discusses the pedagogical implications of encouraging beginner level students to undertake informal language learning activities.

Keywords: Activity Theory, mediation, Japanese pop culture, viewing activities, L1 and L2 subtitles, multimodal texts

1 Introduction

The development of information and communications technology (ICT) has significantly transformed the language learning environment by enabling learners to access a variety of resources, tools and communities to support their language learning regardless of the target language (Benson 2013). In the field of Second Language Acquisition (SLA), therefore, the research on out-of-class language learning has recently been attracting more attention, mainly due to online informal language learning (Sockett 2014; Sundqvist and Sylvén 2016). However, the manner in which language learners engage in authentic language use activities

Miho Inaba, Cardiff University, UK

https://doi.org/10.1515/9783110752441-009

outside of the classroom is relatively underexplored, despite its potential to examine the language learning aspects of these activities.

This chapter aims to discuss how learners of the Japanese language undertake informal language learning activities outside of the classroom. "Informal language learning" here signifies "any activities taken consciously or unconsciously by a learner outside of formal instruction that leads to an increase in the learner's ability to communicate in a second (or other non-native) language" (Dressman 2019). More specifically, it includes any activities involving target language use outside of classes, for instance, watching films in a target language in the learner's private time. These activities are undertaken typically with the intention of entertainment or communication with others, and as a result of engaging in these activities, language learning occurs (Sockett 2014). Indeed, the examples found in previous studies, such as language learning activities in the community of online game players (Chik 2014) and through enjoying pop culture materials (Palfreyman 2011) demonstrated that language learning and leisure activities involving target language use are often inseparable (Dressman 2019).

In this chapter, the relevant studies will firstly be reviewed to identify the gap between the previous studies and this study. Subsequently, the theoretical framework of this study, which is Activity Theory, will be introduced. Activity Theory is one of the strands of Vygotskyan sociocultural theory and enables us to observe out-of-class language learning activities within individual and social contexts (Lantolf and Thorne 2006). Employing the viewpoint of Activity Theory, I will explore what and how learners of Japanese undertake activities involving the Japanese language, including how they utilise their knowledge in the target language, their first language (L1) and second language (L2).

As an example of learning a foreign language other than English, learners of Japanese provide insightful examples due to the increasing popularity of Japanese pop culture overseas in combination with ICT development. This has provided various authentic resources in Japanese, such as *anime* (Japanese cartoons), *manga* (Japanese comic books), and films (e.g., Imura 2018; Williams 2006). Furthermore, increased interest in Japanese pop culture has been a salient motivation to start learning the Japanese language (Sakuma 2006), and as a teacher of Japanese, I have observed that many of my students enjoy Japanese *anime* and films before starting to learn Japanese in formal education settings (e.g., a language course at school or university). For this reason, this chapter discusses the data from five students who learned Japanese in a beginner course at a Swedish University.

2 Previous studies on informal language learning outside the classroom

Research in this area has attracted much attention since the 2000s, due to the affordances of computer technology, which have changed the language learning environment beyond the classroom (Benson 2013; Nunan and Richards 2015; Sockett 2014), and a variety of quantitative studies have explored informal language learning activities outside of the classroom setting, including a series of studies on young Swedish learners of English (Sundqvist 2011; Sylvén and Sundqvist 2012, Sundqvist and Wikström 2015), online informal language learning of English (OILE) by university students in France (Kusyk and Sockett 2012), and a study comparing classroom-based and fully autonomous self-directed learners of English in Brazil (Cole and Vanderplank 2016).

Furthermore, multiple studies have been conducted to examine informal language learning in more depth using a case-study approach (e.g., Hannibal Jensen 2019; Kusyk 2019; Sockett and Toffoli 2012). For instance, Hannibal Jensen (2019) interviewed 15 young Danish learners of English while they engaged in online English activities. Drawing on Activity Theory (Lantolf and Thorne 2006), Hannibal Jensen revealed that their interests in English language activities, and their desire to join a larger online community of English motivated them to engage in their English-mediated activities. In addition, because of their interest and motivation in English activities, they employed various strategies, for instance, inferencing unknown words from context and using online tools (Google Translate) to understand messages in English, which enabled even young learners to create affordances for their language learning (van Lier 2000, 2004; Menezes 2011).

Focusing on learners of Japanese, I comprehensively investigated both out-of-class language learning activities undertaken by 15 students who studied Japanese in the classes of intermediate advanced level at an Australian university (Inaba 2018). Similar to the study of Hannibal Jensen (2019), Activity Theory was employed to analyse the data collected through interviews and diary studies. As for the informal language learning, it was found that the students' interests in Japanese pop culture triggered various types of activities including those via the Internet, such as watching *anime* and listening to Japanese pop songs. Moreover, it was revealed that students strategically utilised linguistic resources not only in English (e.g., English subtitles on Japanese *anime* and Google to search for English translations) but also in the target language (e.g., the vocabulary and grammar items that they learned in the class).

The key findings in these studies are that ICT facilitates students' organisation of their own language learning environment based on their preferences and as a part of their private lives. Students actively utilise linguistic resources to undertake informal language learning activities. However, the majority of studies have analysed learners of English at an intermediate to advanced level, and more research is needed to examine cases of learners who study a foreign language other than English. Research should also include beginner-level learners who are less likely to gain full benefit from the rich language resources available online because these authentic materials are far beyond their target language proficiency (Lai and Gu 2011). In addition to this, learners' concrete actions while they are engaged in their informal language learning activities (such as how they utilise subtitles in videos and online dictionaries) have been relatively underexplored, despite the possibility of these actions to significantly influence L2 development (Cole and Vanderplank 2016). Accordingly, this study will focus on Japanese language learners at a beginner level, and how they engage in their informal learning activities.

3 Activity theory

To explore the manner in which learners engage in out-of-class language learning activities, this study has employed sociocultural perspectives, in particular, Activity Theory. This theory originates from the work of Vygotsky and his colleagues on human mental development and was constructed by Vygotsky's collaborator, Leont'ev (1978). The central notion in Activity Theory is *mediation*, which is Vygotsky's fundamental claim that humans interact with objects in the social-material world through the mediation of artifacts, such as physical and symbolic tools and cultural concepts, including languages (Lantolf 2000; Lantolf and Thorne 2006).

Leont'ev (1978) developed Vygotsky's notion of mediated action and employed the concept of activity. In Leont'ev's framework, an activity is inextricably connected to the concept of motive, which is the biological or social need or desire to lead human activity towards a specific object. Leont'ev also postulated that an activity can be driven by multiple motives, which are "sense-forming motives" and "motive-stimuli" (1978: 123). Where sense-forming motives are regarded as more important motives that provide the main meanings for activities, the motive-stimuli refer to less important motives that provide additional meanings but do not alter the primary meaning of the activity. In the case of informal language learning activities, communication or entertainment are the main aims (Sockett 2014), and can be regarded as a sense-forming motive. However, as I have discussed elsewhere (Inaba 2018), language learners often hold expectations of learning their target language as motive-stimuli even when their main aim is to enjoy authentic materials, and it is highly likely that both types of motives influence how they engage in such activities.

Engeström (1987, 1999, 2001) further developed Activity Theory and proposed an Activity System model by adding three elements to the traditional tripartite conceptualisation (subject, mediating artifacts, and object) of mediated activity: the community or communities in which the subject is embedded; the rules and norms that regulate the activity; and the division of labour among members of the community. In this Activity System model, a subject's action towards the object of each activity is mediated by all these factors which are potentially interrelated.

In Engeström's activity system model, a central activity system (targeted activity system) is linked to multiple neighbouring activities, which influence the elements of the activity system, such as subject, rules, material and symbolic tools, and additionally future activity in which the outcomes of a central activity are embedded (Engeström 1987, 1999; Lantolf and Thorne 2006). For instance, in the current study, learners' informal language learning outside of the classroom may be situated in different activity systems, including not only students' personal activities (e.g., enjoying pop culture as hobbies) but also language classes at the university as the participants in this study were learning the language at the university during the data collection period. Thus, informal language learning might be mediated through other factors in such activity systems.

From an Activity Theory perspective, students' Japanese language skills can be understood as a mediating artifact (tool) to undertake informal language learning activities, for instance, watching *anime*. However, for learners of Japanese at a beginner level, there is generally a significant gap between the participants' language skills and the required level of the target language for the activities that they wish to undertake. In Activity Theory, this gap is interpreted as a "contradiction" (Engeström 2001: 135). Contradictions have been defined as "a misfit within elements, between them, between different activities, or between different developmental phases of a single activity" (Kuutti 1996: 34) and are considered to be an impetus for change and development in activity systems. They are essential to understand what prompts individuals' concrete actions within an activity system (Barab et al. 2002). In the case of language learners, they have to compensate this contradiction between their L2 skills and the object (e.g., enjoying *anime*) by utilising other mediational means available in their activity system(s) under the influence of their motives for the activities (Inaba 2018; Spence-Brown 2004, 2007).

As outlined above, Activity Theory thus shares common ground with the Complex Dynamic Systems (CDS) perspective, which views any change and development in a system as emerging out of the dynamic interaction of multiple components and their connected systems (Larsen-Freeman and Cameron 2008). Although CDS perspective has often been cited as a theoretical basis for informal language learning,

Activity Theory provides researchers with a more concrete analytical lens, such as motives, mediating artifacts, and communities, to investigate how learners engage in informal learning activities.

Therefore, this study employs Activity Theory to investigate how learners of Japanese engage in informal learning activities, by examining the following research questions:
1. What tools do the participants use to support these language learning activities, and
2. How do they engage in their language learning activities utilising such tools under the influence of individual and contextual factors?

As will be introduced in the following section, the participants of the current study are students attending a Japanese course at university. Consequently, their Japanese classes are regarded as one of the factors influencing the their informal language learning activities. Therefore, through exploring these research questions, this study also aims to identify the influence of language classes with the purpose of providing pedagogical suggestions.

4 Methodology

The present study is a continuation of my previous research conducted in Australia (Inaba 2018), and investigates the informal language learning undertaken by beginner-level students studying Japanese at a Swedish university. This section will firstly describe the Swedish context for learning Japanese before introducing the participants. Subsequently, the data collection method will be outlined.

4.1 The Swedish context of learning Japanese

Due to the popularity of Japanese pop culture in Sweden, an increasing number of institutions, such as secondary schools and other educational institutions (e.g., lifelong learning centres), have begun to offer Japanese lessons/courses. Therefore, Japanese has become more accessible for school children than ever before, although universities are still the main providers of Japanese language education (Japan Foundation 2017). Indeed, all of the participants in this study started learning Japanese at a tertiary level, though they enjoyed Japanese pop culture materials, such as *anime* and video games before learning Japanese at university.

4.2 Participants

The participants are five students who studied Japanese at a beginner level in a Swedish university. As mentioned previously, I chose students of this level because the informal language learning of beginner-level students is underexplored. However, the examples from my previous study (Inaba 2018), which investigated out-of-class language learning activities undertaken by intermediate to advanced level Japanese learners in Australia, are partially utilised in this chapter for comparison.

The participants were recruited in February 2014 through emails targeted at students of a Japanese program at a Swedish university. There are five participants: Ida, Fredrik, Lucas, Johanna and Elin (pseudonyms). All the participants except Elin were born in Sweden. Elin is German and moved to Sweden when she was seven years old. In the interview, Elin explained that she was comfortable with both German and Swedish, but she only spoke German with her family.

At the start of the data collection period, all the participants were enrolled in the same first year course of the Japanese studies programme at the university, which is equivalent to CEFR A1–A2. Table 1 below provides basic information on the participants.

Table 1: Background of the participants.

Name (pseudonym)	Ida	Fredrik	Lucas	Johanna	Elin
Nationality	Swedish	Swedish	Swedish	Swedish	German
Japanese study before university	None	Self-directed study	One year distance course	One year at a life-long learning centre	One year at a high school in Sweden and one year exchange at a Japanese high school
Length of Japanese study at university before the data collection	6 months (1 year interruption after the first semester)	11 months	6 months	6 months	6 months
Experience in Japan (before the data collection period)	None	Short trip (a couple of weeks)	None	None	One year exchange at a Japanese high school

Table 1 (continued)

Name (pseudonym)	Ida	Fredrik	Lucas	Johanna	Elin
Major	Psychology	Engineering	Japanese	Japanese	Japanese
Home language	Swedish	Swedish and Cantonese	Swedish	Swedish	Swedish and German

As shown in the table, all the participants except Ida had learning experiences of Japanese in a variety of manners before attending university, for instance, self-study using mobile apps (Fredrik), a distance course (Lucas), and study at a lifelong learning centre (Johanna). Having said that, their learnings through these prior experiences were limited to, for instance, greetings and Japanese characters including a small number of *kanji*. However, Elin was an exception because she had an immersion experience at a Japanese high school, participating in a one-year exchange programme. Indeed, she was able to maintain conversations in Japanese with me on daily topics, and based on this observation, it is reasonable to say that her proficiency level was close to B1, though she was required to take this beginner-level course for her degree. Interestingly, however, there was no significant difference in the ways in which Elin and the other participants undertook their informal language learning activities, as will be discussed in the following sections.

In relation to their learning experiences, all the participants remarked that their exposure to Japanese pop culture media was a catalyst for their interest in the Japanese language. In Sweden, a number of TV shows, TV drama serials and films from the UK and the USA are broadcasted in English with Swedish subtitles. However, a couple of Japanese *anime* TV series dubbed in Swedish, such as Pokémon and Sailor Moon, were broadcast on TV when the participants were school children. The participants watched these TV series as children, which they later understood to be *anime* in their teenage years and started watching them under the influence of their friends at school, subsequently becoming interested in the language. As discussed in the findings, the participants' interest in Japanese pop culture is inextricably connected to their informal language learning outside of the classroom.

Among the five participants, Ida and Fredrik had a major other than Japanese. However, the number of classes they took were the same as the other students, totalling eight contact hours for Japanese language lessons and one Japanese linguistics class per week. This is possible due to the flexibility of the degree system at the Swedish university. For instance, Ida initially studied Japanese for only one semester as a part of her Psychology degree and returned to the Japanese course after completing her degree. Fredrik studied both Engineering and Japanese at the same time – it was possible at the university if students could manage it.

4.3 Data collection

To explore how learners of Japanese engage in informal language learning in detail, this study employs a qualitative research method. Thus, data were collected through semi-structured interviews and language learning diaries for one to two weeks, along with a retrospective type of interview to gather richer data on the participants' informal language learning experiences and influential factors in their learning environments. I employed learning diaries because they are widely recognised in the field of second language acquisition as a useful as well as non-intrusive method of collecting data from an "insider" perspective (Dörnyei 2007: 157). The diaries were written in English, and the interviews were conducted in English because English was a language common to both the participants and the researcher.

The basic data-collection procedure was as follows: (1) a semi-structured interview (60–90 minutes) was conducted to gather information on the participants' backgrounds; (2) the first language learning diary entry was obtained in digital or paper format, and a subsequent interview was conducted; (3) the second diary entry was obtained in the same way as the first diary entry, followed by an interview. All five participants completed the background interview and the first diary study and accompanying interview from March to April 2014, which was their second semester of the Japanese course. Approximately eight to nine months later, the second diary study was conducted between December and January 2015. Only Ida and Lucas fully completed this second round of the diary study, and Fredrik participated in the interview without submitting the diary entries. Although the comparison between the first and second diary studies provided insightful examples, this chapter focuses on the first diary study along with the information from the background interviews to explore informal language learning by beginner-level learners.

The transcribed interview data and the diary entries of each case were coded to determine what types of tools the participants utilised and significant themes related to these tools, based on the factors outlined in Engeström's activity system model (1987, 1999, 2001), including the influence of motives on the participant's choice of tools and the role of the Japanese classes as a linked activity system. Subsequently, the coded data were thematically analysed to examine the way the participants engaged in the informal learning activities outside of the classroom.

5 Findings

The participants of this study reported a number of informal language learning activities despite their proficiency level. Firstly, this section will present the overall picture of their activities involving the Japanese language. Subsequently, I will examine the ways in which the students engaged in such activities, including the linguistic resources they relied on and the possibility of learning the language.

5.1 Overview of the participants' informal language learning activities

The majority of the informal learning activities of Japanese observed in this study were undertaken online or in a digital format. All the students reported viewing activities: watching *anime* (Ida, Lucas, Johanna and Elin), TV drama series (Fredrik), films (Lucas), video clips of TV shows (Fredrik) and TV commercials via video streaming sites (e.g., Netflix, YouTube) or downloaded videos from video-sharing sites (Elin). The *anime*, TV drama series and films were available with English subtitles, including "fansubs" (Leonard 2005: 282) which are voluntarily translated by fans of Japanese pop culture. The participants also reported listening to an *anime* soundtrack (Elin), communicating on Facebook with fellow students and exchange students (Fredrik), reading posts by a favourite *anime* writer on Twitter, and viewing an anonymous imageboard website (Lucas). The activities other than those undertaken online, or in digital format were also reported: talking with exchange students from Japanese universities (Fredrik, Lucas), reading a paper *manga* book (Ida) and watching films at the cinema (Lucas and Johanna).

Among these activities, watching *anime* or a TV drama series online were most frequently reported, from three times to nine times during the two-week diary study. However, the amount of time spent on these viewing activities differed depending on each participant and her/his circumstances (e.g., the amount of homework and time spent on exam preparation). For instance, Lucas reported watching *anime* six times over the two-week period, and often watched two to three episodes in one day (one episode was approximately 30 minutes), and Fredrik reported watching a whole Japanese TV drama series over a weekend (one episode was approximately 45 minutes, with eight to ten episodes for one series).

As previous studies claim (e.g., Sockett 2014; Toffoli and Sockett 2010), it is reasonable to say that the availability of these materials via video streaming sites enables the participants to engage in these activities. In addition to this point, it is worth remembering their initial motivation for learning Japanese. In the first interview, they all explained that they enjoyed Japanese *anime* or video games before learning Japanese, and this was the way that they became interested in the Japanese language. For instance, Ida reported that she started subscribing to other countries' Netflix accounts because more *anime* videos are available on Netflix in English speaking countries than in Sweden. It is thus reasonable to claim that their interests in Japanese pop culture triggered these informal learning activities.

There are also a couple of differences from previous studies. For instance, listening to English songs via on-demand music services was one of the most popular activities in studies in the 2010s (e.g., Kusyk 2017; Sockett and Toffoli 2012), whereas only one participant in this study reported listening to Japanese songs (an *anime* soundtrack). In addition, only two students in this study reported online written communication once over two weeks, though this type of activity was one of the most frequently reported using productive skills (e.g., Kusyk 2017; Sockett and Toffoli 2012).

In-depth discussion about these differences is beyond the scope of this chapter. However, one possible reason might be the difference in the participants' proficiency level. The participants in the previous studies were at an intermediate level (B1–B2), whereas the students in the current study are beginner-level students (A1–A2). For instance, compared to watching *anime* with English subtitles, listening to songs in a target language might be more challenging for beginner-level students because English subtitles are not usually available for this type of media, and students need to seek out different resources, for example, a website with translations of the lyrics, as found in previous studies on intermediate to advanced level learners (Inaba 2018; Sockett and Toffoli 2012). Furthermore, it is also reasonable to assume that the complexity of the Japanese writing system, which is comprised of three different types of characters namely *kanji*, *hiragana* and *katakana*, might prevent students at a beginner level from engaging in online written communication. The following subsections focus on viewing activities and the activity of reading *manga*, for which the students provided detailed examples.

5.2 Online viewing activities with English subtitles

As mentioned previously, all the participants reported that they undertook online viewing activities, such as watching *anime*, TV drama series and films with English subtitles, which are more widely available than those with Swedish subtitles. Although English is a foreign language for the participants, it is a more useful mediating artifact for them than Japanese because of their proficiency level in English.

While watching these materials with English subtitles, the participants paid attention to the language. In the diary entries and the subsequent interviews, all the students except Elin stated that they tried to listen to the Japanese audio as much as possible and noticed grammar items and vocabulary that they learned through their Japanese classes. For example, on watching *anime* on Netflix, Ida commented in her diary as follows: ". . . I try to listen as much as possible and I am delighted every time I hear something I understand, which is more and more. I found myself listening especially for the different verb forms . . ." (23rd of March, 2014).

Johanna also described a particular grammar item, *nichigainai* (no doubt about), which she learned in a Japanese linguistics class, and recognised in an *anime* episode that she watched after the exam:

> We had that article [about this grammar item] in the exam, and when I went home like on weekend, and started watching the first episode, and then I saw, I heard that and that was the first time I heard it like outside the class, so and I I understood it and so clearly clearly understood it. It was amazing, and 'Yes, yes, this is working. I understand something'. (Interview on Johanna's 1st learning diary, 14 April 2014)

These comments imply that the students clearly paid attention to the Japanese language, and viewing activities became an opportunity to enhance what they had learned in class. From the Activity Theory perspective, their Japanese classes can also be seen to play the role of an instrument-producing activity (Engeseteröm 1987), which helped to develop a tool to mediate an activity, in this case, the students' knowledge about the language to enjoy Japanese pop culture for entertainment. In other words, the classes influenced their informal language learning even though they are not directly related to each other.

Here, it is worth noting again that the students' initial motivation for learning Japanese was closely connected to their interest in Japanese pop culture. As Leont'ev (1978) claims, it can be anticipated that this motive would result in their desire to understand the Japanese audio, and notice what they learned in class. Indeed, Ida described her out-of-class activities as 'mixing business and pleasure' (Interview on Ida's first diary).

Interestingly, the participants did not report what they learned through engaging in these viewing activities, except that Fredrik picked up a particular phrase from a Japanese drama. In contrast, a number of the participants in Australia reported that they picked up words and phrases while enjoying Japanese pop culture materials and recognised them in tasks and learning materials in their Japanese classes. In addition, the aforementioned studies on informal English learning also found that the participants learned new vocabulary, expressions and speech styles through their informal language use (e.g., Sockett and Toffoli 2012).

This difference might be caused by the difference in the participants' proficiency levels. The participants in the previous studies, including those in Australia were at an intermediate to advanced level, and therefore, it is anticipated that their language skills should be sufficient to recognise new vocabulary and expressions in authentic materials. On the contrary, as the participants in the current study were at a beginner level, their language skills might not have enabled them to pick up new words and phrases from videos.

From the Activity Theory perspective, a student's target language skills can be viewed as one of the tools used to mediate their informal language learning activities, and this tool in the beginner-level students differs from the tool of the intermediate advanced level students. In other words, their language skills mediate their informal learning activities differently. More precisely, whereas viewing activities can be an opportunity to learn new vocabulary and expressions for the intermediate advanced level learners, the same activity might represent only an opportunity to practice what has been learned in the classroom for the beginner-level students.

5.3 Viewing activities with Swedish subtitles

Two students in the current study, Lucas and Johanna, also reported viewing activities with Swedish subtitles, which were Japanese films at the cinema. Interestingly, both students commented on the quality of the Swedish subtitles in their diary entries. For instance, in his diary entry, Lucas spotlighted the subtitle from one scene in a Japanese *anime* film, *Kaze Tachinu* (The Wind Rises). He stated, "they could have translated that in a more beautiful way" (8th April 2014). In the interview, he explained this translation in more detail:

> The way they wrote it in Swedish was very like, how should I say it, very square, so it's like, it was a very stiff way to convey the message like what actually happened. . . . I mean it's like um she was swept away like the wind or something like it was the way said in Japanese was more was more beautiful than the way it was written in Swedish. (Interview on Lucas' first learning diary, 14 April 2014).

Similarly, Johanna reported watching the Japanese drama film, *Soshite Chichi ni Naru* (Like Father, Like Son), remarking that "at many times I felt that the translation was not at all reflecting the depth of the Japanese language" (Johanna's diary entry on 7th April 2014). Johanna further commented on this point in the interview as follows: "maybe maybe feel like 'OK, that's what they said, but that's not what they mean', so when they're just heard like, really careless translation" (Interview on Johanna's first learning diary, 14 April 2014).

Given that only 43% of the original lines of visual materials are translated into subtitles due to space limitations (de Linde and Kay 2009), it is reasonable to anticipate that even beginner-level students can notice differences between the subtitles and the original audio. Interestingly, however, the comparisons between the Japanese language and the subtitles were observed only in the viewing activities with Swedish subtitles, but not in those with English subtitles.

From the Activity Theory perspective, this difference in the viewing activities can be explained by the influence of the mediating artifacts. Lantolf (2006) reviews the findings in studies on L1 and L2 private speech in cognitively difficult tasks and claims that fluency and proficiency in the L2 for social interaction does not mean that the L2 can be utilised as a mediational means to regulate cognitive activities, because the L2 is likely to occupy a certain amount of the speaker's attention. Although Sweden has been consistently ranked as one of the top countries in the EF English proficiency index (EF Education First 2020), it is reasonable to anticipate that comparing the Japanese expressions to English subtitles, while understanding the content, might be more cognitively demanding than just following the storyline with English subtitles. Moreover, none of the participants had a prolonged experience in English-speaking countries. It is highly likely that the participants view English as their foreign language, and this attitude toward English might inhibit them to comment on the English subtitles.

Another interpretation of this difference is the influence of their learning experiences in the Japanese classes, which is one of the activity systems linked to their informal language learning outside of the classroom. As part of their reading exercises, the participants studied and translated Japanese texts into Swedish in Japanese classes. This learning experience might lead their attention to a comparison between the Japanese language in films and the Swedish subtitles.

5.4 Viewing activities with Japanese subtitles

On video sharing sites, it is possible to access video clips of Japanese TV shows with Japanese subtitles. However, the Japanese subtitles mentioned here are not the same as those which are utilised for translations of foreign languages on TV dramas and movies, nor the closed caption services for people with hearing impediments. Particularly in Japanese variety shows, the Japanese subtitles have frequently been employed to clarify the main points made by cast members; showing what they say or placing an emphasis on particular parts of their speech (Suto 2008).

In my previous studies in Australia (Inaba 2018), two participants reported that they watched videos of Japanese variety shows with such subtitles. One of these students is Lisa, who studied in the advanced class, and regularly watched her favourite Japanese variety shows by relying on Japanese subtitles in order to understand the content. Considering the fact that Lisa had never visited Japan, she might not have acquired sufficient listening skills or colloquial expressions to understand authentic Japanese conversations.

In the current study on Swedish students, only Frederik reported watching videos of Japanese TV shows which included Japanese subtitles. However, he explained that he relied more on the audio than the subtitles, and added the following comments: "[I read the subtitles] sometimes. It depends. If it is a really long caption with katakana [a type of Japanese characters], I don't really read them." (Interview on Fredrik's 1st diary 4th April 2014).

This difference between Lisa and Fredrik might again stem from the differences in their proficiency level, in particular, their reading skills. As Lisa studied at the advanced level of the classes, it is reasonable to say that she could read Japanese texts with good speed. In contrast, Fredrik was in the beginner course, and his comment above implies that reading long subtitles was challenging for him.

In his research on the effectiveness of watching videos with L2 subtitles, Vanderplank (1988) suggested that L2 subtitles would be beneficial for learners with weaker L2 listening skills and stronger reading skills. This claim is applicable to Lisa's case because she was at the advanced level, and had good knowledge of *kanji* (a Japanese version of Chinese characters) as a heritage speaker of Chinese. Although Fredrik is also a heritage speaker of Chinese, he explained that he only utilised Chinese verbally with his parents and he had learned only basic Chinese characters. In addition, Fredrik has been a fan of Japanese pop culture since high school and continued watching *anime*. Given this fact, his listening skills might be stronger than his reading skills. In other words, the effectiveness of tools may vary depending on the level of each language skill.

5.5 Reading *manga*

Manga is one of the best-known types of Japanese pop culture media. However, reading *manga* in Japanese was reported by only one student in the current study, Ida. A similar result was found in my previous study on Australian students (Inaba 2018), where only three out of 15 participants reported reading *manga* in Japanese. One of the possible reasons for this result is the availability of translated *manga* books. For instance, Elin, who is bilingual in Swedish and German, reported that she often purchased *manga* books translated into German when she visited Germany because they were cheaper than those in Sweden.

Although no participants in the current study reported accessing digitised *manga* translated by fans, these are widely available via online fan communities and are regarded as a factor in the successful popularisation of *manga* overseas (Lee 2009; Fabbretti 2017).

More importantly, *manga* in Japanese are written for native speakers, and therefore include a large amount of *kanji* as well as colloquial expressions and unusual writing conventions, which are not fully taught in Japanese classes. Consequently, even the students at intermediate to advanced levels from my previous study reported difficulty in reading *manga* in Japanese (Inaba 2018). Given all of these features that relate to *manga* as authentic Japanese language, it is reasonable to claim that reading *manga* in Japanese is challenging for learners, in particular, for beginners. Indeed, Ida explained her reading activity of a *manga* book which she borrowed from her friends in the intermediate classes: "When I started out reading it, I looked up every word that I didn't know and I read like two or three pages per night, but it was too slow". (Interview on Ida's first diary, 15th April 2014).

Ida started reading this *manga* book because "I always read something for a sleep, so why not something Japanese" (Ida's interview on her first diary, 15th April 2014), in other words, to relax before sleep. However, the above excerpt implies that reading the *manga* book became a time-consuming task. Consequently, Ida altered her way of reading the *manga*, utilising the features of this media as a multimodal text: "It's fun to read for a bit and when I don't understand the words I at least get the gist of it from the pictures and the words I do understand" (Ida's diary entry on 31st March 2014).

In the interview, Ida further explained this diary entry: ". . . I just kept on reading without exactly knowing what they meant so sometimes they come like whole um this um a lot of stuff that I don't know but then I can understand from the pictures, what's going on and so" (Interview on Ida's first diary, 15th April 2014). From the Activity Theory perspective, it can be argued that Ida changed her choice of mediational means from a dictionary to the pictures of *manga* in order to meet her motive, that is to relax before bedtime.

It is also worth noting that Ida still paid attention to the Japanese language, as you can see in her comment: "It's fun to see when they change the way of speaking depending of the situation" (Ida's diary entry on 1st April 2014). In the same interview, she explained that she had just learned polite expressions of Japanese in class, and this was the reason that she "could tell the difference" (Interview on Ida's first diary, 15th April 2014).

This example of Ida is insightful not only for utilising the feature of *manga* as a multimodal text, but also for her attention to the language while enjoying the *manga* for relaxation. In addition, as observed in the viewing activities, the knowledge that Ida gained through the Japanese classes was utilised as a tool to understand the content, that is, the language classes played an important role as an instrument-producing activity in informal learning outside of the classroom.

6 Concluding remarks and implications for language teaching

Drawing on the perspectives of Activity Theory, this study explored the manner in which students engage in informal learning activities in their target language, Japanese. To answer the first research question, which is "What tools do the participants use to support these language learning activities?", this work found that the subtitles in English or Swedish were the main tools for the students' viewing activities for entertainment. Given their proficiency in Japanese, this result was predictable. However, viewed from the other side, the availability of such Japanese pop culture materials, in particular, those with English subtitles, enabled beginners to undertake these informal learning activities and consequently increased their exposure to the Japanese language. In relation to this point, it is also worth remarking that subtitles in the target language might not be an effective tool for beginner-level learners, as Fredrik's comment indicates. It is reasonable to claim that subtitles in the L1 or fluent L2 are more effective tools in order to expand informal learning opportunities.

Another interesting finding is Ida's utilisation of pictures in her *manga* reading, as this is an example of an informal learning activity that didn't rely on mediation by English or Swedish. As Hannibal Jensen (2019) found, the features of multimodal media support learners to undertake informal learning activities as mediating artifacts and expand the language learning affordances outside of the classroom.

To answer the second research question, that is, "How do the participants engage in their informal language learning activities utilising such tools under the influence of individual and contextual factors?", the analysis revealed that the students still paid attention to the Japanese language while they were engaging in the activities with the support of tools, such as the subtitles and the pictures of *manga*. This attention to the language might be influenced by their motive of learning Japanese even though their main aim was enjoying the content, as Ida's comment indicates. Furthermore, this finding implies that language learning might be an outcome of conscious engagement in informal language learning rather than being simply a by-product of a communicative intention (Sockett 2011), at least for the participants in the current study.

It is also noteworthy that L1 subtitles (Swedish) and L2 subtitles (English) might function differently as mediating artifacts. As the examples of Lucas and Johanna show, the L1 subtitles triggered comparisons between the subtitles and the Japanese language of the films, though such comparisons were not observed in the viewing activities with English subtitles. In other words, it is highly probable that subtitles in different languages might influence the way in which learners engage in their viewing activities, and consequently, generate different types of learning opportunities; for instance, deeper understanding about the difference in the mode of expressions between their first language and the target language. Given that video streaming sites such as Netflix and Amazon Prime have recently begun to offer more Japanese movies and anime with subtitles not only in English but also in different languages including Swedish, it might be worth pursuing the ways in which different subtitles affect the learner's attention to the Japanese language as well as their language development.

Furthermore, it was revealed that the Japanese classes played an important role in informal language learning in that the participants often noticed the vocabulary and the grammar items that they learned in class. It is also anticipated that the translation exercises might influence the students' attention to the subtitles, as discussed in Lucas' and Johanna's examples of watching films with Swedish subtitles. All these findings indicate that the linguistic knowledge (e.g., vocabulary and grammar items) and skills (e.g., translation skills) acquired in Japanese classes were utilised as tools, at least partially, to enjoy the Japanese pop culture materials.

These findings have clear pedagogical implications to encourage beginner-level learners to undertake informal learning activities outside of the classroom. Firstly, given that the students often noticed the vocabulary and grammar that they learned in the classes during viewing or reading activities, arranging similar opportunities in the classroom could enable learners to realise the benefit of using their leisure time for learning opportunities. In order to achieve this, it is crucial to choose materials which students are interested in and are related to the content of the language classes, so that they can easily notice the words and the grammar that they learned in class.

Secondly, the example of Ida's *manga* reading suggests that beginner students can enjoy *manga* in the target language if they effectively utilise the features of *manga* as a multimodal text. However, given that not only Ida but also Eric, an advanced level learner in my previous study (2018), relied on dictionaries, teacher intervention might be necessary: for instance, in arranging reading activities utilising *manga* in the classroom and practicing inferring meanings from the language as well as the pictures. By doing so, students might be able to improve their ability to read *manga* and possibly learn new vocabulary and expressions which the Japanese classes and textbooks do not usually cover.

Thirdly, it is important to recommend appropriate tools to students, as Fredrik's comment on the Japanese subtitles suggest. Compared to Japanese subtitles, reading English subtitles might be less challenging for English learners at a beginner level. Having said that, it is still challenging for beginners to read the subtitles in a target language because they disappear quickly from the screen. In this case, the subtitles in their L1 or more fluent L2 are more effective for viewing activities in that they expand language affordances outside of the classroom.

This study has several limitations. The case study offered here is comprised of only five students and therefore the findings are not generalisable to a larger population. It is also important to note that this study only analysed university students who were studying Japanese as a foreign language. Thus, it would be helpful to investigate cases of learning different languages within different contexts. In particular, it is worth exploring examples of those who learn a third language and how the support of their L1 and more proficient L2 affect their informal learning activities in their third language.

Furthermore, this study spans a limited time of only one semester; in other words, it was not sufficient to fully examine the developmental aspect of informal learning activities. It is highly probable that learners alter not only the types of language learning activities they undertake outside of the classroom, but also the ways in which they engage in these activities as their target language skills are improved, including what mediational means they utilise. Longitudinal data (for example, throughout a degree program at a university) would be required to explore how students' language skills and their informal learning activities evolve at a deeper level. Despite these limitations, however, the current study does demonstrate the manner in which beginner-level learners undertake informal language learning activities and the potential of language learning in these activities outside of the classroom.

Finally, the study also clearly shows that Activity Theory is potentially an effective framework to investigate informal language learning activities. As presented above, this theory enabled me to explore each activity involving the target language with consideration of various factors, such as the linguistic resources students rely on, motivational factors and the influence of language classes. This framework may be worth utilising for other studies of informal language learning, particularly those employing qualitative research methods.

References

Barab, Sasha A., Michael Barnett, Lisa Yamagata-Lynch, Kurt Squire & Thomas Keating. 2002. Using activity theory to understand the systemic tensions characterizing a technology-rich introductory astronomy course. *Mind, Culture and Activity* 9(2). 76–107.
Benson, Phil. 2013. Learner autonomy. *TESOL quarterly* 47(4). 839–843.
Chik, Alice. 2014. Digital gaming and language learning: Autonomy and community. *Language Learning and Technology*. 18(2). 85–100.
Cole, Jason & Robert Vanderplank. 2016. Comparing autonomous and class-based learners in Brazil: Evidence for the present-day advantages of informal, out-of-class learning. *System* 61. 31–42.
de Linde, Zoé & Neil Kay. 2009. *The Semiotics of Subtitling*. Manchester: St Jerome.
Dörnyei, Zoltan. 2007. *Research Methods in Applied Linguistics*. Oxford: Oxford University Press.
Dressman, Mark. 2019. Introduction. In Mark Dressman & Randall Sadler (eds.), *Handbook of Informal Language Learning*, 1–12. Hoboken/Chichester: Wiley-Blackwell.
EF Education First. 2020. EF English Proficiency Index. https://www.ef.se/epi/regions/europe/sweden/ (accessed 26 August 2021)
Engeström, Yrjö. 1987. *Learning by Expanding: An Activity-Theoretical Approach to Developmental Research*. http://lchc.ucsd.edu/mca/Paper/Engestrom/expanding/toc.htm
Engeström, Yrjö. 1999. Activity theory and individual and social transformation. In Yrjö Engeström, Reijo Miettinen & Raija-Leena Punamäki (eds.), *Perspectives on Activity Theory*, 19–38. New York: Cambridge University Press.
Engeström, Yrjö. 2001. Expansive learning at work: toward an activity theoretical reconceptualization. *Journal of Education and Work* 14(1). 133–156.
Fabbretti, Matteo. 2017. Manga scanlation for an international readership: the role of English as a lingua franca. *The Translator* 23(4). 456–473.
Hannibal Jensen, Signe. 2019. Language learning in the wild: A young user perspective. *Language Learning & Technology* 23(1). 72–86.
Imura, Taeko. 2018. A portrait of Japanese popular culture fans who study Japanese at an Australian university: Motivation and activities beyond the classroom. *East Asian Journal of Popular Culture* 4 (2). 171–188.
Inaba, Miho. 2018. *Second Language Literacy Practices and Language Learning Outside the Classroom*. Bristol: Multilingual Matters.
Japan Foundation. 2017. *Survey Report on Japanese-Language Education Abroad 2015*. Tokyo: Japan Foundation. https://www.jpf.go.jp/j/project/japanese/survey/result/dl/survey_2015/Report_all_e.pdf
Kusyk, Meryl. 2017. The Development of Complexity, Accuracy and Fluency in L2 Written Production through Informal Participation in Online Activities. *CALICO Journal* 34(1). 75–96.
Kusyk, Meryl. 2019. Informal English Learning in France. In Mark Dressman & Randall Sadler (eds.), *Handbook of Informal Language Learning*, 333–348. Hoboken/Chichester: Wiley-Blackwell.
Kusyk, Meryl & Geoffrey Sockett. 2012. From informal resource usage to incidental language acquisition: language uptake from online television viewing in English. *ASp. La Revue du GERAS* 62. 45–65.
Kuutti, Kai. 1996. Activity theory as a potential framework for human-computer interaction research. In Bonnie A. Nardi (ed.), *Context and Consciousness: Activity Theory and Human-Computer Interaction*, 18–44. Massachusetts: The MIT Press.

Lai, Chun & Mingyue, Gu. 2011. Self-regulated out-of-class language learning with technology. *Computer Assisted Language Learning: An International Journal* 24(4). 317–335.

Lantolf, James P. 2000. Introducing sociocultural theory. In James P. Lantolf (ed.), *Sociocultural Theory and Second Language Learning*, 1–26. Oxford: Oxford University Press.

Lantolf, James, P. 2006. Sociocultural theory and L2: State of the Art. *Studies in Second Language Acquisition* 28(1). 67–109.

Lantolf, James, P. and Steven L. Thorne. 2006. *Sociocultural Theory and The Genesis of Second Language Development*. Oxford/New York: Oxford University Press.

Larsen-Freeman, Diane & Lynne Cameron. 2008. *Complex Systems and Applied Linguistics*. Oxford: Oxford University Press.

Lee, Hye-Kyung. 2009. Between fan culture and copyright infringement: manga scanlation. *Media, Culture & Society* 31(6). 1011–1022.

Leonard, Sean. 2005. Progress against the law: Anime and fandom, with the key to the globalization of culture. *International Journal of Cultural Studies* 8(3). 281–305.

Leont'ev, Aleksie N. 1978. *Activity, Consciousness and Personality*. Engelwood Cliffs: Prentice Hall.

Menezes, Vear. 2011. Affordances for language learning beyond the classroom. In Phil Benson & Hayo Reinders (eds.), *Beyond the Language Classroom*, 59–71. Basingstoke: Palgrave Macmillan.

Nunan, David & Jack C. Richards. 2015. Preface. In David Nunan & Jack C. Richards (eds.), *Language Learning Beyond the Classroom*. New York: Routledge.

Palfreyman, David M. 2011. Family, friends, and learning beyond the classroom: Social networks and social capital in language learning. In Phil Benson & Hayo Reinders (eds.), *Beyond the Language Classroom*, 17–34. Basingstoke: Palgrave Macmillan.

Sakuma, Katsuhiko. 2006. Kaigai ni manabu nihongo kyōiku: Nihongo gakushū no tayōsei [Learning from overseas institutions and teaching in Japanese language education: Diversity of Japanese learning]. In Kokuritsu Kokugo Kenkyūjyo (ed.), *Nihongo Kyōiku no Aratana Bunmyaku: Gakushū Kankyō, Sesshoku Bamen, Komyunikēshon no Tayōsei* [The New Context of Japanese Language Education: Learning Environment, Contact Situation and Diversity of Communication], 33–65. Tokyo: Aruku.

Sockett, Geoffrey. 2011. From the cultural hegemony of English to online informal learning: Cluster frequency as an indicator of relevance in authentic documents. *ASp. La Revue du GERAS* 60. 5–20.

Sockett, Geoffrey. 2014. *The Online Informal Learning of English*. Basingstoke: Palgrave Macmillan.

Sockett, Geoffrey & Denyze Toffoli. 2012. Beyond learner autonomy: A dynamic systems view of the informal learning of English in virtual online communities. *ReCALL* 24(2). 138–151.

Spence-Brown, Robyn. 2004. *Authentic assessment? The implementation of an 'authentic' teaching and assessment task*. Melbourne: University of Melbourne dissertation.

Spence-Brown, Robyn. 2007. Learner motivation and engagement in a pedagogic and assessment task. In Helen Marriott, Tim Moore & Robyn Spence-Brown (eds.), *Learning Discourses and Discourses of Learning*, 1–15. Melbourne: Monash University ePress.

Sundqvist, Pia. 2011. A possible path to progress: Out-of-school English language learners in Sweden. In Phil Benson & Hayo Reinders (eds.), *Beyond the Language Classroom*, 106–118. Basingstoke: Palgrave Macmillan.

Sundqvist, Pia & Liss K. Sylvén. 2016. *Extramural English in Teaching and Learning: From Theory and Research to Practice*. London: Palgrave Macmillan.

Sundqvist, Pia & Peter Wikström. 2015. Out-of-school digital gameplay and in-school L2 English vocabulary outcomes. *System* 51. 65–76.

Suto, Hideaki. 2008. Teroppu ga shichōsha ni ataeru eikyō [Influences of telops on the receivers' interpretation]. *Informatics* 1(2). 13–20.

Sylvén, Liss K. & Pia Sundqvist. 2012. Gaming as extramural English L2 learning and L2 proficiency among young learners. *ReCALL* 24(3). 302–321.

Toffoli, Denyze & Geoffrey Sockett. 2010. How non-specialist students of English practice informal learning using web 2.0 tools. *ASp. La Revue du GERAS* 58. 125–144.

van Lier, Leo. 2000. From input to affordance: Social interactive learning from an ecological perspective. In James P. Lantolf (ed.), *Sociocultural Theory and Second Language Learning*, 245–259. Oxford: Oxford University Press.

van Lier, Leo. 2004. *The Ecology and Semiotics of Language Learning: A Sociocultural Perspective.* Dordrecht: Kluwer Academic Publishers.

Vanderplank, Robert. 1988. The value of teletext sub-titles in language learning. *English Language Teaching Journal* 42(4). 272–281.

Williams, Kara L. 2006. *The impact of popular culture fandom on perceptions of Japanese language and culture learning: The case of student anime fans.* Austin: University of Texas dissertation.

Stefanie Cajka, Ed Griffiths, Nikolay Slavkov, Eva Vetter

10 Linguistic risk-taking and informal language learning in Canada and Austria

Perspectives on moving from print to digital

Abstract: In this chapter, we address informal language learning through the pedagogical practice of Linguistic Risk-Taking (Slavkov 2020; Slavkov and Séror 2019), conceived at a Canadian bilingual post-secondary institution and subsequently developed at an Austrian university. The practice is designed to bridge classroom learning and leisure-based, real-life practice. Linguistic risks are opportunities for language learners to execute authentic communicative acts with an affective slant in the target language, outside the classroom. To encourage informal learning through linguistic risk-taking, we developed a passport (in Canada) and a booklet "Riskier was!" (in Austria) with extensive lists of risks involving everyday life and leisure activities in the learners' target languages. In this chapter, we report initially on the development of these paper tools across both sites. Through interviews conducted with participating learners, we show the way in which students perceived a digital version of the initiative as potentially leading to improvements across three dimensions: proximity, personalised experience, and interaction. We proceed to document the development of a mobile linguistic risk-taking app for Android and Apple in Canada. Our work points to considerable benefits of developing a digital linguistic risk-taking app as the next logical step to supplement the paper-based initiative, incorporate the affordances of modern mobile technology, and further foster informal language learning through linguistic risk-taking.

Acknowledgements: We would like to acknowledge all participants, teachers, and contributors to the Linguistic Risk-Taking Initiative in Canada and the "Riskier was!" Booklet in Austria. Special thanks are due to Gurpreet Kaur Saran for developing the version of the digital app discussed in this article and to Laura Bürger for the transcriptions (GAT 2) of the interviews conducted in Austria. We also acknowledge the following funders: Social Sciences and Humanities Research Council of Canada (SSHRC), Canadian Heritage, and the University of Ottawa as well as the University of Vienna, the unit "Language Teaching and Learning Research" and the Language Center of the University of Vienna for their support.

Stefanie Cajka, Eva Vetter, Universität Wien, Austria
Ed Griffiths, Nikolay Slavkov, University of Ottawa, Canada

https://doi.org/10.1515/9783110752441-010

Keywords: Linguistic Risk-Taking, App Development, Multilingualism, Informal Language Learning, MALL, Materials Design

1 Introduction

In this chapter we follow a research and development model where we report on the development of a pedagogical initiative and its subsequent adaptations and modifications, while at the same time-sharing learner feedback data from qualitative interviews and relating those data to the developments. We illustrate how our pedagogical approach termed *linguistic risk-taking* represents informal language learning and offers interesting new avenues for discussion and practical solutions. Building on previous studies examining risk-taking and the language learner (e.g., Beebe 1983; Cervantes 2013), we created the *Linguistic Risk-Taking Initiative* at the University of Ottawa (Griffiths and Slavkov 2021; Rhéaume, Slavkov, and Séror 2021; Slavkov 2020; Slavkov and Séror 2019) and subsequently at the University of Vienna (Cajka 2021). The initiative was designed to supplement classroom activities with real-life and leisure-based informal learning. Slavkov and Séror (2019) defined linguistic risks within the initiative as authentic everyday communicative acts that take place outside of the language classroom and involve meaningful target language use. Accordingly, linguistic risks include many leisure activities like singing karaoke, exploring museums or making social media posts in the target language (see Appendix). A linguistic risk involves both an element of nervousness or anxiety about using the target language in an unknown or potentially challenging situation, and an element of pleasure or feeling of achievement from overcoming the challenge.[1] Central to the implementation of the Linguistic Risk-Taking Initiative was the production of paper passports (in Canada) and a booklet (in Austria) containing pre-determined risks which could be taken in the target language (see Sections 3 and 4).

In this chapter, we move beyond describing the activities learners are engaging in outside the classroom to focus on how the informal language learning practice of linguistic risk-taking can be improved. In line with the digital theme of this volume, we argue that the aim of linguistic risk-taking to encourage informal language learning was improved by the development of a digital version. Data across the two sites – Canada and Austria – support this claim.

---

[1] For a detailed description of the theoretical framework behind the Linguistic Risk-Taking Initiative and its initial operationalisation, please see Slavkov and Séror (2019).

In Section 2, we explain how we position linguistic risk-taking within an informal language learning framework and how theories of mobile-assisted language learning informed our digital development. In Section 3, we describe the bilingual French/English linguistic context at the University of Ottawa in which this initiative was developed and detail its operationalisation through the creation of a Linguistic Risk-Taking Passport. Section 4 looks at how the initiative was adapted to the context of German language learners in Austria. In Section 5, we report on interviews conducted with participating learners across both sites and highlight areas for improvement that emerged from these conversations, focusing on learners' views on realising the initiative in a digital space. Finally, in Section 6, we describe how the initiative has been adapted as an Android and iPhone app in Canada. In our conclusion in Section 7, we summarise our arguments and offer an outlook for further research.

Different studies have been carried out in the two countries using different participants and different methodologies, so in this chapter we do not present the work as a single study with common research questions and methodologies or as a comparison between the two initiatives (in Austria and in Canada). What unifies us is the goal of pedagogical innovation and enhancing informal language learning experiences as well as developing an iterative research process, where we continue to develop a new tool while piloting and receiving feedback from it. We report on these processes here.

2 Literature review

In this section, we show how the initial development of the Linguistic Risk-Taking Initiative relates to existing literature on informal language learning, especially learning beyond the classroom (LBC), and how the subsequent development of the Linguistic Risk-Taking App can be situated within the field of Mobile Assisted-Language Learning (MALL).

2.1 Linguistic risk-taking and informal language learning

All risks in the Linguistic Risk-Taking Initiative were designed to be taken beyond the walls of the language classroom. Therefore, we found Benson's (2011) LBC framework to be a useful schema for positioning linguistic risk-taking. Benson (2011) employed Livingstone's (2006: 211) definition of informal learning as "anything people do to gain knowledge, skill, or understanding from learning about their health or hobbies, unpaid or paid work, or anything else that interests them outside of organised courses".[2] This aligns with the aims of the Linguistic Risk-Taking Initiative.

Benson (2011) developed a preliminary model of four central dimensions of informal learning: location, formality, pedagogy, and locus of control (see also Reinders and Benson 2017). In Table 1, we characterise the Linguistic Risk-Taking Initiative according to these criteria. Although overlap may exist between these categories (cf. Sockett and Toffoli 2020), we find this a useful heuristic within which to place our initiative.

Table 1: Description of the practice of linguistic risk-taking within Benson's (2011) framework.

Dimension	Description[a]	Linguistic risk-taking
Location	Where and when the learning takes place	Out of class learning; learners have a wide range of optional activities to choose from.
Formality	The degree to which learning is linked to educational qualifications or structured by educational institutions	Learning is informal in that risks are taken outside of organised courses (see above); students are given free rein to choose risks according to their interests; risks are not assessed.
Pedagogy	The degree to which teaching is involved	The initiative is introduced and supported in the classroom. Teachers are free to decide the level of classroom support. Learners may discuss their risk-taking experiences in class; teachers may choose to initiate rehearsal tasks or discuss strategic responses (Griffiths and Slavkov 2021).
Locus of control	How decisions are distributed between the learner and others	Learning is self-directed in that learners choose to take risks freely. These may be naturalistic opportunities which occur as part of an individual's routine, or they may be opportunities sought out by the learner explicitly for the purpose of risk-taking. Learning is not entirely independent; teachers suggest participation in the initiative. Some teachers assign credit for participation in the initiative overall, but students choose risks according to their own schedules and interests.

Notes: [a]Descriptions are taken from Reinders and Benson (2017: 562).

---

[2] Benson contrasted informal learning with both formal classroom learning and non-formal learning (classroom-based projects taken for the sake of interest), while acknowledging that the line between informal and non-formal learning was "not always clearly made" (2011: 10).

Dressman (2020: 4) defined informal language learning as referring to "any activities taken consciously or unconsciously by a learner outside of formal instruction that lead to an increase in the learner's ability to communicate in a second (or other, non-native) language". This definition aligns with linguistic risk-taking because the major objective of the latter is to engage in authentic communication in the second language and potentially explore new domains for L2 use. It should be noted that correlating participation in the Linguistic Risk-Taking Initiative with proficiency outcomes is not at present an empirical question considered by the project. Nevertheless, it is assumed that students participating in the initiative are actively seeking out and creating situations where learning can take place. Furthermore, the results of a regression analysis by Lai, Zhu, and Gong (2015) found that the most important factors in the learning outcomes of out-of-class learning may have been whether activities were varied and meaning-focused (to complement in-class focus-on-form activity). The risks in the Linguistic-Taking Initiative clearly represent a variety of meaning-focused activities.

We believe that the Linguistic Risk-Taking Initiative adds to current discussions within the field of informal language learning, since informal language learning is on the rise due to globalisation and especially digitalisation (Dressman 2020) and questions arise in regard to how it affects formal language learning (cf. Dressman 2020; Sockett and Toffoli 2020) and what its pedagogical implications are (cf. Schwarz 2020). In the literature, the development of pedagogical innovations that simplify the connection between formal and informal language learning are considered an important focus (Sockett and Toffoli 2020: 479), and bridging classroom and informal language learning is considered necessary (cf. Schwarz 2020; Hubbard 2020). The Linguistic Risk-Taking Initiative can serve as a link between formal and informal learning, since it is introduced to learners in the classroom but concerns their target language use in the outside world. In this way, it serves as a bridge between the two domains (Griffiths and Slavkov 2021). This also speaks to a call for a move away from employing an in/out-of-class dichotomy to "a continuum or integrated approach" (Sockett and Toffoli 2020: 472). Since the actual process of taking linguistic risks in this initiative happens outside the classroom in the learners' free time, its relation to the classroom might at first not be obvious.[3] However, Rhéaume, Slavkov, and Séror (2021) showed that support in the classroom is needed for learners to engage in linguistic risk-taking, as introducing the passport without classroom support led to low engagement levels. Therefore, a connection to the formal side of language

---

[3] We acknowledge that linguistic risks may also take place in the classroom. However, we assume classrooms to be generally "safer spaces" where learners receive support from teachers and peers. Thus, our interest for this project is in linguistic risks taken in authentic out-of-class settings.

learning is necessary, which again supports our positioning of linguistic risk-taking as a link between in-class and informal language learning.

2.2 Linguistic risk-taking and mobile-assisted language learning

A review of MALL – a rich area of growth for informal language learning, due to its 'anywhere, anytime' appeal (Burston 2014) – will serve as preliminary background for the Linguistic Risk-Taking App (see Section 6). In Burden and Kearney's (2018) iPAC framework of mobile learning, three concepts are central: personalisation, collaboration, and authenticity. Pegrum (2019: 25) relates MALL to these constructs as follows:

> MALL can conceivably increase personalisation, as students use their own devices in self-determined ways; it can increase collaboration, as students' autonomy is supported by interactions with peers and mentors via mobile media; and most importantly, perhaps, it can increase authenticity as students participate in embodied, embedded tasks which go well beyond and significantly augment the simulated language practice typical of formal language classrooms.

The mobile phone is not just a technological object, but also a social one, which has created 'technological intimacy' between a user and their device (Srivastava 2005). Far from merely shrinking existing content to a mobile device, MALL recognises the concept of the mobilised learner, which necessitates reconsideration of "how people actively create sites for learning as they move across locations, and how to support sustainable communities of learners equipped with powerful personal technologies" (Sharples, Taylor, and Vavoula 2016: 63). This has not always been put into practice in mobile learning products. Kim and Kwon (2012) surveyed 87 language learning apps and noted that most of them drew on cognitive learning styles such as recognition and recall, as opposed to socio-cognitive styles such as experiential learning. Generally, the apps surveyed were thought to be "weak in realising mobility as a more situated, field-dependent, and collaborative learning opportunity" (Kim and Kwon 2012: 53). It is within this gap that we position the Linguistic Risk-Taking App. It has also been argued that "learning becomes more real and permanent when tied to learners' lives outside the academic environment . . . mobile devices are a great way to achieve that goal" (Godwin-Jones 2011: 7). The Linguistic Risk-Taking App described in this article allows learners to move beyond recognition and recall activities to situations where they personalise their learning experience and independently use various resources as they navigate a number of different real-life situations and engage their target language skills authentically beyond the classroom. However, before discussing the implementation of the initiative in the digital sphere, we will present its conception as an analogue tool in the following two sections.

3 Canada: The Linguistic Risk-Taking Passport

The University of Ottawa is a bilingual (French-English) university in Canada's capital city. The university's campus and the location of the city of Ottawa on the provincial border of Ontario and Québec provide many excellent opportunities for French and English learners to practice and improve their second official language.[4] Ottawa is located in Ontario, officially an English-speaking province, while neighbouring Québec is officially French-speaking. Ottawa's proximity to Québec, together with numerous bilingual government workers and a significant Franco-Ontarian minority population, combine to make Ottawa a functionally bilingual city in many ways (Jezak and Carrasco 2017). Courses at the university are offered in both English and French. Campus staff are proficient in both languages and students can expect to communicate in either French or English at the library, cafeterias, and other facilities. This does not, however, mean that all students are bilingual, and traces of the 'two solitudes' (Cummins 2008; MacLennan 1945) of the Canadian linguistic landscape, in which French and English speakers lead separate unilingual existences side-by-side, can still be perceived. Nonetheless, many students choose to benefit from their time at this institution by taking language courses to improve their French or English skills. The Linguistic Risk-Taking Initiative acknowledges that students need to be encouraged out of their comfort zone and into real-life target language use situations. We also recognise that it takes effort, encouragement, and perseverance to engage with a target language outside of class.

At the heart of the Linguistic Risk-Taking Initiative is a printed passport (see Figure 1) containing over 80 pre-determined risks to be taken in the learners' target language (either English or French): order food at the cafeteria, interact with a professor/authority figure, compose an email, take a job interview, switch the language on their mobile device, sing karaoke, and so forth.[5] Risks draw on all areas of the traditional four skills of language learning: verbal interaction, listening, reading and writing; that is, not all risks are production-based. As such, changing the language of a smartphone or watching the TV news in a target language may constitute

---

[4] A second official language may of course represent one of many languages in a multilingual student's repertoire (e.g., L_X, as proposed by Dewaele, Bak, and Ortega 2021).
[5] As this is a dynamic and evolving project, the number of risks has grown since the first implementation of the initiative, and the current number of risks keeps growing with new cohorts of learners.

a risk because of potential practical consequences or feelings of inadequacy due to misunderstanding. These risks also have the characteristic flip-side benefits of feelings of success or belonging.

Passports are available in both French and English and learners use the version corresponding to the language they are learning.[6] In the classroom, learners are asked to identify risks in the passport that are relevant to them and set weekly risk-taking targets; then, in their daily lives outside the classroom, learners take risks and check them off in their passports. When learners return to the classroom, they reflect and build on the risks they have taken and identify new ones, continuing this iterative process over the course of a semester (Rhéaume, Slavkov, and Séror 2021). Most risks in the passport can be taken up to three times for continuous learning and reinforcement purposes.

Learners are also asked to indicate the perceived level of risk for each item they check, using a high-medium-low self-report scale (H-M-L) at the time they take the risk (see Figure 2). Comments can also be included with each risk taken or added at the end of the passport. Furthermore, learners can propose new risks not included in the passport. Learners can choose which risks to take, how often, in which order, and in which contexts or modalities (in person, online, on the phone).

Figure 1: Cover page of the English version of the Linguistic Risk-Taking Passport.

---

6 Digital copies of the latest version of the passports are available to download at https://ccerbal.uottawa.ca/linguistic-risk/ [accessed 24 August 2021].

LINGUISTIC RISKS		
Most risks can be repeated up to three times (see number of checkboxes by each risk); no particular order is required; please rate each risk as High (H), Medium (M) or Low (L) each time you undertake it.	3. I used English at uOttawa's Health Services.	☐..... ☐..... ☐.....
	4. I sent an email to a uOttawa professor in English.	☐..... ☐..... ☐.....
Example: I read the rules of engagement of the linguistic risk-taking passport. ☑ L ☐..... ☐.....	5. I sent an email to a uOttawa staff member in English.	☐..... ☐..... ☐.....
1. I attended an event on campus (e.g. activity, lecture, etc.) in English ☐..... ☐..... ☐.....	6. I spoke English at the Julien Couture Resource Centre (MHN 02).	☐..... ☐..... ☐.....
2. I ordered food on campus in English. ☐..... ☐..... ☐.....	7. I borrowed English material from the Julien Couture Resource Centre.	☐..... ☐..... ☐.....
Comments:	Comments:	

Figure 2: Sample risk-taking pages in the English version of the Linguistic Risk-Taking Passport.

Learners who 'complete' the passport with a minimum of 20 risks can submit it to a draw for prizes. A brief self-evaluation questionnaire is included in the passport and is designed for completion at the end of the semester. The questions ask learners to report whether participation in the initiative increased their perceived level of confidence, competence and engagement with the target language (see Figure 3). Our data indicate that a total of 76% of the participants who responded to this section of the passport agreed or strongly agreed that they were more likely to communicate in the target language as a result of using the tool, 79% agreed or strongly agreed that the passport helped them discover new opportunities for practicing the target language, and 91% agreed or strongly agreed that they felt inspired by the initiative (see Slavkov 2020 for a more detailed analysis).

The passport also includes a page of motivational statements to encourage learners to celebrate their target language competence and adopt a risk-taking profile (see Figure 4). These statements encourage learners to make peace with the idea of having an accent or making errors. Bilingualism is positioned not as perfect mastery of an additional language; rather it is the state of being an active user of that language.

SELF-ASSESMENT

After having completed the passport...

1. I am more comfortable speaking English with strangers.
Strongly Disagree – Disagree – Neutral – Agree – Strongly Agree

2. I am more comfortable speaking English with people I know.
Strongly Disagree – Disagree – Neutral – Agree – Strongly Agree

3. Overall, I am more comfortable taking risks in English.
Strongly Disagree – Disagree – Neutral – Agree – Strongly Agree

4. I am more likely to communicate in English outside of the classroom.
Strongly Disagree – Disagree – Neutral – Agree – Strongly Agree

5. I am inspired to use English more often.
Strongly Disagree – Disagree – Neutral – Agree – Strongly Agree

6. My confidence in English has improved.
Strongly Disagree – Disagree – Neutral – Agree – Strongly Agree

7. This passport has helped me discover new opportunities for practising English.
Strongly Disagree – Disagree – Neutral – Agree – Strongly Agree

8. Overall, this experience had a positive impact on my English skills.
Strongly Disagree – Disagree – Neutral – Agree – Strongly Agree

Figure 3: Self-assessment page in the passport.

LINGUISTIC RISK-TAKER PROFILE

I am eager to use my second official language everywhere on campus and beyond!

I am not a native speaker of this language and I am okay with that!

Yes, I may have an accent but that's what makes me unique!

I am not afraid of making errors; they are natural and normal in language use!

I consider myself bilingual in French and English (even if one of my two official languages may be stronger than the other one).

Figure 4: Motivational statements included in the passport.

Learners typically participate formally in the initiative for one semester but are encouraged to continue beyond this period and draw on the ideas and habits developed with the passport engaging in life-long language learning. Overall, the passport is a tool that supplements classroom learning with creative ideas on how to apply language knowledge and skills to real-life situations. It promotes awareness, authentic practice, and community engagement. At the time of writing in summer 2021, the Linguistic Risk-Taking Initiative has been run in five semesters since Fall 2017. 554 language learners at the University of Ottawa have used the passports (296 French learners and 258 English learners). They have recorded a total of 27410 risks (10706 in French and 16704 in English).

The passport has been designed so that it can be adapted to numerous contexts and has generated a high level of interest from various other post-secondary institutions, K-12 institutions, and government organizations. A Linguistic Risk-Taking Initiative was also developed at the University of Ottawa's clinic to support individuals who stutter, regardless of whether they are monolingual, bilingual or multilingual. Additionally, for language learners we have forged partnerships across Canada, in Japan (MacDonald and Thompson 2019), and in Europe, and expanded this pedagogical approach significantly to such new contexts. In the following section, we report on the adaptation of the passport to an Austrian post-secondary context.

4 Austria: The "Riskier was!" Booklet

In recent years, Austria has become an increasingly popular place of study for international students. In the winter semester of 2019/2020, 28.8% of all regular students at public universities came from abroad, an increase from 21.3% in winter 2009/10 (Statistik Austria 2020). At the University of Vienna, which is the oldest university in the German-speaking world and the largest educational institution in Austria, prospective students need proof of German language proficiency for admission to degree programs with German as the language of instruction (University of Vienna n.d.). When applying for admission, proof of German language proficiency at the Common European Framework of Reference for Languages (CEFR) level A2 is required; for admission to all diploma and bachelor's programmes and most of the master's programmes, proof of German proficiency at level C1 is necessary (University of Vienna n.d.). To obtain the required C1 level, students have the opportunity to participate in a German course of the University Preparation Programme of the Vienna Universities (VWU; University of Vienna n.d.). The Language Center of the University of Vienna is a cooperating partner of the VWU and offers German courses within this program (Sprachenzentrum Universität Wien n.d.). These courses aim to prepare students for their supplementary examination in German ('Ergänzungsprüfung Deutsch' [EPD]), which will be the required proof of German language proficiency in order to be admitted to a specific degree program. After a maximum of four semesters, students have to pass the EPD (Sprachenzentrum Universität Wien n.d.). Therefore, students have to improve their German proficiency from level A2 to C1 within two years.

In this context, the Linguistic Risk-Taking Initiative seemed to be well-suited to support the learning process of prospective students and to raise their awareness of everyday opportunities to use their target language, and was therefore adapted for German language learners in this context. Central to this adaptation process was the development of a German counterpart to the Linguistic Risk-Taking Passport, the "Riskier was!" Booklet.[7]

"Riskier was!", which means "Take a risk!" in English, was chosen to directly address and appeal to learners. While the concept of risk is present in the title, the concept of a passport was not carried into the German counterpart. One reason for this decision was the possibility of confusion with the European Language Passport (see European Union n.d.). Furthermore, a passport might not necessarily be perceived as something positive, especially in the European context of migration, where it might create a sense of legitimisation or exclusion.

The developmental process of the "Riskier was!" Booklet started by translating different versions of the Linguistic Risk-Taking Passport into German. Subsequently, the risks were compiled, selected according to appropriateness for the Austrian context and some new risks were added. The list of potential risks was discussed with the Language Center of the University of Vienna and their feedback was taken into account. The "Riskier was!" Booklet (see Figure 5) has 14 pages and contains 65 risks.[8] Most of them can be repeated up to three times (see Figure 6). Learners are asked to complete as many risks as possible and indicate their perceived risk level by checking the corresponding box (High, Medium, Low), as was the case with the Canadian initiative.

The "Riskier was!" Booklet also includes two pages where learners can propose their own risks. As in the Canadian Linguistic Risk-Taking Passport, there is also a page with motivational slogans (see Figure 7).

Even though the "Riskier was!" Booklet resembles the Linguistic Risk-Taking Passports in many ways, there are some differences. The booklet does not contain a self-assessment page or any comment sections because qualitative and quantitative data were collected separately. An improvement in the check-box design of the Austrian booklet (as compared to the earlier versions of the Canadian passport) was

---

7 More details about the Austrian context, the development of the "Riskier was!" Booklet and the implementation of the Linguistic Risk-Taking Initiative in Austria can be found in Cajka (2021).
8 A digital copy is available to download at https://lehrerinnenbildung.univie.ac.at/fileadmin/user_upload/p_lehrerinnenbildung/SLLF/Riskier_was_-Heft.pdf [accessed 17 August 2021].

Figure 5: Cover page of the "Riskier was!" Booklet.

also implemented, in order to prevent learners from forgetting to indicate risk-levels (High, Medium, Low) while checking off risks they have completed.

The "Riskier was!" Booklet was piloted in summer semester 2019 in two VWU German courses at the Language Centre of the University of Vienna. Accordingly, two teachers and around 40 learners were involved. Before the start of the initiative, there was an individual briefing with the teachers where the Linguistic Risk-Taking Initiative was explained, and they were provided with possible ways to include it in class. However, the teachers were free to decide to what extent they wanted to include it. The initiative was then presented in class and the booklets were distributed. After eight weeks, a questionnaire survey was conducted in class and learners could submit their booklets. In addition, individual interviews with both teachers and two learners per course were conducted. More details about the pilot study can be found in Cajka (2021).

5 Canadian and Austrian participant viewpoints

In line with our wider research aim of continually improving the initiative, language learner participants were interviewed both in Canada and in Austria as part of separate research studies. However, having the same research interest, namely finding out more about learner experiences concerning their participation in the Linguistic Risk-Taking Initiative, allows for some comparability between the data

Riskier was!

Die meisten Risiken können bis zu drei Mal wiederholt werden; es gibt keine Reihenfolge, in der die Risiken eingegangen werden sollen; bitte bewerte jedes Risiko mit hoch (**H**), mittel (**M**) oder niedrig (**N**), indem du nach jedem Versuch das entsprechende Kästchen ankreuzt.

Beispiel: Ich habe die Regeln zur Teilnahme an der Linguistic Risk-Taking Initiative gelesen.

	H	M
1	X	
2		
3		X

1. Ich habe eine deutschsprachige Veranstaltung an der Universität (Vortrag, Vorlesung etc.) besucht.
2. Ich habe mein Essen auf Deutsch bestellt.
3. Ich habe eine E-Mail an eine Lehrperson auf Deutsch geschrieben.
4. Ich habe eine E-Mail an eine Mitarbeiterin/einen Mitarbeiter vom Sprachenzentrum auf Deutsch geschrieben.
5. Ich habe ein neues Vokabel verwendet während ich mit jemandem Deutsch gesprochen habe.
6. Ich habe 24 Stunden lang nur Deutsch gesprochen.
7. Ich habe mir fünf deutschsprachige Lieder angehört.
8. Ich habe ein Telefonat auf Deutsch geführt.
9. Ich habe jemandem eine Sprachnachricht auf Deutsch hinterlassen.
10. Ich habe eine Textnachricht auf Deutsch geschrieben.
11. Ich habe bei der Vereinbarung eines Termins (z.B. bei einer Ärztin/einem Arzt etc.) Deutsch gesprochen.
12. Ich habe in meiner Freizeit ein deutschsprachiges Buch gelesen, das ich nicht für den Unterricht lesen musste.
13. Ich habe in meiner Freizeit einen Artikel in einer deutschsprachigen Zeitschrift oder Zeitung gelesen, den ich nicht für den Unterricht lesen musste.
14. Ich habe während einer Pause mit einer Kollegin/einem Kollegen nur Deutsch gesprochen.
15. Ich habe mit einer Freundin/einem Freund Deutsch gesprochen während wir gemeinsam unterwegs waren.
16. Ich habe einen Bankomaten auf Deutsch verwendet.
17. Ich habe die Sprache auf meinem Handy oder meinem Tablet einen Tag auf Deutsch gestellt.

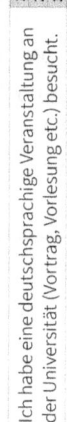

Figure 6: Sample risk-taking pages in the "Riskier was!" Booklet.

Das Profil einer Linguistic Risk-Takerin/eines Linguistic Risk-Takers

- Ich verwende die Sprache Deutsch gerne in meinem Alltag!
- Ich bin keine Native Speakerin/kein Native Speaker des Deutschen und das ist okay für mich!
- Ja, ich habe vielleicht einen Akzent, aber das macht mich einzigartig!
- Ich habe keine Angst davor, Fehler zu machen; das ist ganz normal!

14

Figure 7: Motivational slogans included in the "Riskier was!" Booklet.

from both sites. Therefore, in this chapter we aim to offer sample findings from both contexts. The goal is to present suggestions that emerged in terms of digital solutions regarding the initiative as well as identifying reasons why learners wish for them.

In the Austrian context, interviews (Misoch 2015; Meuser and Nagel 2009; Bogner and Menz 2002, etc.) were conducted by Cajka with four German language learners (two learners per course) who participated in the initiative. German learners were interviewed in German in May 2019 as part of an Austrian pilot study (Cajka 2021). In Canada, semi-structured interviews were conducted by Griffiths with eight French learners who had participated in a Canadian pilot study in the academic year 2018/19. All interviews were audio-recorded. Over 242 minutes of recordings with learners in Canada and over 184 minutes of recordings with learners in Austria were made in total. The interviews with German learners were transcribed using the transcription convention GAT 2 (Selting et al. 2009) and then analyzed using qualitative content analysis (Mayring 2014). More specifically, the procedure of inductive category formation was used, focusing on suggestions for improvement mentioned by participants in regard to the Linguistic Risk-Taking Initiative. Five categories were inductively formulated, of which one related to the possible development of an app. In Canada, the interviews were transcribed using broad general transcription with the goal of executing content and thematic analysis (Auerbach and Silverstein 2003; Boyatzis 1998). For the analysis presented here, the Canadian data were coded for the same categories that emerged from the Austrian data.

In line with the digital theme of this volume, only interview data relating to the category of the app will be reported here. The participants in Austria are identified as A1–A4; participants in Canada are identified as C1–C8. For the purposes of this chapter, Austrian data were translated from German into English and summarised.

Since development of the app had already begun in Canada, some learners were aware of the app already and one had taken part in a trial. However, this was not the case in Austria. There, two German language learners directly suggested the development of an app. German learner A1 described the form of a booklet as very good but stated that having it on the phone would be 'next level'.

Why do learners think having a digital risk-taking app would be an improvement of the initiative? To explore this question further, a secondary step of causation coding (Saldaña 2016) was added. We analysed reasons brought up by learners and three major themes emerged, which are summarised below.

5.1 Proximity

The first theme is 'proximity'. The corresponding transcript sections indicate that learners think a digital version of the passport/booklet would feel and be kept closer to them than the printed version. C1 thought they would use an app more frequently than a printed product because it would always be on them.

Example 1: I'd probably look at [the app] a bit more. Because then it's on you, right? I really didn't carry the book around. (C1)

This was also brought up in Austria. A1 emphasised that they always have their phone on them and use it frequently. Therefore, taking frequent looks at the risk-taking app would not be much of an effort.

Example 2: There are a lot of possibilities to do something, because I've got my phone always on me, you've got your phone always on you, I don't need a pen. I use it [phone] anyway to send a message, then I can take a short look, everything is there. (A1)

A similar point was made by C2, who mentions that more regular checks of the passport would be possible online. This example suggests that the usage of a digital risk-taking product would be easier than the usage of the paper passport/booklet.

Example 3: I think it would've been easier if it had been online because then I could check up on it more regularly. I misplaced it halfway through the semester. (C2)

The increased proximity of a digital risk-taking product was thought to promote easier accessibility. This was mentioned by both A1 and A4. A1, for example, explained that in order to get the "Riskier was!" Booklet, they somehow have to get to the University of Vienna. If it was an app, they could be abroad and would still be able to download it.

Example 4: With a booklet, I have to get to the University of Vienna somehow to get a booklet. If it was an app, I could be in *country* and download it. (A1)

The proximity of a mobile app does not only concern more regular or easier usage and accessibility, but also a potential social dimension. As C8 explained, having a digital risk-taking product would allow them to talk to their friends about language learning. This again suggests increased closeness to a digital product, as well as spontaneity and a feeling that an app is noteworthy or desirable:

Example 5: I think . . . it would be . . . fun to show my friends, like whip out my phone, say, oh, look what I'm doing. (C8)

As indicated in the examples above, proximity is one reason why learners see advantages in having a risk-taking app. Proximity to a digital version of the passport/booklet was addressed by learners in several ways, like always having the phone (and therefore the app) on them, being able to check in more regularly, easier accessibility, and easier ways to share it with friends.

5.2 Personalised experience

The second theme that was identified was 'personalised experience'. This suggests that learners saw an improvement in having a digital risk-taking product because it might allow an even more personalised risk-taking experience. C7, for example, mentioned that they crossed off risks in the passport that they were not going to undertake, which equals a rudimentary attempt to personalise it. They thought that any kind of digital version could help with this problem of risks that were not applicable to them.

Example 6: I crossed off [risks] I knew I really wasn't going to do . . . But because it's in a book, you kind of have to look through it . . . maybe if there was a big sheet with all of them to just look at, or an electronic copy. So that kind of would be neat, because you could just have that – even look at it on your phone or something. (C7)

A similar point was made by C6. They thought that an app would help filter risks that they knew they would not take.

Example 7: There's certain risks that I basically won't be able to do because I'll never use that service . . . I'm not sure if that's a function of the app . . . There are so many [risks] because it's just that some of them don't apply [to me], but it might apply to other people. So the app would help. (C6)

A sense of filtering the risks as a key factor in personalising content emerges from the data. Learners wish to select tasks which are relevant to their own lives. In Austria, A1 addressed having a more personalised risk-taking experience by suggesting the creation of different packs (e.g., job pack, leisure pack).

Example 8: The one idea with the phone is that you could also create packs with these things [risks]. There's a job pack and a leisure pack. Then I can say, 'Well, I don't have a job, so I won't take the job pack.' So now I have some more personal content that suits me. (A1)

The Linguistic Risk-Taking Initiative aims to offer learners the opportunity to create a personalised experience since they may choose different risks to undertake. However, as suggested by the examples, learners seem to wish for an even more personalised experience. Having a risk-taking app could facilitate that, for example, by potentially filtering risks or offering thematic packs.

5.3 Interaction

The third theme regarding reasons for suggesting the development of an app was 'interaction'. Learner interviews mentioned the incorporation of interactive elements in the risk-taking process. In Austria, A1 suggested the implementation of a scoring system, connected to rewards like receiving a trophy (a 'crown') once a certain number of points was achieved.

Example 9: Maybe you could make a scoring system, like in games that say, 'Oh yeah now you've got a crown because you got so many points.' (A1)

A1 also suggested that notifications could remind learners to take risks or praise them for their achievements. Moreover, some risks (especially cultural activities like visiting a museum or a theatre) could be connected with links to websites, so learners would know where to go in order to undertake a risk. It was also suggested that the app could show certain offers for some activities or even a combination of what was mentioned before: once a person gained a certain number of points, they receive an offer for a museum, etc. A1 argued that this would raise motivation to engage more actively in risk-taking.

Interaction not only concerns what happens between learners and the app, but also digital interactions between learners. A1, for example, mentioned that the app could be built by members of the community through sharing their own risks. In Canada, C4 mentioned that in their government job, there was a day of the week on which employees were encouraged to speak their second official language. This participant raised this idea later in the interview as a way in which linguistic risk-taking could be extended further from the classroom as a possible initiative or social media hashtag which could be run across the university.

Example 10: At work there's actually like a 'Speak your Second Language Wednesdays' or something like that. We'll have signs around the office where people will have on their desk or on their office door or something that say, "Speak to me in French." [. . .] I think it's a good place to start [risk-taking] in the classroom, for sure, but I think that if it expanded beyond that could cause- I kind of like the idea of the social media thing where it's like 'Speak your Second Language Wednesday' or hashtag. (C4)

Having a social media hashtag would allow learners to present themselves as risk-takers online, sharing their experience with friends, fellow learners, and their online community.

As the third theme has shown, allowing a more interactive risk-taking experience is another reason for creating a digital risk-taking app. Interaction might be achieved through digital solutions (notifications, scoring/reward systems, links to websites, etc.) as well as personal interaction in the digital sphere (sharing risks, social media hashtags).

However, it should be noted for balance that not all participants in Canada and Austria intuitively oriented to a digital version of the passport. This is particularly noteworthy since one could easily assume that learners – who are in our case mostly young adults – prefer digital to paper solutions. It also suggests that a digital risk-taking product should not replace but rather complement the printed passport/ booklet, further enhancing accommodation of individual learner style differences.

Nonetheless, the overall impression of learner opinions points to considerable benefits in developing a risk-taking app. An analysis of the reasons behind their suggestions showed that these can be categorised in three major themes, namely proximity, personalised experience, and interaction. This seems highly compatible with the iPAC framework (Burden and Kearney 2018, see Section 2.2) of personalisation, authenticity and collaboration. Personalised experience maps to the dimension of personalisation, while many of the interactive features target a collaborative element. In addition, the Linguistic Risk-Taking Initiative in general targets authenticity since learners engage in meaningful everyday activities. How the development of the Linguistic Risk-Taking App corresponds to the three themes that emerged from learner interviews will be reported in the next section.

6 The Linguistic Risk-Taking App

Development of the app version of the Canadian Linguistic Risk-Taking Passport began in Ottawa in summer 2018 in line with long term plans to explore digital options, which was supported by many of the opinions expressed by participants in subsequent interviews (see Section 5). For the development of the app, a graduate student developer from the University of Ottawa's computer science department joined the research team, capitalising on the kind of collaboration suggested by Barcomb, Grimshaw, and Cardoso (2017), which takes advantage of the talent and skills available in the student population.

The app was first specified by Slavkov to take advantage of the affordances of MALL (see Section 2.2). The app was initially developed for Android.[9] Beta-testing was implemented with learner volunteers in the Fall 2018 semester using an Android APK (pre-download) version only. In addition to an initial evaluation by the

---

9 Implemented in Ionic Angular + Node.js technologies, hosted on Amazon AWS EC2 server, database hosted by MongoDB. Privacy policies and terms generated using Iubenda.

research team, at this stage a small-scale user experience pilot survey was also conducted with 18 learners who beta-tested the app in the Fall 2018 semester, in line with Nesbitt's (2013) recommendation to consult the end-user throughout a digital design process. Recommendations from the learner interviews described in Section 5 were also incorporated at this stage. The Android app was made available through Google Play in April 2019, and development of the Apple iOS app began. It went live in the App Store in October 2019.[10] The descriptive text in both Google Play and the Apple App Store specified that the app is currently designed for use as a supplementary tool for designated language classes at the current institution only.

Users of the app are greeted by the app's splash screen (see Figure 8a) and asked whether they will take risks in French or English.[11] An English/French language switch button was not provided so the app exclusively displays the selected language, providing an immersive experience in the user's target language. After language selection, users are asked to specify their name, email address, a password, and their course code in a one-time registration process. This affords the research team access to data on which risks have been taken, in which language, how many times, and so on (cf. 'data mining' opportunities for teachers creating their own mobile resources; see Barcomb, Grimshaw, and Cardoso 2017; Stockwell 2013). Data are anonymised and kept confidential following ethics protocols.

Following registration, users land on a home screen called *My Risk Hub* (Figure 8b).

On the Risk Hub, there are four central options underneath the initiative's logo (Figure 8b). Option 1, *All Linguistic Risks* leads to the scrollable list of 74 risks which are identical to those in the paper passport. As learners take a targeted risk in real life (e.g., "I spoke French at the university health service") they tap on it in the list (Figure 9a) and are asked to mark it as High, Medium or Low (Figure 9b) according to their experience at the time of taking it. A digital stamp styled as the yellow linguistic risk-taking logo appears against each numbered attempt for a risk taken (Figure 9b). The user can also add optional comments about each experience to be used as an aide-memoire or for class discussion later on. The rules of engagement are the same as those used for the paper passport; i.e., users are asked to attempt at least twenty risks before the passport is eligible

---

[10] The availability of the app was suspended at the beginning of the COVID-19 pandemic since opportunities for in-person language interactions were severely restricted. A new release of the app with updated interface and features is scheduled for the 2022–23 academic year.
[11] Figures from the Linguistic Risk-Taking Passport demonstrate a French-learning experience. French content is translated descriptively in English in the surrounding paragraph text. The acronym FLS visible at the top of the screenshots in Figures 8b to 10c stands for *français langue seconde* "French as a second language", a term commonly used in Canada.

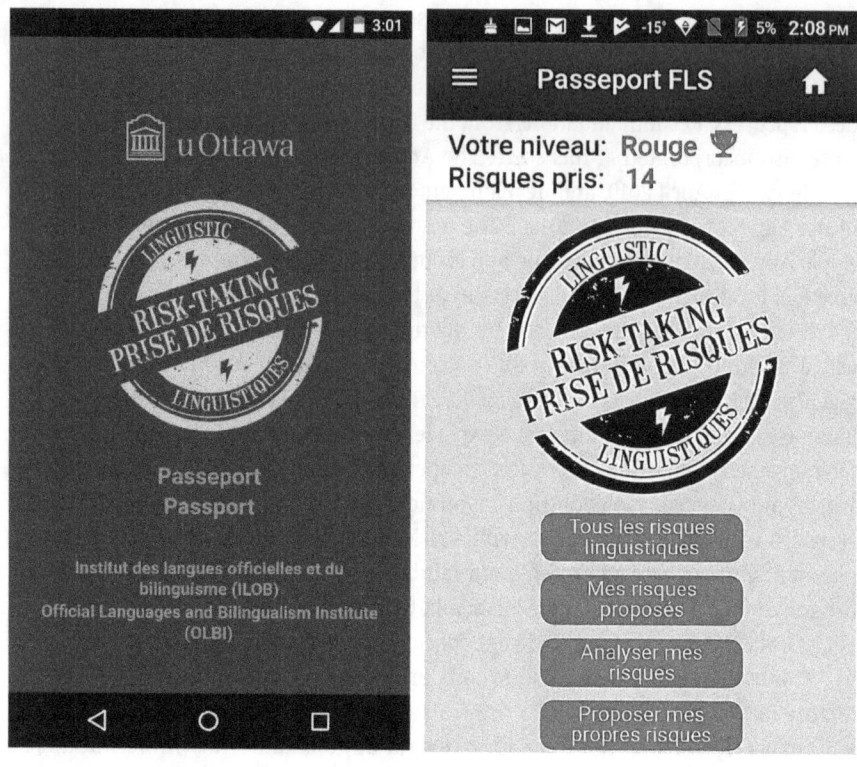

Figure 8a, b: Splash Screen, My Risk Hub (Home Screen).

for submission to an end-of-semester prize draw. The *Submit My Passport* menu option allows app users to submit the app virtually.

A key aspect of the Linguistic Risk-Taking Initiative is encouraging participants to propose their own risks and tailor the concept of linguistic risk-taking to their own lives and experiences. Option 4 (*Propose My Own Risks*) on the Risk Hub allows users to engage with this module. Users can also view their own tailored list of proposed risks by navigating to Option 2 (*My Proposed Risks*). Tapping on Option 3 (*Analyze My Risks*) from the Risk Hub leads to user statistics that show number of risks over time, by type of skill (e.g., reading, writing, spoken interaction, listening), and by thematic domain (on campus, academic, everyday activities, leisure), as indicated in Figure 10a–c, respectively.

We now examine more closely how the development of the app corresponds to the three themes (proximity, personalised experience, and interaction) which emerged from learner interview data in Section 5.

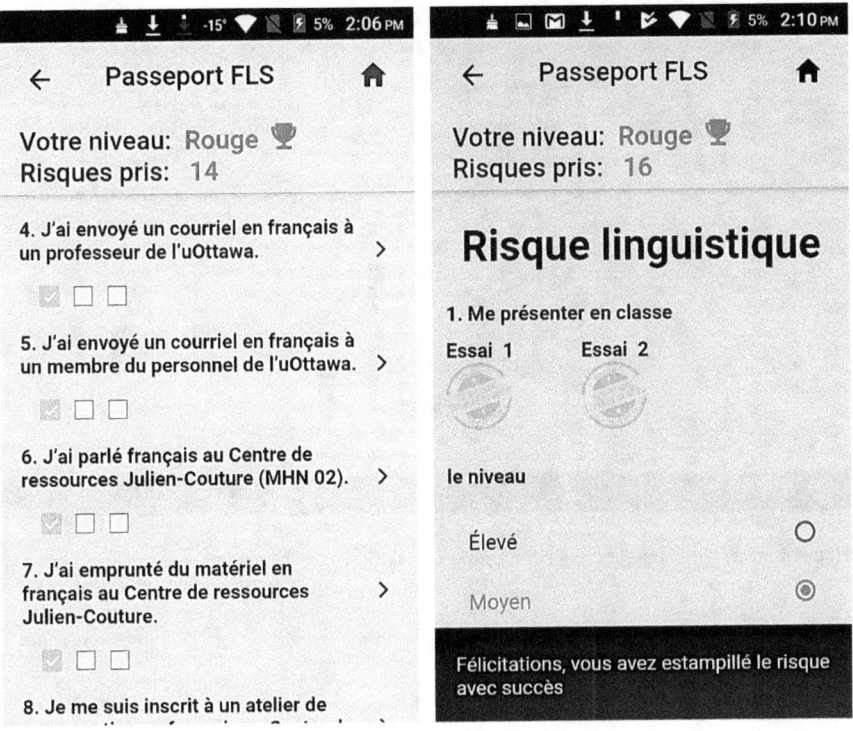

Figure 9a, b: List of Risks (partial view of scrollable screen), Taking a Specific Risk.

6.1 Proximity

As illustrated by learner interview data, learners reported not carrying or misplacing the paper passports, whereas they were more likely to have their phones handy at all times (cf. Examples 3–5). The app has obvious benefits in this area. Checking off risks and marking them as H-M-L is a more straightforward user experience in the app and yields better completion patterns (a study of data collected via Canadian paper passports with 554 participants by Slavkov found that around 17% of users simply ticked off risks without providing a value on the H-M-L scale; this issue is eliminated in the app via mandatory fields). In this way, greater proximity could lead to a greater level of engagement with the initiative.

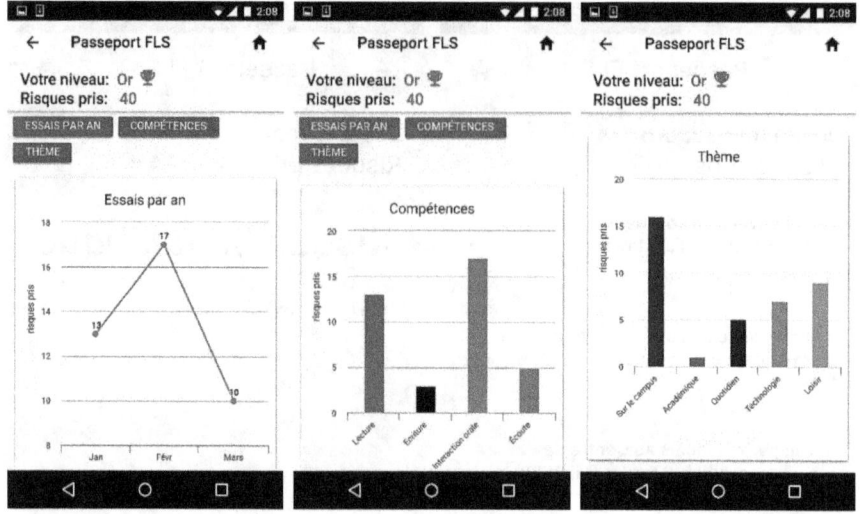

Figure 10a–c: Number of Risks over Time, Risks by Skill, Risks by Theme.

6.2 Personalised experience

A major item in the initial development of the app was the inclusion of usage statistics that may raise motivation and awareness (e.g., self-analysis of skills and themes could result in targeting underused skills and settings). Personalised experience was also further targeted following beta testing of the app by adding a search function. For example, searching for 'professor' brings up the two risks which specifically pertain to communicating with a professor (via email or in person) in the target language. In addition, a two-way filter was installed which allows users to narrow down the list of risks to traditional skill categories (reading, writing, spoken interaction, listening) and thematic categories (on campus, academic, everyday life, technology, leisure). It was also clear from participant interviews that learners wished for a more personalised risk-taking experience by filtering out risks that are not applicable to them. The filters in the app allow for the long list to be reduced significantly based on learner needs and interests. Users can also target specific skills and situate their learning within different areas of their lives. The ability to use both filters concurrently would allow a user who, for example, wanted to work on their French writing in their everyday life to find risks responding to these criteria. The filters also complement the availability of user statistics in the app, which can serve as a diagnostic (i.e., users can determine which skills or thematic domains are underused in their daily life and then search for relevant risks to fill such gaps).

6.3 Interaction

The non-linear navigation which is possible in the app makes for a more dynamic user experience compared to linear flipping through the pages of a passport. Another important innovation in terms of interactivity is found in the *Propose My Own Risks* feature, which was not shareable in the paper passport but can be shared via the app. When proposing a risk, a user can consent to sharing and, if approved by a moderator, it is added to the list of risks in the app for the entire cohort of users. The ability to share risks through mobile technology supports the view of Sharples, Taylor, and Vavoula (2016) that the mobile learner can easily create communities of learning and speaks to the views of learners that an app would increase interactivity. In the app, students have the option to document and encounter risky situations which may not have occurred to the creators or to other participants in the initiative. Finally, a visual/motivational improvement is the introduction of stamps for risks taken, where in the paper passport learners only placed checkmarks.

Following beta testing, it was also decided to develop the idea of user levels similar to those found in video game play, in order to encourage the reader to keep progressing and take more risks (cf. Example 9). Different colour levels (green, yellow, blue, bronze, silver, gold, platinum, etc.) corresponding to a specified number of risks taken were introduced and are continuously displayed in the top status bar of the app to remind the user of their status and allow classmate users to compare levels of engagement. These levels are visible in all Figures 8–10 and replaced an older progress metric (number of risks taken out of total number of risks possible) in the top status bar. The user levels represent only an initial and relatively limited gamification (cf. Flores 2015) commensurate with our timeline and resources; future developments in this area are pending. It was also felt necessary in line with feedback about interactivity that the app had some kind of voice to stand in for the encouraging teacher or friend, and therefore short messages and emojis (e.g., "Well done! Keep going!") were introduced after each risk has been logged. Messages also tell the user how many more risks they must take before proceeding to the next level, helping them to strive to keep going.

It should be acknowledged that not all participant feedback has been actioned. For example, the way that the app interacts with a participant's social media (cf. Example 10) has not yet been fully explored due to budgetary concerns and restrictions on available resources within the team. Other ideas were considered and rejected, e.g., the permanent filtering of risks that participants thought did not apply to them (cf. Example 7) was not deemed as conducive to promoting a growth mindset in which risks open up as possibilities as participation evolves over time.

We have shown in this section how the iterative app development process relates to the themes of proximity, personalised experience and interaction raised by learners. Increased proximity allowed for a greater level of engagement with the initiative, while allowing users to personalise their experiences responded to a perceived need to be able to filter and tailor risks to individual needs. Finally, development of interactive features allowed for the introduction of some gamification, as well as the sharing of ideas for risks across users.

7 Limitations, future research and conclusion

In the sections above, we have detailed an ambitious multi-site multi-modal project designed to encourage learners to move out of their comfort zones to engage in informal language learning beyond the classroom. It was noted at the beginning of the chapter that we do not report here on the individual risks taken by learners or on the effect of risk-taking on language proficiency outcomes. These are intended avenues for future investigation, alongside the way in which risk-taking interacts with many individual differences (e.g., anxiety, autonomy and willingness to communicate).

In this chapter, we have introduced linguistic risk-taking as an informal language learning practice that we believe contributes to the growing discussion of how the classroom may create bridges to informal language learning in the outside world. We then outlined the key points in our path towards pedagogical innovation and enhancing informal language learning experiences by presenting the original Canadian French/English passport and its adaptation to the context of German learners in Austria.

Interview data findings from both sites supported the development of a digital risk-taking app. This suggests that the digital sphere is not merely where learners engage in informal language learning activities but may also be a space where the seeds for engaging in such activities can be sown. This supports the approach we are taking and also highlights further directions which the project may take. For example, the development of a risk-taking app for the Austrian context would be the next logical step. Increasing the learner's ability to personalise their experience and interact with the app could further strengthen communities of learners (cf. Sharples, Taylor, and Vavoula 2016) across a variety of contexts. For example, study-abroad cohorts could use the app to share risk ideas with each other in their target country. In foreign language learning contexts, lists of linguistic risks can be further tailored to digital and context-specific activities. It may even be possible to create a 'white-label' version of the app in which core risks (e.g., I went to the movie theatre to see a film in my target language) are supplemented by relevant risks suggested by local project leaders (e.g., I spoke Japanese in the convenience store next to our school). Such developments would support the growth of this initiative and its objective to encourage informal language learning. Finally, while the app currently has only a modest level of gamification (Roodi and Slavkov 2022), future developments planned in this regard will target new features and game-thinking with the purpose of increasing learner engagement levels even further.

Appendix – Sample: Potential leisure-based risks

Leisure-based risks are here defined as informal learning opportunities (see Section 2.1) which learners may engage with for recreation outside of their studies.

The Linguistic Risk-Taking Passport (University of Ottawa)

I listened to 5 songs by Canadian artists in English/French.
I read a book or a magazine in English/French.
I read a news article in English/French.
I used English/French at a campus recreation location (e.g., gym, pool, etc.).
I subscribed to a podcast feed in English/French.
I listened to a radio station in English/French for an hour.
I watched a movie or a show at home in English/French with French/English subtitles.
I watched a movie or a show at home in English/French without subtitles.
I watched a YouTube video in English/French.
I saw a movie at a movie theatre in English/French.
I watched my favourite sport on TV in English/French.
I checked out apt613.ca/ to find an event or activity in English/French.
I went to a party and spoke English/French there.
I went to karaoke and sang a song in English/French.
I used English/French when traveling in Canada or abroad.
I made a social media post in English/French.

"Riskier Was!" Booklet (University of Vienna)

Ich habe mir fünf deutschsprachige Lieder angehört.
Ich habe in meiner Freizeit ein deutschsprachiges Buch gelesen, das ich nicht für den Unterricht lesen musste.
Ich habe in meiner Freizeit einen Artikel in einer deutschsprachigen Zeitschrift oder Zeitung gelesen, den ich nicht für den Unterricht lesen musste.
Ich habe bei einem Museumsbesuch die Infotexte auf Deutsch gelesen.
Ich habe bei einem Museumsbesuch, einem Ausflug, einer Tour etc. meinen Audioguide auf Deutsch benutzt.
Ich habe beim Sport bzw. im Fitnessstudio Deutsch gesprochen.
Ich habe einen deutschsprachigen Radiosender gehört.
Ich habe ein deutschsprachiges Theaterstück besucht.
Ich habe mir ein Youtube-Video auf Deutsch angesehen.
Ich habe ein Social-Media-Posting auf Deutsch verfasst.
Ich habe mir im Kino einen Film auf Deutsch angesehen.
Ich habe ein Videospiel auf Deutsch gespielt.
Ich habe beim Spielen eines Online-Videospiels auf Deutsch kommuniziert.
Ich bin zu einer Party gegangen und habe dort Deutsch gesprochen.
Ich habe gekocht und dabei ein deutschsprachiges Rezept verwendet.
Ich habe beim Reisen durch Österreich oder im Ausland Deutsch gesprochen.[12]

---

12 English translation:

    I listened to five songs in German.
    In my free time, I read a book in German that I didn't have to read for class.
    In my free time, I read an article in a German-language magazine or newspaper that I didn't have to read for class.
    I read the information texts in German while visiting a museum.
    I used my audio guide in German while visiting a museum, being on an excursion, a tour etc.
    I spoke German while doing sports or in the gym.
    I listened to a German-speaking radio station.
    I went to see a play in German.
    I watched a Youtube video in German.
    I made a social media post in German.
    I saw a movie at a movie theatre in German.
    I played a videogame in German.
    I communicated in German while playing an online videogame.
    I went to a party and spoke German there.
    I used a recipe in German while cooking.
    I spoke German while travelling through Austria or abroad.

References

Auerbach, Carl F. & Louise B. Silverstein. 2003. *Qualitative Data: An Introduction to Coding and Analysis*. New York: New York University Press.

Barcomb, Mike, Jennica Grimshaw & Walcir Cardoso. 2017. I can't program! Customizable mobile language-learning resources for researchers and practitioners. *Languages* 2(3). 1–15. https://doi.org/10.3390/languages2030008

Beebe, Leslie M. 1983. Risk-taking and the language learner. In Herbert W. Seliger & Michael H. Long (eds.), *Classroom Oriented Research in Second Language Acquisition*, 39–66. Rowley: Newbury House.

Benson, Phil. 2011. Language learning and teaching beyond the classroom: An introduction to the field. In Phil Benson & Hayo Reinders (eds.), *Beyond the Language Classroom*, 7–16. Basingstoke: Palgrave Macmillan.

Bogner, Alexander & Wolfgang Menz. 2002. Das theoriegenerierende Experteninterview: Erkenntnisinteresse, Wissensformen, Interaktion. In Alexander Bogner, Beate Littig & Wolfgang Menz (eds.), *Das Experteninterview: Theorie, Methode, Anwendung*, 33–70. Opladen: Leske + Budrich.

Boyatzis, Richard E. 1998. *Transforming Qualitative Information: Thematic Analysis and Code Development*. Thousand Oaks: Sage Publications.

Burden, Kevin & Matthew Kearney. 2018. Designing an educator toolkit for the mobile learning age. *International Journal of Mobile and Blended Learning* 10(2). 88–99. https://doi.org/10.4018/ijmbl.2018040108

Burston, Jack. 2014. The reality of MALL: Still on the fringes. *CALICO Journal* 31(1). 103–125. https://doi.org/10.11139/cj.31.1.103-125

Cajka, Stefanie. 2021. *Die Linguistic Risk-Taking Initiative für Deutschlernende in einem österreichischen Universitätskontext*. Wien: University of Vienna Master's thesis.

Cervantes, Irene M. 2013. The role of risk-taking behavior in the development of speaking skills in ESL classrooms. *Revista de Lenguas Modernas* 19. 421–435.

Cummins, Jim. 2008. Teaching for transfer: Challenging the two solitudes assumption in bilingual education. In Jim Cummins & Nancy H. Hornberger (eds.), *Encyclopedia of Language and Education*, Vol. 5, 65–75. Boston: Springer.

Dewaele, Jean-Marc, Thomas H. Bak & Lourdes Ortega. 2021. Why the mythical "native speaker" has mud on its face. In Nikolay Slavkov, Sílvia Melo Pfeifer & Nadja Kerschhofer-Puhalo (eds.), *The Changing Face of the "Native Speaker": Perspectives from Multilingualism and Globalization*, 23–43. (Trends in Applied Linguistics 31). Berlin: De Gruyter Mouton.

Dressman, Mark. 2020. Introduction. In Mark Dressman & Randall William Sadler (eds.), *The Handbook of Informal Language Learning*, 1–12. Hoboken/Chichester: Wiley-Blackwell.

European Union. n.d. "What happened to the Europass Language Passport?". https://europa.eu/europass/en/what-happened-europass-language-passport (accessed 20 June 2021).

Flores, Jorge Francisco Figueroa. 2015. Using gamification to enhance second language learning. *Digital Education Review* 27. 32–54.

Godwin-Jones, Robert. 2011. Mobile apps for language learning. *Language Learning & Technology* 15(2). 2–11. https://doi.org/10125/44244

Griffiths, Ed & Nikolay Slavkov. 2021. Linguistic risk-taking: A bridge between the classroom and the outside world. *Canadian Journal of Applied Linguistics* 24(2). 127–158. https://doi.org/10.37213/cjal.2021.31308

Hubbard, Philip. 2020. Leveraging technology to integrate informal language learning within classroom settings. In Mark Dressman & Randall William Sadler (eds.), *The Handbook of Informal Language Learning*, 471–487. Hoboken/Chichester: Wiley-Blackwell.

Jezak, Monika & Encarnacion Carrasco. 2017. Integration trajectories of adult (im)migrants in minority and minoritised contexts: Ottawa and Barcelona. In Jean-Claude Beacco, Hans-Jürgen Krumm, David Little & Philia Thalgott (eds.), *The Linguistic Integration of Adult Migrants: Some Lessons from Research*, 97–104. Berlin/Boston: De Gruyter Mouton.

Kim, Heyoung & Yeonhee Kwon. 2012. Exploring smartphone applications for effective mobile-assisted language learning. *Multimedia-Assisted Language Learning* 16(1). 31–57.

Lai, Chun, Weimin Zhu & Gang Gong. 2015. Understanding the quality of out-of-class English learning. *TESOL Quarterly* 49(2). 278–308. https://doi.org/10.1002/tesq.171

Livingstone, Devon W. 2006. Informal learning: Conceptual distinctions and preliminary findings. In Zvi Bekerman, Nicholas C. Burbules & Diana Silberman-Keller (eds.), *Learning in Places: The Informal Education Reader*, 203–27. New York: Peter Lang.

MacDonald, Ewen & Nicholas Thompson. 2019. The adaptation of a linguistic risk-taking passport initiative: A summary of a research project in progress. *Relay Journal* 2(2). 415–436. https://doi.org/10.37237/relay/020216

MacLennan, Hugh. 1945. *Two solitudes*. Toronto: Collins.

Mayring, Philipp. 2014. *Qualitative Content Analysis: Theoretical Foundation, Basic Procedures and Software Solution*. Klagenfurt: SSOAR. https://nbn-resolving.org/urn:nbn:de:0168-ssoar-395173

Meuser, Michael & Ulrike Nagel. 2009. Das Experteninterview – konzeptionelle Grundlagen und methodische Anlage. In Susanne Pickel, Gert Pickel, Hans-Joachim Lauth & Detlef Jahn (eds.), *Methoden der vergleichenden Politik- und Sozialwissenschaft: Neue Entwicklungen und Anwendungen*, 465–479. Wiesbaden: VS Verlag für Sozialwissenschaften.

Misoch, Sabina. 2015. *Qualitative Interviews*. Berlin/Munich/Boston: De Gruyter.

Nesbitt, Danielle. 2013. Student evaluation of CALL tools during the design process. *Computer Assisted Language Learning* 26(4). 371–387. https://doi.org/10.1080/09588221.2012.680471

Pegrum, Mark. 2019. *Mobile Lenses on Learning: Languages and Literacies on the Move*. Singapore: Springer.

Reinders, Hayo & Phil Benson. 2017. Research agenda: Language learning beyond the classroom. *Language Teaching* 50(4). 561–578. https://doi.org/10.1017/S0261444817000192

Rhéaume, Martine, Nikolay Slavkov & Jérémie Séror. 2021. Linguistic risk-taking in second language learning: The case of French at a Canadian bilingual institution. *Foreign Language Annals* 54(4). 1214–1237. https://doi.org/10.1111/flan.12561

Roodi, Farhad & Nikolay Slavkov. 2022. Gamification in L2 teaching and learning: Linguistic risk-taking at play. *OLBI Journal* 12(1). 185–205. https://doi.org/10.18192/olbij.v12i1.6000

Saldaña, Johnny. 2016. *The Coding Manual for Qualitative Researchers*, 3rd edn. Los Angeles: Sage Publications.

Schwarz Marlene. 2020. *Beyond the walls: A mixed methods study of teenagers' extramural English practices and their vocabulary knowledge*. Wien: University of Vienna dissertation

Selting, Margret, Peter Auer, Dagmar Barth-Weingarten, Jörg Bergmann, Pia Bergmann, Karin Birkner, Elizabeth Couper-Kuhlen, Arnulf Deppermann, Peter Gilles, Susannenthner Günthner, Martin Hartung, Friederike Kern, Christine Mertzlufft, Christian Meyer, Miriam Morek, Frank Oberzaucher, Jörg Peters, Uta Quasthoff, Wilfried Schütte, Anja Stukenbrock & Susanne Uhmann. 2009. Gesprächsanalytisches Transkriptionssystem 2 (GAT 2). *Gesprächsforschung – Online-Zeitschrift zur verbalen Interaktion* 10. 353–402.

Sharples, Mike, Josie Taylor & Giasemi Vavoula. 2016. A theory of learning for the mobile age. In Caroline Haythornthwaite, Richard Andrews, Jude Fransman & Eric M. Meyers (eds.), *The SAGE Handbook of E-learning Research*, 2nd edn., 63–81. London: Sage Publications.

Slavkov, Nikolay. 2020. Where the magic happens: Fostering language learning, bilingualism and multilingualism through linguistic risk-taking. In Thomas Tinnefeld (ed.), *The Magic of Language: Productivity in Linguistics and Language Teaching*, 47–69. (Saarbrücken Series on Linguistics and Language Methodology 11). Saarbrücken: htw saar. https://drive.google.com/file/d/1p2mlq5_wT6zMfY3wlqLtW5l1Na6cXTqh/view

Slavkov, Nikolay & Jérémie Séror. 2019. The development of the Linguistic Risk-Taking Initiative at a bilingual post-secondary institution in Canada. *Canadian Modern Language Review* 75(3). 254–271. https://doi.org/10.3138/cmlr.2018-0202

Sockett, Geoffrey & Denyze Toffoli. 2020. Last words: Naming, framing, and challenging the field. In Mark Dressman & Randall William Sadler (eds.), *The Handbook of Informal Language Learning*, 471–487. Hoboken/Chichester: Wiley-Blackwell.

Sprachenzentrum Universität Wien. n.d. "German courses for the University Preparation Programme (VWU)". https://sprachenzentrum.univie.ac.at/en/german-courses/german-courses-for-vwu/ (accessed 10 August 2021).

Srivastava, Lara. 2005. Mobile phones and the evolution of social behaviour. *Behaviour & Information Technology* 24(2). 111–129. https://doi.org/10.1080/01449290512331321910

Statistik Austria. 2020. "Ordentliche Studierende an öffentlichen Universitäten 1955–2019". https://www.statistik.at/web_de/statistiken/menschen_und_gesellschaft/bildung/hochschulen/studierende_belegte_studien/021631.html (accessed 24 August 2021).

Stockwell, Glenn. 2013. Tracking learner usage of mobile phones for language learning outside of the classroom. *CALICO Journal* 30. 118–136. https://doi.org/10.1558/cj.v30i0.118-136

University of Vienna. n.d. "Proof of German language proficiency". https://studieren.univie.ac.at/en/admission/german-language-proficiency/ (accessed 10 August 2021).

Section 4: **Psychological dimensions**

Linlin Liu, Ju Seong Lee

11 Why does IDLE make EFL learners gritty?
The mediating role of enjoyment

Abstract: This study examines the role of IDLE (e.g., watching English-language films) in L2 enjoyment and whether L2 enjoyment, in turn, predicts grit. The data were collected through online questionnaires from 656 Chinese EFL university students. A follow-up, semi-structured interview also was conducted to enrich quantitative findings. The Structural Equation Model results show that L2 enjoyment in general mediated the relationship between IDLE and grit. The interview analysis also confirms that IDLE plays a positive role in enhancing L2 enjoyment (e.g., feeling more joyful and confident about learning and using English), which in turn positively influences grit (e.g., becoming more diligent in learning English). These findings suggest that IDLE is an essential factor for boosting enjoyment in learning English, and an approach that can potentially nurture grit in EFL learners in China or similar EFL contexts.

Keywords: Informal Digital Learning of English, grit, L2 enjoyment, Chinese EFL learners

1 Introduction

Informal Digital Learning of English (IDLE) is a growing phenomenon observed around the globe (Dressman and Sadler 2020; Lee 2022a). Lee (2019a) defines IDLE as self-directed English learning in an extramural digital context that is unrelated to formal instruction. In recent review papers on IDLE-related studies (Soyoof et al. 2021; Zhang et al. 2021), IDLE was found to play a positive role in affective dimensions of language learning outcomes.

To investigate the role IDLE would play in language learning, Lee and his colleagues have explored a link between IDLE and two positive, non-cognitive variables, namely, L2 enjoyment and grit. These studies mainly investigate EFL learners in Asia who generally do not enjoy and are not passionate about learning

Linlin Liu, The Education University of Hong Kong, Hong Kong SAR, China; Yibin Vocational and Technical College, Yibin, Sichuan, China
Ju Seong Lee, The Education University of Hong Kong, Hong Kong SAR, China

https://doi.org/10.1515/9783110752441-011

English (Dewaele and MacIntyre 2014; Lee 2022b). The research findings have shown that IDLE activities are linked to EFL learners' L2 enjoyment (Lee and Lee 2021; Lee, Xie and Lee 2021) and grit (Lee 2020; Lee and Drajati 2019; Lee and Chen Hsieh 2019).

Nevertheless, it remains to be seen whether IDLE plays a role in L2 enjoyment and whether L2 enjoyment, in turn, predicts grit. Further, missing from much of the work on IDLE is the perspective of EFL university learners in mainland China. This is surprising because today's Chinese university students are increasingly engaging in IDLE by using mobile devices (Peng et al. 2020). To address these gaps and advance this line of research, this study set out to investigate the mediating role of L2 enjoyment in the relationship between IDLE and grit as it pertains to Chinese EFL university students.

2 Literature review

2.1 Informal digital learning of English (IDLE)

Situated within CALL, IDLE has received increasing attention, along with several other newly emerging concepts (Lee 2022a). These notions include language learning and teaching beyond the classroom (Benson and Reinders 2011; Reinders and Benson 2017), informal language learning (Dressman and Sadler 2021), informal second language learning (Arndt and Woore 2018), fully autonomous self-instructed learning (Cole and Vanderplank 2016), recreational language learning (Chik and Ho 2017), Extramural English (Sundqvist and Sylvén 2016), CALL in the digital wilds (Sauro and Zourou 2019), out-of-class autonomous language learning with technology (Lai 2018) and online informal learning of English (Kusyk 2017; Sockett 2014; Toffoli 2020; Toffoli and Sockett 2013).

IDLE has received the lion's share of attention from researchers based in Asian EFL contexts (e.g., South Korea and Indonesia), in which language learners rarely use English with an actual interlocutor in everyday life. To illustrate, Soyoof and his associates (2021) reported that nearly 40% of the papers on the subject of IDLE were published in Asian EFL contexts between 1980 and 2019. Lee (2021) provided a brief summary of twelve pedagogical advantages of IDLE, most of which are related to affective states (see Table 1). Correspondingly, many of the studies on IDLE have been devoted to investigating whether IDLE could bring psychological benefits to EFL learners (see review papers on IDLE-related studies; Soyoof et al. 2021; Zhang et al. 2021). This approach makes sense because Asian L2 learners (mostly EFL learners) reported the lowest levels of L2 enjoyment, but the highest levels of L2 communication anxiety among L2 learners from around the world (Dewaele & MacIntyre 2014). This may be in part attributed to Asia's unique socio-educational context, which often overemphasises the value of high stakes English tests, such as school exams and national university entrance examinations (Lee 2020).

Table 1: Twelve pedagogical advantages of IDLE (Lee 2021: 2–3).

Advantages	Descriptions
1. Autonomy	Students feel a strong sense of control about their IDLE activity because they can make decisions about their own materials and strategies.
2. Authenticity	IDLE learners can be exposed to authentic English while interacting with other English users in real-life situations.
3. Identity	IDLE learners often assume a new identity as English users rather than English learners.
4. Motivation	IDLE activities are generally triggered by intrinsic motivation (e.g., self-interest) rather than extrinsic motivation (e.g., a test).
5. Investment	IDLE learners, who perceive themselves as English users, are likely to invest in practicing English in extramural digital contexts.
6. Flow	IDLE learners (e.g., watching Netflix in English) tend to lose track of time and experience a flow state.
7. Grit	IDLE learners exert continuous effort in learning and using English while maintaining their personal interests.
8. Community of practice	IDLE learners feel connected to others from online communities (e.g., fan fiction or gaming communities) that share the same interests.
9. Affective filter	Since there are no teachers or classmates, IDLE learners often practice English in a low affective filter situation.
10. Multimodality	IDLE activities often involve various modalities, such as text, images, audio, videos, and music.
11. Comprehensive input	IDLE helps learners grasp the meaning of words and sentences.
12. Accessibility	Since there are no time or space limitations on the Internet, English is continuously available to IDLE learners.

Empirically, several studies have shown that IDLE-related activities are positively associated with affective aspects of L2 learning, including motivation (Lee and Lee 2020, 2021), and confidence (Lai et al. 2015; Lee and Drajati 2019), as well as lack of anxiety (Lee and Chen Hsieh 2019; Lee and Drajati 2019; Lee and Lee 2020). This suggests that IDLE activities, which are different from classroom-based English activities, appear to provide EFL learners with several psychological advantages (Lee 2022b; Soyoof et al. 2021; Zhang et al. 2021). In the subsequent sections of this paper, the two particular types of affective variables, namely L2 enjoyment and grit, are discussed in relation to IDLE.

2.2 IDLE and L2 enjoyment

Although cognitive views have dominated the field of SLA during the past half-century, some researchers have been consistently devoted to research on the topic of L2 emotions (Barcelos 2015). More recently, in tandem with emerging research trends on the 'affective/emotional turn' (Pavlenko 2013; Prior 2019), L2 emotions have increasingly attracted attention from SLA scholars. Concurrently, influenced by the movement of positive psychology (Seligman and Csikszentmihalyi 2000), SLA researchers have begun paying increasing attention to positive psychology in SLA (MacIntyre et al. 2019). Positive psychology in SLA is primarily based on Fredrickson's (2001) broaden-and-build theory – that is, positive emotions (e.g., joy) enlarge the scope of one's attention, widen the range of one's behaviors, and enable an individual to become more tolerant and open minded regarding new and innovative ideas and experiences. Over time, an individual with a broader mindset can continue to develop and accumulate more skill and knowledge and become more resilient. MacIntyre and Gregersen (2012) echoed the finding that an individual's positive emotions with regard to a foreign language, such as enjoyment in learning English, play a vital role in "broaden[ing] a person's perspective [and] opening the individual to absorb the language" (193).

The emerging trend of positive psychology in SLA has prompted researchers to shift their main attention from negative emotions (e.g., anxiety) to positive ones (e.g., enjoyment and grit). Since positive emotions are found to influence other affective aspects (e.g., L2 WTC) of L2 learning (Lee 2022b), the past five years have witnessed a particular interest in L2 enjoyment in exam-oriented Asian EFL contexts, such as China (Jiang and Dewaele 2019; Li 2019; Li, Jiang, and Dewaele 2018) and South Korea (Lee 2020; Lee and Lee 2021). In relation to IDLE, a positive association between IDLE-related activities and L2 enjoyment has recently been identified among contemporary Asian EFL learners.

In one such pioneering work, Lai, Zhu, and Gong (2015) found that Chinese EFL secondary learners who reported regular engagement in out-of-class English learning using technology tended to also report a higher level of L2 enjoyment. Similarly, Lee (2019b) found that Korean EFL university students who regularly practiced IDLE activities showed a higher level of L2 enjoyment. Regrettably, a single-item scale of L2 enjoyment was adopted in both Lai et al. (2015) and Lee (2019b). However, Lee and Lee (2021) have recently addressed this methodological limitation by developing ten items of an L2 enjoyment scale based on Dewaele and MacIntyre's (2014) Foreign Language Enjoyment scale. Using this newly developed L2 questionnaire, Lee and Lee (2021) found a positive relationship between IDLE and L2 enjoyment in a study that involved Korean EFL secondary and university students. This finding is congruent with that of Lai et al. (2015) and Lee (2019b). Contrary to Lee and Lee (2021), who adopted a broad L2 enjoyment scale (a combination of classroom L2 enjoyment and L2 enjoyment in general), Lee (2020) employed a narrow facet of the L2 enjoyment scale by focusing on classroom L2 enjoyment. It was found that Korean EFL secondary students' classroom L2 enjoyment was significantly associated with grit, which is another important positive, non-cognitive construct in the field of SLA.

2.3 IDLE and grit

Grit is defined as "perseverance and passion for long-term goals" (Duckworth et al. 2007: 1087). This notion consists of two sub-constructs, namely, *perseverance of effort* and *consistency of interests*. The former refers to the ability to make a continuous effort despite difficulties or setbacks. The latter term indicates the ability to sustain interests in the face of challenges or failures. Extensive studies have shown that individuals who scored higher on a grit scale were likely to work harder and more persistently, thereby achieving superior performance in various domains (Duckworth 2017; Eskreis-Winkler et al. 2014). These overall findings suggest that individual differences in grit could predict to what extent one may put forth effort and achieve long-term goals in spite of various challenges along the way.

In the field of Second Language Acquisition (SLA), several cross-sectional studies have demonstrated that grit is positively linked with levels of multilingualism (Wei et al. 2020), L2 enjoyment (Lee 2020; Teimouri et al. 2020; Wei et al. 2019; Wei et al. 2020), L2 motivation (Lan et al. 2021; Lee and Drajati 2019; Lee and Lee 2020), L2 self-confidence (Lee and Drajati 2019; Lee and Lee 2020), L2 risk-taking (Lee and Lee 2020), L2 willingness to communicate in face-to-face settings (Lan et al. 2021; Lee 2020; Lee and Lee 2020), English proficiency (Wei et al. 2019; Wei et al. 2020), and digital storytelling performance in the L2 (Chen Hsieh and Lee 2021). However, other studies have reported no significant relationship between grit and L2 learning variables, such as L2 speaking anxiety (Lee and Lee 2020), L2 willingness to communicate in digital settings (Lee and Lee 2020), self-perceived proficiency (Khajavy et al. 2020), and L2 achievement (Khajavy et al. 2020). Due to such conflicting results, more research is needed to better understand the role of grit in L2 learning.

In connection with IDLE, Lee and Drajati (2019) provided some of the first evidence that IDLE was linked to grit. In that particular study, IDLE was composed of two types of activities: receptive IDLE activities (consuming something in English; e.g., watching English-language films) and productive IDLE activities (producing something in English; e.g., chatting with other English users on social media). The researchers showed that both types of IDLE activities correlated significantly with grit among Indonesian EFL learners. More recently, in a study involving Korean EFL university students, Lee and Lee (2020) found a positive and significant relationship between IDLE (particularly related to intercultural experiences) and grit. These studies suggest that EFL learners who regularly engage in IDLE activities are likely to remain passionate and persistent in pursuing long-terms goals, such as mastering a foreign language. In that regard, grit appears to provide a valuable affective benefit for EFL learners in extramural digital contexts, who often learn and use English without the supervision of teachers.

3 Research models and hypotheses

Based on current studies, we schematised a conceptual model, as shown in Figure 1, which engenders three hypotheses (H) to be investigated. As IDLE was found to positively correlate with grit (Lee and Drajati 2019; Lee and Lee 2020), the first hypothesis was formulated as:

H1: IDLE positively predicts grit.

Second, classroom L2 enjoyment was positively associated with both IDLE (Lee and Drajati 2019) and grit (Lee 2020). Based on these findings, a second hypothesis was established:

H2: Classroom L2 enjoyment mediates the relationship between IDLE and grit.

Third, L2 enjoyment in general is positively linked to IDLE (Lai et al. 2015; Lee 2019b; Lee and Lee 2021) and grit (Lee and Lee 2020). This led to the formulation of the third hypothesis:

H3: L2 enjoyment in general mediates the relationship between IDLE and grit.

Additionally, with reference to previous research (Lee et al. 2021; Lee and Drajati 2019), four sub-models, which include four sub-categories of IDLE, are also developed and tested for a deeper analysis (see Figure 3 in Section 4).

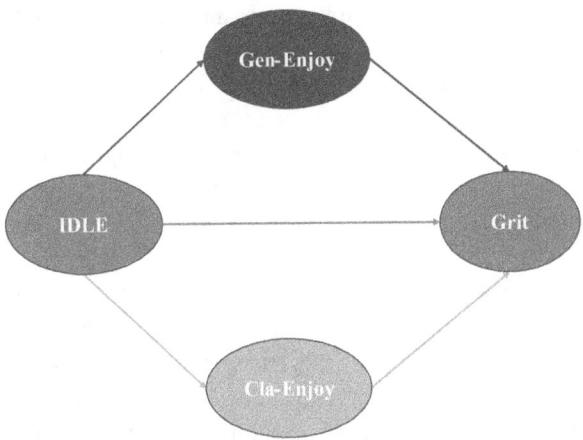

Figure 1: Conceptual model.
Note: Gen-Enjoy = L2 enjoyment in general; Cla-Enjoy = Classroom L2 enjoyment

4 Method

4.1 Participants and context

Data were conveniently collected from 656 freshmen Chinese EFL learners (Male = 232, 35%; Female = 424, 65%; ages from 19 to 24), who were enrolled in a prestigious public vocational college in southwestern China. During the 2020–2021 academic year, all potential respondents were invited to take part in an online survey. The research participants majored in a variety of non-English disciplines (e.g., social studies, finance, agriculture, architecture, and manufacturing) but enrolled in the same course (named 'College English'). At the time of this study, 99.4% of the students (n = 652) reported no overseas experience in English-speaking countries. In the sample, nearly 85% of the participants (n = 552) had been learning English for more than five years. The participants were all grouped at the B1 level (lower-intermediate) according to their scores on the college entrance test, as referred to CEFR criteria.

4.2 Measures

The online questionnaire consisted of four parts. The first part was designed to elicit students' demographic data, such as gender, age, length of time studying English, and overseas experience. In the second part, participants were asked to respond to 29 items concerning the types and frequency of IDLE activities (Lee et al. 2021). Answers to these questionnaire items were rated on a five-point Likert scale, ranging from 1 "Never" to 5 "Very often (many times per day)." In the third part, 18 questionnaire items were employed to assess participants' level of L2 enjoyment on a five-point Likert scale, ranging from 1 "Strongly disagree" to 5 "Strongly agree" (Dewaele and MacIntyre 2014; Lee and Lee 2021). Lastly, 11 question items were used to evaluate EFL learners' grit, using a five-point Likert scale, ranging from 1 "Not like me at all" to 5 "Very much like me" (Duckworth et al. 2007; Lee and Lee 2020). All questionnaire items are presented in the Appendix. Concerning the limits of the access to some online activities for Chinese EFL learners, the first author (a native Chinese speaker) translated the original English questionnaire items into Chinese and then back-translated them into English, resulting in modifying a few items (e.g., "I watch English-language YouTube videos." was modified to "I watch English-language videos on YouKu, Tudou, or Tencent"). Next, the second author, whose expertise is IDLE and positive psychology in SLA, confirmed the face and content validity of the questionnaire. Finally, in order to avoid any misunderstanding due to low English language competence, the questionnaire was presented in both Chinese and English versions (see Appendix).

4.3 Data collection

After the Institutional Review Board's approval had been obtained, the first author informed potential participants of the purposes, steps, benefits and risks of the study. The operational definition of IDLE along with its relevant examples was given on the front page of the survey, so that all participants would have the same understanding of IDLE. Only volunteer informants were allowed to fill out the survey. Next, all survey respondents were invited to voluntarily take part in follow-up, semi-structured interviews. However, since the interview was arranged during the online pandemic period, only one student took part in the interview. This audio-recorded online interview was conducted in Chinese for approximately 15 minutes.

4.4 Data analysis

Six steps were taken to analyse the research questions by using IBM SPSS Statistics 25 and IBM SPSS Amos 22, through the measurement model and structural model assessment. First, the normality of data distribution (the mean, standard deviation, skewness and kurtosis) was checked (see Table 3). Second, the loading values of each item for the corresponding construct and sub-constructs were examined for the reliability of individual items. Based on a principal axis factor analysis with the varimax rotation technique, seven latent factors with loadings of greater than 0.5 (ranging from 0.50 to 0.91) were identified through Exploratory Factor Analysis (Table 2). To be precise, Factor 1 consisted of six items related to text-based IDLE practice. A specific example is, "I read English news online." Factor 2 consisted of four items related to game-based IDLE practice, for example, "I play digital games in English." Factor 3 consisted of nine items concerning IDLE practice in leisure time, such as "I listen to songs in English". Factor 4 consisted of nine items related to IDLE practice for social communication, such as, "I talk with native English speakers via social media."

Factors 5 and 6 counted for the measurement of EFL learners' enjoyment in learning English. Specifically, Factor 5 consisted of eight items related to learners' enjoyment in learning English in general, such as "I can be creative using English", while Factor 6 consisted of ten items concerning learners' enjoyment in learning English in the classroom, such as "I have learned interesting things in English class." The last factor consisted of eleven items concerning learners' grit level in learning English. The item includes "I set a goal to learn English and continue to pursue that goal." Consequently, the construct validity of seven constructs was acceptable.

Third, values of Cronbach's alpha ranged from 0.89 to 0.96, indicating that the internal reliability of the questionnaire was acceptable (see Table 2). Fourth, values of Composite Reliability (above 0.8) and Average Variance Extracted (above 0.5) were observed, thereby verifying convergent validity (Fornell and Larcker 1981).

Fifth, the conceptual model, which represents three hypotheses, was tested through SEM. Lastly, four additional models were developed and tested through SEM to delve into the association between four different types of IDLE, L2 enjoyment in general, Classroom L2 enjoyment, and grit (see Figure 3). With respect to qualitative analysis, the first author initially transcribed and translated the interview data into English, followed by confirming the accuracy of the translation through member checking.

Table 2: Construct validity and internal reliability.

Construct		Item	Sample (N = 656)			
			Loading (>0.5)	α (>0.8)	CR (>0.8)	AVE (>0.5)
IDLE	Text-based IDLE	IDLE 1	0.80	0.89	0.85	0.50
		IDLE 2	0.84			
		IDLE 3	0.81			
		IDLE 4	0.62			
		IDLE 5	0.56			
		IDLE 6	0.50			
	Game-based IDLE	IDLE 7	0.81	0.91	0.82	0.54
		IDLE 8	0.73			
		IDLE 9	0.76			
		IDLE 10	0.62			
	Leisure-based IDLE	IDLE 11	0.67	0.92	0.88	0.50
		IDLE 12	0.74			
		IDLE 13	0.72			
		IDLE 14	0.65			
		IDLE 15	0.77			
		IDLE 16	0.56			
		IDLE 17	0.68			
		IDLE 18	0.61			
		IDLE 19	0.67			
	Social-based IDLE	IDLE 20	0.65	0.96	0.95	0.67
		IDLE 21	0.80			
		IDLE 22	0.84			
		IDLE 23	0.84			
		IDLE 24	0.88			
		IDLE 25	0.85			
		IDLE 26	0.88			
		IDLE 27	0.81			
		IDLE 28	0.80			
L2 enjoyment in general		ENJ 1	0.77	0.93	0.91	0.57
		ENJ 2	0.55			
		ENJ 3	0.78			
		ENJ 4	0.83			
		ENJ 5	0.84			
		ENJ 6	0.82			
		ENJ 7	0.68			
		ENJ 8	0.75			

Table 2 (continued)

Construct	Item	Sample (N = 656)			
		Loading (>0.5)	α (>0.8)	CR (>0.8)	AVE (>0.5)
Classroom L2 enjoyment	ENJ 9	0.79	0.95	0.95	0.68
	ENJ 10	0.72			
	ENJ 11	0.73			
	ENJ 12	0.85			
	ENJ 13	0.84			
	ENJ 14	0.76			
	ENJ 15	0.80			
	ENJ 16	0.91			
	ENJ 17	0.91			
	ENJ 18	0.91			
Grit	GRIT 1	0.89	0.96	0.97	0.74
	GRIT 2	0.80			
	GRIT 3	0.89			
	GRIT 4	0.88			
	GRIT 5	0.78			
	GRIT 6	0.88			
	GRIT 7	0.90			
	GRIT 8	0.85			
	GRIT 9	0.90			
	GRIT 10	0.81			
	GRIT 11	0.84			

Note: α = Cronbach's alpha, CR = Composite Reliability, AVE = Average Variance Extracted

5 Results

5.1 Descriptive data

Descriptive data analysis (see Table 3) shows that respondents reported below-neutral levels of text-based IDLE (M = 2.34, SD = .83), game-based IDLE (M = 1.75, SD = .86), leisure-based IDLE (M = 2.25, SD = .78), social-based IDLE (M = 1.61, SD = .78), L2 enjoyment in general (M = 2.69. SD = .87), and grit (M = 2.77, SD = .86), as the mean score was less than 3 (neutral agreement) on a five-point Likert scale. This indicates that Chinese EFL learners had generally low levels of engagement in different kinds of IDLE activities, and enjoyment with respect to studying English in general settings. In particular, the value of game-based IDLE and social-based IDLE scored the lowest (both below 2), which implies that Chinese EFL learners are less likely to participate in learning or using English through online games or social communication. However, the value of classroom L2 enjoyment (M = 3.14, SD = .95) suggests that students had generally higher levels of enjoyment with respect to studying or using English in the classroom, as the mean score was above 3 on a five-point Likert scale.

Table 3: Descriptive statistics.

Constructs	Items	h^2	Skew	Kurt	M (SD)	M (SD) for all items
Text-based IDLE	1	.71	.34	−.52	2.72 (1.13)	2.34 (.83)
	2	.79	.59	−.05	2.47 (1.05)	
	3	.74	.42	−.38	2.54 (1.06)	
	4	.71	.98	.84	1.89 (.92)	
	5	.64	.78	.19	2.03 (.98)	
	6	.61	.58	−.06	2.37 (1.03)	
Game-based IDLE	1	.78	1.18	.70	1.84 (1.05)	1.75 (.86)
	2	.82	1.16	.88	1.77 (.95)	
	3	.81	1.24	.92	1.71 (.94)	
	4	.78	1.25	.99	1.69 (.91)	
Leisure-based IDLE	1	.66	.78	.08	1.98 (.97)	2.25 (.78)
	2	.57	−.11	−.89	3.33 (1.17)	
	3	.62	.94	.38	1.86 (.95)	
	4	.59	1.02	.52	1.94 (1.02)	
	5	.66	.32	−.63	2.67 (1.14)	
	6	.59	.86	.32	2.02 (.99)	
	7	.64	.63	−.16	2.34 (1.09)	
	8	.60	.73	−.19	2.13 (1.08)	
	9	.66	.89	.40	2.00 (1.00)	
Social-based IDLE	1	.72	1.03	.59	1.88 (.99)	1.61 (.78)
	2	.79	1.43	1.55	1.62 (.92)	
	3	.80	1.49	1.71	1.58 (.88)	
	4	.79	1.38	1.45	1.61 (.87)	
	5	.84	1.73	2.42	1.50 (.86)	
	6	.81	1.58	2.13	1.53 (.82)	
	7	.86	1.54	1.96	1.56 (.87)	
	8	.77	1.33	1.17	1.65 (.91)	
	9	.73	1.36	1.12	1.60 (.88)	
L2 enjoyment in general	1	.59	.51	.22	2.39 (.97)	2.69 (.87)
	2	.43	.22	−.35	2.75 (1.07)	
	3	.72	.19	−.50	2.78 (1.12)	
	4	.80	.20	−.35	2.78 (1.07)	
	5	.67	.48	−.09	2.40 (1.02)	
	6	.78	.22	−.37	2.82 (1.10)	
	7	.68	.09	−.56	2.97 (1.13)	
	8	.63	.23	−.40	2.67 (1.07)	

Table 3 (continued)

Constructs	Items	h²	Skew	Kurt	M (SD)	M (SD) for all items
Classroom L2 enjoyment	1	.77	.33	−.33	2.64 (1.09)	3.14 (.95)
	2	.83	.07	−.41	2.96 (1.09)	
	3	.86	.21	−.38	2.76 (1.08)	
	4	.85	.09	−.53	2.92 (1.11)	
	5	.80	−.14	−.51	3.31 (1.12)	
	6	.79	−.04	−.55	3.15 (1.13)	
	7	.82	−.13	−.60	3.21 (1.14)	
	8	.90	−.29	−.64	3.43 (1.17)	
	9	.88	−.39	−.68	3.57 (1.19)	
	10	.89	−.35	−.60	3.50 (1.18)	
Grit	1	.79	.00	−.08	2.80 (.97)	2.77 (.86)
	2	.65	.20	−.04	2.59 (.96)	
	3	.79	.50	−.22	2.85 (1.03)	
	4	.77	.00	−.06	2.86 (.99)	
	5	.61	.08	−.19	2.94 (1.04)	
	6	.78	.29	.00	2.64 (.98)	
	7	.80	.11	−.16	2.75 (1.00)	
	8	.73	.11	−.32	2.86 (1.06)	
	9	.80	.18	−.08	2.72 (1.00)	
	10	.66	.19	−.31	2.59 (1.02)	
	11	.70	.08	−.27	2.86 (1.05)	

5.2 Correlation analysis

Pearson's correlation analysis was performed to examine correlations among different variables and all the correlation values were based on the composite scores. As presented in Table 4, grit correlated significantly with all the affective variables, which means grit was positively related to different types of IDLE activities, including text-based IDLE, game-based IDLE, leisure-based IDLE and social-based IDLE. Meanwhile, grit was also positively linked with L2 enjoyment in general and in classroom L2 enjoyment. In particular, grit had a higher positive correlation with L2 enjoyment in general ($r = .762, p < 0.01$) than Classroom L2 enjoyment ($r = .673, p < 0.01$). In addition, grit had strong positive correlations with both text-based IDLE ($r = .572, p < 0.01$) and leisure-based IDLE ($r = .504, p < 0.01$), but moderately positive correlations with game-based IDLE ($r = .327, p < 0.01$) and social-based IDLE ($r = .393, p < 0.01$).

Table 4: Correlations among variables.

	1	2	3	4	5	6	7
1. Text-based IDLE	1	.534**	.738**	.569**	.569**	.429**	.572**
2. Game-based IDLE		1	.641**	.712**	.297**	.149**	.327**
3. Leisure-based IDLE			1	.653**	.503**	.394**	.504**
4. Social-based IDLE				1	.366**	.167**	.393**
5. L2 enjoyment in general					1	.775**	.762**
6. Classroom L2 enjoyment						1	.673**
7. Grit							1

Note: ** $p < 0.01$ (two-tailed)

5.3 Structural equation modelling (SEM)

A total of five different SEMs were formulated to test our hypotheses. In light of modification indices, some correlated errors were added to the models. As summarised in Table 5, all five models demonstrated a good fit with the data: χ^2 divided by the value of degree of freedom (χ^2/df) was less than 3; the root mean square of approximation (RMSEA) was less than or equal to 0.08; the adjusted goodness-of-fit index (AGFI) was above 0.85; and the goodness-of-fit index (GFI), the normed fit index (NFI), and the comparative fit index (CFI) were above 0.9 (Hair, Tatham, Anderson, and Black 1998).

Table 5: A summary of goodness-of-fit indices of the five SEM models.

	χ^2/df	RMSEA	AGFI	GFI	NFI	CFI
Basic mediation model	1.76	0.03	0.87	0.91	0.94	0.97
Sub-model 1	2.40	0.05	0.87	0.91	0.95	0.97
Sub-model 2	3.83	0.05	0.86	0.90	0.95	0.96
Sub-model 3	2.23	0.04	0.87	0.90	0.95	0.97
Sub-model 4	2.12	0.04	0.88	0.91	0.96	0.98
Recommended value	< 3	≤ 0.08	> 0.85	> 0.9	> 0.9	> 0.9

To be specific, a five-factor SEM demonstrated that IDLE positively influenced grit both directly ($\beta = 0.20$, $p < 0.01$) and indirectly through the mediations of L2 enjoyment in general ($\beta = 0.40$, $p < 0.001$; see Figure 2). However, Classroom L2 enjoyment did not mediate the relationship between IDLE and grit ($\beta = 0.02$, $p > 0.05$).

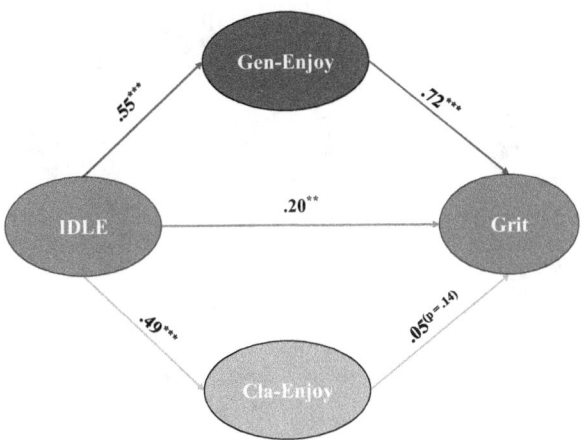

Figure 2: Estimated results of basic mediation model.
Note: Gen-Enjoy = L2 enjoyment in general; Cla-Enjoy = Classroom L2 enjoyment
*** $p < 0.001$ (two-tailed), ** $p < 0.01$ (two-tailed)

To further analyse the association between different types of IDLE practice, enjoyment and grit, four different sub-models were developed and tested through SEM. Intriguingly, four different types of IDLE practice have the same direct effect ($\beta = 0.14$, $p < 0.001$) on grit as displayed in Figure 3. In terms of the indirect effect concerning different types of IDLE on grit through the mediating role of enjoyment, it was found that the indirect effect of text-based IDLE practice on grit through enjoyment in general settings ($\beta = 0.44$, $p < 0.001$) topped the rank, with the indirect effect of leisure-based IDLE on grit through L2 enjoyment in general ($\beta = 0.33$, $p < 0.001$), the indirect effect of social-based IDLE on grit through L2 enjoyment in general ($\beta = 0.29$, $p < 0.001$) and the indirect effect of game-based IDLE on grit through L2 enjoyment in general ($\beta = 0.12$, $p < 0.001$) coming in sequenced order. With respect to the indirect effect of different types of IDLE practice on grit through Classroom L2 enjoyment, only a slight impact was identified. Among these types, leisure-based IDLE practice ($\beta = 0.03$, $p < 0.001$) showed a relatively higher indirect effect on grit through Classroom L2 enjoyment when compared to the other three categories. Moreover, the indirect effects of both text-based IDLE practice and social-based IDLE practice were insignificant.

Qualitative data further supported the first model – namely, that a Chinese EFL learner who regularly engages in IDLE is likely to enjoy learning English, which in turn helps her become gritty. For example, Sandy, a 19-year-old female freshman majoring in Marketing Management explained her experience thus:

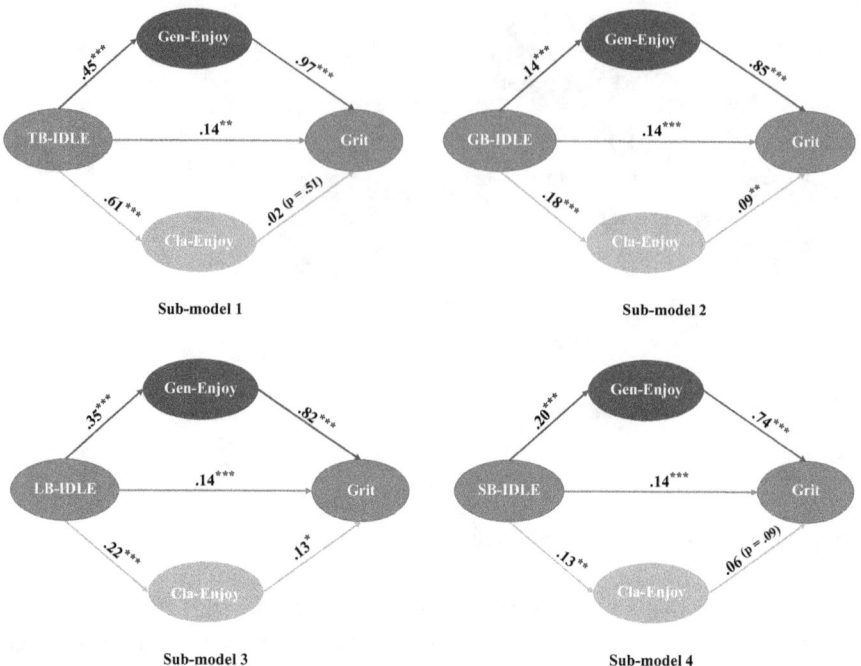

Figure 3: SEM analyses on the sub-models.
Note: TB-IDLE = Text-based IDLE activities, GB-IDLE = Game-based IDLE activities, LB-IDLE = Leisure-based IDLE activities, SB-IDLE = Social-based IDLE activities, Gen-Enjoy = L2 enjoyment in general; Cla-Enjoy = Classroom L2 enjoyment;
** $p < 0.01$ (two-tailed), *** $p < 0.001$ (two-tailed).

> I enjoyed a lot when I do IDLE activities . . . I love listening to English songs [and] watching English films . . . I felt no pressure, and I enjoyed doing these kinds of activities very much. And I found that the more I do, the more I become confident in singing English songs in my dormitory or in Karaoke in front of my friends . . . Most importantly, the more I use English, the more positive feedback I get from the interlocutors, such as teacher, friends and classmates. They keep telling me that I am improving my English. This positive affirmation makes me feel tremendously wonderful, which helps me become more diligent in learning English.

6 Discussion

Our SEM analyses offer several important insights. First, IDLE positively predicted grit, which provides support for H1. This finding is in line with previous studies, which have demonstrated a positive link between IDLE and grit among Indonesian and Korean EFL learners (Lee and Drajati 2019; Lee and Lee 2020). This suggests that Chinese EFL learners who more frequently engage in IDLE were more likely to remain passionate about and persistent in learning and mastering English. Since IDLE learners generally learn and practice English independently in extramural digital settings, it seems probable that they develop a capacity for consistent effort (while maintaining interest) in learning English in the face of challenges or setbacks.

It is important to note that previous studies investigated Indonesian EFL learners' two types of IDLE (i.e., receptive and productive IDLE activities; e.g., Lee and Drajati 2019) and Korean EFL learners' four types of IDLE (i.e., receptive, productive, form-focused, and game-based IDLE activities; Lee et al. 2021). However, the current study, which involved Chinese EFL students, was able to identify more types of IDLE activities, namely: text-based, game-based, leisure-based, and social-based IDLE activities. This suggests that IDLE activities can be differently categorised depending on EFL learners' contexts. A deeper analysis revealed a positive link between these four types of IDLE and grit. This indicates that regardless of type of IDLE activities, participants who regularly engaged in IDLE tended to score high on grit.

In addition, L2 enjoyment in general mediated the relationship between IDLE and grit, which could provide support for H2 that *Classroom L2 enjoyment mediates the relationship between IDLE and grit*. However, classroom L2 enjoyment did not play a mediating role between IDLE and grit, which rejects H3. These findings suggest that L2 enjoyment in general settings rather than L2 enjoyment in classroom settings, as facilitated by IDLE, play a significant role in helping Chinese EFL learners become grittier. This makes sense because IDLE has been found to offer several psychological benefits to EFL learners who learn English using technology outside the classroom (Soyoof et al. 2021; Zhang et al. 2021). According to Lee (2022b), IDLE learners, as English users, report that they tend to feel a high sense of autonomy (e.g., selecting their favorite L2 resources), easily interact with real English users in authentic situations (e.g., fan-fiction communities based on their respective interests), and experience a flow state (e.g., watching interesting movies/dramas on Netflix). Therefore, EFL learners who more frequently practice IDLE are likely to report feeling a higher sense of L2 enjoyment (particularly L2 enjoyment in general), which subsequently helps them become more persistent about learning English while maintaining a positive attitude about learning that particular language.

These findings are consistent with previous studies that have identified several associations, but separately: a positive link between classroom L2 enjoyment and IDLE (Lee and Drajati 2019); a positive link between L2 enjoyment in general and IDLE (Lai et al. 2015; Lee 2019b; Lee and Lee 2021); and a positive association between L2 enjoyment in general and grit (Lee and Lee 2020). It is worth noting that our research provides some of the first mediating models, demonstrating a fuller range of associations between IDLE, L2 enjoyment in general, and grit. Thus, it seems plausible to argue that IDLE can make EFL learners gritty through the mediation of L2 enjoyment in general. However, our findings are contrary to Lee (2020), which reported a positive association between classroom L2 enjoyment and grit. This contradiction merits further investigation on this topic.

A deeper analysis also revealed that various types of IDLE appear to have different effects on L2 enjoyment and grit. For instance, our SEM results showed that text-based and leisure-based IDLE activities, compared to game-based and social-based IDLE activities, were found to be more associated with grit as well as L2 enjoyment in general. This suggests that text- or leisure-types of IDLE activities seem to offer more psychological benefits to Chinese EFL learners. These findings are consistent with Lee and Lee (2021), who reported a positive link between IDLE and L2 enjoyment among Korean EFL secondary and university students. However, the content of IDLE practices was of a general nature because Lee and Lee (2021) combined various types of IDLE activities into one construct. In contrast, the present study elucidated four specific types of IDLE activities (e.g., text-based IDLE), with examples for each (e.g., I read English news online). Thus, our findings can offer more specific pedagogical insights for EFL educators.

Qualitative data, albeit only one case (a Chinese EFL university student), can support and elaborate this interpretation: Sandy engaged regularly in IDLE, especially leisure-based IDLE (e.g., listening to English-language songs or watching English-language films). While engaging in IDLE activities, she did not feel any negative emotions, such as anxiety. In light of the affective filter hypothesis (Krashen 1981), IDLE appears to help Sandy remain safe emotionally and to practice English with a low affective filter. Sandy also claimed that the more she became involved in IDLE, the more she felt confident and became willing to use English (e.g., singing English songs in Karaoke in the presence of others). Further, she received positive affective support from her social groups (e.g., teacher, friends and classmates), which helped her exert continuous effort in learning and using English.

From the perspective of grit, IDLE (including the four different types identified here) was a positive and significant predictor for grit. Previous studies reported mixed findings on the association between L2 learning variables and grit, with some reporting a positive relationship (e.g., Lee 2020; Lee and Drajati 2019; Teimouri et al. 2020; Wei et al. 2019; Wei et al. 2020), but others not observing such a relationship (Khajavy et al. 2020; Lee and Lee 2020). In this regard, our findings could bring additional evidence to the ongoing discussion on this topic. At the methodological level, previous SLA research reported conflicting findings on the validity of grit scale: some researchers (Lee and Chen Hsieh 2019; Lee and Drajati 2019) adopted a comprehensive scale of grit (a combination of perseverance of effort and consistency of interest). In contrast, others (Lee 2020; Lee and Lee 2020; Temouri et al. 2020) employed only one dimension of grit (perseverance of effort) due to the types of validity concerns raised by Credé et al. (2017). Consistent with the findings reported in Taiwanese and Indonesian EFL contexts (Lee and Chen Hsieh 2019; Lee and Drajati 2019), our study found that compound measures of a grit scale are valid and reliable in the Chinese EFL context.

7 Limitations and implications for research

The strengths of the current study notwithstanding, three limitations are acknowledged, and some directions for future research are provided. First, since it is an observational study, the survey data was collected over a short period of time, with the interview component limited to a single participant. Similarly, even though we recruited a large sample size (N = 656), covering different academic majors, the quantitative findings were based on self-reported data. According to Dörnyei (2007), respondents' subjective opinions or inaccurate recollections about the phenomena could affect accuracy. Thus, future studies should consider collecting data through multiple sources, for example, focus groups and observations or in-depth interviews with additional participants, to ensure data reliability and accuracy. Second, this study investigated only EFL university learners in mainland China; thus, it can be argued that the findings may not be applicable to participants from different age or linguistic and cultural backgrounds. Hence, future research should consider selecting participants from different levels of institutions and diverse socio-cultural backgrounds to gather extra proof to support the findings of the present study. Third, emotions, both positive and negative, could also affect IDLE practices and EFL learners' behaviors. Therefore, negative emotions such as anxiety and boredom should also be taken into consideration in future research.

8 Conclusions

This study empirically tested a model of the pathways from IDLE to Chinese EFL learners' grit, involving two types of L2 enjoyment as mediators. Our SEM analyses supported the first two hypotheses, which suggest that EFL learners tend to become grittier (or exert more effort while maintaining their interest in learning English) when their sense of L2 enjoyment in general is enhanced through regular practice using IDLE activities. Our findings may offer context-specific pedagogical insights for EFL practitioners. EFL teachers in China or in similar EFL contexts may encourage students to engage in IDLE activities, especially text-based and leisure-based IDLE activities. This approach is likely to help students to enjoy learning English and become more resilient while sustaining a more positive attitude toward learning the language.

Appendix

Part 1: Demographic Information

*For each question below, please choose the appropriate answer.
   1. **How old are you?**
   2. **What is your gender?**
      1) male, 2) female
   3. **What languages can you understand and use? (Indicate all options)**
      –Chinese
      –Cantonese
      –English
      –Spanish
      –French
      –Japanese
      –Korean
      –Others
   4. **How were you first exposed to English?**
      1) Media (TV, Internet, Radio)
      2) School
      3) Private Institute
      4) Overseas experience (e.g., travel and study)
      5) Communication with other English users
   5. **How long have you been studying English?**
      1) 1–2 years
      2) 3–4 years
      3) 5–6 years
      4) 7–8 years
      5) 9–10 years
      6) More than 10 years

6. If you have ever lived in English-speaking country, how long have you lived there?
   1) None
   2) Less than 1 year
   3) 1–2 years
   4) More than 3 years
7. How many hours did you spend daily on IDLE activities in the past 3 months (e.g., watching YouTube videos in English, listening to English songs, playing games in English, chatting with others in English, searching information in English, etc)?
   1) None
   2) Less than 1 hour
   3) 1–2 hours
   4) 2–3 hours
   5) More than 3 hours
8. How would you rate your English proficiency?
   1) 1, 2) 2, 3) 3, 4) 4, 5) 5, 6) 6, 7) 7, 8) 8, 9) 9, 10) 10
9. What grade did you get in your last English exam? (out of 100)

Part 2: Informal Digital Learning of English Type/Frequency

*How often do you engage in the following IDLE activities?
1. Never; 2. Rarely (Once a week); 3. Sometimes (2 or 3 times per week); 4. Fairly Often (Once a day); 5. Very Often (Many times per day)

Items English	Chinese
IDLE	非正式数字化英语学习活动
1. I use online dictionary.	1. 我使用在线词典查单词。
2. I learn English vocabulary using apps.	2. 我利用在线软件或平台来学习词汇。
3. I use search engine to check grammar and vocabulary.	3. 我使用搜索引擎来学习语法和词汇。
4. I read English news online.	4. 我阅读在线网络英语新闻。
5. I read English content via social media such as WeChat, Sina Weibo, Tencent QQ, Tencent Video, and Douban.	5. 我在社交媒体上阅读英语文章,如微信、新浪微博、腾讯QQ、腾讯视频或豆瓣网。

(continued)

Items English	Chinese
IDLE	非正式数字化英语学习活动
6. I read entertaining contents (e.g., shopping, comics, traveling, movies) online.	6. 我在网络上阅读与娱乐活动相关主题的文章 (如: 购物、动画、旅行、电影等)。
7. I play digital games in English (e.g., StarCraft, FIFA, Overwatch, Call of Duty, The Sims, Diablog, Lineage).	7. 我玩以英语语言为主的网络游戏 (如: StarCraft 星际争霸, FIFA足球在线, Overwatch 守望先锋, Call of Duty 使命召唤, The Sims 模拟人生, Diablog 暗黑破坏神, Lineage 天堂)。
8. I read comments in online game communities (e.g., NeoGAF, GameFAQS, IGN, Gamespot, Reddit) and get some information.	8. 我阅读在线网络游戏论坛中的留言并从中获得相关信息(如: NeoGAF, GameFAQS, IGN, Gamespot, Reddit)。
9. I talk to other players in English while playing games.	9. 我在玩在线网络游戏时用英语和其他玩家交流。
10. I leave comments or ask questions in online game communities.	10. 我在网络游戏论坛中用英语留言或询问信息。
11. I listen to English language news programs online or TV.	11. 我通过在线平台或电视听英语新闻。
12. I listen to songs in English.	12. 我听英文歌曲。
13. I listen to English podcasts.	13. 我听英文广播。
14. I watch sports events in English online or TV.	14. 我通过在线平台或电视看英文体育赛事活动。
15. I watch English language movies or dramas with subtitles in English online or TV.	15. 我通过在线平台或电视看带字幕的英文电影或电视剧。
16. I watch English language movies or dramas without any subtitles online or TV.	16. 我通过在线平台或电视看不带字幕的英文电影或电视剧。
17. I watch English cartoon online or TV.	17. 我通过在线平台或电视看英文动画片。
18. I watch YouTube or DouYin videos in English.	18. 我在YouKu 网站或抖音上看英文视频。
19. I watch educational English contents (e.g., TED Talks, lecture, documentary) online or TV.	19. 我通过在线平台或电视看教育类的英文视频 (如: TED 演讲、讲座、纪录片等)。
20. I chat with others in English via social media such as WeChat, Sina Weibo, Tencent QQ.	20. 我在社交媒体上用英语与他人交流 (如: 微信、新浪微博、腾讯 QQ 等)。

(continued)

Items English	Chinese
IDLE	非正式数字化英语学习活动
21. I talk with native English speakers (e.g., American, British) via social media.	21. 我在社交媒体上与以英语为母语的人交流 (如: 英国人、美国人等)。
22. I talk with non-native English speakers (e.g., Singaporean, Malaysian, Thai, Filipino, Korean) via social media.	22. 我在社交媒体上与不以英语为母语的外国人交流 (如:新加坡人、马来西亚人、泰国人、菲律宾、韩国人等)。
23. I write comments in English on social media such as Zhihu.	23. 我在社交媒体上用英文留言,如:知乎等。
24. I live stream on social media in English.	24. 我在社交媒体上用英文做直播。
25. I talk to chatbots (e.g., Xiaoice, Julie or Pandora Vince) in English.	25. 我使用英语与聊天机器人交谈, 如: Xiaoice, Julie or Pandora Vince。
26. I chat with intelligent personal assistants (e.g., AliGenie, Google Assistant, Apple's Siri, or Amazon's Alexa)	26. 我使用英语与智能社交媒介交谈, 如: AliGenie, Google Assistant, Apple's Siri, Amazon's Alexa 等。
27. I share English contents online.	27. 我在网络上分享英文主题内容。
28. I send an email to others in English.	28. 我用英文写邮件与他人沟通和交流。

Part 3: English Enjoyment

*Please respond to the following statements on a five-point Likert scale.
1. Strongly disagree; 2. Disagree; 3. Neutral; 4. Agree; and 5. Strongly agree*

Items English	Chinese
L2 Enjoyment	学习英语的愉悦度
1. I can be creative using English.	1. 我可以很自然地使用英语。
2. I can laugh off embarrassing mistakes in English.	2. 我可以对使用英语时犯的尴尬的错误一笑而过。
3. I don't get bored with English.	3. 我觉得英语一点也不枯燥。
4. I enjoy learning English.	4. 我很享受学习英语的过程。
5. I can express myself better in English.	5. 我更倾向于使用英语来表达观点。
6. It is fun to learn English.	6. 我认为学习英语很有乐趣。

(continued)

Items English	Chinese
L2 Enjoyment	学习英语的愉悦度
7. Making errors is part of the English learning process.	7. 我认为在英语学习过程中犯错误也是一种学习。
8. I act as though I am a different person during the English class.	8. 我在英语课堂学习中感觉自己是变成了另一个人。
9. I am a worthy member of the English class.	9. 我认为我在英语课堂中是非常重要的一员。
10. I have learned interesting things in English class.	10. 我在英语课堂中学习了很多有趣的知识。
11. In English class, I feel proud of my accomplishments.	11. 我在英语课堂的学习中有很大的成就感。
12. English class has a positive environment.	12. 我的英语课堂是个积极向上的学习环境。
13. The classmates are nice in English class.	13. 我的同学们非常互助友好。
14. There is a good atmosphere in English class.	14. 我的英语课堂学习气氛非常好。
15. We laugh a lot in English class.	15. 我的英语课中经常有欢快的笑声。
16. The English teacher is encouraging.	16. 我的英语老师很善于激励学生学习。
17. The English teacher is friendly.	17. 我的英语老师很友好。
18. The English teacher is supportive.	18. 我的英语老师可以给学生提供很多帮助。

Part 4: Grit in learning English

*Please respond to the following statements on a five-point Likert scale
1. Not like me at all; 2. Not much like me; 3. Somewhat like me; 4. Mostly like me; 5. Very much like me

Items English	Chinese
L2 Grit	学习英语的毅力
1. I have overcome difficulties to improve my English communication.	1. 我克服许多困难来不断提升我的英语沟通能力。

(continued)

Items English	Chinese
L2 Grit	学习英语的毅力
2. I have no difficulty in learning new English vocabulary every day.	2. 我现在对于每天新单词的学习感觉不到有任何压力。
3. Difficulties don't discourage me to practice my English skills.	3. 困难不会让我退却练习使用英语的步伐。
4. I work hard to improve my English ability.	4. 我非常努力地提高我的英语交际能力。
5. I have learned English continuously for several years.	5. 我已经坚持学习英语很多年。
6. I am diligent in practicing English.	6. 我坚持练习使用英语进行沟通交流。
7. I set a goal to learn English and continue to pursue that goal.	7. 我定下了学习英语的目标并且不断努力实现目标。
8. I have maintained interest in learning English for many years.	8. 很多年来,我一直对学习英语很感兴趣。
9. I have learned new English words regularly because it is interesting to me.	9. 我坚持学习英语词汇,因为我对它很感兴趣。
10. It is easy to maintain my focus on reading an English book that takes more than a few weeks to complete.	10. 尽管需要花几周的时间才能读完一本英文书,但我还是可以坚持读完。
11. Once I become interested in improving my English through a certain method, I often sustain that interest for a long time.	11. 一旦我找到某种我感兴趣的方法来学习英语,我就会一直对它感兴趣。

References

Arndt, Henriette L. & Robert Woore. 2018. Vocabulary learning from watching YouTube videos and reading blog posts. *Language Learning and Technology* 22(3). 124–142.

Barcelos, Ana Maria Ferreira. 2015. Unveiling the relationship between language learning beliefs, emotions, and identities. *Studies in Second Language Learning and Teaching* 5(2). 301–325.

Benson, Phil & Hayo Reinders (eds.). 2011. *Beyond the language classroom*. New York: Palgrave Macmillan.

Chen, Jun Hsieh & Ju Seong Lee. 2021. Digital storytelling outcomes, emotions, grit, and perceptions among EFL middle school learners: Robot-assisted versus PowerPoint-assisted presentations. *Computer Assisted Language Learning*. https://doi.org/10.1080/09588221.2021.1969410

Chik, Alice & Jenifer Ho. 2017. Learn a language for free: Recreational learning among adults. *System* 69. 162–171. https://doi.org/10.1016/j.system.2017.07.017

Cole, Jason & Robert Vanderplank. 2016. Comparing autonomous and class-based learners in Brazil: Evidence for the present-day advantages of informal, out-of-class learning. *System* 61. 31–42. https://doi.org/10.1016/j.system.2016.07.007

Credé, Marcus, Michael C. Tynan & Peter D. Harms. 2017. Much ado about grit: A meta-analytic synthesis of the grit literature. *Journal of Personality and Social Psychology* 113(3). 492–511. https://doi.org/10.1037/pspp0000102

Dewaele, Jean-Marc & Peter MacIntyre. 2014. The two faces of Janus? Anxiety and enjoyment in the foreign language classroom. *Studies in Second Language Learning and Teaching* 4(2). 237–274.

Dörnyei, Zoltán. 2007. *Research Methods in Applied Linguistics*. Oxford: Oxford University Press.

Duckworth, Angela. 2017. *Grit: Why Passion and Resilience are the Secrets to Success*. London: Penguin Random House.

Duckworth, Angela L., Christopher Peterson, Michael D. Matthews & Dennis R. Kelly. 2007. Grit: Perseverance and passion for long-term goals. *Journal of Personality and Social Psychology* 92(6). 1087–1101.

Dressman, Mark & Randall William Sadler (eds.). 2020. *The Handbook of Informal Language Learning*. Hoboken/Chichester: Wiley-Blackwell.

Eskreis-Winkler, Lauren, Elizabeth P. Shulman, Scott A. Beal & Angela L. Duckworth. 2014. The grit effect: Predicting retention in the military, the workplace, school and marriage. *Frontiers in Psychology* 5. 1–12. https://doi.org/10.3389/fpsyg.2014.00036

Fornell, Claes & David F. Larcker. 1981. Structural equation models with unobservable variables and measurement error: Algebra and statistics. *Journal of Marketing Research* 18(3). 382–388. https://doi.org/10.1177/002224378101800313

Fredrickson, Barbara L. 2001. The role of positive emotions in positive psychology: The broaden-and-build theory of positive emotions. *American Psychologist* 56(3). 218–226.

Hair, Joseph F., William C. Black, Babin J. Barry, Rolph E. Anderson & Ronald L. Tatham. 1998. *Multivariate Data Analysis*, 5th edn., 207–219. Upper Saddle River, NJ: Pearson Prentice Hall.

Jiang, Yan & Jean-Marc Dewaele. 2019. How unique is the foreign language classroom enjoyment and anxiety of Chinese EFL learners? *System* 82. 13–25. https://doi.org/10.1016/j.system.2019.02.017

Khajavy, Gholam H., Peter D. MacIntyre & Jamal Hariri. 2020. A closer look at grit and language mindset as predictors of foreign language achievement. *Studies in Second Language Acquisition* 43. 379–402. https://doi.org/10.1017/S0272263120000480

Kusyk, Meryl. 2017. The development of complexity, accuracy and fluency in L2 written production through informal participation in online activities. *CALICO Journal* 34(1). 75–96. https://www.jstor.org/stable/10.2307/90014679

Krashen, Stephen D. 1981. *Second Language Acquisition and Second Language Learning*. Oxford/London: Pergamon Press.

Lai, Chun. 2018. *Autonomous Language Learning with Technology: Beyond the Classroom*. New York: Bloomsbury Publishing.

Lai, Chun, Weimin Zhu & Gang Gong. 2015. Understanding the quality of out-of-class English learning. *TESOL Quarterly* 49(2). 278–308. https://doi.org/10.1002/tesq.171

Lan, Guoxing, Larisa Nikitina & Wai Sheng Woo. 2021. Ideal L2 self and willingness to communicate: A moderated mediation model of shyness and grit. *System* 99. https://doi.org/10.1016/j.system.2021.102503

Lee, Ju Seong. 2019a. Informal digital learning of English and second language vocabulary outcomes: Can quantity conquer quality? *British Journal of Educational Technology* 50(2). 767–778.

Lee, Ju Seong. 2019b. Quantity and diversity of informal digital learning of English. *Language Learning and Technology* 23(1). 114–126.

Lee, Ju Seong. 2021. Teacher as change agent: Integrating informal learning into formal education. Paper presented at the *International Conference of Teacher Training and Education (ICTTE)*, Surakarta, Indonesia. 25–26 August, 2021.

Lee, Ju Seong. 2022a. *Informal Digital Learning of English: Research to Practice*. New York: Routledge.

Lee, Ju Seong. 2022b. The role of grit and classroom enjoyment in EFL learners' willingness to communicate. *Journal of Multilingual and Multicultural Development* 43(5). 452–468. https://doi.org/10.1080/01434632.2020.1746319

Lee, Ju Seong & Jun Chen Hsieh. 2019. Affective variables and willingness to communicate of EFL learners in in-class, out-of-class, and digital contexts. *System* 82. 63–73.

Lee, Ju Seong & Nur Arifah Drajati. 2019. Affective variables and informal digital learning of English: Keys to willingness to communicate in a second language. *Australasian Journal of Educational Technology* 35(5). 168–182.

Lee, Ju Seong & Kilryoung Lee. 2020. Affective factors, virtual intercultural experiences, and L2 willingness to communicate in in-class, out-of-class, and digital settings. *Language Teaching Research* 24(6). 813–833.

Lee, Ju Seong & Kilryoung Lee. 2021. The role of informal digital learning of English and L2 motivational self-system in foreign language enjoyment. *British Journal of Educational Technology* 52(1). 358–373.

Lee, Ju Seong, Qin Xie & Kilryoung Lee. 2021. Informal Digital Learning of English and L2 willingness to communicate: Roles of emotions, gender, and educational stage. *Journal of Multilingual and Multicultural Development*. 1–17. https://doi.org/10.1080/01434632.2021.1918699

Li, Chengchen. 2019. A positive psychology perspective on Chinese EFL students' trait emotional intelligence, foreign language enjoyment and EFL learning achievement. *Journal of Multilingual and Multicultural Development* 41(3). 246–263.

Li, Chengchen, Guiying Jiang & Jean-Marc Dewaele. 2018. Understanding Chinese high school students' Foreign Language Enjoyment: Validation of the Chinese version of the Foreign Language Enjoyment scale. *System* 76. 183–196.

MacIntyre, Peter D. & Tammy Gregersen. 2012. Emotions that facilitate language learning: The positive-broadening power of the imagination. *Studies in Second Language Learning and Teaching* 2(2). 193–213.

MacIntyre, Peter D., Tammy Gregersen & Sarah Mercer. 2019. Setting an agenda for Positive Psychology in SLA: Theory, practice, and research. *Modern Language Journal* 103(1). 262–274.

Pavlenko, Aneta. 2013. The affective turn in SLA: from 'affective factors' to 'language desire' and 'commodification of affect'. In Danuta Gabryś-Barker & Joanna Bielska (eds.), *The Affective Dimension in Second Language Acquisition*, 3–28. Bristol: Multilingual Matters.

Peng, Hongying, Sake Jager & Wander Lowie. 2020. A person-centred approach to L2 learners' informal mobile language learning. *Computer Assisted Language Learning*. 1–22. https://doi.org/10.1080/09588221.2020.1868532

Prior, Matthew T. 2019. Elephants in the room: An "affective turn," or just feeling our way? *Modern Language Journal* 103(2). 516–527.

Reinders, Hayo & Phil Benson. 2017. Research agenda: Language learning beyond the classroom. *Language Teaching* 50(4). 561–578.

Sauro, Shannon & Katerina Zourou. 2019. What are the digital wilds? *Language Learning & Technology* 23(1). 1–7. https://doi.org/10125/44666

Seligman, Martin EP. & Mihaly Csikszentmihalyi. 2000. Positive Psychology: An introduction. *American Psychologist* 55(1). 5–14.

Sundqvist, Pia & Liss Kerstin Sylvén. 2016. *Extramural English in Teaching and Learning: From Theory and Research to Practice*. Basingstoke/London: Palgrave Macmillan.

Sockett, Geoffrey. 2014. *The Online Informal Learning of English*. Basingstoke/London: Palgrave Macmillan.

Soyoof, Ali, Barry Lee Reynolds, Boris Vazquez-Calvo & Katherine McLay. 2021. Informal digital learning of English (IDLE): A scoping review of what has been done and a look towards what is to come. *Computer Assisted Language Learning*, 1–33. https://doi.org/10.1080/09588221.2021.1936562

Teimouri, Yasser, Luke Plonsky & Farhad Tabandeh. 2020. L2 grit: Passion and perseverance for second language learning. *Language Teaching Research* 26(5). https://doi.org/10.1177/1362168820921895

Toffoli, Denyze. 2020. *Informal Learning and Institution-wide Language Provision: University Language Learners in the 21st Century*. Chem: Palgrave Macmillan.

Toffoli, Denyze & Geoff Sockett. 2013. University teachers' perceptions of Online Informal Learning of English (OILE). *Computer Assisted Language Learning* 28(1). 7–21. https://doi.org/10.1080/09588221.2013.776970

Wei, Hongjun, Kaixuan Gao & Wenchao Wang. 2019. Understanding the relationship between grit and foreign language performance among middle school students: The roles of foreign language enjoyment and classroom environment. *Frontiers in Psychology* 10(1508). 1–8. https://doi.org/10.3389/fpsyg.2019.01508

Wei, Rining, He Liu & Sshijie Wang. 2020. Exploring L2 grit in the Chinese EFL context. *System* 93. 1–9. https://doi.org/10.1016/j.system.2020.102295

Zhang, Ruofei, Di Zou, Gary Cheng, Haoran Xie, Fu Lee Wang & Oliver Tat Sheung Au. 2021. Target languages, types of activities, engagement, and effectiveness of extramural language learning. *PLoS ONE* 16(6). https://doi.org/10.1371/journal.pone.0253431

Artem Zadorozhnyy, Baohua Yu

12 Preservice English language teachers and informal digital learning of English (IDLE) in Kazakhstan

Reconciling two identities

Abstract: Given that existing digital affordances offer contemporary language learners ample opportunities to be exposed to authentic language and culture learning experiences in online environments, this chapter adopts a critical approach for examining how undergraduate preservice English teachers negotiate and balance their language learner and language teacher identities. To do so, we adopt a qualitative research design informed by 32 semi-structured interviews with prospective English language teachers from Kazakhstani universities. Research findings allow us to address beliefs about the concept of informal digital learning of English (IDLE) and to provide possible clarifications for the results obtained. In addition, we discuss plausible explanations for the contradictions expressed by interviewees and propose further research pathways.

Keywords: informal digital learning of English, L2 teacher identity, preservice English language teachers, metacognitive awareness, Khazakstan

1 Introduction

The globalisation of liberal arts education (Lewis 2018) and exponential growth of digital technology as a result of the fourth industrial revolution (Gleason 2018) has resulted in the emergence of vast opportunities for learners to be widely exposed to their target languages. In alignment with these trends, researchers emphasise that contemporary language learners have access to numerous digital affordances that provide students with an extensive collection of language learning materials and offer individuals meaningful opportunities to become immersed in the language learning process (Colpaert 2020). The availability of multimodal digital resources has attracted considerable attention from researchers who study language learning activities beyond the classroom level (Gong et al. 2019; Kusyk 2017; Lai 2017; Toffoli 2020). What is more, the recent COVID-19

Artem Zadorozhnyy, Baohua Yu, The Education University of Hong Kong, Hong Kong SAR, China

https://doi.org/10.1515/9783110752441-012

outbreak and the resulting rise in emergent remote schooling practices in online spaces as a response to the imposed lockdown measures worldwide (Hodges et al. 2020) have further sparked researchers' interest and efforts to pursue this line of inquiry.

Given the number of concurrent conceptualisations that reflect out-of-class computer-assisted language learning processes, for this chapter, we propose utilising one of the most cited definitions introduced by Lee (2020), who defined informal digital learning of English (IDLE) as "learning English autonomously in extramural digital contexts independent of formal English instruction" (156). While referring to the concept of IDLE, this study primarily concentrates on the aspects of behavioural engagement pertaining to informal L2 experiences, as opposed to the multidimensional framework utilised by Arndt (see Chapter 14). Hence, in discussing IDLE activities in this chapter, the term 'engagement' will be used interchangeably with 'participation' and 'involvement' to depict informal language learning behaviours with digital resources.

Overall, the objective of this study is to investigate perceptions of prospective nonnative English language teachers regarding the multitude of emerging digital tools and platforms, including social media applications and blogs (Aloraini & Cardoso 2020), mobile technologies (Ma 2017) and online role-playing games (Sundqvist 2019), to name a few, that can be used for increased exposure to the English language. In addition, this study seeks to depict how prospective language teachers negotiate and balance their language learner and language teacher identities. To achieve these goals, given the scarcity of IDLE data from the Central Asian region, this study provides empirical findings obtained through semi-structured interviews with prospective English language teachers in Kazakhstan.

2 Literature review: Perceptions about IDLE

With the rapid development of digital technologies and the breadth of emerging opportunities for students to practice their target language in online spaces, many scholars have started to pay attention to the myriad of existing informal digital learning practices and perceptions about them (Chik 2020; Toffoli and Sockett 2015; Trinder 2017; Zadorozhnyy and Yu 2021). For instance, a research inquiry about non-formal language learning applications (e.g., Duolingo and Babbel), conducted by Arvanitis (2019), demonstrated that students considered them useful due to the availability of personalised feedback, the quality of visual and sound effects and the adaptive content delivery. Favourable perceptions about the digital affordances of Duolingo were also revealed by Chik (2020), who reported that integration of social networking components into language teaching motivated students to be persistent in learning the target language. Similarly, Hung (2011) and Lin et al. (2016) observed positive language learning outcomes associated with engagement of students in social networking sites and vlogging activities, respectively. In a similar vein, positive impact was discovered concerning informal reading activities (Suk 2016), overall exposure to authentic language materials (Sockett 2014), L2 writing performance (Hsu and Lo 2018), L2 digital literacies (Zadorozhnyy and Yu 2021), engagement in video games (Sundqvist 2019; Sundqvist and Wikström 2015), and participating in blogging and vlogging activities (Arndt and Woore 2018; Hung 2011), to name a few.

Trinder (2017) studied the perceived usefulness of informal learning practices among L2 learners in Austria. Detailed examination of students' opinions showed their positive predisposition towards informal learning activities. Students reported being frequently engaged in receptive informal language learning activities (e.g., watching movies and TV series) with the explicit goal of improving their English language abilities. Such findings correspond to those of Salomon (1983), who stated that perceptions about learning activities influence the amount of effort that students invest in learning a language. In other words, perceptions about IDLE activities were conducive to students' actual intentional self-directed IDLE engagement.

A more deliberate description of students' perceptions can be found in the study of Lai et al. (2017), who analysed the experience of undergraduate foreign language learners enrolled at higher education institutions in Hong Kong and the United States. The cross-regional study demonstrated that students' perceptions and their subsequent involvement in self-directed language learning practices with technologies depended on L2 teachers' recommendations of tools along with relevant guidance (i.e. teacher capacity support). In addition, Hong Kong students' attitudes were found to be impacted by affective and teacher behaviour support. This also corroborates the findings of Hu (2014) on the cultural predisposition of Asian students to perceive teachers as credible authorities. As seen from the findings of the outlined studies, scholars have made successful attempts to depict the variety of existing informal language learning tools and resources, their potential influence and students' attitudes across a variety of contexts (Jurkovič 2019; Lai et al. 2017; Lee 2020; Toffoli 2020; Trinder 2017).

Likewise, prior studies have sought to investigate perceptions of L2 educators about the phenomenon of informal learning and the place of such perceptions in their teaching practices (Lai, Yeung, and Hu 2016). Following this line of investigation, a detailed qualitative research inquiry was conducted by Toffoli and Sockett (2015) to understand whether university language instructors in France perceive informal learning practices as useful for language acquisition. Their findings demonstrate that although teachers lack understanding about the scale of students' engagement in informal online language learning activities, they consider that such practices might positively influence students' in-class behaviours and overall level of English.

A significant gap in previous research on informal learning exists due to a lack of attention paid to the sample of prospective English language teachers. Given a growing role of English as a modern *lingua franca* and its ubiquitous presence online (Galloway and Rose 2015), the attention of researchers is directed to the perceptions and experiences of nonnative language teachers who are assumed to balance their language learning and language teaching identities (Chun et al. 2016; Dewey 2020). For instance, prior publications highlighted the responsibility of teachers in shaping students' language learning beliefs and their actual behavioural, cognitive, linguistic, and affective engagement in L2 learning activities (Arndt 2019; Lai et al. 2015; Shelton-Strong 2020). Considering the findings of earlier research, non-native language instructors are anticipated to perceive potentially problematic circumstances more fully than native language instructors by imitating their own learning experiences (Sutherland 2012).Therefore, it might be assumed that good language learners have a higher likelihood of becoming successful language instructors. Based on this line of thought, we can speculate that prospective non-native language teachers should be capable of balancing their language learning and language teaching identities.

However, although the role of L2 teachers regarding informal learning has been recognised (Andrei 2017; Bruggeman et al. 2021), previous research into the phenomenon of informal learning has disregarded the role of *future* language educators as well as their perceptions and informal learning experiences. Given the growing interest in IDLE, this chapter aims to explore perspectives about engagement in IDLE activities among nonnative preservice L2 teachers. In doing so, we will draw on the experiences of prospective English language teachers in the context of the Central Asian country of Kazakhstan to provide responses to the question: How do students' experiences in engaging in informal digital language learning activities affect their development as future L2 teachers?

3 Methodology

As engagement in a target language community of practice is bound to complex issues surrounding learner identity formation, a qualitative data collection approach was adopted in order to discover student teachers' perceptions about the informal learning phenomenon. Specifically, the data were drawn from a sample of undergraduate university students pursuing their bachelor's degrees at Kazakhstani Pedagogical Institutions. Given the paucity of data obtained in the Central Asian region, this study aimed at filling the existing gap. In addition, owing to the relatively low level of English language proficiency in Central Asian countries we deliberately chose to conduct the study with reasonably advanced students whose interest in English language acquisition and overall level of proficiency were expected to be higher than average by default due to the students' choice of educational path. That is, this study was expected to contribute to the existing literature by focusing on multiple existing identities of prospective nonnative English language teachers.

Before implementation, the project was approved by the Human Research Ethics Committee (HREC) of the Education University of Hong Kong. The qualitative research design was informed by 32 semi-structured interviews with preservice English language teachers who studied English as their first FL while double majoring in French or German. All of the students were born in Kazakhstan and were fluent in Russian, despite the fact that the Kazakh language was indicated as participants' first language in a few cases. The data were gathered through face-to-face and online semi-structured interviews which lasted for an average of one hour. All students were enrolled in the program entitled "Foreign languages: two foreign languages", which is dedicated to training future foreign language teachers in Kazakhstan. Altogether, the sample consisted of seven male and twenty-five female students, among which there were five freshmen, five sophomores, sixteen third year, and six fourth-year students, representing six state academic institutions.

Interview questions were divided into two main sections: (1) questions about students' actual engagement in various informal learning activities, their beliefs, and associated benefits and (2) considerations about the impact of informal L2 learning activities on prospective and ongoing teaching practices. Upon completion, all interviews were transcribed verbatim for further analysis. Identification codes were used to conceal the participants' identities and related details to respect their privacy. The process of interview coding was performed with NVIVO software for facilitating and structuring data management (Creswell and Clark 2017). The initial analytic techniques were guided by a deductive approach based on prior knowledge regarding the topic of informal L2 learning, followed by inductive analysis procedures related to the identification of newly emerging subthemes (Elo and Kyngäs 2008).

To distinguish frequent from non-frequent IDLE users, given that this study was initially informed by quantitative data, the frequency of students' engagement in informal learning was evaluated by calculating average means of engagement in productive and receptive IDLE practices. Both types of informal learning activities were evaluated on a 6-point Likert scale ranging from 1 (never) to 6 (very often, multiple times a day; Lee and Drajati 2019); hence, students were regarded as frequent IDLE users in cases when the average means were equal to, or greater than 4 (sometimes, = 2–3 times per week).

4 Perceived effects of informal practices

Amongst the most frequently mentioned skills, all the interviewees indicated positive connection between engagement in diverse informal activities, such as watching movies, playing games, and listening to music and podcasts, and the development of listening skills. Primarily positive perceptions were emphasised when evaluating the effect of engagement in social media on the development of communicative competence. Depending on students' interests, some interviewees shared their experience of practicing English with other people via communication-oriented applications (e.g., Tandem, Hi Native and Slowly), whilst others exemplified the popularity of social networks (e.g., Instagram, Facebook, and Twitter) in facilitating communication and positively influencing their confidence.

Reported availability of open access resources and awareness about digital affordances were seen to impact students' engagement in social-oriented technological experiences within global social media platforms. Frequent IDLE users were found to consider themselves part of a global community of L2 learners that allows them to be exposed to authentic language content. Interviewees reported being more engaged in receptive (e.g., reading and listening-centered activities) rather than in productive informal learning practices and underlined perceived benefits connected to the development of L2 digital literacies. That is, some suggested examples demonstrate that engagement in digital spaces helped students understand digital genre-specific norms better.

> *English is an old language, so there are many old-style words. Young people come up with their own slang and words, it seems to me, it only makes the language better. It would be too boring to use academic language for everyday communication. One of the slang features is to use the abbreviation of words. Americans are very fond of abbreviations. For example, they use "u" instead of "you", "so much" is just "SM", "talk to you later" is "TTYL". I noticed that they do not like to write long words. Teachers need to pay attention to such things. For sure.*
> (Student K)

In addition, exposure to different views and opinions was said to facilitate students' critical reflection of the content by considering perspectives brought by people of different origins and cultural backgrounds. In other words, participating in IDLE activities was linked to the development of skills for critically evaluating information, recognising the situated nature of literacies, and establishing meaningful communication in various circumstances.

The most remarkable and noticeable experience was supplied by Student G, a freshman who possesses a favourable perception regarding the impact of IDLE practices on his English language development. This interviewee graduated from a mainstream state school, wherein no particular emphasis is given to the development of English, has never travelled overseas, and claims that among his relatives only his elder brother shares the interest in improving English skills. This interviewee began his story by sharing that his involvement in online gaming resulted in creating personalised and learner-centred space, the exposure to which was conducive to the development of his language skills.

> Once I played a game, it was called BlockLand. There were no Russian speakers among players, but I needed to communicate with other people, hence I needed to learn English. That time I had terrible English, I did not know anything, I couldn't link sentences, although I was aware of some basics. I had to learn the language to continue playing. And so, I continued [playing]. Over some time, I began playing other games. I switched on Russian subtitles and listened to original English voice acting, so that I could hear English and immediately see the translation. I immediately saw how the sentences were built; what words were used. Translation helped me to see the full picture. And so over time, I began developing some language skills, some understanding. I started feeling the language. (Student G)

The interviewee provided a detailed description of his path towards learning English by playing multiplayer videogames (e.g., Destiny 2, Blockland and Starbound), during which he constantly participated in multiple communicative situations. The participant noted that his interest and need in utilising English in authentic learning situations were the most crucial factors in developing his language capabilities. To support his favourable perceptions of IDLE practices, Student G mentioned that he perceives his English language skills to be derived entirely from his informal activities. As evidence of his progress, he recalls winning first place in the national state English language contest during his senior year of high school. To summarise, while no generalisations can be drawn from the single case of Student G, his experience can be utilised as a vivid illustration of how involvement in online environments might assist language development.

4.1 IDLE users as learners

The analysis of interviews identified several critical features of informal learning practices amongst preservice teachers. First, the interviewees indicated that in comparison with receptive practices (e.g., listening to music, watching movies, series, and videos in social media), engagement in productive informal practices was limited. Secondly, students overwhelmingly underscored their engagement in interest-based and meaning-making practices. In particular, students reported initiating language learning activities based on their interest in a certain topic rather than on the improvement of their language abilities, which was a feature of the study's key idea, i.e., IDLE in extramural situations. Almost all students reported similar patterns of watching movies in their original language and underlined their gradual evolution from native (e.g., Russian) subtitles to foreign language captions, followed by the final stage of disabling them entirely. In contrast to the majority, two male students (Year 1 and Year 3) recommended watching movies without subtitles, following a "sink or swim" language-learning approach. One interviewee stated: "When you go abroad, you develop the language faster because its presence surrounds you. What we can do [in informal environments] is we can imitate such situations online" (Student D). Through this quote, the participant indicates that engaging with audio and video materials might be an alternative for authentic language environments by providing extensive exposure to the target language.

Interviewees acknowledged that engagement in different informal learning activities helped them to construct personalised and learner-centred spaces. For instance, one male student explained how his interest in playing multiplayer videogames helped him to construct his vocabulary knowledge:

> Let's say it is a team game, then you have a voice chat. You know that this object, hero or item in the game has a particular name. There is no Russian translation of this name. It can be translated, but no one will call it that. You say the name of this item, "tower" for example, and then you add "go". Let's say you don't even know the meaning of the word "tower". But English-speaking players understand you, so they go with you. And when they say "go kill bear", even if you don't know what the word "kill" means, but you know that the word "bear" means "that monster in the forest", and you see that they suddenly kill it, you understand what the word "kill" means. And so, step by step, you learn things. (Student G)

Another example of personalised practices was suggested by Student E, who noted her attachment to informal online communities in various social media platforms. For example, Student E was a moderator of a Russian K-Pop (Korean popular music) online community where her duties included content generation for one year. As it was hard to find information about K-pop culture in Russian, she spent her time translating news, stories, fanfiction archives, and social media comments from English, which subsequently helped her develop vocabulary knowledge.

While most students emphasised the general unstructured nature of their informal learning activities, only five students (N = 5) reported integrating structured activities that followed the usual patterns of their classroom behaviours. That is, students offered examples of selecting short stories from online sources with subsequent completion of corresponding tasks, engagement in a manual compilation of vocabulary lists with word-by-word translation, and completion of structured online grammar textbook exercises, to name a few. Engagement in other informal L2 learning activities was, for the most part, perceived by such students as impractical unless specific efforts were initiated to establish continuity or repetition of formal classroom activities.

> Student A: I searched for YouTube videos on the topics that I didn't understand. For example, the prepositions "in", "at", "on". I watched 3–4 videos and then completed assignments.
>
> Interviewer: Was it a kind of a digital lecture?
>
> Student A: That's right. Digital lecture with explanations, whiteboard, marker, and a teacher . . . It was important for me to understand information and then to practice it. To strengthen my knowledge, I performed grammar tasks. You know, there are such online tasks when you write and they say to you: "Here it is wrong, try again", such grammatical tasks.

In contrast, the opinions of frequent informal English language learners considerably varied, with three students who stated that language learning is a vivid process that should not depend fully on structured learning activities. Among frequent informal language learners, Student G highlighted the importance of engaging in authentic online learning environments. He provided an interesting point by comparing the language to a dynamic system that could not be learnt by following the textbooks and suggested that one should pay more attention to practicing the language rather than learning the rules:

> I never studied English with the textbooks [before university], I don't like it. It's like reading an instruction, I don't think that the language has its instruction. I believe that the language can either be learned by learning its rules or it can be felt. But to follow the instructions, this is somehow neither so nor so. I don't like to learn languages by instruction. (Student G)

In contrast to positive opinions about the impact of informal learning practices, an overall negative opinion was presented in connection with non-formal language learning practices such as engagement in non-formal, structured language learning applications like Duolingo, Babbel, Rosetta Stone and Mondly. The arguments against using them were connected to their predominantly formal inclination, limited access to free-of-charge features (i.e., limited and restricted levels in Duolingo, disabled "near me" function in Tandem) and the lack of engaging activities for intermediate or advanced language students. To sum up, the findings reported here shed new light on the degree of engagement in IDLE practices among Kazakhstani student teachers; the students showed awareness about diverse IDLE practices and provided rationales for their extensive engagement.

4.2 IDLE users as teachers

Most interviewees pointed out their positive attitude towards the role of informal learning practices for improving foreign language skills. Students acknowledged the current responsibilities of teachers in explaining to students how to utilise devices wisely and sustainably. The willingness and aspirations of interviewees to consider informal learning strategies in their teaching practice were reflected in their desire to embed informal learning elements into their future lesson plans during the internship period. Student E, for instance, emphasised that as a private tutor, she tries to start her lessons by discussing the latest news that is of interest to her students for raising their interest in getting involved in further informal activities. Although not many students expressed their genuine interest in teaching, they still underlined the need for future teachers to be more innovative in their teaching approaches. One female interviewee stated:

> *I am working on creating my methodology for which I am already compiling a database of useful webpages and materials from the internet. It seems to me that all textbooks [which are used in schools and universities] are outdated, they do not reflect contemporary language. Hence, I think that informal environments could provide us with more authentic language samples.* (Student P)

Interestingly, the participants, who reported more engagement in IDLE activities through their responses, perceived more importance in bridging informal and formal activities by promoting and facilitating students' awareness regarding informal activities and emerging digital resources. When describing themselves as prospective language teachers, interviewees mostly agreed that informal practices should be perceived as a continuation of formal education.

> *I think, we should connect them [informal and formal learning]. Based on my experience that's what our teachers did. Maybe I connected it by myself naturally. We have to connect them. We need more informal ways to study English and fewer formal ones. Informal ways have more weight than formal. They have to be together in order to work . . . . Okay, you get knowledge following formal practices but then you should do something to develop this knowledge. I did not know that before, but I have been doing it naturally. To develop this knowledge, you have to listen and watch more in English.* (Student W)

Many students emphasised that their schoolteachers lacked skills and consistency in aligning digital resources to students' interests, scaffolding their usage or revisiting the same tools. Considering themselves to be future L2 teachers, interviewees pointed out the need to promote the usage of digital resources in out-of-class settings and the establishment of brainstorming activities to retrieve alternative approaches for their implementation. Likewise, interviewees highlighted the need to integrate more up-to-date resources.

In contrast to extensive critiques of the school language education system, students were mainly positive about the roles of university teachers in recommending informal learning activities and supplied some illustrative examples. Students C and D offered examples of how brainstorming in-class exercises and discussions about how to utilise specific digital resources (e.g., corpus learning webpages, vlogging activities) led to the adoption of some webpages and applications into their IDLE repertoire. To extend this line of thought, students pointed out their role as future teachers in bridging formal and informal modes of practice by facilitating the usage of platforms and applications and by introducing activities that will assist students in exploring effective ways to implement various digital resources to learn the language autonomously.

Although still pursuing their undergraduate degree, several senior students exemplified how they shape their language teaching identity in informal environments. For instance, Student P stated that her behaviour in social networks is directly connected to her identity as a prospective teacher:

> *All content that I publish is exclusively in English. I know that this is better than using Russian language, especially for my friends and subscribers. People got used to posts in Russian, and it's not interesting to them. But when you do it [post information] in English, they will look for answers themselves and remember new words. For example, when I post stories on Instagram about my life, I always add English words or hashtags. It is useful for me as I practice my skills and for my friends who might not know some words or expressions. They have thanked me many times for that.* (Student P)

This view was echoed by other frequent informal language learners who tend to recommend useful resources and language learning strategies to their friends. Half of the participants in the present study reported adopting the role of language mentors for which they advise relevant L2 materials and occasionally collect evaluative feedback.

> *Classmates may come up to me and ask how to do this task in English, "Can you explain?" And I explain. During my English classes when we have some assignments I am often asked [by teachers] to check what my classmates are doing, so that I can explain them their mistakes, as well as rules and tips to avoid these mistakes. Once a classmate approached me, she told me that she has a poor knowledge of English, and she wanted me to help her. I agreed. For quite a long time she sent me various tasks that she could not complete on her own, and I explained them to her. And now she practically does not send them to me at all because she can complete them all by herself . . . Sometimes they [classmates] just ask, "How did you learn English?" I say, "By and large I dit it thanks to my brother and video games I play." They say, "Games? How come?". And then I begin to explain that I merely wanted to understand what I was seeing and what was happening [in the game]. To do this, I had to know the language. Well, I think I have learned it because I played a lot.* (Student G)

> I've recently had such a case when a friend of mine made a similar request [asked to recommend how to learn the language informally]. I told him that the first thing he has to do is to learn the most important English words, so that he can understand basic texts. You don't need to learn grammar right away because you would not understand it anyway. Then I recommended him watching short cartoons in English and listening to music in English. He told me that he is good at it, but it is not enough. Now we are studying together. Every day he sends me a small report on the work he has done. For example, how many words he has learned. Now I already have three such people who improve their knowledge day by day. I love this teaching process. (Student L)

These two quotes exemplify how the foreign language learner identity of interviewees helps the interviewees to construct their L2 teacher identity. Students perceive that, while formal textbooks tend to become outdated, constantly updated content in online environments exposes language learners to authentic language materials and various communicative situations. Similarly, other interviewees emphasised the need for constructing personalised, student-centered language learning approaches (Student G and Student J) and the need for teachers to be aware of emerging digital resources by adapting teaching activities to students' interests (Student B). Finally, teachers were seen as influential in directing students to be creative in their language learning practices (Student W). Thus, taken together, these findings suggest that prospective Kazakhstani language teachers work on constructing their teaching identity based on an assessment of their personal L2 learning paths.

4.3 Contradicting identities

Unexpected findings of our study are associated with the discrepancies between the opinions of several students about informal language learning activities. For instance, despite a positive opinion regarding the influence of informal practices and perceived gradual development of abilities which several students exemplified, the same interviewees also remained sceptical about the impact of informal learning on a large scale. As such, Student I and Student A underlined that they were not certain to what degree their knowledge derived from either formal or informal language learning practices. Furthermore, three interviewees also emphasised that the actual influence of unstructured activities is elusive.

> I can spend an hour and a half a day on social media, but it is for entertainment purposes only. . . I wouldn't say that social media is useful for language learning. People on Instagram write using English language varieties. They use words that we, as teachers, do not teach our students, and which our teachers do not teach us. My goal is to learn original British English. And only then, when there is an opportunity to go to the country and plunge into the environment of the language, you can learn slang and idioms. (Student A)

The quote from the interview illustrates the position of a senior student (year 4) who spends a significant amount of time in online environments. Surprisingly, the interview subject emphasises the superiority of one language variety over another and underestimates the impact of exposure to non-standard language forms. Although the exposure to online environments implies encountering the complexities inherent in global English varieties, the position of this student provides an example of apparent disconnection between traditional forms of language taught in formal education programmes and actual varieties in use.

Furthermore, even though almost all students, except one freshman, had teaching practicum and/or private tutoring experience, we observed some further contradictions. For instance, Student H explicitly pointed out his regular engagement in watching sports activities, movies and series in English although denying the impact of these activities on his language abilities:

> *I don't think that it [informal language learning] particularly affected my skills. I think it might only affect my everyday language skills. Of course, there is a chance that such practices might change the language level, but I would not say that there will be any big changes. For example, when you watch the review of a basketball match . . . the only thing you can remember is how they [presenters] speak using Present Simple tense to describe what the player does and what happens during the game. Probably, this could add some sport terminology to your knowledge, but it will not have any good or bad effect on your skills.* (Student H)

A contradiction might be noticed when juxtaposing the above-cited quote with the student's claims regarding his regular engagement in informal learning. For instance, the interviewee noted that although it was difficult to comprehend the original audio track of movies and videos without embedded subtitles during the first year of his studies, frequent engagement in receptive informal activities resulted in a gradual development of listening skills. In addition, the participant claimed that he used to "lookup for the meaning and definitions [of words] and even created a separate notebook", which has been used for memorising new words and their further application during formal language learning sessions. Therefore, apparent discrepancies might have resulted from the lack of metacognitive skills or difficulties associated with balancing L2 student and L2 teacher identities.

Another contradiction was noted from the perceptions of Student D who initially claimed that he developed his level of English due to extensive engagement in the context-oriented practices in online games rather than because of rote memorisation:

> *When you are playing a video game, you are literally the main character, and no matter what you are told, it will always influence you. So, for example, let's say you were poisoned, and you don't know what it means. Then you see that HP bar [Health bar] above, it turns green*

> *and starts decreasing slowly. At that moment you realise that something, probably, has happened to your character and it might be connected to the poison because this is usually how poison is shown in games. And then you seem to have realised what the word "poison" means.* (Student N).

This example demonstrates the instance of using contextual and semantic encoding strategies to guess the meaning of words from the context (Gu and Johnson 1996). To support this argument, Student N acknowledged that engagement in different informal learning activities helped him to construct his vocabulary knowledge. However, while answering the questions regarding his perceptions of IDLE practices as a future language teacher, the interviewee contradicted his statements and noted that L2 students need to rely on explicit vocabulary acquisition strategies. Surprisingly, the interviewee dismissed the value of previously mentioned contextual vocabulary learning techniques and music listening activities and underlined that grammar could only be acquired through rote memorization of tenses.

> *Researcher: If you are approached by one of your students who asks to recommend some out-of-class language learning activities, what would you advise him/her?*
>
> *Student N: It depends on the person and on what he/she likes the most. If he/she likes watching films, let him/her watch films. First, he/she could use Russian subtitles as a support. I would even recommend the movies, which he/she has already watched – to make sure he/she loves the movie. The plot is already clear so student would not get lost while checking subtitles. But he/she needs to pay attention to what each word means. If needed, he/she should stop the movie to clarify things. Also, listening to the music in English but honestly, not I am sure if it helps. All my life I have been listening to music in English, and I don't think that it helped me . . . About grammar. It needs to be learnt by heart, crammed, just like in school, it cannot be learned in any other way.*

To summarise, the foregoing examples show that, while students are found to include many IDLE activities into their repertoires and report positive perceptions, they exhibit some inconsistencies when asked to reflect on their L2 teaching beliefs.

5 Discussion and conclusions

The purpose of this chapter was to investigate the perspectives of aspiring non-native L2 educators from Kazakhstan regarding the effects of IDLE activities. Overall, our results strengthen the idea that the availability of digital resources in online environments provides students with numerous opportunities for language learning depending on their interests and needs. Although most interviewees were positive regarding the importance of bridging informal and formal learning, most interviewees acknowledged insufficient attention to informal digital practices in public school and, to some extent, in the university setting. That is, in concurrence with the arguments of Lai (2017), research participants in the study emphasised the need to support L2 learners in discovering effective methods for implementing diverse digital resources beyond the classroom. This support could include assistance in retrieving alternative methods of implementing digital resources and increasing students' interest and motivation to get involved in informal language learning activities.

In line with previous studies, such as that of Toffoli and Sockett (2015), prospective language teachers recognise the need to adapt their teaching strategies to contemporary realities. However, compared to only two-thirds of French university teachers (N = 30) who were reported to have a high level of awareness regarding IDLE practices, participants in the current study were found to be more informed. This finding could be explained by the fact that the interviewees in our study best fit the description of 'digital natives', as opposed to 'digital immigrants' who acquired computer skills at some point in their adult lives (Prensky 2001).

Qualitative findings revealed that the new generation of English language teachers in Kazakhstan is not reluctant to changes in the language education system. Interviewees believe that both school and university curricula should recognise the affordances of online exchanges and adopt various informal learning approaches and strategies. The interview results extend this stance and suggest that motivated modern-day language learners are determined to grasp and search for additional strategies to enrich their language learning strategies in contexts beyond the classroom settings. The majority of prospective teachers believe that language educators have the power to guide students in the right direction by providing the resources and initial tasks that may further lead to students' engagement in personalised informal digital learning activities in subsequent stages. Such findings corroborate the previously reported results of Lai (2015) and Shelton-Strong (2020). The authors emphasised the connection between self-directed informal activities and teacher-induced practices with authentic language resources by asserting the responsibility of teachers in forming students' language learning beliefs.

However, the opinions of interviewees in our study regarding the roles of L2 teachers in forming students' out-of-class language learning habits should be considered in accordance with contextual peculiarities of Kazakhstan. To some extent, contemporary language teaching in Kazakhstan is still attuned to Soviet foreign-language teaching methodology (Akimenko 2017). This connection is particularly apparent when considering the prevalence of teacher-centred language pedagogies (Goodman and Karabassova 2018). In addition, it is important to underline that in collectivist societies, such as Kazakhstan, teachers are viewed as the 'authority, parent and font of knowledge' which usually leads to adapting their positions and viewpoints (De Mooij and Hofstede 2010: 906). Therefore, the viewpoints of students about the roles of L2 teachers should be treated with some caution and research into the perspectives of prospective language teachers from more individualist societies is needed.

Finally, possible causes behind the expressed contradictions among interviewees should be addressed. Among the plausible explanations for the encountered inconsistencies, we can refer to participants' metacognitive awareness that might range in regard to formal and informal language learning activities (Bozorgian and Alamdari 2018). Given the majors of interviewees, it might be expected that prospective L2 teachers dedicate considerable time to explore formal language teaching methodology and approaches. However, the description of formal language instruction provided by participants does not indicate that much attention is paid to the deconstruction of personalised informal learning practices. Hence, the lack of metacognitive awareness pertaining to language learning processes occurring in out-of-class spaces could be considered as a possible reason behind the discovered contradictions.

Given these arguments, the responsibility of aspiring language teachers in Kazakhstan is not only to impart knowledge but also to critically assess their own language learning ideas and experiences before sharing their recommendations and knowledge with EFL students. That is, owing to contextual peculiarities, prospective Kazakhstani L2 educators should be aware of their influence as role models for their tutees or potential students. Hence, to support student teachers, contemporary formal teacher training programmes in Kazakhstan are advised to have a purposeful and consistent focus on developing metacognitive skills and awareness about informal L2 learning strategies.

In contemporary realities, language teachers should no longer be perceived as only the mediums of knowledge (De Mooij and Hofstede 2010). Teachers' roles are becoming increasingly multifaceted and complex in today's world; hence, formal L2 teacher training programmes should seek to aid students in acquiring metacognitive skills, so that they can independently evaluate language learning resources and practices in formal classroom spaces and beyond. This should be done to better prepare student teachers to balance and manage their L2 teaching and L2 learning identities, as well as to focus their attention on developing cognitive and metacognitive language learning skills.

6 Limitations and possible further research pathways

Although the chosen data collection method was thoroughly discussed and critically addressed before implementation, there were some limitations which should be reported. As many aspects of informal learning are incidental and unconscious, it is important to acknowledge that interview participants might not be completely accurate in describing their experience owing to some cognitive biases, known as the *availability heuristic* (Schwarz et al. 1991). In other words, while personal statements should be considered, one should recognise that perceptions are formed based on emotional stimuli, facts, and images that leave a lasting impression in individuals' minds and might project a distorted reality due to personal biases. In addition, due to the voluntary participation in the data collection procedures, it is important to acknowledge that the chosen sample might represent students who are more interested and experienced in exploring the digital wilds than average student teachers. Hence, due to the relatively small sample size, careful consideration should be made before generalising our findings.

While our study aimed to depict the complexity of perceptions about IDLE activities among prospective language teachers, constant emergence of new digital tools should be seen as a foundational rationale for extending this line of inquiry. An important and exciting direction of future research would be to broaden our qualitative approach for comparing perceptions about the impact of IDLE practices among school and university L2 teachers in Kazakhstan and globally. This might be done to compare and contrast the views about informal learning held by educators working with different groups and levels of students around the world. Similarly, special attention may be devoted to comprehending the extent to which nonnative and native language teachers may hold similar or opposing perspectives on the phenomenon. These investigations could potentially yield additional insights regarding the relationship between informal and formal L2 learning activities, thereby aiding educators in aligning their teaching to expand students' IDLE repertoire.

Given current trends of internationalisation in higher education (Seeber, Meoli, and Cattaneo 2020), further studies on the change in perceptions and the actual engagement in IDLE activities among participants of international academic exchange programs appears to be another promising research direction. Thanks to multiple educators who acknowledge the direct and indirect impact of studying overseas on the involvement in informal practices (Arndt 2019; Lee 2022) and willingness to engage in L2 communication in IDLE spaces (Kang 2014), this research direction might facilitate understanding of these influential processes.

Finally, future research could examine whether remote schooling practices implemented in response to the COVID-19 outbreak influenced students' and SLA teachers' perceptions of informal digital language learning.

References

Akimenko, Olessya. 2017. Investigating the effectiveness of private small group tutoring of English in Kazakhstan: Perceptions of tutors and students. *NUGSE Research in Education* 2(1). 16–26. https://nugserie.nu.edu.kz/index.php/NUGSERIE/article/download/55/8

Aloraini, Nouf & Walcir Cardoso. 2020. Social media in language learning: A mixed-methods investigation of students' perceptions. *Computer Assisted Language Learning*. 1–24. https://doi.org/10.1080/09588221.2020.1830804

Andrei, Elena. 2017. Technology in teaching English language learners: The case of three middle school teachers. *TESOL Journal* 8(2). 409–431. https://doi.org/10.1002/tesj.280

Arndt, Henriette L. 2019. *Informal second language learning: The role of engagement, proficiency, attitudes, and motivation*. Oxford: University of Oxford dissertation.

Arndt, Henriette L. & Robert Woore. 2018. Vocabulary learning from watching YouTube videos and reading blog posts. *Language Learning & Technology* 22(3). 124–142. https://doi.org/10125/44660

Arvanitis, Panagiotis. 2019. Self-paced language learning using online platforms. In Mark Dressman & Randall William Sadler (eds.), *The Handbook of Informal Language Learning*, 117–138. Hoboken/Chichester: Wiley-Blackwell.

Bozorgian, Hossein & Ebrahim Fakhri Alamdari. 2018. Multimedia listening comprehension: Metacognitive instruction or metacognitive instruction through dialogic interaction. *ReCALL* 30(1). 131–152.

Bruggeman, BramJo Tondeur, Katrien Struyven, Bram Pynoo, Anja Garone & Silke Vanslambrouck. 2021. Experts speaking: Crucial teacher attributes for implementing blended learning in higher education. *The Internet and Higher Education* 48. https://doi.org/10.1016/j.iheduc.2020.100772

Chik, Alice. 2020. Motivation and informal language learning. In Mark Dressman & Randall William Sadler (eds.), *The Handbook of Informal Language Learning*, 13–26. Hoboken/Chichester: Wiley-Blackwell.

Chun, Dorothy, Richard Kern & Bryan Smith. 2016. Technology in language use, language teaching, and language learning. *The Modern Language Journal* 100(S1). 64–80. https://doi.org/10.1111/modl.12302

Colpaert, J. 2020. Editorial position paper: How virtual is your research? *Computer Assisted Language Learning* 33(7). 653–664. https://doi.org/10.1080/09588221.2020.1824059

Creswell, John W. & Vicki L. Plano Clark. 2017. *Designing and Conducting Mixed Methods Research*. Los Angeles: Sage publications.

De Mooij, Marieke & Geert Hofstede. 2010. The Hofstede model: Applications to global branding and advertising strategy and research. *International Journal of Advertising* 29(1). 85–110. https://doi.org/10.2501/S026504870920104X

Dewey, Martin. 2020. English language teachers in context: Who teaches what, where and why? In Andy Kirkpatrick (ed.), *The Routledge Handbook of World Englishes*, 609–623. London: Routledge.

EF Index. 2021. *Education First English Proficiency Index 2021*. https://www.ef.co.th/epi/

Elo, Satu & Helvi Kyngäs. 2008. The qualitative content analysis process. *Journal of Advanced Nursing* 62(1). 107–115.

Galloway, Nicola & Heath Rose. 2015. *Introducing Global Englishes*, 1st edn. London, UK: Routledge. https://doi.org/10.4324/9781315734347

Gleason, Nancy W. 2018. Introduction. In Nancy W. Gleason (ed.), *Higher Education in the Era of the Fourth Industrial Revolution*, 1–11. Singapore: Palgrave Macmillan.

Gong, Qian, Kyoko Kawasaki, Wai Ling Yeung, Grace Zhang & Toni Dobinson. 2019. Students' perceptions of the use of video recording in additional language oral assessments. In Toni Dobinson & K. Dunworth (eds.), *Literacy Unbound: Multiliterate, Multilingual, Multimodal*, 133–152. Cham: Springer.

Goodman, Bridget & Laura Karabassova. 2018. Bottom up and top down: Comparing language-in-education policy in Ukraine and Kazakhstan. In M. Chankseliani & Iveta Silova (eds.), *Comparing Post-Socialist Transformations: Education in Eastern Europe and Former Soviet Union*, 147–166. Oxford: Symposium Books.

Gu, Yongqi & Robert Keith Johnson. 1996. Vocabulary learning strategies and language learning outcomes. *Language Learning* 46(4). 643–679.

Hodges, Charles, Stephanie Moore, Barb Lockee, Torrey Trust & Aaron Bond. 2020. The difference between emergency remote teaching and online learning. *EDUCAUSE Review*. http://hdl.handle.net/10919/104648.

Hsu, Hsiu-Chen & Yun-Fang Lo. 2018. Using Wiki-mediated collaboration to foster L2 writing performance. *Language Learning & Technology* 22(3). 103–123. https://doi.org/10125/44659

Hu, Ran. 2014. Learning about the challenges of teaching in two worlds. In W. Ma (ed.), *East Meets West in Teacher Preparation: Crossing Chinese and American Borders*, 7–23. Columbia University: Teachers College Press.

Hung, Shao-Ting. 2011. Pedagogical applications of vlogs: An investigation into ESP learners' perceptions. *British Journal of Educational Technology* 42(5). 736–746. https://doi.org/10.1111/j.1467-8535.2010.01086.x

Jurkovič, Violeta. 2019. Online informal learning of English through smartphones in Slovenia. *System* 80. 27–37. https://doi.org/10.1016/j.system.2018.10.007

Kang, Dae-Min. 2014. The effects of study-abroad experiences on EFL learners' willingness to communicate, speaking abilities, and participation in classroom interaction. *System* 42. 319–332. https://doi.org/10.1016/j.system.2013.12.025

Kusyk, Meryl. 2017. The development of complexity, accuracy and fluency in L2 written production through informal participation in online activities. *CALICO Journal* 34(1). 75–96. https://doi.org/10.1558/cj.29513

Lai, Chun. 2015. Modelling teachers' influence on learners' self-directed use of technology for language learning outside the classroom. *Computers & Education* 82. 74–83. https://doi.org/10.1016/j.compedu.2014.11.005

Lai, Chun. 2017. *Autonomous Language Learning with Technology: Beyond the Classroom*. London/New York: Bloomsbury Publishing.

Lai, Chun, Xiaoshi Li & Qiu Wang. 2017. Students' perceptions of teacher impact on their self-directed language learning with technology beyond the classroom: Cases of Hong Kong and U.S. *Educational Technology Research and Development* 65(4). 1105–1133. https://doi.org/10.1007/s11423-017-9523-4

Lai, Chun, Yuk Yeung & Jingjing Hu. 2016. University student and teacher perceptions of teacher roles in promoting autonomous language learning with technology outside the classroom. *Computer Assisted Language Learning* 29(4). 703–723. https://doi.org/10.1080/09588221.2015.1016441

Lai, Chun, Weimin Zhu & Gang Gong. 2015. Understanding the quality of out-of-class English learning. *TESOL Quarterly* 49. 278–308.

Lee, Ju Seong & Nur Arifah Drajati. 2019. Affective variables and informal digital learning of English: Keys to willingness to communicate in a second language. *Australasian Journal of Educational Technology* 35(5). 168–182. https://doi.org/10.14742/ajet.5177

Lee, Ju Seong. 2020. The role of informal digital learning of English and a high-stakes English test on perceptions of English as an international language. *Australasian Journal of Educational Technology* 36(2). 155–168. https://doi.org/10.14742/ajet.5319

Lee, Ju Seong. 2022. *Informal Digital Learning of English: Research to Practice*. Routledge.

Lewis, Pericles. 2018. Globalizing the liberal arts: Twenty-first-century education. In Nancy W. Gleason (ed.), *Higher Education in the Era of the Fourth Industrial Revolution*, 15–38. Singapore: Palgrave Macmillan.

Lin, Chin-Hsi, Mark Warschauer & Robert Blake. 2016. Language learning through social networks: Perceptions and reality. *Language Learning & Technology* 20(1). 124–147. https://www.learntechlib.org/p/176113/

Ma, Qing. 2017. A multi-case study of university students' language-learning experience mediated by mobile technologies: A socio-cultural perspective. *Computer Assisted Language Learning* 30(3–4). 183–203. https://doi.org/10.1080/09588221.2017.1301957

Prensky, Marc. 2001. Digital natives, digital immigrants. *On the Horizon* 9(5). 1–6. https://doi.org/10.1108/10748120110424816

Salomon, Gavriel. 1983. The differential investment of mental effort in learning from different sources. *Educational Psychologist* 18(1). 42–50.

Schwarz, Norbert, Herbert Bless, Fritz Strack, Gisela Klumpp, Helga Rittenauer-Schatka & Annette Simons. 1991. Ease of retrieval as information: Another look at the availability heuristic. *Journal of Personality and Social Psychology* 61(2). 195–202.

Seeber, Marco, Michele Meoli & Mattia Cattaneo. 2020. How do European higher education institutions internationalise? *Studies in Higher Education* 45(1). 145–162. https://doi.org/10.1080/03075079.2018.1541449

Shelton-Strong, Scott J. 2020. Advising in language learning and the support of learners' basic psychological needs: A self-determination theory perspective. *Language Teaching Research* 1(23). 1–23. https://doi.org/10.1177/1362168820912355

Sockett, Geoffrey. 2014. *The online informal learning of English*. UK: Palgrave Macmillan.

Suk, Namhee. 2016. Teacher and student perceptions of extensive reading activities. *Modern English Education* 17(1). 69–88

Sundqvist, Pia. 2019. Commercial-off-the-shelf games in the digital wild and L2 learner vocabulary. *Language Learning & Technology* 23(1). 87–113. https://doi.org/10125/44674

Sundqvist, Pia & Peter Wikström. 2015. Out-of-school digital gameplay and in-school L2 English vocabulary outcomes. *System* 51. 65–76. https://doi.org/10.1016/j.system.2015.04.001

Sutherland, Sean. 2012. Native and non-native English teachers in the classroom: A re-examination. *Arab World English Journal* 3(4). 58–71.

Toffoli, Denyze. 2020. *Informal Learning and Institution-wide Language Provision: University Language Learners in the 21st Century*. Cham: Palgrave Macmillan.

Toffoli, Denyze & Geoff Sockett. 2015. University teachers' perceptions of online informal learning of English (OILE). *Computer Assisted Language Learning* 28(1). 7–21. https://doi.org/10.1080/09588221.2013.776970

Trinder, Ruth. 2017. Informal and deliberate learning with new technologies. *ELT Journal* 71(4). 401–412. https://doi.org/10.1093/elt/ccw117

Zadorozhnyy, Artem & Baohua Yu. 2021. Addressing the impact of informal language learning practices in digital wilds on the development of L2 digital literacies. In Naouel Zoghlami, Cédric Brudermann, Cedric Sarré, Muriel Grosbois, Linda Bradley & Sylvie Thouësny (eds.), *CALL and professionalisation: Short papers from EUROCALL 2021 Conference*, 307–311. https://doi.org/10.14705/rpnet.2021.54.9782490057979

Denyze Toffoli
13 Learner profiles and ISLL trajectories
Indicators and learner-documented evidence

Abstract: This study analyses initial learner profiles, in terms of language level in English, learner autonomy, attachment and self-determination, of 174 students, with metrics established using previously validated instruments. It then documents 9 of these students' contacts with English and their progress in the language over the 10 months of their first year in higher education, using logbook and classroom observation data. Using a self-determination framework and referring to constructs such as attachment, motivation and autonomy, it examines possible relations between initial profiles and subsequent learning trajectories, in and out of the classroom, over the course of the year. The 9 case-studies are shown to be representative of the cohort and lead to the emergence of three learner profiles: the pawn, the independent user and the good language learner.

Keywords: Autonomy, attachment, self-determination, informal second language learning, logbook data

1 Introduction

Informal Second Language Learning (ISLL), as we have chosen to call it in this volume, has attracted substantial attention from researchers in Applied Linguistics worldwide (as attested by recent handbooks such as Dressman and Sadler 2020 or Reinders et al. 2022) or indeed the present book. While much of such research has covered areas including the diversity of practices, the widespread nature of such learning and specific types of acquisitions that may be attributed to it, this chapter, similar to Alm's hereafter, is interested in the link between learner profiles and ISLL trajectories. In this case, the interactions between motivation, as a self-determination construct implying autonomy, attachment and L2 competence, and ISLL practices will be examined. This chapter explores these elements as they concern a small cohort of first-year university students, via questionnaires and evidence provided by online course material and personal narratives in learning logbooks over the course of an academic year. The findings here do concord with a growing body of research that implies that ISLL transforms additional language development and provides

---

Denyze Toffoli, Université de Toulouse III – Paul Sabatier, France

new affordances to people who might otherwise experience difficulty moving from a "good classroom learner" posture to a "good independent learner" posture and, perhaps further along, to becoming "fully independent users". They also indicate that the definition of a good language learner could be very broad, embracing a large number of qualities and approaches to learning.

I have previously argued (Toffoli 2020) that learner autonomy, attachment and competence in the development of additional languages are highly interconnected motivational factors and significant for learning outcomes, based essentially on three preliminary studies that examined them separately: autonomy – Toffoli and Speranza 2016; attachment – Toffoli 2016; competence as a component of self-determination – Toffoli and Perrot 2017. The object of this chapter is to present empirical evidence to support this position, by examining questionnaire data on these three variables, backed-up by logbook citations and teacher observations over a 1-year period, giving further insight into the articulation of these psychological constructs when looking at informal language learning.

2 Theoretical framework

Self-determination theory, "*a contemporary, empirically based approach to motivation and development*" (Ryan and Deci 2017: 202) has been recognised as one of the most operational theories of motivation, particularly with regards to learning, with several hundred experimental studies to support its hypotheses (Ryan and Deci 2013: 194), including many in the areas of education (Deci et al. 1991; Ryan and Deci 2013; Milyavskaya and Koestner 2011) and more specifically of language learning (Oga-Baldwin et al. 2017; McIntosh and Noels 2004; Liu, Wang and Ryan 2016). Self-determination theory conceives of motivation as being regulated along a continuum from total lack of motivation (a-motivation) through various degrees of external, and progressively more internalised motivation, to fully internalised intrinsic motivation (Figure 1):

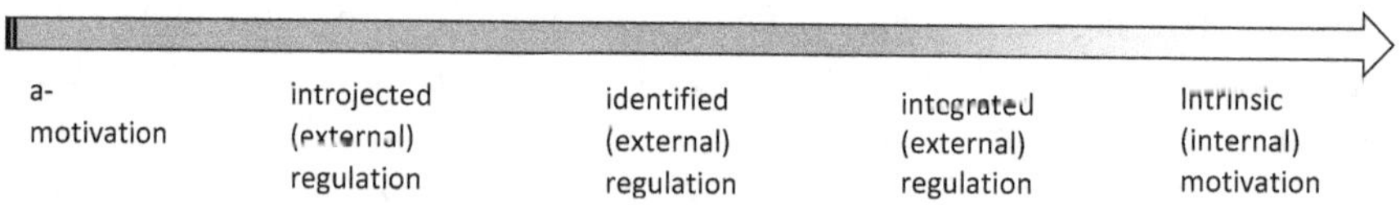

| a-motivation | introjected (external) regulation | identified (external) regulation | integrated (external) regulation | intrinsic (internal) motivation |

Figure 1: The progressively internalised continuum of motivation according to self-determination theory.

A recurring hypothesis in ISLL literature (Arndt 2019; Cole 2015) is that people engaging in ISLL would have highly internalised motivation, but also that informal language activities themselves might increase motivation for learning an L2 (Cole 2015; Lamb and Arisandy 2020). Several studies have argued that learner motivation would have a significant influence not only on the types of activities learners are involved in, but also on how intensive their informal practices are and how efficient for language acquisition (Arndt 2019; Cole 2015; Lamb and Arisandy 2020; Lee and Chen Hsieh 2019; Lee and Lee 2020).

The informal development of additional (second or foreign) languages can thus usefully be understood within the conceptual framework of self-determination theory (Deci and Ryan 2002), both as regards the motivational continuum above and as a global framework, which posits that three basic psychological needs – autonomy, relatedness and a sense of competence – foster motivation and that their satisfaction is in fact central to the process of internalisation depicted above (Ryan and Deci 2017). The framework of self-determination theory provides a pertinent and global understanding of many of the affective and cognitive factors weighing in on informal language learning. Moreover, each of these three basic psychological needs has received theoretical attention on its own merit in L2 learning-related research, as I shall indicate below, although autonomy and competence have garnered more attention than relatedness, or than relatedness in the guise of attachment, as I have chosen to study it.

As attachment as such has been little exploited in applied linguistics research, I will provide more extensive background on the theory of attachment than on theories of autonomy and competence, which have been widely researched in the field. For the originators of self-determination theory, attachment is the foundation of relatedness (Ryan and Deci 2017) and as such can be viewed within the self-determination framework, as pictured in Figure 3 in conclusion to this section. Initially developed by John Bowlby and Mary Ainsworth in the mid-twentieth century, in recognition of the importance of relationship to a primary caregiver in early infancy, attachment has been referred to in explanation of many aspects of human development and behaviour, including resilience (Cyrulnik 2009), classroom behaviour (Geddes 2006), social skills (Dereli and Krakus 2011) and language development (Day 2007; van IJzendoorn, Dijkstra and Bus 1995). While early childhood attachment was traditionally felt to determine trait-like aspects of personality (Bartholomew and Horowitz 1991; Rholes and Simpson 2006), adult attachment has more recently been considered to be a situated psychological component of human activity, in particular as related to learning (Fleming 2008; Fraley et al. 2011; Riley 2011).

The attachment construct is conceived of as an interaction between levels of anxiety on the one hand, and degrees of avoidance on the other (Bartholomew and Horowitz 1991; Fraley et al. 2011). Measures of these are used to indicate attachment types. Figure 2 depicts the interaction of these two variables to create specific types of attachment in each of the quadrants.

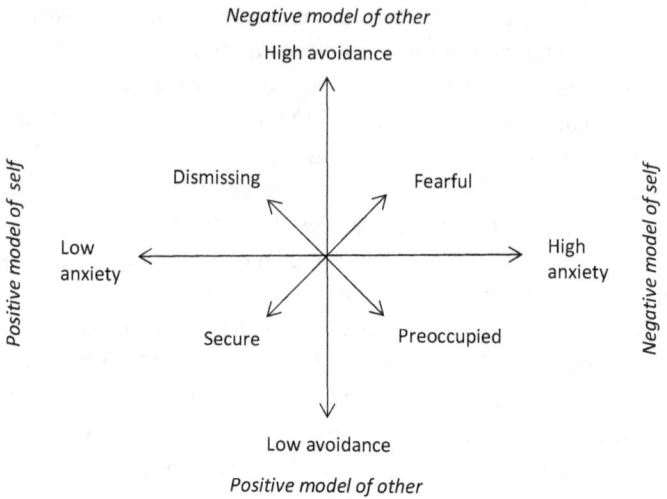

Figure 2: Attachment model, as developed by Bartholomew and Horowitz 1991.

Secure attachment is thus the result of both little anxiety and little avoidance. My 2016 publication (Toffoli 2016) pointed to the possible pertinence of the attachment construct for language learning, through the case study of a French university student in her relationship to the German language and to the people she interacted with in German over a 6-month period. Her logbook brought to light evidence of all four attachment types seen in the model above. In this study, I will look at attachment with regards to a significant other using the L2 and with regards to the L2 itself. Positing the need for strong and secure attachment, in order for autonomy to flourish (Bartholomew and Horowitz 1991; Dereli and Krakus 2011; Geddes 2006; Rholes and Simpson 2006), attachment bridges both the relatedness and the autonomy dimensions of self-determination.

Autonomy has been widely studied in second language development, as both a psychological characteristic of learning and as its goal (Little, Dam and Legenhausen 2017). It has been considered as a set of skills to be acquired for language learning, as well as a factor of personal liberation (Holec 1979) and has been linked to questions of learner identity (Macaro 2002) and problematised with regards to both self-instructed learning and technology-based learning (neither being conditions for autonomy – Benson 2011). Three aspects of language learner autonomy have been considered particularly important and interrelated in the literature (Benson 2012): general or personal autonomy (the autonomy of self-determination theory and of psychological theories of the person), learner autonomy (regulating how an individual takes charge of their own learning, organisationally, cognitively and procedurally (Albero 2000; Stephanou et al. 2004), and finally L2 autonomy (the capacity to function on one's own in a foreign or second language – Little 2013). These interact in co-adaptive and dynamic ways (Toffoli 2020). Learner autonomy is probably the most accessible of these to measurement, via the notion of self-direction (first defined by Knowles 1975), sometimes referred to as independence of learning (Benson and Voller 1997; Macaskill and Taylor 2010), or the capacity to identify one's own goals and objectives and to work towards them independently (Holec 1979). It is this aspect of autonomy that will be adopted in the study below.

For Deci and Ryan, the competence dimension of self-determination theory involves the sentiment of personal efficacy, in that, to feel truly competent, we must consider ourselves responsible for our competence and feel that it belongs to us fully (Ryan and Deci 2017: 95). It is this perception of competence and the feeling of efficacy that it procures that drives motivation and therefore action. Again, this has received much attention in studies on additional language development, notably through researchers who have worked with Bandura's (1977) concept of self-efficacy (Graham 2022). According to Ryan and Deci, to "develop a true sense of perceived competence, . . . people must feel ownership of the activities at which they succeed (2017: 95).

While many skill-sets could be included in the competence dimension of language learning, from communicative and linguistic competence, to digital literacy and its related skills, to, perhaps, even the behavioural aspects of learner autonomy, such as knowing how to set goals or find appropriate materials, in this study, we are concerned primarily with L2 competence as it has been defined by the Council of Europe (2000; 2018) and declined into five communicative skills (listening, reading, speaking, writing, interaction) and three linguistic dimensions (grammar, vocabulary, pronunciation). However, in order to consider it as motivational impetus, a measurement of language proficiency is likely to prove inadequate. For budding L2 users, how they feel about what they are able to do in an additional language, their sense of ownership and the feeling of efficacy that it procures, is paramount.

In conclusion, our theoretical framework adopts self-determination theory as a means of understanding much of the complex interrelatedness between several concepts relevant to additional language development. This is depicted in Figure 3:

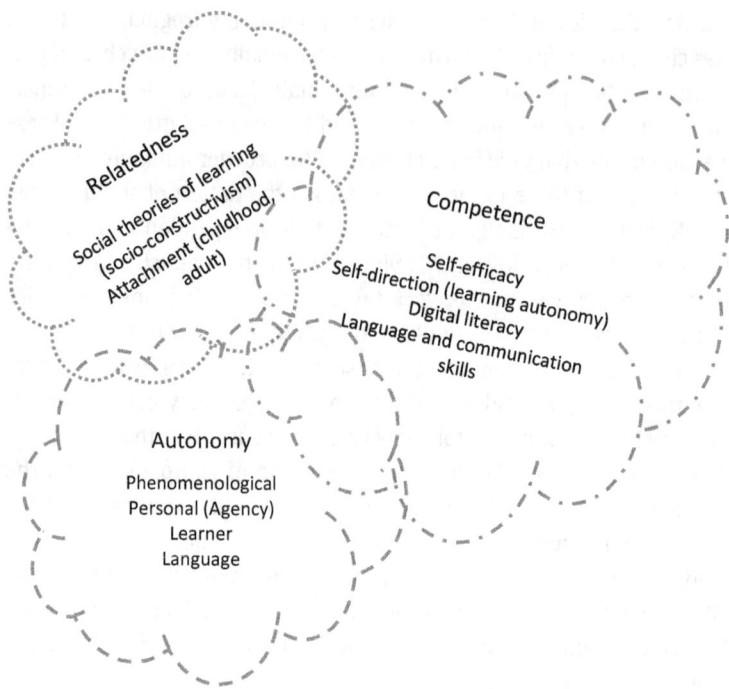

Figure 3: Related Concepts and Theories, within a Self-determination Framework.
From: Toffoli, Denyze, *Informal Learning and Institution-wide Language Provision: University Language Learners in the 21st Century*, 2020, Palgrave Macmillan. Reproduced with permission of Springer Nature Switzerland.

3 The present study

The objective of this study is to uncover correspondences between instruments targeting the three motivational constructs of autonomy, attachment and competence on the one hand and documented learner activities in English that demonstrate aspects of these same constructs on the other. I have therefore examined questionnaire, logbook and observation data from 89 1st-year university students, providing information about time spent on ISLL practices, proficiency in English, independence of learning, attachment and self-determination. I examine possible relations between students' profiles as determined by their responses to the survey instruments and their learning trajectories over the course of a year, in order to better understand the interactions between the two.

4 Methodology

With the aim of more closely apprehending how the salient characteristics of autonomy, attachment and self-determined motivation might influence an individual's ISLL, these characteristics were surveyed using exiting instruments, which will be described below.

4.1 Setting and participants

The initial sampling concerned 177 first-year students enrolled in a commerce/management programme in a University Institute of Technology (IUT) in Toulouse, France. This convenient sampling, like some 67% of all samples in Applied Linguistics research (Plonsky and Derrick 2016), consists exclusively of college or university students. All of the participants are between 17 and 22 years old. There are about equivalent numbers of men and women in the complete academic cohort, which is approximately 200 strong per year. However, 64% of the respondents in the present data are women. The response rate is close to 80%, but as will be seen, not all students provided data for all of the aspects analysed.

4.2 Instruments and data collection

To obtain an indication of autonomy, a questionnaire developed by Macaskill and Taylor (2010) was used, which evaluates *Independence of learning and Study habits*, which the authors claim to be "a brief measure of learner autonomy." In it, twelve statements are evaluated on a 5-point Likert scale, seven referring to independence of learning (for example "I am open to new ways of doing familiar things") and five to study habits (for example "I plan my time for study effectively"). These are referred to as the "autonomy" scales.

For motivation, the *Language Learning Orientations Scale*, developed by Noels, Pelletier, Clément, and Vallerand (2000), which positions language learners' motivation on the self-determination continuum was used. In this questionnaire, students are asked to select a maximum of nine statements, from a list of 21, which best answer the question "why are you learning English?". Analysis of the items selected allows an interpretation of the predominant motivations at play, from a-motivation to intrinsic motivation. I refer to results from this instrument as the "motivation" scale.

For attachment, the *Adult Attachment Questionnaire* established by Fraley, Heffernan, Vicary and Brumbaugh, which provides "a method for assessing attachment orientations across relationships" (2011: 615), was chosen. It requires subjects to assess 9 statements, with regards to a specific relationship, on a 5-point Likert scale, from "strongly disagree" to "strongly agree". Statements assess anxiety and avoidance, the two interacting vectors of attachment. These three instruments were combined into a *Language learner motivation survey*.

Moderate changes were introduced to a few items in the interest of clarity or precision. For example, some questions from both the learner autonomy and adult attachment questionnaires were reworded so as to focus attention on (English) language learning. For instance, the statement "I usually discuss my problems and concerns with this person" was transformed to "I usually asked this person questions about my problems or difficulties with learning the language." The adult attachment questionnaire, which was designed to be used with "each interpersonal target" (Fraley et al. 2011) was duplicated, taking as its first target "a person who is important to you and with whom you speak English." We asked students to assess each statement with that person in mind. We also asked them to do the questionnaire a second time, thinking about "the English language" as a target.[1] The final version of the survey was formatted in *Limesurvey* and pretested for comprehensibility (with eighteen first-year university students from a different establishment).

Language level was measured by means of a widely-used adaptive commercial off-the-shelf test (ELAO – originally "Efficient Language Assessment Online"), which is calibrated to CEFR levels (Council of Europe 2000) and purports to measure grammatical accuracy, passive and active general vocabulary knowledge and listening comprehension. The four scores are averaged to give a level of general English. Students were also asked to self-assess, using 5 can-do statements.

Finally, a 39-item questionnaire called *My use of English*, designed and tested by Perrot (2022), examines the students' self-declared ISLL activities. It asks specific questions about the activities students are involved in (watching videos, with or without subtitles or captions, reading, listening to music, playing video games and other), requiring for each an estimation of frequency. It also proposes a few open questions, notably asking why students choose to do these activities in English and asking for specific examples. There are several options for comments.

---

[1] The validation of considering one's relation to a language as a relationship has yet to be established and is the object of further study at present.

4.3 Specific instructions for participants

Other data were collected through formal learning activities that students were required or requested to engage in for their compulsory (44-hour) English course. These involved ad hoc teacher/researcher observations during class time, learning analytics collected from the *Moodle* platform where much of their coursework was housed, and a logbook, where students were asked to write in English, at least once a week, on topics of their choice. They were told that this could be about their English learning, but could also be about anything they were particularly interested in. The objective was to write interesting content, not to document ISLL or other learning, however, many students did use it in this way. It was suggested that log entries be around a paragraph for A1–A2 learners and a page or more for higher levels. Students were at liberty to answer the questionnaires or not, nonetheless, the logbook and some Moodle activities were compulsory for course completion as stated above and this may well have influenced the type of information provided.

4.4 Logbook selection and analysis

89 logbooks were received for marking at the end of the academic year. The classroom marking process itself allowed for an overview of all of them and their sorting into three categories: complete (whether or not the request for regular writing had been respected), interesting (what I subjectively deemed to relate to my research questions[2]) and whether or not the student had requested their logbook to be given back. With one exception, the latter were eliminated, as they would not be available for further consultation.

Using purposeful sampling (Uztosun 2022) I then selected nine participant records presenting complete data sets (answers to all of the questionnaires, plus a logbook), targeting both "standard" examples (whose scores regarding the variables that interested me were close to the average for the overall sampling) and "extreme" examples (whose scores for these same variables were at or near the upper or lower limits. Using a content analysis approach (Hall 2022), the logbooks of these participants were then reread and tagged for mentions pertaining to the autonomy, attachment and self-determined motivation factors under study here. Other elements, such as amount of writing, completion of other assignments and

---

2 On this basis, I rejected logbooks that were purely reiterations of daily or weekly routines or events and that involved no further commentary or signs of investment.

choice of topics were also examined and will be included in the discussion. Successive readings brought to light three main profiles that exemplified specific orientations with regards to autonomy, motivation and attachment.

The nine learners whose logbook work is examined here are 7 women and 2 men. They all grew up in France and speak French at home. They have been learning English at school for 6 to 10 years. I have named them the LOGBOOK9 cohort and they will be identified individually as Leonor, Ophelia, Gaby, Breana, Oriane, Olivier, Khawla, Nicolas et Nadine (not their real names).

5 Quantitative results, comparisons and representativity

In all, 174 data sets (of the 177 collected) from the questionnaire instruments are exploitable, however, as explained above, many of these are incomplete for one or several of the metrics, as the questionnaires and tests were administered at different times[3] and as only about half of the logbooks were available. In this section, I will present some descriptive results from the surveys, illustrated at times by additional findings from the logbook or class data of the LOGBOOK9 cohort. The section has been organised so as to present the data related to proficiency levels, investment in ISLL and motivational variables separately, with the quantitative data orienting choices for the presentation of qualitative data. Descriptive statistics and analyses of distributions within the group as a whole allow for claims of representativity of the nine participants selected above for further qualitative analysis. I will therefore present comparative data for the different variables between the overall cohort and the LOGBOOK9 cohort, but also provide detailed results for the LOGBOOK9 participants, to give sufficient background for the qualitative analyses to follow.

5.1 ELAO scores and self-assessment

Seventy-seven students took the ELAO test at the beginning of the year. The distribution of their proficiency score (the average of the sub-tests) is depicted in the graph below (Figure 4).

---

[3] The n value therefore varies from one question, table or graph to another and so is indicated for each.

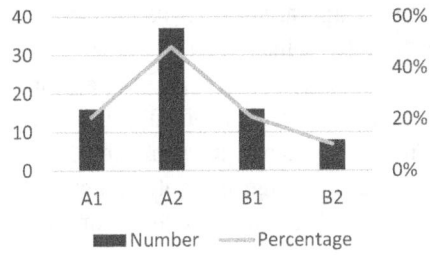

Figure 4: Distribution of ELAO test results of all participants.

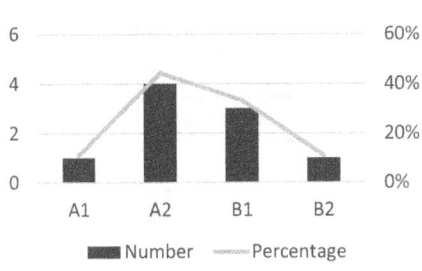

Figure 5: Distribution of ELAO test results for the LOGBOOK9 cohort.

For comparison, the distribution for the LOGBOOK9 cohort can be seen in Figure 5. Table 1 gives details of all ELAO results for these nine learners.

Table 1: English levels of LOGBOOK9 cohort.

	CEFR level[4]	Grammar	Active Vocabulary	Passive Vocabulary	Listening	Self-assessment
Leonor	A1 (75)	B1	A1 (75)	A1 (75)	A1 (50)	know a few phrases
Oriane	A2 (50)	A2 (50)	A2 (25)	A2 (50)	B1	simple conversation
Nadine	A2 (50)	A2 (25)	A2 (50)	A2 (75)	A2 (75)	simple conversation
Ophelia	A2 (50)	A1 (75)	A2	A2 (50)	B1 (25)	simple conversation
Olivier	A2 (50)	A2 (25)	A1 (75)	A2 (50)	B1	complex conversation
Khawla	B1	B1	A2 (50)	B1 (50)	A2 (75)	simple conversation
Breana	B1	A2 (50)	B1	B1 (50)	B1	simple conversation
Gaby	B1 (25)	B1 (50)	A2 (75)	B1 (25)	B1 (75)	simple conversation
Nicolas	B2 (75)	B1 (75)	B2 (50)	C1 (25)	C1 (25)	complex conversation (without difficulty)

---

4 The ELAO test sub-divides CEFR levels into quartiles, which are annotated in parentheses. The lowest quartile is without annotation, the next are incrementally (25), (50) and (75).

Although ELAO scores give relatively detailed appraisals of English proficiency, all students also estimated their own levels on a five-point scale: I only know a few words or phrases, I can give or get some simple information, I can have a simple conversation, I can have a complex conversation, but with some difficulty, I can have a complex conversation, with no difficulty. These have been included in Table 1.

Further statistics for ELAO test scores are presented in Table 2, alongside data of students' declared frequency of ISLL activities, to allow for comparison between the overall and LOGBOOK9 cohorts.

Table 2: Comparison between overall and LOGBOOK9 cohorts for ELAO and ISLL.

	ELAO scores	Frequency ISLL/ academic year
valid N overall cohort	77	148
valid N LOGBOOK9	9	9
overall mean	11.53	625,54
LOGBOOK9 mean	12.44	632,22
overall SD[5]	3.440	497,917
LOGBOOK9 interval	12	2090
overall minimum	A1	0
LOGBOOK9 minimum	A1(75)	10
overall maximum	B2(75)	2400
LOGBOOK9 maximum	B2(75)	2100

As can be seen regarding both elements, the cases chosen for the LOGBOOK9 cohort are close to both the general average of the main cohort and present cases approaching the minimum and maximum extremities, thereby confirming their relevance for further study.

5.2 ISLL activities

In the *My use of English* questionnaire, students were asked to declare the frequency with which they practice various informal activities in English (such as watching videos, listening to music or playing video games). The declared frequencies were multiplied to a 10-month equivalent (the duration of the academic year)

---

[5] Standard deviations were not provided for the LOGBOOK9 cohort, as the sampling is too small for them to be relevant. In place, the interval between minimum and maximum values is provided, which does not allow for comparison, but does give an order of magnitude.

and the different activities added together, so as to have an order of annual magnitude. The totals cover a wide range, from 0 to 2400 activities. For the most active students this corresponds to an average of eight activities per day, each of which could involve anything from a few minutes to a few hours of practice.

In much of the literature on ISLL, time spent online doing activities in English has been seen as a useful way to measure the level of investment or interest students may have in using English outside the classroom (Moffat 2022; Sockett 2014). Similarly, (lack of) competence in English can often (stymie or) favour such participation. The interactive nature of these two variables is also confirmed in our data from the sub-set of 77 respondents who completed the relevant questions (see Figure 6):

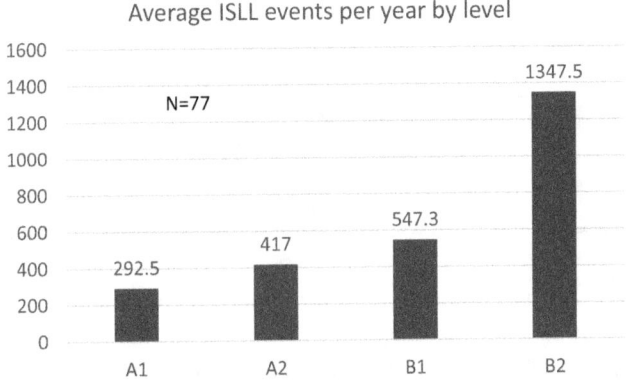

Figure 6: Average declared ISLL events per year, by CEFR level (ELAO test results).

Figure 6 shows that CEFR level and declared amount of ISLL tend to be incremental, which confirms studies such as Kusyk and Sockett (2012), based on self-assessment, or Lee (2020), who uses the results of a standardised test. Among the many reasons why more advanced students would spend more time on leisure activities in English (ease of access, unimpeded comprehension and so on), effects of authentic as opposed to dubbed voices or access to different and more diversified content may also encourage less proficient users of English to spend time on these activities, thereby creating a virtuous spiral of increased practice leading to increased competence, leading to increased practice, etc.

Details of declared ISLL activities for each of the members of the LOGBOOK9 cohort are specified in Table 3, along with figures concerning their logbook production and notations (Y=yes, N=no) regarding coursework and supplementary course activities.

While the range of participation in ISLL activities from around 1 per month (Oriane) to 7 or 8 per day (Nicolas) is extremely wide, the average is just over 2

Table 3: ELAO, ISLL, logbook and course completion data for the LOGBOOK9 cohort.

	CEFR level	Declared ISLL activities (academic year)	Estimated ISLL hours (academic year)	Logbook entries (N)	Word count per entry (approx.)	Completion of online course requirements	Attempted supplementary course activities
Leonor	A1 (75)	340	57	7	60	N	N
Oriane	A2 (50)	10	2	10	80	Y	Y
Nadine	A2 (50)	900	150	24	63	Y	Y
Ophelia	A2 (50)	1060	177	?[6]	?	Y	Y
Olivier	A2 (50)	350	58	20	105	Y	N
Khawla	B1	690	115	23	53	Y	Y
Gaby	B1 (25)	200	33	27	127	Y	Y
Breana	B1	40	7	27	100	Y	Y
Nicolas	B2 (75)	2100	350	9	100	Y	Y

such activities per day, or 632 per academic year for the LOGBOOK9 and 625 for the larger cohort (see Table 2).

In the specific examples of ISLL given in answer to the questionnaire, seven mention watching videos, series or films in first place. Gaby does not answer the question and Nicolas specifies only discussing with friends or working with anglophone partners on various projects. Leonor indicates occasionally watching with French subtitles and having begun to watch in English only in the current year, whereas the eight others all indicate having begun to watch videos in English at least three years prior. Moreover, in line with the profile that will be presented below, Leonor indicates doing this only about once every two months, where Nadine and Ophelia declare "mostly every day" and Nicolas states "all the time and on all sorts of topics". Three of the cohort watch in English to improve their practice of the language, but the others state it is because they prefer hearing the actors' real voices or just that they prefer the language. Among other English

---

[6] Ophelia's logbook having been returned to her on her request, I do not have access to the specific number and length of entries. However, the several quotations, images and the overall extent of her writing were recorded before its return.

language activities, all mention listening to music, two listening to podcasts, three reading books, two writing and only one playing video games.

Both how and what participants answer to open questions in the *Use of English* survey can be indicative of their use of English. Six members of this group answer exclusively in French; Ophelia and Olivier answer exclusively in English and Khawla primarily in English, with one answer in French. Leonor and Ophelia give the longest single answers, Leonor to explain an online game she plays in English (she is the only one to do so) and Ophelia to explain her progression in watching English-language videos. Gaby, Oriane and Ophelia report "non-formal" learning (Sockett 2014), mentioning *Duolingo*, *Tandem* and an unnamed flash-card app. Four of the nine indicate intentionality, specifically citing the desire to learn or improve their English as a reason for engaging in ISLL. Only two have studied abroad: Khawla in Ireland and South Africa and Nicolas in the USA.

5.3 Cognitive and affective variables

Table 4 recaps comparative statistics between our purposeful sampling and the whole cohort for the cognitive and affective variables. It allows assumption of representativity of the LOGBOOK9 cohort for the autonomy, motivation and attachment scales.

Table 4: Comparison between overall and LOGBOOK9 cohorts for cognitive and affective variables.

	Independence of Learning (autonomy)	Study Habits (autonomy)	Motivation	Anxiety (person)	Avoidance (person)	Anxiety (language)	Avoidance (language)
valid N overall cohort	58	58	59	58	58	58	58
valid N LOGBOOK9	9	9	9	9	9	9	9
overall mean	71.4	71.2	2.97	2.19	2.57	2.79	3.26
LOGBOOK9 mean	75.5	79.5	3.33	2.58	2.5	2.68	3.06
overall SD	9.43	15.85	1.01	0.54	0.65	0.75	0.55

Table 4 (continued)

	Independence of Learning (autonomy)	Study Habits (autonomy)	Motivation	Anxiety (person)	Avoidance (person)	Anxiety (language)	Avoidance (language)
LOGBOOK9 interval	31.43	48	2	2.33	2.2	2.33	1.2
overall minimum	54.3	20	0	1.11	1.4	1.22	2.1
LOGBOOK9 minimum	62.9	48	2	1.67	1.5	1.44	2.4
overall maximum	97.1	100	4	4	4.2	4.22	4.4
LOGBOOK9 maximum	94.3	96	4	4	3.7	3.78	3.6

Table 5 details the results for cognitive and affective variables for the restricted cohort. I will return to many of these figures when presenting learner profiles using the qualitative data from the logbooks.

Table 5: Cognitive and affective variables for the LOGBOOK9 cohort.

	Independence of learning score (autonomy ≥24/35)	Study Habits score (autonomy ≥17/25)	Motivation (amotivation=0 intrinsic=4)	Anxiety (person) >3	Avoidance (person) >3	Anxiety (language) >3	Avoidance (language) >3
Leonor	22 N	12 N	external / introjected	2.56 N	2.8 N	3.56 Y	3.3 Y
Oriane	26 Y	20 Y	intrinsic	2.44 N	3.6 Y	3.33 Y	3.5 Y
Nadine	26 Y	21 Y	integrated	1.67 N	1.9 N	1.67 N	3.6 Y
Ophelia	27 Y	15 N	internal / intrinsic	4 Y	3.7 Y	2.44 N	2.5 N

Table 5 (continued)

	Independence of learning score (autonomy ≥24/35)	Study Habits score (autonomy ≥17/25)	Motivation (amotivation=0 intrinsic=4)	Anxiety (person) >3	Avoidance (person) >3	Anxiety (language) >3	Avoidance (language) >3
Olivier	28 Y	22 Y	intrinsic	2 N	2.5 N	2 N	3 Y
Khawla	25 Y	23 y	internal / intrinsic	2.22 N	2.6 N	3.11 Y	3 Y
Gaby	25 Y	24 y	intrinsic	2.44 N	1.9 N	2.78 N	3.2 Y
Breana	26 Y	19 Y	external / intrinsic	3.44 Y	2 N	3.78 Y	3 Y
Nicolas	33 Y	23 Y	introjected / intrinsic	2.44 N	1.5 N	1.44 N	2.4 N

Based on this overview of the quantitative data and having established a statistical representativity for the LOGBOOK9 cohort, I will now present more detailed, qualitative insights for these individuals.

6 Three learner profiles

6.1 Leonor, fearful pawn?

Leonor stands out in the LOGBOOK9 group as the person with the weakest test results (A1) and the lowest self-assessment. She also has the lowest autonomy scores, significant language anxiety and language avoidance scores, positioning her relationship to English in the "fearful" quadrant (see Figure 2 above). In her reasons for learning English she has checked wholly instrumental answers such as "to get a more prestigious job" or "a better salary", which qualify as introjected motivational regulation, but also "the ability to speak more than one language" or "personal development", which are more internalised and have been linked to identified regulation (see Figure 1). She has not chosen any of the answers pointing towards intrinsic motivation, nor even those indicating integrated regulations. This type of motivation for learning English can perhaps explain the (relatively little) time she spends on it and her lack of investment in the logbook activity (see below). Nonetheless, she declares equivalent or more implication in ISLL activities than half of this cohort (see Table 3: 340 activities, estimated at around 60 hours per academic year).

Her ELAO test results for grammar are the only ones in the group that are higher than her overall score (B1 as compared to A1). Does this indicate a grammatical approach to learning English (as opposed to more communicative and meaning-based approaches for the other students)? Could it be an anomaly in the test and therefore due to chance? Does it explain her difficulty in producing English, as evidenced by her logbook?

Leonor's logbook presents several factors that can be seen to support the elements that emerge from her questionnaires and assessments. Less than five pages long, the first three and a half are composed of impersonal summaries of episodes of the BBC's *English at Work* series that she was required to watch for her course. Much of this appears to be copied directly from the website but could be considered relevant cognitive processing for someone at an A1 level with very basic listening and vocabulary skills (see Table 1). The final page and a half, written at the end of second semester, recount two personal events: April vacation and getting her drivers' license. The style is based on French syntax, yet the vocabulary appears to be machine-translator assisted, in that some expressions which often pose problems to French students (for example "s'en occuper" => "take care of it"; "mettre en pension" => "board") have been translated appropriately:

> She also has a horse since she young that she put in board in an equestrian centre not far from her appartement so that she can take care of it more often. (2/05/21).

Is it possible to consider this logbook as evidence of Leonor's "fearful" attachment with regards to the English language, her external motivation and the "inefficient" study habits that the questionnaires brought to light? It does seem coherent with her somewhat mitigated responses regarding her ISLL, her failure to complete her online course requirements and her rather limited achievement in English thus far, perhaps even of the mismatch between her test results in grammar and her overall competence in English.

None of the eight other students in this cohort illustrate this type of profile, which could be labelled a "pawn" profile, in reference to deCharms, Carpenter and Kuperman's (1965) characterisation of externally driven individuals.[7] While there seem to be some indications of a desire to make progress in English, and some effort to use the language, there is also a lack of knowhow, motivation,

---

[7] I thank Antonie Alm for her suggestion of this term.

impetus or strategies to transform this into actual results, at least at this point in the process.

6.2 Nicolas and Olivier, independent users

Nicolas's level, activities and motivational data place him in stark opposition to Leonor for use of English. With the highest tested level among the LOGBOOK9 cohort at nearly a C1, Nicolas considers himself capable of holding complex conversations in English with no difficulty. He declares around 2100 ISLL activities per academic year (the second-highest number of the entire sampling), estimated at well over 350 hours.[8] Nicolas's year in the USA on a study-abroad programme undoubtedly influences his language skills and attitude. His combined autonomy scores are the strongest in the cohort, his language anxiety and avoidance the lowest. His commentaries in the questionnaire[9] indicate using English "for pleasure and for work," watching English-language videos "all the time and on all sorts of subjects," "out of habit and because many of them are not available in French." He is the only one of the nine to declare habit and availability as reasons for his extensive online use of English. He gives examples of reading, writing, watching and listening in English. All of these factors attest to autonomous behaviour. He scores highly for both introjected and intrinsic motivation, again at the opposite end of the continuum from Leonor. Contrary to her, he also not only completes his course requirements, but some (primarily online) supplementary activities as well.

Nicolas's logbook, however, presents only one entry more than Leonor's (although almost twice as many words). It documents his daily use of English to make business contacts and further his entrepreneurial project, for example reading a 230-page book about writing sales letters, running an ad campaign for his e-commerce, meeting a new partner for his business and learning about crypto-currencies. Even so, it presents perfunctory and essentially uninspired writing, finishing at the end of second term with: "I just went back to my logbook and noticed I haven't write much in it. I completely forgot about it . . . ." The logbook could be qualified as an unnecessary and uninteresting exercise for grades and Nicolas's lack of investment could be seen as a logical outcome of his mastery of not only the English language, but also of the necessary means to maintain it as a lifelong skill. In all of his activities Nicolas behaves as a competent user of English and not as a language learner. His entries concern new business opportunities that involve using English. He only

---

8 Again, according to our conservative method of estimation.
9 In French and translated here by me.

mentions learning twice, once with reference to the book on sales letters and once about e-commerce, indicating learning new words in the field. All of these elements attest to autonomous behaviour as regards the use and learning of English. Nicolas seems to epitomise an "independent user" profile, demonstrating his proficiency, but also clearly indicating that he has no need for external guidance, nor for institutionally-provided opportunities for practice.

Olivier, although testing at an A2 level (B1 for listening), has in many ways a profile similar to Nicolas. He self-assesses as being capable of complex conversation. He indicates he has been watching movies and series in English since he was 15 years old and that what he likes about this activity is that "I can learn English without working." While he provides very little other information through the open questions in the *My Use of English* questionnaire, he does declare approximately 350 ISLL activities per year which, as these are mostly series and film, probably add up to significantly more than our estimated 58 hours of viewing time.[10]

Olivier's logbook is composed of 20 highly variable entries in terms of length. Like Nicolas, the activity does not interest him, although at one point he acknowledges that it could be useful for learning:

> Today I don't know what to talk about but writing in English. I find it rather instructive and it's a real reflex to adopt to be able to progress in the language I think. In addition to speaking and watching movies and series in English, it encourages us to look for vocabulary and enriches me a lot. [. . .] Writing is not complicated at all and even if is not interesting, it allows me to look for some words and phrases. (entry #6)

Next to Nicolas, Olivier is the member of the cohort who scores highest on the autonomy scales. His motivation is intrinsically regulated and he scores low for language anxiety and undetermined regarding language avoidance, which could indicate either secure or dismissive attachment to English. Although less marked than Nicolas, Olivier also appears to demonstrate an "independent user" profile.

6.3 Ophelia, a good language learner

Ophelia reveals yet another profile with regards to English. On the motivation scale, her score points to highly internalised motivation: identified and intrinsic. Of 9 possible reasons for learning English, she has chosen 6 from the intrinsic categories, including items such as "the pleasure I experience when surpassing myself in my English studies," or "the enjoyment I experience when I grasp a difficult construct in English." She also scores strongly on the *Independence of*

---

10 30 minutes per session would produce 175 hours.

Learning scale, but much less so for study habits (15/25), with a score of 15 (60%) that is lower than the average in our sampling (mean=71.5% and SD=14.14). Finally, her attachment to the English language indicates both low avoidance of the language and low anxiety in its presence, allowing it to be qualified as secure.

Some reflections of these orientations are also visible in her logbook entries, which she begins thus:

> Hello . . . I'm a little shy because it's the first time I have an English book but I'm also realy excited of this new experience!
> So the object of the game is to write more frequently; I will try to write every day even if regularity is not my strong point. (September 15, 2020)

In this excerpt she thinks of keeping a logbook as a game and the themes of pleasure and leisure are recurrent in her entries. In the early pages, she tells us about some of the ISLL she likes to do. In particular, she discusses watching vloggers, movies, series and reality shows, as in the following examples:

> When coming home after doing my homework (because I'm a good student) I watched some videos on Youtube. I saw the recent video of *Q2HAN* it's two Korean twin sister and in their video they speak English . . .
> [. . .] I also like *Jelien Mercado*[. . .] but also *eve frsr, Jake Warden, Jeffreestar*, [. . .] I love these people for their way of being and their originality. So that way I can learn while having fun. (September 17, 2020)

The reference to being a good student seems pertinent and I will return to it below. As time goes on, Ophelia reports on the diversity of activities she engages in in English, for example listening to music: "Yesterday the album of the new group BlackSwan debuted [. . .] I just heard 2 songs and I love it" (October 19, 2020); or buying and reading three books, including one called *Burn after Writing* (October 31, 2020). Her informal and leisure-related learning activities are not limited to digital content, since these books seem to have been purchased in paper format.

Searching for information online is also a significant part of Ophelia's ISLL activities, as in the following example:

> I search on the Internet [. . .] I read more than twenty sites (in english) [. . .] I looked on google maps using the photos of the loft that I found and after 1 hour I found it (December 11, 2020).

She also reports on a tandem session that was proposed by her English teacher, indicating that the frontiers between learning and leisure, formal and informal may be only implicit for learners.

> Saturday March 20 I did a Zoom session with a student from Miami [. . .]. We noticed that we had a lot in common that make an easiest conversation. (March 23, 2021).

Ophelia apparently considers this online activity to be relevant to her informal learning since the nature of the conversation corresponds to an informal context whereas only the origin of the exchange is formal (classroom-based).

Often, her logbook becomes a qualitative record of her ISLL activities, where she discloses particular techniques that she uses to help with her language learning. Here she talks about another notebook she keeps:

> I have a small notebook where I write the citation or sentences that I hear and touch me, so I will share some with you:
> "Don't take revenge. Let karma do all the work."
> "Three things cannot be long hidden: The sun, the moon, the truth"
> "No one is born ugly, we're just born in a judgemental society"
> (October 11, 2020).

The logbook itself contains other traces of learning strategies, such as the small tags depicted in Figure 7, that she glues into her book and which are seemingly devices that are used to help remember language she has noticed and feels to be important in some way.

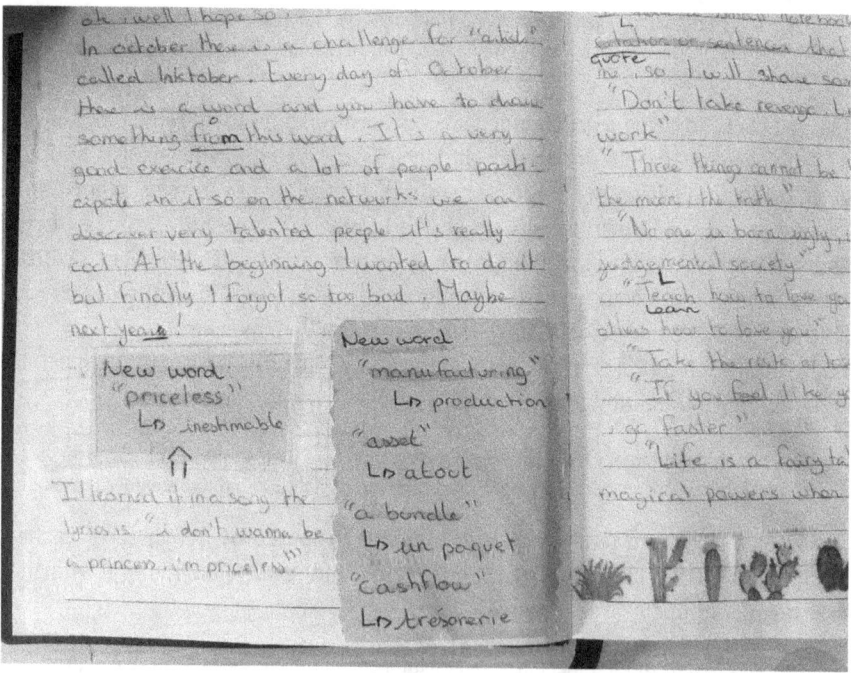

Figure 7: Extract from Ophelia's Logbook.

While these have some systematicity in that they are all the same colour and seem to be semantic indicators, some are single words, others idiomatic expressions or frequent collocations; some are translated, others are noted with an English equivalent and some carry explanatory notes as to where they were found or why they were targeted.

Ophelia's writing is not only record-keeping of her ISLL, it also includes thoughts, opinions and analyses of the material she encounters. In an entry where she discusses her dream home, she describes a loft she saw online, her search to precisely situate its location (cited above – December 11), what exactly she likes about it and how it makes her feel. When discussing a movie, she not only mentions "I just watched the movie Enola Holmes on Netflix (in English with French subtitles)", but also tells us

> why I likes the movie:
> The story is good
> Sherlock Holmes (I love this person)
> Talks about a women in society
> Talks about finding your own way
> British accent (the most beautiful accent in the world. I want to be able to speak with)
> Original because they break the 4th wall.
>
> October 17, 2020

While the description above is informative, there is still much to learn about Ophelia's learning trajectory. Has her ISLL been this intensive since she was 13? If so, how is it that she still scores an A2 level at the beginning of the year? Perhaps a different teaching approach has allowed her to attend to learning English in ways more suited to her personality and even overcome learning difficulties encountered in previous schooling. Her year-end marks would place her with students in the B2 range, both for speaking and writing. Has she been rewarded primarily for her investment and little tags? Ophelia would appear to be spending over 270 hours on ISLL each academic year. Could changes in results be credited to this additional practice? What would happen if she re-took the ELAO test? If she re-self-assessed? As Ophelia states herself (see above – September 17), she would seem to be typical of what teachers might think of as the "good language learner," in the sense first used by Naiman (1978), although her lower-than-average *Study Habits* score seems to contradict such a judgement. Nonetheless, I have chosen her here to personify the "good language learner" profile, as she appears to exemplify it, even if this be a posture that she has recently adopted.

6.4 Gaby, Oriane, Nadine, Khawla and Breana

Separate profiles have not been elaborated for these 5 learners, as they do not present clear illustrations of different sets of characteristics. However, they do display characteristics that group them together, often with Ophelia and even Olivier, but which set them quite apart from Leonor or Nicolas. In this section, I will briefly draw attention to the main features they have in common.

Seven of the LOGBOOK9 test in the mid-A2 to lower-B1 range, which might be referred to as lower intermediate. They all completed their course requirements, including the suggested number of entries in their logbooks, indicating a certain deferral to academic authority and instructions. Nonetheless, all qualify as independent learners, according to the measures used. Other characteristics were dominant in this sub-group, with only single exceptions: investment in supplementary course material (all but Olivier) self-assessments as "capable of a simple conversation", (compare to Leonor "a few words and phrases", Olivier "complex conversations, with some difficulty" or Nicolas "complex conversations, with no difficulty"); intrinsic motivation (all but Nadine); autonomous study habits (all but Ophelia).

Gaby, Oriane, Nadine, Khawla and Breana resemble Ophelia's profile most: earnest, autonomous, motivated, fulfilling requirements and often going beyond, although in different ways: good language learners. This would of course be the logical outcome of their selection on the basis of providing complete data sets for the questionnaires, complete logbooks and other secondary data.

7 Discussion

The contrasting case studies of Ophelia and Leonor are an illustration of how rich data can be helpful in teasing out the complex interactions between autonomy, attachment and ISLL competence. Since Leonor falls into the "fearful" quadrant of attachment for the English language, her propensity for risk-taking is diminished in the informal sphere, leading to her tendency to avoid leisure activities in English, while Ophelia sees the informal sphere as a playground, where she engages in various "games" (leisure activities that others might call work), thus creating the virtuous spiral in which language development is facilitated.

The example of Nicolas, portraying advanced competence and a high degree of autonomy, reminds us that particularly autonomous students may well be those who can't be bothered to comply with their teachers' wishes at all or who are so busy doing their own thing that they see the request to answer questionnaires as an impingement on their autonomy and thus fall completely outside of the researcher's domain of observation. Specific cases that were eliminated from this study for lack of data come to mind and the challenge of how to access such profiles remains open.

The representativity from which I extracted the three profiles presented here allows neither extrapolation (for example that 6/9 students in the overall sampling are also good language learners) nor extension (that all students in the original sampling would fit one of the identified profiles). A glance at test results suffices to eliminate such conclusions, as a student population with 80% good language learners would undoubtedly produce a very large number of learners testing at C1 and C2 levels, instead of A2 and B1.

In a future study the three motivational factors of attachment, autonomy and self-determination could each be re-explored independently and in greater depth, mining the same student data. This could potentially reveal new and pertinent manifestations of each, leading to a readjustment of the profiles proposed here. Another future direction for study could be deeper investigation using statistical methods such as factor analysis and correlations. As a study in applied linguistics, a further question involves the possible use that such information can be to teachers: could access to the motivational profiles of their students facilitate their guidance or influence their suggestions (and perhaps coercions) for different language practice opportunities? This question too remains open for future exploration.

From the perspective of self-determination theory, this study has explored the notion of secure attachment (relatedness) as a source of autonomous behaviour in informal additional language learning contexts and found potential links to different measures of language competence (from various self-assessments to standardised proficiency tests to teacher assessments). In line with self-determination theory I consider autonomy to be a fundamental component of motivation as well as an essential factor in the informal development of additional languages. Approached initially via the "independence of learning" (Benson and Voller 1997; Macaskill and Taylor 2010) measures here, the logbook entries revealed more nuanced features and appear to exemplify Little's conception of the agentic aspects of autonomy channelled through use of the target language (Little 2015), demonstrating "the close link between autonomy, intrinsic motivation and the efficiency of developmental and experiential learning" (Little 2000: 32). The use of the motivation measurement, positioning the internalisation of learners' motivation, helps to clarify these links.

In a global and inter-related manner, these cognitive and affective variables (attachment, competence and autonomy) can be related to concrete outcomes, such as length or depth of involvement in ISLL, proficiency scores or self-assessment, but not in a predictive or strictly correlational manner, re-confirming the complex and dynamic nature of human endeavours such as learning. These issues point to challenges faced (for example) in evaluating proficiency levels using various instruments such as commercial language tests, self-assessment and academic results, which may offer a disparity of outcomes. They also indicate the limitations of conclusions that can be drawn from psychometric instruments, however well they be internally validated.

8 Conclusion

In the introduction I proposed to present empirical data supporting the position that learner autonomy, attachment and self-determination are highly interconnected motivational factors and significant for individual outcomes in the development of additional languages. I purported to present questionnaire data on these three variables, in order to compile learner profiles and relate them to ISLL trajectories, materialised through a separate questionnaire, logbooks, coursework and teacher observations over a 1-academic-year period.

Questionnaire and test data from 174 participants were analysed with reference to a selected cohort of nine individuals, from whose qualitative data three learner profiles emerged: the pawn, the independent user and the good language learner. While these profiles are unlikely to have predictive value for learning trajectories, they can be useful for better understanding the complex interplay of ever-changing variables impacting formal and informal learning along individual paths and notably the highly imbricated nature of attachment, competence and autonomy, as proposed by self-determination theory.

My findings here do concord with a growing body of research that implies that ISLL transforms additional language development and provides new affordances to people who might otherwise experience difficulty moving from a "good classroom learner" posture to a "good independent learner" posture and, perhaps further along, to becoming "fully independent users". They also indicate that the definition of a good language learner could be very broad, embracing a large number of qualities and approaches to learning.

Complex dynamic systems theory (Bot, Lowie and Verspoor 2007; Larsen-Freeman and Cameron 2007) is helpful for comprehending much of the idiosyncratic nature of language learning and development, by apprehending learners, language and learning as interacting sub-systems of a perpetually changing movement, itself subject to outside influences of varying duration and intensity. ISLL trajectories can be thought of as individual learners' paths, on, over, around or through the composite terrain of additional language development. As in all learning considered as a complex dynamic system, a plethora of resources, obstacles,

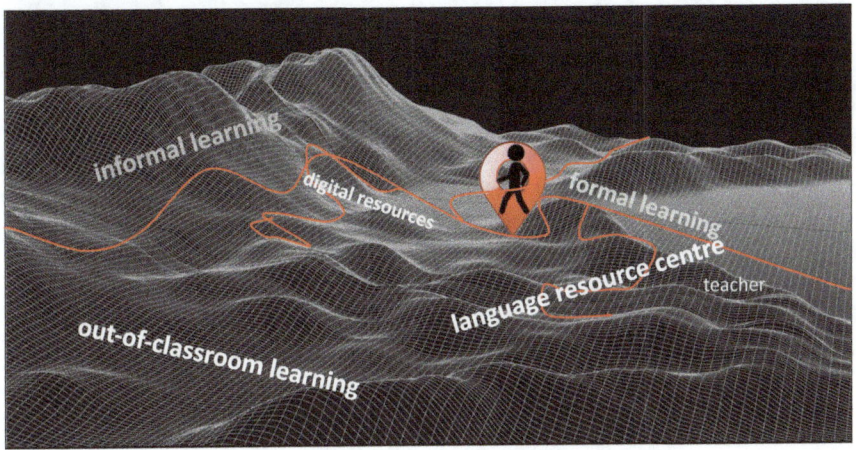

Figure 8: The ISLL learner on their language-learning trajectory.
Source: Toffoli, Denyze, *Informal Learning and Institution-wide Language Provision: University Language Learners in the 21st Century*, 2020, Palgrave Macmillan. Reproduced with permission of Springer Nature Switzerland.

deviations and even dead-ends can be found at various times and places along this far-from-linear path (see Figure 8). The terrain portrayed in Figure 8 could also be superimposed on the conceptual systems depicted in Figure 3. The autonomy, competence and relatedness aspects of motivation discussed above are themselves sub-systems within the system of informal additional language development, influenced by and interacting with the terrain and resources mentioned, the language development such learning promotes and the effects it has or may have on the learner. This once again confirms that informal language learning (with technologies) is open, self-determined and dynamic learning.

Appendix

Language learner motivation survey

The following survey is based on 3 different questionnaires, recognised for their relevance to language learning.

This questionnaire aims to pinpoint some of the important areas that influence your language learning. You are NOT required to complete this survey. It is to be done on a strictly voluntary basis.

We may use your answers anonymously for research into language acquisition and development, but the questionnaire itself is not anonymous.

Please answer the questions honestly, otherwise they are not much use for our research!

You can access the question and answers in either English or French and can change languages as often as you want (or need) during the survey.

Thank you so much for completing this survey.

Part I: Personal information

Name
Email address
Age <18, 18–25, >25
Gender F / M / 0
Where did you grow up?
Year of study
Faculty / Department

Part II: Learning English

A) Language Learning Orientations[11]

Why are you learning English?
1. To show myself that I am a good citizen because I can speak English.
2. Because I think it is good for my personal development.
3. In order to have a better salary later on.
4. Honestly, I don't know, I truly have the impression of wasting my time in studying English.
5. Because I enjoy the feeling of acquiring knowledge about another language community and their way of life.
6. For the pleasure I experience when surpassing myself in my English studies.
7. Because I have the impression that it is expected of me.
8. For the pleasure I get from hearing English spoken by native speakers.
9. For the satisfaction I feel when I am in the process of accomplishing difficult exercises in English.

---

[11] Adapted from Noels et al. 2000.

10. Because I would feel guilty if I didn't know English.
11. I don't know; I can't come to understand what I am doing studying English.
12. For the pleasure that I experience in knowing more about English literature.
13. Because I choose to be the kind of person who can speak a second language.
14. For the "high" I feel when hearing foreign languages spoken.
15. For the satisfied feeling I get in finding out new things.
16. Because I choose to be the kind of person who can speak more than one language.
17. In order to get a more prestigious job later on.
18. Because I would feel ashamed if I couldn't speak to my friends from other cultures in English.
19. For the enjoyment I experience when I grasp a difficult construct in English.
20. I cannot come to see why I study English, and frankly, I don't give a damn.
21. For the "high" feeling that I experience while speaking in English.

B) Autonomous learning[12]

Which of the following best describes you?

1 Not at all like me	2 quite unlike me	3 Neither like nor unlike me	4 quite like me	5 Very like me

1. I enjoy finding information about new topics on my own.
2. I frequently find excuses for not getting down to work.
3. I am good at meeting deadlines.
4. My time management is good.
5. I am happy working on my own.
6. Even when tasks are difficult I try to stick with them.
7. I am open to new ways of doing familiar things.
8. I enjoy being set a challenge.
9. I plan my time for study effectively.
10. I tend to be motivated to work by assessment deadlines.
11. I take responsibility for my learning experiences.
12. I enjoy new learning experiences.

---

[12] Adapted from Macaskill & Taylor 2010.

C) Attachment[13]

Looking back, who is the **one person** who *most influenced* your learning of English?

Please write the relationship you had with this person (parent, (girl)friend, teacher, sibling (brother or sister) or whatever). Be as specific as possible, indicating just one person (for example "my girlfriend (or boyfriend) when I was 15").

Please rate the various aspects of your relationship with the person identified in the previous question:
1 strongly disagree 2 disagree slightly 3 ambivalent 4 agree slightly 5 strongly agree
1. It helped to turn to this person when I had problems with my language learning.
2. I usually asked this person questions about my problems or difficulties with learning the language.
3. I talked easily about the language and language learning with this person.
4. I found it easy to depend on this person.
5. I didn't feel comfortable opening up to this person.
6. I preferred not to show this person how I felt deep down.
7. I often worried that this person didn't really care for me.
8. I was afraid that this person would let me down.
9. I worried that this person wouldn't care about me as much as I cared about him or her.
10. I thought this person was really good in English.

Using the same scale, please rate the various statements about your relationship with English:
1. It helps to use English when I have problems with my language learning.
2. I use English to ask questions about my problems or difficulties with learning it.
3. I easily talk in English about the language and language learning.
4. I can depend on English to express my feelings.
5. I feel comfortable opening up to people in English.
6. I prefer to use a language other than English to show how I feel deep down.
7. I worry that I'm not very good in English.
8. I'm afraid that the English language will trip me up
9. I worry that the English language isn't very kind when we make mistakes.
10. I really like the English language.

---

[13] Adapted from Fraley et al. 2011.

References

Albero, Brigitte. 2000. *L'autoformation en Contexte institutionnel: Du Paradigme de l'Instruction au Paradigme de l'Autonomie*. Paris/Montréal: Éditions L'Harmattan.
Arndt, Henriette L. 2019. *Informal second language learning: The role of engagement, proficiency, attitudes, and motivation*. Oxford: University of Oxford dissertation.
Bandura, Albert. 1977. *Social Learning Theory*. Englewood Cliffs: Prentice Hall.
Bartholomew, Kim & Leonard M. Horowitz. 1991. Attachment styles among young adults: A test of a four-category model. *Journal of Personality and Social Psychology* 61(2). 226–244.
Benson, Phil. 2011. Language learning and teaching beyond the classroom: An introduction to the field. In Phil Benson & Hayo Reinders (eds.), *Beyond the Language Classroom*, 7–16. Basingstoke: Palgrave Macmillan.
Benson, Phil. 2012. Autonomy in language learning, learning and life. In L'Autonomie dans les Pratiques Éducatives [Special Issue], *Synergies France* 2012(9). 29–40.
Benson, Phil & Peter Voller. 1997. *Autonomy and Independence in Language Learning: Applied Linguistics and Language Study*. London: Longman.
Bot, Kees de, Wander Lowie & Marjolijn Verspoor. 2007. A dynamic systems theory approach to second language acquisition. *Bilingualism: Language and Cognition* 10(1). 7–21. https://doi.org/10.1017/S1366728906002732.
Cole, Jason. 2015. *Foreign language learning in the age of the internet: A comparison of informal acquirers and traditional classroom learners in central Brazil*. Oxford: University of Oxford dissertation.
Council of Europe. 2000. *Common European Framework of Reference for Languages: Learning, Teaching, Assessment*. Cambridge: Cambridge University Press. http://www.coe.int/t/dg4/linguistic/Source/Framework_EN.pdf.
Council of Europe. 2018. *Common European Framework of Reference for Languages: Learning, Teaching, Assessment – Companion Volume with new descriptors*. Strasbourg: Council of Europe.
Cyrulnik, Boris. 2009. *Resilience: How Your Inner Strength Can Set You Free from the Past*. London: Penguin.
Day, C. 2007. Attachment and early language development: Implications for early intervention. *NHSA Dialog* 10(3–4). 143–150.
de Charms, Richard, Virginia Carpenter & Aharon Kuperman. 1965. The "origin-pawn" variable in person perception. *Sociometry* 28(3). 241. https://doi.org/10.2307/2786024.
Deci, Edward L. & Richard M. Ryan. 2002. *Handbook of Self-determination Research*. Rochester: University of Rochester Press.
Deci, Edward L., Robert J. Vallerand, Luc G. Pelletier & Richard M. Ryan. 1991. Motivation and education: The self-determination perspective. *Educational Psychologist* 26(3–4). 325–346.
Dereli, Esra & Ozlem Krakus. 2011. An examination of attachment styles and social skills of university students. *Electronic Journal of Research in Educational Psychology* 9(2). 731.
Dressman, Mark & Randall Sadler. 2020. *The Handbook of Informal Language Learning*. Hoboken/Chichester: Wiley Blackwell.
Fleming, Ted. 2008. A secure base for adult learning: Attachment theory and adult education. *Adult Learner: The Irish Journal of Adult and Community Education*. 33–53.
Fraley, R. Chris, Marie E. Heffernan, Amanda M. Vicary & Claudia Chloe Brumbaugh. 2011. The experiences in close relationships – Relationship Structures Questionnaire: A method for

assessing attachment orientations across relationships. *Psychological Assessment* 23(3). 615–625. https://doi.org/10.1037/a0022898.

Geddes, Heather. 2006. *Attachment in the Classroom: The Links Between Children's Early Experience, Emotional Well-being and Performance in School*. Duffield: Worth Publishing.

Graham, Suzanne. 2022. Self-efficacy and language learning – what it is and what it isn't. *Language Learning Journal*. 1–22.

Hall, Graham. 2022. Researching the language classroom through ethnographic diaries: principles, possibilities, and practices. In Dikilitaş, Kenan & Kate Mastruserio Reynolds, *Research Methods in Language Teaching and Learning: A Practical Guide*, 24–40. Hoboken: Wiley Blackwell.

Holec, Henri. 1979. *Autonomy and Foreign Language Learning*. Strasbourg: Council of Europe. http://eric.ed.gov/?id=ED192557. (7 March, 2015).

IJzendoorn, Marinus H. van, Jarissa Dijkstra & Adriana G. Bus. 1995. Attachment, intelligence, and language: A meta-analysis. *Social Development* 4(2). 115–128. https://doi.org/10.1111/j.1467-9507.1995.tb00055.x.

Knowles, Malcolm Shepherd. 1975. *Self-directed Learning: A Guide for Learners and Teachers*. Cambridge: Cambridge Adult Education.

Kusyk, Meryl & Geoffrey Sockett. 2012. From informal resource usage to incidental language acquisition: the new face of the non-specialist learning English. *ASp. La revue du GERAS* 62. 45–65.

Lamb, Martin & Fauziah Eka Arisandy. 2020. The impact of online use of English on motivation to learn. *Computer Assisted Language Learning*. Routledge 33(1–2). 85–108. https://doi.org/10.1080/09588221.2018.1545670.

Larsen-Freeman, Diane & Lynne Cameron. 2007. *Complex Systems and Applied Linguistics*. Oxford: Oxford University Press.

Lee, Ju Seong. 2020. The role of informal digital learning of English and a high-stakes English test on perceptions of English as an international language. *Australasian Journal of Educational Technology* 36(2). 155–168. https://doi.org/10.14742/ajet.5319.

Lee, Ju Seong & Jun Chen Hsieh. 2019. Affective variables and willingness to communicate of EFL learners in in-class, out-of-class, and digital contexts. *System* 82. 63–73. https://doi.org/10.1016/j.system.2019.03.002.

Lee, Ju Seong & Kilryoung Lee. 2020. Affective factors, virtual intercultural experiences, and L2 willingness to communicate in in-class, out-of-class, and digital settings. *Language Teaching Research* 24(6). 813–833. https://doi.org/10.1177/1362168819831408.

Little, David. 2000. Learner autonomy: Why foreign languages should occupy a central role in the curriculum. In Simon Green (ed.), *New Perspectives on Teaching and Learning Modern Languages*, 24–45. Bristol: Multilingual Matters.

Little, David. 2013. Learner autonomy as discourse: The role of the target language. In Anja Burkert, Leni Dam & Christian Ludwig (eds.), *The Answer is Autonomy: Issues in Language Teaching and Learning*, 14–25. Canterbury: IATEFL.

Little, David. 2015. University language centres, self-access learning and learner autonomy. *Recherche et Pratiques Pédagogiques en Langues de Spécialité. Cahiers de l'Apliut* 34(1). 13–26. https://doi.org/10.4000/apliut.5008.

Little, David, Leni Dam & Lienhard Legenhausen. 2017. *Language Learner Autonomy; Theory, Practice and Research* (Second Language Acquisition). Bristol: Multilingual Matters.

Liu, Woon Chia, John Chee Keng Wang & Richard M. Ryan. 2016. *Building Autonomous Learners: Perspectives from Research and Practice using Self-Determination Theory*. Singapore: Springer.

Macaro, Ernesto. 2002. *Learning Strategies in Foreign and Second Language Classrooms*. London: Continuum.

Macaskill, Ann & Elissa Taylor. 2010. The development of a brief measure of learner autonomy in university students. *Studies in Higher Education* 35(3). 351–359.

McIntosh, Cameron & Kimberly Noels. 2004. Self-determined motivation for language learning: The role of need for cognition and language learning strategies. *Zeitschrift für Interculturellen Fremdsprachunterricht* 9(2). https://selfdeterminationtheory.org/wp-content/uploads/2019/06/2004_McIntoshNoels_openaccess.pdf (accessed 2 November 2014)

Milyavskaya, Marina & Richard Koestner. 2011. Psychological needs, motivation, and well-being: A test of self-determination theory across multiple domains. *Personality and Individual Differences* 50(3). 387–391. https://doi.org/10.1016/j.paid.2010.10.029.

Moffat, Andrew D. 2022. *Second Language Use Online and its Integration in Formal Language Learning*. Bristol: Multilingual Matters.

Naiman, Neil. 1978. *The Good Language Learner*. Multilingual Matters.

Noels, Kimberly, Luc Pelletier, Richard Clément & Robert Vallerand. 2000. Why are you learning a second language? Motivational orientations and self-determination theory. *Language Learning* 50(1). 57–85.

Oga-Baldwin, W. L. Quint, Yoshiyuki Nakata, Philip Parker & Richard M. Ryan. 2017. Motivating young language learners: A longitudinal model of self-determined motivation in elementary school foreign language classes. *Contemporary Educational Psychology* 49. 140–150. https://doi.org/10.1016/j.cedpsych.2017.01.010.

Oxford, Rebecca L. 1990. *Language Learning Strategies: What Every Teacher Should Know*. New York: Newbury House.

Perrot, Laurent. 2022. *Pratiques informelles de l'anglais : Une étude exploratoire auprès de collégiens en France*. Paris: Université Paris Cité dissertation.

Plonsky, Luke & Dierdre Derrick. 2016. A meta-analysis of reliability coefficients in second language research. *The Modern Language Journal* 100(2). 538–553.

Reinders, Hayo, Chun Lai & Pia Sundqvist (eds.). 2022. *The Routledge Handbook of Language Learning and Teaching Beyond the Classroom* (Routledge International Handbooks of Education). Abingdon/New York: Routledge.

Rholes, W. Steven & Jeffry A. Simpson (eds.). 2006. *Adult Attachment: Theory, Research, and Clinical Implications*. New York: Guilford Press.

Riley, Philip J. 2011. *Attachment Theory and the Teacher-Student Relationship: A Practical Guide for Teachers, Teacher Educators and School Leaders*. London: Routledge.

Ryan, Richard M. & Edward L. Deci. 2013. Toward a social psychology of qssimilation: Self-determination theory in cognitive development and education. In Bryan W. Sokol, Frederick M. E. Grouzet & Ulrich Müller (eds.), *Self-Regulation and Autonomy* (Interdisciplinary Approaches to Knowledge and Development), 191–207. Cambridge: Cambridge University Press. http://dx.doi.org/10.1017/CBO9781139152198.014.

Ryan, Richard M. & Edward L. Deci. 2017. *Self-Determination Theory: Basic Psychological Needs in Motivation, Development, and Wellness*. New York: Guilford Publications.

Sockett, Geoffrey. 2014. *The Online Informal Learning of English*. Basingstoke: Palgrave Macmillan.

Stephanou, Candice, Kathleen Perencevich, Matthew DiCintio & Julianne Turner. 2004. Supporting autonomy in the classroom: Ways teachers encourage student decision making and ownership. *Educational Psychologist* 39(2). 97–110. http://dx.doi.org/10.1207/s15326985ep3902_2.

Toffoli, Denyze. 2016. Attachment theory: insights into student postures in autonomous language learning. In Christina Gkonou, Dietmar Tatzl & Sarah Mercer (eds.), *New Directions in Language Learning Psychology*. Cham/Heidelberg/New York/Dordrecht/London: Springer.

Toffoli, Denyze. 2020. *Informal Learning and Institution-wide Language Provision: University Language Learners in the 21st Century*. Cham: Palgrave Macmillan. https://doi.org/10.1007/978-3-030-37876-9.

Toffoli, Denyze & Laurent Perrot. 2017. Autonomy and the online informal learning of English (OILE): Relationships between learner autonomy, L2 proficiency, L2 autonomy and digital literacy. In Marco Cappellini, Tim Lewis & Annick Rivens Mompean (eds.) *Learner Autonomy and Web 2.0*, 198–228. Sheffield: Equinox.

Toffoli, Denyze & Lauren Speranza. 2016. L'autonomie comme facteur déterminant dans la réussite d'un enseignement Lansad en sciences historiques. In Linda Terrier, Cédric Sarré, Joanne Pagèze & Dominique Delassalle (eds.), Du secteur Lansad et des langues de spécialité [Special issue], *Recherche et Pratiques Pédagogiques en Langues de Spécialité. Cahiers de l'Apliut* 35(1). https://doi.org/10.4000/apliut.5505.

Uztosun, Mehmet Sercan. 2022. Grounded Theory: A Means to Generate Hyotheses on the Possible Impacts of Student Negotiation in an EFL Speaking Context. *In Research Methods in Language Teaching and Learning: A Practical Guide*, 41–58. NJ: Wiley Blackwell.

Section 5: **Engagement**

Henriette L. Arndt
14 Behaviour, thoughts, and feelings
Informal second language learning through the lens of task engagement

Abstract: This chapter provides an introduction to *task engagement* as a framework for better understanding how individuals participate in and learn from second language activities in their leisure time. Although the concept is relatively new to second language acquisition research, engagement has been extensively studied in educational science, as a way of operationalising different aspects of students' participation in learning activities (Christenson, Reschly and Wylie 2012). Engagement is most commonly defined in terms of behavioural, cognitive, and affective dimensions, referring broadly to the way in which students act, think, and feel in educational contexts (Oga-Baldwin 2019). In order to explore the nature of engagement in informal second language learning (ISLL), the current chapter reviews prior research and presents a selection of novel findings from a large-scale mixed-methods study of engagement in informal activities among students of English as a foreign language in German secondary schools (Arndt 2019). Whereas prior ISLL research focused primarily on behavioural engagement, that is, the quantity and diversity of second language activities in which learners participate in their leisure time, the current study also considered affective and cognitive engagement, or the ways in which students think and feel about informal second language activities. To increase the applicability of the engagement framework to the study of language learning (both in- and outside of the classroom), an additional linguistic engagement dimension is proposed, referring to the extent to which learners consciously focus on processing linguistic features they encounter and improving their language skills. The findings suggest that these four engagement dimensions play different roles in the informal language learning process and that they are highly complex and dynamic, in that engagement can vary between students (alongside, for example, their personal interests and L2 proficiency) and dif-

---

Acknowledgements: I gratefully acknowledge the support and encouragement I received from my PhD supervisors, Dr Robert Woore and Dr Jessica Briggs Baffoe-Djan, while carrying out the research reported here. I would also like to give thanks to the pupils who volunteered to take part in this study and to their teachers who donated their time and effort. The project was funded by the UK Economic and Social Research Council and the Foundation of German Business (Stiftung der Deutschen Wirtschaft).

Henriette L. Arndt, Lund University, Sweden

https://doi.org/10.1515/9783110752441-014

ferent types of informal activities (depending on the medium, linguistic difficulty, narrative complexity, etc.).

Keywords: task engagement, student behaviour, emotion, cognition, attention, focus on form

1 Introduction

With the continuing development and spread of new technologies and the concomitant emergence of increasingly globalised popular culture, many language learners nowadays choose to take part in leisure activities which involve using their second language (L2), but which were not explicitly designed for the purpose of language learning (e.g., watching TV series, listening to music, playing video games, etc.). For the most part, research has found positive correlations between such informal second language learning (ISLL) practices and developing language proficiency, which is generally interpreted as evidence that such activities help learners improve their language skills (De Wilde, Brysbaert, and Eyckmans 2019; Kuppens 2010; Lee and Dressman 2017; Sundqvist 2011). Nevertheless, findings regarding the relationship between informal L2 activities and language skills have not been unanimous. For example, some studies found that the variety of informal activities was more strongly related to proficiency than the time spent on them (Lee 2019; Lai, Zhu, and Gong 2015), whereas others discovered significant correlations only for particular sub-groups of learners (Cole 2015; Sundqvist 2011). Attempts to explain such individual and group differences have generally been vague, with some researchers proposing that variations in learning outcomes occur due to differences in learner motivation, or because different (groups of) learners may *interact with* informal resources in different ways (Cole 2015; Kuppens 2010).

In this chapter, I introduce the theory of *engagement* – a concept derived from educational research (Appleton et al. 2006; Christenson, Reschly, and Wylie 2012; Boekaerts 2016) – as a way of conceptualising the nature of learners' participation in informal second language activities. I argue that thinking of students' participation in L2 leisure activities in terms of their behaviour, thoughts, and feelings will allow ISLL researchers to gain a better understanding of what might make some learners more likely to participate in, and benefit from, informal practices. The introduction of the theoretical framework is followed by a brief review of prior research pertaining to different aspects of engagement in ISLL. Subsequently, I present a selection of research findings from a large-scale mixed-methods study of engagement in informal L2 activities among students of English as a foreign language in German secondary schools (Arndt 2019). Drawing on the Contextual Model of Engagement (Lam et al. 2012), this larger study explored the hypothesis that engagement, as a mediator, can be used to understand the relationships between language learners' past and future motivation and attitudes and their L2 development. The specific findings presented in the current chapter concern the nature of, and relationships between, four different dimensions of engagement in informal activities: affective, behavioural, cognitive, and linguistic.

2 Theoretical background: Student engagement

Engagement is a relatively new concept in research on second language acquisition (see Asoodar et al. 2014; Liu, Wang, and Tai 2016; Akbari et al. 2016), although the term is widely used and readily understood among teachers and has been extensively studied in educational research. Broadly speaking, engagement describes students' participation in educational contexts and the ways in which they interact with learning tasks (Christenson, Reschly, and Wylie 2012; Wang et al. 2016). Engagement has been found to be an important predictor of academic achievement (see contributions in the *Handbook of Research on Student Engagement*, Christenson, Reschly, and Wylie 2012, and reviews by Boekaerts 2016; Lawson and Lawson 2013). It is distinct from motivation, which can be defined as an antecedent to engagement: the psychological force which "moves a person to make certain choices, to engage in action, to expend effort, and to persist in action" (Dörnyei and Ushioda 2011: 3).

Although there is much variation in terminology, definitions, and instruments (Reschly and Christenson 2012), most researchers understand engagement as a meta-construct comprising at least three separate, but closely interrelated dimensions: behavioural, cognitive, and affective engagement (Fredericks, Blumenfeld, and Paris 2004), referring respectively to the ways in which students act, think, and feel (Oga-Baldwin 2019). Some researchers have proposed the addition of other dimensions to this framework, such as social-behavioural engagement (Pekrun and Linnenbrink-Garcia 2012) or student agency (Reeve and Tseng 2011).

Engagement is highly situated, or task dependent. This distinguishes the concept from attitudes, which similarly comprise affective and cognitive (and by some definitions also behavioural) components (Jhangiani, Tarry, and Stangor 2014). Whereas attitudes refer to learners' *general* beliefs about or feelings towards a subject (Tódor and Dégi 2016), engagement describes learners' behaviour, thoughts, and feelings *while doing* a particular activity.

In the field of second language acquisition (SLA), the term engagement has previously been used synonymously with *noticing* or *focus on form* to describe cognitive processes that involve developing language awareness (Ellis 2010; Svalberg 2009; 2018). More recently, however, researchers have suggested that the educational model of student engagement introduced above should be adapted by SLA researchers as a way to acknowledge and study the complex dynamic interactions between affective, cognitive, and behavioural processes in L2 learning (Oga-Baldwin 2019; Philp and Duchesne 2016).

Philp and Duchesne (2016) discussed engagement in the context of task-based language learning and teaching, focusing on how the theory allows for the integration of well-known concepts such as attention, self-regulation, anxiety, and collaboration into one larger, multidimensional framework. Meanwhile, Oga-Baldwin (2019) focused on the distinction between engagement and other related factors, such as language learner motivation, attitudes, and beliefs, which he conceptualised as necessary precursors to student engagement. Both articles also cover basic theoretical and methodological issues related to researching engagement in *classroom-based* language learning and teaching.

While the theory of engagement also provides a useful framework to study language related activities *outside of the classroom*, the ways in which we define and measure engagement will necessarily differ between informal and formal contexts. By definition, language is at the heart of most learning tasks in formal language education. That is, such tasks are designed to support language learning, and many require explicit focus on form. Therefore, engagement in formal contexts often involves engaging with the language itself. By contrast, research suggests that learners who engage in informal second language activities may generally be more meaning- than form-focused, especially if their primary goal is entertainment rather than to improve their language proficiency (Sockett 2014; Sundqvist 2011). However, learners who are not consciously focusing on language features may still be cognitively or emotionally engaged in the activity at hand. As noted by Svalberg (2009: 244), individuals using language "for purely communicative ends may [still] be [. . .] engaged but not *Engaged with language*" (emphasis added).

In the context of informal second language learning, the three dimensions of engagement included in Fredericks et al.'s (2004) original framework can be defined as follows:

(a) *Behavioural engagement*: the observable qualities of engagement in informal L2 activities, including the duration, frequency, and variety of activities.
(b) *Affective engagement*: learners' emotional state while engaging in informal activities, including enjoyment and interest, and conversely boredom and indifference.

(c) *Cognitive engagement*: the extent to which learners are concentrated or focusing on the task at hand as opposed to extraneous stimuli.

To increase the applicability of the engagement construct to the study of language learning (in- and outside of the classroom), I propose the addition of the following dimension:

(d) *Linguistic engagement*: the extent to which learners are focused on processing linguistic features and improving their language skills (e.g., *focus on form* as opposed to *focus on meaning*).

Like cognitive engagement, linguistic engagement also describes learners' mental state. To clarify the difference between them, we may think of learners' mental focus as force represented by a mathematical vector. Cognitive engagement refers to the overall strength of focus or concentration which learners bring to a particular activity (magnitude of the force/length of the vector), whereas linguistic engagement is concerned with how much of that attention is directed specifically at understanding and acquiring new language features versus, for example, the general meaning or narrative thread (direction of the force/vector).

Through the addition of linguistic engagement, this updated engagement framework also connects the current research with two broader areas of enquiry within SLA: incidental language learning and language learning strategies. Incidental learning refers to language acquisition which occurs as a *by-product* of engaging in primarily meaning-focused activities (Hulstijn 2001; Nation 2001), while language learning strategies can be defined as mental processes and behaviours which learners employ to help them in comprehending or learning new linguistic features (Grenfell and Macaro 2007). Both concepts can be framed in terms of linguistic engagement. When learners employ strategies and consciously focus on learning new linguistic features they encounter, they display strong linguistic engagement. By contrast, when learners are primarily focused on meaning, they display little linguistic engagement, even though incidental learning may occur.

3 Engagement in informal second language learning

In the following sections, I discuss findings from studies which have previously addressed different aspects of engagement in informal activities and their links to outcomes of ISLL. Although these studies do not explicitly refer to engagement as defined above, their results will be discussed through the lens of the engagement framework to illustrate its applicability to this area of research and facilitate comparison with the results of the current study.

3.1 Behavioural engagement

Prior research in informal second language learning primarily focused on two aspects of behavioural engagement: the frequency with which learners engage in informal activities (Kuppens 2010; Olsson and Sylvén 2015; Toffoli and Sockett 2010; Schwarz 2020) and how much time they spend on them (De Wilde, Brysbaert, and Eyckmans 2019; Olsson 2011; Sundqvist 2011; Sundqvist and Sylvén 2014). These studies have found positive relationships between the frequency and duration of engagement in informal activities and L2 proficiency, motivation, self-efficacy, and enjoyment. This is generally interpreted as evidence that learners' leisure-time engagement in informal L2 activities positively impacts their language development.

In addition, a smaller number of studies also considered the variety of informal practices in which learners engage. Lai, Zhu, and Gong (2015), for example, investigated the out-of-class L2 activities of 82 EFL learners in China (14 years old) using questionnaires and focus group interviews. *Out-of-class learning* in this study included both informal activities (e.g., watching television, reading, or listening to music) and *non-formal* activities (e.g., attending tutorial classes and engaging in form-focused language practice). The quantitative analyses revealed significant positive correlations between the variety of the participants' out-of-class activities and their English grades, their confidence in themselves as learners of English, and their general enjoyment of language learning. In contrast to the studies cited above, however, Lai, Zhu and Gong did *not* find a significant correlation between these criterion measures and the duration of out-of-class activities.

In a similar study with 94 university-level learners of English in South Korea, Lee (2017; 2019; Lee and Dressman 2017) also investigated the links between the duration and variety of out-of-class activities, language proficiency, and several affective variables. The variety of the activities in which the learners engaged correlated significantly with receptive vocabulary size, productive vocabulary scores, performance on a speaking test, and standardised university entrance English exam scores (TOEIC). Again, the time spent on out-of-school practices did not correlate significantly with any of these measures. Both the duration and variety of informal activities did, however, share significant correlations with the learners' enjoyment of and confidence in language learning.

In trying to explain why the quantity of out-of-school practices significantly correlated to language skills in many prior studies but not his own, Lee (2019: 122) speculated that "quantity may produce different learning outcomes depending on the students' learning contexts". This underscores the importance of simultaneously considering various aspects of engagement in informal L2 activities in order to expand our understanding of the circumstances in which such activities may contribute to language development.

3.2 Affective engagement

Several prior ISLL studies have found positive relationships between informal L2 activities and a range of affective variables, including self-efficacy, confidence, and enjoyment of language learning, anxiety, grit, and willingness to communicate in the L2 (Lai, Zhu, and Gong 2015; Lee 2017; 2019; Lee and Drajati 2019). However, general affective variables related to language learning (e.g., whether learners are typically interested in and enjoy language learning) are not the same as *affective engagement in a specific informal activity* (e.g., emotions learners experience during the activity). Nevertheless, some studies which have focused on learners' motivation for engaging in informal L2 practices can also provide insight into the emotions which are central to learners' experiences with ISLL, namely their levels of enjoyment of and interest in the activity with which they are engaging. Most of the research findings on the topic point towards the conclusion that learners engage in informal L2 activities during their leisure time primarily for entertainment purposes, due to a genuine personal interest in, for example, a particular TV series, musician, game, etc. and not out of a desire to improve their language skills (Olsson 2011; Sockett 2014; Sundqvist 2011; Sundqvist and Olin-Schneller 2013).

What is more, the enjoyment that learners derive from informal L2 activities may actually affect the extent to which these activities contribute to their overall language development. For example, in a study with 84 Brazilian university students, Cole (2015) observed that the *fully autonomous self-instructed learners* (FASILs) in his study regarded informal English activities as one of their main sources of enjoyment in daily life, whereas the *classroom-trained learners* (CTLs) viewed them primarily as learning activities. Overall, 74% of the FASILs (vs. 27% of the CTLs) perceived English as essential to carrying out activities they valued (e.g., reading English-language books or watching TV series and films) or reaching goals linked to their personal identity (becoming part of a global community and/or developing an international identity). Cole also found that, even though learners in both groups spent comparable amounts of time on informal English-language activities during their leisure time, the FASILs' average proficiency was significantly above that of the CTLs (measured by seven tests completed by both groups as part of the study).

Together, these findings suggest that the difference in enjoyment which the FASILs and CTLs derived from informal English activities is one factor which may have contributed to their different levels of language proficiency. In a similar study on ISLL motivation among secondary-school learners of English in Greece, Lyrigkou (2019) also found that students who were motivated to engage with English in their free time because it allowed them to carry out personally valued activities also spent more time engaging in informal activities than students who did not see English-language activities as central to their personal interests.

To reiterate, although the focus of Lyrigkou's (2019) and Cole's (2015) studies was to investigate how general motivation for language learning related to informal second language learning, their findings suggest that it is important to conduct further research into learners' emotional experiences while engaging informal L2 activities (affective engagement). To this author's knowledge there have been no studies which have included more targeted measures of the emotions which learners experience during informal L2 activities and how they relate to informal second language learning outcomes. This is one gap in the literature which the current study aimed to address.

3.3 Cognitive engagement

The attention that learners bring to informal L2 activities has been an important topic of discussion among ISLL researchers. However, due to a lack of clarity in the terms being used, it can sometimes be difficult to understand whether these discussions focus solely on the amount of attention that learners consciously direct at decoding and learning new language features (focus-on-form or linguistic engagement), or whether there is also a consideration of the overall strength of focus or concentration which learners bring to different informal activities, as opposed to other simultaneous activities or distractors (cognitive engagement).

For example, when Sundqvist and Sylvén (2016) reviewed previous findings regarding the types of informal activities that are most popular among learners and their correlations with L2 proficiency, they proposed a distinction between "active" and "passive" informal practices (see also Sundqvist 2011). The active category includes mostly productive language activities (speaking and writing), but also some practices which involve receptive language use, like reading and playing video games. Meanwhile, listening to music and watching TV or films (activities which involve receptive language use) are classified as passive by these researchers. Although their distinction is not based on concrete measures of learner cognition, Sundqvist and Sylvén (2016: 188) suggest that it "takes more effort" to engage in active practices because learners "need to be active" and "rely heavily on their own L2 English language". At the same time, they argue that active practices are also "relatively more important" for gaining L2 proficiency (139). Based on these descriptions, it is unclear whether the researchers propose that active practices are more beneficial to informal language learning because they require learners to focus more on the task at hand and not *zone out* or get distracted by outside stimuli (higher cognitive engagement), or because a larger proportion of the learners' attention is likely to be drawn towards specific language features (higher linguistic engagement) when they are trying to speak, read, or write in their L2 than during activities that primarily involve listening.

3.4 Linguistic engagement

While not previously called *linguistic engagement*, other researchers have proposed that a certain level of focus-on-form and conscious language learning is beneficial, if not necessary, for successful language development in informal contexts. For example, Cole (2015: 339) observed that the more proficient fully autonomous self-instructed learners (FASILs) in his study reported investing more "mental effort" into informal activities than generally less proficient classroom-trained learners (CTLs). Cole defines what he means by the word *effort* more narrowly than Sundqvist and Sylven (2016; cf. Section 3.3), making it clearer that he is talking about linguistic, rather than cognitive engagement: He explains that the FASILs in his study talked more frequently about using intentional learning behaviours in informal contexts, such as looking up unknown words or phrases or trying to infer their meaning through closely reading the subtitles in L2 videos – behaviours which indicate linguistic engagement by the current study's definition. Cole suggested that the more frequent use of such strategies for language learning among FASILs could help to explain the differences in language proficiency he found between the two groups.

Cole also argued that the extent to which FASILs and CTLs focused on conscious language learning while engaging in informal activities may, in turn, be explained by the learners' different *motivation* and *attitudes* towards ISLL in general. He observed that the CTLs generally considered their language classes the most valuable learning resources at their disposal and may thus have perceived informal L2 practices merely as leisure activities – therefore investing less mental effort, and thus learning less. The FASILs, on the other hand, seemed to consider informal activities their most important resources for learning *as well as* enjoyment, which Cole speculates may be what led them to invest more effort into learning new language features and make greater gains in proficiency. In other words, Cole proposed that individuals' attitudes towards informal second language learning affect the amount of effort they invest into decoding and learning novel language features (linguistic engagement) and, in turn, their language development.

Lyrigkou (2019) also explored the amount of "cognitive effort" which the participants in her study invested in understanding and learning language features they encountered in informal practices. Using self-rating scales, the surveyed learners reported how likely they were to, for example, try to guess the meaning of unknown words or phrases from context or search for translations in their first language (behaviours which signify linguistic engagement). Lyrigkou found that cognitive effort correlated negatively with the amount of time participants spent on informal activities, but did not correlate significantly with their scores on a test measuring spoken language proficiency. Therein, her findings contradict Cole's (2015) suggestion that linguistic engagement in informal activities promotes language development, although this could be due to differences in the context of the two studies (the participants' ages, proficiency levels, educational context, etc.).

Similarly, research by Lai, Zhu, and Gong (2015) also suggests that a focus on form may not be essential, or even beneficial, to successful informal learning. In semi-structured interviews with secondary school pupils in China, the researchers observed that less proficient learners tended to report focusing more on linguistic forms than learners with higher proficiency, even in what they call "meaning-focused activities" (*informal* as opposed to *non-formal* activities, see Section 3.1). Thus, the researchers suggest that a focus on *meaning* might be more important to successful language development, enjoyment, and interest in out-of-class learning, because it complements the more form-focused approach of in-classroom learning.

In summary, research on the nature of learners' engagement in informal L2 activities has largely focused on behavioural engagement (frequency, quantity, and diversity). Generally, these studies found positive correlations between behavioural engagement and L2 proficiency, although in some populations the variety of activities in which learners engage may be relatively more important for ISLL than the amount of time spent on them (Lai, Zhu, and Gong 2015; Lee 2019). Meanwhile, even though several researchers have debated the role of attention in informal language learning, and specifically whether a focus on form is beneficial or even necessary (Cole 2015; Sundqvist and Sylvén 2016; Lai, Zhu, and Gong 2015), there is a considerable lack of studies which have actually measured *in-situ* how much attention learners bring to specific informal L2 activities, what portion of it they dedicate to decoding and acquiring novel linguistic forms, and how this relates to informal learning outcomes. In the current chapter, I seek to address these gaps in the literature by presenting findings relating to the nature of learners' behavioural, affective, cognitive, and linguistic engagement in informal second language activities and how these factors relate to one another.

4 Methods

The findings in this chapter stem from a large-scale mixed-methods study on ISLL among students of English as a foreign language in German secondary schools, which was conducted in three stages between spring 2017 and summer 2018 (Arndt 2019). In addition to the nature of, and relationships between, the different dimensions of engagement in informal activities that are discussed in this chapter, the study also explored the relationships between engagement, developing language proficiency, and attitudes towards/motivation for language learning. A total of 506 pupils participated in the study across all three stages. They were between 15 and 17 years old, attended year ten at selective-entry upper secondary schools (*Gymnasien*) in rural Germany, and had been recruited through volunteer sampling. Among them were 286 girls (56.5%), 217 boys (42.9%) and three pupils who self-identified as non-binary. 452 students (90.4%) had been raised monolingually in German and 48 (9.6%) grew up speaking German and at least one other language (most often Russian or Kurdish). Four participants were excluded from the analyses because they were native speakers of English and two because they were new arrivals in Germany who had only recently started to learn the language and therefore seemed to struggle to fully understand the questionnaires. The remaining pupils had mostly been learning English as a foreign language since they were eight years old (third year of primary school), or for about eight years before the start of the study ($M = 7.89, SD = 1.18$). The pupils' English teachers estimated that their students had reached, on average, CEFR B1–B2 level in English, which corresponds to what is stipulated in the state curriculum for this age group (Böwing et al. 2006).

In the first stage of the study, semi-structured focus group (FG) interviews were conducted with 47 pupils about how and why they engaged with informal English-language leisure activities (see interview guide, Appendix 1). The focus group discussions lasted between 40–60 minutes and were conducted in groups of four to six students. The pupils were allowed to choose their own groups (usually mixed gender), with the aim that being with their friends would make them feel more at ease and free to voice their opinions. The focus group discussions were conducted in German, audio-recorded, and later transcribed by the researcher. They were analysed using *directed content analysis*, a method which involves both deductive (exploration of themes previously identified through literature review) and inductive processes (identification of new emergent themes or sub-themes). Finally, the coding framework was refined through discussion with a research assistant who cross-coded one of the nine interviews (87% inter-rater agreement).

The qualitative findings from the FGs informed the subsequent development of instruments for collecting quantitative data on engagement, motivation and attitudes in ISLL during the second stage of the study. All instruments were piloted with a group of 105 learners and further validated in the third stage with data from another 354 pupils. These data were finally used to statistically analyse the relationships between proficiency, engagement, and motivation/attitudes.

Among the novel instruments in this study was the *Informal Second Language Engagement Questionnaire* (ISLE; Arndt 2023), an online questionnaire designed to capture various aspects of the students' engagement in L2 leisure activities. Following an *event contingent diary* design (Bolger, Davis, and Rafaeli 2003), the participants were prompted to complete the ISLE every time they engaged in an informal English-language activity over the course of one week. In comparison to the retrospective questionnaires that have typically been employed in ISLL research, the event-contingent approach is thought to yield data that is rich, highly ecologically valid, and less likely to be affected by recall errors and biases (Arndt, Granfeldt, and Gullberg 2021; Hektner, Schmidt, and Csíkszentimihályi 2007). A range of statistical methods (including Exploratory Factor Analysis, Multilevel Confirmatory Factor Analysis, and Path Modelling) were used to analyse the quantitative data, to gain insight into the students' behavioural, affective, cognitive, and linguistic engagement in English-language leisure activities, and to statistically validate the hypothesised theoretical framework which portrayed these variables as separate but intercorrelated aspects of engagement (Arndt 2019; 2023).

In the next section, I present a selection of (qualitative and quantitative) findings from the first and third stage of the study pertaining to the following research questions:

RQ1: What is the nature of behavioural, affective, cognitive, and linguistic engagement in English-language leisure activities among German secondary school pupils?
RQ2: How do the four dimensions of engagement relate to, and/or mutually influence, one another?

5 Results

In the following sections, I present a selection of findings which address the two research questions above. For RQ1, I will primarily draw on insights from the FG interviews, which are presented together with key quotes from participants that illustrate the main findings. The quotes were translated from German into English, and participants are identified by researcher-assigned pseudonyms matching the students' self-identified gender. The qualitative data are supplemented by insights from a descriptive analysis of the quantitative ISLE data collected during the third phase of the research project (Table 1) and a statistical comparison of the average levels of affective, cognitive, and linguistic engagement associated with different types of informal activities (Table 2).

By contrast, RQ2 will be addressed primarily by looking at the correlations between the different dimensions of engagement which emerged in the Multilevel Confirmatory Factor Analysis (MCFA) of the ISLE data (Arndt 2023). These findings will be supplemented, wherever possible, with insights from the FG interviews.

5.1 Behavioural engagement (RQ1)

Of the 354 pupils who participated in the third stage of this study, 258 (72.9%) submitted ISLE entries documenting their engagement in informal English-language activities (see Table 1). On average, these students engaged in English leisure activities for 108 min/day (1.8 h/day, or 12.6 h/week).[1] Although there was considerable individual variation in this time ($SD = 86$ min/day, $min = 4$, $max = 539$), just over half of the values clustered in the 30–120 min/day range. This average is

---

[1] Behavioural engagement was assessed in terms of time spent on informal activities and the number of different informal activities *per day* because there was some variation in the number of days across which each participant submitted ISLE questionnaire responses (between 1–12 days; 66% of the learners reported across 5 days or more; 8% across only 1 day). It must be acknowledged that the validity of the resulting average values depends heavily on how representative the recorded days' activities were of the student's general informal English-language practices, especially if an individual pupil only submitted questionnaire responses across a small number of days. However, Arndt (2019) showed that the number of days did not significantly predict variations in the different engagement variables, and that the ten participants who had the lowest and highest values for time spent on informal practices per day recorded data across at least three days – showing that the overall patterns of engagement that were observed across the entire sample of students were unlikely to be influenced heavily by outlying values belonging to participants who recorded only a single or two days of unusually short or long engagement in informal L2 activities.

somewhat higher than the estimates provided by the FG participants, which mostly ranged between 30–60 min/day ($min = 15$, $max = 300$). However, many of the interviewed students remarked how difficult they found it to estimate the time they generally spent on informal activities. As the following quote illustrates, a few students speculated that they might be underestimating the time they spend on informal activities because they would often engage in them while also doing something else:

(1) **Finja:** *I don't know, I think I do it more than I realise maybe. Because I watch a lot of beauty YouTubers in English. Quite a lot actually, now that I think about it. [. . .] I will often just put on a playlist when I'm getting ready or something.*

Both the qualitative and quantitative data indicated that the activities in which the pupils engaged most often involved receptive language use, such as listening to English music, streaming series and online videos or, less frequently, reading in English, mostly on social media and other websites. Most pupils communicated very little in English themselves. The FG findings suggested that the only exceptions were pupils who either had personal connections to someone from another country (e.g., extended family members; friends they made on holidays abroad), or those who regularly played online games and communicated in English with other players via text or voice chat.

In general, individual participants' leisure practices were not particularly varied, with most engaging in only one or two unique activities on any given day. This does not mean that they engaged in the same activities every day, but that there was little variation within each day. There was a significant, positive correlation between the quantity and variety of students' informal activities ($r = .52, p < .001$), meaning those who spent more time on informal activities also tended to have more varied repertoires. Both the FG and ISLE data showed that many of the participants who spent the most time on informal activities (more than 2 h/day) tended to listen frequently to music, play video games, or "binge-watch" series or online videos in English for several hours. Meanwhile, the pupils who spent the least time with informal activities (less than 20 min/day) tended to listen only to a few songs in English, or occasionally encounter English-language content on their social media timelines.

Table 1: Summary statistics – behavioural, affective, cognitive, and linguistic engagement.

Item	$n_{students}$	Missing	min	max	M	SD	Skewn.	Kurt.
BEHAVIOURAL ENGAGEMENT								
Quantity: Per participant mean time spent on informal language practices per day (in minutes)	258	92	4	539	108	86	1.50	4.29
Variety: Per participant mean number of unique informal language practices per day	258	92	0.14	4.00	01.29	0.54	1.26	2.31
AFFECTIVE ENGAGEMENT								
All in all, this activity was [boring –entertaining].	256	94	40.60	100	82.80	12.26	−1.25	2.10
The activity was [not at all interesting –very interesting] to me.	256	94	22.06	100	75.75	15.64	−0.91	0.85
I [really did not like –really liked] this activity.	255	95	39.46	100	81.73	12.43	−1.01	1.24
COGNITIVE ENGAGEMENT								
During this activity, I [did not concentrate –concentrated hard] on it.	257	93	8.57	100	62.76	17.99	−0.48	−0.66
All in all, I was [not at all–completely] focused on the content.	256	94	13.96	100	70.45	17.00	−0.95	0.08
LINGUISTIC ENGAGEMENT								
I was [not at all –completely] focused on trying to understand every single word.	257	93	0	100	49.18	20.21	0.07	−1.03
All in all, I was [not at all – completely focused] on the language.	257	93	3.71	100	48.70	19.18	0.02	−0.90
All in all, I thought [very little –a lot] about the language during this activity.	258	92	0	94	39.49	20.02	0.33	−0.78

Affective, cognitive, and linguistic engagement were measured using cognitive differential scales (see Arndt 2023). In the online questionnaire, the terms appearing in square brackets marked the min and max values (0–100) on slider scales, which respondents could move freely to show agreement with each statement.

Table 2: Comparison of sample-wide levels of engagement per activity type.

Activity	$n_{entries}$	Affective engagement Standardised Factor Scores		Cognitive engagement Standardised Factor Scores		Linguistic engagement Standardised Factor Scores	
		Mean rank	Mdn	Mean rank	Mdn	Mean rank	Mdn
Films	35	865.49[b c]	.205	863.14[a b]	-.255	831.80[c d]	-.256
Serials & TV shows	155	983.36[b]	.271	932.94[a b]	.266	783.04[c d]	.046
Video-based social media	262	844.31[c]	.152	917.97[a b]	.269	836.17[c d]	.091
Text-based social media	77	646.33[d]	-.066	833.23[b]	.218	830.85[c d]	.058
Mixed social media	256	754.28[c d]	.103	841.14[b]	.195	823.01[c d]	.089
Writing	65	607.74[d]	-.077	1017.09[a]	.502	1166.57[a]	.653
Speaking	84	725.88[c d]	.123	958.65[a]	.374	1068.22[b]	.554
Music (background)	218	405.26[e]	.380	215.05[d]	-.846	332.27[f]	.508
Music (focused)	428	721.04[d]	.028	562.87[c]	-.176	636.87[e]	.106
Video games	42	921.97[b c]	.256	769.59[b]	.060	702.81[d e]	.054
Video games & communication via text or voice chat	52	1101.10[a]	.366	976.88[a]	.346	674.41[d e]	.111
Reading	79	783.09[c d]	.146	1029.76[a]	.454	959.82[b c]	.314
Listening (spoken word)	62	575.94[d e]	-.214	786.57[b]	.092	910.83[d c]	.155

A series of Kruskal-Wallis tests showed significant overall differences in the levels of affective ($\chi^2[12] = 206.93, p < .001$), cognitive ($\chi^2[12] = 465.29, p < .001$), and linguistic engagement ($\chi^2[12] = 290.03, p < .001$) associated with different types of informal activities. Stepwise step-down post-hoc analyses were used to identify which activities differed significantly from each other in which aspect. The results are coded by the superscripts in the table, with identical letters marking subsets of activities which did *not* significantly differ from each other and different letters marking sets between which significant differences were found ($p < .05$).

5.2 Affective engagement (RQ1)

Affective engagement was defined in this study as the emotions which learners experience while engaging in English leisure activities, including interest and enjoyment. The qualitative data revealed that affective engagement was one of the main driving forces behind participation in informal activities. It seemed that a prospective informal activity had to evoke a certain level of positive emotions (i.e., interest and potential enjoyment) to be considered worth doing, in addition to not being too linguistically challenging. This was best summarised by Jennifer, when she explained why she liked watching daily vloggers on YouTube (creators who share videos about their everyday lives):

(2) *Jennifer: I mean, the content is interesting to you and also the people. If you watch a video, then you like the person or what they do. But that it's in English . . . That doesn't matter if it's easy [enough]. It's not like you want to learn English and then you watch it, or something like that.*

The importance of affective engagement is also reflected in the quantitative data (Table 1): the distributions of all three affective engagement items in the ISLE questionnaire were negatively skewed, meaning that the vast majority of learners reported high levels of interest and enjoyment during the activities in which they engaged. In other words, the participants did not often engage in activities that they did not enjoy.

Moreover, the reported levels of affective engagement were consistently high across all different types of informal activities, although there were still some significant differences (Table 2). *Playing video games and chatting with other players* was associated with significantly higher affective engagement than all other informal practices, followed, at some distance, by watching series and playing video games without inter-player communication. The high emotional engagement in video games, which seemed to be further strengthened through social interactions with other players, is perhaps unsurprising, given that the immersive nature of gaming has been discussed extensively in the literature and led to suggestions of using games as tools for engaging students in learning (e.g., de Freitas 2013). Meanwhile, the high levels of affective engagement evoked by TV series might be reflective of pupils becoming, over time, increasingly immersed in the programmes' narratives and emotionally invested in the lives of the main characters, as this student suggested:

(3) *Linus: I think when I'm watching a series it's more fun – I mean, you get to know the story and such. And then you just get into it more. For example, not like in films, I think.*

5.3 Cognitive engagement (RQ1)

Cognitive engagement describes how much attention learners bring to an informal activity, that is, how strongly they are concentrating on the task itself versus other distractors. In the FG interviews, many students talked about how they would often listen to music or put on an online video "in the background" for entertainment while doing something else, because it did not take a lot of concentration for them to follow what was going on. For example, one student described how she would watch YouTube videos for several hours every day while doing her homework:

(4) **Insa:** *I just watch a lot of YouTube. [With the auto play function] you just put on a video and it keeps going. And then it's just there . . . in English [laughs] during my homework or something. I would say you don't really think about [the fact] that it's in English. It's just . . . It's just really normal. It's normal. You just do it.*

Most of the FG participants who reported regularly engaging in English leisure activities said that, like Insa, they could follow the contents without much effort. Some even claimed that they perceived no difference between watching a video, reading a text, etc. in English and German. By contrast, several of the participants who did *not* frequently engage in informal practices said that this was because they had to concentrate too much to reach a level of comprehension that would allow them to enjoy the activity:

(5) **Jill:** *But when I just want to do something to relax, I wouldn't want to suffer through the English to play a video game. I would just do it in German, so that I can just do it without having to try so hard – I mean, to understand what it's saying and what I have to do.*

(6) **Karin:** *It's sometimes less fun because you have to concentrate more to understand it in English. Otherwise [in German] it's always like . . . You just look at it and understand everything.*

Together, these observations suggest that, in addition to affective engagement, how much focus a learner thought something required (perceived cognitive engagement) also determined, to some extent, whether the students chose to take part in certain informal activities. A similar finding was previously reported by Lai, Hu, and Lyu (2018) in a study with Hong Kong and US-American L2 learners, where the frequency of engagement in out-of-class practices was significantly predicted by the perceived ease of such activities.

There was some disagreement among the FG participants over which types of activities required the most concentration. Some pupils described struggling most with the fast-paced speech and often unfamiliar accents that they would encounter in series or online videos, which meant that in a moment of inattention they could lose the narrative thread altogether. Meanwhile, many others commented on the exceptional focus that reading books required, in part due to narrative complexity, but also the fact that, when one is reading, comprehending the meaning depends solely on understanding the language (i.e., one cannot make inferences from the visual context, such as when watching videos). Indeed, reading books was among the activities which, according to the quantitative data, was associated with the highest average levels of cognitive engagement, together with writing in English, speaking, and communicating with fellow players while playing video games (Table 2).

It is perhaps unsurprising that writing and speaking also required high levels of cognitive engagement, given that language production, in contrast to receptive skills, is generally regarded as more difficult by learners, teachers, and researchers alike. More importantly, however, this finding corroborates Sundqvist and Sylvén's (2016) distinction between "active" and "passive" informal practices (see Section 3.3): the same activities which emerged as requiring greater cognitive engagement in the current study – speaking, writing, reading, and playing video games – were labelled as "active" by Sylvén and Sundqvist, who speculated that these practices required "more effort" from learners.

5.4 Linguistic engagement (RQ1)

The findings presented above suggest that cognitive engagement (the amount of attention that learners bring to a particular activity) is, in part, related to language processing. However, the broader study on which the current chapter is based also explored separately the dimension of *linguistic engagement*, that is the *attention to form* or *conscious focus* on linguistic features. As the following quote illustrates, a vast majority of the FG participants reported that they did not generally focus much on the language in informal activities.

(7) **Eileen:** *To be honest, I don't really pay attention to the language when I'm [. . .] watching a series or something. Because, for example, I'm more interested in what's happening than what they are saying exactly.*

This was also reflected in the quantitative data, as the questions about linguistic engagement in the ISLE produced mean scores well below the cognitive and affective engagement items (Table 1). These findings support the conclusion that the pupils in this study – much like the participants in prior research (Sockett 2014; Sundqvist 2011; Sundqvist and Olin-Schneller 2013) – engaged in informal practices primarily for entertainment purposes (cf. *affective engagement* above) and were not strongly motivated by a desire to improve their language proficiency. Other studies, too, have concluded that most learners do not intentionally and/or strategically engage with unknown language features in informal second language activities (Cole 2015; Lyrigkou 2019). This suggests that any language learning which is found to be associated with informal second language practices is likely to be mostly incidental.

When the FG participants were asked whether they ever focused on a particular word or phrase when engaging in informal activities, most reported that they rarely or never did so. A few learners did, however, concede that they might choose to focus on understanding and remembering a particular word or phrase if it was repeated frequently and/or appeared integral to understanding the overall meaning. In the following example, Lisa describes what she would do in such a situation.

(8) **Lisa:** *Sometimes it's unimportant information and sometimes there are key terms in there, that you have to understand, that come again and again. And if you don't understand those [. . .] then maybe you look them up or something.*

Lisa was the only student who immediately mentioned looking up the meaning of a word or phrase in a dictionary when talking about trying to understand a particular linguistic form. All of the other students who mentioned that they sometimes tried to learn a specific expression said that they would first try to pay closer attention and derive the meaning from either the surrounding text or any available visual cues (e.g., accompanying video or photos). If this failed, they reported using a variety of other strategies, including rewinding a video or re-reading earlier parts of a text, turning on captions (for films and serials), looking up song lyrics, and only as a "last resort" consulting online dictionaries or translation apps.

Even so, with the exception of two pupils, all interviewees stressed that their primary purpose in focusing on particular linguistic features was always to increase their understanding of the overall meaning so that they could enjoy the activity, and not to improve their language skills. The following exchange illustrates how far-fetched the idea of intentionally using informal activities to improve their English skills seemed to many of the interviewed learners:

(9) **Monika:** *But if you hear something over and over again that you didn't understand, and then you look at it again, then I do think that you listen to the language more. Because you would like to understand it. [. . .] I think then you pay more attention.*

> *Interviewer:* But is that about understanding what's going on, or about learning words or phrases, or some grammatical structure?
> *Monika:* No! [laughs] It's definitely just about what's going on generally. [other students join in the laughter and agree]

While the quantitative data confirmed that levels of linguistic engagement were generally low across most of the activities involving receptive language use, they also showed that – perhaps unsurprisingly – the average linguistic engagement was significantly higher during productive language activities (Table 2). Since the learners also reported some of the highest cognitive engagement while writing and speaking, the two dimensions seem to be closely interrelated (more on this below). However, one finding in particular illustrated how these two factors were, indeed, conceptually distinct: whereas *playing video games while communicating with other players* was among the activities with the highest levels of cognitive engagement, the levels of linguistic engagement associated with this activity were significantly *below* all other activities. This suggests that while playing games and connecting with other players, the participants were highly focused on the activity at hand (cognitively engaged) not because it involved language production per se, but because it was a highly immersive experience and required the parallel coordination of many tasks (in addition to producing language), including active gameplay, cooperation, and strategic planning.

This particular finding is valuable in supporting the theoretical distinction between cognitive and linguistic engagement as separate, but closely interrelated variables (which also emerged through factor analyses, see Arndt 2019; 2023): While cognitive engagement captured the overall strength of mental effort that learners dedicated to an activity, linguistic engagement measured how much of that effort was directed towards consciously decoding linguistic forms. Thus, linguistic engagement appears to be predicated on cognitive engagement. If a learner is not attentive while engaging in an activity (such as when playing music in the background while doing something else), it is less likely that any particular language feature would become salient enough to command their conscious attention. Conversely, as the case of *playing video games while chatting with other players* shows, high levels of cognitive engagement do not always result in conscious attention to form.

The findings presented above have served to illustrate the nature of affective, behavioural, cognitive, and linguistic engagement in informal second language activities among the learners in this study. It has been shown that engagement is dynamic, in that it varies between students and different types of informal activities (depending on the medium, linguistic difficulty, narrative complexity, etc.). Furthermore, the findings supported the hypothesis that the proposed four dimensions of engagement are indeed distinct, but closely interrelated. In the next section I will therefore discuss in greater detail what the qualitative and quantitative data revealed about the ways in which the different aspects of engagement seem to influence one another in this context.

5.5 Relationships between the engagement dimensions (RQ2)

The focus in this section is on the correlations between the different engagement variables, which emerged from a Multilevel Confirmatory Factor Analysis (MCFA) of the quantitative data. Due to the nested data structure (multiple ISLE responses per participant), factor analysis was conducted on a multilevel model, which included behavioural, affective, cognitive, and linguistic engagement as separate but correlated variables at both the *activity-level* (within the same set of questionnaire responses, i.e., within one activity) and the *person-level* (across a participants' entire collection of responses, indicating individual tendencies in engagement). The correlations between the four dimensions of engagement are reported in Table 3 and a side-by-side comparison of the statistically significant relationships ($p < .05$) at the activity- and person-level is shown in Figure 1. In the following discussion, these findings will be supplemented with insights from the focus group interviews.

As mentioned previously, the qualitative data indicated that enjoyment and interest were the main motivators for these students' engagement in English leisure activities. This was also borne out in the positive correlation between affective and

Table 3: Correlations of the engagement dimensions at the activity-and participant-levels.

	Affective Engagement	Cognitive Engagement	Linguistic Engagement
PARTICIPANT LEVEL			
Affective Engagement			
Cognitive Engagement	.74 ***		
Linguistic Engagement	.24 *	.66 ***	
Behavioural Engagement (Quantity)	.06	.28 *	− .01
ACTIVITY-LEVEL			
Affective Engagement			
Cognitive Engagement	.54 ***		
Linguistic Engagement	.19 *	.67 ***	
Behavioural Engagement (Quantity)	.18 **	− .12 *	− .17 **

The Pearson's *r*-coefficients are derived from an MCFA with robust Maximum Likelihood estimation and listwise deletion (model fit: $\chi^2_{[47]} = 169.08$, $p < .001$; $n_{obs} = 1505$; $n_{part} = 254$; $CFI = .97$, $TLI = .95$, $RMSEA = .05$; $SRMR_{w/i} = .05$; $SRMR_{b/w} = .05$). Asterisks denote the level of statistical significance of the correlation, where *$p < .05$, **$p < .01$, and ***$p < .001$.

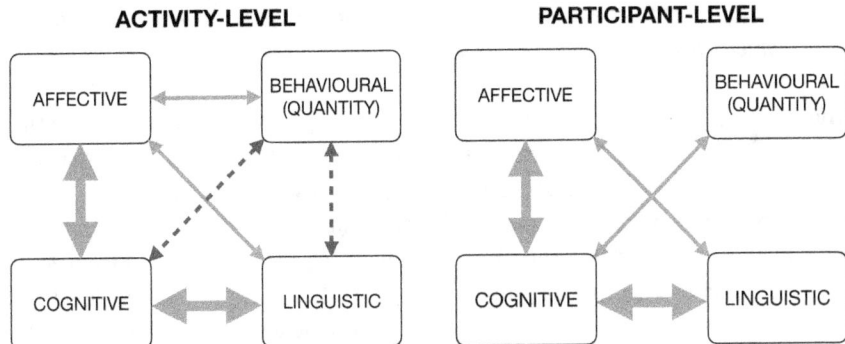

Figure 1: Statistically significant correlations between the four dimensions of engagement. Solid arrows indicate positive and dashed arrows represent negative relationships. The width denotes the strength of the correlation ($r < .30$ vs. $r > .50$).

behavioural engagement at the activity level ($r = .18, p < .01$), which suggests that students tended to spend more time on activities they enjoyed. However, affective and behavioural engagement did not significantly correlate at the participant-level, that is, participants who *in general* derived greater levels of enjoyment and interest from engaging in informal practices did not necessarily spend more time on them. This implies that affective engagement influences the decision to engage in informal practices situationally. Learners seem to decide to engage in an informal activity based on their interest in this specific activity and the enjoyment they expect to derive from it, rather than according to whether they *generally* enjoy informal L2 activities in their leisure time.

In the qualitative data, interest and enjoyment also emerged as determinants of participants' willingness to pay close attention to an activity (cognitive engagement) and to persist in it even if they had to focus closely on some features of the language to understand them (linguistic engagement). This can be seen in the following quotes from two participants explaining why they did not like to engage in English activities very often during their free time.

(10) **Johanna:** *I tried reading articles [on Snapchat] sometimes because they looked interesting. But then I didn't understand what they were writing at all. And then I thought 'Well, somehow it doesn't really interest me anymore' and just left it.*

(11) **Lisa:** *It generally depends on whether the video really interests me or whether I just clicked on it for fun and don't really need to see it. If I can't understand something, I would probably just make it go away [. . .]. But if it*

really interests me, I would maybe rewind and watch it again or look up something.

The quantitative analysis showed that affective engagement was indeed significantly correlated with cognitive engagement at both the activity- and participant-level ($r = .54$ and $.74$, $p < .001$). The correlations between affective and linguistic engagement were weaker, although still significant ($r = .19$ and $.24$, $p < .05$). A possible explanation for the lesser strength of these correlations is that the expected positive effect of affective engagement on linguistic engagement was weakened by a concurrent negative effect of linguistic engagement on affective engagement. In other words, while the FG participants suggested they would be more willing to try and decode unknown words and phrases in a highly enjoyable and interesting activity (positive effect of affective engagement on linguistic engagement), they also agreed that thinking about language features would take away from their enjoyment (negative effect of linguistic engagement on affective engagement), especially during more meaning-focused activities such as watching TV series or online videos.

(12) **Diana:** *I might think about [a word I don't know], but then the action just continues and then you miss something again and . . . I think you won't really understand what's going on and enjoy it, if you think about it so much.*

A second possible explanation is that the direct effect of affective on linguistic engagement is small, because their relationship may be mediated via cognitive engagement. That is, when individuals engage in highly interesting and enjoyable activities, they are more likely to focus closely on these activities (vs. other stimuli), which in turn would make it more likely for them to notice, and try to decode, salient linguistic features. This explanation is supported by the finding in the qualitative data that cognitive engagement seemed to be a prerequisite for linguistic engagement, and the fact that these two factors were highly correlated in the CFA at both the activity- and participant-level ($r = .67$ and $.66$, $p < .001$).

Cognitive engagement was furthermore found to share a weak negative correlation with behavioural engagement at the activity-level ($r = -.12, p < .05$). This may suggest either that learners were gradually losing focus as they engaged in longer activities, or conversely, that they stopped engaging in activities which required higher levels of concentration (cf. Section 5.3). By contrast, at the participant-level, there was a weak positive correlation between cognitive and behavioural engagement ($r = .28, p < .05$), suggesting that participants who generally spent a lot of time engaging with informal L2 activities were also more likely to engage in activities which required higher levels of concentration. Indeed, it was found that of the 29 participants (10%) who recorded the highest overall quantity of engagement in informal activities (more than 1.5 hours/day), ten played video games while chatting with other players for more than 50 minutes per day, which was the activity with the highest average level of cognitive engagement. No such patterns were found, however, regarding the other activities associated with higher cognitive engagement scores (reading, writing, and speaking in English).

Finally, there was a weak but significant negative correlation between behavioural and linguistic engagement at the activity-level ($r = -.17, p < .01$) which seems to suggest that, like affective engagement, linguistic engagement may *situationally* influence learners' decision to engage in informal activities. That is, pupils may be discouraged from spending more time on a particular activity if they need to pay close attention to the language in order to gain good comprehension. This was suggested by one of the FG participants, Sarah, when she explained why she only liked to watch very simple (mostly children's) TV shows in English:

(13) **Sarah:** *In English, if you have to think about the language, then you can't really understand the plot, because you have to think so much about what they even said, and then there's just no point to it.*

Meanwhile, linguistic engagement was not significantly correlated with behavioural engagement at the participant-level, meaning that there were no clear differences in the extent to which students who engaged in informal activities more or less frequently focused on linguistic features they encountered. That is, the current study does not replicate Lyrigkou's (2019) finding of a significant negative correlation between learners' general use of language learning strategies and their overall quantity of informal contact. The contrast between this finding and the current study could be indicative of differences between the studied learner populations (comparable ages, but different national context), but they may also reflect the different methodological approaches. Lyrigkou administered a more general self-report questionnaire in which she asked respondents to reflect on how they *typically* engaged in informal second language practices, whereas the participants in the current study evaluated their levels of linguistic engagement for each individual informal activity they reported.

Altogether, the findings presented in this section show how the different engagement dimensions are dynamically interconnected, seemingly reinforcing as well as inhibiting each other in various ways. However, the observed relationships between the engagement variables were very different when looking at individual activities (within participants) as compared to different learners (between participants). This shows the value of using multilevel modelling techniques to help researchers make sense of the differences between intra- and inter-personal changes in dynamic constructs, such as learner engagement.

At the participant-level (which represents students' general tendencies in engaging with informal activities) affective, cognitive, and linguistic engagement were strongly interconnected. By contrast, behavioural engagement was mostly separate at this level, except for a weak correlation between cognitive engagement and the quantity of informal activities. This implies that the time that learners spend on informal practices and the variety of activities in which they engage neither have a strong effect on, nor are strongly influenced by, the emotions which they generally associate with informal activities (affective engagement) and the extent to which they tend to be consciously preoccupied with the language they encounter (linguistic engagement).

Meanwhile, at the activity-level, which captured relationships between these engagement dimensions *within the same reported activity*, all variables including behavioural engagement correlated significantly, if not always strongly, with one another. Although in general, the participants in this study paid little attention to form during informal practices, the observed correlations suggest that learners are more likely to notice and engage with linguistic features the more focused they are on the activity at hand and the more they enjoy it. Furthermore, while learners seem to be more likely to spend more time engaging in activities they find interesting and enjoyable, their focus also seems to diminish during longer activities and they are less likely to direct much attention towards processing specific linguistic features they encounter.

6 Conclusion

In this chapter, I introduced the concept of *engagement* as a framework for investigating the nature of learners' L2 leisure activities, not merely in terms of what they do, but also their thoughts and feelings. The application of this framework to the study of informal second language learning was illustrated using a selection of research findings from a large-scale mixed-methods study on the English leisure activities of German secondary school learners (Arndt 2019). Qualitative and quantitative data from focus group interviews and an event-contingent engagement questionnaire were analysed to demonstrate how behavioural, affective, cognitive, and linguistic engagement can be defined in the context of ISLL and used to understand the ways in which learners differ in their interactions with informal practices. The findings suggested that these four types of engagement play different roles in the informal language learning process. In particular, I highlighted instances in which it seems important to distinguish between the effects of the general strength and specific direction of learners' conscious attention, which is made possible by the addition of linguistic engagement to the theoretical framework as a dimension separate from cognitive engagement.

Investigating the nature of, and relationships between, the four engagement variables supported the conclusion that engagement is highly complex and dynamic, in that it can vary between students (alongside, for example, their personal interests and L2 proficiency) and different types of informal activities (depending on the medium, linguistic difficulty, narrative complexity, etc.). The larger study (Arndt 2019) from which these results were drawn was concerned primarily with *general* patterns of learner engagement in informal second language practices. Therefore, the collected engagement data were summarised at the participant-level (averaged across activities and time), which provides a macro perspective. However, temporal analysis of the available ISLE data (many responses per participant, spread over several days) could also provide further insight into how engagement can vary longitudinally, across different days and informal activities, and the variables which may influence these changes. Conducting these analyses was beyond the scope of the current study but could be a worthwhile endeavour for future ISLL research. In order to gain a better understanding of engagement in informal L2 activities at a micro-level, future studies should also investigate how learners' thoughts, attention, and emotions fluctuate from moment to moment, within the same informal activity, and the properties which influence these changes. Ultimately, knowing more about learners' behaviour, thoughts, and feelings while engaging in informal L2 activities will help researchers to gain a better understanding of what might make some learners more likely to participate in, and benefit from, informal second language practices.

Appendix

Semi-structured focus group interview guide

- How do you use English in your free time (besides in school or when you're doing homework)?
- What do you like about these activities?
- Could you estimate how much time per week you spend on these activities?
    - Is this more or less the same every week, or does it vary? If so, why?
- Why do you do these activities in English rather than German?
- How do you evaluate your own understanding of English in these circumstances?

- How important is it to you that you understand everything? Why/why not?
- Is there anything you feel you can't do because you don't understand enough?
- Do you ever consciously focus on specific language features – e.g., words, phrases, or grammatical constructions – while you are doing these activities?
  - Why/why not? How often? Can you give examples?
- What do you do when you notice a particular word, phrase, or construction?
  - Do you do anything to learn the words or grammar you encounter, or to remember them better?
- Do you think using English in your free time like this has helped you improve your language skills?
  - Why/why not?
- What do you think are the differences between learning in this way and learning in school?
  - How much of your English knowledge would you say comes from school, and how much from using the language in your free time?
  - Why do you think that you learned more/less in your free time than in school?
- Can you remember anything that you learnt using English outside of class that you don't think you could have learnt in class?

References

Akbari, Elham, Naderi Ahmad, Robert-Jan Simons & Albert Pilot. 2016. Student engagement and foreign language learning through online social networks. *Asian-Pacific Journal of Second and Foreign Language Education* 1(4). 1–22. doi:10.1186/s40862-016-0006-7

Appleton, James J., Sandra L. Christenson, Dongjin Kim & Amy L. Reschly. 2006. Measuring cognitive and psychological engagement: Validation of the student engagement instrument. *Journal of School Psychology* 44. 427–445. doi:10.1016/j.jsp.2006.04.002

Arndt, Henriette L. 2019. *Informal second language learning: The role of engagement, proficiency, attitudes and motivation.* Oxford: University of Oxford dissertation. https://ora.ox.ac.uk/objects/uuid:c579077d-61fd-4b94-bd57-de7063389122

Arndt, Henriette L. 2023. Construction and validation of a questionnaire to study engagement in informal second language learning. *Studies in Second Language Acquisition*. 1–25. Advance online publication. doi:10.1017/S0272263122000572

Arndt, Henriette L., Jonas Granfeldt & Marianne Gullberg. 2021. Reviewing the potential of the Experience Sampling Method (ESM) for capturing second language exposure and use. *Second Language Research* 39(1). 39–58. doi:10.1177/02676583211020055

Asoodar, Maryam, Mahmood Reza Atai, Shahin Vaezi & Seyyedeh Susan Marandi. 2014. Examining effectiveness of communities of practice in online English for academic purposes (EAP) assessment in virtual classes. *Computers & Education* 70. 291–300. doi:10.1016/j.compedu.2013.08.016

Boekaerts, Monique. 2016. Engagement as an inherent aspect of the learning process. *Learning and Instruction* 43. 76–83. doi:10.1016/j.learninstruc.2016.02.001

Bolger, Niall, Angelina Davis & Eshkol Rafaeli. 2003. Diary methods: Capturing life as it is lived. *Annual Review of Pyschology* 54. 579–616. doi:10.1146/annurev.psych.54.101601.145030

Böwing, Corinna, Wilfried Frome, Klaus Gerking, Dieter Haupt & Wilhelm Schulte. 2006. *Kerncurriculum für das Gymnasium Schuljahrgänge 5–10*. Hannover: Niedersächsisches Kultusministerium. http://docplayer.org/10838846-Niedersaechsisches-kultusministerium-kerncurriculum-fuer-das-gymnasium-schuljahrgaenge-5-10-englisch-niedersachsen.html

Christenson, Sandra L., Amy L. Reschly & Cathy Wylie (eds.). 2012. *Handbook of Research on Student Engagement*. New York: Springer. doi:10.1007/978-1-4614-2018-7

Cole, Jason. 2015. *Foreign language learning in the age of the internet*. Oxford: University of Oxford dissertation. https://ora.ox.ac.uk/objects/uuid:db80473a-2075-4e91-bb07-a706bb6a433f

de Freitas, Sara. 2013. *Learning in Immersive Worlds: A Review of Game-based Learning*. Bristol: Joint Information Systems Committee. http://www.jisc.ac.uk/media/documents/programmes/elearninginnovation/gamingreport_v3.pdf

De Wilde, Vanessa, Marc Brysbaert & June Eyckmans. 2019. Learning English through out-of-school exposure. Which levels of language proficiency are attained and which types of input are important? *Bilingualism: Language and Cognition*. 1–15. doi:10.1017/S1366728918001062

Dörnyei, Zoltan & Emma Ushioda. 2011. *Teaching and Researching Motivation*. Harlow: Pearson Education.

Ellis, Rod. 2010. Epilogue: A framework for investigating oral and written corrective feedback. *Studies in Second Language Acquisition* 32(2). 335–349. doi:10.1017/S0272263109990544

Fredericks, Jennifer A., Phyllis C. Blumenfeld & Alison H. Paris. 2004. School engagement: Potential of the concept, state of the evidence. *Review of Educational Research* 74. 59–109. doi:10.3102/00346543074001059

Grenfell, Michael & Ernesto Macaro. 2007. Claims and critiques. In Andrew D. Cohen & Ernesto Macaro (eds.), *Language Learner Strategies: Thirty Years of Research and Practice*, 9–28. Oxford: Oxford University Press.

Hektner, Joel M., Jennifer A. Schmidt & Mihaly Csíkszentimihályi. 2007. *Experience Sampling Method: Measuring the Quality of Everyday Life*. London: Sage Publications. doi:10.4135/9781412984201

Hulstijn, Jan H. 2001. Intentional and incidental second language vocabulary learning: A reappraisal of elaboration, rehearsal and automaticity. In Peter Robinson (ed.), *Cognition and Second Language Instruction*, 258–286. Cambridge: Cambridge University Press. doi:10.1017/CBO9781139524780.011

Jhangiani, Rajiv, Hammond Tarry & Charles Stangor. 2014. Exploring Attitudes. In *Principles of Social Psychology – 1st International Edition*. Victoria: BCcampus.

Kuppens, An H. 2010. Incidental foreign language acquisition from media exposure. *Learning, Media and Technology* 35(1). 65–85. doi:10.1080/17439880903561876

Lai, Chun, Xiao Hu & Boning Lyu. 2018. Understanding the nature of learners' out-of-class language learning experience with technology. *Computer Assisted Language Learning* 31(1–2). 114–143. doi:10.1080/09588221.2017.1391293

Lai, Chun, Weimin Zhu & Gang Gong. 2015. Understanding the quality of out-of-class English learning. *TESOL Quarterly* 49(2). 278–308. doi:10.1002/tesq.171

Lam, Shui-fong, Bernard P. H. Wong, Hongfei Yang & Yi Liu. 2012. Understanding student engagement with a contextual model. In Christenson, Sandra L., Amy L. Reschly & Cathy Wylie (eds.), *Handbook of Research on Student Engagement*, 403–420. Boston: Springer.

Lawson, Michael A. & Hal A. Lawson. 2013. New conceptual frameworks for student engagement research, policy and practice. *Review of Educational Research* 83(3). 432–479. doi:10.3102/0034654313480891

Lee, Ju Seong. 2017. Informal digital learning of English and second language vocabulary outcomes: Can quantity conquer quality? *British Journal of Education Technology*. doi:10.1111/bjet.12599

Lee, Ju Seong. 2019. Quantity and diversity of informal digital learning of English. *Language Learning & Technology* 23(1). 114–126. doi:10125/44675.

Lee, Ju Seong & Nur Arifah Drajati. 2019. Affective variables and informal digital learning of English: Keys to willingness to communicate in a second language. *Australasian Journal of Educational Technology* 35(5). 168–182. doi:10.14742/ajet.5177

Lee, Ju Seong & Mark Dressman. 2017. When IDLE hands make an English workshop: Informal digital learning of English and language proficiency. *TESOL Quarterly* 52(2). 435–445. doi:10.1002/tesq.422

Liu, Chen-Chung, Pin-Ching Wang & Shu-Ju Diana Tai. 2016. An analysis of student engagement patterns in language learning facilitated by Web 2.0 technologies. *ReCALL* 28(2). 104–122. doi:10.1017/S095834401600001X

Lyrigkou, Christina. 2019. Not to be overlooked: agency in informal language contact. *Innovation in Language Learning and Teaching* 13(3). 237–252.

Nation, I. S. Paul. 2001. *Learning Vocabulary in Another Language*. Cambridge: Cambridge University Press. doi:10.1017/CBO9781139524759

Oga-Baldwin, W. L. Quint. 2019. Acting, thinking, feeling, making, collaborating: The engagement process in foreign language learning. *System* 86. 1–10. doi:10.1016/j.system.2019.102128

Olsson, Eva. 2011. *"Everything I read on the Internet is in English" – On the impact of extramural English on Swedish 16-year-old pupils' writing proficiency*. Gothenburg: University of Gothenburg dissertation.

Olsson, Eva & Liss Kerstin Sylvén. 2015. Extramural English and academic vocabulary: A longitudinal study of CLIL and non-CLIL students in Sweden. *Journal of Applied Language Studies* 9(2). 77–103. doi:10.17011/apples/urn.201512234129

Pekrun, Reinhard & Lisa Linnenbrink-Garcia. 2012. Academic emotions and student engagement. In Christenson, Sandra L., Amy L. Reschly & Cathy Wylie (eds.), *Handbook of Research on Student Engagement*, 259–282. Boston: Springer. doi:10.1007/978-1-4614-2018-7_12

Philp, Jenefer & Susan Duchesne. 2016. Exploring engagement in tasks in the language classroom. *Annual Review of Applied Linguistics* 36. 50–72. doi:10.1017/S0267190515000094

Reeve, Johnmarshall & Ching-Mei Tseng. 2011. Agency as a fourth aspect of students' engagement during learning activities. *Contemporary Educational Psychology* 36. 257–267. doi:10.1016/j.cedpsych.2011.05.002

Reschly, Amy L. & Sandra L. Christenson. 2012. Jingle, jangle, and conceptual haziness: Evolution and future directions of the engagement construct. In Christenson, Sandra L., Amy L. Reschly & Cathy Wylie (eds.), *Handbook of Research on Student Engagement*, 3–20. Boston: Springer. doi:10.1007/978-1-4614-2018-7_1

Schwarz, Marlene. 2020. *Beyond the walls: A mixed methods study of teenagers' extramural English practices and their vocabulary knowledge*. Wien: University of Vienna dissertation.

Sockett, Geoffrey. 2014. *The Online Informal Learning of English*. Basingstoke: Palgrave MacMillan. doi:10.1057/9781137414885

Sundqvist, Pia. 2011. A possible path to progress: Out-of-school English language learners in Sweden. In Phil Benson & Hayo Reinders (eds.), *Beyond the Language Classroom*, 106–118. New York: Palgrave Macmillan. doi:10.1057/9780230306790_9

Sundqvist, Pia & Christina Olin-Schneller. 2013. Classroom vs. extramural English: Teachers dealing with demotivation. *Language and Linguistics Compass* 7(6). 329–338. doi:10.1111/lnc3.12031

Sundqvist, Pia & Liss Kerstin Sylvén. 2014. Language-related computer use: Focus on young L2 English learners in Sweden. *ReCall* 26(1). 3–20. doi:10.1017/S0958344013000232

Sundqvist, Pia & Liss Kerstin Sylvén. 2016. *Extramural English in Teaching and Learning*. London: Palgrave MacMillan. doi:10.1057/978-1-137-46048-6

Svalberg, Agneta Marie-Louise. 2009. Engagement with language: Interrogating a construct. *Language Awareness* 18(3–4). 242–258. doi:10.1080/09658410903197264

Svalberg, Agneta Marie-Louise. 2018. Researching language engagement; current trends and future directions. *Language Awareness* 27(1–2). 21–39. doi:10.1080/09658416.2017.1406490

Tódor, Erika-Mária & Zsuzsanna Dégi. 2016. Language attitudes, language learning experiences and individual strategies: What does school offer and what does it lack? *Acta Universitatis Sapientiae, Philologica* 8(2). 123–137. doi:10.1515/ausp-2016-0022

Toffoli, Denyze & Geoffrey Sockett. 2010. How non-specialist students of English practice informal learning using web 2.0 tools. *ASp. La revue du GERAS* 58. 125–154. doi:10.4000/asp.1851

Wang, Ming-Te, Jennifer A. Fredricks, Feifei Ye, Tara L. Hofkens & Jacqueline Schall Lin. 2016. The math and science engagement scales: development, validation, and psychometric properties. *Learning and Instruction* 43. 16–26. doi:10.1016/j.learninstruc.2016.01.008

Geoffrey Sockett
15 Learner engagement and learner change under lockdown

Abstract: Having established the widespread existence of informal second language learning in a range of activities such as video viewing, social networking and gaming, research is now focusing on the different ways in which learners engage with the affordances of such activities, asking why they may experience different effects of exposure to and interaction with a target language. After reviewing some recent publications relating to this area, this chapter examines the informal learning practices of a cohort of students who were in their final year of high school during the 2020 COVID lockdown. It presents qualitative data on cognitive/linguistic, behavioural, social and affective engagement profiles identified in the cohort of some 200 students and seeks to consider how such profiles relate to self-declared language level. From a complex dynamic systems (CDST) perspective, the chapter then examines to what extent the lockdown was a key moment of change in informal practices and engagement profiles for some learners. Among the findings, it is suggested that engagement profiles may be dynamic, with phases of cognitive and behavioural engagement being experienced at lower levels which may enable learners to engage socially and affectively in informal practices once higher skill levels have been attained.

Keywords: COVID19 confinement, change, engagement types, IDLE practices, individual differences

1 Introduction

This chapter is based on the opening talk given at the Learning through leisure symposium at AILA 2021. It suggests that having established the widespread existence of IDLE, in a range of activities such as video viewing, social networking and gaming, research is now focusing on the different ways in which learners engage with the affordances of such activities in an informal context, asking why they may experience different effects of exposure to and interaction with a target language. After reviewing some recent publications relating to this area, the chapter presents, as an example of this variability, a survey of some 200 first year

Geoffrey Sockett, Université Paris Cité, France

https://doi.org/10.1515/9783110752441-015

university students. It takes in the period in which students were locked down because of the COVID 19 crisis and therefore reflects on the way in which informal digital activities came to the forefront during this time. In a world in which such activities give each learner a unique repertoire of contents and interactions overlaid on their own psychological and social specificities, it is likely that the search for meaningful patterns within an overall picture of variability will become a major focus of IDLE research in the years to come.

2 Overview of the field

Every person engaged in IDLE has a unique range of practices and interactions based on their own individual characteristics, which may include learning style and strategies, degree of extraversion, various types of motivation, age, gender, language aptitude etc. These characteristics interact with the repertoires of activities available to the learner. Current research into the nature of learner engagement probably sits at the interface between individual differences and a study of the affordances of informal activities, observing how certain individual traits interact with certain materials. A more sociable personality may for example find the learner more involved in networking activities which offer affordances for language learning. Inevitably this complexity means that informal learning is not a magic bullet, opening a door to painless and highly efficient language acquisition for all, but is associated with great variability in terms of outcomes. In order to begin to address the issue of variability in informal learning, my own research has adopted a complex dynamic systems theory (CDST) perspective, which has variability at its heart. As our own work (Sockett 2014) and Godwin-Jones (2018, 2019) have suggested, a complex systems perspective takes a holistic view of the learner rather than focusing on one aspect of learner language development. Such an approach allows for research which both points to the individual pathways of each learner and looks for patterns of change within nested sets of data.

The fifteen chapters of this book contain many helpful perspectives on the existing literature in the field of language learning and leisure. Since non-native speakers around the world increasingly have access to their L2 through online leisure content and interactions, researchers who may once have limited their study of SLA to the classroom or to other formal contexts have begun in the past 15 years to investigate this phenomenon. Indeed, significant collections of studies on informal language learning have appeared in the past five years. Three such collections, offering a particularly comprehensive view of the field are CALICO Journal 34(1) from 2017, entitled *Computer-Assisted Language Learning (CALL) in Extracurricular/Extramural*

Contexts, edited by Liss Kirsten Sylvén and Pia Sundqvist, Language Learning and Technology 23(1) from 2019 entitled *CALL in the Digital Wilds*, edited by Shannon Sauro and Katerina Zourou, and Mark Dressman and Randall Sadler's *Handbook of informal language learning* (2019). One way to offer an insight into both the predominant areas of focus and the emerging linguistic conventions of the field is to perform a corpus analysis of collocations on the empirical studies in these publications. A ranking of the most frequent collocations (with the number of occurrences) of the word *informal* from this corpus is presented in Table 1.

Table 1: Collocations of *informal*.

informal language learning	59
informal activity/activities	35
informal English learning/learning of English	34
informal sphere/spheres	14
informal learning of + lang	13
informal source/sources/resources	10
informal context/contexts/environment	10
informal digital learning of English	9
informal language user	8
informal usage	8
informal practices	5
informal/formal/non-formal	4
informal habits	3

This list offers a guide to the major preoccupations in the field of informal language learning. As mentioned in the introduction to this book, these may be categorised as: what informal learners do (*activities, practices, habits, sources* and *usage*), where they do it (*informal spheres, contexts/environments*), the particularities of the language involved (*informal English, language*), the nature of any language development (*learning*) and the links between informal and formal learning contexts. It is also possible to observe a focus on *informal language users* themselves.

It is this final category of learner characteristics which will be a particular focus of this chapter. From a CDST perspective, it is important to observe that these areas are in interaction with each other, as contexts offer affordances for activities which may offer opportunities for language development both inside and outside the classroom, all of which may mould learner characteristics which in turn lead to choices to explore other contexts and activities.

2.1 The informal language user

I have previously (Sockett 2014) suggested that those engaging in informal activities are best described as language users, or at least fledgling language users, rather than just as language learners, since they report hours of leisure activities in the target language, usually well in excess of time spent in the classroom. Indeed, having established that informal activities occur in a range of contexts, that they often involve English, that some language acquisition results and that this has consequences for English language learning and teaching in general, it is important to look more closely at the question of the individual and their specificities which may lead to differing experiences and outcomes of informal practice.

Many existing studies of IDLE and related fields reference, for example, individual differences relating to activity choice, which from a CDST perspective may be seen to be in interaction with learners' individual profiles. Beyond the collections in Table 1, some helpful perspectives in this area include Sundqvist and Sylvén's (2016: 139) *EE House*, illustrating differing levels of effort and reward involved in different activities, or Muñoz's (2020) study of which activities are predominantly engaged in by boys and girls. Focusing holistically on the informal language user is an opportunity to consider how some of these characteristics may be seen in the ways in which learners engage in informal activity.

2.2 Recent approaches to individual differences in informal learning

Two recent PhDs, Arndt (2019; see also Henriette Arndt's chapter in this volume) and Peng (2021) have adopted an approach to the characteristics of informal language users, focusing on engagement profiles. This notion was discussed in a classroom context by Philp and Duschesne (2016) and considers that learners may be characterised by one of four engagement types when carrying out classroom activities: cognitive/linguistic, behavioural, affective (or emotional) and social. Such a breakdown of approaches divides L2 user experiences into broad groups which might be termed thinking about it, just doing it, loving it and sharing it. While Philp and Duschesne conceived of these categories to characterise how learners engaged in classroom activities, it is possible to consider how they might also characterise IDLE practices.

Cognitive or linguistic profiles involve active thought about the language activity and the linguistic forms involved. In informal contexts, the issue of whether the language is studied consciously (focus on form) or whether the acquisition is merely a by-product of leisure activities (focus on meaning) has been discussed extensively (Lai and Lyu 2019). In IDLE contexts, cognitive or linguistic engagement can be operationalised as just such a focus on form. The presence of the two terms *cognitive* and *linguistic* in this profile is a reminder that the learner may be actively focusing on problem solving in digital activities which may not only be linguistic in nature, as Ellis et al (2019) remind us in their review of learning tasks.

Behavioural engagement in a classroom context involves just carrying out the activity regularly. Since, in informal learning, the length of time learners spend on activities is different for each learner rather than prescribed by a teacher, the concept of behavioural engagement can be used in IDLE contexts to focus on learners who spend a particularly long time engaging in informal activities. Many informal activities are associated with extensive exposure. In the field of online gaming, Las Vergnas (2017) suggests that many committed gamers are using English for 20–35 hours per week, while binge-watching videos and using social media are examples of how many teenagers reach their average of some 7 hours per day of screen time.[1]

Affective, or emotional engagement, as the name suggests, involves learners experiencing the activity as an emotional one and describing their experience of enjoyment or love for the activity. L2 media use in free time, such as viewing, gaming and social networking can be seen as means of escape from the harsh realities of life, work or school. An emotional connection with characters in a series, vloggers, singers, or real online friends can be a significant dimension in the IDLE experience.

Finally, social engagement, while clearly overlapping with affective engagement where social networking with friends is involved, views any IDLE activity as an opportunity to be engaged in interaction with other people. The wide range of social networking activities and multiplayer games as well as opportunities to watch media with other people or interact with the authors and other fans are examples of the social affordances of informal contexts.

3 Engagement types in IDLE activities

Since complex dynamic systems theory is at the heart of our understanding of the informal digital learning of English, there are many layers of dynamics to be observed in any given situation. It is likely that individual learners will not only

---

[1] https://www.commonsensemedia.org/sites/default/files/research/report/2019_8-18-infographic_final-release.pdf.

correspond to a range of engagement types, but that these types may be impacted by moments of major change in the life of language users. Indeed, CDST suggests that it is the interactions between changes in situations and individual pathways in learning, rather than the state of language development at a given time which are of particular interest. The 2020 Covid 19 lockdown is an example of such a radical change. Since many people were required to stay at home for extended periods and be online for activities which would normally happen face to face, it is possible that IDLE practices also changed during this period, increasing to combat boredom, decreasing to reduce screen time, or changing in focus in a more complex manner. It may be hypothesised that many learners experienced changes in their informal practices over this period.

During this period, a new intake of first year students in the Economics department of Université Paris Cité were asked to respond to open questions relating to their experience of informal learning and lockdown via an online questionnaire administered in September 2020, approximately six months after the beginning of the lockdown of March 2020. Out of some 250 students surveyed, 208 completed the whole questionnaire. The questionnaire was presented on Moodle at the beginning of an online English course. It included indications about the learners' backgrounds and perceived levels of English.

Alongside this study of reported change in practices, the learners' open responses about their experience of lockdown also represent an opportunity to code these responses according to the four categories suggested by Philp and Duchesne (2016), as discussed above, as a way of suggesting which learners may be characterised by some of these engagement profiles. In order to explore how the cognitive/linguistic (C/LE), behavioural (BE), affective (AE) and social (SE) categories may be operationalised in informal contexts, a number of further hypotheses can be formulated.

In the case of cognitive/linguistic engagement, for a listening activity such as viewing a television show, the learner would be actively focusing on understanding the meaning of particular words in the show and may even be writing them down or looking them up in a dictionary. Since this form-focused awareness of the contents suggests that the learner experiences the language in conditions of controlled rather than automatic processing (Sinclair 1995), it may be hypothesised that many of these learners would situate themselves at lower levels in the CEFR. Higher level learners may be more likely to experience IDLE as a meaning-focused activity with mostly implicit acquisition of new vocabulary.

Arndt's (2019) suggestion that behavioural engagement is best operationalised as extensive listening leads one to look for examples of extensive hours of series and vlog viewing for example, with evidence that these practices were not part of a broader picture including speaking/chatting activities. Many researchers, including

Sundqvist and Sylvén (2016) have pointed out that practices involving no opportunity for language production are likely to be less helpful in leading to language development than production activities such as speaking, writing, or text chatting online. With this in mind, it may be hypothesised that learners characterised by behavioural engagement may have lower language levels than those in the social engagement category.

The fourth category suggested by Philp and Duchesne involves affective or emotional engagement. For listening activities, this suggests enjoyment of the implicit emotional content of fictions and vlogs. In social media, it also implies developed relationships with other people online, exchanging points of view and expressing feelings. Much of this language relates to the higher (B2–C1) levels of the CEFR. One might therefore consider that affective engagement, like social engagement, could be associated with higher language levels than behavioural engagement and cognitive/linguistic engagement.

Since my work views IDLE from a CDST perspective, one might wish to further hypothesise as to the dynamics of these four categories. Cognitive/linguistic engagement is mentally tiring and prohibits the very extensive exposure times found in behavioural engagement. It is likely that cognitive/linguistic engagement is necessary to allow the phase transition towards behavioural engagement which many learners report as the shift between the conscious and unconscious processing of audio input when 95–98% of vocabulary in a given input is known. If cognitive/linguistic engagement often precedes behavioural engagement, then it is also likely that the extensive exposure to and familiarity with the language offered by behavioural engagement can lead either to a focus on the enjoyment of listening contents (affective engagement) or to opportunities to engage socially. These different hypotheses will be explored in the following sections.

3.1 Levels

The sample in this study at Université Paris Cité was made up of 100 male and 108 female students. 171 stated that they were French, while 37 listed other nationalities or dual nationalities. In order to obtain a general idea of their perception of their level in English, the students were asked to read (in French) four descriptors of the CEFR for reading, writing, listening and speaking and to assess themselves in these four areas.

The results are illustrated in Table 2. When presented graphically in Figure 1 (as percentages), it is possible to observe that the learners consider themselves to be around a B1–B2 level for most skills with As and Cs making up around 15% of the sample each.

Table 2: Sample by levels.

	Listening	Reading	Speaking	Writing
A1	6	6	10	10
A2	16	18	32	18
B1	84	80	86	91
B2	66	71	52	62
C1	24	28	22	22
C2	12	5	6	5

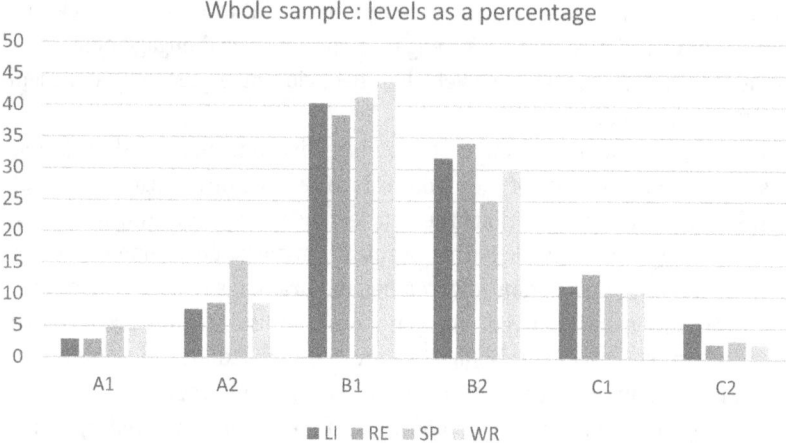

Figure 1: Levels of whole sample, expressed as a percentage.

3.2 Abstention from informal activities

Since this study relates to individual differences in informal learning, a fundamental starting point is to identify respondents who claim to participate little in such activities. Indeed, while the literature in this field suggests that a great majority of young people engage in IDLE activities, there are always a small number who, for a variety of reasons, report very few such practices. To observe whether non-IDLErs consider themselves to have weaker language skills than the others, in Figure 2, the reported CEFR levels of these 22 learners are indicated

Comparison with the other 186 respondents (Figure 3) indicates that many non-participants in informal activities (referred to here as "non-IDLErs") situate themselves at B1 level, while some 30% place themselves at B2 level for reading and writing. Only some 20% consider themselves to be B2 or above in listening.

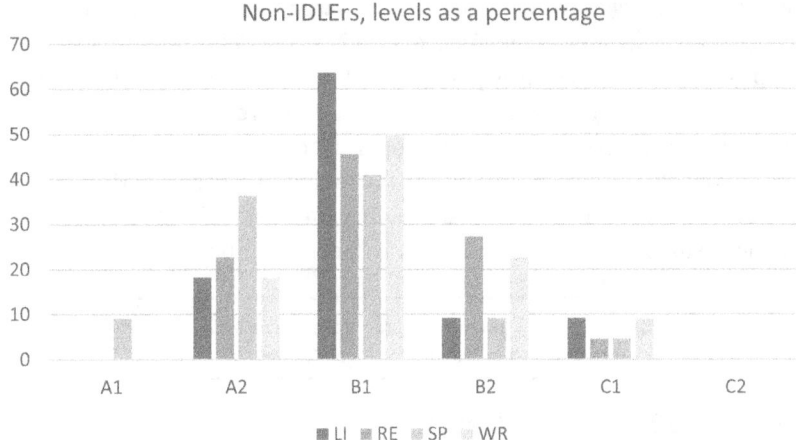

Figure 2: Levels of "Non-IDLErs", expressed as a percentage.

This is in stark contrast to the rest of the sample in which more than 50% consider themselves to be B2 or above in listening. Statistically, the difference between the reported levels in four skills for the non-IDLEr group and those of the 186 other respondents is highly significant (T=0.0004). It is also of interest to observe that the non-IDLEr group considered themselves marginally better at reading and writing in English than at listening, whereas the rest of the sample ranked listening above reading and writing.

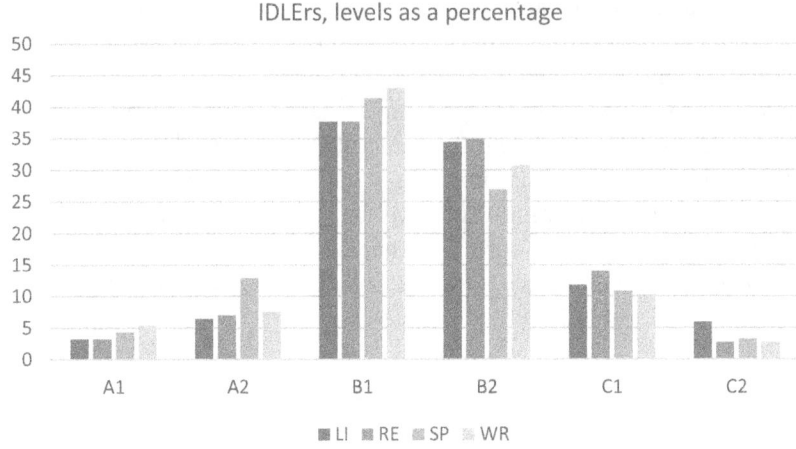

Figure 3: Levels of "IDLErs", expressed as a percentage.

While the data suggests that lower listening comprehension levels interact significantly with abstention from informal activities, the qualitative data also reveals a range of reasons why participants may not have engaged in such activities during the 2020 lockdown. The following example is offered as an illustration of how for some higher-level learners, abstention from IDLE activities can sometimes be far removed from an unwillingness or inability to engage. Here, FH, a gamer, mentions that avoiding informal activities was their deliberate choice due to the addictive nature of such activities at a particularly difficult time.

Example 1: But during the confinement, I wanted to stop video games because I knew it would be my only activity of the day, and it couldn't be like this for 2 months. (FH)

FH avoids gaming because of their awareness of the risk of addiction. It is also interesting to observe that FH considers gaming to be part of their everyday life ("it couldn't be like this") and not just an occasional activity.

3.3 The watchers versus the speakers

In order to explore the hypothesis that speaking and chatting activities, and indeed social engagement characterised by exchanges with others, are associated with higher CEFR levels than listening only, the relative levels of those who report production activities during lockdown and those who report only listening activities may be compared. In Figures 4 and 5, the reported CEFR levels of the 52 students engaging in production activities are compared to the reported CEFR levels of the 122 students engaging only in comprehension activities. These values are expressed as percentages.

While the two graphs appear broadly similar, taken as a whole, the reported difference in levels in the four skills is significant (T=0.014). The most significant distinction between the two distributions appears in the C levels, indicating that some 20% of the speakers are at C1/C2 level but only 10% of the watchers. In order to better understand this outcome, a number of examples of learner comments may be analysed. Examples 2, 3, and 4 were coded as "watching only".

15 Learner engagement and learner change under lockdown — 369

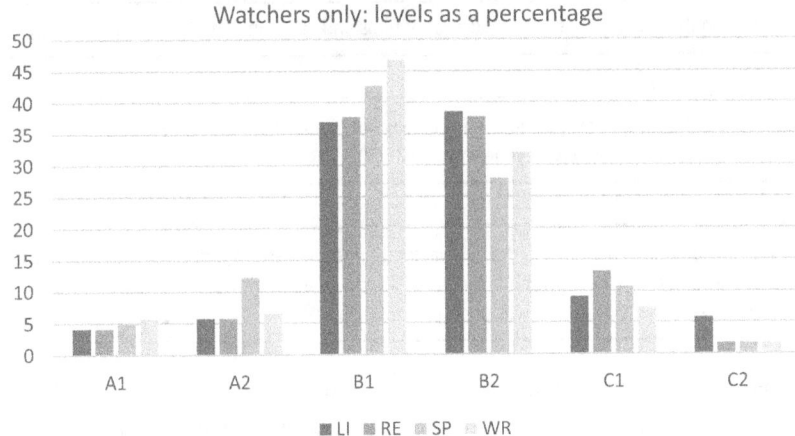

Figure 4: Levels of "Watchers only", expressed as a percentage.

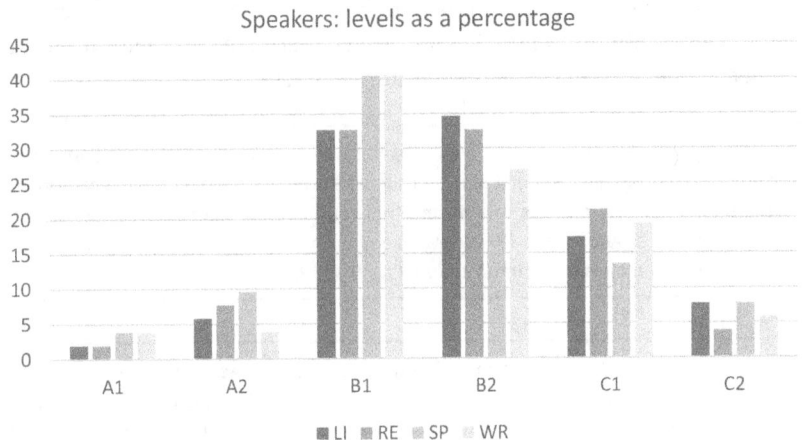

Figure 5: Levels of "Speakers", expressed as a percentage.

Example 2: During the confinement I watched a lot of films and series in English that's all. (AN: A1)

Example 3: I basically watched movies and series all day long haha, in addition I fell fan of the series "the handman's stale" that I advise everyone since (GM: A2)

Example 4: It was a good experience. Indeed, I watched films and series more than usually because I had the time for it. I had also more time to listen music and so english music. I think that these are the two best ways to learn english so it was good for me! (OA: B1)

In example 2 above, AN, a self-assessed A1 level student for listening comprehension indicates that watching films and series was not only a frequent activity but also the only activity in which they engaged. In example 3, GM uses the term "all day long" to indicate the high volume of viewing while also hinting at affective dimensions of their engagement. Example 4 suggests that OA had more time to view and listen and considers these activities to be good opportunities for learning. In contrast, in examples 5 and 6 below, there are clear indications of production activities as well as comprehension activities.

Example 5: During the confinement I saw a lot of series and films I also played **a lot of video games with my friends**. Recently a friend of mine counted the number of series and film episodes in Vostfr *(Eng with Fr subtitles)* **that we saw during this confinement**, the number is titanic: 126 episodes . . . + 3 sagas . . . Add to that a whole evening of online video games on European servers with **English as the only means of communication**. (VQ: B1)

Example 6 . . . sometimes I don't understand a few words and have to **ask my buddies online to repeat**. I think it's due to the fact that I haven't trained my ear enough . . . On the positive side, I think I've gotten more used to it and have gotten better because I now understand easier than I did before the confinement, **talking to my friends online in English has helped me out a bunch**. (JMD: C1)

In example 5, VQ indicates that online gaming provides an opportunity to connect with other gamers via English as a language of communication. It is also possible to observe the social orientation of VQ's activities in that even their viewing activities appear to have taken place with other people. In example 6, JMD refers to online friends who talk to each other and ad hoc correction processes such as asking to repeat. It is clear that JMD believes the volume of activities possible during confinement has contributed to language development in this context, while the use of general American English vocabulary in the response may also be an indication of informal acquisition in a context where British English is most commonly taught in schools.

Amongst the categories of engagement suggested by Philp and Duchesne (2016), one may seek to observe whether cognitive/linguistic engagement is an indicator of a lower language level while affective engagement or social engagement may be indications of a higher level. In Figures 6 and 7, those coded for cognitive/linguistic engagement, referred to here as "learners", are contrasted with those who make comments coded as "affectives". It is apparent that while the largest group of "learners" is at the B1 level, the largest group of "affectives" is at the B2 level. There is also a significant proportion of C level learners in this group (some 25%) and very few A level learners.

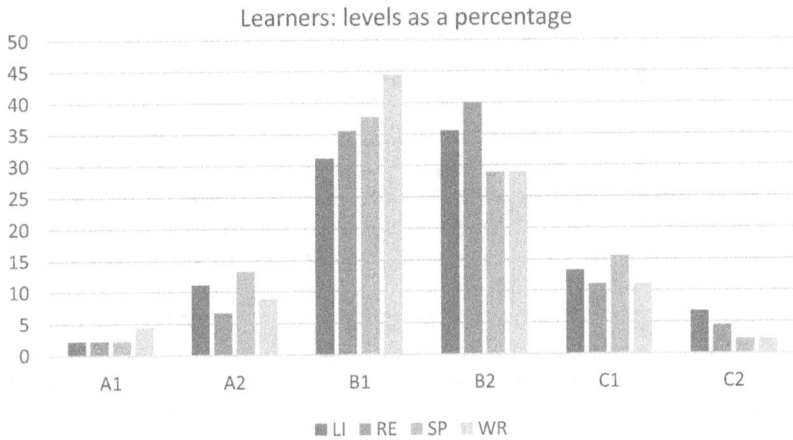

Figure 6: Levels of "Learners", expressed as a percentage.

Analysis of a number of examples from the corpus may be helpful in understanding these differences. Examples 7, 8 and 9 were coded as instances of cognitive/linguistic engagement.

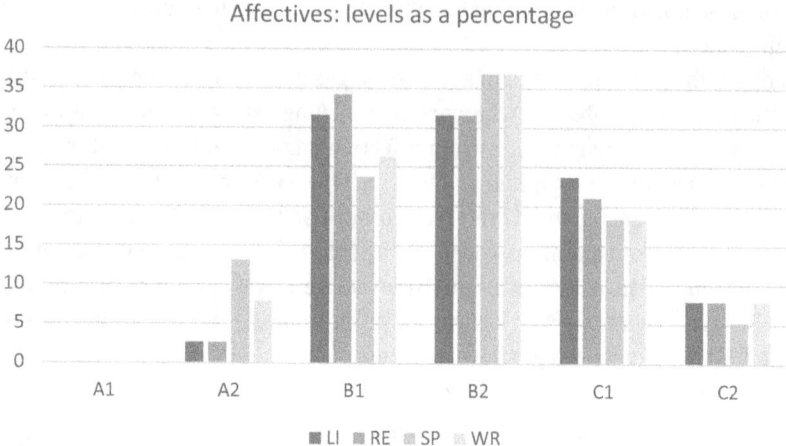

Figure 7: Levels of "Affectives", expressed as a percentage.

Example 7: During the confinement, I watched a lot of series in English with subtitles to **not stop practicing English while enjoying myself**. It allowed me to continue listening to English and **to learn some words**. In the same idea I listened to music in English, **trying to understand** as many things as possible for me. In fact, I tried to **listened to old music that I knew** to try **to understand other words** that I didn't understand. (CFD: A2)

Example 8: These informal activities are fun and help me progress in English. So, as well as being entertainment, I am aware that it helps me to progress . . . I like to understand the lyrics of a song so when I don't know certain words, **I look for their translation on internet**. (RG : B2)

Example 9: I watched a lot of series and I tried to improve my English in a new way: everytime I did not understand a specific word, **I pressed the pause** bouton to write the later **on a piece of paper**. The following day, **I learnt the list of words** (CD: B2)

The learner in example 7 claims to be using informal activities as a way of continuing to learn English in the absence of face-to-face English lessons during lockdown. This is evidenced in the terms in bold which indicate that CFD believes they are learning by listening. The dual aims of learning and enjoyment are not seen as contradictory by CFD but as complementary, as is the case in example 8. The decision to listen to music which they already know well indicates that CFD is using the strategy of reducing cognitive load by allowing focus on form where the meaning is already known. In examples 8 and 9, the learners use other explicit strategies such as using online resources ("look for their translation"), pausing the recording, making notes and delayed recall learning ("the following day I learnt the list of words"). Research into cognitive learning strategies such as Cohen (2011) continues to provide a helpful framework for analysing this type of naturally occurring behaviour. While examples 7 and 8 are also coded as affective engagement, due to the references to fun, entertainment and enjoyment, there is no indication of this in example 9.

The following further examples of affective engagement offer insights into this category beyond the notions of fun and entertainment:

Example 10: As i previously said i used to watch a lot of movies and tv shows **to calm and relax myself from all this stress** . . . I also watched a lot of videos on Tiktok and since my "for you" page mainly consists of American creators it allowed me to discover more about myself **and be more open about the world** (since i have met people with different beliefs, culture and style). (AKA: B2)

Example 11: No matter what i do, i use 90% of **english in my life** cause **i would like to live in London** and work there too . . . So when i play any video game or watch movie i used to do it in English (BB: C1)

In example 10, the role of informal activities as a way of relaxing in the uncertain times of the 2020 lockdown can be seen, while AKA also credits viewing TikTok videos from other countries with improving their degree of openness to other cultures. Philp and Duchesne (2016: 57) state that "emotional engagement relates to motivation and refers to the affective nature of learners' involvement." In example 11, the motivation of the learner is clearly at the root of their day-to-day choices to use English in a variety of contexts.

One of the aims of this study was to observe examples of changes in informal practices in the descriptions given by the respondents. Unsurprisingly, more than half of the respondents (105/208) indicated that they had spent more time engaging in IDLE activities than normal during the confinement, with only 27 indicating that they had spent less time than before. Reasons for this change predictably related to having more free time and boredom because of restrictions on other activities. Beyond the change in quantity of IDLE activities, changes in activity type could also be observed by coding the open responses for references to new or different activities. In Figure 8, the reported levels of the 67 respondents coded as referring to such changes are presented.

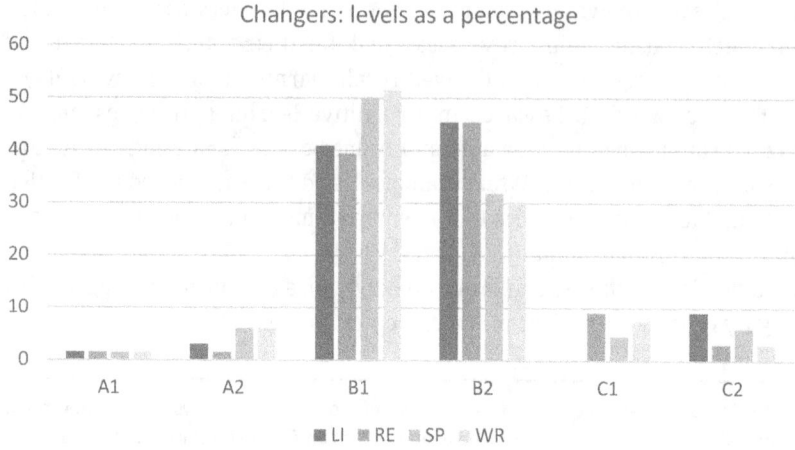

Figure 8: Levels of "Changers", expressed as a percentage.

This graph indicates that references to change came mostly from the B1/B2 levels, with very few A or C level respondents represented. In an effort to understand the reasons for such an outcome, a number of examples of responses can be analysed.

Example 12: before I watched in VF *(dubbed)* because I love to watch my series and do other things at the same time (tidy up, put on makeup etc.) **but during confinement** I did almost nothing so I started to watch in VOSTF *(Eng with Fr subtitles)* and since then I love it! (GM:A2)

Example 13: During the lockdown, I have used my phone a lot to watch YouTube during the day, and in the evening, I watched movies on **Netflix, which I installed at the beginning of the lockdown**. I think that listening to English during this period helped me to understand, **easier than before**, the English language, **even without subtitles** (in French or in English). So, I can say that I am quite proud of myself. (IH: B1)

Example 14: I started talking to people online through apps such as discord so that I have informal conversations with people. (LMS: C1)

Since most informal practice continues to take the form of viewing audio-visual materials, it is not surprising that two of these examples relate to subtitling. The learner in example 12 is at the beginning of an informal learning experience, watching television series in English rather than French for the first time and using French subtitles to aid comprehension, which is consistent with their self-evaluation of an A2 level in listening comprehension. In example 13, the change is from French subtitles to English subtitles, or occasionally no subtitles. These changes are associated with positive outcomes for both learners, as indicated by terms such as "I love it", "I am quite proud of myself". There are also instances of co-adaptation with contextual changes in examples 12 and 13 which mention increased focus on the contents instead of "do (ing) other things at the same time" and installing Netflix at the beginning of the lockdown. Example 14 shows that LMS began using chat applications in English, leading to what they call *informal conversations with people*. Therefore, it can be observed that changes during the lockdown period were not only quantitative, but also qualitative, as learners adopted new activities, including shifting from the category of "watchers only" to that of "speakers".

4 Discussion

It can be argued from the findings presented above that engagement types offer an interesting snapshot of some of the different ways in which learners interact with English online in their leisure time. Rather than being a "one size fits all" experience, learning through leisure involves differing degrees of mental effort, differing time commitments, varied emotional expressions and contrasting use of opportunities to engage with other people. These are important first steps in understanding some of the variability inherent in the impact of leisure time activities on learning. It might however be argued from a complexity perspective that since informal learning is inherently a dynamic process, these engagement profiles reveal only part of the landscape. In CDST perspectives, it is the direction and manner of travel rather than the position in a system at a given time which is primarily of interest. It is therefore necessary to consider whether for many learners, cognitive, behavioural, social and affective engagement are stages through which many learners pass on their journey through IDLE. The 2020 confinement can indeed be seen as a period of change, with more than half of the respondents reporting quantitative changes in IDLE and around a third indicating qualitative changes.

To emphasise the complexity inherent in IDLE activities, in a final example from the corpus used in this study, one of the students claiming to have had very little engagement with English during the 2020 lockdown made the following comment:

Example 15: "I used to watch a lot of series back in the days, and i think I've done like an OD of series, I can't watch 2 episodes in the row of the same series now because it's getting boring . . . " (DW: C1)

It is apparent that DW would at one time have been categorised as an example of behavioural engagement, but they have become bored with the binge-watching lifestyle. This is an indication that observing IDLE at a given point offers only a limited view of what is happening in the dynamic system of informal language learning.

It is also apparent from the examples reviewed above that cognitive or linguistic engagement is a necessary step on the path to behavioural engagement, since actively focusing on understanding every word of several hours of media contents would involve considerable cognitive overload and fatigue. This view of behavioural engagement, which would allow for viewing as leisure, only becomes possible when the learner encounters sufficient islands of reliability (Sinclair 1995) in the contents to guess the meaning of most of the rest of what is going on.

Once the learner can experience prolonged listening to English as a leisure activity, it is possible that affective or social engagement may then develop, as the emotional content of speech becomes accessible and the necessary skills to engage meaningfully with others are mastered. Highly introverted learners may express affective engagement with their preferred media but do not necessarily experience the need to interact with others in this context. One might therefore suggest that behaviourally engaged learners have the necessary platform of skills to develop social engagement or affective engagement according to their particular psychological profile.

As ever, the challenge of such hypotheses is that longitudinal research, or at the very least retrodictive methodologies, are necessary in order to observe such long-term changes. Moreover, the extent to which awareness of evolution through such engagement types is accessible to introspection may prove particularly difficult.

5 Conclusion

This chapter has aimed to contribute to the ongoing study of individual differences in the informal digital learning of English. Much excellent work has already been undertaken in the characterisation of different engagement profiles and the data presented in this chapter can only contribute to this body of work in a very limited way. Indeed, the choice of a methodology relying both on learner self-evaluation of language level and researcher categorisations of answers to open questions can be seen as unlikely. However, IDLE itself is learner-centred and emic approaches are likely to be the only ones able to observe what is going on in the private worlds of learners, while their characterisations of the nature of their engagement are inevitably idiosyncratic. The argument that many IDLErs pass through a number of engagement profiles in the course of their language development may offer opportunities for further study in this dynamic field of second language acquisition.

References

Arndt, Henriette L. 2019. *Informal second language learning: The role of engagement, proficiency, attitudes and motivation*. Oxford: Oxford University dissertation. https://ora.ox.ac.uk/objects/uuid:c579077d-61fd-4b94-bd57-de7063389122

Cohen, Andrew D. 2011. *Strategies in Learning and Using a Second Language* (Longman Applied Linguistics). 2nd edn. Harlow/New York: Pearson Longman.

Common Sense. 2019. The common sense census: Media use by tweens and teens. https://www.commonsensemedia.org/sites/default/files/research/report/2019_8-18-infographic_final-release.pdf (accessed 18 December 2022)

Dressman, Mark & Randall William Sadler (eds.). 2019. *The Handbook of Informal Language Learning*. Hoboken/Chichester: Wiley Blackwell.

Ellis, Rod, Peter Skehan, Shaofeng Li, Natsuko Shintani & Craig Lambert. 2019. *Task-Based Language Teaching: Theory and Practice* (Cambridge Applied Linguistics). Cambridge: Cambridge University Press. https://doi.org/10.1017/9781108643689.

Godwin-Jones, Robert. 2018. Chasing the butterfly effect: Informal language learning online as a complex system. *Language Learning & Technology* 22(2). 8–27. http://scholarspace.manoa.hawaii.edu/handle/10125/44643 (accessed 26 January 2021).

Godwin-Jones, Robert. 2019. Future directions in informal language learning. In *The Handbook of Informal Language Learning*, 457–470. Hoboken/Chichester: Wiley Blackwell.

Lai, Chun & Boning Lyu. 2019. Hong Kong and informal language learning. In *The Handbook of Informal Language Learning*, 271–287. Hoboken/Chichester: Wiley Blackwell.

Las Vergnas, Olivier & Laboratoire CIREL-Trigone (eds.). 2017. Le e-learning informel? des apprentissages diffus, noyés dans la participation en ligne. Symposium presented at the colloquium "*La e-formation des adultes et des jeunes adultes*" organisd by the CIREL-Trigone laboratory, Université de Lille, 3–5 June 2015. Paris (France): Éditions des Archives contemporaines.

Muñoz, Carmen. 2020. Boys like games and girls like movies: Age and gender differences in out-of-school contact with English. *Revista Española de Lingüística Aplicada/Spanish Journal of Applied Linguistics* 33(1). 171–201. https://doi.org/10.1075/resla.18042.mun.

Peng, Hongying. 2021. *A Holistic Person-Centred Approach to Mobile Assisted Language Learning*. Gröningen: University of Gröningen dissertation. doi:10.33612/diss.172696334.

Peng, Hongying, Sake Jager & Wander Lowie. 2022. A person-centred approach to L2 learners' informal mobile language learning. *Computer Assisted Language Learning* 35(9). 2148–2169. https://doi.org/10.1080/09588221.2020.1868532.

Philp, Jenefer & Susan Duchesne. 2016. Exploring engagement in tasks in the language classroom. *Annual Review of Applied Linguistics* 36. 50–72. https://doi.org/10.1017/S0267190515000094.

Sauro, Shannon & Katerina Zourou. 2019. What are the digital wilds? *Language Learning & Technology*, 23(1). 1–7. http://scholarspace.manoa.hawaii.edu/handle/10125/44666. (accessed 23 March 2020).

Sinclair, John. 1995. *Corpus, concordance, collocation*. Oxford: Oxford University Press.

Sockett, Geoffrey. 2014. *The Online Informal Learning of English*. Basingstoke: Palgrave Macmillan.

Sundqvist, Pia & Liss Kerstin Sylvén. 2016. *Extramural English in Teaching and Learning from Theory and Research to Practice*. Basingstoke: Palgrave Macmillan.

Sylvén, Liss Kerstin & Pia Sundqvist. 2016. Computer-assisted language learning (CALL) in extracurricular/extramural contexts. *CALICO Journal* 34(1). i–iv. https://doi.org/10.1558/cj.31822.

Antonie Alm
16 Engaging with L2 Netflix
Two in(tra)formal learning trajectories

Abstract: This chapter presents a descriptive case study of two language students, Alisha and Carol, who watched self-selected German Netflix series as an out-of-class activity. Both participants had a similar academic profile but differed in their prior experiences of informal learning with Netflix. Alisha had been watching Netflix for years, including German series, whereas Carol was new to Netflix and had never contemplated watching a German programme before. Their opposing experiences are presented and discussed with reference to the concept of willingness to engage (Wang and Mercer 2021) and the forms of engagement (agentic, cognitive, affective, social) they exhibited during the six-week viewing period. The chapter concludes with pedagogical suggestions for the inclusion of informal learning activities in formal educational contexts to enhance learner engagement.

Keywords: Netflix, German, informal learning, intraformal learning, engagement, case study

1 Introduction

When my students returned to campus in May 2020 after six weeks of lockdown, they were welcomed back with a poster campaign reminding them that "Wi-fi's not just for Netflix". At university, wi-fi is supposed to be used for academic purposes, or in times of a pandemic, for contact tracing. However, while confined at home for the preceding six weeks, wi-fi was a lifeline for many, providing contact to the outside world, friends, lectures and online entertainment. In other words, the spaces for engagement with learning and leisure merged into one. Given a choice, many students might have opted for leisure, watching Netflix, which reached a record high in subscriptions in April 2020, rather than for learning and attending online lectures. Coincidentally, the students of my intermediate German class had just started watching German Netflix series as an out-of-class learning activity when the pandemic hit. In their case, the choice was not between online lectures or online leisure (at least for their German class) but between watching German Netflix with a focus on learning or a focus on leisure.

Antonie Alm, University of Otago, New Zealand

https://doi.org/10.1515/9783110752441-016

Living conditions under the pandemic have highlighted the customary division of spaces associated with learning and with leisure activities and further between engagement in formal and informal learning. It might have been the inability to travel or the gamified nature of many language apps, but informal language learning was at an all-time high during the first month of lockdown (Whitebloom 2020). Like Netflix, the popular language learning app Duolingo had a huge surge after the World Health Organization declared a global pandemic on 16 March 2020, with new users doubling that month (Blanco 2020). Yet, the appeal of combining learning with leisure has preceded the pandemic. Language learners exploring the "digital wilds" (Godwin-Jones 2019) to practice their languages in engaging ways have been studied for over a decade, described with catchy acronyms such as OILE (Online Informal Learning of English), IDLE (Informal Digital Learning of English), or more inclusive of languages other than English, as YELL (Young Extramural Language Learning) or ISLL (Informal Second Language Learning). The use of streaming services to watch television shows or to listen to music in a second language, or the use of social media sites to communicate with speakers of other languages to develop their language skills either intentionally (with a focus on learning) or incidentally (when learning results as a by-product of the language activity), however, is not a prerogative of learners of English. When Netflix released the fourth season of *La Casa de Papel* in April 2020, it was the most watched show worldwide (Katz 2020). While many will have chosen to watch the show synchronised in their first language or relied entirely on subtitles, many others have taken the opportunity to refresh their Spanish or start learning Spanish while enjoying a good show (Butler 2021).

Informal language learning describes a wide spectrum of learning experiences outside the boundaries of formal education. It can be intentional or non-intentional and incidental. For example, an informal learner of Spanish might watch a Netflix series with the intent of learning Spanish or with the intent of being entertained, whereby language learning becomes a non-intentional by-product. Further, intent can change over time. For example, a person watching a Netflix series in Spanish to learn Spanish sets up a regular viewing schedule and a system to record and revise phrases from the episodes. At times, however, the routine changes. They skip episodes, or to the contrary, they get so involved in the plot that they forget to look up words and binge-watch a few episodes. Informal language learning is self-initiated, self-regulated and dynamic, shifting in degrees of intent to learn and in degrees of intensity. It differs fundamentally from formal learning, which similarly encompasses a wide range of learning experiences but is other-initiated (by the curriculum, the teacher), other-regulated (through tasks and assignments) and static (to provide consistency for measurable learning outcomes).

The dynamics described in the example of the informal learner illustrate the presence of learning strategies informed by formal learning practices, such as self-initiated routines for viewing and note keeping. Conversely, a formal learning environment can integrate activities associated with informal learning practices. Over a decade ago, Thorne and Reinhardt (2008: 558) proposed the pedagogical concept of bridging activities. Designed to enhance learner engagement by incorporating students' informal online L2 experiences (e.g., chatting, blogging, gaming), it supported students in developing the digital literacies for learning contexts relevant to them. In other words, the bridge symbolised a two-way street between formal and informal learning practices, one enriching the other. Similarly, Godwin-Jones (2019: 8) has argued more recently that formal and informal learning should not be seen as a dichotomy but rather as a "yin–yang relationship of mutual dependence and interaction". To label this space emerging between formal and informal learning practices, I propose the term *intra-formal language learning*.

To shed light on the dynamic nature of learner engagement in intra-formal learning, this chapter presents a descriptive case study of two language students, Alisha and Carol, who watched self-selected German Netflix series as an out-of-class activity. Both participants had similar academic profiles but differed in their prior experiences of informal learning with Netflix. Alisha had been watching Netflix for years, including German series, whereas Carol was new to Netflix and had never contemplated watching a German programme before. Their respective experiences are presented and discussed with reference to the concept of willingness to engage (Wang and Mercer 2021) and the forms of engagement (agentic, cognitive, affective, social) they exhibited during the viewing period. The chapter concludes with pedagogical suggestions for the inclusion of informal learning activities in formal educational contexts to enhance learner engagement.

2 Netflix

With over 200 million subscribers, Netflix is one of the world's leading entertainment services. The introduction of media streaming in 2007 disrupted the television programming model by letting people decide how to consume video content. As pointed out in the company's annual report, "[m]embers can watch as much as they want, anytime, anywhere, on any internet-connected screen" (Netflix annual report 2020: 1). Netflix turned into a global online TV provider when it started its international expansion in 2010. The production of local content since 2013 resulted in popular shows such as *Elite* (Spain), *Dark* (Germany), *The House of Flowers* (Mexico) and *Lupin* (France), which, some geo-blocking notwithstanding, are available around the globe in 190 countries. International content is made accessible to speakers of different languages through dubbing and subtitling options, enriching people's viewing choices, as well as establishing new TV viewing experiences. For example, closed captions, which were initially introduced for the deaf and hard-of-hearing (National Association of the Deaf), are now commonly used as an additional input channel to increase comprehension, examples being: to better understand unfamiliar accents or unclear speech, or to compensate for lack of understanding due to a noisy environment (Gernsbacher 2015). Captions also enable people to view videos with the volume turned down, as is useful in public spaces etc. Captions with audio descriptions provide an additional soundtrack with descriptive information for the visually impaired, enabling viewers to follow a show without paying close attention to the screen, for example, during multitasking. These functions extend viewing options and give people control over their viewing experiences. They "can play, pause and resume watching" across devices (Netflix annual report 2020: 1). Finally, Netflix has been associated with the phenomenon of "binge-watching", which evolved through a combination of compelling ("binge-worthy") content and the release of entire series at once (McAlone 2016). Communication scholars Rubenking and Bracken (2021: 2) have defined binge-watching as "[l]ong periods of focused, deliberate viewing of sequential television content that is generally narrative, suspenseful, and dramatic in nature". Binge-watching by now, as an established viewing norm, may well be the ultimate form of recreational engagement for some people.

2.1 Netflix for language learning

Language learners in particular benefit from this development in consumer-oriented and controlled video consumption. The access to international content, particularly popular TV series, and the control over language options (audio and subtitles) and playback make Netflix an appealing choice for recreational language learning. Even mainstream media such as the Guardian, with an article entitled *No habla español? How Netflix could transform the way we learn languages* (Tapper 2019), presents the streaming service as a game-changer for language education. Furthermore, a number of apps and browser extensions add functionalities to the features provided by Netflix to support language learning. For example, the chrome extension *Language Reactor* (formerly called *Language Learning with Netflix*) offers optional dual language subtitles, a popup dictionary (glosses), additional video playback controls and word-saving features when watching films and series on Netflix. For a more detailed list of the features of the extensions see Table 1.

Table 1: Features of Chrome extension *Language Reactor* (*Language Learning with Netflix, LLN*).

Feature	Description
Dual subtitles	Two sets of subtitles, one in the language of the video (also called caption), and an additional one in the language chosen by the viewer (the subtitle).
Hidden subtitles	Two sets of subtitles. The caption is displayed, but the subtitle is greyed out. A click on the greyed-out area reveals the translation.
Auto-pause	Automatically pauses playback at the end of every subtitle.
Transcript	A window with the running transcript is displayed on the right side of the screen.
Video playback control	Adjustable speed 0.5, 0.75, 0.875, normal, 1.25, 1.5, 1.75
Popup dictionary	Left click on word in caption displays dictionary with translation, sound file, and a list with all occurrences of the word in the show. This clickable feature is also referred to as glosses.
Saving words	Right click to save word. Saved words can also be coloured and sorted by language, type and colour.
Saving phrases	Clicking on the star next to the caption saves the subtitle
Export words	Saved words and phrases can be exported in HTML, Excel, Anki, CSV, JSON

The popularity of TV series for language learning precedes Netflix and is well documented in in-class (Webb and Rodgers 2009) and out-of-class settings (Kusyk and Sockett 2012). An activity associated with entertainment, L2 viewing has been compared to L2 reading. Some of the benefits of L2 viewing are, according to Durbahn et al. (2020), that fewer words are needed to follow a programme than for reading a book and words are repeated more often, especially when learners engage in the viewing of multiple episodes of a TV series. As Vanderplank (2016) pointed out, repeated exposure familiarises learners with characters and their relationships in a programme, helping them to understand better "complicated dialogue, rapid speech and accents" (218). In addition, visual clues help learners infer meaning and increase general understanding (Yeldham 2018).

Subtitles (translated text of audio) and captions (text version of audio in the same language) have become increasingly available in online viewing environments (e.g., TED talks, YouTube, Netflix) providing additional support for L2 viewing. They can draw the learner's focus to form and linguistic detail, enhancing cognitive engagement with the language. Research has demonstrated the effectiveness of captions and subtitles for increasing comprehension (Gass et al. 2019;

Rodgers and Webb 2017) and vocabulary learning (Pujadas and Muñoz 2019; Rodgers and Webb 2020). Winke, Gass, and Sydorenko (2010) have shown that captions can increase learners' attention to input, whereas some learners use subtitles as a crutch. Comparing the effect of subtitles as opposed to captions on language development indicates that subtitles lead to better comprehension and recall, whereas captions support lexical learning (Pujadas and Muñoz 2020). Frumuselu et al. (2015) found that subtitles can reduce the affective filter in learners with lower proficiency levels, and Pujadas and Muñoz (2019) observed that higher proficiency generally relates to higher vocabulary gains with either subtitle or caption support. Peters and Muñoz' (2020) recent special issue on language learning from multimodal input shows that research into captioned L2 viewing is developing in scope, addressing different types of captioning (e.g., glossed captions), different viewing conditions (intentional learning or incidental learning) and time conditions (intensive or extensive viewing), focusing on different components of language learning (comprehension and vocabulary).

Dizon and Thanyawatpokin (2021) and Fievez et al. (2021) explored additional subtitle options that are available through the Chrome extension *Language Learning with Netflix (LLN)*. Dizon and Thanyawatpokin (2021) compared how subtitles, captions and dual subtitles (in two languages) differed in their impact on vocabulary learning and listening comprehension. Three groups of participants, EFL learners in Japan, watched an episode of a Netflix show under the three different subtitling conditions. Findings suggested that captions are least effective for vocabulary learning and listening comprehension, which is more likely to be supported by subtitles or dual subtitles. Fievez et al. (2021) investigated the effects of the glossed captions feature of *LLN* (the use of the popup dictionary embedded in the captions) on incidental vocabulary learning. Learners watched six episodes of a French Netflix series in an out-of-classroom context, and results showed that the use of the feature positively influenced lexical development.

The research into L2 viewing in the above examples demonstrates the cognitive benefits of multimodal input for language learning in experimental studies, with participants assigned to specific viewing conditions. However, as language learners increasingly initiate L2 viewing on their terms, making their content and subtitling choices, the scope of investigation widens. Online streaming services such as Netflix enable language learners to engage in L2 viewing with a sense of agency as they "can watch as much as they want, anytime, anywhere" with control over playback to "play, pause and resume watching" (Netflix annual report 2020: 1). Additionally, strategic use of tools such as the *LLN* extension provide further options to support comprehension as well as strategic use of the features and enhance lexical development. Engagement provides a useful framework to conceptualise how language learners engage with L2 viewing.

3 Engagement

Described in Mercer and Dörnyei (2020: 1) as "the holy grail of learning", the psychological concept of engagement has been applied in a wide range of educational disciplines (Fredricks, Blumenfeld and Paris 2004; Linnenbrink and Pintrick 2003; Matos et al. 2018; Reeve and Tseng 2011; Reschly and Christenson 2012; Skinner et al. 2009), including in second language acquisition (Baralt et al. 2016; Mercer 2019; Oga-Baldwin 2019; Philp and Duchesne 2016; Svalberg 2009).

Engaged learners display a number of characteristics, which have been theorised and broken down into distinct categories. Observable actions, such as the time spent on task and the quality of a learner's contributions, are captured in the *behavioural dimension*. Internal aspects like focused attention and mental effort are subsumed in the *cognitive dimension*, and the emotional disposition of a learner during an activity represents the affective or *emotional dimension*. The three dimensions are interrelated (Fredricks, Blumenfeld and Paris 2004) and operate within a social context (Mercer 2019). To put it simply, a learner interested in a topic (emotion) is more likely to interact with peers actively (social), think things through (cognition) and stay on task (behaviour). Conversely, a negative experience in one dimension (e.g., task difficulty or anxiety) can reduce the involvement in the other areas. Thus, engagement is an alterable and dynamic state that emerges from the constantly evolving interactions between its components.

Although researchers agree on the multidimensional nature of engagement, they differ in their views on the number, types and conceptualisations of engagement dimensions. Mercer (2019: 646) argues that "true engagement necessitates all three components". She gives the example of a student who, for compliance's sake, goes through the motions of an activity, displaying external behavioural signs of engagement without involving themselves emotionally or intellectually. While for Mercer, behavioural engagement on its own indicates shallow engagement, Oga-Baldwin (2019: 4) considers that it could serve "as a key step in the learning process ... catalys[ing] other aspects such as emotion, cognition, and agency". Others again reject the behavioural category altogether, like Barkley and Major (2020: 10), who view behaviours not as a "type of engagement but rather as the outcome of engagement", limiting their model to two dimensions, or Svalberg (2021: 42) who argues that "all dimensions of engagement are manifested behaviourally". Her model of Engagement with Language (EWL; Svalberg 2009) subsumes behavioural engagement under cognitive, affective, or social engagement.

Some models, particularly those relating to language learning, include a social dimension. Social engagement captures the relationships among learners that enable social interaction to develop language awareness (Svalberg 2021) or language practice (Philp and Duchesne 2016). The social aspect also relates more broadly to the social context in which learning occurs (Reeve 2012: 152), a reason for Mercer (2019) not to consider social engagement as a separate dimension in her conceptualisation. As she put it (2019: 646), "all aspects of cognition and affect are socially situated and behaviour typically involves others in social settings". A few scholars (Oga-Baldwin 2019; Reeve 2012) argue for the inclusion of agentic engagement as a fourth aspect of engagement. Reeve (2012), who approaches learner engagement through the lens of self-determination theory, argues that concepts composed of behavioural, emotional, and cognitive dimensions depict learners' reactions to teacher-initiated tasks but don't take into account how learners shape the learning environment by asking questions, offering input and making suggestions. He explains that "students not only react to learning activities but they proact on them" (162), proactively enriching and transforming the learning environment. A desirable attribute in formal learning contexts, agentic engagement is a crucial component in informal learning contexts, where it is up to learners to create and adjust their own learning environment to their developing learning needs.

The concept of engagement is closely related to motivation. Mercer (2019: 645) describes the question about their difference or similarity as "perhaps the thorniest definitional issue". However, engagement scholars seem to agree that motivation is the "precursor of engagement" (Christenson et al. 2012: 814). In other words, motivation is perceived as the intent to act, whereas engagement reflects the action itself (Mercer 2019). Motivational theories have been used to understand the psychological antecedents to support student engagement.

Self-determination theory (SDT), in particular, has served in many studies as an analytical framework for the understanding of learner engagement in formal learning contexts (Mercer 2019; Noels et al. 2019; Reeve 2012). The theory suggests that humans have three psychological needs that underlie growth and development. The basic needs are *autonomy* (the feeling one has a choice and willingly endorses one's behaviour), *competence* (the desire to be effective in one's own activity) and *relatedness* (the desire to feel connected with others; Ryan and Deci 2002). When these needs are nurtured and fulfilled, people are more autonomous in their behaviours and feel better overall. The self-determination continuum describes distinct types of motivation, ranging from *amotivation*, the complete lack of personal intention to fulfil an action (when none of the basic needs are met), to *intrinsic motivation*, a motivational state that emanates from inherent interest and enjoyment. Between those two poles are several types of extrinsic motivation, a motivational state caused by external factors. Depending on the level of support for their basic needs, people act with different degrees of self-determination. An externally motivated person on the bottom scale will act out of obligation ("going through the motions", as Mercer put it), whereas an internally motivated person on the top scale endorses requested actions, perceiving that personal goals are met, and needs are fulfilled.

The theory explains how conditions in formal learning environments can support (or hinder) intent to act (motivation) and engagement (motivation in action). Furthermore, it illustrates that engagement in an educational context is an expression or product of external forms of motivation. Regardless of whether learners engage reluctantly or enthusiastically with a task, it is always a response to external stimuli. Task designs that support learners in their basic psychological needs increase their level of self-determination, resulting in a high-quality and sustainable motivation that brings out volitional engagement in learners.

In informal learning contexts, intrinsic motivation plays a predominant role. Driven by internal rather than external incentives, informal learners act from an internally perceived *locus of causality* (DeCharms 1968). With the understanding that motivation is the precursor of engagement, this raises the additional question about the conditions that influence a person's readiness to engage in learning. To address this issue, and to explore the factors leading to learner engagement in informal language contexts, Wang and Mercer (2021) have introduced the concept of Willingness to Engage (WTE). Inspired by the model of Willingness to Communicate (WTC; MacIntyre et al. 1998) and the notion of Willingness to Participate (WTP; Kubanyiova and Yue 2019), Wang and Mercer (2021: 264) propose that a learner's WTE is a necessary antecedent state that occurs prior to actual engagement. They relate individual and social factors to the fulfilment of the learners' need to regulate learning experiences and the ability to make decisions that match personal interests (autonomy), their experience of being effective in a learning activity (competence), and to feel connected and to belong to a community (relatedness). The findings of their study – an autoethnographic account of Wang's experiences of learning German when arriving in Austria – highlight the importance of the social context and opportunities for language engagement. They argue that without opportunities for language use, "WTE would remain potentially unfilled" (268). They found further that learner beliefs play a crucial role in the uptake of learning opportunities. Merging their findings into a model, Wang and Mercer (2021: 273) describe WTE as a *"conglomerate* of motivational, cognitive, affective, social, contextual and behavioural factors", suggesting that WTE emerges through the dynamic interactions of these components.

Intra-formal learning contexts provide yet again different conditions for engagement. Students' willingness to engage in informal learning within a formal learning context might be met with resistance or taken up as an opportunity to extend existing practices in a formal context. Further, their engagement patterns might differ from those observed in predominantly formal learning environments. The current study aimed to investigate the conditions and nature of engagement of two German language students who viewed Netflix series as an out-of-class activity. The research questions guiding the inquiry were:

- What are the factors that determine language learners' willingness to engage with L2 viewing?
- How do language learners engage with the viewing activity?

4 The study

4.1 Method

The research design used in this study is a (descriptive) case study investigating the engagement trajectories of two language learners. A case study is an empirical method that provides an in-depth and contextualised understanding of the phenomenon, with the case being an exemplar of the phenomenon under investigation (Yin 2018). Case study research is well established in applied linguistics, particularly in the area of language learning, providing insights into learners' experiences, performances and developmental pathways within a particular context (Duff 2014). A growing number of case studies can be found in studies on learners of languages other than English, as pointed out by Duff (2014), but also in student engagement (e.g., Koltovskaia 2020) and informal language learning (e.g., Kusyk 2020).

4.2 Participants

The participants of the study were two university students of an intermediate-level (B2) German language course of 11 students. The choice of the two focal case participants was determined by the similarity of their academic profiles and difference in experiences with Netflix prior to and during the project. Alisha and Carol (pseudonyms) studied German towards a major in Language & Linguistics; they were high-achieving students, receiving top marks (As) in all their classes, they both had grown up in New Zealand, and their first language was English. Alisha had already studied German in high school, whereas Carol started her German studies at beginners' level at university. They were in the same German language class, Alisha in her second year at university and Carol in her third year. While their academic background was quite similar, their experiences with Netflix were on the opposite sides of the spectrum. Alisha had extensive experience and had been subscribed to the streaming service since it was released in New Zealand in 2015. She spent much of her time watching Netflix series, including a German one, when she was in high school. Carol, on the other hand, claimed to have had no experience with Netflix at all. Both gave consent for their data to be used for this project (see Table 2).

Table 2: Participants' profiles.

Name	Age	First language	Schooling	Major	Academic standing	Netflix user
Alisha	20	English	New Zealand	Language & Linguistics	High achieving	yes
Carol	21	English	New Zealand	Language & Linguistics	High achieving	no

4.3 Task

Eleven students of the German language class were instructed to watch a German Netflix series for six weeks. Prior to the task, they discussed their personal experiences with Netflix (in German) in class. They then decided individually on a show they wanted to watch. They were asked to view a minimum of two episodes a week (regardless of length), and to write in German about their viewing experiences in their weekly blogs. They received prompts for each entry (week 1 Netflix experiences, week 2 choice of series, week 3 viewing routines, week 4 use of subtitles, week 5 focus on vocabulary learning, week 6 German Netflix: entertainment or study?) and were encouraged to read and to comment on each other's blog entries. In week 3, the chrome extension *LLN* was introduced and made available to all class members. At the conclusion of the viewing activity, they were asked to write a report, also in German, on their learning experiences. In the report, they reviewed the series (did they like it, would they recommend it), wrote about their viewing strategies (e.g., subtitling choices) and evaluated their own learning.

The task was a regular class activity. Yet, the nature of the task was intra-formal, as it considered and supported pre-existing social practices (online streaming habits) and enabled learners to embed their viewings in their everyday routines. Learners were free to choose their series and their preferred viewing modes (e.g., types of subtitles, playback speed). While learners were instructed to view a series and were provided with the tools to do so, informal practices (e.g., increased viewing times, viewing for leisure) developed over time, especially when the formal aspect receded due to the lockdown environment.

4.4 Data collection

Research data were collected by means of questionnaires, semi-structured interviews, learner journals (blogs) and a written report during and after the intervention. An online questionnaire was administered prior to intervention to obtain information about students' prior use of Netflix in languages other than English (the students' first language), and perceived benefits of watching Netflix for language learning. This was followed by semi-structured interviews to elicit more detailed information from participants on their experiences, views and expectations of engaging with Netflix for language learning. The data collected from the questionnaire and the interviews were in English. The data from the blogs, blog entries and comments, and the report were in German. At B2 level, students were able to express their experiences and reflections in the target language. The data used is not corrected and contains some grammatical errors. The errors are not reflected in the translation. A preliminary thematic analysis of the blogs informed the second round of interviews conducted in German. Like the previous interviews, the interviews were transcribed with the transcription tool Otter and cleaned up by a research assistant. The interview data were then imported into NVivo to extend the thematic analysis. The analysis informed the design of the final online questionnaire (see Table 3).

Table 3: Research data.

Pre-intervention (end February)	Questionnaire 1	11
Pre-intervention (early March)	Follow up interviews	5
During intervention (March-April)	6 blog entries and 1 report	11
Post-intervention (May)	Semi-structured focus group interviews	5
Post-intervention (June)	Questionnaire 2	9

4.5 Data analysis

For the case study, data from the larger study was extracted and triangulated. Triangulation entails the corroboration of different sources and types of data for analytical purposes (Denzin 1970). The data from the questionnaire (treated as structured interviews), the two interviews, the blog entries and reports were analysed for instances of engagement related to the research questions, following the protocol outlined by Ellis and Barkhuizen (2005) for thematic coding. The questionnaire was reduced to the items relevant to the themes from the qualitative analysis, contrasting the responses of both participants. All items were measured on a Likert-scale for agreement (5 strongly agree – 1 strongly disagree), except for the items on *LLN* (which were 5 extremely useful – 1 not useful at all). The questionnaires are attached in the appendix. The findings, which result from the iterative process of reading and re-reading the qualitative data while comparing the themes emerging from the data of the different sources, are presented as two narratives. The following abbreviations were used to identify the sources of the data: A for Alisha, C for Carol, B for blog, B1 for blog entry 1, B2 for blog entry 2 etc., REP for report, FGI1 for focus group interview 1, FGI2 for focus group interview 2, OT1 for Questionnaire 1, OT2 for Questionnaire 2, Q for Question (of Questionnaire 2), Q1 for Question item 1, etc., *LLN* for question items relating to *LLN*. For example, C/B2 refers to Carol's second blog entry.

5 Two trajectories

The two trajectories describe how Alisha's and Carol's prior viewing experiences and language learning beliefs influenced their choice of learning opportunities and shaped the nature of their viewing and learning engagement.

5.1 Alisha's trajectory

Alisha described herself in her blog as "Netflix-Profi", a professional in all things Netflix. She had been watching Netflix since she talked her father into subscribing to the online streaming service as a teenager when it first became available in New Zealand in 2015, claiming she needed to watch a film for a school assignment. The educational purpose was quickly forgotten as watching Netflix became a recreational pastime with a social rather than cognitive orientation. She reported enjoying watching Netflix with friends, on her own, when seeking comfort and finding company with her favourite programmes, *"wenn ich traurig bin, kann ich ein Kömodie finden"* [when I am sad, I can find a comedy] (A/B1), or just as background noise (Q1–3). In her final year of high school, when she "was getting less and less motivated" (FGI1) in her German class, Alisha started watching the German Netflix series *Dark*.

Alisha's familiarity with Netflix and her prior German viewing experience made her feel well prepared for the Netflix project. She had watched *Dark* for enjoyment rather than for learning, describing herself in retrospect as "a stupid year 13 student" (FGI2). She conceded that she was reading the English subtitles rather than paying attention to the German, which she was "hearing" rather than "listening" to.

This time, she decided to rely less on English subtitles and listen actively to improve her German. She set up a viewing routine, that allowed her to balance recreation and concentration, "*Ich schaute am Donnerstagnachmittag mit einen Kaffee auf der Sofa die erste Folge, und obwohl ich es oft anhalten muss, habe ich fast alles verstanden. Ich denke dass die Kaffee hilft mir auf der Sprache zu konzentrieren.*" [I watched the first episode on Thursday afternoon with a coffee on the sofa, and although I have to pause it often, I understood almost everything. I think the coffee helps me to concentrate on the language.] (A/B2). The positive impact of an informal and relaxed learning environment for learning has been described as "zengagement" by Hunter and Cox (2014), with "zen" referring to a relaxed frame of mind. In Alisha's case, it is her coffee (recurringly mentioned in her blog) that helped her reach this relaxed state and sharpened her focus.

Alisha prepared for her L2 viewing by creating a comfortable environment (Q19) and selecting a series she could relate to. The high school drama *Wir sind die Welle* [We are the wave] caught her interest as it reminded her of her own teenage years. In this series, she encountered people like her (Q29), who talked about topics relevant to her, using the type of language, "casual and colloquial", she was eager to acquire (Q28). Alisha felt that she needed to practice her speaking to improve, and that learning expressions from the series could support her goal of becoming more fluent and developing a better accent (A/B1), "*Ich habe das Gefühl, dass mein Deutsch nicht besser wird, wenn ich nicht mehr spreche, aber diese Serie hilft mir dabei, mehr Vokabeln zu lernen, die ich in einer lockeren Situation und mit jungen Deutschen benutzen kann.*" [I feel like my German doesn't get better when I don't speak more, but this series helps me learn more vocabulary to use in a casual situation and with young Germans.] (A/B2).

Her high school experience with *Dark* had taught Alisha that English subtitles distracted her from listening. She described their effect as "washing over what you're hearing" (FGI1). Using German captions instead of English subtitles improved her focus (Q10) and helped her understand the words better (Q11). She paused the video to check on words (Q7), or when the characters spoke too fast, ensuring to capture the phrases: "*Manchmal, wenn die Charakteren einen Streit haben und schnell sprechen beginnen, verstehe ich weniger, also muss ich mich zurückhalten, und zurück gehen, um die Sprache zu wirklich verstehen.*" [Sometimes, when the characters have an argument and start talking fast, I understand less, so I must pause and go back to really understand the language.] (A/B2).

Alisha used the features of the *LLN* extension purposefully to focus on colloquial phrases. Instead of displaying the dual subtitles, which she found distracting (Q14), she opted for the hidden subtitles (LLN4). This feature displays the captions but greys out (hides) the English subtitles, which can be activated by moving the cursor on the space where they are hidden. Alisha displayed the English subtitles only when she needed a translation for idiomatic expressions. Colloquial phrases were not captured in the glossed captions of *LLN* (which provided literal translations of individual words). The ability to check out expressions that seemed relevant without having to process a screen full of text (with two tracks of subtitles) was particularly appealing for Alisha (A/B3).

She further used the slowed-down playback feature (LLN5), which she described as "VERY helpful" (A/B4). It allowed her to exercise some control over the speed and understanding by listening rather than reading, decreasing her dependency on captions and translations. The glossed captions enabled her to review the words she wanted to learn. The feature permits viewers to select and colour words, which then reappear highlighted when they come up again in the transcript. Alisha used this tool (LLN7, 8) for filler words, which are difficult to translate as they take different meanings in different contexts. The ability to review these filler words in other sentences supported her goal of developing fluency. *"Ich habe interessante Sätze und wichtige Wörter aufgenommen, insbesondere Sätze mit Füllwörtern, die den Satz nicht verändern, aber sind noch wichtig um flüssig zu werden, wie ‚ja', ‚doch' und ‚gern'. Dieser Wörter und andere bestimmter Sätze haben oft auftauchen, deshalb konnte ich mit ihnen vertraut machen."* [I have included interesting sentences and important words, especially sentences with filler words that do not change the sentence but are still important to become fluent, such as 'ja ', 'doch' and' gern'. These words and other specific phrases have come up often, so I was able to familiarise myself with them.] (A/B4).

Alisha recorded her favourite phrases in her blog to apply and consolidate her knowledge. Relating them to her personal context, she jokingly remarked in one entry, *"Vokabeln wie ‚Spinnst du?!' und ‚Ihr seid echt total Irre' sind sehr hilfreich wenn man in Selbstisolation mit der Familie ist!"* [Vocabulary like 'Are you crazy?!' and 'You guys are really nuts' are very helpful when you're in self-isolation with the family!] (A/B4). While it is unlikely that Alisha actually used these German phrases with her English-speaking family during lockdown, she might well have rehearsed them in her mind. This would align with her responses in questionnaire 2, *After watching L2NF I spoke to myself in my L2* (Q33), and *After watching L2NF I was thinking in my L2* (Q34). These indications of self-talk and her strong agreement with the statement, *Watching L2NF makes me want to use my L2 more* (Q32), as well as her comments indicate in fact that she seized on various opportunities to apply the words and phrases she learned in different modalities: by writing her blog, by chatting on the tandem app *Hellotalk* (B5) and by talking to German-speaking friends (Q36).

Alisha's practice of using her blog to apply her newly learned phrases also sheds light on the emotional dimension of her viewing experience. In her fourth blog entry she describes the context of her *"Lieblingssatz"* [favourite line], of an episode: *"Einer der Protagonistin war geschossen . . . ich war sehr beängstigend! Meine Lieblingssatz von dieser Folge war sehr dramatisch: als Lea zu Tristan sagte „Du bist das Einzige, was schiefgegangen ist". . . . sehr brutal!* [One of the protagonists was shot . . . I was very scared! My favourite line from this episode was very dramatic: when Lea said to Tristan "You are the only thing that went wrong" . . . very brutal!] (A/B4). Through her use of language, in particular of the adjectives dramatic, brutal and scared, she expresses the emotional impact the scene had on her.

Having chosen a short series with only six episodes, Alisha decided to start a new series, *Parfum*, as she was re-watching *Wir sind die Welle*. She reported that she had to pause less at the repeated viewing since she was familiar with the vocabulary, and able to look away from the screen and just listen, concluding *"Es ist besonders hilfreich wenn man eine singuläre Folge ein anderer Mal schaut, sodass man die Sprache wirklich hören kann, und wirklich konzentrieren."* [It is especially helpful to watch a singular episode another time so that you can really hear the language and really concentrate.] (B5).

Over the six weeks, Alisha explored a range of strategies to optimise her L2 viewing, but even during the period when she was watching *Wir sind die Welle*, her focus on language varied. For example, when she had to return to her parents' house in a different city during lockdown and found her old bedroom transformed into a guestroom, she initially struggled to recreate the comfortable viewing environment she had in her student flat. She explained that when under stress, she was more likely to keep the cursor on the hidden subtitles to read the English text rather than focusing on the German (FGI2). Also, her plan to watch two series towards the end of the project did not quite work out. She did not enjoy the new series as much as the first one, and she did not continue with the plan of re-watching the old one. A few months later, during the second interview, however, she had picked up a new series. At that stage, she seemed to have settled for the middle ground between learning and leisure, watching a German series mainly for pleasure while actively focusing on the language. Her final conclusion was, "as long as you are concentrating, you are getting something out of it" (FGI2).

5.2 Carol's trajectory

Carol did not have any experience with Netflix prior to the project. She described her family as *"ziemlich altmodisch"* [pretty old fashioned] (C/B1), watching movies hired from the local DVD store or on TVNZ on demand, the online streaming service of the national television channel. Carol had never watched any German programmes and struggled with the idea of using entertainment for language learning. *"Da das Anschauen von etwas normalerweise eine Möglichkeit ist, mich zu entspannen, mache ich mir Sorge, dass ich nicht in der Lage sein werde, mich genug zu engagieren, um mich das Deutsche zu konzentrieren."* [Since watching something is normally a way to relax, I worry that I won't be able to engage enough to focus on the German.] (C/B1). Her response in the first questionnaire, however, indicates that she could see some benefit in watching German series to improve her listening comprehension, although she was concerned that "they speak too fast" (QT1). Also, when she started looking for a series for the project, she remembered that a friend had watched *Dark*, indicating that she had some awareness of Netflix and its German content. She decided to watch the series, coincidentally the same one that Alisha enjoyed as a high school student, hoping she would be able to fully engage with it.

After the first two episodes, Carol admitted in her blog that she enjoyed the series and was looking forward to her subsequent viewing sessions (C/B2). She resolved to focus on her listening skills (C/REF) and worked through a number of strategies to this effect. Using the *LLN* extension, she developed what she labelled her *"Lesemethode"* [reading method] (C/REF). She found it useful to have the transcript (LLN2) of the dialogues displayed on the right side of the screen. This enabled her to process first the written input and then attend to the aural. As she explained: *"Dies bedeutet, dass ich vorauslesen und dann versuchen kann, prognostizieren, welche Aktion folgen wird."* [This means that I can read ahead and then try to predict what action will follow.] (C/B2). In the following week, she tried out a variation of her approach. Instead of first reading and then listening, she decided to first listen, and then read the dual subtitles (LLN1), starting with the German: *"Diese Woche habe ich versucht, nicht so viel vorauszulesen und sondern mich konzentriert, echt Audio zu hören bevor ich die deutschen Untertitel und dann die englischen überprüft habe."* [This week I tried not to read ahead so much and instead concentrated on really listening to the audio before checking the German subtitles and then the English.] (C/B3).

Carol's approach of attending sequentially to input highlights her cognitive capacity to process multiple inputs. She increased the cognitive load even further when she started using the captions with audio descriptions (LLN3), designed for the visually impaired. Having activated them accidentally, she was first confused by the suddenly appearing narration but described the situation with the German saying *"Glück im Unglück"* [lucky in disguise]. Recommending the feature to a classmate, she explained in a blog comment, *"@Kristy, es beschreibt die Landschaft, was die Charakter tun, usw. . . . es hilft mir, die Serie zu verstehen!"* [@Kristy, it describes the landscape, what the characters do, etc. . . . it helps me understand the series!] (C/B3). Carol felt that the audio narration forced her to listen more attentively since the absence of textual support prevented her from "cheating" (C/REF), as she put it. Instead of relying on the subtitles, she focused on the visuals that the narrator described. As an add-on, she seemed more relaxed about comprehension, *"Ich lasse die Hörgeschädigte [sic] über mich fließen, ohne mir zu viele Sorgen darüber zu machen, alles zu verstehen."* [I let the hearing impaired [sic] flow over me without worrying too much about understanding everything.] (C/B3).

Once she had overcome her initial reservations about using entertainment for learning and worked out a strategy that help her to deal with comprehension, Carol started watching a lot, *"Ich werde zugeben, dass ich letzte Woche viel mehr als die geforderten zwei Folgen angeschaut habe!"* [I will admit that I watched a lot more than the required two episodes last week!] (C/B5). In fact, she watched two entire seasons of *Dark* (18 x 50-minutes episodes), eagerly awaiting the release of the third season. Carol not only binge-watched her series; the intensity of her viewing experience indicates that she was fully focused when engaging in her series, *"Ehrlich jedes Mal, wenn ich eine Folge anschaue, fühlt es sich an, als würde mein Gehirn schmelzen."* [Honestly every time I watch an episode it feels like my brain is melting.] (C/B3). The positive experience of her intense viewing is supported by her strong agreement with Q24, *I enjoyed the cognitive challenge of watching a L2NF series*. The focus she brought to her viewing contrasts her habit of media multitasking (Loh and Lim 2020) when watching English programmes on TV on demand, *"weil ich einer dieser schrecklichen Menschen bin, die fast immer gleichzeitig etwas auf ihrem Handy machen"* [because I'm one of those horrible people who is almost always doing something on their phone at the same time] (C/B1). For her L2 viewing, she fully immersed herself in the activity (Q23), deploying her cognitive resources to process the multi-modal input. However, Carol acknowledged that her viewing experiences were not homogenous. At times, she explained, she couldn't wait to watch the next episodes, whereas, at other times, she found it more of a struggle to watch with full attention. Especially when she was tired, she found it harder to focus and was more likely to read English subtitles (Q17). Similarly, she felt that her listening comprehension fluctuated, *"Ich finde, dass mein Hörverständnis je nach Tag und Müdigkeit dramatisch variieren."* [I find that my listening varies dramatically depending on the day and how tired I am.] (C/B5).

Carol's engagement with the project resulted in a shift of her learning beliefs. She described her viewing experience as a "nice contrast" to the grammar approach she was used to (C/REF). Her use of the glossed captions (LLN8), which she coloured according to word category, illustrate her attempt to "grammatise" her learning, *"grün für Verben, gelb für Substantive, blau für Adverbien und rot für Adjecktive"* [green for verbs, yellow for nouns, blue for adverbs and red for adjectives] (C/B3). Yet, it also testifies to her willingness to explore different tools in the new learning environment. She systematically worked through different tools and approaches, demonstrating her metacognitive awareness. She knew that to maximise learning benefits she could view an episode more slowly, pause and replay more, replay whole episodes, or even a whole season (C/REF). Yet, waiting for the third season of *Dark*, and a long list of series and movies on her Netflix list, she decided after the conclusion of the project to continue her German Netflix trajectory more passively, for entertainment (C/REF).

6 Discussion

6.1 Willingness to engage in L2 viewing

The first research question related to the factors that affect language learners' willingness to engage with L2 viewing.

The two trajectories show a range of individual, social and contextual factors that impacted on the participants' willingness to engage in L2 viewing. Alisha and Carol's trajectories differed in terms of prior experiences, motivation, language learning beliefs and learning goals, all of which determined how they approached the actual viewing activity. Alisha's immediate willingness to engage, building on past experiences, contrasts with Carol's initial unwillingness or reluctance to engage. While Alisha declared herself an authority in all things Netflix, readily sharing her prior Netflix experiences with her peers in her blog, Carol portrayed herself as a hesitant adopter of technology. Alisha had already figured out in high school that she wanted to *use* German in authentic contexts rather than *study* grammar and revise vocabulary. In contrast, Carol, who started studying German at university, had so far only experienced a grammar-based approach to language learning. Their difference in prior experiences and language learning beliefs far outweighed their similarities, as two female students of similar age and similar academic level and language proficiency in the same intermediate-level German class. Their different backgrounds shaped their motivations and expectations of the benefits and limitations of L2 viewing for their language development. Both prepared for the actual viewing, Alisha by arranging her physical environment, creating a space for "zengagement", and Carol by figuring out how to calibrate the *LLN* extension. Their individual approaches were driven by different learning goals. Alisha had the aim of developing her fluency. She sought out ways to increase her exposure to colloquial language through her choice of series and selection of *LLN* tools which directed her focus on relevant words and phrases. Her approach was guided by her language learning beliefs, the importance of comprehensible input and speaking practice, and the goal to increase her fluency. Carol, on the other hand, was driven by intellectual curiosity. She believed in a structured approach to language learning and arranged her viewing sessions systematically to optimise her goal of improving her listening comprehension.

The trajectories illustrate the relevance of opportunities and social context for engagement. In Alisha's case, the use of Netflix in her social circles triggered her interest, and even Carol chose *Dark* because she knew a friend had enjoyed it. Within this context, their learning beliefs shaped their WTE and the way they approached their viewings. Carol was initially held back by her negative anticipations (too difficult to understand, too hard to engage), whereas Alisha was positively disposed and able to seize on affordances for the development of her fluency. Throughout her trajectory, she explored and engaged in learning opportunities conforming to and confirming her beliefs. Carol, on the other hand, was initially not able to relate her beliefs to the task. Still, by pursuing a strategic approach (which suited her learning style), she was able to uncover affordances and was even open to those that appeared accidentally (the captions with audio descriptions). Her trajectory shows the interplay between engagement and willingness to engage. As she actively engaged in L2 viewing and started to enjoy it, her WTE re-formed, leading to a different type of engagement.

The dynamic nature of WTE is demonstrated in the two trajectories. Both describe the effect of physiological changes on their willingness to engage. When Alisha had to move to her parent's place during lockdown, she didn't feel as comfortable in her viewing environment, and Carol felt that her concentration dropped when she was tired. Both were more likely to revert to reading the English subtitles instead of focusing on the German when they felt emotionally unbalanced. Their willingness to engage also fluctuated from moment to moment as the difficulty of the language and their interest in the story changed from episode to episode or even from scene to scene. The contextual and temporal dynamics constantly reconfigured their WTE, with positive viewing experiences generating further WTE. Their respective WTE determined how they engaged with the viewing.

6.2 Engaging with L2 viewing

The second research question addressed the learners' actual engagement during the viewing activity. The trajectories illustrate the emergence of agentic, social, cognitive, and emotional forms of engagement which are interconnected and individual in their composition to each learner.

6.2.1 The agentic dimension

Both participants exercised their agency by proactively exploring and creating learning opportunities to fully engage in L2 viewing. They enriched their learning situation by transforming the L2 viewing into something interesting (Alisha, by creating a social context) and making it optimally challenging (Carol, by maximising auditory input). They also modified the task by adapting *LLN* tools to suit their learning needs. They personalised it by engaging in ways that aligned with their developing learning beliefs and goals all manifestations of agentic engagement as listed by Reeve (2012: 62). Looking back on her initial experiences with Netflix, Alisha described herself as a "stupid year 13 student", not being able to perceive the affordances for language learning that became obvious to her once she started sharing her experiences with her peers and explored *LLN*. Similarly, Carol changed her approach once she realised that she was able to control her viewing and follow a German programme. She adjusted her learning beliefs and started enjoying what she called "informal learning". Both exercised their agency, developing different engagement profiles.

6.2.2 The social dimension

Netflix had an established social function in Alisha's life. It was through her social practice (Barton and Potts 2013) of watching programmes with friends and on her own that she discovered *Dark*. During the project, she felt that watching German series brought her closer to German culture, everyday life, and most importantly German as spoken by people of her age group. This aligned well with her learning belief that learners need to be exposed to a lot of comprehensible input and speaking practice to progress. The series provided her with a social context (Mercer 2019) for her language practice, first through exposure (as she was watching), followed by language production (through mental rehearsal or actual verbal interactions; Philip and Duchesne 2016). This social dimension is interrelated with her emotional engagement, as her enthusiasm for Netflix and the series triggered initial uptake, regulated viewing, and influenced subsequent language engagement (Svalberg 2021). This included her engagement in self-talk. The manifestation of private speech demonstrates, according to Sang and Hiver (2021), cognitive engagement. In other words, her social and emotional engagement shaped the nature of her cognitive engagement. In sum, Alisha could be described primarily as a socially engaged L2 viewer.

6.2.3 The cognitive dimension

Carol, who displayed no obvious signs of social engagement, would better fit in the category of a cognitively engaged L2 viewer. She approached the task strategically, making use of her cognitive ability to consciously sequence auditory and visual inputs. The variation in information processing between her and Alisha, who found the dual subtitles and audio descriptions overwhelming, can possibly be explained by differences in working memory capacity (Gass et al. 2019). Her cognitive engagement is also interrelated with her enjoyment of watching the series, as the frequency and intensity of her viewing episodes demonstrate. She enjoyed its cognitive challenge, which led her to seek further viewing opportunities.

6.2.4 The emotional dimension

The participants' emotional engagement during the viewing (as opposed to the role of emotions in their WTE) relates to their social or cognitive engagement. Both enjoyed their L2 viewing because it was entertaining, Alisha enjoyed the social aspect (hearing people similar to herself speaking German), and Carol took pleasure in the cognitive challenge. Alisha expresses her emotional involvement and a sense of relatedness, when she relived the dialogues between the characters of a scene, whereas Carol describes viewing as a brain melting sensation. Fully immersed in the viewing through intense concentration, high interest, and enjoyment, she might have temporarily entered a state of flow (Csikszentmihalyi 1997), reaching the perfect balance between emotional and cognitive engagement. The difference in their experiences further highlights the individuality of each person's engagement profile.

7 Conclusion and pedagogical implications

Alisha's and Carol's trajectories illustrate how engagement develops and the different ways in which it can manifest itself in L2 viewing. Prior experiences and language learning beliefs played an essential role in their uptake of the activity and in the ways they engaged in the viewing. Displaying different types of engagement, both profiles demonstrate the multidimensional nature of meaningful engagement.

There are a number of pedagogical implications that can be drawn from this investigation for language education. As language learners are increasingly exposed to informal language learning opportunities in their social circles, they bring different skill sets and expectations to their language classes. Prior informal learning experiences need to be acknowledged and addressed in their distinctiveness. While some students might be able to draw on extensive experiences, others might not have had the same opportunities and even be reluctant to engage in learning activities that do not align with their expectations of formal language instruction. Schwarz (2020) found that some students with informal learning experience resent being asked to engage in L2 viewing with a focus on language learning rather than (just) entertainment.

A pedagogical framework, based on the understanding that learners seek to fulfil basic psychological needs opens opportunities for intra-formal learning with language learners from different backgrounds and informal L2 experiences. An *intra-formal* pedagogy of language learning, supporting the needs of autonomy, competence and relatedness enables learners to draw on and share prior informal language learning experiences, and extends their practices through collaborative discovery and self-reflection. The engagement that emerges from this approach is dynamic, channelled by emotional forms of engagement, supported by social engagement and stimulating cognitive engagement. Such a pedagogy of support and meaningful L2 engagement is ultimately a pedagogy of wellbeing that understands engagement in language learning as personal growth, rather than language development as a measurable achievement.

Appendix

Appendix A: Questionnaire LLN Items.

	Perceived usefulness of LLN extension		
		Alisha	Carol
1	Dual subtitles	4	5
2	Transcript display	0	5
3	Audio description	1	5
4	Hidden subtitles	5	4
5	Slow down speed	5	4
6	Dictionary (glossed subtitles)	5	5
7	Saving words and phrases	5	5
8	Colour-coding words	4	3

Note: (5 – very useful – 1 not useful at all)

Appendix B: Questionnaire Engagement Items.

	Engagement with L2 Netflix		
	Pre-project	Alisha	Carol
1	I watch Netflix for entertainment.	5	1
2	I watch Netflix to relax.	5	1
3	I often listen to Netflix in the background while I do something else.	5	1
4	I searched Netflix for interesting L2 series and movies.	4	1
5	I have enjoyed watching L2NF for some time.	5	1
6	People in my social circles watch L2 Netflix.	4	2
	During Project		
19	I choose a comfortable place to watch my series.	5	5
20	I enjoy watching L2NF because it is entertaining.	5	5
21	I am watching L2NF for entertainment.	4	4
22	I am watching L2NF to relax.	2	2
23	I am watching L2NF in the background while I do something else.	1	1
	Post Project		
37	I have gained confidence watching L2NF.	5	4
38	I am watching L2NF at the moment.	4	5
39	I am looking at other sources (beyond Netflix) to practice my L2.	4	4
41	When watching L2NF I mainly use L2 subtitles.	4	4
42	When watching L2NF I mainly use L1 subtitles.	2	2
43	I am now able to watch L2NF without subtitles.	1	1

	Engagement with L2 Netflix		
	Cognitive engagement (controlling playback)	Alisha	Carol
7	I used pause to check on words.	5	4
8	I used rewind because I find it helpful to hear something again.	5	5
9	I often looked up words I don't understand.	5	4
	Cognitive engagement (affected by captions)		
10	L2 subtitles allow me to focus better on the language.	4	5
11	L2 subtitles help me to understand the words better.	5	5
12	I remember words and phrases better when I have L2 subtitles.	4	4
13	When reading L2 subtitles I stop listening.	4	4
14	I find the dual subtitles distracting.	4	2
15	I find audio-descriptions a bit overwhelming.	4	3
	Cognitive engagement affected by emotional factors		
16	When I was really interested in the story I paused less to look up words.	5	2
17	I relied more on L1 subtitles when I was tired.	5	5

Appendix B (continued)

	Engagement with L2 Netflix		
	Pre-project	**Alisha**	**Carol**
18	Sometimes I watched for entertainment, other times I focused more on the language.	5	5
	Emotional engagement affected by cognitive factors		
24	I enjoyed the cognitive challenge of watching a L2NF series.	4	5
25	I enjoyed the series because I felt I was using my L2.	4	5
26	It was a satisfying experience to be able to watch L2NF.	5	5
	Emotional engagement affected by social factors		
27	I enjoyed learning phrases for L2 interactions.	5	3
28	Watching L2NF teaches me good phrases to use in conversations with L2 speakers.	5	3
29	I identified with some of the characters in the show.	4	1
30	Watching a L2NF brought me closer to the target culture.	5	1
31	I enjoyed learning about everyday life in the L2 culture.	5	2
	Willingness to Engage after L2 viewing		
32	Watching L2NF makes me want to use my L2 more.	5	3
33	After watching L2NF I spoke to myself in my L2.	4	1
34	After watching L2NF I was thinking in my L2.	4	1
35	After watching L2NF I found it easier to speak in my L2.	5	3
36	I used some phrases I learned in conversations with other L2 speakers.	5	2
	Willingness to Engage after NF project		
37	I have gained confidence watching L2NF.	5	4
38	I am watching L2NF at the moment.	4	5
39	I am looking at other sources (beyond Netflix) to practice my L2.	4	4
40	I continue to use LLN to watch L2NF.	5	5
41	When watching L2NF I mainly use L2 subtitles.	4	4
42	When watching L2NF I mainly use L1 subtitles.	2	2
43	I am now able to watch L2NF without subtitles.	1	1

	Engagement with L2 Netflix		
		Alisha	**Carol**
1	I watch Netflix for entertainment.	5	1
21	I am watching L2 NF for entertainment.	4	4
2	I watch Netflix to relax.	5	1
22	I am watching L2NF to relax.	2	2
3	I often listen to Netflix in the background while I do something else.	5	1
23	I am watching L2NF in the background while I do something else.	1	1

Appendix B (continued)

	Engagement with L2 Netflix	Alisha	Carol
4	I searched Netflix for interesting L2 series and movies.	4	1
5	I have enjoyed watching L2NF for some time.	5	1
6	People in my social circles watch L2 Netflix.	4	2
	During Project		
19	I choose a comfortable place to watch my series.	5	5
20	I enjoy watching L2NF because it is entertaining.	5	5
21	I am watching L2NF for entertainment.	4	4
22	I am watching L2NF to relax.	2	2
23	I am watching L2NF in the background while I do something else.	1	1
	Post Project		
37	I have gained confidence watching L2NF.	5	4
38	I am watching L2NF at the moment.	4	5
39	I am looking at other sources (beyond Netflix) to practice my L2.	4	4
41	When watching L2NF I mainly use L2 subtitles.	4	4
42	When watching L2NF I mainly use L1 subtitles.	2	2
43	I am now able to watch L2NF without subtitles.	1	1

References

Baralt, Melissa, Laura Gurzynski-Weiss & Y. Kim. 2016. Engagement with the language: How examining learner's affective and social engagement explains successful learner-generated attention to form. In Masatoshi Sato & Susan Ballinger (eds.), *Language Learning & Language Teaching. Peer Interaction and Second Language Learning. Pedagogical Potential and Research Agenda*, 209–240. Amsterdam: John Benjamins.

Barkley, Elizabeth F. & Claire H. Major (eds.). 2020. *Student engagement techniques: A handbook for college faculty*. John Wiley & Sons.

Barton, David & Diane Potts. 2013. Language learning online as a social practice. *TESOL Quarterly* 47 (4). 815–820.

Blanco, Cindy. 2020. Changes in Duolingo usage during the COVID-19 pandemic. *Duolingo blog*. https://blog.duolingo.com/changes-in-duolingo-usage-during-the-covid-19-pandemic/

Butler, Bethonie. 2021. 'Money Heist' flopped on Spanish TV. On Netflix, it became a global phenomenon. *The Washington Post*. https://www.washingtonpost.com/arts-entertainment/2021/09/03/money-heist-final-season/

Christenson, Sandra, Amy L. Reschly & Cathy Wylie (eds). 2012. *Handbook of research on student engagement*. Vol. 840. New York: Springer.

Csikszentmihalyi, Mihaly. 1997. *Finding Flow: The Psychology of Engagement with Everyday Life*. New York: Basic Books.

Deci, Edward L. & Richard M. Ryan (eds.). 2002. *Handbook of Self-determination Research*. Rochester: University of Rochester Press.

DeCharms, Richard. 1968. *Personal Causation: The Internal Affective Determinants of Behavior*. New York: Academic Press.

Denzin, Norman K. 1970. *The research act: A theoretical introduction to sociological methods*. Chicago: Aldine.

Dizon, Gilbert & Benjamin Thanyawatpokin. 2021. Language learning with Netflix: Exploring the effects of dual subtitles on vocabulary learning and listening comprehension. *Computer Assisted Language Learning Electronic Journal* 2 (3). 52–65.

Duff, Patricia A. 2014. Case study research on language learning and use. *Annual Review of Applied Linguistics* 34. 233–255. https://doi.org/10.1017/S0267190514000051

Durbahn, Marion, Michael Rodgers & Elke Peters. 2020. The relationship between vocabulary and viewing comprehension. *System* 88. 102–166.

Ellis, Rod & Gary Barkhuizen. 2005. *Analysing Learner Language*. Oxford: Oxford University Press.

Fievez, Isabeau, Maribel Montero Perez, Frederik Cornillie & Piet Desmet. 2021. Promoting incidental vocabulary learning through watching a French Netflix series with glossed captions. *Computer Assisted Language Learning* 1–26. https://doi.org/10.1080/09588221.2021.1899244

Fredricks, Jennifer A., Phyllis C. Blumenfeld & Alison H. Paris. 2004. School engagement: Potential of the concept, state of the evidence. *Review of Educational Research* 74 (1). 59–109. https://doi:10.3102/00346543074001059

Frumuselu, Anca Daniela, Sven De Maeyer, Vincent Donche & María del Mar Gutiérrez Colon Plana. 2015. Television series inside the EFL classroom: Bridging the gap between teaching and learning informal language through subtitles. *Linguistics and Education* 32. 107–117.

Gass, Susan, Paula Winke, Daniel R. Isbell & Jieun Ahn. 2019. How captions help people learn languages: A working-memory, eye-tracking study. *Language Learning & Technology* 23 (2). 84–104.

Gernsbacher, Morton Ann. 2015. Video captions benefit everyone. *Policy Insights from the Behavioral and Brain Sciences* 2(1). 195–202. https://doi.org/10.1177/2372732215602130

Godwin-Jones, Robert. 2019. Riding the digital wilds: Learner autonomy and informal language learning. *Language Learning & Technology* 23 (1). 8–25.

Hunter, Jonathan & Andrew Cox. 2014. Learning over tea! Studying in informal learning spaces. *New Library World*. https://www.emerald.com/insight/content/doi/10.1108/NLW-08-2013-0063/full/html

Katz, Brandon. 2020. Why Netflix's 'Money Heist' is the most in-demand show in the world. *Observer*. https://observer.com/2020/04/netflix-money-heist-la-casa-de-papel-most-watched/

Koltovskaia, Svetlana. 2020. Student engagement with automated written corrective feedback (AWCF) provided by Grammarly: A multiple case study. *Assessing Writing* 44. 100450. https://doi.org/10.1016/j.asw.2020.100450

Kubanyiova, Magdalena & Zhen Yue. 2019. Willingness to Communicate in L2: Persons' Emerging Capacity to Participate in Acts of Meaning Making with One Another. *Journal for the Psychology of Language Learning* 1 (1). 42–66.

Kusyk, Meryl. 2020. Informal English learning in France. In Mark Dressman & Randall William Sadler (eds.), *The Handbook of Informal Language Learning*, 333–348. Hoboken/Chichester: Wiley-Blackwell.

Kusyk, Meryl & Geoffrey Sockett. 2012. From informal resource usage to incidental language acquisition: language uptake from online television viewing in English. *ASp. La revue du GERAS* 62. 45–65.

Linnenbrink, Elizabeth A. & Paul R. Pintrich. 2003. The role of self-efficacy beliefs in student engagement and learning in the classroom. *Reading & Writing Quarterly* 19 (2). 119–137.

Loh, Kep Kee & Stephen Wee Hun Lim. 2020. Positive associations between media multitasking and creativity. *Computers in Human Behavior Reports 1*. 100015.

McAlone, Nathan. 2016. Netflix's streaming service exploded when it figured out a big weak spot in the TV business. *Business insider*. https://www.businessinsider.com/how-netflix-invented-binge-watching-2016-6

MacIntyre, Peter D., Richard Clément, Zoltán Dörnyei & Kimberly A. Noels. 1998. Conceptualizing willingness to communicate in a L2: A situational model of L2 confidence and affiliation. *The Modern Language Journal* 82 (4). 545–562.

Matos, Lennia, Johnmarshall Reeve, Dora Herrera & Mary Claux. 2018. Students' agentic engagement predicts longitudinal increases in perceived autonomy-supportive teaching: The squeaky wheel gets the grease. *The Journal of Experimental Education* 86 (4). 579–596.

Mercer, Sarah. 2019. Language learner engagement: Setting the scene. In Xuesong Gao (ed.), *Second Handbook of English Language Teaching*, 643–660. Cham: Springer. https://doi.org/10.1007/978-3-030-02899-2_40

Mercer, Sarah & Zoltán Dörnyei. 2020. *Engaging Language Learners in Contemporary Classrooms*. Cambridge: Cambridge University Press.

Netflix annual report 2020. https://ir.netflix.net/financials/annual-reports-and-proxies/default.aspx

Noels, Kimberly A., Nigel Mantou Lou, Dayuma I. Vargas Lascano, Kathryn E. Chaffee, Ali Dincer, Ying Shan Doris Zhang, and Xijia Zhang. 2019. Self-determination and motivated engagement in language learning. In Martin Lamb, Kata Csizér, Alastair Henry & Stephen Ryan (eds.), *The Palgrave Handbook of Motivation for Language Learning*, 95–115. Cham: Palgrave Macmillan.

Oga-Baldwin, W. L. Quint. 2019. Acting, thinking, feeling, making, collaborating: The engagement process in foreign language learning. *System* 86. 1–10. https://doi.org/10.1016/j.system.2019.102128

Pekrun, Reinhard & Lisa Linnenbrink-Garcia. 2012. Academic emotions and student engagement. In Sandra Christenson, Amy L. Reschly & Cathy Wylie (eds.), *Handbook of Research on Student Engagement*, 259–282. Boston: Springer. https://doi.org/10.1007/978-1-4614-2018-7_12

Peters, Elke & Carmen Muñoz. 2020. Introduction to language learning from multimodal input [Special issue]. *Studies in Second Language Acquisition* 42 (3). 489–497.

Philp, Jenefer & Susan Duchesne. 2016. Exploring Engagement in Tasks in the Language Classroom. *Annual Review of Applied Linguistics* 36. 50–72. https://doi.org/10.1017/S0267190515000094

Pujadas, Geòrgia & Carmen Muñoz. 2019. Extensive viewing of captioned and subtitled TV series: A study of L2 vocabulary learning by adolescents. *The Language Learning Journal* 47 (4). 479–496.

Pujadas, Geòrgia & Carmen Muñoz. 2020. Examining adolescent EFL learners' TV viewing comprehension through captions and subtitles. *Studies in Second Language Acquisition* 42 (3). 551–575.

Reeve, Johnmarshall. 2012. A Self-determination theory perspective on student engagement. In Sandra L. Christenson, Amy. L. Reschly & Cathy Wylie (eds.), *Handbook of Research on Student Engagement*, 149–172. Boston: Springer. https://doi.org/10.1007/978-1-4614-2018-7_7

Reeve, Johnmarshall & Ching-Mei Tseng. 2011. Agency as a fourth aspect of students' engagement during learning activities. *Contemporary Educational Psychology* 36 (4). 257–267.

Reschly, Amy L. & Sandra. L. Christenson. 2012. Jingle, jangle, and conceptual haziness: Evolution and future directions of the engagement construct. In Sandra L. Christenson, Amy L. Reschly & Cathy Wylie (eds.), *Handbook of Research on Student Engagement*, 3–20. Boston: Springer.

Rodgers, Michael P. H. & Stuart Webb. 2017. The effects of captions on EFL learners' comprehension of English-language television programs. *CALICO Journal* 34 (1). 20–38.

Rodgers, Michael PH & Stuart Webb. 2020. Incidental vocabulary learning through viewing television." ITL-International Journal of Applied Linguistics 171 (2). 191–220.

Rubenking, Bridget & Cheryl Campanella Bracken. 2021. Binge watching and serial viewing: Comparing new media viewing habits in 2015 and 2020. *Addictive Behaviors Reports* 14. 100356. https://doi.org/10.1016/j.abrep.2021.100356

Sang, Yuan & Phil Hiver. 2021. Engagement and companion constructs in language learning: Conceptualising learners' involvement in the L2 classroom. In Phil Hiver, Ali H. Al-Hoorie & Sarah Mercer (eds.), *Student Engagement in the Language Classroom*, 17–37. Bristol/Blue Ridge Summit: Multilingual Matters.

Schwarz, Marlene. 2020. *Beyond the walls: A mixed methods study of teenagers' extramural English practices and their vocabulary knowledge*. Wien: University of Vienna dissertation.

Skinner, Ellen A., James G. Wellborn & James P. Connell. 1990. What it takes to do well in school and whether I've got it: A process model of perceived control and children's engagement and achievement in school. *Journal of educational psychology* 82 (1). 22–32.

Skinner, Ellen A., Thomas A. Kindermann, James P. Connell & James G. Wellborn, 2009. Engagement and disaffection as organisational constructs in the dynamics of motivational development. In Kathryn R. Wentzel & David B. Miele (eds.), *Handbook of Motivation at School*, 223–245. New York: Routledge.

Svalberg, Agneta M. L. 2009. Engagement with language: Interrogating a construct. *Language Awareness* 18 (3–4). 242–258. https://doi.org/10.1080/09658410903197264

Svalberg, Agneta M. L. 2021. Engagement with language in relation to form-focused versus meaning-focused teaching and learning. In Phil Hiver, Ali H. Al-Hoorie & Sarah Mercer (eds.), *Student Engagement in the Language Classroom*, 38–55. Bristol/Blue Ridge Summit: Multilingual Matters.

Tapper, James. 2019. No habla español? How Netflix could transform the way we learn languages. *The Guardian*. http://www.theguardian.com/education/2019/mar/02/netflix-languages-education

Thorne, Steven L. & Jonathon Reinhardt. 2008. "Bridging activities," new media literacies, and advanced foreign language proficiency. *CALICO Journal* 25 (3). 558–572.

Vanderplank, Robert. 2016. *Captioned Media in Foreign Language Learning and Teaching: Subtitles for the Deaf and Hard-of-hearing as Tools for Language Learning*. Chem: Springer.

Wang, Isobel Kai-Hui & Sarah Mercer. 2021. Conceptualising willingness to engage in L2 learning beyond the classroom. In Phil Hiver, Ali H. Al-Hoorie & Sarah Mercer (eds.), *Student Engagement in the Language Classroom*, 260–279. Bristol: Blue Ridge Summit: Multilingual Matters. https://doi.org/10.21832/9781788923613-017

Webb, Stuart & Michael PH Rodgers. 2009. Vocabulary demands of television programs. Language Learning 59 (2). 335–366.

Webb, Stuart. 2015. Extensive viewing: Language learning through watching television. In David Nunan & Jack C. Richards (eds.), *Language Learning Beyond the Classroom*, 175–184. New York: Routledge.

Whitebloom, Sarah. 2020. Lockdown surge in language learning. Offord News Blog. https://www.ox.ac.uk/news/arts-blog/lockdown-surge-language-learning

Winke, Paula, Susan Gass & Tetyana Syodorenko. 2010. The effects of captioning videos used for foreign language listening activities. *Language Learning & Technology* 14 (1). 65–86.

Yeldham, Michael. 2018. Viewing L2 captioned videos: what's in it for the listener? *Computer Assisted Language Learning* 31 (4). 367–389.

Yin, Robert K. 2018. *Case Study Research and Applications: Design and Methods*. 6th edn. London: Sage Publications.

Geoffrey Sockett, Denyze Toffoli, Meryl Kusyk
17 Conclusion

Abstract: The final chapter of *Language Learning and Leisure* summarises the contents of the book under 6 headings: language, learning, informality, learner characteristics, activities and engagement, before examining the methodological orientations that emerge from this collection of chapters regarding future research into this area. Finally, it recalls the opportunities and challenges of research into informal additional language development, suggesting not only that such studies should contribute to a comprehensive understanding of these phenomena, but also that informal and leisure-based learning cannot be ignored when studying other aspects of second language acquisition.

Keywords: language learning, learner characteristics, learner activities, informality, future directions

1 A corpus approach to what has been said

In the introduction to this book we identified issues such as what informal learners do, where they do it, the role of the target language, the nature of acquisition and the relationship to classroom learning as being key dimensions of the field of informal second language learning (ISLL) or "language learning and leisure", as we have called it in the title. These areas can clearly be seen to have not only links to SLA but also to language didactics (teaching and learning of languages) and, more broadly, to the study of human behaviour. We began by suggesting that, in some ways, schooling and leisure have not always been seen as opposites and that indeed some problem solving in the context of leisure pursuits could be an effective form of σχολή (*schole*). How may we now sum up the evidence for this assertion gleaned from the preceding chapters? We will conclude in two parts: first by structuring the main dimensions of language learning and leisure as seen through recurrent keywords in the fifteen chapters and second by looking at the five subsections of the book, specifically regarding methodologies, with a view to making suggestions for the future of the field.

Geoffrey Sockett, Université de Paris Cité, France
Denyze Toffoli, Université de Toulouse III – Paul Sabatier, France
Meryl Kusyk, Karlsruhe University of Education, Germany

Table 1: Ranking of keywords in the contributed chapters of the book.

rank	occurrences	keyword
8	1060	language
10	1030	learning
15	715	English
17	592	informal
19	584	activities
25	466	students
27	444	engagement
30	429	learners
38	344	study
43	327	idle

A cursory count of keywords in the fifteen contributed chapters (Table 1) hints at a general overview of the themes encountered.

This table shows the ranking of individual words in the fifteen chapters once functional words (articles, prepositions, conjunctions, etc.) have been removed, leaving only keywords. The second column shows the number of occurrences of each keyword.

1.1 Language

The unsurprisingly high frequency of three of the four words that compose the acronym ISLL and their ranking at the top of the most recurring content words in the texts highlight the main topics of this book: *language* as a focus of study, the personal development which is inherent in *learning* and specifically that which has been qualified as *informal* or leisure-related. Interestingly, the word *leisure* itself does not seem to have caught on, even among the chapters retained. The language referred to in the acronym ISLL is often English, which itself is the third most frequently occurring word in Table 1. Studies of other languages, such as Japanese, which may have a comparable media presence, are therefore helpful in understanding the extent to which some informal second language learning activities (such as reading mangas or watching telenovelas) are themselves tied to a particular language and culture. This matter is most simply illustrated in the range of acronyms used to designate informal learning varieties, several of which focus only on one language (Extramural English, Informal Digital Learning of English and Online Informal Learning of English), while the more general label of Informal Second Language Learning allows for a range of languages to be considered. In this volume, Inaba's study of learning Japanese, Alm's study of learning

German and Cajka et al's work regarding learning of French and German are therefore particularly helpful as starting points to consider which aspects of ISLL are relatively constant, even when the target language changes. Benson (155) refers to such constants as a "broad framework" within which variation is observed. One such constant is the presence of video watching in contexts as different as Japanese learners in Sweden (Inaba), German learners in New Zealand (Alm) and English learners in Kazakhstan (Zadorozhnyy and Yu).

The opening three chapters of the book explore dimensions of language through the lenses of Anthropology, Second Language Acquisition (SLA) and Computer Assisted Language Learning (CALL). In considering the nature of Language Learning and Leisure, three relevant adjectives emerge from the chapters by Mark Dressman, Meryl Kusyk and Robert Godwin-Jones: *messy, incidental* and *complex*. These interrelated terms in some ways encapsulate recurring ideas from the rest of the book and so we shall first examine how each is presented in this theoretical section, before using them as a lens for the remainder of the book.

Adopting an anthropological perspective, Dressman reminds us that the study of IDLE (his chosen term) is "messy", in part because it involves the development of students' personal, cultural, and social identities. We might argue that this messiness therefore largely springs from the fact that fledgling users of English are perhaps more in the business of answering questions such as "who would I like to be, what do I value and how would I like to relate to others?" than they are strictly in the business of language learning. Transferring this notion of messiness to Kusyk's analysis of the implicit-explicit continuum we can observe both the wide range of reasons for engaging in informal activities as well as the diversity of levels of awareness of the possible language development in progress. From Kusyk's SLA-focused perspective, this means that while it is possible, although difficult, to pursue the measurement of acquisition from ISLL as one would in a less messy, controlled context, acquisition itself remains only one dimension of the developing language user's engagement in informal activities. Kusyk argues that the language development emerging through ISLL is both complex, involving differing degrees of intention and awareness, and dynamic, in that these variables are likely to change over time and according to the variety of ISLL in question.

Godwin-Jones also emphasises the inherent messiness of ISLL when he reminds us that "the dynamics of that process need to be understood not from the perspective of linear development or cause and effect, but rather as part of a complex web of interactions the L2 user-learner has with both people and non-human actors" (81). Indeed, the identities of the user-learner develop along a unique trajectory of interactions with people, media and devices best understood from a complex dynamic systems (CDS) perspective. The *complexity* and interconnectedness of all the varied aspects of ISLL are therefore at the heart of our understanding of the field. These insights can also be helpful in our understanding of the other frequently occurring terms in this volume.

1.2 Learning

The authors of this volume characterise learning, development or acquisition in informal contexts within the broader framework of other facets of development which may be taking place. Since ISLL can be seen as a subfield of both SLA and language didactics, it is important to note that some studies are more acquisition focused, seeking to measure what has been learned, and others more pedagogy focused, situating ISLL with regards to classroom practice. Chapters four and five examine acquisition as it manifests in two aspects of language production, discourse marker use and pronunciation. These dimensions of ISLL have been underrepresented in a field which has in the past often focused on comprehension skills, both in terms of specific vocabulary and of more general comprehension. These studies also exemplify the messy, incidental and complex nature of ISLL.

To take an example from listening skills, we might adopt as a hypothesis that ISLL viewing begins with L1 subtitling to support lower levels of oral comprehension, before moving on to viewing with target language captions or no subtitles at all at higher proficiency levels. In this case, Lyrigkou's observations that three key activities (frequent viewing without subtitles, spoken production and spoken interaction) are significantly related to changes in discourse marker use, raises questions about how language level relates to informal acquisition and also brings into focus questions of identity. It is easy to see how the practices of imitating the speech patterns of actors from favourite series reported by Lyrigkou is both a next step in the process of leaving behind a reliance on first language subtitles and moves messily into the kind of cultural and personal identity development suggested by Dressman. The incidental nature of these developments is also prevalent in this study and consideration of how the three key activities identified by Lyrigkou interact with the other twenty activities reported by her sample further underlines the complexity of the ISLL phenomenon.

Yibokou's study of pronunciation also considers the incidental nature of the uptake of specific sounds related to accent, and identifies considerable messiness in terms of inter and intra individual variability, while his comments about cultural affiliation and identity are also very much in line with Dressman. Awareness of contexts of production is also a key notion here, with a clear need for data from naturalistic settings which may show how priming from sources such as favourite series, as Lyrigkou identifies, leads to productions which reflect and construct cultural and personal identities in informal contexts.

1.3 Informality

As merely the opposite of formal, this label runs the risk of telling the reader more about what informal is *not* than what it *is*. Similarly, "extramural" tells us that activities do not take place in a school, but does not tell us precisely where, how, or why they do take place. This notional fuzziness surrounding the term "informal" and the semantic relationship between informal and formal mean that many studies seek to identify the boundaries of ISLL. This may be in terms of context, including the role of formal learning, or of awareness or intentionality, for example the extent to which the activity fulfils learning objectives.

Studies in this collection which look specifically at the interface between formal and informal learning include Cajka et al.'s approach to risk-taking, Benson's work on spatial factors, Zadorozhnyy and Yu's study of preservice teachers and Alm's work on Netflix as a study aid. Taken with the term "students", which is the sixth most frequently occurring term in our list, the paradox of the informal learner and student can be observed. Since informal learning takes place outside any educational structure, the learner cannot be considered as a student, and yet, in order to study informal learning, we require respondents who are most often accessible to researchers because they are enrolled in (higher) education. Although most ISLL research takes place in universities, in reality, this particular tip of the iceberg may not be entirely representative of what lies beneath, in the day-to-day lives of Netflix viewers and multiplayer gamers who do not have a language class coming up the following day. While the word "user" does not make it into the top ten, the word "learners", the eighth most frequent keyword in Table 1, is a helpful counterpoint to "student". It is also a reminder that many of these issues relate closely to the identity of the developing user/learner/student of the language in question. Indeed, how the person sees themself or would qualify themself with respect to their ISLL activity clearly interacts with issues such as whether and how learning is taking place, why activities are taking place and how formal learning is involved in the process.

1.4 Learner characteristics

The relationship between the informal learner and other learner characteristics is clearly a growing area of interest, as witnessed by the chapters relating to psychological factors, which encourage the reader to consider how feelings such as enjoyment, confidence or anxiety, may interact with ISLL.

The messiness exhibited in the contradicting identities of pre-service teachers, as pointed out by Zadorozhnyy and Yu, indicates that the construction of identities inherent through ISLL practices can lead learners in several different directions at once. For example, the professional identity of a pre-service teacher might believe that teachers play a central role in facilitating informal learning, whilst the learner identity is aware of having developed language skills without such assistance. Toffoli's study using attachment theory introduces dimensions such as fearfulness or dismissiveness, emotions which are often present in formal education but rarely feature in leisure activities. Do fears associated with formal learning carry over into the informal sphere, or do learners conceive of them as two separate experiences? In this case also the connectedness of formal and informal learning is at issue.

Liu and Lee's study of the relationship between grit (an ability to persevere) and enjoyment, again lead the reader to the interfaces between formal and informal, implicit and explicit, cognitive and affective. Their finding that classroom L2 enjoyment did not play a mediating role between IDLE and grit and that different ISLL activities had different associations with a willingness to persevere in English offer a multitude of questions for further study. Indeed, the finding that gaming and social media had a less positive influence on formal learning than text-based activities, for example, allows us to consider ranking ISLL activities by resemblance to classroom activities rather than by opportunity for interaction, since although multiplayer gaming offers opportunities for endless hours of spoken interaction, it bears little resemblance to a language class focusing on listening or reading comprehension.

1.5 Activities

The term "activities" is the fifth most frequent in Table 1. Individual activities are helpful entries into the complex world of ISLL for the researcher, enabling pre-existing methodologies to be brought to bear on language users engaged in listening, reading, viewing, etc. in order to consider outcomes such as fluency or vocabulary acquisition. Studies such as Yibokou's on pronunciation or Schwarz's on vocabulary acquisition strategies are examples of this kind of approach. While this allows the researcher to focus on a single area, the very interconnectedness of ISLL phenomena requires constant and careful consideration of how the individual activity or dimension relates to the greater whole. One may associate with the issue of activities another element of context contained in the final word in the list, "IDLE". This acronym, standing for Informal Digital Learning of English, was first suggested by Dressman and Lee (2017), and is to some extent in competition with ISLL as a potential name for the present field of study. In addition to being wedded to English as the language of study, IDLE also contains the key notion of digital practices and emphasises the links between informal learning and the vast fields of gaming and social media in particular. The perception that ISLL activities take place overwhelmingly in virtual spaces, using digital media, is a further indication of how ISLL relates to CALL, moving that field away from a study of tools created by the researcher and towards a study of the affordances of the learners' chosen tools and practices, as exemplified by Godwin-Jones' "complex web".

1.6 Engagement

The reader will have observed that the concept of "engagement" (the seventh keyword in Table 1) in ISLL practices receives particular attention in this volume, the final three contributions looking at different ways of characterising the engagement of learners in ISLL. While one may conclude that engagement is just another way of saying what learners do, the notion of differing engagement types is an important step in teasing apart some of the messiness of ISLL by asking what is at stake in the different activities of different learners. Etymologically, the word "engage" has its origins in the French *"un gage"*, which is a stake, pledge or forfeit. Hence the dimensions of behavioural, cognitive, social and affective engagement bring to light the learner's investment in the process and perhaps their hopes for a return on that investment. The implicit/explicit continuum is again a pertinent concept here, reminding us that while learners are sometimes thinking about language learning as they engage in ISLL activities, they are also thinking about their feelings, their friends, or just their need to fill time. Inter and intra-personal differences in learning outcomes will clearly be exhibited when what learners are focusing on can be so different in a given activity. How learning outcomes are differentially impacted when the stakes change can be seen most clearly in Arndt's work, focusing on "the nature of learners' L2 leisure activities, not merely in terms of what they do, but also their thoughts and feelings" (352). Her findings relating to variations in the role of conscious linguistic attention are of relevance to the implicit-explicit axis of ISLL, while her observation that longitudinal analysis of ISLL, including levels as detailed as intra-activity variability, again point to the relevance of emic approaches in future studies. Sockett suggests that there may be a large framework in which four dimensions of engagement, behavioural, cognitive, affective and social, evolve as a function of language level. Such a view also invites the study of variability within this framework. Alm's study offers an opportunity to observe the interconnectedness of the different dimensions of engagement in individual learners and offers the kind of fine-grained observation needed as the study of engagement types in ISLL develops. The individual pathways of a learner used to encountering foreign languages on Netflix and another for whom this was a new experience illustrate two key aspects of complex and dynamic systems theory: the unique starting points of each learner and the impact of these differences on the evolution of the system.

Finally, the term "study" (item nine in Table 1) offers an opportunity to consider how the field of language learning and leisure may move forward as a result of this volume. The issues of what studies could now be developed and what methodologies may be most effective for each of the sub-themes into which we have chosen to divide the book will bring to a close this concluding chapter.

2 Future methodological orientations from five areas of ISLL

The fifteen chapters of this volume have taught us a great deal about the characteristics of ISLL, and these characteristics are most richly understood when the field is viewed from a number of perspectives. In the editorial process, we have chosen to identify some of these perspectives by dividing the book into five sections: The nature of ISLL, language outcomes, learner activities, psychological dimensions and engagement.

It is apparent in reviewing the book that the inherent issues of messiness, degrees of intentionality and complexity require attention to methodology in order to design innovative and insightful studies that will move the field forward. It is equally apparent that such methodologies will vary according to each focus of study. We have already referred to emic approaches allowing first-hand accounts of ISLL engagement, production data from naturalistic settings and longitudinal data identifying variability within and between activities for a given learner. Considering the fifteen chapters by subsection allows for further suggestions as to which methodological approaches may be most appropriate for different types of study.

2.1 The nature of ISLL

Future directions for research into the theoretical basis of learning through leisure are hinted at in the chapters offered by Dressman, Kusyk and Godwin-Jones. The range of their work, pointing the reader in the directions of anthropology, psycholinguistics and CALL, presents both challenges and opportunities. On the one hand this involves the search for unifying topics of study. On the other, it is also clear that most research into additional language development needs to increasingly consider its prevalence in informal settings, as identities emerge through use of different tools and with differing degrees of awareness.

Dressman's chapter is an appeal to the adoption of ethnographic methodologies in the study of ISLL, on the basis that they need to involve the same four major components as anthropological studies: participant observation, artefact collection and analysis, narrative and thick description and longitudinal case studies. He claims that such tools, along with introspection and "confession" (in the sense of admission of fallibility) should be the privileged instruments of ISLL, allowing researchers to avoid reductionism and foster the emergence of theory.

Godwin-Jones' chapter, through his foray into the technological affordances of Intelligent Personal Assistants (IPAs), claims that investigations into the person/machine relationship for language development can most efficiently be made within the frameworks of ecological SLA, sociomaterialism and complex dynamic systems. The methodologies that he recommends include the examination of both linguistic interactions and the particular dynamics of an interaction with machines (such as the use of voice systems) at varying distances and levels of detail. While recognising that datamining may well be a valuable orientation for future investigations into these areas, he also warns against the ethical questions raised by the indiscriminate collection of various types of online data and suggests that qualitative studies are likely to offer the most enlightening results, by tracing individual learning trajectories, perhaps drawing on retrodictive qualitative modelling (Dornyei 2014). Such an approach would involve identifying prototypical informal learner profiles, selecting an appropriate sampling of each profile, collecting qualitative data (often via interviews) and conducting qualitative analyses of the language learning narratives of these learners, similar to Toffoli's approach herein.

Looking specifically to identify evidence of implicit knowledge when examining the nature of informal learning, Kusyk suggests several methodological approaches. This is relevant due to the absence of classroom contexts in which explicit knowledge may be acquired. Such approaches include focusing on measures of fluency, measuring frequency effects through collocations or formulaic knowledge and employing timed oral grammaticality judgement tests. In order to target implicit learning, Kusyk suggests employing think-aloud protocols and longitudinal designs, as studies that investigate learning over shorter periods may be inherently biased against implicit learning. Along with other authors in this book, Kusyk too proposes studying the nature of learning in ISLL within a complex and dynamic systems framework, as the constructs examined (awareness, incidental learning, explicit and implicit learning systems, . . .) involve constantly evolving and highly complex variables, sub-systems and systems.

These studies point to opportunities for adopting protocols as yet underrepresented, such as real-time video-recording of ISLL learner activity and think-aloud or stimulated-recall protocols. These would offer insights into not only the nature of ISLL but also individual differences and acquisitional data, which may differ from those available retrospectively through diary studies, interviews and questionnaires.

The matter of the names used to describe ISLL also falls under the remit of theoretical studies. A broad consensus would make ISLL more readily identifiable to other researchers and indicate the maturing of this emerging area. The jingle-jangle phenomenon (Reschly and Christenson 2012) relates to occasions when two terms are used to refer to the same phenomenon (jangle), and those where two phenomena are given the same name (jingle). In the case of ISLL, questions such as whether non-formal learning from purpose-made materials falls within the scope of informal learning, or whether informal, extramural learning and autonomous learning with technology outside the classroom should be taken as synonyms are examples. A key practice in developing and updating research in the informal sphere would be to continue to carry out meta-studies, such as the scoping review produced by Soyoof et al. (2021). A forthcoming series of studies based on a systematic review involving several authors of this book will offer the broadest possible perspectives on this fast-moving field.

2.2 The acquisition studies

While acquisition studies in formal settings seek to obtain data from classroom or even laboratory settings, ISLL acquisition studies aim to measure the process and product of a phenomenon that usually takes place in the L2 user's private sphere. A major challenge in setting up acquisition studies for informal contexts is thus obtaining data from naturalistic settings. This demands creativity from researchers as they are confronted with challenges such as recruiting participants, controlling variables, respecting privacy and facilitating logistics. While convenient sampling has most often been used in ISLL studies, it may be more difficult to recruit participants from under-represented demographics. Control of variables such as activity frequency or content, may change both the relationship to that activity and possible learning outcomes. Respecting privacy is clearly a key issue since this research involves forays into private habits or relationships that could raise feelings of embarrassment or uneasiness and potentially impact relevant variables. Logistical issues include where, if not in the classroom, data collection should be carried out and how the participants' natural L2 usage timetable can be fully considered.

In the context of studies of pronunciation, many opportunities exist to obtain recordings of learners in naturalistic settings since making and posting video and audio files is a significant aspect of social media use today. Comparing pronunciation characteristics of informal learner productions to those of native speaker corpora would offer such an opportunity in social media contexts. In his contribution on pronunciation in the present volume, Yibokou emphasises the need for both larger-scale studies and for investigating additional segmental (individual sounds) and suprasegmental (intonation, stress) features. In order to grasp a more complete picture of phonological development he also recommends longitudinal studies, which would give a more fine-grained view of participants' informal usage and allow the researcher to more reliably explore associations between variables such as frequency of viewing, pronunciation, engagement or aptitude.

Lyrigkou's chapter on the acquisition of discourse markers (DMs), also underlines the need to expand the number of variables investigated in order to obtain clearer results. She suggests, for example, creating sub-corpora that contain the L2 content that learners use or are exposed to in a leisure context (transcripts of television series, of interactions with friends or voice-recordings from the users themselves). This would allow researchers interested in L2 pragmatics acquired within the informal sphere to better understand DM exposure and usage not only from a quantitative, but also qualitative (functional), perspective.

2.3 Learner activities and strategies

The four chapters relating to learner activities and strategies offer relatively homogenous perspectives on future research methodologies, pointing essentially to the direct observation of learner activities. In a world in which smartphones log our every action, Benson and Cajka et al.'s use of apps to automatically record aspects of informal learning in a study abroad context can be seen as a natural progression from manually logging activities in a diary. Such apps may in return offer learning tips or suggest nearby opportunities for interaction.

It has in the past appeared logical that classroom observation be an essential part of data gathering on learner strategies and activities in a formal context, however any attempt to spy on the private worlds of informal learners would doubtless result in a significant change in their behaviour. The area of leisure and the guilty pleasures which might fill it seem a difficult context in which to request study participants to allow researchers to log hours spent viewing hair and makeup videos, dating sites or other activities which fall into categories identified by Sundqvist (2019: 101) as "please don't tell my Dad". However, as suggested by Schwarz, direct observations of actual practices would offer a useful complement to regular interviews with learners in a longitudinal approach. So Inaba's view that the activity, as operationalised in activity theory, is a useful unit of informal learning, may lead to a renewed focus on what learners are actually doing in real time.

It is likely that a microscopic approach to informal learning, using technologies such as eye tracking, would, in the past, have required placing learners in laboratory conditions, which again would have hindered access to the activities they may have engaged in naturalistically at home. Perhaps in a world in which the smartphone screen is the predominant mode of access to informal contents and interactions, such a need to know precisely where on the screen the learner is looking is of less importance than logging the more easily accessible swipes and taps which characterise smartphone use.

It is therefore possible that while direct observation of activities may have been rejected as impractical or unweildy in early ISLL research, learners may be more likely to agree to participate in such studies today. Current projects such as the Lang Track App at Lund University, as well as the work reported on in this volume by Benson and Cajka et al., are valuable steps towards setting up such methodologies and also stress the importance of technological R&D for this type of research. While researchers currently have little experience of such an approach, it is likely that there will be a place for such studies going forward, as part of a range of tools building up the complex picture of learning through leisure.

2.4 Psychological dimensions

The chapters on psychological dimensions study a number of individual differences, including grit and enjoyment (Liu and Lee), teacher beliefs and identity (Zadorozhnyy and Yu) and autonomy, attachment, and L2 competence as aspects of self-determined motivation (Toffoli), yet all evoke similar methodological difficulties and envisage similar methodological perspectives. Investigating perceived contradictions within and among participants and comparing individuals with differing characteristics are all felt to be important avenues of exploration. While all five of these authors rely on retrodictive protocols, they simultaneously all bemoan the relative (un)reliability of self-report data. Liu and Lee warn that such data, which may be composed of opinions and inaccurate recollections, could affect both the accuracy and reliability of even quantitative studies, such as their own.

Suggestions for offsetting these types of biases involve mixed method data collection and triangulation, such as that attempted by Toffoli in chapter 13, who draws on test scores, grades, questionnaire data from four different instruments targeting different learner variables, learner assertions (in the form of both answers to open questions and logbook entries) and teacher observations. However, while such instruments are useful in approaching individual experiences, all such self-report data, whether verbal or written, are subject to fundamental biases. These are inherent in what Kahneman (2011) refers to as "System 1 thinking", that which comes to us easily, but is often lacking in precision or logic and can be (un)intentionally manipulated by minute factors, of which the investigators themselves are often unaware. Zadorozhnyy & Yu refer, for example, to Schwarz et al.'s (1991) *availability heuristic*, one of the biases of System 1 thinking.

Another means to offset these biases is to diversify participant demographics, in terms of age or linguistic and cultural backgrounds. In reference to de Mooij and Hofstede (2010), Zadorozhnyy & Yu recommend comparing data collected from societies with different cultural biases. For example, when studying teacher beliefs or beliefs about teachers, this would involve investigating both individualist and collectivist societies, as they suspect that the differently experienced role of teachers as figures of authority in these contexts would significantly influence the other factors examined.

2.5 Engagement studies

The three studies in the subsection entitled *Engagement* offer complementary views of the path ahead for this type of research. Indeed, the presence of a number of studies in this collection taking up engagement as a way of analysing learner practices is in itself an indication of a developing orientation of ISLL research. Arndt's distinction between cognitive engagement, relating to meaning in informal contents, and linguistic engagement, relating to the form of the language, makes the framework suggested by Philp and Duchesne (2016) easier to apply to informal contexts. Indeed, informal learners are facing the competing demands of both these aspects without explicit external guidance on which dimensions of engagement to prioritise at any given time.

Arndt's conclusion that engagement is highly complex and dynamic is a reminder that, as research methodologies seek to take a more longitudinal view of learner engagement in informal activities, there are many fractal timescales to observe. These include variation within the timeframe of a single activity, variation over a few days and long-term shifts such as those from cognitive, linguistic and behavioural engagement towards affective and social engagement suggested by Sockett. In the shorter timescales, it may be particularly useful to design protocols able to identify under what circumstances linguistic engagement comes in and out of focus as learners either become aware of or choose to put into practice a greater focus on form. The role of focus on form is central to Alm's work on engagement, as the key issue of how to create interfaces between formal and informal is considered. Identifying the promotion of autonomy, competence and relatedness as key aspects of such an interface, Alm also observes that the relationship between engagement types is dynamic, reflecting personal growth rather than merely language acquisition. As such, it is inevitably important to observe the ways in which identities are tied up with engagement in thoughts, feelings and relationships mediated through informal activities.

Methodologically speaking, dynamic engagement studies will therefore require a range of longitudinal approaches which may include real time think-aloud protocols to identify the relationship between linguistic and cognitive engagement, as well as retrodictive studies looking at how contrasting profiles such as those in Alm's study impact present and future engagement in informal practices. How such think-aloud protocols may be put into practice in informal settings is again a difficult question. Possible solutions may include the use of smartphone technologies of the kind suggested in Section 2. They may also be approached from the perspective of looking for examples of form-focused utterances in informal contexts. These may include requests for correction in exchanges between gamers on multiplayer platforms, or longitudinal interviews with those concerned, to review their examples of linguistic engagement.

3 Final words

This book is a testimony to the health of ISLL as an emerging field of research. The inaugural ISLL conference in Oxford in 2018 was followed by a successful symposium at AILA 2021, the contributions to which make up the majority of the chapters of this collection. At the time of writing, a further symposium at AILA 2023 is in preparation, focussing on methodology.

It is worth recalling, in closing, the opportunities and challenges of our area of study. It is a field in which acquisition, technology and anthropology pursue differing if complementary aims. As such it is important for researchers adopting each of these perspectives to see the value of the others for the field as a whole. All avenues of the study of second language learning and teaching now need to include an ISLL focus; indeed, it is difficult to make sense of a learner's limited hours of the formal study of a language without factoring in the limitless varieties of informal exposure.

In many ways, all of the studies included in this volume express the necessity of a comprehensive view of ISLL, while at the same time recognising the difficulty of such a view, given the complex nature of human beings and the fact that their actions and discourses vary in a natural and social world which is itself infinitely complex. We look forward to the next episode in this popular series as creative and enthusiastic researchers continue to expand our understanding of language learning and leisure.

References

De Mooij, Marieke & Geert Hofstede. 2010. The Hofstede model: Applications to global branding and advertising strategy and research. *International Journal of Advertising* 29(1). 85–110.
Dörnyei, Zoltan. 2014. Researching complex dynamic systems: 'Retrodictive qualitative modelling' in the language classroom. *Language Teaching* 47(1). 80–91.
Kahneman, Daniel. 2011. *Thinking Fast and Slow*. New York: Farrar, Straus and Giroux.
Lee, Ju Seong & Mark Dressman. 2017. When IDLE Hands Make an English Workshop: Informal Digital Learning of English and Language Proficiency. *TESOL Quarterly*. 435–445. https://doi.org/10.1002/tesq.422.
Philp, Jenefer & Susan Duchesne. 2016. Exploring engagement in tasks in the language classroom. *Annual Review of Applied Linguistics* 36. 50–72.
Reschly, A. L. & S. L. Christenson. 2012. Jingle, jangle, and conceptual haziness: Evolution and future directions of the engagement construct. In S. L. Christenson, A. L. Reschly & C. Wylie (eds.), *Handbook of Research on Student Engagement*, 3–20. Boston: Springer.
Schwarz, Norbert, Herbert Bless, Fritz Strack, Gisela Klumpp & Annette Simons. 1991. Ease of retrieval as information: another look at the availability heuristic. *Journal of Personality and Social Psychology* 61. 195–202.
Soyoof, Ali, Barry Lee Reynolds, Boris Vazquez-Calvo & Katherine McLay. 2021. Informal digital learning of English (IDLE): A scoping review of what has been done and a look towards what is to come. *Computer Assisted Language Learning*. 1–33. https://doi.org/10.1080/09588221.2021.1936562
Sundqvist, P. 2019. Commercial-off-the-shelf games in the digital wild and L2 learner vocabulary. *Language Learning and Technology* 23(1). 87–113. http://scholarspace.manoa.hawaii.edu/handle/10125/44674

Index

accent 11, 108, 122, 124, 126, 129–40, 215, 313, 392, 412
Activity Theory 185–190, 196–198, 200, 201, 203, 204
adolescent learners 12, 91, 162
affective engagement 14, 272, 329, 333–334, 343–345, 349–352, 359, 363, 365, 371, 373, 375, 376, 415
American English 121, 125, 127, 134, 370
authenticity 212, 226, 243

behavioural engagement 270, 327, 329, 332, 336, 349–352, 359, 363–365, 376, 385, 422
British English 123–126, 371

Canada 207, 208, 213, 217, 219, 225
case study 8, 21, 26, 29, 149, 294, 379, 381, 388, 390
cognitive engagement 327, 331, 334, 335, 344, 345, 347, 349–353, 383, 399–401, 421, 422
collaboration 212, 226, 330

discourse markers 11, 91, 92, 118, 419

emotional 75, 78, 80, 124, 244, 258, 285, 362, 386, 398, 400, 401
explicit knowledge 48, 50, 417
explicit learning 43, 45, 48–51, 60, 61
Extramural English 3, 10, 33, 42, 44, 45, 52, 55, 91, 160, 163–165, 169, 242, 410

focus on form 330, 331, 336, 362, 372, 422
formal learning 7, 9, 39, 60, 100, 210, 278, 283, 299, 361, 379–381, 386, 387, 401, 413, 414, 418
French 4, 7, 14, 36–38, 42, 55, 87, 121–123, 127, 130, 132–136, 161, 164, 171, 180, 209, 213, 214, 217, 221, 225, 227, 230, 232–234, 262, 273, 283, 294, 300, 304, 305, 308, 309, 313, 321, 365, 374, 384, 411, 415

gamification 76, 231–233, 235
German 4, 7, 15, 55, 73, 127, 164, 166, 191, 199, 209, 222, 217–22, 232, 273, 294, 327, 329, 337–339, 344, 352, 353, 379, 381, 387–395, 397–400, 411
Greek 41, 91, 94, 97, 104, 107

IDLE 3, 10, 13, 21–42, 53, 56, 58–60, 63, 122, 143, 158, 241–60, 269–279, 282, 283, 285, 359–360, 362–367, 373, 375, 376, 380, 411, 414, 415
implicit knowledge 48–50, 62, 417
implicit learning 44–51, 53, 57, 58, 60–63, 417
incidental acquisition 45, 51, 52, 55–58, 60, 95, 96, 109
incidental learning 10, 43, 50–53, 60, 62, 95, 331, 384, 418
individual differences 5, 8, 14, 121, 126, 134, 136, 178, 232, 245, 359, 360, 362, 366, 376, 418, 420
intentional learning 32, 43, 45, 57, 59, 60, 95, 96, 98, 109, 335, 384
intraformal 9, 15, 381
ISLL 3–58–15, 43, 44, 52–55, 57–62, 91, 92, 94–110, 113, 159, 162, 177, 178, 291, 293, 296–317, 327, 328, 331–338, 352, 353, 380, 409–418, 420–423

Japanese 4, 7, 12, 23, 28, 125, 149, 185–203, 205, 233, 262, 410

language teachers 9, 14, 269, 270, 272, 273, 278, 280, 283–285
LBC 52, 53, 56, 58, 60, 63, 209
learner autonomy 7, 56, 291, 292, 294, 295, 297, 298, 316
learning strategies 15, 121, 159, 162, 177, 184, 278, 279, 283, 284, 312, 331, 351, 373, 381
leisure activities 2, 10, 12, 14, 43, 121, 148, 149, 153, 155–156, 159, 165, 166, 169, 171, 175, 178, 186, 207, 208, 303, 314, 328, 335, 337–339, 343, 344, 349, 352, 362, 380, 414, 415
linguistic engagement 14, 327, 329, 331, 334–339, 341, 342, 345, 347–352, 363–365, 371, 372, 376, 421, 422

linguistic risk 207–211, 225, 227, 228, 232, 236
longitudinal 8, 30, 62, 83, 91, 97, 136, 376, 415–420, 422

mediation 5, 53, 135, 185, 188, 201, 254, 255, 258
motivation 13, 14, 28, 44, 53, 62, 77, 93, 173, 175, 179, 186, 187, 194, 196, 225, 230, 243–245, 283, 291–293, 295, 297–299, 305, 307–310, 314, 315, 317, 328–330, 332–335, 337, 338, 360, 373, 386, 387, 397, 420
multimodal 72, 83, 173, 185, 200, 202, 243, 269, 384
music 2, 4, 6, 25, 32, 55, 69, 133, 135, 165, 195, 243, 274–276, 280, 282, 298, 302, 305, 311, 328, 332, 334, 340, 344, 347, 370, 372, 380

Netflix 15, 104, 194–196, 202, 243, 257, 313, 374, 375, 379–384, 387–391, 394, 397–399, 402, 413, 416
non-formal 9, 32, 52, 54, 135, 210, 270, 277, 305, 332, 336, 361, 418

OILE 3, 52, 55, 56, 58–60, 63, 121, 122, 143, 187, 380

personalization 72, 212, 226
pop culture 185–187, 190, 192, 194, 196, 199, 201, 276
pragmatics 27, 76, 84, 88, 91, 93, 106, 108, 110, 419
pronunciation 11, 30, 44, 53, 70, 72–74, 80, 121–129, 132–136, 168, 169, 174, 295, 412, 414, 419

qualitative data 136, 162, 163, 178, 272, 300, 306, 316, 339, 343, 349, 350, 359, 367, 391, 417

quantitative data 159, 163, 218, 273, 300, 307, 338, 340, 343, 345, 347, 348, 352

self-determination 14, 15, 291–297, 315, 316, 386, 387
social engagement 14, 74, 363, 365, 368, 371, 376, 385, 386, 400, 401, 422
social media 32, 33, 43, 56, 70, 95, 98, 144, 165, 169, 208, 225, 226, 231, 234, 246, 249, 270, 274–276, 280, 340, 342, 363, 365, 380, 414, 415, 419
study abroad 2, 12, 85, 117, 143–149, 151, 155–157, 419
subtitles 7, 12, 103, 104, 106–108, 126, 133, 161, 185, 187, 188, 192, 194–199, 201–203, 233, 275, 276, 281, 282, 298, 304, 313, 335, 370, 372, 374, 380, 382–384, 389, 391, 392, 394–396, 398, 400, 412

television series 55, 121, 124, 126, 133, 135, 136, 419, *see* TV series
TV series 110, 123, 135, 192, 271, 328, 333, 343, 350, 382, 383
TV watching 91, 95, 106

variability 11, 13, 14, 49, 101, 126, 129–131, 134, 359, 360, 375, 412, 415, 416
video games 2, 43, 55, 135, 190, 195, 271, 279, 298, 302, 305, 328, 334, 340, 343, 345, 347, 351, 367, 370
vocabulary acquisition 12, 30, 51, 67, 122, 160, 162, 163, 168, 173, 178, 179, 182, 282, 414
vocabulary learning 59, 68, 159–162, 164, 167, 168, 173, 174, 176–178, 180, 184, 282, 384, 389

www.ingramcontent.com/pod-product-compliance
Lightning Source LLC
Chambersburg PA
CBHW061925220426
43662CB00012B/1803